C

The Middle East: Oil, Conflict & Hope

The Middle East: Oil, Conflict & Hope

Critical Choices for Americans

Volume X

Edited by

A. L. Udovitch

Lexington Books
D.C. Heath and Company
Lexington, Massachusetts
Toronto

Library of Congress Cataloging in Publication Data

Main entry under title:
   The Middle East.

   (Critical choices for Americans; v. 10)
   "Prepared for the Commission on Critical Choices for Americans."
   Includes index.
   1. Near East—Addresses, essays, lectures. 2. Near East—Politics and
government—Addresses, essays, lectures. I. Udovitch, Abraham L. II. Com-
mission on Critical Choices for Americans. III. Series
DS42.4.M47   956   75-44728
ISBN 0-669-00424-3

Published simultaneously in Canada.

Printed in the United States of America.

International Standard Book Number: 0-669-00424-3

Library of Congress Catalog Card Number: 75-44728

Foreword

The Commission on Critical Choices for Americans, a nationally representative, bipartisan group of forty-two prominent Americans, was brought together on a voluntary basis by Nelson A. Rockefeller. After assuming the Vice Presidency of the United States, Mr. Rockefeller, the chairman of the Commission, became an ex officio member. The Commission's assignment was to develop information and insights which would bring about a better understanding of the problems confronting America. The Commission sought to identify the critical choices that must be made if these problems are to be met.

The Commission on Critical Choices grew out of a New York State study of the Role of a Modern State in a Changing World. This was initiated by Mr. Rockefeller, who was then Governor of New York, to review the major changes taking place in federal-state relationships. It became evident, however, that the problems confronting New York State went beyond state boundaries and had national and international implications.

In bringing the Commission on Critical Choices together, Mr. Rockefeller said:

As we approach the 200th Anniversary of the founding of our Nation, it has become clear that institutions and values which have accounted for our astounding progress during the past two centuries are straining to cope with the massive problems of the current era. The increase in the tempo of change and the vastness and complexity of the wholly new situations which are evolving with accelerated change, create a widespread sense that our political and social system has serious inadequacies.

We can no longer continue to operate on the basis of reacting to crises, counting on crash programs and the expenditure of huge sums of money to solve our problems. We have got to understand and project present trends, to take command of the forces that are emerging, to extend our freedom and wellbeing as citizens and the future of other nations and peoples in the world.

Because of the complexity and interdependence of issues facing America and the world today, the Commission has organized its work into six panels, which emphasize the interrelationships of critical choices rather than treating each one in isolation.

The six panels are:

Panel I: Energy and its Relationship to Ecology, Economics and World Stability;

Panel II: Food, Health, World Population and Quality of Life;

Panel III: Raw Materials, Industrial Development, Capital Formation, Employment and World Trade;

Panel IV: International Trade and Monetary Systems, Inflation and the Relationships Among Differing Economic Systems;

Panel V: Change, National Security and Peace;

Panel VI: Quality of Life of Individuals and Communities in the U.S.A.

The Commission assigned, in these areas, more than 100 authorities to prepare expert studies in their fields of special competence. The Commission's work has been financed by The Third Century Corporation, a New York not-for-profit organization. The corporation has received contributions from individuals and foundations to advance the Commission's activities.

The Commission is determined to make available to the public these background studies and the reports of those panels which have completed their deliberations. The background studies are the work of the authors and do not necessarily represent the views of the Commission or its members.

This volume is one of the series of volumes the Commission will publish in the belief that it will contribute to the basic thought and foresight America will need in the future.

WILLIAM J. RONAN
Acting Chairman
Commission on Critical Choices
for Americans

Members of the Commission

LEO CHERNE
  Executive Director, Research Institute
  of America, Inc.

JOHN S. FOSTER, JR.
  Vice President for Energy Research
  and Development, TRW, Inc.

LUTHER H. FOSTER
  President, Tuskegee Institute

NANCY HANKS
  Chairman, National Endowment for the Arts

BELTON KLEBERG JOHNSON
  Texas Rancher and Businessman

CLARENCE B. JONES
  Former Editor and Publisher,
  The New York Amsterdam News

JOSEPH LANE KIRKLAND
  Secretary—Treasurer, AFL-CIO

JOHN H. KNOWLES, M.D.
  President, Rockefeller Foundation

DAVID S. LANDES
  Leroy B. Williams Professor of History
  and Political Science, Harvard University

MARY WELLS LAWRENCE
  Chairman and Chief Executive Officer,
  Wells, Rich, Greene, Inc.

SOL M. LINOWITZ
  Senior Partner of Coudert Brothers

EDWARD J. LOGUE
  Former President and Chief Executive Officer,
  New York State Urban Development Corporation

EDWARD TELLER
  Senior Research Fellow, Hoover Institution
  on War, Revolution and Peace,
  Stanford University

ARTHUR K. WATSON*
  Former Ambassador to France

MARINA VON NEUMANN WHITMAN
  Distinguished Public Service Professor
  of Economics, University of Pittsburgh

CARROLL L. WILSON
  Professor, Alfred P. Sloan
  School of Management,
  Massachusetts Institute of Technology

GEORGE D. WOODS
  Former President, World Bank

Members of the Commission served on the panels. In addition, others assisted
the panels.

BERNARD BERELSON
Senior Fellow
President Emeritus
The Population Council

C. FRED BERGSTEN
Senior Fellow
The Brookings Institution

ORVILLE G. BRIM, JR.
President
Foundation for Child Development

LESTER BROWN
President
Worldwatch Institute

LLOYD A. FREE
President
Institute for International Social Research

*Deceased

Preface

For many Americans, the Middle East was not a pressing fact of life until the oil embargo in late 1973. It was no longer only a region caught up in squabbles among its member nations, but a region that could touch the life of every American and threaten our life-style. The Middle East is today an arena of intense local and superpower rivalry with the traditional strategic importance of the area now enhanced by its vast economic and financial power. It is, as the title of this volume implies, a region of great natural resources, of great diversity where conflict and instability abound; and the ultimate issues of world war or world peace will be affected by what transpires there over the next decade.

The Middle East: Oil, Conflict, & Hope is one of seven geographic studies prepared for the Commission on Critical Choices for Americans, under the coordination of Nancy Maginnes Kissinger. Companion volumes cover Western Europe, the Soviet Empire, China and Japan, Southern Asia, Africa, and Latin America. In myriad ways, America's goals, interests, and prosperity over the next decade will depend significantly on its relations with, and the shape of, the world around it. In recent decades, the world has grown closer together and more interdependent as this country and other nations find it impossible to solve domestic problems in isolation.

The studies that A.L. Udovitch has brought together are a comprehensive report based on expert research. By analyzing the basic factors at work within each of the states of the Middle East and within the region as a whole, these essays help us identify the problems America should be concerned with and the policy options available to us. Developments within this area will have a crucial impact on the economic welfare of the United States, its allies in the free world, the Communist world and the Third World. The critical choices we face as Americans in our relationship with this region must be based on an informed understanding of the area's current realities and future prospects.

W.J.R.

Acknowledgments

The planning, preparation, and editing of this volume has benefited from the help, counsel, and hard work of a number of people whose names do not appear on its pages. I would like to express my sincere thanks to Anne Boylan and Charity Randall of the Commission staff; to Grace Edelman and Mary Craparotta of Princeton for devoted secretarial help and more; to Professors Sidney Alexander (M.I.T.), L. Carl Brown (Princeton), Bernard Lewis (Princeton), Ragaei el-Mallakh (Colorado), William Quandt (Pennsylvania), and Frederic Shorter (Population Council) for their participation in a discussion meeting on the early drafts of the papers in this volume in June 1975.

A.L.U.

Contents

List of Tables

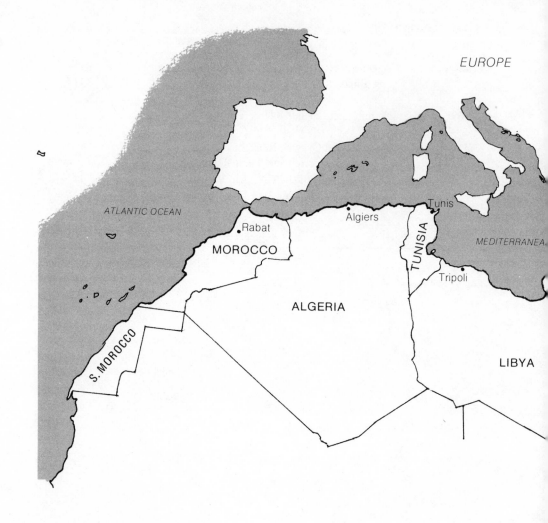

EUROPE

ATLANTIC OCEAN

MEDITERRANEA

Tunis

Algiers

Rabat

MOROCCO

TUNISIA

Tripoli

ALGERIA

S. MOROCCO

LIBYA

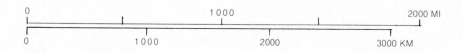

NORTH AFRICA and the MIDDLE EAST

0	1000	2000 MI
0	1000	2000	3000 KM

I   Introduction

A.L. Udovitch

In myriad ways, America's goals, interests, and prosperity over the next decade or so will depend significantly on its relations with, and the shape of, the world around it. With respect to the Middle East, events of the past several years have dramatically demonstrated the area's crucial importance for America's security and economic well-being and for the well-being of Europe and Japan, areas which are obviously vital to American interests and security over the next decade. The critical choices America faces in its relationship to the countries of the Middle East must be based on an informed understanding of the area's current realities and future prospects.

Within the framework of the Commission on Critical Choices for Americans, the aim of the Middle East Panel has been to facilitate the deliberations of the Commission and its various panels by providing a set of reports identifying the major trends and issues in the area and spelling out, as far as possible, their implications for American foreign policy.

Since the area comprises national units of varying ethnic, linguistic, and religious composition, differing political systems and ideologies, widely uneven distribution of economic and human resources, a significant proportion of the reports in this volume are devoted to individual country studies. In addition, a number of reports are devoted to general political and economic problems relevant to America's future relations with the Middle East which are common to all or to many of the countries of the area.

The contributors to this volume are among the leading Middle East experts in the United States, Western Europe, and the Near East. On the basis of present perceptions and discernible trends, they were charged with determining the critical choices facing the United States and the world in the Middle East and indicating the range of desirable and realistic objectives for the United States in this region of the world over the next several decades. From varying perspectives, each contributor seeks to identify the elements essential to attain these objectives and to recommend immediate actions and policy directions which will advance the likelihood of their achievement.

Predicting human behavior, be it on an individual or on a social and political level, is a risky, not to say futile, enterprise. The multiplicity of actors, factors, and motives and their range of possible combination is very great indeed. With respect to the Middle East, one faces an additional complication in that the starting point of any analysis or attempt at informed prediction is shifting and elusive. More than most regions of the world, the Middle East in the past several years has experienced rapid changes of uncertain consequences within its constituent states, within the region as a whole and in its political and economic relations with the rest of the world. Even within the period of the gestation of this volume, perspectives have to a great extent shifted; a variety of problems— old and new—which two years ago loomed large and urgently menacing, are now perceived in a somewhat more relaxed manner and seen in more manageable and realistic human proportions. In view of these rapidly shifting circumstances and the inherent complexity of the problems themselves, the absence of unanimity in the recommendations of the contributors to this volume should come as no surprise. Even within the context of each individual contributor's conclusions and projections, the degree of qualifications and reservations is considerable. Nevertheless, when taken together, the insights and recommendations articulated in the reports which make up this volume do represent the most informed exposition of the range of policy and objectives and policy choices which confront the United States in the Middle East.

If there is no unanimity among our contributors regarding the details of the solutions to the problems confronting the Middle East itself and those facing American policy in the Middle East, there does emerge from all the reports a broad consensus concerning the major problems to which American policy will have to address itself.

In early 1974, when the papers in this volume were first being planned, the Middle East had just emerged from another costly but inconclusive Arab-Israeli war. Its political and economic consequences appeared to be far more profound for the area and the world than any following upon previous conflicts. Some observers in the Middle East and elsewhere saw in the aftermath of this war the beginning of a new era in Middle Eastern and world politics. The Arab states emerged from this war with high political expectations for a favorable settlement of their conflict with Israel. The unity and coordination among the Arab states was a high point, with new alliances among Egypt, Syria, and Saudi Arabia. The oil producing countries were beginning to acquire vast riches as a result of the steep increase in oil prices and the prospect of a powerful concentration of financial power in the Middle East seemed a certainty. Conversely, a threat to the economic and especially the financial stability of the industrialized Western world seemed imminent.

Two and a half years later, all of these factors are still present and all of the problems are still with us. Yet, their urgency has subsided and the pace at which they are working themselves out has become less frantic and, above all, new and unexpected destabilizing situations have emerged. Lebanon is a good case in point. All were aware of the communal and social tensions in that country and of the tenuous and fragile nature of its governmental authority. But in early 1974 few observers would have predicted that the crisis in Lebanon would come so soon or that its political breakdown would be as prolonged, bloody, and tragic as has turned out to be the case in 1975 and 1976.

In the Middle East, as in most other parts of the world, the twists and turns of events may not be predictable, but the general problems in the context of which these occur have been with us for a long time and are likely to remain with us. The constants, then, are precisely these long-term issues and problems upon which the contributors to this volume have achieved a broad consensus. While I can only speak for myself in this regard, I believe that within the constantly changing constellation of events in the Middle East, three basic problems are the fixed stars which should guide an effective American foreign policy in this region for the next decade or two. These issues are:

1. The formulation and adherence to a realistic, broadminded U.S. policy tied to U.S. interests in all their variety with particular attention to maintaining America's position in the area's balance of power.
2. A stable and reliable arrangement with respect to the availability of oil and to the nondisruptive recycling of the area's financial resources in excess of those invested regionally.
3. Providing impetus and expertise which will enhance prospects for favorable and rational economic development in face of the overwhelming demographic problems the Middle East will have to contend with in the next two decades.

Virtually all the day-to-day policy questions confronting our government can be subsumed under one or another of these three major issues and might be profitably evaluated according to the degree to which they further our own interests and those of the region itself in terms of these three considerations.

The three general issues I have enumerated are, of course, interrelated in many ways. Each corresponds to a major component of our overall national interest. Prospects of continued peace or recurrent local wars in the Middle East and the consequences of each eventuality have a direct bearing on our global security posture vis-à-vis the USSR and Europe. The oil resources and the financial resources of the region bear directly on our economic prosperity and well-being and have profound social and political implications for the political and social stability of the United States, Western Europe, and Japan. The manner in which these financial resources are utilized within the region itself and the ability of the countries within the region—especially the larger oil-poor states—to cope with their rapid, not to say galloping, demographic growth will, more than any other factor, affect the political shape of the area, its stability and well-being, and its relations to the rest of the world.

The divisions—social, political, economic, religious, and ethnic—which characterize the contemporary Middle East make the likelihood of continued local and regional conflicts over the next two decades very great. In addition to the Arab-Israeli conflict, one could point to the confrontation between Turkey and Greece over Cyprus, the still unresolved and potentially explosive civil war in Lebanon, the smoldering insurgencies in the Persian Gulf and the developing showdown between Algeria and Morocco over the succession to the Spanish Sahara. Other areas of potential local and regional conflict abound. The political order of the area is fragile and a change in regime of any of the major countries of the Middle East (e.g., Saudi Arabia, Egypt or Iran) could lead to unpredictable short-term complications, aggravations, and realignments.

At the present time, and in the most recent past, the Arab-Israeli conflict has been the most prominent issue and has received the lion's share of attention from the international community. The issues involved in this conflict are, as a number of reports in this volume make amply clear, extremely difficult and possibly intractable. As desirable as any reduction in the level of tension or danger of war in this conflict would be, it is not the only pressing danger spot in the Middle East, nor necessarily the most important when viewed within the time frame of the two decades ahead. Nor can one entertain the hope that any partial or reasonably full resolution of this vexing problem would lead to a trouble-free era of U.S.-Middle Eastern relations. By these remarks I do not in any way intend to minimize the importance of American and Western efforts to take an active role in accelerating the resolution of this conflict. Rather, the intention is to highlight a continuing dilemma for American policy and to suggest at least one or two basic guidelines in coming to terms with it.

In most of the overt conflicts enumerated above and in those which are likely to flare up in the Middle East in the foreseeable future, the United States has clear national interests in maintaining friendly and effective relations with all parties involved. While the time has long since passed when we could hope to influence decisively the policies and actions of even the smallest countries in the region, our political presence and influence in terms of the global balance of power in the area is absolutely essential. Any perception on the part of the states in the Middle East that our political will has weakened or that our political and other capabilities are insufficient to protect them from the aggressive designs (direct or indirect) of a rival superpower would quickly lead to disastrously destabilizing political and economic consequences seriously adverse to our national interests. In our continuing active efforts to resolve or at least defuse the various political-military conflicts in the area, we must go beyond palliatives which do not address the basic questions at issue between the various opposing parties. Our national interest lies in a stable and durable peace in the area, be it between Israel and the Arab confrontation states, between Turkey and Greece, or between Morocco and Algeria. There are no easy or quick formulas which can be prescribed. Only a steadfast adherence to this long-term goal is likely to contribute to the achievement of the painful changes and adjustments necessary for an equitable and durable peace in the Middle East.

By the year 2000 the population of the Middle East (213 million in 1975) will be approaching 450 million people. By the end of this century, Egypt's population, for example, will reach a figure of 75 million; and this projection is based on very conservative demographic assumptions. How the Middle East is going to feed its population twenty years hence, and how its national and regional economies are going to provide an adequate and dignified way of life for twice their present number is the overriding critical issue confronting the Middle East and the world. By comparison, all political questions are dwarfed. It is this problem in all its ramifications which should be high on the agenda of the world's chanceries. Unless these problems receive timely and consistent attention, we face the prospect that Professor Boutros-Ghali points to in the conclusion to his own report: that the population explosion on the banks of the Nile and on the flanks of the Atlas mountains will sweep aside any formula for regional peace and stability that we devise.

II

Population Growth in the Middle East and North Africa: Selected Policy Issues

Allan G. Hill

The Political and Economic Importance of Population Policy

Heightened concern about the social and ecological effects of continued economic and population growth both at home and abroad has brought the topic of population size and growth firmly into the center of the political arena. The widespread public interest generated in connection with the work of the Commission on Population and the American Future[1] has been fueled by the publicity surrounding World Population Year and the deliberations of national governments at the World Population Conference in Bucharest, August 1974.[2] In addition, the current shortage of food grains in the world, discussed in detail at the recent Food and Agricultural Organization (FAO) sponsored World Food Conference in Rome, October 1974,[3] and the continuing upward pressure on the price of energy are perceived by many as further evidence of the need for strenuous efforts to slow population growth around the world. Although slower or zero population growth will not lead directly to lower levels of consumption or pollution, nevertheless many lobbyists, including Zero Population Growth, Inc., and the Sierra Club, insist that slower population growth is of prime importance in preserving the quality of the environment and the condition of mankind. The "doom and gloom" lobby in the United States, however wrong-headed, is a force with which policymakers have been forced to reckon because of the breadth of their support and the effectiveness of their propagandists, especially Paul Ehrlich.[4]

Few would criticize the domestic achievements of this group of people who have been instrumental in introducing new legislation on, for example, pollution

7

controls and the use of public lands, but there are dangers when these strongly held views spill over into foreign affairs. For example, the suggestion that coercive policies are necessary to radically alter the large-sized family norm[5] may be acceptable in principle and practice in some states, but difficulties arise when these concepts are taken from one country to another in a propagandist fashion. Deciding a country's "proper" rate of population growth and its "proper" population size is ultimately a national decision in which external interference is generally not welcomed, both because national sovereignty is involved and also because ethnic, religious and linguistic subgroups are generally suspicious of a vigorously pursued population policy, which to them may seem like a novel form of genocide. In any case, there can be no *single* optimum population size or optimum rate of growth for individual countries; rather, what we are usually faced with is a number of apparently optimal conditions each of which is in turn dependent on the subjective choice of a particular welfare function.[6]

In the Middle East these considerations assume a new poignancy because of the extremely high per capita incomes and high rates of natural increase in the less populous oil-producing countries. For these countries, at least at the macroeconomic level, it is more difficult to argue that rapid population growth is inhibiting national economic growth, but of course when we introduce the issue of individual welfare, the case for slower growth is stronger. Second, the argument that rapid population growth in the Middle East is resulting in the speedy depletion of the regions nonrenewable resources is simply not tenable since the very existence of some of the Middle Eastern states is a function of the industrialized world's thirst for oil. Third, all the states of Arabia (except for the Yemen Arab Republic), Libya, and Algeria have small populations both in relation to their total land areas and to their financial resources. An additional factor is that in some of the Gulf states, immigration and not natural increase accounts for over half the total population growth. This influx of population has had positive effects on the region as a whole besides contributing a great deal to the development of the Gulf states themselves. For all these reasons, the bald assertion that Zero Population Growth (ZPG) is a desirable goal in all countries of the Middle East is quite inappropriate.

Despite the difficulties, the decision by some rich countries to shy away from direct involvement in the field of population policy in the less developed countries (LDCs) and especially in the Middle East is regrettable. Countries such as Britain spend as much as possible of their foreign aid on population affairs by giving to the multilateral agencies such as the International Planned Parenthood Federation or the UN Fund for Population Activities, hence buffering themselves from possibly adverse criticism. This policy does not make good sense in the Middle East since, more so than most other world regions, its economy is closely bound up with the Western market economy because of its strategic location and especially because of its huge oil reserves. All the great powers are thus willy-nilly bound up with the economic development of the Middle East and current political arrangements reflect this involvement. One only has to consider the possibility of a Jordan without the United States and the United Kingdom, an Egypt without U.S. grain shipments and a Saudi Arabia without a market for its oil to realize the extent of this interdependence. For Western nations who thus have a vested interest in the economic prosperity and the political stability of the Middle East to abandon the issue of rapid population growth as an impediment to faster economic growth appears to be bordering on the verge of irresponsibility.[7]

The central question or the critical choice facing us is therefore (a) how to assist the Middle East countries appreciate the indirect as well as the direct effects of rapid population growth and (b) how to help these countries take action designed to slow population growth and to mitigate the adverse effects of current rates of natural increase without losing the allegiance and trust of the countries concerned. Some sociologists feel that radical changes in economy and society are a prerequisite for slowing population growth,[8] but it seems desirable to at least attempt to accomplish some of these changes without advocating the inconvenience of full-scale revolution. There are of course doctrinaire objections to this position from the Marxists and other groups,[9] but from the little evidence we have from some Middle Eastern countries which have accomplished a fall in fertility (Egypt, Tunisia, Turkey), the remarkable thing is that revolutionary changes in the sense of the Russian revolution have so far not been, necessary and in fact the direct action that has been taken is relatively mild in relation to the drops in fertility realized. Past policies have tended to focus on one or two components of fertility (e.g., the provision of contraceptives or changing the legal age for marriage), ignoring the surprising range of quite feasible policy alternatives to hand. The World Population Conference in Bucharest may have moved us a little along the road away from the purely family planning approach to slowing population growth, but it remains to be seen if the wise words of the World Plan of Action can be translated into actions and results in the field.

The Demographic Situation in the Middle East and North Africa in the Mid-1970s

In 1975, the area under study contained an estimated 213.3 million people, of whom over one-half lived in Egypt, Iran, and Turkey. As Table II-1 indicates, the demographic circumstances of each individual country differ in detail although there are some broad regional similarities.

1. In every country except Israel and the Occupied Territories,[a] the rate of

aThe "administered territories" is the term used by the Israelis for the Jordanian territory captured during the 1967 June War.

Table II-1
Selected Demographic Parameters for the Countries of the Middle East and North Africa

(Millions) (Rates Per Thousand)	Estimated Population 1975	Birthrate	Death Rate	Rate of Natural Increase	Infant Mortality Rate	Years to Double the Population with Current Rate of Growth
Algeria	16.8	48.7	15.4	32	128	22
Egypt	37.5	37.8	14.0	24	103	29
Libya	2.3	45.0	14.8	30	130	23
Morocco	17.5	46.2	15.7	29	149	24
Sudan	18.3	47.8	17.5	30	141	23
Tunisia	5.7	40.0	13.8	22	128	31
Bahrain	0.3	49.6	18.7	31	138	22
Iran	32.9	45.3	15.6	30	139	23
Iraq	11.1	48.1	14.6	34	99	20
Israel	3.4	26.5	6.7	29	21	24
Jordan-East	1.9	47.6	14.7	33	99	21
Kuwait	1.0	43.6	5.3	38	44	18
Lebanon	2.9	35.0	9.9	25	59	28
Occupied Territories	1.1	47.6	14.7	33	99	21
Oman	.8	49.6	18.7	31	138	22
Qatar	.1	49.6	18.7	31	138	22
Saudi Arabia	5.4	49.5	20.2	29	152	24
Syria	7.3	45.4	15.4	30	93	23
Turkey	39.9	39.4	12.5	25	119	28

U.A. Emirates	.2	49.6	18.7	31	138	22
Yemen Rep.	5.2	49.6	20.6	29	152	24
P.D.R. Yemen	1.7	49.6	20.6	29	152	24
Total =	213.3	Mean = 45.3	Mean = 15.3	Mean = 43	Mean = 116	Mean = 23

Sources:
1. Population Reference Bureau Data Sheets.
2. UN, *Population and Vital Statistics Reports*, Series A.
3. Population Council, *Reports on Population/Family Planning*, No. 2 (December 1974).
4. Supplemented with more accurate data available for Lebanon, Kuwait, and P.D.R. Yemen.

natural increase is close to 3 percent per annum, implying a doubling time of just over twenty-three years if present growth rates continue. This rate is one of the highest values currently on record for any major world region.[10]

2. Many of the populations of the regions, as a result of unchanged or even rising fertility and steadily declining mortality, are very young and bear a high dependency ratio as a result of their youthful age structures. As Table II-2 illustrates, there is a direct relationship between the dependency burden and the rate of population growth: in a stable population with an expectancy of life at birth of forty-five years and a rate of increase of 3 percent per annum, each person of working age is supporting himself and an additional dependent.

3. Partly as a result of this rapid population growth, the urban centers of the Middle East and North Africa have grown at 4.3 percent per annum between 1960 and 1970[11] so that some countries (such as Israel, Kuwait, Lebanon and

Table II-2

Selected Stable Population Parameters Associated with Given Levels of Mortality and Fertility (females only)

$e_o^o = 45$	Annual Rate of Natural Increase						
	0.0	1.0	2.0	2.5	3.0	3.5	4.0
Mean Age	33.9	29.3	25.2	23.4	21.7	20.2	18.8
GRR ($\bar{a} = 29$)	1.55	2.05	2.72	3.12	3.58	4.46	5.15
Dependency Ratio	66	72	84	91	100	111	123
$e_o^o = 55$							
Mean Age	36.0	31.1	26.7	24.8	22.9	21.3	19.7
GRR ($\bar{a} = 29$)	1.31	1.74	2.31	2.65	3.04	3.49	4.0
Dependency Ratio	68	72	81	88	96	105	116
$e_o^o = 65$							
Mean Age	38.0	32.8	28.1	26.0	24.0	22.2	20.6
GRR ($\bar{a} = 29$)	1.15	1.54	2.04	2.34	2.69	3.09	3.54
Dependency Ratio	71	73	80	86	93	102	112

Notes:

1. GRR is the gross reproduction ratio, the average number of daughters born per woman passing through the childbearing ages assuming that her fertility experience will be the same as the recorded period fertility rates.

2. Dependency ratio is the number of persons aged 0-14 plus those over 60 divided by the number of persons aged 15-59, all times 100.

3. The values shown above assume a "South" age-specific pattern of mortality. See A.J. Coale and P. Demeny, *Regional Model Life Tables and Stable Populations* (Princeton, N.J.: Princeton University Press, 1966).

Bahrain) have close to 90 percent of their populations in urban areas, although in the three largest countries the proportion in urban areas is about 40 percent.[12] Hence it is in the cities rather than in the countryside that the effects of the recent rapid increases in population are most apparent.

4. Apart from the universal trend in migration from rural to urban areas, two additional migrations have further contributed to the rapid growth of urban centers and to the problems associated with this growth. The first concerns the emigration of Arabs from Israel and the occupied territories after each of the four Arab-Israeli wars. The numbers are not known precisely but the volume is substantial. In June 1974, the United Nations Relief Works Agency (UNRWA) registered refugees (those displaced by the 1948 hostilities and their descendents) totaled 1,583,646, of whom 38 percent were located in east Jordan.[13] Many refugees have been displaced two or three times but, as a result of the 1967 war, as many as 500,000 people—half of them already refugees—may have fled from their homes.[14] Thousands moved in with friends and relations, mainly in Amman. The war of October 1973 caused fewer dislocations, but the overall effect was to create a feeling of insecurity in rural areas particularly those close to armistice lines, and thus to increase the volume of migration to the urban areas.

Another factor contributing to the mobility of the population of the Arab world has been the growth of the oil producing countries in the Persian Gulf which have attracted Palestinians and northern area Arabs to the region in thousands.[b] The back-flow of information and remittances has been a factor of great but so far unquantified importance in broadening the horizons of residents of remote and poor rural areas and possibly making them receptive to the idea of migration or of social change.

In addition, the migration of workers, especially those with education and skills, from Turkey and North Africa to the European countries has been a significant factor in both the demography and the economic growth of the emigrant countries. For example, it is estimated that there are at least 700,000 Algerians living in Europe, the majority in France. The value of their remittances is estimated to exceed Algeria's export revenue from wine or citrus fruits. Had there not been this emigration, unemployment would have been an extremely serious problem even without the disruptive effect of the war of independence and the subsequent exodus of one million settlers and 500,000 French troops. In the business of exporting labor for foreign exchange, very little is known about the relative gains for the parties concerned, but since international migration to Europe is already closely controlled, in principle it should be possible to develop new policies designed to protect the interests of the migrants and those of the labor exporting country.

[b]In 1970, Kuwait alone contained 147,696 Palestinians and Jordanians, Qatar had 9,583 and Bahrain had 1,338 in 1971. Approximately 50,000 Jordanians and Palestinians live in Saudi Arabia.

5. A final common attribute which all the countries of the Middle East and North Africa share is an enormous potential for future growth resulting from their youthful age structures and the widespread pattern of early and almost universal marriage.[15] To illustrate this point, let us consider a country with a growth rate of 2.6 percent per annum in 1965-1970, a net reproduction rate of 2.07 and a female e_0^0 of 51 years (the average figures for all less developed countries). Reducing fertility to replacement level (NRR 1.0) by 1970-1975 would still result in a 68 percent enlargement in the size of the existing population and a population which in fact would not cease to grow in size until 2095-2100.

Recent Trends in Mortality and Fertility and Their Interpretation

Mortality

The main cause of the high rates of population growth in the Middle East is undoubtedly the rapid post-1945 fall in mortality. For example, in 1937 in Egypt the expectancy of life at birth (e_0^0) for females was 42.1 years; in 1960, the figure was 53.8 years. In Kuwait, the change is even more rapid: the value of e_0^0 for females rose from about 51 in 1955 to 70.6 in 1970.

There is no doubt about the reasons for this spectacular rise in the expectancy of life which is the introduction of Western medicine and Western standards of hygiene into the region. Omran describes in detail the changing causes of death in Egypt,[16] including the recession of the five epidemic diseases of cholera, plagues, typhus, smallpox, and relapsing fever. The World Health Organization describes how the vectors of disease and the diseases themselves were attacked on a systematic basis by outsiders.[17] One of the most important demographic effects has been over the reduction of infant mortality through the control of diarrhea and gastroenteritis; this more than the reduction in adult mortality is producing enlarged cohorts of potential mothers and thus a strong inertial force for continued growth.

Some UNRWA figures bear out the importance of the multilateral agencies: in 1961-63, infant mortality rates per thousand live births were around 100 in camps in Lebanon and Syria, 128 in Gaza. By 1970-72, these figures had been reduced to around 50 and around 80 respectively.[18]

Mortality, however, is a variable which for a number of reasons can only be moved in one direction. As Notestein points out,[19] these reasons include:

1. Survival in good health is the primary objective of any humanitarian activity.
2. Productive and innovative people are not produced from debilitated and disease-ridden stocks.

3. Reduction of infant mortality seems to have the effect of lowering fertility.
4. On a less tangible level, a higher probability of survival between any two ages does seem to reduce the strength of fatalistic attitudes towards life.

Without reservation it is recommended that a forceful attempt be made to further reduce mortality both for its own ends and for the indirect effects it can have on fertility and attitudes towards problem-solving in general. Even in the Gulf states and Kuwait, where per capita expenditures on health and welfare services is as high as anywhere in the world, there is still considerable room for improving the level of infant mortality. At present, the age pattern of mortality is similar but not identical to that of Spain and Portugal early in this century due to the common features of a high incidence of gastroenteritis and diarrhea. Reduction in the importance of these diseases of early infancy can have an effect on fertility by guaranteeing the survival of a small number of offspring to adulthood and thus making redundant the practice of producing a large number of live births to ensure an adequate number of survivors.

Fertility

The level of fertility in any human population is a function of three main variables: the pattern of nuptiality, the level of fecundity, and the extent of contraceptive practice. A highly fecund population in which marriage is early and universal and in which the degree of contraception is small produces the highest level of fertility possible. In the Middle East and North Africa, these three conditions are closer to being met than in many other developing countries, but one must remember that even the levels of fertility indicated in Table II-1 are both well below any theoretical "biological maximum" (if such a thing exists) and below some of the levels achieved in certain European and North American populations in the nineteenth century. Thus the prevailing levels of fertility in the Middle East are the end products of a complex interaction involving, on the one hand, social customs such as those that regulate the age of entry into marriage and the proportions ever-marrying, and, on the other hand, the biological determinants of fertility, such as the health and nutritional status of the population.[20] These two sets of factors are not entirely independent: for example, the conventional minimum age of marriage in the Middle East has been the age of menarche, which in poorly fed populations can occur as late as age eighteen. Among Kuwaiti women, the age of menarche is currently 12.4 years because of improvements in health and nutrition,[21] but we know that in this case, the age of marriage has not fallen with the age of menarche. The practice of lactation, too, is largely a function of social custom. Where breast feeding is widespread and prolonged, inter-birth intervals in a noncontracepting society are longer than in a society which discourages its mothers from lengthy lactation.

For the reasons given above, we can assume that, in the long run, all governments and societies are concerned about increasing the health and nutritional status of their populations so that any reversal of this trend will be unacceptable. Thus, we can be certain that fecundity will be rising steadily throughout the Middle East in the decades ahead, which means that we must hope that changes in social norms will more than compensate for the rising fertility which increased fecundity implies.

The Social Context of Childbearing

It seems reasonable to begin from the stance suggested by Ryder[22] that the level of fertility is determined by the interests of those affected by reproductive decisions and represents an adjustment to prevailing levels of mortality and especially child survival. Hence the high fertility in the Middle East can be interpreted as a rational response to the prevailing ecological and social circumstances *of the past*, but because of lags, it is out of step with the new conditions which prevail today. Following Ryder, it seems plain that in the Middle East in the past, the "intergenerational contract" has been strongly in favor of the parents and society. In other words, the arrangements worked out to ensure high fertility have tended to stress what the child can offer its parents (labor, status, security in old age, and so on) rather than what the parents can offer the children. To parents in the Middle East, the value of children has been and still is high for sound economic and social reasons and at the same time having more children increases these benefits with less than proportional increases in liabilities.[23] Thus what is needed to attain lower fertility is an intervention by society on behalf of children (since children have no rights and little power under existing arrangements) to produce a more equable intergenerational contract.

Before considering ways in which this adjustment can be achieved, let us give some thoughts to the existing social context of fertility in the Middle East.

The context in which individual couples make their reproductive decisions is complex, but possibly it is this very complexity which is responsible for the stability of the outcome through time.[24] From a policy standpoint, the statement is depressing since it points to a difficult task—the manipulation of a host of variables themselves linked to important social subsystems and unlikely to respond in the same way to external changes, such as an increase in the material standard of living or a sharp fall in the level of infant mortality.

If there is any factor of central importance it would seem to be the social role of women. The low independent status of women produces a chain of effects which inevitably result in a high level of fertility. For example, substantial numbers of women have only recently begun to work outside the home in most Arab countries (Table II-3). Deprived of an independent career by social custom,

Table II-3
Status of Women in Selected Countries of the Middle East and North Africa

Country	Date	% Women Aged 10 and Over Illiterate or with No Schooling	% Women Aged 15+ Economically Active	% Women with Secondary or Higher Education
Kuwait				
Kuwaitis	1970	62.7	2.1	2.5
Non-Kuwaitis		34.8	17.4	16.5
Egypt	1966	78.9	6.0	3.7
Lebanon	1970	79.3	14.0	2.1
Israel				
Jews	1971	13.5	32.5	80.1
Non-Jews		34.6*	7.8	52.0*
Syria	1970	73.2	8.5$^+$	0.2
Bahrain^o	1971	53.3	4.1	1.8
Algeria	1971	92.9	6.0	1.5
Iraq	1965	84.4	N.A.	1.0
Jordan	1961	66.0^b	4.4^a	3.6
Iran	1966	81.6	12.2	4.6
Libya	1966	90.9	4.1	0.2
Morocco	1971	94.0	4.5	N.A.
Turkey	1969	67.3	56.8	3.6
Tunisia	1966	89.1	5.5	1.4
U.A.E.	1968	91.1	2.1	N.A.

N.A. − Not available

  * − Both men and women

  + − Aged 10 and over

  o − Bahrainis

  a − Aged 14 and over

  b − Aged 15 and over

Sources:
National censuses supplemented from:
  UN *Demographic Yearbook 1972*, Table 8.
  UN *Demographic Yearbook 1971*, Tables 18 and 19.
  N.H. Youssef, *Women and Work in Developing Societies*, Population Monograph Series # 15 (Berkeley: University of California, 1974).

most girls are accustomed to marrying at an early age and to producing children as soon as possible after marriage. Failure to produce children is likely to lead to divorce: in Syria between 1963 and 1972, almost two-thirds of the divorces registered by Shari'a religious courts concerned childless couples and similar or higher figures are available for other Arab countries. A woman's social status is enhanced by births, especially of sons, so that there is no fixed minimum number of births which a woman is expected to achieve. Society, and in particular the extended family, maintains this pronatalist pressure on the couple right up to the end of the women's childbearing age-span unless clear-cut medical reasons for stopping are apparent. Thus, if forced to select a single factor for the continued high fertility in the region, it would be the social system structured on the assumptions that the independent social role of women must be closely circumscribed; that the prime function of women is to produce and raise children; and that one important measure of her efficiency in performing this task is the number of her offspring, especially sons.

Clearly this is a social system devised and maintained by a male-dominated society. It sounds contradictory but it is nonetheless true that the private interfamilial role of women is important, but the obstacles placed in the way of such women fulfilling this more dominant function in public are formidable.

It may be that the process of modernization is the most important way to simultaneously modify the entire suite of social factors which have a bearing on fertility. In course of modernization, one of the adjustments normally made is the raising of the social status of women, but there are conflicting ideas on how this necessary social change should be accomplished. On the one hand, it is suggested that all vestiges of the old order have to be destroyed before change can come about. Others assert that traditional social systems have already accommodated a great deal of change and are capable of maintaining their basic structures intact while at the same time incorporating some behavioral modifications from the outside. On present evidence, it seems that where society has been sufficiently secularized, or at least where the religious objections to family planning have been met head-on (as in Egypt or Tunisia), Middle Easterners fully appreciate the advantages of smaller families. In Harik's study of a small Egyptian village, most villagers were aware that a large number of children conflicted with their main goals of health, education, and economic security for themselves and their families.[25] He attributed the weakness of the family planning program in his village to organizational factors and indeed, since he was talking both to individuals and to groups, it is noteworthy that the villagers' attitudes and practices were sustained even when exposed to criticism of their peers. The central policy question would seem to be whether Middle Eastern social systems are capable of further adaptation to the extent that they allow the individual, and especially women, a larger public role and more diverse opportunities apart from childrearing.

Prospects for Change

While the description of the current demographic situation in the Middle East presents fewer problems than it used to because of the increase in the quality and the quantity of the available demographic data, it is still extremely difficult to produce firm conclusions about the trends in fertility and their causes. Generalizing from scanty data, it seems that in the twentieth century most of the countries of the Middle East have experienced a slow but steady rise in fertility up to the 1960s. The principal cause of this increase in fertility, we surmise, was the improvement in the health and nutritional status of the population, especially females. In some countries, (e.g., Saudi Arabia, Qatar, and Oman) still at a relatively early stage in the reduction of mortality and morbidity, the birthrate still has some way to go before reaching the very high level achieved in Kuwait. Much of the increase in fertility is thus due to a rise in fecundability and this effect is felt throughout the childbearing age span. Healthier and better-fed women are capable of earlier conception, are subject to higher probabilities of conception and a prolonged period at risk due to the later onset of menopause. An additional factor contributing to rising fertility in recent years has been the tendency for women to wean earlier and to breast-feed for shorter periods than was previously the case. Their reasons for doing this are mixed and include fashion and the propaganda advanced by the makers of dried milk and baby foods, although the makers of powdered milk have now agreed to include in their advertizing a statement that breast milk is a superior source of nutrition for babies. In any case, the net effect of earlier weaning is to reduce the length of the period of postpartum amenorrhea and to shorten the inter-birth intervals in a noncontracepting population.

These effects cannot continue to raise fecundability indefinitely, but at present it seems that the effects of more widespread contraceptive use are being overshadowed as a result of rising fertility in the early years of marriage. Thus, whether a country is experiencing a fall in fertility or not depends both on the stage it has reached in terms of the reduction of morbidity and improvement in nutrition and on the extent of contraceptive use in the population. To illustrate from the example of the Kuwaitis, it seems that their fertility rose steadily from the early 1960s and reached a peak in the late 1960s due to the achievement of extremely low levels of mortality and remarkable levels of nutrition.[26] This high level of fecundability was combined with almost no contraceptive use producing a birthrate in the low fifties. In the 1970s, fecundability has apparently continued to rise but so has the use of contraception among older, high-parity women. At present, the effect of the use of contraceptives has been to slightly reduce fertility and to offset some of the effects of rising fecundability.

Of course not all the populations in the Middle East are like the Kuwaitis, but the general principle of improvements in health and welfare contributing positively to fertility through the biological component of reproduction and the social changes contributing negatively to fertility through increased use of contraception has considerable generality. The timing of the changes (biological and social) is critical in the determination of the period fertility rates of the population.

In addition to these two sets of factors which affect marital fertility, we have to remember that changes in the size of the population at risk also affect fertility. In almost all of the countries of the region, Algeria being a notable exception, the mean age of marriage for girls is rising and the proportions ever marrying are gradually falling. There seems no reason to expect any reverse in the direction of these changes: in fact, unless the proportions marrying alter fairly considerably in the future, we are unlikely to see a significant drop in fertility because of the imperfections involved in the methods and practice of contraception. At the same time, it is difficult to imagine most Middle Easterners moving to a situation where celibacy is the norm rather than the exception and policies designed to foster this change would undoubtedly collide head-on with a number of traditional and strongly-held views in most sections of society.

In conclusion, since it seems that mortality and especially infant mortality will continue to decline and possibly at an accelerated rate, the ratio of natural increase for the population of the Middle East as a whole is unlikely to fall dramatically in the near future. For countries like Algeria, Egypt, and Syria, already having difficulty accommodating their annual population increment, the problems will probably become worse before they get any better. It is important to appreciate the magnitude of the effects of continued growth before considering the opportunities for intervention.

The Course of Future Growth

Projecting Population Growth

It is clearly impossible to predict with any great degree of accuracy the size and composition of any of the national populations of the Middle East. Apart from the problem of predicting the future course of mortality and fertility, we are up against the highly volatile factors of migration and shifting political boundaries which are much more of a problem in the highly interdependent and strife-prone Middle East than in some other world regions. What we can do, however, is to make a number of clearly defined assumptions about the course of future growth and to incorporate these assumptions into a number of projection models. One of the most important assumptions will be to exclude international migration in most of the projections with the important exceptions of the Gulf states (including Kuwait), Israel, and Turkey. This is not to suggest that external migration is neither a possibility nor a policy variable: in certain cases, such as Egypt, external migration could bring numerous regional and domestic benefits and in several countries (like Turkey, Kuwait, and Algeria), migration (both immigration and emigration) is already making a positive contribution to economic development. In most cases however, it is felt that a greatly increased volume of international migration within the Middle East is likely to create a number of additional political complications which at present the Arab states are not prepared to accept. The most difficult population to project is the Palestinians, many of them refugees three times over. Until we have the results of the mooted census of the Palestinians, and some further political decisions on their long-term future, projections for them based on present data have a spurious accuracy.

In the projections, it has been assumed that the political boundaries as they stand at present will persist in the foreseeable future, i.e., the thirty years ahead covered by the projections. This may not hold in several parts of the region, especially in the Levant. To deal with this problem, separate projections are presented for the total refugee population of Palestine at present registered with the UN Relief and Works Agency (UNRWA). There are a large number of different categories into which refugees are placed by UNRWA in an attempt to distinguish degrees of need, and the statistics are often misleading and inaccurate: indeed some refugees are completely self-sufficient but they are still registered with the agency while others eligible for registration are not in fact registered. The value of projecting the registered UNRWA population is that it does provide some indication of the total number of the persons the international community, including the Arabs and the Israelis, must consider in their future plans. For the same reasons, the populations of the occupied territories have been treated separately since it is not out of the question that they may form the core of a new state in the near future.

The Future Course of Mortality

In the projections, it has been assumed that mortality levels will continue their downward trend. This may seem rash in view of the current concern about the world's food resources, but with the great wealth of many of the Arab countries it seems most unlikely that they will be unable to purchase foodstuffs on the world market even if their own agricultural production was affected in some catastrophic way. Agricultural production in the Middle East is on the whole not very high and the potential for extending and intensifying production is very great everywhere except in Egypt.[27] Thus major Malthusian checks to the downward trend in mortality are unlikely in the next thirty years.

Broadly the same can be said about the checks stemming from disease epidemics and pandemics. With a large amount of foreign assistance, the Middle

Eastern countries have taken a wide variety of public health measures, such as routine inoculations and improvements in sanitation, which make the recurrence of the age-old killers such as cholera, smallpox, yellow fever, typhoid, and others less and less likely as the century proceeds.

The Future Course of Fertility

The future trend of fertility in any human population is very much more difficult to foresee than the trend of mortality. For one reason, there are many more factors involved, some of them social and psychological in nature, which rarely follow a simple pattern of change. Another reason is that there are as yet only inadequate models for describing fertility experience so that in dealing with populations which have poor or deficient statistics, there is no foolproof way of filling in gaps in the information which we need for our population projections. A third reason for uncertainty is that changes in fertility occur simultaneously to cohorts and to the population at large considered at a single moment in time. Thus, an overall improvement in welfare, particularly in the level of nutrition, is going to raise the fecundity of all women simultaneously, but a trend towards a later age of first marriage will affect younger cohorts of women much more than older cohorts. These technicalities are unfortunately very important since the effect of fertility on the size and composition of a population is much more pronounced than the effect of mortality.[28] Some further explanation of the general procedures adopted in making the projections is needed here: more specific descriptions for individual countries are presented in Appendix IIA.

Two basic pieces of information are needed for population projections based on the components of growth procedure. First, one needs an overall level of fertility for each of the time periods under consideration: the usual measure is total fertility which, during a period of unchanging fertility, is equivalent to the average number of children ever born to women at their menopause. Second, one needs an indication of the distribution of fertility by age. Two populations with the same total fertility but with different age patterns of fertility grow at different rates: the one with the lower mean age of its fertility schedule grows more rapidly. For most countries of the Middle East, it is possible to obtain a reasonable estimate of total fertility using indirect methods as well as published statistics.[29] The age distribution of fertility is harder to discover. There is a method for constructing model fertility schedules by making assumptions about the values of three important components of fertility—the youngest age at which childbearing begins, the rate of entry into marriage relative to some standard, and the degree of contraception practiced by the population.[30] Sadly, the model schedules obtained have to be revised to take account of cohort effects, particularly delays in the age of marriage and contraception amongst older women, but they have proved useful in making the projections for the region. In general, the observed age pattern of fertility has been used at the outset, but it has been assumed that later marriage, a slower rate of entry into marriage, and an increasing degree of control over conception will all make themselves felt in the region in the next thirty years, although of course at very different rates for individual countries.

The projections are an attempt to present the most likely outcome given present policies and the present degree of provision for the future. An alternative and equally valid procedure would have been to project the populations assuming that fertility as it stands at present would remain unchanged in the future. This choice is useful if the aim of the projection is to demonstrate the implications of present policies, presumably in the hope that the projections themselves will be instrumental in modifying these policies. Here it was assumed that we are aware of the implications of a continuation of present trends,[31] and that the main aim of the projections was, first of all, to demonstrate the approximate size and nature of the populations of the Middle East in the future, and second, to show what kind of extra effort would be needed to achieve radically different results from those which are contained in the projections. A subsidiary aim is to indicate the importance of the momentum effect in population growth, including the implausibility of some of the targets adopted by the governments of Middle Eastern countries for their future growth.

Projection Results

The process of population projection yields a large amount of useful information, only a small part of which can be used and referred to here. Summaries of the projection results are attached at the end of this section.

By the year 2000, almost all of the Arab populations of the region will have at least doubled in size (Table II-4). Even already crowded Egypt will have a population double its present size, and that assumes that fertility will fall fairly steeply in the decades ahead. The overall impression reached is that the gross imbalance between area, population, and wealth which exists today will be greatly exaggerated by the year 2000, so much so that it is difficult not to foresee a large degree of international migration as the only possibility for achieving a more equable distribution in the long run. It seems unlikely that countries like Saudi Arabia (870,000 square miles) or Libya (679,000 square miles) will be able to resist the political, moral, and physical pressures of the overcrowded and relatively poor demographic giants, such as Turkey and Egypt, in the decades ahead. One of the most positive measures which the Arab countries as a bloc could consider concerns not only the redistribution of wealth but also the redistribution of people. At present, there are considerable political difficulties involved in large-scale international migration, but in this region the populations have a greater cultural cohesion than in areas such as Southeast Asia.

Table II-4
Estimated Future Populations of the Middle East and North Africa*
(Millions)

	1975	1980	1985	1990	1995	2000
Algeria	16.40	19.51	22.93	26.44	29.89	33.04
Egypt	37.70	42.46	47.90	53.57	58.67	62.82
Iran	33.35	39.35	46.41	54.35	63.16	72.48
Iraq	10.45	12.28	14.49	16.97	19.71	22.70
Israel: Jews	2.97	3.49	3.98	4.46	4.92	5.35
Israel: Non-Jews	.53	.64	.77	.92	1.09	1.26
Jordan: East	1.92	2.27	2.70	3.17	3.68	4.23
Jordan: West and Gaza	1.11	1.27	1.48	1.71	1.95	2.20
Kuwait	.80	.93	1.09	1.26	1.46	1.67
Lebanon	2.46	2.78	3.11	3.48	3.84	4.18
Libya	2.14	2.48	2.86	3.28	3.74	4.23
Morocco	17.86	20.45	23.60	27.42	31.70	36.13
Palestine Refugees	1.66	1.92	2.22	2.59	3.03	3.57
Syria	7.33	8.57	10.01	11.64	13.45	15.42
Tunisia	5.86	6.63	7.51	8.62	9.74	10.84
Turkey	40.53	44.63	48.47	52.54	56.99	61.64
Other countries either with small populations or with poor demographic data for which projections are less reliable						
Bahrain	.25	.30	.35	.42	.50	.60
Oman	.76	.89	1.03	1.20	1.39	1.62
Qatar	.13	.16	.19	.22	.27	.32
Saudi Arabia	5.60	6.40	7.40	8.60	9.90	11.50
South Yemen	1.69	1.96	2.28	2.65	3.08	3.58
U.A.E.	.24	.29	.35	.43	.53	.65
Yemen	5.40	6.20	7.20	8.30	9.60	11.10
Grand Total	197.14	225.86	258.33	294.24	332.29	371.13

*For notes on sources and assumptions, see Appendix IIA.

There is of course great cultural and ethnic diversity in the Middle East, but the possibilities for arranging profitable and acceptable exchanges of people seem much brighter in the Middle East than elsewhere.

Another important conclusion from the projections is the importance of slowing the rate of natural increase, if only because of the beneficial effects which it has on the age structure of a population: there are obvious and causal links between the statistics presented in Tables II-5 and II-6. In the latter table, we find that in the year 2000, the average Lebanese worker will be supporting

Table II-5
Projected Population Growth Rates in the Middle East and North Africa, 1965-2000*
(Percentage per annum)

	1965-70	1975-80	1985-90	1995-2000
Algeria	3.2	3.5	2.8	2.0
Egypt	2.4	2.4	2.2	1.4
Iran	2.8	3.3	3.2	2.8
Iraq	2.6	3.2	3.2	2.8
Israel: Jews	3.3	3.2	2.2	1.7
Israel: Non-Jews	4.0	3.8	3.6	3.0
Jordan: East	3.2	3.4	3.2	2.8
Jordan: West and Gaza	2.6	2.8	2.9	2.4
Kuwait	9.1	3.1	3.0	2.7
Lebanon	2.3	2.3	2.2	1.7
Libya	2.8	2.9	2.7	2.5
Morocco	2.3	2.7	3.0	2.6
Palestine Refugees	2.8	2.9	3.0	3.1
Syria	3.2	3.1	3.0	2.7
Tunisia	2.5	2.5	2.7	2.1
Turkey	2.7	1.9	1.6	1.6

*For sources and notes, see Appendix IIA.

just 0.61 dependents, whereas his Syrian counterpart will be carrying a much greater dependency burden—0.79 dependents on average. Further, the potential for future reproduction remains very high in the countries with slowly falling fertility. The gross reproduction rate (Table II-7) tells us how many daughters will on average be born to each woman assuming no mortality among mothers or daughters. Thus, even by the year 2000, it seems that each Iraqi woman will still be producing 2.49 daughters and potential mothers although we must remember that this figure would be higher if we are to consider the number of daughters born to married women instead of daughters born to all women.

Finally, it is worth looking closely at the estimates for the future populations of the Levant. From the standpoint of the Israeli Jews, it would seem that their pronatalist population policy is proposing unrealistic and unobtainable goals. Any attempt to outgrow the neighboring Arabs is clearly doomed to failure regardless of the volume of Jewish immigration. Even with an optimistic figure for annual immigration (say 70,000 *per annum* forever), the total Jewish population of pre-1967 Israel would amount to only 4.86 million people at the end of 1990.[c]

[c]Immigration in 1974 fell to just over 32,000 while emigration rose to 18,000, making the point that the volume of immigration to Israel is both volatile and subject to factors largely beyond Israeli control.

Table II-6

Projected Dependency Ratios in the Middle East and North Africa, 1970-2000*

(Persons aged 0-14 and 65+ per person 15-64)

	1970	1980	1990	2000
Algeria	1.01	1.01	.91	.67
Egypt	.85	.78	.73	.59
Iran	.92	.92	.93	.81
Iraq	1.06	.91	.94	.84
Israel: Jews	.59	.68	.68	.57
Israel: Non-Jews	1.16	1.05	.94	.83
Jordan: East	1.00	.99	.94	.80
Jordan: West and Gaza	1.19	.84	.78	.71
Kuwait**	1.18	1.04	.86	.72
Lebanon	.96	.79	.69	.61
Libya	.92	.89	.83	.75
Morocco	1.20	1.02	.81	.80
Palestine Refugees	.84	.86	.84	.85
Syria	1.10	.98	.88	.79
Tunisia	.96	.83	.79	.73
Turkey	.84	.82	.60	.56

*For sources and notes, see Appendix IIA.
**Kuwaitis only

Selected Country Positions on Population Policy

In the Middle East and North Africa, ten countries have a firm population policy which is stated explicitly and is being acted on. Five of these countries (Morocco, Tunisia, Egypt, Turkey, and Iran) all want to reduce their population growth rates: Israel, Qatar, Libya, Algeria, and Saudi Arabia are officially pronatalist. In the other countries of the region there may be no explicitly stated population policy but the actions and statements of the government and other semi-official agencies can be interpreted as an implicit position on population policy (Table II-9).[32]

Israel

Following the enactment of the Law of Return shortly after the founding of the state in 1948, Israel has tried to build up the Jewish population in the Middle East both as a response to external factors such as the loss of at least five million Jews in the holocaust of the Second World War, but also in response to the need

Table II-7
Projected Values for the Gross Reproduction Rate in the Middle East and North Africa, 1975-2000*

	1975-1980	1985-1990	1995-2000
Algeria	3.66	2.68	1.71
Egypt	2.62	2.19	1.46
Iran	3.12	2.76	2.19
Iraq	3.51	2.98	2.49
Israel: Jews	1.66	1.51	1.32
Israel: Non-Jews	3.41	2.83	2.24
Jordan: East	3.07	2.63	2.19
Jordan: West and Gaza	2.54	2.19	1.85
Kuwait**	3.05	2.41	1.78
Lebanon	2.44	1.95	1.46
Libya	3.09	2.63	2.19
Morocco	3.23	2.75	2.26
Palestine Refugees	2.58	2.58	2.58
Syria	3.49	2.83	2.29
Tunisia	3.02	2.39	1.90
Turkey	2.15	1.37	1.22

*For notes on sources and assumptions, see Appendix IIA.
**Kuwaitis only

to settle the newly acquired territory in Palestine. The principal method of population growth has of course been immigration: between independence in 1948 and the end of 1971, 60 percent of the growth of the Jewish population was due to immigration. Despite this impressive achievement, the small size of the Jewish population (2.6 million) is still a matter of national concern, particularly as there is a strong indication that the Jewish population in Israel is moving towards the norm of smaller families and hence a lower level of fertility which is unlikely to be revised upwards in the foreseeable future.[33] This trend also applies to the new immigrants, including those from Asia and Africa who displayed high fertility in their area of origin.

By comparison, the non-Jews in Israel have been growing at very high rates of natural increase. Period rates can be deceptive, but let us compare the gross reproduction rates of the Jews and non-Jews in recent years. Since the mid-1950s, the GRR for the Jews has been hovering at about 1.65 while the rate for the non-Jews has fluctuated a little but has always been between 3.5 and 4.1. Thus the doubling time for the Jewish population of Israel is about thirty-nine years at present rates of natural increase and assuming no further migration, whereas the doubling time for the non-Jews is just over seventeen years. By the

Table II-8
The Population of the Levant in 1985
(Thousands)

	Jews	Arabs	Total
Israel (pre-1967 area)	3,983	1.985	5,968
West Bank and Gaza occupied since 1967	–	1,477	1,477
Palestinians outside these areas	–	2,222	2,222
East Jordan	–	2,697	2,697
Lebanon	–	3,110	3,110
Total	3,983	11,491	15,474
Percentage	25.7	74.3	100

year 2020, non-Jews will constitute half of the population of Israel as defined by the pre-1967 boundaries, assuming no change in the present rates of natural increase.

It is in response to these kinds of challenges that the government of Israel has been forced to frame a population policy, although it must be remembered that there is a strong body of religious feeling which supports a larger world Jewish population as well as an enlarged population of Jews in Israel and which predates the formulation of a national policy. The main aim of this policy, whose origins are traced in detail by Friedlander,[34] has been to encourage the growth of the Jewish population of Israel by supporting immigration and by trying to prevent further falls in the birthrate. Unfortunately, the influx of immigrants is not easy to control since the rate of immigration depends very much on external factors. It seems, too, that the birthrate will continue its downward track despite the efforts of the Natality Committee set up in 1962. In its report published in April 1966 and summarized in English by Friedlander,[35] the most important discussion centered on the issue of induced abortion. At present, contraceptive services are not officially promoted by the government although most private physicians can provide them for their patients. The abortion laws are, however, fairly liberal so that many women (we do not know how many) are using induced abortion as a way of achieving a small completed family size. The Demographic Center in the Prime Minister's Office has, as one of its projects, the investigation of the problem of large numbers of induced abortions. Whether any major change in the law will stem from these inquiries remains to be seen.

In any event, the domestic policy of the Jews in Israel on abortion and contraception is not a topic of major concern to outsiders. If the Israelis do want to begin a program of family planning through contraception rather than by abortion, they have both the technical and the administrative resources to carry it through. Of much more concern to outsiders is the control of immigration to

Table II-9

Summary of Official Policy and Action Concerning Population Policy

Type of Policy	Strength of Policy Implementation:		
	Weak	Moderate	Strong
Strongly in favor of slower growth	Morocco	Egypt Iran	Tunisia Turkey
Mildly in favor of slower growth	P.D.R. Yemen Yemen	Syria Jordan Lebanon	
Mildly in favor of continued rate of growth	Oman Iraq	Kuwait Bahrain U.A.E.	
Strongly in favor of continued or more rapid growth	Libya PLO	Saudi Qatar Algeria	Israel (Jews)

Sources:

1. Reports on Population/Family Planning, No. 2 (September 1973).

2. Reports on Population/Family Planning, No. 15 (January 1974).

3. *Studies in Family Planning* 5,1 (January 1974): 2-12.

4. World Population Conference 1974, *Report on the Second Enquiry Among Governments on Population and Development*, UN Economic and Social Council, E/CN.9/303.

5. "A Report on Bucharest," *Studies in Family Planning* 5,12 (December 1974).

6. UN, ECWA, *Final Report of the Post-World Population Conference Consultation for the ECWA Region*, 1975.

Israel: both the great powers and the inhabitants of the Middle East are more concerned with the influx and distribution of new Jewish settlers than with the issue of family planning for the Israelis. Future Israeli policy on Jewish settlements on the West Bank and on the Golan Heights are of much greater significance since this policy touches on the core of the Middle East problem, which is the national aspirations of the Palestinians and their quest for the territorial expression of those aspirations.

Egypt

While the case of Israel serves to illustrate the point that quite strong political, moral, and religious inducements cannot force couples to raise their family size norms when they clearly intend to do otherwise, the example of Egypt shows that couples are capable of lowering their fertility even when the official government family planning program is both small and relatively inefficient. Official statistics show that there has been a steady decline in the birthrate in Egypt since 1963, although the official figures probably underestimate the absolute level of the birthrate by about one point per thousand because of uncertainties about the size of the denominator. In 1960, the crude birthrate was estimated at 45 per thousand.[36] The last full census was taken in 1960, while the census taken in 1966 was taken only on a sample basis. The trend in fertility does seem to be downward although at a slow rate: in the mid-1970s the crude birthrate was about 38 per thousand, still large enough to give a rate of natural increase of about 2.4 percent per annum. Only a small part of the decline can be attributed to the government family planning program since the decline had set in before the program took to the field early in 1966 and at present only about 6 percent of the target population of married women aged 15-45 have been covered by the program.[37] Dropout rates are high and administrative inefficiencies are widespread, some of them due to external factors. For instance, a major problem associated with the severing of relations with the United States in 1967 was the interruption in the supply of contraceptive materials and a consequent loss of clients. But there are some basic weaknesses inherent in the government's program which will be difficult to eradicate in the future. One of the ways in which doctors were persuaded to participate in the family planning program was to allow them to make a small commission on the sale of pills and to receive a payment for the insertion of an IUD. The pills were sold in clinics at £E0.05 per cycle compared to a charge of £E0.20 in pharmacies, while the fee paid to doctors for the insertion of an IUD was £E1.00, a sum usually split among other assistants at the clinic as well as the doctors. Most program administrators now regret the introduction of the incentive system, which introduced a number of malpractices into the system including the falsification of records, but perhaps more important, which prevented the family planning services from becoming an integral part of the health services provided by the state.[38]

Nevertheless, official endorsement of family planning did a lot to overcome the resistance of the traditionalists and raise the level of public awareness about the population problem in general and about family planning in particular. The discussion of the subject since the 1952 revolution and the overall reorientation of public and private attitudes in the years following the revolution has created an atmosphere in which people are both willing and eager for contraceptive services and advice. Perhaps the most telling manifestation of these new attitudes is the rash of induced abortions which the city hospitals are having to deal with in the 1970s—some of the cases stemming from clumsy attempts by mothers to terminate their own pregnancies.[39] In such circumstances, one would expect a family planning program to be certain of success, but there are some considerable difficulties facing the official program.

First, within the Supreme Council for Population and Family Planning, there is a feeling that the family planning program has in the past in some way neglected the broader issues of social and economic development which must accompany the trend towards reduced fertility. In part, this attitude is a reflection of attitudes prevalent in some Socialist or radically-oriented Third

World countries which were aired at some length at the World Population Conference in 1974. Another reason for the development of these attitudes is the relatively poor response which the family planning program was able to elicit in some rural areas. Dr. Wafiq Hassouna, chief expert in social planning in the Institute of National Planning, concludes from some of his own studies that the time is not yet ripe to take family planning services to the people.[40] Other straws in the wind mentioned by government officials included the desire by the people to produce soldiers for the war with Israel, the responsibilities of Egypt to provide the Arab world with skilled persons and to fill the "vacuum" which surrounds the country. Regardless of their illogicality, it is important to realize that the emergence of these reasons is in itself evidence that the family planning program is running into opposition among senior officials in the government. The reasons for the opposition, a better word would be indifference, are complex and stem from the domestic political problems facing Egypt. The ten year plan (1973-1982) for the National Population and Family Planning Policy looks like an attempt to decentralize the whole family planning movement by making each of the factors referred to in the National Plan the responsibility of individual ministries.[41] This is probably a reflection of sincerely held beliefs rather than a political maneuver, but it raises some questions about the future control of the family planning movement. In particular, it suggests a long-term focus when what is apparently needed is a short-term orientation. In the cities and among high parity women, the demand for family planning services is strong: witness the rising incidence of induced abortion and the strong demand for family planning services encountered by the volunteer Egyptian Family Planning Association and some government clinics.[42]

For the future, it seems that we sorely need some high quality research on the effectiveness of family planning services in Egypt: an illuminating comparison would be between the government services and the unofficial programs.[d] This research is urgently needed since it looks as if the official program may be dumped or sidelined for the wrong reasons. Egypt seems to be a prime example of a country where outside help is needed to evaluate the work already carried out and to examine priorities for the future. A coherent program of education, research, and technical assistance would go a long way to redirect indigenous efforts and to eliminate some of the wrong-headedness which seems to be creeping into official policy.

Turkey

In the Turkish case, the decision to support family planning services dates from April 1965, when the state reversed the earlier policy of support for an enlarged

---

[d]A crude comparison of the costs per new acceptor in 1973 is illuminating: in the national program, each new acceptor "cost" about E234.66 while in the private program, the comparable figure was E1.86.

population, which was in part a response to the heavy war losses incurred in connection with both world wars. The 1965 law permits the promotion and sale of contraceptives, but outlaws castration and sterilization. Abortion is only permissible for medical reasons and a list of these acceptable reasons was published in 1967.[43]

One of the central problems facing the organizers of the Turkish family planning program is the size and dispersion of the population. As a result of the sheer size of the country (301,302 square miles), there are strong regional variations in income, educational levels, and other socioeconomic indicators which produce widely differing fertility levels and attitudes to family planning. The birthrate in the rural areas of the east was estimated at 56 per thousand in 1960 whereas the figure for the metropolitan areas was only 23.7.[44] As a response to these geographical difficulties associated with spreading family planning throughout Turkey, the General Directorate of Family Planning, a section within the Ministry of Health, decided to try to supply contraceptive services and advice to the rural population by means of mobile teams of educators and physicians. An additional 572 fixed clinics have been set up. In both facilities, the main contraceptive recommended has been the interuterine device (IUD). In addition to the government program, independent agencies, such as the Turkish Family Planning Association and the Development Foundation of Turkey, have been extensively involved in the delivery of family planning services.[45] Despite their efforts, it seems that only 2.5 percent of the married women aged 15-44 were contraceptive users in 1974.[46]

From the demographic standpoint, there does seem to be convincing evidence that the Turkish birthrate is declining and at a moderate rate. Not all of this effect can be attributed to the family planning program, but undoubtedly it has been instrumental in making control easier for some women and also in preparing the way for other women to become contraceptive users. Naturally, it will be some time before the farmers of the east reduce their fertility to the levels which prevail in Turkey's urban areas today, but there seems no reason not to expect the diffusion of family planning to follow the route prepared by other eastward-moving innovations.[47] Turkey has experienced a much longer and possibly more radical period of social and economic change than either Iran or Egypt, which is why in the projection, fertility is predicted as falling rapidly in the decades ahead.

Lebanon

Public and official interest in population policy is growing steadily in Lebanon where it has become conventional not to discuss population questions because of their strong political overtones.[48,49] The first and last complete census conducted in 1932 by the French formed the basis for the compilation of the political constituencies for the Lebanese Chamber of Deputies and since then there has been little effort made to overhaul the confessional balance in the Chamber, especially amongst the Christians, despite drastic demographic changes.[50] An additional barrier to a free discussion of population policy is the position of the Maronite Christians on birth control: their doctrinal attitude is now identical to that of the Church of Rome. Despite these institutional difficulties, some good demographic information is now available for Lebanon because of a series of sample surveys conducted by the government statistical service.[51] In addition, the Lebanese Family Planning Association, itself operating illegally in the country, has just finished a survey of fertility and contraceptive practice with the assistance of the statistical service.[52]

These data clearly show what we had previously suspected: that the Lebanese probably lead the Arab world in the effective use of contraceptive techniques. The control of conception coupled with the more "Western" nuptiality patterns (later age of first marriage and a larger proportion permanently celibate than in the rest of the Arab world) produces a rate of natural increase which is quite modest (2.4 percent per annum) and likely to decline in the near future.

At present, assistance to couples who want contraceptive advice is unevenly spread throughout the country because of the law against the dissemination of contraceptive techniques and devices. In fact, many of the clinics of the Lebanese Family Planning Association are attached to government hospitals or clinics and the Minister of Health has been cooperating with the Association in a number of unofficial ways. The law itself is not the prime obstacle preventing the further spread of family planning in the state. Much more important are the political factors implicit in any discussion of population growth and distribution. A new draft bill, covering both induced abortion and family planning, has been on the president's desk for over a year, but he refuses to sign it because of the opposition it is likely to generate from among the ranks of the Maronites, the president's most powerful and important supporters. The present situation is tolerable for the middle and upper classes and for those sections of the urban poor who happen to live close to a hospital or clinic in which the Family Planning Association is active, but for large sections of the population who, according to the results of the fertility study, generally want fewer children than they have, the situation is very unsatisfactory. Quite how much opposition the new bill is likely to encounter is uncertain: like many aspects of life in Lebanon, it seems that there is a wide gap between official attitudes and actual practice. In the past, the Lebanese solution has been to let sleeping dogs lie until a crisis situation develops. At present, the crisis of population growth is dwarfed by the internal and external security question so that there is little to be gained from increasing pressure on the government to change the law on abortion and family planning: it seems more important to assist the Family Planning Association to expand the range and capacity of its services within existing arrangements.

A problem of at least equal significance to the Lebanese is the position and numbers of foreigners resident in the state. These fall into two main groups: first, there are the immigrants from the Arab countries, especially the Syrians and the Palestinians, who carry with them a very heavy political freight and create enormous difficulties for the Lebanese. Second, there are the other aliens, many of them Europeans and Americans, who are in Beirut because of the city's location, climate, and regional importance. Both groups are growing annually (178,000 in 1970) and are largely beyond the control of the Lebanese government, even if control was deemed necessary. Of the two groups, the first is of course of much greater immediate significance: many Lebanese would like to restrict the military and political strength of the Palestinians but find it impossible because of political pressures from the other Arab countries, particularly Syria. The position of the Palestinians will depend very much on the situation on the west bank of Jordan. Presumably some of the camp population of refugees could be persuaded to move to an independent Palestinian state on the west bank but it seems less likely that the Palestinians living outside the camps in Lebanon would want to start a new life in uncertain political and economic circumstances.

The civil strife of 1975 has complicated the problems in a number of ways. On the one hand, the Israeli incursions on the south have contributed to the migration from the south of poor farmers, mostly Shi'a Muslims. Certainly, policies designed to reduce the exodus of migrants or migration to Beirut, or the whole topic of a national population policy, are not issues which can be discussed at present. One suggestion emerging from the chaos is that the Muslims may drop their demands for a census and consequent reallocation of political power in exchange for a 50:50 share in the government and administration. The demography of Lebanon is very much a live issue but no one wants his judgment clouded by facts at the present stage of negotiation.

Kuwait

Since the discovery of oil in 1938, Kuwait has been heavily dependent on all types of expatriate labor in the oil industry and in the economy as a whole. After 1948, when the number of Palestinians in the state started to grow significantly, the Kuwaitis introduced a number of controls over immigration which have remained largely unaltered to the present day. They include a system of work permits and residence visas and a policy of careful discrimination between the native born Kuwaitis and the immigrant population within the state. Almost none of the immigrants have been offered Kuwaiti nationality, the major exception to this rule being the foreign wives of Kuwaitis.[53] Much of the immigration policy is conducted on an ad hoc basis and consists of trying to maintain a balance between the citizens and the aliens in the ratio of 45:55, while at the same responding to outside pressures to accept as many as possible of the northern area Arabs, especially the Palestinians. After each war, for example, there is a surge of people into Kuwait, but thereafter the numbers are gradually reduced by the simple expedient of not reissuing the necessary work permits or visas. The work permit is an effective method of control since over one-third of all jobs are in the public sector.

Offering Kuwaiti nationality to some of the immigrants would seem an obvious solution to many of Kuwait's problems, but it remains a fairly remote possibility for a number of reasons. First, the largest single immigrant group most eligible for nationalization because of their long association with Kuwait is composed of the Jordanians and Palestinians. In 1975, they comprised about 40 percent of the non-Kuwaiti population (210,000 people), over one-fifth of the total population of Kuwait. Many immigrants, such as the Jordanians and the Palestinians, are better educated and more skilled than their Kuwaiti counterparts, who occupy more senior positions and therefore stand to be displaced by nationalized non-Kuwaitis. Finally, the cost of extending citizenship would be substantial since all the benefits available to the Kuwaitis (home loans, higher salaries, early retirement schemes, free medical and education schemes, etc.) should also have to be extended to the newly naturalized.

In its attitudes towards contraception and abortion, the government seems to have tacitly accepted the need for both types of service despite the lack of enabling legislation. Contraceptives are on open sale in supermarkets and pharmacies, but these are probably not the principal sources of such material. The all-embracing and free government health service provides devices and information to both Kuwaitis and non-Kuwaitis through its extensive network of clinics and hospitals. There is no attempt to promote the use of contraceptives in any propagandist manner but, nevertheless, older high parity women seem to be adopting contraception of their own volition. Few of the younger and newly married Kuwaitis show much inclination to limit their family sizes so far. There is some reluctance among physicians in the state to administer induced abortions for both ethical and religious reasons, but the maternity hospital specializing in complicated maternity cases is seeing some cases arising from self-induced abortion attempts.[54] At any rate, there seems to be no legal obstacle to the effective spread of contraception in the state although the issue of abortion is likely to be much more contentious.

Kuwait thus seems to be providing us with a model which is of considerable interest to the rest of the Middle East since its implicit population policy is one to which many nations pay lip-service. From the developmental point of view, the interesting feature of Kuwait is that younger women, despite their increased independence and education, have not as yet broken away from the strongly pronatalist pressures stemming from the extended family and the broader social system. With low mortality and an excellent health service including a fully integrated system of family planning clinics, one is faced with what would seem ideal conditions for the successful adoption of the smaller family norm. The failure of this norm to take root in Kuwait so far is one of the reasons why one must be concerned at the high rates of population growth elsewhere in the Middle East.

Other Countries

Even for the Middle Eastern countries which have taken a stance on population matters, there is a considerable gap between expressed policy and its implementation. Four countries have come out strongly in favor of continued growth—Saudi Arabia, Qatar, Algeria, and Libya—and to this group we must add the Palestinian Liberation Organization (PLO). The Saudis, partly as a result of the disappointingly small number of Saudis discovered by the census of September 1974, have banned contraceptive imports and have pronounced (erroneously) that contraception under all circumstances is contrary to the teaching of Islam. These measures alone are probably inadequate to greatly affect fertility: the reduction of infant and general mortality will probably contribute more to the growth of Saudi population. So far, no more effective measures (such as increasing the volume of immigration and nationalizing some of the existing migrants) have been taken to increase population size, largely because of concern about changing the nature of the Saudi state. Qatar adopts a similar position to Saudi Arabia, but again its policy implementation is extremely weak. Qatar, too, refuses to publish its first and only census since less than 40 percent of the total population consisted of Qatari nationals. The Algerians were among the most vociferous nations at the World Population Conference and were instrumental in altering the whole nature of the Draft Plan.[55] Their high annual growth rate (±3.5 percent) is a reflection of a fall in the average age of marriage for females—high proportions married and a reduction in mortality in recent decades—rather than a result of deliberate policy. The curious feature about the Algerian position on population growth adopted at the World Population Conference is that in Algeria there is considerable official support for demographic training and research and at the same time several United Nations agencies, including the United Nations International Children's Emergency Fund (UNICEF), and the World Health Organization (WHO), are involved in projects which include the provision of family planning services.

The PLO publicly supports the idea that each Palestinian couple should produce at least four children, but the effect of the statement on an already high level of fertility is probably unimportant. The UNRWA health services include contraceptive services and advice and, of course, the better-off Palestinians living outside the camps are practicing contraception, but neither the national family planning associations in the host countries nor UNRWA itself is in a position to actively promote the use of contraceptives. This problem more than anything else has stalled the development of a Jordanian population policy since even the geographical distribution of mother and child health clinics and the base for the Jordanian Family Planning Association (Amman or Jerusalem) are live political issues.

The position of Iraq is again somewhat ambiguous since officially family planning is approved only for the purposes of "birth spacing" and for reasons of health. Population growth itself is not considered an obstacle to development although the extremely rapid growth of Baghdad is often referred to as a problem. Family planning has been officially supported since 1972, however, and there is an Iraqi Family Planning Association and contraceptives can be imported duty-free. A few years ago this was also the Syrian position, but partly as a result of the 1970 census, which showed that natural increase was about 3.2 percent per annum, official support for contraceptive services provided through mother and child health clinics increased in importance. One very recent development is the growing Syrian interest in demographic training and research: for example, the United Nations Fund for Population Activities (UNFPA) is assisting the University of Aleppo to expand its demographic training program. This and similar developments now have strong official support since the government economic planners appreciate the value of good demographic data and are seriously concerned at the current rate of population growth.

Morocco and Iran both have official policies to reduce the population growth rate and have instituted national family planning associations and have incorporated measures to reduce population growth into their respective national plans. Iran, for example, wants to reduce the population growth rate to 1 percent over twenty years, and has eased the laws on induced abortion in 1973 and uses the Literacy, Health and Development Corps to spread knowledge of contraceptive use.[56] Morocco wants to achieve a crude birth of thirty-five per thousand by 1980-85 and has established a National Family Planning Center in 1974 to extend the existing, moderately successful family planning program.

Tunisia, of all the Arab countries, has adopted the most forthright policy to reduce population growth.[57] The 1973-74 Plan, for example, states that Tunisia aims to reduce the general fertility rate by 2.5 points per annum. The Tunisians have abolished polygamy (1956), restricted family allowances to only four children (1960), legalized the importation and sale of contraceptives (1961), raised the minimum age of marriage for males to twenty and for females to seventeen (1964), and have legalized induced abortion with very few restrictions for women in the first twelve weeks of their pregnancy (1973). Undoubtedly the Tunisian birthrate is falling and natural increase, although still high, has been reduced to about 2.5 percent per year. The independent effect of the family planning measures on fertility is difficult to measure because of the other factors involved (such as rising educational levels and increasing urbanization) but the promising feature of the Tunisian experience has been that population growth has been slowed despite relatively modest rates of overall economic development.

Opportunities for Intervention

Framework

In most of the fertility surveys and censuses taken in the region, we find that, for example, better-educated couples living in cities with urban-based jobs have fewer children than people without these characteristics. The question remains: do these data provide enough evidence to prove that fertility is declining and will continue to decline as a result of rising educational standards and further urbanization and that these attributes of the couples with low fertility are themselves policy variables?

This point is crucial, and yet one still awaits a definitive answer. For poor and populous countries, such as Egypt, it is small comfort to discover (even if it were true) that slowing the rate of population growth is dependent on covering Egypt with factories and cities and filling them with well educated citizens. This basic dilemma confronts one and explains why less conventional remedies (such as mass vasectomy camps or nonclinical distribution of pills) have been proposed and adopted in certain countries.

The argument advanced in this chapter begins from the standpoint that neither the social systems nor the economic systems of the Middle East (which together have a great deal to do with the rate of population growth) are free-standing entities: they are artifacts erected in some cases by a consensus and in other cases by an élite. While the majority of countries in the Middle East do not have a distinct and well-orchestrated population policy, they have, by dint of the whole assemblage of past decisions and legislation, enacted a policy which in most cases is pronatalist. For example, welfare payments to parents with large families, while achieving the valuable goal of equalizing income distribution, also provides a reason for couples with large families to use as a justification for not contracepting. Equally important are the host of decisions taken centrally which generally result in far higher levels of social service provision in the cities than in the rural areas. Migrants, for a variety of reasons, can pass on their costs of moving to society by insisting on access to urban services, especially housing, provision of which once again relieves the pressure on individual couples to restrict their number of births.

Thus, the nub of the argument is that fertility can be reduced by reversing some of these past decisions, and in particular, paying close attention to the ways in which individual couples pass-on their childbearing and rearing costs to society and, at the same time, internalize their childbearing and rearing benefits. This means working on a general front, sorting through the maze of collective decisions which constitute a de facto policy in population and establishing the significance of the effects of each of the measures on population growth. This is different from proposing wholesale industrialization and urbanization and different again from proposing vigorous and possibly coercive family planning programs.

Intermediate Variables Affecting Fertility

We know that the biological capacity to reproduce, including the amount of fetal wastage, the length of the fertile lifespan for females, and the regularity of ovulation, can all be directly influenced by a number of environmental factors such as the level of nutrition and the general health of the population.[58] Neither the health nor the nutritional status of the population are policy instruments in that deliberately slowing or even reversing current trends (which are mostly in a positive direction) cannot be seriously advocated. There is, however, one socially determined custom—the duration of breast feeding—which could be thought of as a policy measure since prolonged lactation lengthens the period of postpartum amenorrhea and vice versa. It is worth noting that research has shown that the quality of the breast milk is maintained even among poorly fed mothers[59] and that the risks of infection are lower for breast-fed babies.

Of much greater significance from the policy standpoint are the factors which determine the size and the age composition of the population "at risk" (usually the currently married population). Clearly, the proportion never-marrying (which varies considerably from one society to another) has a direct effect on fertility as does the age at which couples first marry. The age composition of a closed population is very largely determined by fertility and mortality in the recent past but the age distribution itself affects these rates. In a population where marriage is early and contraception is unimportant, the mean length of generation is short and the growth rate of the population is faster than in a population with the same mortality and fertility levels but with a later mean age of childbearing. We know too that older spouses are less fecund than younger ones, that coital frequency declines with age, that fetal wastage and that infant mortality are greater among older women, *ceteris paribus*. Thus, there are many sound reasons for attempting to affect the proportions marrying and the age of marriage.

Finally, the extent of contraceptive knowledge and use has a great deal to do with fertility. To contraception, we might add the use of induced abortion as a means of dealing with contraceptive failures or mistakes apart from its more neutral use in cases where the health of the mother or of the unborn child are at risk. The technical aspects of contraception are much less important than the task of providing potential users with a suitable motivation for limiting their family size. In addition to the use of contraception to prevent further births once the desired number have been achieved, we must remember that controlling the timing of births also has an effect on fertility since couples who space their children end up with smaller families than those who do not and spacing also has the more subtle effect of lengthening the mean length of generation, thus slowing population growth.

Affecting fecundity, nuptiality and the extent of contraceptive practice are the three main fields of population policy. These topics cannot be approached directly, however, so one must give some thought to the range of feasible policy measures which will affect the three main determinants of fertility and population growth.

Health-Related Policy Measures

Improving general mortality and especially infant mortality has a number of indirect effects as well as altering the probabilities of survival. On the one hand, with falling mortality and constant fertility, the proportion of the population under any age rises although the mean age of the population increases, resulting in an increased dependency burden for the working population. On the other hand, the introduction of scientific approaches to health care can have spin-off effects in other fields producing an increased awareness in the efficacy of individuals and reducing the significance of fatalism.[60]

A national insurance scheme or some other form of national health service is an important component of the effort to reduce mortality and fertility since in most countries the distribution of health services and especially of hospitals and doctors is very uneven. In fact, it is not at all uncommon to find the bulk of the health services in the areas of smallest need which are of course the most profitable places for doctors to work. It is for this reason that some form of state intervention is necessary to equalize the spread of health services and skilled health personnel. Again, the provision of a basic health service with some form of associated welfare scheme for the elderly and the disabled is an important factor in convincing people that it is unnecessary to produce large numbers of children to substitute for these welfare services.

An additional consideration is the effect of high parity on both the mother and the already born children. Apart from pointing out that high parity women experience greater rates of fatal loss and of maternal death than other mothers,[61] there are some more subtle effects of large families on child development. There are some significant relationships between educational achievement and birth order and there are some psychological effects on children largely reared by their siblings.[62]

Finally, as a basic part of the health service, it would be worth spending more time explaining what we know of the reproductive process, particularly with respect to the workings of several of the modern means of contraception.

Education-Related Policy Measures

Just providing education facilities for girls on a par with those for boys and teaching both sexes together has a great deal to do with altering the status of women. Improving the syllabus by emphasizing the development of critical judgment at the expense of rote learning usually leads to a reexamination of some of the society's accepted mores, many of which concern the relationships between the sexes and attitudes toward marriage and the family. Discussion of traditional religious beliefs in an open and not necessarily skeptical manner can do a great deal to produce a better understanding and possibly a reappraisal of some of the beliefs which have a bearing on fertility. In the Middle East, despite the pronouncements of the Shaikhs of Al-Azhar and the conclusions of a conference on Islam and family planning,[63] there is still an ingrained conviction that contraception is against the teaching of Islam in all circumstances—a point which had been further confused by recent Saudi assertions to this effect.

At higher levels, the development of population studies centers where research into the causes and effects of rapid population growth and the training of skilled demographers and demographic-economic planners can take place must be a high priority. The dearth of skilled manpower is the most important factor which is holding up the improvement of the analysis of demographic-economic relationships in the region. Very little expertise exists in the region in the important area of population and development planning although there are signs that several institutions in the Western Asia region will soon be improving the quality of their instruction in this field.[e] The demand for these services and skills is very strong and the list of projects suggested by the twelve Western Asian countries is well beyond the current resources of existing institutions in the region.[64]

Labor Force-Related Policy Measures

It appears to be axiomatic that women, when offered an alternative to a career of childbearing and child-rearing, accept the alternative with alacrity. There are a number of ways of providing women with alternatives of which the most obvious is the provision of female employment opportunities. In the Middle East, female labor force participation rates are extremely low. There are social and institutional barriers to the employment of women but they are not insurmountable obstacles. The overall structure of the labor force is important since it is easier for women to work if there are a number of light industries or service industries which do not have a large manual labor component. In addition, if the job opportunities are widely distributed and close to home, more women will work. Sex segregated offices and unequal rates of pay are institutional barriers which can be removed by legislation, but care is necessary to avoid being over-generous to women and thus (as in the case of Egypt) making it more expensive and inconvenient for employers to employ women than men.

---

[e]Both the Universities of Aleppo and Jordan are establishing population studies programs.

Social Welfare-Related Policy Measures

The range of policy opportunities in this field is extremely wide and includes the following:

1. revising the inheritance laws to favor the oldest child regardless of sex;
2. restricting family allowances to the first N children (n Tunisia, N equals 4);
3. introducing savings schemes or educational bonds which give extra rewards to small families without penalizing the larger ones;
4. revising housing priorities so that the largest families are not given the highest priority;
5. providing old age and disablement pensions;
6. spreading welfare, educational, and health services evenly among the population regardless of location, sex, class or ethnic group;
7. facilitating migration, especially for single women.

Economic Development

All the changes and policy measures outlined above are a great deal easier to implement when the national income is growing and there are new sources of income being generated in order to finance health, education, and welfare facilities. How each state in the Middle East realizes its potential for economic growth is beyond the scope of this chapter, but it should be plain that rapid population growth (at least by natural increase alone) is probably a net impediment to achieving long-term prosperity, and that devoting some small fraction of the total budget of a development plan to population matters will probably produce a sizable net gain over the long run. Simply calculating the losses or gains due to population growth using both macroeconomic and microeconomic approaches has a number of beneficial side effects. Demands for good quality data increase when economic planning passes beyond the stage of wishful thinking and this in turn generates demands for skilled personnel capable of greater objectivity. Thereafter, once the general goal of trying to maximize economic and social welfare for both individuals and society at large has been accepted, the issue of a population policy passes from the stage of being a statement of aims to being a coordinated attempt to draw together the various strands of social and economic planning into a policy which is unidirectional and unequivocal in its aims and intentions.

Conclusion

Future involvement by the West in the population problems of the Middle East is inevitable. The World Population Conference of 1974 and the meetings concerned with the New Economic Order politicized the population issue and forced the agencies involved in providing population assistance in one form or another to think of population problems in an economic development context. This, of course, is as it should be since the purely family planning approach to population problems was not succeeding in its aims nor was it proving popular in a number of countries. Thus, once we accept that the West as a whole has an interest in promoting economic development in the LDCs and that slowing population growth is an important part of these efforts, we have to make a number of critical choices concerning our links with the Middle Eastern countries in the future.

Degree of Involvement. The rich countries have to decide how strong a stance they wish to take on rapid population growth. At present, classical economic analysis indicates that relatively small gains flow from slowing population growth in the short term although these benefits are much greater in the long run. So far, the amount of microeconomic research carried out in LDCs, especially in the Middle East, is extremely small, but there are strong indications that the benefits from slowing population growth are much greater at this level. We know very little about situations where the marginal productivity of labor is zero or negative and about how to measure labor productivity when we have large nonmoney sectors. Thus, the stance of the rich countries on population growth is based on a slender statistical base and the degree of commitment to slowing population growth in the Middle East depends more on faith or on conclusions drawn from other situations than on empirical work carried out in the region. For countries like Egypt, Turkey, Iran, and Tunisia, which have already committed themselves to a policy of slowing population growth by a wide variety of measures including family planning, external assistance is needed most to undertake research into the efficacy of current policies and to search for new policy instruments. For the more conservative regimes such as Saudi Arabia and the lower Gulf states, there is a greater need for careful analysis of existing relationships between economic development and population growth, leaving the issue of intervention open for now. Development of health, education, and welfare facilities will inevitably lead to the reappraisal of the social justice of a pronatalist stance since such a policy, to be really effective, involves the reversal of some extremely powerful trends (e.g., encouraging earlier rather than later marriage; denying educational opportunities to women; and preventing girls from entering the labor force).

The World Population Plan of Action approved at Bucharest in 1974 and the resolutions passed by the African and Western Asian regions subsequently offer the best available overall framework for action. The Plan itself is very flexible and while it is not necessary to move from the position generally accepted in the West that population growth in the less developed countries does constitute an obstacle to more rapid economic growth, it does allow external aid donors to vary the stress put on measures designed to directly affect population growth (such as contraceptive services and abortion on demand) according to the wishes of the receiving country.

Type of Involvement. There are a variety of opportunities for intervention, some of which are ineffective or politically unacceptable to certain countries. On the most sensitive issues (e.g., induced abortion), very few countries in the Middle East relish the thought of well-financed outsiders becoming heavily involved. On less sensitive issues (e.g., improving the quality of infant and maternal health care), outsiders are more welcome. Unfortunately, we are still in the dark about which of the policy measures do most to improve welfare and to slow population growth. Does a dollar invested in a family planning program produce an equivalent effect on the birthrate as a dollar invested in health clinics, and how long do we have to wait for each of the effects to be felt? Thus, it is imperative that more research by *Middle Easterners* working in the Middle East is carried out to clarify these issues. It may mean that some of the research conclusions reached in the West will have to be rediscovered in the Middle East, but the results will have a much greater impact if the work is produced by indigenous research workers. Without changing their basic position on the interrelationships between economic development and population growth, it is recommended that major aid givers and especially the U.S. Agency for International Development (AID) shift their programmatic emphasis away from family planning and towards helping Middle Easterners discover the causes of their own demographic circumstances.

Means of Involvement. There are three ways in which rich countries can become involved in the economic development and population growth problems of the Middle East. The first is through the bilateral aid-giving agencies such as the U.S. AID and the British Overseas Development Administration. Support from these sources tends to be volatile since political factors are of greater significance than need in allocating support to LDCs. In addition, since some aspects of population policy can prove unpopular both in the donor and in the receiving country, this approach to population problems is not the most satisfactory.

An alternative to bilateral assistance is provided by the various UN agencies which have grown in significance in the population field since the UN Fund for Population Activities was established in 1962. The UN agencies have achieved a great deal but the disadvantage of the UN is that its procedures are slow, bureaucratic, and cumbersome and that it can only give support at the governmental level. It is quite common for a university or a health ministry to have its application for support blocked or badly delayed in the government agency through which all external applications for financial support must be channeled. At present, the UN agencies have more money available for population matters than ever before but they can only respond to country requests for assistance and cannot become too actively engaged in the development of grant applications. One solution to the clumsiness of the UN system is follow the guidelines of the Taylor report and to decentralize as much of the regional responsibility as possible. The UN agencies which have greater freedom in the Middle East, such as the UN Relief and Works Agency for the Palestinian Refugees and the Population Division of the Economic Commission for Western Asia, have made a very great contribution to both improving individual welfare and to raising the awareness of population problems in the Middle East.

Finally, we come to the private foundations and to the charitable institutions, many of which (especially in the Levant and Palestine) have been represented in the region for a very long time. These organizations are less hidebound by bureaucratic procedures and, generally speaking, their overheads are much less than those of the UN or of the bilateral aid-giving institutions. They are in a position to develop projects and they can fund individuals or institutions whose views or approach do not correspond with the publicly expressed government view but whose research is nonetheless given tacit support. There are a large number of worthwhile proposals which could help in the search for policy instruments in the field of population and development planning and the major obstacle to the completion of this research is lack of funds. For rich countries wanting an indirect route into supporting population activities in the Middle East, supporting some of the foundations could be a more profitable means of achieving this aim than giving the money to one of the United Nations' agencies.

Appendix IIA
Technical Description
of the Assumptions
and Input Data for the
Population Projections

Projection Procedure

All the projections were made with the projection package outlined in the Population Council book by F.C. Shorter, *Computational Methods for Population Projections with Particular Reference to Development Planning.* New York: Population Council, 1974. This extremely versatile set of routines allows one to make estimates of the future course of mortality and fertility in the usual way, but in addition makes provision for the inclusion of migrants who are then subjected to the prevailing mortality and fertility regime.

The life tables used were the model life tables produced by Coale and Demeny. In every case except two, the South model of mortality was employed because this age pattern of mortality best fitted the available data for the region. The South pattern is characterized by a high level of infant and child mortality relative to the level of mortality in adulthood. For the Israeli Jews and for the Palestinians registered with UNRWA, the West pattern of mortality was used. For the Jews, it was plain that this pattern best fitted the good quality registration data. For the Palestinians, some surveys of infant mortality recently completed by UNRWA indicated that the emphasis on infant and child care in the UNRWA health services may have produced a larger decrease in infant mortality than in adult mortality. Other evidence, based on the age structure and the rate of increase of the Palestinian population, indicated that the West model of mortality was most appropriate.

Once the age pattern of mortality was determined, the level prevailing at the start of the projection period was fixed usually by indirect methods since the registration of mortality is very incomplete in the majority of Arab countries.

The sources of these estimates varied: many of them came from the Cairo Demographic Center book, *Demographic Measures and Population Growth in Arab Countries*, 1970. Others were drawn from special demographic surveys and a few were estimated for the first time. Overall, the level of mortality was everywhere expected to improve in the future but at different rates depending on the initial level of mortality. Where two estimates of the level of mortality at two different points in time were available, it was assumed that the future trend in the expectancy of life at birth (e_o^o) could be modeled by fitting the logistic growth curve to the two observed values. This model was selected because we know that elsewhere the trend in mortality has, generally speaking, followed this pattern. In effect, the model simply says that when mortality is high, as in most poor countries, the annual increase in the expectancy of life will be greater than when mortality is already at a low level. For practical reasons, the limits for the expectancy of life were assumed to lie between 30 and 77.5 years—the latter representing level 24 in the Coale and Demeny model life tables. Where two estimates of the level of mortality at two dates were unavailable, the future trend in mortality was taken from the model values calculated from another country, usually one with similar mortality prospects.

The initial level of total fertility was estimated in a similar fashion, relying in the main on indirect estimates and on the few reliable figures which can be extracted from the region's vital registration statistics. A useful source of information is another Cairo Demographic Center book, *Fertility Trends and Differentials in Arab Countries*, 1971. The reported age pattern of fertility was accepted in almost every case, but frequently adjustments were made to the level of fertility. For the projections, the future age patterns of fertility were taken from the model fertility schedules compiled by Coale and Trussell (*Population Index* 40, 2 (1974): 185-258) with reasonable assumptions about the future rate of entry into marriage and the degree of contraceptive use. Further details are explained in the section dealing with individual countries.

Algeria

The initial age structure was taken from the 1966 census and smoothed by hand as in Cairo Demographic Center, 1970, p. 22. The initial level of fertility and the age specific fertility schedule came from Etudos Sociales Nationales de la Population, *Resultats de l'Enquete Nationale de la Population*, November 1972, Series B, vol. 2. Total fertility was expected to fall slowly to 3.5 by 1995-2000 due to the relatively lukewarm official interest in family planning, which at the moment is supported only to facilitate "child spacing." Some pediatric clinics provide family planning advice but this is restricted to women with four or more children. The future age pattern of fertility was chosen to match this pattern of control initiated by older, high parity women.

Egypt

A revised age structure, based on the comparison of the size of the same cohorts at different points in time was taken from V.G. Valaoras, *Population Analysis of Egypt*, Cairo Demographic Center, Occasional Paper 1, 1972, table 5. The initial age specific fertility schedule came from the same source, table 17. Fertility was assumed to fall steadily to a value of 3.0 in 1995-2000 based on extrapolation of present trends and the assumption that parities of five and over would gradually disappear over the next thirty years. The age specific pattern of fertility was modified on this assumption since we have tables showing parities by age of mother.

Iran

The revised age structure was taken from Shorter, *Computational Methods*, p. 62, with the total adjusted to include the nomads and tribesmen. The same source provided the initial age specific fertility schedule (p. 54) later adjusted from the model schedules by Coale and Trussell. A modest assumption was made about total fertility which was projected to fall to 4.5 in 1995-2000. This corresponds to a NRR of 1.0 in 2020 and is in fact much higher than the Shah's proclaimed target. Other sources (see Frejka's *Country Prospects for Iran* produced by the Population Council) also indicate the difficulty of achieving the announced fertility aims.

Iraq

The unaltered age distribution was taken from the published results of the 1965 census, table 5, which look as if they have been smoothed before publication. The total excluded Iraqis abroad. Iraqi vital statistics are of very poor quality so that indirect estimates were taken from Cairo Demographic Center (1970), pp. 46-47. The Iraqi government, in the reply to the ECWA questionnaire sent round in 1974 prior to the World Population Conference, said that they favored the continuation of the present level of fertility to 1980, after which it would begin to fall. This seems realistic and was used in the projections. The level of total fertility in 1995-2000 emerges as 5.1.

Israel

The Israeli statistics are of good quality and were used unaltered in any way in the projections. For the Jews, it was assumed that total fertility would continue its steady downward trend reaching 2.5 in 2000-2005 and that immigration would continue at the rather optimistic value of 40,000 per annum until 1980-85 when it would fall to 30,000 per annum until 1995-2000. Thereafter, the volume was fixed at 20,000 per annum. For the Arab population of pre-1967 Israel, it was assumed that their fertility would decline slowly reaching 4.0 in 2000-2005 because of the restriction on the supply of contraceptives by the Israeli government and the greater difficulty faced by Arabs in obtaining an abortion. No migration was allowed for and no boundary changes were anticipated. Future age patterns of fertility were taken from model schedules.

Jordan-East Bank

The Jordanian government published an official figure for the population of the East Bank which for want of a better alternative, was divided up in the same proportions as in the census of 1961. The values used were those derived by H. Wander, *Analysis of the Population Statistics of Jordan*, Department of Statistics, 1966, Appendix p. 6. The age specific fertility rate and total fertility were taken from the same source, table 6, p. 9.

Jordan-West Bank and Gaza Excluding Jerusalem

The Statistical Abstract of Israel, 1972, Chapter 26, was the principal source of initial age structure for the occupied territories. These figures are based on the census of 1967 which has been updated in the light of recorded vital events and smoothed to allow for age misreporting. Vital rates were taken from the same source, Chapter 3. In the projections, model age specific fertility schedules were employed.

Kuwait

The 1970 census was revised by applying the appropriate stable population parameters and allowing for a period of destabilization which occurs following a fall in mortality. Vital registration is good in Kuwait so that the published rates were accepted at face value. For the migrants, only the gross totals were projected since we have incomplete information on the age characteristics of the arrivals by calendar year.

Lebanon

A sample census was held in November 1970. The results from this census have been modified by Y. Courbage and P. Fargues in a recent book, *La Situation*

Demographic au Liban (Beirut: Université Libanaise), 1974. Their revised estimates were accepted, including their assessment of fertility. In the projection, it was assumed that total fertility would fall to 2.5 in 2000-2005.

Libya

The age distribution reported in the 1964 census was corrected as in the Cairo Demographic Center book, 1970. The pattern of fertility was taken from Algeria and because of official indifference to family planning, it was assumed that total fertility would fall to just 4.5 by the period 1995-2000.

Morocco

C. Paulet in an unpublished paper prepared at Princeton in May 1974 produced some estimates of the vital rates in Morocco using census and vital registration data. These estimates were used in the projection, including a revised age structure for females. The male age distribution was estimated by using the sex ratios in a stable population with the appropriate vital rates.

Syria

The modified age structure based on the 1970 census was taken from N. Khoury, *La Situation Demographique en Syrie*, University of Paris, Doctorat de Specialite, (Ph.D. thesis) 1974, 3eme cycle, lere annee. It was assumed that total fertility would fall by 10 percent every five years starting in 1975-80.

Tunisia

All estimates come from U.S. Department of Commerce, Bureau of the Census *The Population of Tunisia*, Series P-96, No. 3, 1971. It was assumed that fertility would fall from 6.9 to 3.5 by 2000-2005. Model age specific fertility schedules were employed during later phases of the projection.

Turkey

Shorter (*Computational Methods*) has produced a revised age distribution for the 1970 census together with some estimates of the vital rates. These were used at the outset. It was assumed that the population policy of the Turks would prove to be very effective and that total fertility would fall to 2.5 by 2000-2005. External migration was assumed to account for a net loss of 100,000 people per annum initially, falling to 40,000 per annum in later phases of the projection.

UNRWA Registered Refugees

The age distribution supplied by UNRWA was used since there is no consistent way to modify such a distribution to take account of age misreporting errors. Vital rates were estimated for the first time from some additional UNRWA statistics, notably a report by the director of health on child mortality (January 11, 1974, HD/P/140 and HD/P/150). The level of fertility was fixed at 5.3 and does not vary throughout the projection. The same age specific fertility was used as is observed for the Arabs living in Israel.

Notes

1. A final report and seven volumes of research papers have been published by the Commission covering diverse aspects of the U.S. population. A review of the Commissions' work and effectiveness by C. Westoff, its executive director, appears in *Population Index* 39, 4 (October 1973): 491-502. A more accessible summary of report, *Population and the American Future*, was published by the New American Library, Signet Special 1972.

2. The main statements by President Ford and the U.S. delegation together with the final version of the World Plan of Action are published in the Department of State Bulletin, Publication 8783, International Organization and Conference Series 116, October 1974, Office of Media Sources, Bureau of Public Affairs. An excellent discussion of the Plan and its text appeared in *Population and Development Review* 1, 1 (September 1975): 87-146, 163-181.

3. Details are provided in the papers prepared by the UN World Food Conference Secretariat. Especially noteworthy are the papers *Assessment of the World Food Situation, Present and Future* (E/Conf. 65/3) and *World Population and Food Supplies: Looking Ahead* (E/Conf. 60/CBP/19), the latter written by Lester Brown.

4. Ehrlich's most dramatic exposition of the effects of population growth was called *The Population Bomb* (1968). ZPG Inc. was founded in 1968 and following its promotion by Ehrlich on television, had attained a membership of 40,000 in 400 chapters by 1971. The Ehrlichs' newer book called *Population, Resources, Environment* (San Francisco: Freeman, 1970) also contains a strong plea for a stationary US and eventually, world population. Many demographers disagree with their diagnosis of the problem and their recommended solutions. See Ansley Coale's review entitled "Disastrous Numbers," in *Science* 170 (October 23, 1970): 428-429.

5. Kingsley Davis and Judith Blake Davis have adopted this stance. See their articles in *Science*, vol. 158, No. 3802 (November 10, 1967): 730-739 and vol. 164, No. 3879 (May 2, 1969): 522-529.

6. S.F. Singer (ed.), *Is there an optimum level of population?* (New York, McGraw-Hill, 1971).

7. For a good summary of the case for slower growth see: *Rapid Population Growth* (1971) published by Johns Hopkins for the National Academy of Sciences, 2 vols. A classic in this area is the book by A.J. Coale and E.M. Hoover (Princeton, Princeton University Press, 1958) *Population Growth and Economic Development in Low Income Countries*, especially pp. 332-335.

8. N.B. Ryder, Realistic pathways to fertility reduction in developing countries, Presidential Address, Population Association of America, New York, April 1974.

9. J.L. Frinkle and B.B. Crane, "The Politics of Bucharest: Population Development and the New International Economic Order," *Population and Development Review* 1, 1 (September 1975): 87-114.

10. The 1965-72 rate of increase for South Asia as a whole was 2.8 percent but Southwest Asia alone had a growth rate of 2.9 percent, according to the UN *Demographic Yearbook 1972*, Table 1. Latin America had a similar growth rate whereas the population of North Africa grew at 3.1 percent over the same period.

11. Kingsley Davis (1969) *World Urbanization 1950-1970*, v. I, *Basic Data for Cities, Countries and Regions*, University of California, Table D.

12. UN, *Demographic Yearbook* 1972, Table 5.

13. *Report of the Commissioner-General of the UN Relief and Work Agency for Palestine Refugees in the Near East*, July 1, 1972-June 20, 1973, General Assembly, 28th Session, Supplement No. 13 (A/9013), Tables 1 and 7.

14. About 17,000 registered refugees left the Golan Heights in June 1967 together with about the same number of Syrians. Approximately 215,000 people who were registered refugees fled from the West Bank in 1967 of whom about 8,000 have been permitted to return. In June 1974, UNRWA distributed rations to 205,000 displaced persons on the East Bank who were not registered UNRWA refugees on behalf of the government of Jordan. See *Report of the Commissioner-General UNRWA*, July 1, 1973-June 20, 1973, General Assembly, 29th Session, Supplement No. 13 (A/9613), especially paragraphs 20 and 50-72.

15. See table 1 in "Explaining cross-cultural variations in age at marriage and proportions never marrying," by Ruth B. Dixon in *Population Studies* 25 (1971): 215-233.

16. A.R. Omran in *Egypt: Population Problems and Prospects* (1973) University of North Carolina at Chapel Hill.

17. *Men and Medicine in the Middle East* (1967) by Jan Simon.

18. UNRWA document HD/P/140-150, *Children Mortality Report*, January 11, 1974.

19. Letter to Advisory Group on the World Plan of Action, August 1974.

20. Recent work on nutrition and fecundity is producing results which indicate a strong causal link. See R. Frisch, "Menstrual cycles: fatness as a determinant of minimum weight for height necessary for their maintenance and onset," *Science* 185 (September 1974), and a summary of current knowledge produced by John Bongaarts for the Population Council in October 1974.

21. Hassan Hathout and Mohammed Selim, "Menstrual survey of girls schools," *Journal of the Kuwait Medical Association* 6 (1972): 141-158.

22. *Realistic pathways to fertility reduction in developing countries*, Presidential address at the Population Association of America, Annual Meeting in New York City, April 1974.

23. There are abundant references which document these attitudes. Amongst the best are: W. Goode *World Revolution in Family Patterns* (Free Press, 1970), Paperback edition; M. Berger, *The Arab World Today* (Anchor Books, 1964), Chapter 4; E.T. Prothro and L. Diab, *Changing Family Patterns in the Arab East* (Syracuse University Press, 1974).

24. The notion that complexity is an important factor in producing stability is best developed in ecology. See the work by Robert MacArthur in, for example, *The Theory of Island Biography* (Princeton, 1967); or the synopsis given by E.P. Odum, *Fundamentals of Ecology* (Saunders, 1959).

25. I.F. Harik, *The Political Mobilization of Peasants: A Study of an Egyptian Village* (Bloomington: Indiana University Press, 1974).

26. A.G. Hill, "The demography of the Kuwaiti population of Kuwait," *Demography* 12, 3 (1975): 537-548.

27. M. Clawson et al., *The Agricultural Potential of the Middle East* (American Elsevier, 1971).

28. For a theoretical discussion of the effects of mortality and fertility on the structure of populations, see A.J. Coale, *The Growth and Structure of Human Populations: A Mathematical Investigation* (Princeton University Press, 1972).

29. See: UN (1967) "Methods of estimating basic demographic measures from incomplete data," Manual IV, Population Studies 42, ST/SOA/Series A/42. Cairo Demographic Center (1970) *Demographic Measures and Population Growth in Arab Countries*, Research Monograph 2.

30. A.J. Coale and T.J. Trussell, "Model fertility schedules: variations in the age structure of childbearing in human populations," *Population Index* 40, 2 (April 1974): 185-258.

31. See the UN projections for comparison in: UN, Department of Economic and Social Affairs (1973) *World population prospects as assessed in 1968*, ST/SOA/Series A/53, Table A.6.4. Or see: Cairo Demographic Center (1970).

32. See the Population Council's publications: Population and Family Planning: A Factbook, *Reports on Population Family Planning*, No. 2 (December 1974), especially table 8. An additional source are the *Country Profiles* currently available for the following Middle East countries: Iran, Morocco, Israel, Turkey

and Egypt. As part of the documentation for World Population Year, the Committee for International Co-ordination Of National Research in Demography (CIDRED) sponsored country monographs, which will soon be available for most countries of the Middle East.

33. D. Friedlander in *Population Policy in Developed Countries*, edited by B. Berelson, a Population Council book published by McGraw-Hill (1974), pp. 71-73. See also J. Matras, "Matchmaking, marriage and fertility in Israel," *American Journal of Sociology* 79, 3 (1973): 364-371.

34. Friedlander, *Population Policy*, pp. 52-69.

35. Ibid., pp. 61-69.

36. The corrected series are given in A.R. Omran (ed.), *Egypt: Population Problems and Prospects* (University of North Carolina at Chapel Hill, 1973), p. 75, table 1, but see *Population Index* 41 (1975): 207-208 for new estimates.

37. Omran, *Egypt*, pp. 421-425. The Annual Report of the Supreme Council for Population and Family Planning, August 1974, shows on table 1 that overall only 6.2 percent of the eligible women 15-45 were users in June 1974. The figure for the urban areas, however, was almost 12 percent.

38. Laila el-Hamamsy has described the shortcomings of the program in two papers based on survey work in an urban area and in a village. The papers, published by the Social Research Center of the American University in Cairo, are called: *Availability of contraceptives: why go beyond?* (May 1974) and earlier one called *Egypt's family planning program from the social perspective*. An additional reference is Saad Gadalla, *Population problems and family planning programs in Egypt*, paper presented at the 8th International Congress of Anthropological and Ethnological Sciences, Tokyo, 3-10 September 1968.

39. Two abortion studies are presented in Omran, *Egypt*, pp. 387-408. A book published by the International Planned Parenthood Federation, Middle East and North Africa region in 1972 and called *Induced Abortion: A Hazard to Health?* has three papers which indicate that the incidence of induced abortion in Egypt is high and growing: the papers are by Larsen, Foda and I. Kamal with others. Older, high parity women, many of them from low income backgrounds, were the most common abortion cases seen.

40. See his paper, "The impact of small and large numbers of children on the health and welfare of individual families: a micro-case study," The Institute of National Planning, May 1972, memo No. 1011, especially pp. 36-37.

41. A Ministry of Health paper, written by the Minister, M.M. Mahfouz in February 1973, called, *Conceptualization of a National Plan for Family Planning in the Arab Republic of Egypt* makes a number of points in parallel with Bindary's paper. On pp. 3-6, the national goals to solve the population problem are listed as lowering infant mortality, changing the rural economy, emphasizing cultural, religious and ideological development, social development, political awareness of the population problem and preparing the cadres for solving the problem. The shortcomings of family planning as a method of slowing population growth are discussed on pages 1 and 2.

42. See the *Annual Reports* of the Egyptian Family Planning Association which show that in the 1970s, new acceptors totalled about 65,000 women every year. The total budget of the Association is only about E136,000.

43. A good background source is N.H. Fisek, "Prospects for fertility planning in Turkey," in S.J. Behrman et al. (eds.), *Fertility and Family Planning* (University of Michigan Press, 1971). Most of this section is adapted from L.S. Anderson's, *Turkey, Country Profiles*, The Population Council, January 1970.

44. F.C. Shorter, "Information on fertility, mortality and population growth in Turkey," *Population Index* 34, 1 (1968): 3-21.

45. This description is adapted from Aykut Toros, "Tarsus II: a social experiment in fertility regulation," Ph.D. thesis, Princeton University, 1974, pp. 11-17.

46. D. Nortman, "Population and Family Planning Programs: A Factbook," *Reports on Population/Family Planning*, 1974, table 22.

47. For a description of these patterns, see R.C. Treadway, "Gradients of metropolitan dominance in Turkey: alternative models," *Demography* 9, 1 (1972): 13-33.

48. See W. Kewenig, *Die Ko-existenz der Religiongemeinschaft in Libanon*, University of Koln, Walter de Gruyter and Co., Berlin, 1965.

49. H.F. Fayyad, "The effect of sectarianism on the Lebanese administration," M.A. thesis, American University of Beirut, 1956. ˙

50. A good summary of these changes appears in Y. Courbage and P. Fargues, *La Situation Demographique au Liban*, vol. 2 (Lebanese University Publication, 1974), pp. 9-25.

51. Ministere du Plan, Direction Centrale de la Statistique (1972), *L'Enquete-par Sondage sur la Population Active au Liban*, 2 volumes.

52. Jam'iya tanzim al-usra fi libnan, *Al-usra fi Libnan: tahqiq ihsa'i bi al-'aina haziran 1971*, 2 volumes (Beirut: 1974).

53. More details appear in G.E. French and A.G. Hill, *Kuwait: Urban and Medical Ecology* (Springer Verlag, 1971).

54. See the papers by Hassan Hathout expressing Kuwait's position, e.g., "Looking at abortion material," in *Induced Abortion: A Hazard to Public Health* (1972), IPPF Conference Proceedings, Beirut 1971, edited by J.R. Hazor.

55. See "A Report on Bucharest" by W. Parker Mauldin et al., *Studies in Family Planning* 5, 12 (The Population Council, December 1974).

56. Asayeah, K.A., *Iran* and *Family Planning in Iran* (North Carolina: Population Center, 1974).

57. See R.J. Lapham, "Family planning and fertility in Tunisia," *Demography* 7 (1969): 241-530; and J. Vallin and R. Lapham, "Place du planning familial dans l'évolution récente de la natalité en Tunisie," *Revue Tunisienne des Sciences Sociales* 17-18 (1969): 379-413.

58. For a good summary of evidence, see Rose E. Frisch, "Demographic implications of the biological determinants of female fecundity," paper presented to the Population Association of America, New York, April 1974.

59. Rose E. Frisch, "Does malnutrition cause permanent retardation in human beings?" *Psychiatria, Neurologia, Neurochiurgia* 74 (1971): 463-479.

60. See A. Inkeles and D. Smith, *Becoming Modern* (Harvard: 1974); and an unpublished paper by A. Inkeles and K. Millar on fertility and individual modernization, 1975.

61. D. Nortman, "Parental age as a factor in pregnancy outcome and child development," *Reports on Population/Family Planning*, No. 16 (August 1974); and J.D. Wray, "Population pressure on families: family size and child spacing" in National Academy of Sciences, *Rapid Population Growth* 2 (1971): 403-461.

62. See the discussion and references provided by J.A. and S.R. Clausen, "The effects of family size on parents and children," in J.T. Fawcett (ed.), *Pavchological perspectives on population* (Basic Books, 1973).

63. See the two volumes edited by I. Nazer for IPPF, Near East Region, *Islam and family planning* (Beirut, 1974); *Muslim attitudes towards family planning*, edited by Olivia Schieffelin (The Population Council, 1967); B.F. Musallam, "The Islamic sanction of contraception" in *Population and its problems: A plain man's guide*, edited by H.B. Parry (Claredon, Oxford, 1974).

64. For details, see the recent *Population Bulletins* published by the Economic Commission for Western Asia, Beirut.

III The Economy of the Middle East and North Africa: An Overview

Charles Issawi

Recent Trends

Growth in 1960-71

In the recent development of the economy of the region a dividing point is constituted by the Tripoli-Tehran agreements of 1970-1971, which greatly increased the oil revenues of the oil producing countries and started a new chapter in the relations between governments and oil companies. Another important event was the economic impact of the October 1973 War and quadrupling of oil prices, the consequences of which have by no means yet worked themselves out.

The estimates of real growth in Gross National Product and per capita incomes made by the International Bank for Reconstruction and Development and published in *World Bank Atlas, 1973* are shown in Table III-1.

This shows marked contrast between the Asian and African subregions. First, per capita incomes are distinctly higher in the fifteen Asian than in the six African countries. The median figure in 1971 was $450 in the former and about $290 in the latter; and the mean figures $461 and $337, respectively; for both subregions combined, the median was $370 and the mean $405. Secondly, the Asian economies have, in general, been growing appreciably more rapidly than the African. The median rate of per capita increase in the period 1960-71 was 3.1 percent per annum in the former and 2.2 percent in the latter. Lastly, between 1960-65 and 1965-71 no less than nine of the fifteen Asian countries accelerated their per capita rate of growth while five reduced it; the group that raised its rate of growth consists of: Bahrain, Iran, Israel, Kuwait, Lebanon,

59

Table III-1

Gross National Product, Per Capita Income, and Rate of Growth in the Middle East and North Africa, 1960-71

	Population 1971 (000)	GNP 1971 ($ million)	Per Capita Income 1971 (US $)	Annual Rate of Growth (%) 1960-1971 GNP	Per Capita	1965-1971 GNP	Per Capita
Asia							
Bahrain	216	140	640	6.6	3.2	9.9	7.1+
Iran	29,780	13,420	450	9.5	6.5	10.7	7.7+
Iraq	9,750	3,560	370	5.6	2.4	4.6	1.4−
Israel	3,010	6,600	2,190	7.9	4.7	7.9	5.2+
Jordan	2,380	620	260	5.3	2.0	−0.1	−3.5−
Kuwait	830	3,200	3,860	7.7	−2.5	7.7	−2.1+
Lebanon	2,804	1,840	660	3.3	0.7	3.4	0.8+
Oman	600	270	450	17.0	15.0	27.7	25.1+
Qatar	127	300	2,370	12.3	2.9	15.4	5.8+
Saudi Arabia	7,487	4,010	540	9.8	8.1	9.1	7.4−
Syria	6,509	1,900	290	6.4	3.1	6.4	3.1
Turkey	36,160	12,160	340	6.2	3.7	6.5	4.0+
United Arab Emirates	235	740	3,150	29.7	20.6	27.8	17.8−
Yemen, North	5,900	480	90	4.2	2.0	4.6	2.4+
Yemen, South	1,470	170	120	−1.3	−4.5	−4.3	−7.2−
	107,258	49,410					
Africa							
Egypt	34,080	7,540	220	4.1	1.6	2.7	0.2−
Sudan	16,135	1,950	120	2.8	−	1.9	−0.9−
Libya	2,010	2,930	1,450	21.3	17.6	11.8	8.1−
Algeria	14,438	5,260	360	6.7	3.5	8.0	4.8+
Tunisia	5,245	1,670	320	4.9	2.8	5.7	3.6+
Morocco	15,379	4,040	260	3.8	1.1	5.2	2.5+
	87,287	29,390					
Grand Total	194,545	78,800					

Note: (+) indicates that the rate of per capita growth was higher in 1966-71 than in 1960-65, and (−) indicates that it was lower.

Source: Adapted from IBRD, *World Atlas, 1973.*

Oman, Qatar, Turkey, and North Yemen, i.e., all the major economies except for Iraq and Saudi Arabia. By contrast, in the African subregion only three countries accelerated their rate of growth (Algeria, Tunisia, Morocco) while three reduced it, including what was by far the largest economy, Egypt.

Per capital incomes in the Middle East and North Africa are still below those of Latin America but compare favorably with those of other developing regions.[a] As regards per capita rates of growth, the median for the Asian subregion was 3.1 percent in 1960-71 and 4 percent in 1965-71; for the African subregion it was about 2.2 percent and 3.1 percent, respectively. Here the Middle East compares favorably with other developing regions, but North Africa does not fare so well: for 1960-71, the median rate for Latin America was 2.3 percent per annum, for Asia 1.8 percent and for Africa 2.2 percent.

One further point should be noted: these high rates of economic growth in per capita incomes were achieved in spite of a very high rate of population increase—2.5 to 3 percent, or even more, per annum (see below, "Developments 1972-74"). In addition, the massive influx of people into the small oil-producing countries (Kuwait, Qatar, the United Arab Emirates and, to a much smaller extent, Libya) greatly raised their rate of population increase, resulting in a *decline* in per capita income in Kuwait and a very small rise in Qatar, in spite of high rates of growth in their GNP.

Finally, a few words may be said about the countries that had negative or very low rates of growth. In South Yemen, when the economy rested heavily on the Port of Aden with its British garrison, oil refinery, and bunkering facilities, the closing of the Suez Canal and the withdrawal of the British troops in 1967 was a crippling blow. In North Yemen, the civil war that dragged on through most of the 1960s was also a severe strain. In the Sudan, the civil war in the South drained the country's resources and resulted in a decline in per capita income in 1965-71 that wiped out the small gain achieved in 1960-65. In Jordan, the 1967 war converted what had been a very respectable rate of growth into a sharp decline, and the war was also partly responsible for the low growth rates of Egypt and Lebanon. And Algeria's long war of independence and the immense disruption caused by the exodus of one million Europeans, caused a sharp drop in GNP which has been made up only by the rapid growth of recent years.

Physical Indexes

In the Middle East and North Africa, as in other developing regions, the figures used to compute GNP, price deflators and even in many countries population size and growth, are very tentative. It is therefore necessary to complement and check them by some physical measures of economic activity, and five such indexes are given in Table III-2.

The rate of growth in the indexes is, in the main, somewhat higher than

[a]The median per capita income of the twenty-one Latin-American states in 1971 was $450. The Latin-American mean is relatively still higher, since the four largest economies (Brazil, Mexico, Argentina, and Venezuela) lie above the median. For the twenty-seven countries of Asia, including both China and Japan, the median figure was $150 and for the forty-eight countries of sub-Sahara Africa it was $160; in both continents, the mean was above the median if the exceptionally developed countries (Japan and South Africa) are included, but

Table III-2
Physical Indexes of Economic Activity

Country	Per Capita Energy Consumption (Kgs. of coal)		Per Capita Steel Consumption (Kgs.)		Cement Production (000 tons)		Electricity Output (million kwh)		Commercial Vehicles (000)	
	1959	1972	1960	1972	1960	1972	1960	1972	1960	1972
Iran	332	954	25	59	797	3,600	(1,000)	9,100	44	88
Iraq	456	642	33	47	813	1,856	852	2,261[a]	20	46
Israel	1,135	2,712	170	234	806	1,545	2,313	7,639	24	85
Jordan	179	331	..	15	165	662	(95)	249	5	6
Kuwait	..	10,441	..	206	—	1,499[a]	249	3,295	(10)	43[a]
Lebanon	644	889	107	144	854	1,626	422	1,545	9	19
Saudi Arabia	198	900	12	69	60	910	44	1,000	(26)	50[b]
Syria	256	455	23	42	489	1,004	368	1,223	12	20
Turkey	239	564	22	55	2,038	8,421	2,815	11,242	68	164[a]
Yemen North	6	13	..	..	..	..	..	19[a]	..	..
Yemen South	1,265	423	..	..	..	..	144	139	2	4[a]
Total					6,022	21,123	8,302	37,712	220	525
Algeria	241	533	52	48	1,062	964[a]	1,325	2,270	75	82[a]
Egypt	240	324	30	30	2,047	3,921[a]	2,639	8,030	20	39
Libya	299	4,407	..	224	—	72[a]	107	508[a]	10	45[b]
Morocco	126	223	14	21	580	1,542	1,012	2,196	47	91[a]
Sudan	52	119	..	5	91	189[a]	74	259[a]	14	18[a]
Tunisia	154	349	13	57	405	629	316	1,013	24	47
Total					4,185	7,317	5,473	14,276	190	322
Grand Total					10,207	28,440	13,775	51,988	410	847

[a]1971
[b]1970

Source: Adapted from *United Nations Statistical Yearbook*, various issues; figures in brackets estimated.

that of GNP or per capita income, but the general ranking is similar.[b] Comparison with the figures for other regions confirms the fact that the Middle East and North Africa grew much more rapidly than did the world as a whole and other developing areas.

It remains, briefly, to mention the forces that have pushed the Middle Eastern, and at a slower pace the North African, economies along this path of growth. In recent years, the most powerful single factor has been the spectacular expansion of the petroleum industry. Prior to the growth of the oil industry, foreign aid was the major force in many countries. The third, and most immediate, cause of growth was the rise in investment rates, made possible in most countries by the increase in petroleum revenues or the inflow of foreign aid. The fourth factor was the provision of infrastructure and the development of human resources, starting in the 1920s and greatly accelerating in the last two decades.[1]

Consumption and Income Distribution

It is necessary to inquire how this increase in incomes was used. Since, except in countries with enormous oil revenues, such as Kuwait, Libya, and Saudi Arabia (see below), savings ratios generally remained constant or rose very little until about 1970, it may be taken that total consumption advanced at much the same pace as income. Within this field, government consumption grew far more rapidly than did private—generally about twice as fast—and its share in the total rose significantly in almost every country through the 1950s and 60s. Defense accounted for the bigger part of this increase (see below), but a large part was used for social services—education, health, cheap urban housing, provision of drinking water to the villages, and rudimentary welfare services such as old age pensions and other forms of assistance—which were of direct benefit to the poorer classes.

Luxury consumption also increased rapidly, as the rise in the number of passenger automobiles, (see Table III-3) upper and middle class housing, travel and various forms of luxury imports attests. The level of living of the masses has also somewhat improved, as is shown by the increased consumption of such staples as sugar, tea, textiles, shoes, and, at a somewhat higher level, radios, printing and writing paper, and bicycles (see Table III-3). No one who remembers conditions in the region either before or immediately after the Second World War can doubt that the urban working class, and at least part of

[b]Excluding the abnormal cases of Oman and United Arab Emirates, the highest growth in per capita income in 1960-71 is shown by Libya, followed by Saudi Arabia, Iran, Israel, and Turkey, in that order. In three of the indexes (energy, steel, and commercial vehicles) Libya also ranks first; Saudi Arabia ranks first in electricity and second in energy and steel and Iran second in electricity and third in energy and steel. Turkey is among the top five countries in all series. These similarities in rank order inspire some confidence in the rates of growth shown in Table III-1.

Table III-3
Indexes of Consumption

	Sugar		Tea		Textiles		Paper		Radios		Cars	
	1963	1971-72	1963-65	1968-70	1961-62	1971-72	1960	1970-71	1960	1972	1960	1972
Asia												
Bahrain	..	..	..	..	..	..	..	..	82	335	6[a]	13
Iran	18	28	821	843	4.3	5.1	0.6	3.9	45	229	92	394
Iraq	24	33	2,327	2,202[a]	4.5	4.5	1.1	1.3	13	106[a]	40	76
Israel	46	65	..	..	8.1	13.3	6.0	12.0	194	221	27	201
Jordan	..	..	903	1,250[a]	4.2	4.1	1.2	1.0[a]	38	203	6	18
Kuwait	..	..	..	..	..	..	3.0[b]	9.1	270	132[a]	30[b]	131[c]
Lebanon	..	..	..	..	8.9	9.9	..	7.0	61	211[a]	47	165
Saudi Arabia	..	..	..	..	..	..	0.1	0.9	12	11[a]	31[d]	65[e]
Syria	18	26	567	506[a]	4.8	6.8	0.3	1.2	57	374	17	32
Turkey	15	20	336	664[b]	4.9	6.7	0.8[b]	1.5	49	107	46	147[e]
South Yemen	..	..	..	..	..	..	..	0.3	52	..	9	13[c]
Africa												
Algeria	20	17	322	281	1.9	4.6	2.6	2.7	54	47	170	135[c]
Egypt	16	16	907	803	4.1	4.6	1.6	1.5	58	143	71	152
Libya	..	..	..	..	2.9	9.7	0.4	0.9	62	46	18	100[e]
Morocco	33	29	794	863	2.9	3.0	0.9	0.8[a]	46	95	125	242[c]
Sudan	12	17	748	1,074[b]	2.4	2.9	0.1	0.3	1	80	15	30[c]
Tunisia	..	..	1,043	888	2.5	3.1	2.7	1.0[a]	41	74	44	80

Notes:

1. Sugar: kilograms per capita per annum

2. Tea: grams per capita per annum; a. 1969-71; b. 1970-72.

3. Textiles: Cotton, wool, flax, and other natural and man-made fibres, kilograms per capita per annum.

4. Paper: Printing and writing paper, not including newsprint, kilograms per capita per annum; a. 1970; b. 1965.

5. Radios per 1,000 inhabitants; Israel, Turkey, Algeria, Egypt, Libya, Morocco, Sudan, Tunisia: licensed sets; other countries estimated number in use; a. 1971.

6. Passenger cars, thousands; a. 1963; b. 1961; c. 1971; d. 1962; e. 1970.

Sources: Adapted from United Nations *Statistical Yearbook, 1973*; UNESCO, *Statistical Yearbook, 1972*; FAO "Per Caput Fibre Consumption Levels."

the peasantry, live somewhat better than before. This is surely true of the Middle Eastern subregion and probably also of former French North Africa where the decline in per capita consumption is attributable to the mass exodus of the European population that lived at a far higher level than the Arab.

However, as in other parts of the world which have experienced rapid economic growth, a disproportionately large share of the increment in income and wealth has gone to the upper classes, and the degree of inequality of income has widened. Reliable figures on income distribution are scarce, but it would seem that in such typical countries in Egypt, Iraq, Lebanon, Syria, and Turkey, the top 5 percent of the population receives one-third or more of total income, a figure similar to that prevailing in other underdeveloped regions but distinctly higher than the one-fifth to a quarter found in Western Europe and the United States. Moreover, in most countries the factors furthering inequality seem to have outweighed those reducing it. The chief leveling factors have been the expropriation and exodus of the foreigners who owned such a large proportion of the wealth of Egypt, Libya, and French Africa, the land reforms that transferred large areas and income flows from landlords to peasants in Egypt, Iraq, Syria, and Iran in 1952-63, and the nationalizations and expropriations in Egypt, Iraq, and Syria in the 1960s.

Offsetting these equalizing factors has been the rapid growth of the oil industry which has had a profoundly unequalizing impact. In the first place, for a long time the bulk of the enormous revenues flowing from oil accrued to the ruling clans and their dependents. Later, when a distinction was made between the ruler's privy purse and the government budget, a very large share of oil revenues was absorbed by the army and bureaucracy, especially in their higher ranks. The same was true of the other countries of the region, where the huge expansion in the numbers and pay of the army and bureaucracy is reflected in the rapid growth of public consumption.

The same factors, together with the more rapid rate of growth in industry and other urban activities than in agriculture and their more privileged position (see below), explain the increasing inequality in levels of living between town and country. This is particularly true of the capital city, which tends to account for most manufacturing, commercial, and financial activities and to contain a large fraction of the bureaucracy. Finally, as in other developing countries, economic progress tends to widen the gap between certain regions that become "growth poles" and the rest of the country, e.g., the Aegean provinces in Turkey, the Caspian in Iran, the Eastern (oil) province of Saudi Arabia, and the Gezira region in Sudan.

This process of increasing inequality is most noticeable in what were formerly the most equalitarian societies of the region, i.e., the tribal societies of Arabia and Libya and countries like Israel, Lebanon, Sudan, and Turkey, where wealth, and more particularly land, was fairly widely diffused. In all these countries the level of the masses has appreciably risen, but the concentration of wealth and incomes at the top has increased even more and consequently inequality has widened. In such countries as Egypt, Iraq, Syria, and Iran, a great measure of inequality had prevailed for at least a hundred years longer; it is possible that the land reforms in these countries, and the expropriations in the first three, may have somewhat reduced it.

Savings and Investment

Rapid economic growth presupposes a high rate of investment, and sustained growth requires, in addition, a high rate of saving. Until the Second World War, both prerequisites to growth were low and, since there was practically no flow of foreign capital into the Middle East except to the oil industry and Palestine, they were roughly equal. In the 1930s, the gross investment rate was probably around 5 to 8 percent in Egypt, Iraq and Syria, somewhat higher in Iran and about 10 percent in Turkey; all of this was covered by domestic savings. In Palestine, an investment rate as high as 30 percent was more than covered by the inflow of Jewish funds, giving a negative rate of savings. Large Italian government funds in Libya and private French capital in Morocco also produced relatively high investment rates.

During the Second World War the vast Allied military expenditures, the sharp decline in imports and the general shortage of goods and the consequent rise in prices led to a decline in consumption and an increase in forced savings, mainly in the form of sterling, franc and gold balances. After 1945 these were drawn down and helped to raise investment rates. By the late 1940s or early 50s, a savings rate of around 10 percent obtained in Egypt, Lebanon, and Turkey, and a somewhat larger figure was attained in Iraq and Syria, while investment rates rose correspondingly, or slightly more. The overall rate continued to be zero or negative in Israel and close to zero in Jordan; in both countries savings were positive in the private sector and negative in the public. Large foreign aid to both countries, however, resulted in an investment rate close to 10 percent in Jordan and 25 percent or more in Israel.

In the 1950s, the revenues of oil producing countries rose dramatically (see Table III-4) and most of the other countries began to receive increasing amounts of foreign aid. This made it possible to raise investment rates sharply without a corresponding rise in the savings rate or a slowing down of the growth of consumption. As Table III-4 shows, by the mid-1960s investment ran at 15 to 20 percent of GDP, but the Arab-Israeli arms race, accelerated by the 1967 war, reduced it very considerably in some of the countries concerned, such as Egypt, Lebanon, and Syria. These same factors also affected savings in these states as well as in Israel and Jordan.

Four groups of countries may be distinguished in Table III-4. In Kuwait, Libya, and Saudi Arabia—and also in Abu Dhabi and Qatar—as a result of large

Table III-4

Gross Saving and Investment Ratios (as percentages of Gross Domestic Product)

	1957 or 1958[a]		1960-62		1966-68		1970	
	I	S	I	S	I	S	I	S
Kuwait	20	45	12	84	18	73	15[b]	52[b]
Libya	19	10	49	12	20	42	25[c]	55[c]
Saudi Arabia	..	..	15	30	16	36	21[c]	60[c]
Algeria	..	..	24	11	18	17	30	26
Iran	17	16	15	15	19	19	19[a]	15[a]
Iraq	23	27	19	18	16	22	17[d]	21[d]
Egypt	14	12	17	13	19	18	12[e]	9[e]
Morocco	..	..	11	10	14	12	15	10
Sudan	9	9	16	13	10	11	14[b]	11[b]
Syria	20	20	17	11	17	17	14[a]	11[a]
Tunisia	..	..	19	8	22	11	22	16
Turkey	13	13	15	11	17	16	18[a]	16[a]
Israel	29	13	26	12	19	5	25	1
Jordan	13	0	17	9	16	4	20[c]	0[c]
Lebanon	16	15	22	15	23	8	18[c]	4[c]

[a]Percent of GNP.

[b]1969.

[c]1968.

[d]1969, percent of GNP

[e]1968/69, percent of GNP.

Source: Adapted from United Nations, *World Economic Survey, 1969-1970* (New York, 1970), pp. 209-210, and others.

oil revenues savings were abnormally high, amounting to over half of GDP or GNP. Although domestic investment was high, it could absorb only a fraction of savings, and the balance was transferred abroad in the form oil grants, loans or foreign exchange reserves.

The second group of nations consists of those oil producing countries with relatively large populations and abundant natural resources. Here oil revenues, although large, could until the last year or two be easily absorbed at home. In fact, both Algeria and Iran drew largely on foreign resources in the 1960s to supplement their domestic savings.

The third group includes four of the five most populous countries of the region and accounts for some three-fifths of its population. In these nations, as in other developing countries, domestic savings covered only three-quarters to four-fifths of investment, the balance was met from foreign grants, loans or investments. Declining saving rates or a decreased inflow of foreign funds, or both, combined to reduce investment rates in most of the countries of this group in the late 1960s and early 70s.

Lastly, there are the three contiguous states of Israel, Jordan, and Lebanon. All three have traditionally relied rather heavily upon outside funds and, in the last twenty years, this dependence has increased. Thus, by 1970, domestic savings were negligible in all of them and almost the whole of investment was met by foreign resources.

In the mid-1960s the performance of the Asian part of the region compared very favorably with that of other underdeveloped areas with respect to savings and investment as did the African subregion.[2] The next few years saw a deterioration in several countries. But the enormous rise in oil revenues has clearly put the oil producers in a special category: in all the ones listed in Table III-4 the savings ratio is bound to rise to well over 50 percent of GDP, and in many it will be far higher. For the nonproducing countries, however, the initial impact of the rise in oil and other prices has been unfavorable, and their savings ratio is sure to be sharply reduced. Whether their investment rate will fall correspondingly will depend on how much aid they receive from foreign sources—either the oil producing states or the advanced countries, or both. What is certain is that their dependence on outside help has greatly increased and will remain high in the foreseeable future.

Composition of GNP

Table III-5 brings out both the distinctive pattern and the trend of the composition of GNP in the Middle East and North Africa. The main characteristics of the pattern—apart from the high and rapidly growing contribution of oil—are the small share of agriculture and the large share of services, compared to other developing regions with equal per capita incomes.[3] The small share of agriculture is explained by the aridity of the region, the neglect of'agriculture and underpricing of its products (see below), and the large size of the oil and services sectors. The services sector is swollen by income which accrues as a result of location (e.g., Suez Canal, dues on oil pipelines); by pilgrimage and tourism; by the very large size of the government sector; and by the receipt of massive foreign aid (see below) which has enabled the beneficiaries to import food and other goods rather than produce them at home and has made possible a disproportionate growth in services.

The main trends are the decline in the share of agriculture and rise in services in practically every country; the expansion of the oil sector; and the sharp increase in the industrial sector. In Israel, Egypt, Turkey, and Tunisia manufacturing, mining (excluding oil), construction and power account for well over a quarter of GDP, and in Iran, Lebanon, Algeria, and Morocco for well over a

Table III-5
Percentage Composition of Gross Domestic Product

	1950				1971			
	A	M	O	S	A	M	O	S
Algeria[e]	33	24	–	43	12	26	18	44
Egypt[a,e]	35	13	–	52	25	25	–	50
Iran[b]	31	14	17	38	15	20	28	37
Iraq[a,e]	22	10	40	28	21	15	32	32
Israel	11	30	–	59	6	30	–	64
Jordan[b]	16	14	–	70	17	13	–	70
Kuwait	–	–	–	–	–	6	67	27
Lebanon	20	18	–	62	8	21	–	71
Libya[b]	10	14	23	53	2	9	61	28
Morocco	30	24	–	46	31	28	–	41
Saudi Arabia[c,f]	9	8	54	29	6	12	48	34
Sudan[d,e]	61	11	–	28	35	16	–	49
Syria[a]	44	15	–	41	22	24	–	54
Tunisia[b]	25	25	–	50	17	22	–	61
Turkey	49	16	–	35	28	28	–	44

A – Agriculture, Forestry, Fishing.
M – Manufacturing, Mining, Power, Construction.
O – Oil.
S – Services.

[a]1953.   [d]1956.
[b]1960.   [e]1970.
[c]1963.   [f]1969.

Sources: Adapted from IBRD, *World Tables*, table 4; United Nations, *Statistical Yearbook, 1973*; other sources.

fifth. These trends will continue, for in all countries the rate of growth of oil, manufacturing, and services is far greater than that of agriculture—usually about twice as high—and there is no sign that the governments are changing their basic economic strategy which has stressed industry, construction and certain public services.

Petroleum

No industry has ever risen so suddenly to a commanding position in the world economy as Middle Eastern petroleum. At present, the Middle East accounts for

55 percent of world reserves and 58 percent of exports, North Africa account for 7 and 10 percent, respectively. The growth in both output and oil revenues is shown in Table III-6. Significant oil revenues have also accrued to nonproducing countries: in the late 1960s, Syria received some $60 million a year from pipeline tolls, Lebanon $15 million and Jordan $5 million. The figures are now higher; and, until the closure of the Suez Canal in 1967, Egypt earned over $200 million a year in tanker dues.

The huge expansion in oil revenues is partially the result of the increase in production, but is related even more closely to the steep rise in the producing governments' revenue per barrel. Until 1950, most concession agreements provided for a fixed royalty payment of 20-25 cents per barrel of oil produced; this meant that some 20 percent of the gross income produced in the Middle Eastern oil industry accrued to the governments and 80 percent to the companies.[4] In 1950-52, this arrangement was replaced by the so-called 50-50 profit sharing agreements, which raised the governments' take per barrel to 70-80 cents, and their share to a half, or over, of gross income. Thanks to various concessions obtained by the Organization of Petroleum Exporting Countries (OPEC) from the oil companies in the 1960s, the governments' take had risen to some 87 cents a barrel by 1970, and their share to about 60 percent of gross income and over 70 percent of net income (i.e., after deduction of 10-20 cents representing costs of production). The Tripoli-Teheran agreements of 1970-71 raised the take per barrel to about $1.25 in 1971 and $1.40 in 1972 and the share of net income to some 80 percent. The 1973 rise in price and taxes, and subsequent developments, including the acquisition of oil company equity, mean that today, the host governments receive about $9 to $10 per barrel, and absorb over 95 percent of both gross and net income.

The petroleum industry is by far the largest sector of the region's economy, both in terms of its importance for the rest of the world and its contribution to GNPs. But until quite recently, its impact on the national economies was limited. This was partially due to a number of factors: the highly capital intensive nature of the industry, which kept its labor force rather small; its self-sufficiency, which reduced the need to provide overhead capital that could have served a wider segment of the economy; the isolated and inhospitable location of the oil fields and low economic and social level of the surrounding populations, which prevented the industry from being integrated in the local economies and made it dependent on imported inputs as well as preventing the utilization of such valuable by-products as natural or refinery gases. Nevertheless, even by the 1950s the large oil revenues had become of crucial importance.

By the late 1960's employment in the oil industry in Algeria, Iran, and Iraq represented less than 1 percent of the labor force, and in Kuwait, Libya, and Saudi Arabia some 2 to 3 percent. Petroleum's share in GDP had risen to 20-30 percent or over in the three larger countries and 60 percent or more in the smaller ones. Oil revenues constituted more than 50 percent of total government

Table III-6
Petroleum Production (millions of metric tons) and Government Revenues (millions of dollars)

		1938	1948	1960	1970	1973	1974[c]	1975[c]	1980[c]
Abu Dhabi	P	—	—	—	33	63			
	R	—	—	—	233	1,000	4,800	6,580	14,750
Iran	P	10	25	53	191	293			
	R	15	75	285	1,136	3,900	14,930	17,100	30,700
Iraq	P	4	3	48	77	97			
	R	10	9	266	521	1,500	5,900	7,550	16,750
Kuwait	P	—	6	86	151	152			
	R	—	14	415	895	2,100	7,990	10,050	12,850
Qatar	P	—	—	8	18	27			
	R	—	—	54	122	400	1,425	1,650	2,900
Saudi Arabia	P	—	19	66	189	378			
	R	2	53	346	1,200	4,900	19,400	22,850	43,450
Total Middle East[a]	P	16	55	262	688	1,045			
	R	28	153	1,379	4,257	14,850	66,090	78,700	139,400
Algeria	P	—	—	9	49	51			
	R	—	—	—	325	1,000	3,700	4,250	5,750
Libya	P	—	—	—	160	105			
	R	—	—	—	1,295	2,200	7,990	10,050	12,850
Total North Africa[b]	P	0.2	2	12	237	174			
	R	—	—	—	1,620	3,200	11,690	14,300	18,600
Grand Total	P	16	57	274	925	1,219			
	R	28	153	1,379	5,877	18,050	77,780	93,000	158,000

[a]Includes Bahrain, Oman (beginning in 1967) and Dubai (beginning in 1969).
[b]Includes Egypt, Tunisia, and Morocco.
[c]Estimates.

Sources: Charles Issawi and Mohammed Yegareh, *The Economics of Middle Eastern Oil* (New York: Praeger, 1963); *Petroleum Press Service*, November 1973 and May 1974; IBRD estimates for 1973-80, as quoted in *Middle East Economic Digest*, January 25, 1974; United Nations, *Statistical Yearbook, 1949-50, BP Statistical Review of the World Oil Industry.*

revenues in the former group and 80 to 90 percent, or over, in the latter. Except in Iran and Algeria, oil exports provided practically all the foreign exchange earned by the producing countries and, directly or indirectly, accounted for the bulk of capital formation.

No figures which show the effect of the huge expansion in oil revenues that took place in 1973 and 1974 on the economies of the producing countries are available. Its magnitude is, however, indicated by Table III-7, which compares estimated oil revenues in 1974 with estimated GNP in 1973. Even in the largest country, Iran, the oil industry overshadows the rest of the economy, and this situation is likely to prevail for many years, until the oil revenues begin to decline in absolute terms and the investments made in the other sectors come to fruition.

Agriculture

As Table III-8 shows, in 1961-72 total agricultural and food production in the Middle East and North Africa rose distinctly faster than in other developing regions, or in the world as a whole. On a per capita basis, the region also did a little better than other developing areas, though less well than the world. In the Middle East, per capita output fell considerably in Jordan, Syria, and North Yemen, and in North Africa in Algeria; particularly noteworthy increases were registered in Israel, Lebanon, Sudan, and Morocco. However, it should be noted that in the previous decade (1951-60) the region's performance had been much less satisfactory.

Table III-7
Estimated Petroleum Revenues, 1974 and GNP, 1973
(Millions of dollars)

	Oil Revenues	GNP	Ratio of Revenues to GNP
Abu Dhabi	4,800	1,200	4.0
Iran	14,900	22,700	0.7
Iraq	5,900	4,500	1.3
Kuwait	8,000	4,200	1.9
Qatar	1,400	450	3.1
Saudi Arabia	19,400	5,800	3.3
Algeria	3,700	5,800	0.6
Libya	8,000	4,300	1.9

Source: 1973 GNP for Iran, Kuwait, and Saudi Arabia from U.S. Department of Commerce, *The Near East Market* (Washington, D.C.: GPO, July 1974); other figures by extrapolation from 1971.

Table III-8
Index Numbers of Agricultural Production
(1961-65 = 100)

| | Total Agricultural | | | | Food | | | |
| | Total | | Per Capita | | Total | | Per Capita | |
	1961-62	1971-72	1961-62	1971-72	1961-62	1971-72	1961-62	1971-72
Iran	99	133	103	105	99	133	103	105
Iraq	101	153	106	115	101	155	106	116
Israel	89	174	95	138	88	170	94	136
Jordan	85	74	90	57	84	72	89	56
Lebanon	90	142	93	111	90	141	94	111
Saudi Arabia	96	128	99	102	96	128	99	102
Syria	92	111	96	85	94	111	98	85
Turkey	95	132	97	106	96	130	100	104
North Yemen	99	107	103	86	99	108	103	85
South Yemen	96	124	99	99	97	127	101	101
Algeria	98	109	101	84	98	107	96	83
Egypt	92	128	96	102	93	131	97	104
Libya	93	138	98	103	92	139	98	104
Morocco	88	146	91	115	88	147	91	115
Sudan	96	158	100	123	93	158	98	122
Tunisia	83	134	87	104	83	135	87	105
World	96	124	99	106	96	126	99	107
Near East	95	132	99	104	96	131	100	104
Africa	95	125	99	101	95	125	99	102
Latin America	95	124	100	97	95	126	100	99
Far East	98	123	101	100	98	123	101	100

Source: Adapted from Food and Agricultural Organization, *Production Yearbook*, 1972 (Rome, 1973).

Weather conditions, and more particularly rainfall, are still the major factor affecting crops, but the rise in output reflects some of the structural, organizational and technical changes that have taken place in the region's agriculture. In recent years, the bulk of the increase has come from intensification of production rather than the extension of farmland. Between 1948-52 and 1963-64 the total area planted to cereals (mainly wheat, barley, millet, maize, rice, and oats, in that order, which account for some four-fifths of the cultivated area) in the Near East[c] increased by 43 percent, while the yield of wheat and barley rose by only 15 percent. By contrast, between 1961-62 and 1971-72, total area rose from 32,500,000 to 34,600,000 hectares, or by only 6 percent, total output from 34,900,000 to 46,300,000 metric tons, or 33 percent, and overall yield from 1,072 to 1,340 kilograms, or 25 percent.

But in spite of this increase, yields are still very low in the Middle East and even lower in North Africa. Wheat yields per hectare are about 500 kilograms or less in Algeria, Libya, and Tunisia but somewhat higher in Morocco and Sudan. Egypt is a striking exception, with wheat yields of nearly 3,000 kilograms and correspondingly high maize and cotton yields. Lebanon, Iran and Syria approach the 1,000 kilogram mark, Israel, Turkey, and the cultivated parts of the Arabian peninsula exceed it, and Iraq falls well below it. For comparison, in Western Europe yields exceed 4,000 kilograms, and in the United States and Japan they are over 2,000.

This rise in yields has resulted from greater inputs of labor, due to population growth, and capital. Higher input of capital has taken many forms. First, there is the extension of irrigation which raises yields, allows double cropping and thus raises output per acre by three to six times and reduces its annual fluctuations. Secondly, there is the sharp increase in the use of chemical fertilizers. Between 1961-65 and 1971, the Near East's consumption of nitrogenous fertilizers rose by 148 percent, of phosphates 196 percent, and of potash 92 percent.[5] But except in Egypt, Israel, and Lebanon, where use of fertilizers per acre is at the West European level, application of fertilizers is still very restricted and confined to the more valuable cash crops. Other forms of capital input include a large increase in the use of pesticides and selected seeds. Lastly, there is mechanization. The number of agriculatural tractors in the Near East more than doubled between 1961-65 and 1971, rising from 96,000 to 202,000,[6] but here too, except in Israel, the ratio of machines to cultivated area is still extremely low. And, generally speaking, in all the above-mentioned respects, and with the exception of Egypt, North Africa stands well below the Middle East.

One more trend should be mentioned, though it has so far made little contribution to increasing total agricultural output—the shift to more valuable cash crops. These include cotton, sugar beets, rice, and fruits and vegetables. But

[c]The area designated as the Near East by the FAO includes the Asian part of the region, plus Afghanistan and Cyprus, as well as Egypt, Sudan and Libya, i.e., it covers the Middle East and North Africa except for Algeria, Morocco and Tunisia.

the region still has not taken advantage of the possibilities offered by its climate and proximity to both Western and Eastern Europe, which enable it to supply both markets with early ripening fruits, vegetables and flowers. Indeed, one major country, Algeria, has moved in the opposite direction, tearing up its vineyards and replacing them with food crops.

The basic pattern of Middle Eastern and North African agriculture may be described in two statements: low output per man, except in Israel; and low output per acre, except in Egypt, Israel, and Lebanon. In the 1960's, net agricultural output per farm worker was between $300 and $500 in practically every country except Israel, where it stood at around $2,000. And net output per hectare of arable land ranged between $50 and $100 except for Egypt, Israel and Lebanon where it stood at $500-$600. Both sets of figures are in line with those of other developing regions to which the Middle East compares somewhat more favorably than North Africa.[7]

The low level of output in the region is due not only to unfavorable climate—notably the scarcity and extreme variability of rainfall—and poor techniques, but also to defective organization and unfavorable land tenure systems. In the last twenty-five years the governments of the region have attempted, with varying degrees of success, to supply more agricultural credit, improve country roads, build storage facilities, and provide agricultural credit and extension services. Major land reforms have been implemented in Egypt (1952), Syria and Iraq (1958), Iran (1963) and, mainly as part of decolonization, Algeria, Tunisia, and Morocco. Of these, the Egyptian and Iranian programs have been most successful. Land reform demonstrates the growing awareness of the importance of agriculture, but that sector is still far from receiving the attention it deserves. In several countries prices paid to farmers are set at low levels, in order to keep down the cost of living in the towns. In all of them agricultural credit, compared to that available to other sectors, is still very inadequate. And in all, the share of agriculture in total investment is much too small, compared to its contribution to GNP, employment and exports; available figures for 1961-67 range from 20-25 percent in Sudan and Egypt, through 15-20 percent for Tunisia, Syria and Turkey, to 10 percent or less for Israel, Iraq, and Algeria.[8] Clearly, agriculture remains a neglected sector and one that will demand far greater attention and efforts in the next decades.

Manufacturing

In the past twenty years, manufacturing has, in real terms, been the fastest growing sector of the region's economy. In the 1960s, output in the four leading industrial countries (Turkey, Egypt, Israel, and Iran) increased at over 10 percent per annum, and similar rates were registered in Jordan, Saudi Arabia, and Libya. Other countries that also advanced fairly fast (6-7 percent) were

Lebanon, Iraq, Syria, and Kuwait. In North Africa, Morocco, and Tunisia grew at only about 4 percent per annum, but Algeria, after a prolonged stagnation following independence, has recently been expanding its industrial output very rapidly.[9]

This rapid growth reflects the high level of investment in manufacturing. Some 20 to 30 percent of total investment has gone to manufacturing in Egypt, Turkey, Israel, Iran, Algeria, Iraq, and Syria, a proportion far higher than that devoted to agriculture, which is still so much more important in terms of employment, exports and, in most countries, contribution to GNP. Indeed the only countries that seem to be investing more in agriculture than in industry are Sudan and Tunisia, which put only 10 to 15 percent of their total investment in manufacturing.[10]

This high level of investment reflects the determination of the governments to industrialize their countries at all costs. But in spite of a marked modernization of equipment, capital investment per worker is still low, typically some $3,000 in the 1960s, except in the largest and most recently installed plants. Similarly, although output per worker has risen appreciably, it still remains low. In 1963, value added per worker was around or slightly above $1,000 a year in Egypt, Algeria, Morocco, Tunisia, Libya, Iran, and Turkey, less in Iraq and Syria, about $2,000 in Lebanon and nearly $3,000 in Israel; it may be assumed that the present levels are approximately twice as high. In 1963, the comparable figure in India was $250, in Latin America typically $1,500-$2,000 and in Western Europe $2,500-$4,000.

The growth in industrial output has gone mainly to the home market, since all the countries have followed a policy of import substitution and have given their industries a very high degree of protection. As a result, in many industries costs are far above world levels, and in some the value added is negative, i.e., the value of the products (estimated at world prices) is lower than the sum of the values of the inputs. Only a few industries are competitive in foreign markets and, except in Israel—and to a far lesser degree Lebanon, Egypt, and Iran—the share of nonresource-based manufactures in commodity exports is very low.

As in other developing regions, industrialization started with three main sectional groups: food processing, textiles, and building materials. Since then, as elsewhere, other industries have grown much more rapidly, particularly petrochemicals, basic metals, and engineering, Israel has developed a wide variety of precision instrument and science-based industries. Nevertheless, taking the region as a whole, the earlier and simpler industries are still predominate.

Balance of Payments

Until the late 1960s, all the countries, except for those with small populations and with large oil revenues such as Kuwait, Saudi Arabia, and Libya, had deficits in their accounts, and generally the deficits were large. Excluding oil, every country usually had an import surplus and although tourism and other services met part of the trade deficit in certain countries (Israel, Lebanon, Tunisia) they were far from covering the whole. In the early postwar years, several countries such as Egypt, Turkey, Israel, Lebanon, and Syria drew on the sterling and other balances they had accumulated during the Second World War. In the 1950s and 60s, foreign aid played the major role. As Table III-9 shows, from 1945 through 1972 United States grants and loans to the region exceeded

Table III-9
Economic Aid Disbursed or Committed
(Millions of dollars)

	Disbursements from Developed Market Economies and Multilateral Institutions[1] (Average 1970-72)	United States[2] 1945 through 1972	Centrally Planned Economies[3] 1954 through 1972
Iran	12	1,238	1,401
Iraq	11	44	965
Israel	73	1,810	−
Jordan	70	752	−
Kuwait	−3	25	−
Lebanon	12	106	−
Saudi Arabia	3	76	−
Syria	15	55	587
Turkey	(30)	2,559	(250)
North Yemen	13	48	141
South Yemen	4	48	
UNRWA	−	621	83
Algeria	116	192	907
Egypt	39	1,227	2,327
Libya	11	206	−
Morocco	103	781	85
Sudan	13	103	283
Tunisia	112	696	143
	(634)	10,539	(7,172)

1. Average annual disbursements of official development assistance.

2. Grants and credits.

3. Commitments; a little over half the total was provided by the Soviet Union and the balance by East Europe and China.

Sources: Adapted from *Statistical Abstract of the United States, 1973; United Nations Statistical Yearbook, 1973.*

$10 billion and went to every single country; the main beneficiaries were Turkey, Israel, Iran, and Egypt, in that order, followed by Morocco, Jordan and Tunisia. Commitments of aid by the Sino-Soviet bloc in 1954 through 1972 exceeded $7 billion, and actual disbursements may have been around $5 billion; a little over half of this sum came from the Soviet Union. Here the main beneficiaries were Egypt, Iran, Iraq, Algeria, and Syria; the number of recipients was much smaller than those which received United States aid. Neither set of figures includes military aid, which both the United States and the USSR may have individually extended in excess of $10 billion. Further large sources of aid were France for North Africa; Germany and various Jewish agencies for Israel; Britain for Jordan, and various other countries, as well as the International Bank for Reconstruction and Development (IBRD) and the United Nations and its agencies. In 1970-72 aid from the Western countries and the multilateral institutions averaged over $600 million per annum. In addition, large amounts from Kuwait, Saudi Arabia, and Libya flowed to various Arab countries.

In the early 1970s important shifts took place, which are reflected in Table III-10. First, oil revenues increased rapidly, and all producers except Algeria had substantial surpluses in their current accounts. Several of them, notably Libya, Kuwait, Saudi Arabia, and Abu Dhabi, used this surplus to help Egypt, Jordan, and other Arab countries, enabling them to convert a large deficit in their merchandise and services account into an overall surplus on current account. Tourism played an increasingly important role in Israel, Lebanon, Tunisia, and Morocco. Lastly, two countries with chronic deficits, Turkey and Algeria, began to receive massive remittances from their workers in Germany and France—over $1,000 million for Turkey in 1973, giving it an overall surplus, and some $250 million for Algeria; workers' remittances were also significant in Jordan, Morocco and Tunisia. Thus, with two major exceptions, Algeria and Israel, and three minor ones—Syria, Tunisia, and Lebanon—the region had emerged as a large surplus area. The rise in the price of oil, food and other commodities in 1974 has, however, changed this situation drastically, as will be described below.

Developments 1972-74

North Africa

Algeria. During the Four Year Plan, 1969-73, GDP is estimated to have grown at 7 percent per annum, in real terms, and would have done even better if there had not been a slowdown in 1971, following the nationalization of the oil industry. Consumption rose at almost 9 percent per annum but investment rose at 18 percent, pushing up the ratio of gross domestic savings to GDP from 27 percent in 1969 to the exceedingly high rate of 33 percent in 1973, and the investment ratio rose from 30 to 37 percent. Agriculture showed no increase over the

Table III-10
Main Items in Balance of Payments, 1973
(Provisional) (Millions of SDR)

	Imports	Exports	Other Major	Net Current Account
Algeria	1,717	1,469	253[a]	−356
Egypt	1,318	840	532[b]	65
Iran	3,308	5,597	−1,623[c]	339
Iraq[1]	696	1,538	−619[c]	188
Israel	2,279	1,288	1,846[d]	−312
Jordan	278	62	157[b]	32
Kuwait	(800)	(1,800)	..	(500)
Lebanon[2]	621	288	133[f]	−15
Libya	2,674	4,169	−1,904[e]	−863
Morocco	867	764	206[f]	87
Saudi Arabia	1,518	7,399	−2,802[c]	2,265
Sudan	308	373	..	21
Syria	410	195	109[g]	−58
Tunisia	213	332	108[f]	−24
Turkey	1,588	1,107	1,052[a]	468

1. 1971.
2. 1970.
[a]Mainly workers' remittances.
[b]Unrequited government transfers.
[c]Mainly oil investment income.
[d]Unrequited private (677 million) and government (1,169 million) transfers.
[e]Of which 744 millions mainly oil investment income and 1,160 million unrequited government and private transfers.
[f]Tourism.
[g]Mainly pipeline dues.
Source: International Monetary Funds, *Balance of Payments Yearbook; International Financial Statistics*, Central Bank of Kuwait, *Quarterly Statistical Bulletin*.

period, partly because of the conversion of vineyards to wheat cultivation, but manufacturing rose at some 10 percent per annum and petroleum and natural gas at over 15 percent. As a result, the share of agriculture in GDP fell from 19 percent in 1969 to 8 in 1973, that of petroleum and gas rose from 15 to 20 percent, and that of manufacturing remained unchanged at 13 percent. The 1974-77 plan provides for an annual increase of at least 10 percent in GDP, largely as a result of the growth of the manufacturing and oil and gas sectors.[11]

Morocco. During the 1968-72 Five Year Plan Morocco's real annual rate of growth was 5.7 percent; the 1971 figure was 5.2; and the 1972 figure, 4.5 percent. This was partly due to a series of good crops, which raised agricultural production by 6 percent per annum, while manufacturing and handicrafts rose by 5.3 percent and commerce and services by 5 percent. The Five Year Plan for 1973-77 provides for a real growth rate of 7.5 percent. This is to be achieved mainly by a growth in mining and manufacturing of 11 percent per annum, raising that sector's share in GDP from 29 percent in 1973 to 33 percent in 1977; the main components of this growth are phosphoric acid, phosphates and metal fabrication. The tertiary sector is to grow at 6.9 percent, largely because of tourism; and agricultural growth is planned at only 3.6 percent.[12] It may be added that the tripling of the price of phosphates at the beginning of 1974 and the subsequent increase by another 50 percent in July has greatly eased Morocco's foreign exchange situation: in 1974 phosphates were expected to earn about $1,000 million, over four times the 1973 figure, and to account for 65 percent of export proceeds. It is planned to raise output from about 22 million tons in 1974 to 46 million by 1987.[13]

Tunisia. Tunisia's economy still fluctuates widely, in response to weather conditions. In 1965-71, the average annual growth was 5.7 percent; in 1972, it was 16.8 percent, but in 1973 only 2.8 percent, mainly because of the sharp rise and subsequent decline in agricultural output. Fixed capital formation amounted to 23 percent of GDP in 1973, and of this some two-thirds was covered by domestic savings. Preliminary data for 1974 indicate a rise in agricultural production and a decline in manufacturing and mining.[14]

Libya. No recent national accounts are available, but the trend may be gauged from data on the oil sector, which dominates the economy. Output has been cut back every year since 1970, in all by about 50 percent, but this has been more than offset by the sharp rise in prices; total revenues have greatly increased. The 1972-75 Three Year Plan, as modified in 1973, projected a 10.5 percent annual growth rate, including 17.5 percent for nonpetroleum sectors; for agriculture this rate is 16 and for manufacturing 26 percent.[15]

Egypt. In 1965-71 Egypt's GNP rose at an annual rate of only 2.7 percent, or just ahead of its population growth of about 2.5 percent. In 1972, it rose by 5 to 6 percent and in 1973 somewhat less, but the 1974 budget envisaged an increase of 6.7 percent for the year. The Ten Year Plan for 1972-82 sets an annual growth rate of 7.2; 30 percent of investment is to be allocated to industry, 20 percent to transport and communications, 10 percent to agriculture and 10 percent to housing.[16]

Sudan. The Sudan's performance in recent years has been extremely disappointing, largely because of the civil war in the South but also because of the disruption caused by political instability in 1969-71, when most industrial enterprises were nationalized. In 1965-71 GNP rose at less than 2 percent per annum and per capita income actually declined, but in 1972 growth was distinctly higher. A Five Year Plan for 1970/71-74/75, increasing GDP by 7.6 percent a year, was prepared but it is not clear to what extent it is being implemented. Agricultural output is, however, steadily growing, mainly by extension of the cultivated area and the introduction of new crops, such as sugar cane, rice and coffee.[17]

Asia

Iran. Iran's performance during the Fourth Plan (1967/68 to 1972/73) was exceptionally good. Real GNP rose by 11.6 percent per annum, the rates accelerating to 12.9 in 1971/72 and 14.2 percent in 1972/73. Agriculture grew at the modest rate of 3.9 percent, but manufacturing and mining expanded at a rate of 13 percent, oil at 15 and services at 14 percent. As a result, the share of agriculture in GNP fell from 23 percent in 1968/69 to 16 in 1972/73, that of manufacturing rose from 22 to 23 and that of "national oil" from 17 to 20 percent. Consumption increased slightly less rapidly than GNP, and the savings ratio rose slowly to 20 percent, while the ratio of fixed investment advanced to 24 percent; of the latter 57 percent came from public investments and 43 from private. The 1973-78 Plan has been revised to provide for an annual growth of 25.9 percent, raising per capita income to $1,521 by 1978; this high rate was based on an actual 33 percent growth in 1973/74, and an estimated 52 percent in 1974/75, followed by 16 percent in each of the succeeding years. Oil and gas are expected to grow by 52 percent a year, followed by industry and mines with 18, services with 16 and agriculture with 7 percent. By the end of the Plan, "national oil" is expected to account for 49 percent of GNP, compared to 20 percent in 1972.[18]

Iraq. Iraq's economy has been subjected to severe shocks in the last fifteen years: The 1958 Revolution; the frequent and bloody *coups* that followed; the civil war with the Kurds that has just ended; border disputes with Iran and Kuwait; the mismanaged land reform that disrupted agriculture; and the disputes with the oil companies that resulted in a sharp decline in oil production. It has been estimated that fixed capital formation declined from 24.7 percent of GDP in 1962 to 14.4 in 1969, and in 1965-71 the annual rate of growth was put at only 4.6 percent. The sharp rise in oil income in 1973 and 1974 has, however, made it possible to allocate much larger amounts to development and the current 1969-74 Plan envisages an annual growth rate of 7.1 percent. Heavy emphasis is being placed on industrialization, and major irrigation and drainage schemes are being implemented.[19]

Israel. Israel's growth rate in 1971-73 was close to its 1965-71 trend of 8 percent per annum: real GNP rose by 8.2 percent in 1971, 10 percent in 1972, but only 6.3 percent in 1973, because of the strain imposed by the October War. Manufacturing was the fastest growing sector, averaging 12 percent in 1971-73, while agriculture, after rising by 12 percent in 1971/72 fell by 3.6 percent in 1972/73, because of frost and drought. The number of tourists, after increasing by 49 percent in 1971 and 11 percent in 1972, fell by 9 percent in 1973 because of the October War. The balance of payments deficit widened appreciably, and the share of total resources provided by imports rose from 34 percent in 1972 (66 percent coming from GNP) to 39 percent in 1973. The gross investment rate declined slightly, from 20.5 percent of total resources in 1972 to 19.9 in 1973. Available information for 1974 shows an upward movement in production (a GNP increase of about 7 percent) and exports, but an accentuation of the trends in inflationary pressures and balance of payments deficits.[20]

Jordan. Until 1967 Jordan achieved a remarkably high rate of growth—some 7 to 8 percent per annum—but the Arab-Israeli War in that year, and its aftermath, reduced the growth rate to zero in 1965-71 and, partly because of the influx of refugees, the per capita rate fell to minus 3.5 percent. In 1972 overall growth was put at 3 to 5 percent but, because of drought, crops were very poor in 1973, and GNP must have suffered accordingly; however, available data show an expansion in agriculture and industry in 1974. One of the few promising prospects is mineral production. Output of phosphates has risen from 700,000 tons in 1972 to an estimated 1.8 million in 1974 and capacity is being expaned to reach 3.0 million by 1976, and prices have risen sharply. Sizable copper reserves have also been discovered and some export may be possible.[21]

Lebanon. Lebanon's growth rate, as given in the *World Atlas*, was only 3.5 percent in GNP and under 1 percent per capita in 1965-71. This is probably an understatement, and the available data for 1972 show a higher rate of growth. The Six Year Plan 1972-77 provides for an annual rate of growth of 7 percent in GDP, based on the following sectoral rates: industry, 9 to 10 percent per annum; agriculture, 4 to 5 percent; construction, 6 percent and services and transport, 6 to 7 percent. The total investment required is put at $2.7 billion.[22]

Saudi Arabia. Economic growth has accelerated rapidly in the last few years. In constant prices, GDP rose by 9.7 percent in 1970, 4.2 in 1971, 15.5 in 1972, and 22.5 percent in 1973.

The bulk of the growth came, of course, from the oil sector's contribution, which doubled between 1970 and 1973 and which increased its share in the total from 55 percent in 1970 to 66 in 1973. No accurate figures are available on investment but actual government expenditures on projects doubled between 1970 and 1973.

Syria. Syria's economy has shown sharp fluctuations, partly because of its military involvement and burden and partly because of the great variations in its agricultural sector caused by the weather. However, in 1970-71 it averaged about 6.5 percent per annum and in 1972 its GNP is believed to have risen by over 10 percent. Expansion is taking place in several sectors. Agricultural output is slowly rising, mainly because of the extension of the irrigated area made possible by the Euphrates dam and minor works. Oil production is increasing and may reach 12.5 million tons by 1975, compared to 5.7 million tons in 1972. Manufacturing output, which was disrupted by the nationalizations of 1964-65, is resuming its upward trend. The 1970-75 Five Year Plan aims at an annual growth rate of 8.2 percent.[23]

Turkey. Turkey's recent growth in GDP has been at a respectable, if not outstanding, rate: 9.4 percent in 1971, 6.1 in 1972 and 4.8 in 1973. The deceleration is attributable to the decline of agricultural production, which fell by 0.2 percent in 1972 and 8.8 percent in 1973, reducing agriculture's share in GNP to 21 percent. Industry on the other hand rose rapidly, by 11.5 percent in 1972 and 13.1 in 1973, and its share advanced to 20 percent of GNP. Other sectors also increased quite rapidly and income from abroad (mainly remittances of workers in Europe) shot up in a spectacular way, raising the rates of growth in GNP to 10.7 percent in 1971, 7.6 in 1972 and 6.4 in 1973—or slightly above the 1965-71 average of 6.5 percent. Consumption has been increasing steadily, but somewhat more slowly than GNP, and the savings rate rose to the high level of 20.2 percent of GNP in 1972 and 21.0 in 1973. Investment has kept slightly ahead of savings, equalling 20.5 percent of GNP in 1972 and 22.0 in 1973.[24]

North and South Yemen. Practically no data are available for either country. Both have announced development plans: South Yemen a Five Year Plan for 1974-79, with a total outlay of about $250 million, and North Yemen a Three Year Plan with an outlay of $180 million. For both, investment funds will come largely from outside sources: mainly Iraq, Libya, and Kuwait for South Yemen and the United States, Saudi Arabia, and other Arab sources for North Yemen.[25]

Projections

At best of times, economic projections are subject to great uncertainties, and this is particularly true of a region where data are lacking, the political situation is constantly changing, and no clear answer can be given regarding the use of the accumulated oil revenues. Comparison of earlier projections made by excellent economists with the actual course of events[26] induces great modesty. At best, one can make some tentative extrapolations, based on recent performance and having a certain plausibility.

Oil Producing Countries

A distinction must first be made between the oil producers and the other countries. For the former, one of the major constraints on development has been removed: shortage of capital. Several economists have discussed development with unlimited supplies of labor: here we have the hitherto unique possibility of development with almost unlimited supplies of capital. Another potentially favorable factor is the great technological backwardness of these countries. This means that investment can be used as a means of infusing not only capital but also a large amount of more advanced technology. The combination of the two factors should, with proper management, ensure a very high rate of growth.

Within this group three large and well-endowed countries stand out: Iran, Algeria, and Iraq. Their population is relatively big—ranging from 10 to over 30 million. They have an abundance of natural resources other than oil: water, fertile land, and various minerals. Their human resources are relatively developed: their governmental and administrative structure is more efficient and they have a large and rapidly growing stock of the skills needed to run a modern economy and society. The same characteristics are true of their infrastructures, particularly that of Algeria, which are being constantly improved. They have a rapidly expanding industrial nucleus, which may be expected to maintain or even accelerate its recent rate of growth. Given a reasonable amount of political stability very rapid overall growth may be projected: an annual rate of 10 percent per capita through and beyond 1985 seems rather conservative, even granted that such a rate has never been sustained for any length of time by an country other than Japan. Its main components could be an overall growth rate of not over 5 percent in agriculture; up to 20 percent in manufacturing, mining, power, and construction combined; about 5 percent in oil; and perhaps 15 percent in transport and services; in addition, there may be some income from foreign investments.

The other oil producing countries—Saudi Arabia, Libya, Kuwait, United Arab Emirates, and Qatar—are in a different situation. In them, capital is even more abundant, but there are other, more formidable constraints. Their populations are very small. They lack almost all other natural resources, including the most important of all, fresh water. Their agriculture is exiguous and backward. Their industrial development has only just begun. Their infrastructure is grossly inadequate and, given the sparseness of their population and the hugeness of the area of Saudi Arabia, Libya, and Oman, costly to develop. Their harsh climate, which takes a great toll in depreciation of machinery and structures, is a further handicap. Lastly, their supply of skills is extremely limited and, with the best will in the world, cannot be expanded beyond a certain rate.

Of course, capital and technology can break bottlenecks. Managers, administrators, technicians, and workers can be trained. Cheap energy can be used to desalt sea water and establish a wide range of petrochemical and energy intensive industries. Minerals are being discovered in significant quantities in Saudi Arabia and elsewhere, and it is likely that more will be found as better methods of prospecting are used, transport is improved and water supplies become more abundant. But, for the next decade or more, the overall rate of growth of the Gross Domestic Product will be determined primarily by the expansion of the oil industry, which—given the efforts that are being made everywhere to reduce consumption—is not likely to exceed 5 percent per annum. Other sectors—notably petrochemicals and other industries and construction—should, however, grow much more rapidly, bringing the overall rate of growth of GDP to perhaps 7 to 8 percent. Moreover, returns on the enormous investments being made abroad should make a large contribution to Gross National Product if not to Gross Domestic Product. An overall rate of growth in GNP of about 10 percent, and in per capita income of, say 7 to 8 percent, seems therefore a reasonable guess.

Nonoil Producers

Except for Morocco, which in 1974 quadrupled the price of the phosphates that constituted about a quarter of its exports, all of these countries are faced with a very painful fact: the price of their imports has risen much more than that of their exports, their import surplus is growing rapidly and the balance that many of them had managed to achieve in their international current accounts has been upset. This means that their dependence on outside capital has greatly increased. For Israel, the only available source is the United States, supplemented perhaps by a smaller West European contribution.[d] The same is true of Turkey, except that the European share may be *relatively* greater and there may be a further contribution made by the Soviet bloc. For the other countries, all of which are Arab, the obvious source is the surplus Arab oil states—though it is worth noting that Iran has already advanced a large sum to Egypt. The following projections rest on the rather optimistic assumption that outside assistance will be sufficiently large to reduce greatly the foreign exchange constraint and make possible the resumption of the recent growth trend.

Israel. In the next decade, and postulating that a large amount of foreign aid will be forthcoming and that the defense burden will not become unbearably heavy, a rate of 8 percent and a per capita rate of 5 percent have been assumed.

Turkey. Assuming that remittances from Turkish workers in Europe do not fall off greatly and that additional foreign aid will be available, Turkey may hope to maintain its recent rate of 6.5 percent, or 4 percent per capita.

[d]In 1974 U.S. grants to Israel were about $900 million and loans $400 million; a further $600 million came from World Jewish funds, for a total of $1.9 billion. But this covered only half the deficit, estimated at $3.5 billion. (*The Economist*, November 16, 1974).

The nonoil Arab countries may be divided into three groups. The first consists of those countries with a large agricultural sector, Egypt, Morocco, Sudan, and Syria, which offers possibilities of growth; and where, moreover, the first two nations have a relatively developed industry. The second consists of three small countries in which the provision of services, rather than the production of goods, plays a very large part: Lebanon, Jordan, and Tunisia. The last consists of two very underdeveloped countries with few known natural resources, North and South Yemen.

Egypt. It is difficult to envisage a high growth rate for Egypt in the coming decade. For even if it should receive a very large amount of capital from the oil-rich Arab countries, much of that will be absorbed by the sheer effort of reconstructing and renovating the infrastructure (see below). An overall rate of 5 to 6 and a per capita rate of 3 percent are probably too optimistic, but will be used here.

Morocco. A long-term rate of 7 percent, and per capita increase of 4 percent are not unrealistic in view of the country's potential and of the sharp rise in the price of its phosphate exports.

Sudan. Although Sudan's performance in recent years has been extremely disappointing, largely because of the civil war in the South, an overall rate of growth of 4 to 5 percent, and a per capita rate of 2 percent, are not unreasonable, given the country's enormous potential.

Syria's economy has shown sharp fluctuations, due partly to its military burden and partly to the great variations in its agriculture caused by the weather. In view of its recent rate of growth, a projection of 7 percent in GNP and 4 per capita seem reasonable.

Passing on to the second group, *Tunisia's* recent performance has been quite satisfactory. Population growth has been brought down to just over 2 percent and it seems likely that, with outside aid, Tunisia can sustain an overall growth rate of 6 and a per capita rate of 4 percent for the next decade.

Lebanon's future is highly problematic. On the one hand, its import bill has greatly risen and its earnings from European and American tourism are likely to decline. On the other, some of the enormous accumulation of wealth in the Arab oil countries is almost certain to spill over into Lebanon, in the form of demand for exports, payments for tourist and other services, bank deposits and investment in real estate and other branches. A guess of a long-term growth rate of 4 to 5 percent and per capita income of 2 percent may therefore be plausible.

Jordan's future is equally problematic, and it is difficult to envisage a rate higher than 5 percent for GNP and 2 percent per capita.

Lastly, there are the two *Yemens*, for which no reliable data exist; hence a purely arbitrary figure of 2 percent per capita has been assumed.

The per capita incomes for 1974 have been arrived at as follows: For the nonoil countries, the 1971 figures have been extrapolated forward at the 1965-71 rate of growth, except for Egypt, Jordan, Sudan, and the two Yemens where an annual growth of one percent has been assumed. For the oil countries, the figures for 1973 and the estimated oil revenues for 1975 (Table III-7) have been added to obtain the 1974 GNP. Needless to say, the figures are rough.

The resulting projections are shown in Table III-11. Its most striking feature is, not surprisingly, the great widening of the gap between the oil producing

Table III-11
Projected Per Capita Rate of Growth to 1985
(In U.S. dollars)

Country	Estimated Per Capita GNP 1974	Projected Rate of GNP	Projected Rate Per Capita	Per Capita GNP 1985
Large Oil Countries				
Iran	940	12-13	10	2,700
Algeria	530	12-13	10	1,500
Iraq	930	12-13	10	2,700
Small Oil Countries				
Saudi Arabia	2,900	10-11	8	6,800
Libya	5,800	10-11	8	13,500
Kuwait	8,500	10-11	8	20,000
UAE	over 10,000	10-11	8	over 23,000
Qatar	over 10,000	10-11	8	over 23,000
Oman	1,000	10-11	8	2,300
Non-Oil				
Israel	2,900	8	5	5,000
Turkey	375	6.5	4	580
Egypt	225	5-6	3	310
Morocco	280	7	4	430
Sudan	125	4-5	2	160
Syria	300	7	4	460
Tunisia	350	6	4	540
Lebanon	675	4	2	840
Jordan	270	5	2	340
North Yemen	100	5	2	125
South Yemen	125	5	2	160

countries and the others. The projected figures for the smaller oil producers—Kuwait, United Arab Emirates, Qatar, and Libya, as well as Saudi Arabia—range between $7,000 and $60,000, or well above the level of *any* country in the world today. Israel would be at the level of today's most advanced countries. The larger oil countries—Iran, Algeria, Iraq, and also Oman (which between them include over fifty million inhabitants or more than a quarter of the region's population) range between roughly $1,700 and $3,500, or say the present level of Ireland and France, respectively. This does not, of course, mean that, in real terms, these countries will be at the present-day economic—much less social—level of Western Europe. The third group, which has some one-hundred million inhabitants or just over half the region's population (Turkey, Egypt, Morocco, Syria, Tunisia, and Jordan), ranges between about $350 and $550, or somewhat below the typical Latin American level of today and (except for Albania!) far below the poorest of the Western and Eastern European countries. The last group consists of three very poor countries, Sudan and the two Yemens, whose per capita income stands well below $200, or say today's Asian level.

Composition of GNP

The projected increase in GNP will be accompanied by important changes in its composition. The sharp decline in the relative share of agriculture (Table III-5) will continue. For even if, as they should, the governments make an all-out effort to improve the agricultural sector, its rate of growth can hardly exceed 5 percent per annum, as compared to the present 3 percent. This is well below the projected rate for all but the slowest growing economies, and should reduce agriculture's share in most countries to the proportion prevailing in Western Europe today; in the oil producing countries, 10 percent or even less; in the medium countries (Turkey, Egypt, Morocco) 15 to 20 percent; and in the low income countries 20 percent or more. But, unlike what happened in the West, the decline in the share of agriculture will not be accompanied by a corresponding rise in productivity per man or per acre, and the gap in output per person employed in agriculture and in other sectors should widen considerably.

Manufacturing, on the other hand, is likely to accelerate its rate of growth far above the present 10 percent rate, and in many countries a 15 to 20 percent annual growth is not unlikely. This should raise the share of manufacturing, mining and power in GNP to 30 percent or more in all but the small oil states and the very backward economies. This rate, too, is not much below that prevailing in Western Europe but here, too, for reasons discussed below, productivity will continue to be far lower than in Europe. However employment in industry is likely to rise far less than output, and its share in the labor force, at present usually around or below 10 percent, is unlikely to exceed 15 or, exceptionally, 20 percent.

Construction should also grow very rapidly and raise its share of GNP. Residential housing will have to be greatly expanded to accommodate the increase in population and the massive migration towards the cities. In most countries, the population of the larger towns has been growing at 5 to 10 percent per annum, and in the smaller oil countries even faster.[27] In addition, higher living standards will result in the demand for larger and better housing. No less important will be nonresidential construction, taking the form of offices, shops, factories, roads, dams, ports, airports, and other works.

Power, water supplies, and other public utilities should also increase very rapidly and their share of GNP may also be expected to rise. So should that of transport.

The share of oil has, of course, expanded enormously as a result of the increase in oil revenues. Hereafter, however, barring unforeseen circumstances, world demand for oil may be expected to rise rather slowly and the growth in oil revenues should also slow down. The share of oil in GNP should therefore gradually decline.

Lastly, the service sector should, as in the past, grow somewhat faster than GNP and its share should slowly increase. The demand for services of all kinds in the region—education, health, professional, personal—is immense and growing. And government services, in the form of both the armed forces and the civilian bureaucracy, may be expected to flourish and proliferate as in the past.

Distribution of GNP

Three important shifts may be expected in the distribution of GNP in the next decade: an enlargement of the public sector; a widening of the gap between town and country; and a more unequal distribution of incomes and wealth. All three represent an accentuation of the trends of the past twenty or thirty years (see above).

Typically, in the late 1960s government tax revenues equaled about 25 percent of national income, a figure well above that of underdeveloped countries but lower than that of the United States and Western Europe; for several countries, however—Jordan, Lebanon, Morocco, Sudan, Syria, and Turkey—it was close to 15 percent. Government expenditure constituted a distinctly higher fraction of GDP, since it included foreign aid. And the government's share of total resources was, generally, between a quarter and a third, or even more. The enormous expansion in oil revenues has greatly raised those shares, and the aid that the nonoil countries may receive should have a similar effect. In other words, the economic role of the state is bound to become increasingly important.

One particular aspect of this is the government's enormously increased share of investment. Until some fifteen or twenty years ago, the bulk of investment in the region was provided by private enterprise, foreign or domestic, and the government's share was generally restricted to infrastructure. The expropriation of foreign capital in the 1950s and 60s and the nationalization of large sectors of the economy in such countries as Algeria, Egypt, Iraq, Libya, Syria, and Tunisia, and the great expansion of the state sector in all the oil producing countries, have however greatly changed this picture. By the late 1960s, the government's share of total investment was two-thirds or more in all but a handful of countries such as Israel, Jordan and Lebanon. And there is every reason to expect this trend to continue.

The same is true of the gap between town and country, which has been widening and may be expected to widen further. For, as in other underdeveloped regions, the townsmen have been favored at the expense of the farmers. Urban wages are relatively higher than rural and social services are far more developed in the towns. Moreover, both government and private investments have tended to concentrate on the cities.

For much the same reasons inequality of incomes is likely to increase, unless checked by drastic measures. The immense flow of oil revenues and foreign aid accrues to a small group at the top, and the opportunities for receiving a share of this money are very unequal. It is a sad aspect of the history of the last two centuries that economic development has, in its initial stages, increased inequality of incomes and wealth—not by making the poor poorer but by providing vast new sources of enrichment. And where there is a massive and rapid influx of funds, the likelihood of this happening is greatly enhanced.

A Viable Economy?

One last question remains: to what extent can the Middle Eastern and North African economies become viable, if not by 1985 then in the following ten or fifteen years? Three constraints may be noted: skills, savings, and foreign exchange.

Skills. There is no doubt that every country is making a great effort to develop its human resources and generate the skills required for running a modern economy and society, e.g., the number of students in higher education in the Arab countries rose from 20,000 in 1945 to some 400,000 in 1971 and was expected to double again by 1980.[28] Similar developments have taken place in Iran, Israel, and Turkey. In addition, there are some 30,000 Arabs studying in Europe and the United States, and an approximately equal number from the three other countries. Even allowing for the fact that, in most institutions, the quality of education is extremely poor, and also for the brain-drain which may absorb a quarter or more of the students sent abroad,[e] the potential addition to the stock of skills represented by these figures is truly impressive.

---

[e]This proportion is likely to decline sharply in the next ten years for two reasons: rapidly expanding opportunities in the region and tightening markets in the United States and Europe.

Perhaps a better illustration is provided by engineering. In 1945, there were five engineering colleges in the whole Arab world; but by 1973 there were thirty-four. In 1968, 5,500 engineers graduated in the Arab countries or 50 for every million inhabitants. For Egypt the ratio was 125, for Israel, 271, Turkey, 42 and Iran, 25. This compares with 530 in Japan, 265 in the United States, 20 in India, and 12 in Pakistan.[29] If the upward trend continues; if extensive on-the-job training is given in the innumerable new projects being implemented; if a larger number of students is sent abroad; and if extensive use is made of foreign experts, there is no reason to fear that the viability of the region's economies will be seriously impaired by a shortage of skills in the critical ten or fifteen years lying ahead.

Savings and Foreign Exchange. The two other constraints present themselves very differently in the oil and nonoil countries, respectively. With incomes rising, albeit slowly, the nonoil countries' capacity to save should increase. Whether it will do so in fact depends on several factors, mainly extra-economic and centering on the willingness and ability of the governments concerned to divert resources from private and even more public consumption to saving and investment. Clearly, the task can be accomplished: By 1985 practically all these countries should have reached a level that makes it possible to have a savings rate of 20 or even 25 percent of GNP while ensuring an adequate subsistence for the mass of the population and modest incentives for the middle class. Equally clearly, this demands unpopular measures, and the very fact that foreign aid has been available will constitute a strong temptation to postpone such austerity.

A closely connected question is whether these countries can achieve balance in their external transactions. Except for a few where tourism may take a significant contribution (Israel, Jordan, Lebanon, Morocco, Tunisia, and, perhaps, Turkey) or where other substantial service income may be available (worker remittances in Algeria and Turkey, Suez Canal dues in Egypt), this means, more specifically, whether exports can be increased fast enough to cover their rapidly growing imports. In some countries, notably Sudan, Syria, and Morocco, but to a smaller extent also Egypt, Tunisia, and North Yemen, it should be possible to expand agricultural output sufficiently not only to cover the greater needs of a growing population and a rising level of living but also to provide a substantial export surplus. But most of the increment in exports will probably have to consist of manufactured goods—this is certainly true of Israel, Lebanon, Egypt, and Morocco, and to a lesser degree of the others. And this, in turn, presupposes that the local industries can be improved so that both the quality of their products and their costs of production make them competitive in world markets. This is a formidable, though not impossible, task as South Korea, Taiwan, and other countries have shown. It is also one that faces the oil producers.

The problem facing the oil producing countries may be stated as follows: to develop their economies and provide alternative exports to sustain their greatly increased import needs by the time oil ceases to earn significant amounts of foreign exchange. All that can be done here is to provide a few illustrative figures, showing the dimensions of the problem.

First there is the question of oil reserves. At the beginning of 1975 the ratio of *proved reserves* to output ranged between twenty and eighty years: it stood at seventy-seven for Kuwait, fifty-five for Saudi Arabia, fifty for Iraq, forty-seven for Abu Dhabi, forty-three for Libya, thirty for Qatar, thirty for Iran and twenty-four for Algeria.[30] But these figures have to be adjusted in two opposite ways. First, given an annual growth rate of 6 percent, production would double in less than twelve years and the time it would take to exhaust the reserves would be halved. However, "proved reserves" represent only a fraction of potential reserves and the rise in the price of oil will surely stimulate exploration, so that the amount of "proved reserves" may well double in the next decade.[f] Assuming that these two factors cancel each other out, a time span of twenty to thirty years may be postulated for Algeria and Iran, considerably more for Iraq, and forty to sixty for the less populous countries.

As regards nonoil exports and imports, two illustrations may be given. In Saudi Arabia, exports other than oil are negligible and are likely to remain so for a long time to come. Imports, however, have risen rapidly at a compound rate of some 16.5 percent per annum in 1969-73, 30 percent in 1973, and nearly 100 percent in 1974. To meet such an expanded volume of imports out of the proceeds of nonoil exports is clearly impossible: at best the products of some petrochemical and other energy using industries may be increased, and some minerals, notably iron or even steel, may be developed on a large scale. Oil tanker and other shipping income may also help. But the main source of finance will have to remain first oil exports and then, after three or four decades when they may begin to drop off sharply, the income from investments made abroad during the next couple of decades. With minor changes, what has been said of Saudi Arabia applies to the other small oil countries.

Iran may be taken as representative of the larger oil producers. Between 1968/69 and 1972/73, its exports (other than oil and gas) grew at an·annual rate of 20 percent, imports at 17 percent, and the import surplus at 16 percent. Since the growth of imports is accelerating, exports will have to be stepped up much more rapidly if the gap is to be closed by the late 1980s or early 1990s, when the contribution of oil will probably fall off sharply. Moreover, Iran, like Algeria and Iraq, and unlike the smaller countries, is not by then likely to have a large income from foreign investments.

Of Iran's nonoil exports, "Traditional and Agricultural" goods, e.g. carpets, cotton and dried fruits, have been growing at 15 percent per annum and "new industrial" goods, mainly textiles, clothing, shoes, and simple chemical products, at 46 percent. At present, Iran's industries—like those of the other countries—are

---

[f]"There are high-placed officials in Saudi Arabia who claim privately that the country's true reserves amount to at least 450 billion barrels, i.e., over twice proved reserves." (*The Economist*, December 7, 1974, p. 86).

very heavily protected and uncompetitive. In fact, in several the cost of inputs is higher than is the price of the finished product in world markets. Moreover, quality is poor, and it is no coincidence that the bulk of industrial exports go to the Socialist countries, which are willing to accept goods that would be rejected in Western markets. These facts point clearly the appropriate policy: the gradual exposure of local industry to foreign competition, to force it to improve quality and reduce costs, along with every possible aid—technical, financial, and other—in doing so. If this is done, and agriculture is raised from its very low level and the great mineral wealth is exploited, a viable economy can be achieved by the time oil ceases to play such a predominant role. With minor qualifications, the same may be said of Algeria and Iraq, the constraints on the former being much more severe.

The Role of the United States

United States Handicaps

In no part of the world is the United States' freedom of action as circumscribed as in the Middle East and North Africa. In addition to the handicaps under which the United States is operating elsewhere, there are some reasons specific to the region. First, the United States has to incur the hostility of at least one side—and more generally of both—in any flare-up of the long smouldering and intense local hatreds and enmities: the recent example of Cyprus has shown this only too clearly. Second, the United States has become the heir and legatee of all the resentments accumulated against the previous foreign rulers of the region. Third, the United States can command only limited and lukewarm support from its European and Japanese allies for its Middle Eastern policy. Fourth, the Arabs—who constitute nearly two-thirds of the region's population—see in the United States the main supporter, financier, and arms supplier of Israel and react accordingly. Fifth, the region's proximity to the Soviet Union imposes particular restraint in dealing with it. And last, and perhaps most important, for the first time in nearly 150 years, the United States is facing an area that is richer than it is—not, of course, in the sense of real wealth, or means of production, or accumulated skills or levels of living, but in command over liquid funds that can be made to serve specific economic or political purposes. This greatly reduces the leverage that the United States can hope to exert. Elsewhere, United States funds may make such a difference to a country's balance of payments, budgetary balance or capital formation that its government may be willing to go a long way in meeting United States wishes. Clearly this is not true of the oil countries, some of which suffer from an embarrassment of funds and all of which have more than enough for their needs. It may not even be true of the nonoil Arab countries, which can hope to meet their financial needs from their rich Arab neighbors—indeed it should be a major aim of United States policy to encourage and facilitate such transfers between Arab countries.

Another weakness is inherent in the fact that, except for oil, the United States is not a major market for any Middle Eastern or North African product. Whereas Western Europe can absorb large amounts not only of oil but also of fruits, cotton and other agricultural produce, and is making appropriate arrangements for this purpose by associating the Maghreb, Turkey, Iran, Israel, and other countries with the European Economic Community (EEC), the United States meets all its own needs in these and other products. And whereas the region's industrial goods can easily be sold in the Soviet bloc, and may occasionally be acceptable in Western Europe, they are of too low a quality to compete in United States markets.

United States action is also limited by the fact that the major problems from which the region suffers are ones for which an outside state can give very little help, because the difficulties are so deeply imbedded in the social and political structure. Three examples will illustrate this. First, there is the population explosion. This development is highly undesirable, but inevitable: the mothers of the 1970s-90s are already born, and all that can be done is to persuade them to have fewer children. But this is a matter over which national governments have very little influence. And the most that a foreign government can do is to offer advice, suggestions and, if called upon, various birth control techniques.

Hardly less difficult is the question of agriculture which has been a lagging sector and almost everywhere should have the first priority in development plans. Agricultural efficiency is so closely bound up with matters like land tenure, which in turn are one of the main strands in the social fabric, that outside interference is likely to be neither welcome nor effective.

Another example is that of armaments. Perhaps the greatest service the outside world could render to the Middle East would be to help it reduce its enormous arms burden—a burden which, in terms of percentage of GNP going to defense, is greater than anywhere in the world.[31] Military expenditures have risen sharply since 1967 and show no sign of slackening, not only in the countries directly involved in the Arab-Israeli conflict, particularly Egypt, Israel, and Syria, but even more in those bordering the Gulf: Iran, Iraq, and Saudi Arabia.[g] In North Africa, however, defense still absorbs only a small part of total resources. Of course, the decision on such matters has to be taken by the governments concerned, and all that outsiders can do is to offer advice, help, and good offices. At the moment the outsiders, including the United States and Soviet Union, far from helping the Middle Eastern countries to reduce their armaments, are doing all they can to supply them with the latest weapons—for cash or on credit.

[g]Even Kuwait has announced an arms program of $1.5 billion, and the expenditure on weapons by Abu Dhabi and Oman is relatively enormous.

United States Advantages

This long list of handicaps must, however, be followed by an enumeration of the advantages at present enjoyed by the United States in its dealings with the Middle East. Paradoxically, some of these stem from the weakening of the United States position in the region. Thus, the virtual take-over of the oil companies has meant that the most important hostage held by the local governments has now been disposed of. And the greatly increased involvement of the Soviet Union has brought with it commensurate resentment and antagonism—not only from the Egyptians and Syrians who strongly dislike their Soviet "advisers" but from the Iraqis, who saw the oil they sold to the Soviets (in repayment for arms) at $6 a barrel being resold to Germany at $18, or from the Iranians, who receive for the gas they send to the Soviet Union half the price the latter charges for gas sent to Poland or Czechoslovakia.[32]

The proximity and growing power of the Soviets also enhances the attraction of the United States as a diplomatic counterweight. This applies most obviously to Israel, which relies almost exclusively on the United States; to Turkey and Iran, which have long lived under the Russian threat; and to the conservative Arab governments, such as those of Saudi Arabia, Jordan, Lebanon, Tunisia, and Morocco. But it is also true of the radical Arab governments, which do not enjoy the propsect of being left tête-à-tête with the Soviets. For the same reason, the United States' capacity to supply the most up-to-date weapons greatly adds to its power of manoeuvre.

There are also some very important economic assets. American goods, designed for an affluent domestic market, are more highly prized than those of other countries. The United States is the only major country with a food surplus, a very important fact in a world where food is, next to oil, the scarcest commodity. It has a set of so-called multinational corporations that can, better than anyone else, carry out some of the projects that the governments are so eager to implement. More particularly, it has the oil companies, which still have an important part to play. More easily than anyone else, too, these corporations can find outlets for the new goods these countries are planning to produce, such as petrochemicals, some of which may indeed be absorbed in the huge United States market. But perhaps most important of all are United States financial institutions and technology.

American financial institutions are playing a dual role. First, there are the American banks, brokerage houses, and other firms operating in the region. For a long time they tended to concentrate in Beirut, but more recently they have greatly increased their activity in Cairo, Tehran, Jiddah, and other places. At first their main activity was taking deposits and handling individual customer's investments but now their fund management includes multimillion deals, e.g., an $800 million steel complex, half owned by the Saudi Arabian Petromin and half by a group of American, European, and Japanese companies, a $100 million loan to a Canadian electricity authority, and other similar transactions. Of course, European and Japanese banks are also very active in this business.

The other, and more important, aspect is the absorption of the Organization of Petroleum Exporting Countries (OPEC) funds in the United States money markets which has so far been on a small scale, though United States banks are tapping a very large share of the oil money that is going to the Eurodollar market. Much remains to be done if larger amounts of oil funds are to be attracted to the United States. This should be done for two reasons. First, it will ease the strain on the United States' balance of payments and recycle some of these funds, avoiding a potentially disastrous liquidity shortage. Second, it is only if the oil producers become more closely involved in the Western economy and their stakes in it are greatly increased that they will become concerned with its well being and take positive measures to ensure its continued functioning. It has been said that what the Arabs want is "Liquidity, Anonymity and Security," i.e., security against both political action and depreciation of the monetary asset.[33] But they and the Iranians want more: access to Western technology and assurance of continued supplies of essential industrial products; this explains the Iranian purchase of a 25 percent interest in Krupp and, possibly, Kuwait's acquisition of 14 percent of Daimler Benz. Means should be found of making similar minority participations possible in United States industries, although, of course, precautions should be taken to safeguard essential national interests.

As for technology, the United States is particularly well placed to extend aid in four fields that are of special concern to the region: agriculture, nuclear power, desalination, and solar energy. It has been repeatedly stressed here that agriculture has been the weakest spot in the region's economy, and will continue to be in the foreseeable future. Now if there is one field in which the United States has far surpassed all other countries, it is agriculture. American achievements, such as "miracle" wheat and rice, are well known all over the world. The United States has also much to teach in range management, forestry and other branches, in the prevention of soil erosion and in other ecological matters. Experts from its arid regions have a vast fund of experience in water conservation. And its hydraulic engineers are second to none, and have already made a significant contribution to some of the region's major projects, such as the Dez dam.

Nuclear power is another area in which the United States starts with important advantages, although here the competition of such countries as Britain and France is intense. Several countries, notably Israel, Iran and Egypt, have shown interest in nuclear reactors, and atomic power will almost certainly be generated on a significant scale in the coming decade.

Desalination of salt or brackish water offers more hope to the Middle East and North Africa than to any other part of the world, since it is the most arid portion of the globe. An immense expanse of good land is available, which needs only water to produce adequate crops. In this field the United States has carried out more experimentation than any other country and here too it has a leading role to play, preferably in cooperation with the Middle Eastern countries themselves.

Finally, there is the utilization of solar energy. The United States has done much work on this subject, but other countries, notably the Soviet Union, Israel, and France, have also accomplished a good deal. The current energy shortage has turned the attention of Americans to the importance of this clean and inexhaustible source of heat and power, and in the next few years noteworthy advances are likely to be made. Such developments are of vital concern to the region since, more than any other part of the world, it has abundant and unfailing supplies of sunshine! In this field also, cooperation between the United States and the various countries could be of mutual benefit.

A Few Suggestions

A few specific suggestions may be made, but first a threefold distinction must be drawn between the oil producing countries; the nonoil Arab countries; Israel and Turkey.

Israel will continue to depend to an overwhelming extent on United States financial support. There is every indication that both the United States government and the American Jewish community are fully aware of this and are prepared to shoulder the burden. The idea of setting up two agro-industrial complexes, one in Israel and one in Egypt, using nuclear energy to process a wide range of metals and the heat to desalt sea water for agriculture, was seriously considered by various United States agencies a few years ago; it should be reconsidered.

Turkey also needs United States financial help, but here the main burden may, more properly, be carried by Western Europe with which Turkey is becoming more closely associated through EEC. The Soviet Union may also play an increasingly important role. But the United States has much to offer in the way of capital and technical and, particularly in agriculture.

Perhaps the most useful act the United States can perform is to use its influence to persuade Saudi Arabia and other rich countries to channel some of their surplus funds to the nonoil producing Arab countries. The nations most in need of funds are Egypt, Sudan, and Jordan, but Syria, Tunisia, Lebanon, and the two Yemens also need money. A combination of Arab money and United States technology and organization could make an enormous contribution to their development.

As for the oil producers, the United States would probably be well advised to follow the suggestion made by the Shah and the example set by France in its $7 billion agreement with Iran. This includes the setting up of two nuclear energy plants of 900 megawatts; construction of a subway in Tehran for $650 million; sale of French color television process; turbo-trains and railroad equipment; a fleet of ships to carry liquified natural gas; an ammonia plant; oil refinery equipment; gas exploration and telecommunications. Similar deals, worth $3 billion each, have been reported with Algeria and Iraq.[34] Both the type of arrangement and the items offered indicate the lines along which the United States should be acting.

In conclusion, two or three more specific possibilities will be examined. First there is Egypt, which needs literally billions of dollars for reconstruction. This includes the clearing, dredging and eventual enlarging of the Suez Canal and the rebuilding of the cities of Suez, Ismailiya and Port Said, at a total estimated cost of $8 billion.[35] It also includes the rebuilding of much of Egypt's infrastructure—water supplies, sewage, streetcars, telephones, and other utilities. Some decades ago these were by far the best in the region but in recent years they have deteriorated to a dangerously low level.[36]

Unlike Egypt, which is greatly dependent on outside funds, Algeria is in a position to meet its own capital needs, at least for the immediate future. The progress achieved in the last few years has been remarkable, and the prospects are good. But there are serious weaknesses in the economy, particularly in agriculture. Despite its Socialist rhetoric and the very active anti-Western role it has played in the United Nations, Algeria has shown itself very eager to do business with capitalist countries, and several American companies are actively engaged in very large projects there. United States private capital has an important part to play in bringing technology and organization and carrying out mutually profitable trade; American help in agriculture and water development could also be very useful.

As for the Persian Gulf countries, two main lines present themselves. First there are petrochemicals, including fertilizers. Over the next three or four years, the Arab countries and Iran will be adding 3 million tons a year of ammonia and 3.3 million of urea capacity. But in the longer term, decisions to invest some $15 billion in chemical plants, refineries and gas liquefaction plants have been taken, and another $25 billion's worth of plants is under consideration.[37] Clearly, the Gulf is becoming the center of the world's petrochemical industry and it looks as though its enormous gas resources, hitherto almost entirely wasted, will be put to use. There is much that American corporations can do to further this development, by building and operating the plants and marketing the products, but the competition will be stiff.

The second possibility is provided by the enormous development plans being implemented by the oil states, and running into several billions of dollars. They range from a great variety of civil engineering projects—housing, roads, ports, airports, etc.—to various industries and the installation of very advanced equipment. Here, too, competition from Europeans and Japanese will be intense, but an enormous field remains open and the opportunities are immense.

Notes

1. For details, see Charles Issawi "Economic Development in the Middle East," *International Journal* (Toronto), Autumn 1973.

2. See table in *United Nations, World Economic Survey 1969-1970* (New York, 1970), p. 210.

3. See the table based on the regression analysis of Chenery et al. in Barbara Ward et al. (eds.), *The Widening Gap* (New York: Columbia University Press, 1971), p. 30.

4. For more details, see Charles Issawi and Mohammed Yeganeh, *The Economics of Middle Eastern Oil* (New York: Praeger, 1963) and Charles Issawi, *Oil, the Middle East and the World* (New York: The Washington Papers, Library Press, 1972).

5. FAO, *Production Yearbook*, 1972.

6. Ibid.

7. U.S. Department of Agriculture, *Changes in Agriculture in 26 Developing Nations* (Washington, D.C.: GPO, 1965), Marion Clawson et al., *The Agricultural Potential of the Middle East* (New York, Elsevier, 1971), p. 87 and FAO *Production Yearbook*.

8. IBRD, *World Tables*, table 5.

9. IBRD, *World Tables*, table 4, and IBRD, *Industry*, April 1972.

10. IBRD, *World Tables*, table 5.

11. *IMF Survey*, November 4, 1974 and Economist Intelligence Unit (henceforth EIU), *Algeria Annual Supplement*, 1974.

12. *IMF Survey*, May 20, 1974; Banque de Maroc, *Rapport*, 1972; EIU *Quarterly Economic Review, Morocco*, No. 3, 1974.

13. *The Economist*, May 11, 1974.

14. *IMF Survey*, August 5, 1974, and EIU, *Quarterly Economic Review*, Libya, Tunisia, Malta, No. 3, 1974.

15. Ibid, and *Annual Supplement, 1973.*

16. National Bank of Egypt, *Economic Bulletin* No. 1, 1974; United Nations *World Economic Survey, 1972* (New York, 1973), p. 92, EIU *Egypt, Sudan, Annual Supplement*, 1973; *Quarterly Economic Review* No. 1, 1974.

17. Ibid, and Democratic Republic of Sudan, *Economic Survey 1973* (Khartoum, 1974).

18. Bank Markazi Iran, *Annual Report 1351*, EIU *Quarterly Economic Review, Iran*, No. 3, 1974.

19. EIU, *Iraq Annual Supplement 1974*, ibid., *1973; Quarterly Economic Review*, No. 3, 1974.

20. Bank Leumi, *Economic Review*, Annual Issues, 1973 and 1974; EIU *Israel, Annual Supplement, 1974.*

21. Royal Scientific Society, Amman, "Economic Conditions in Jordan," August 1974. United Nations, *World Economic Survey, 1972*; EIU *Saudi Arabia and Jordan, Annual Supplement*, 1974.

22. Saudi Arabian Monetary Agency, *Annual Report* 1392-93 A.H., EIU, *Saudi Arabia and Jordan, Annual Supplement* 1974.

23. United Nations, *World Economic Survey, 1972*; EIU *Syria, Lebanon, Cyprus, Annual Supplement*, 1973.

24. The Central Bank of Turkey, *Annual Report*, 1973.

25. EIU, *Quarterly Economic Review, The Arabian Peninsula*, No. 2, 1974.

26. In Charles A. Cooper and Sidney S. Alexander (eds.), *Economic Development and Population Growth in the Middle East* (New York: Elsevier, 1972).

27. United Nations Economic and Social Office in Beirut, *Studies on Selected Development Problems* (New York, 1970), p. 76.

28. M. Ali Kettani, "Engineering Education in the Arab World," *Middle East Journal*, Autumn 1974.

29. Kettani, "Engineering Education."

30. *Oil and Gas Journal*, December 30, 1974.

31. See the International Institute for Strategic Studies, *The Military Balance*.

32. *The Economist*, August 3, 1974.

33. Susan Strange, "Arab Oil and International Finance," *The Ditchley Journal*, Autumn 1974, report of a conference held at Ditchley in December 1973.

34. *New York Times*, December 27, 1974.

35. *The Economist*, February 2, and March 9, 1974.

36. Ibid., November 2, 1974.

37. Ibid., October 19, 1974.

IV

The Accumulation of Financial Capital by Middle East Oil Exporters: Problems and Policies

Bent Hansen

Despite a general accelerating increase of the world price level, with a substantial increase in world demand for oil, oil prices fell from 1957 to 1970. From the latter year, the situation changed. With the Libyan price increases of 1970 and the subsequent Tehran-Tripoli agreements of 1971 between the Organization of Petroleum Exporting Countries (OPEC), it became clear that oil prices would tend strongly upwards, and that the major oil exporters were to experience large surpluses on current account in their balances of payments. Although oil prices at that time were modest, judged by present standards, and there was not yet a question of threats to the foreign payments position of the major developed oil consumers, already in the summer of 1973, U.S. Treasury Secretary George Shultz expressed concern about the financial accumulations of the oil exporters in the Middle East and the changing outlook for the international financial markets and the international monetary system with the Middle East oil exporters as major creditor countries. With the exorbitant oil price increases at the end of 1973 and the beginning of 1974, what was thus already considered a big problem suddenly developed into a huge problem. This chapter discusses its financial aspects, its dimensions, its consequences for international capital movements and monetary relations, and possible policies and reforms that might be adopted by developed countries—the United States in particular—in order to cope with the problem.

The Dimensions of the Problem

As early as 1973 the major oil exporters enjoyed a current account surplus of US$5 billion. So-called developed countries had a surplus of $12 billion while less developed countries, other than oil exporters had a deficit of $9 billion (Communist countries not included).

For 1974, preliminary estimates show a surplus for the oil exporters by about $60 billion. The surplus of the developed countries has changed into a deficit of about $35 billion and the deficit of other less developed countries increased to about $30 billion.

For 1975, the surplus of the oil exporters is at present expected to be some $40-45 billion. The deficit of other less developed countries may increase further while that of the developed countries will fall dramatically. These predictions were made before the new increase of crude prices of September 1975, which may lead to a revenue increase by some $5-10 billion for the oil exporters.

The longer term outlook is uncertain and the grossly exaggerated predictions of developments until 1985 made during the summer of 1974 by authorities like the World Bank and the U.S. Treasury Department warn against our having much confidence in such predictions. The course of the future current account surplus of the oil exporters hinges partly upon oil revenues, partly upon their willingness and ability to spend these revenues on imported goods and services. The uncertainties are very substantial both on the revenues and the spending side.

1. Future gross *oil revenues* depend upon the OPEC countries price policies and the development of world demand for oil from these countries. The gross revenue of about $95 billion in 1974 is likely to be about the same in 1975, the combined result of the slow recovery of the world recession, increasing response of demand to the oil price increase and mild winter weather in the Northern Hemisphere. Two of these factors are presumably temporary, but demand response will increase, partly depending upon the oil consumers' domestic energy supply policies. With the latter still shrouded in cloud, particularly in the United States, predictions of OPEC oil revenues are bound to be equally uncertain. The future price policies of the cartel depend partly upon the course of world inflation. The stability of the cartel and its reactions to political pressures is another factor of uncertainty. It makes little sense at the present moment, therefore, to venture upon predictions beyond 1980. Everything considered, it appears likely that the total annual gross revenues of the OPEC countries may increase to some $150 billion in 1980. Of these gross revenues, more than one-half may accrue to Arab Middle East countries.

2. Oil exporters' *expenditure on foreign goods and services* is increasing rapidly. From 20 billion in 1973 it rose to 37 billion in '74 and may reach 55 billion in '75. Some of the OPEC countries—Indonesia and Nigeria, in particular, but also Iran, Iraq, Algeria, and Venezuela—have large poor populations and substantial domestic investment outlets and may be capable of letting expenditure on imports quickly catch up with the increase in oil revenues. But the oil exporters in the Arab peninsula have relatively small populations, and profitable domestic investment outlets are limited. For these countries petrochemical

industries at home and facilities "downstream" (ports, tankers, pipelines, the Suez Canal, and so forth) seem to be the most important *profitable* investment outlets, and these can at most absorb a minor part of the future oil revenues. Public consumption may grow fast, in particular if sophisticated weaponry continues to be made available on a large scale to Iranian and Middle East Arab governments. Increasing private consumption is another way of making imports follow the growth of the oil revenues. Governments have, for that purpose, to distribute oil revenues as transfers and direct or indirect subsidies to the population of their countries. However, against such a policy speaks the fact that the known oil reserves of all these countries are uncertain and should the reserves be exhausted, per capita income and consumption would have to fall back to the very low levels existing before the oil prices were increased, unless savings and investments have been made that will secure continued revenues. This consideration—clearly on the mind of the rulers of the Arab oil exporting countries—should prevent these nations from using current oil revenues exclusively for consumption purposes, although it should not, on the other hand, rule out very substantial increases in the present low level of per capita consumption of the general population in a country like Saudi Arabia. In fact, Kuwait and Libya do pursue this kind of welfare policy; it serves as an insurance premium against revolution or as an expression of genuine concern for the people. Other oil-exporting countries may choose to follow their example.

The experience so far has been a surprisingly fast increase of foreign purchases by all the OPEC countries. Imports of all kinds of goods have soared, in many cases limited only by the capacity of transportation facilities. Large scale weapons contracts, in some cases with advance payments, have been signed with both West and East. Development plans have been set up by several countries, visualizing a complete domestic absorption of the oil revenues over the next five years. Thus Saudi Arabia has announced a Five Year Plan according to which $500 billion expected oil revenues will be spent entirely upon domestic projects. It goes without saying that the speed with which the oil revenues can be invested profitably is limited and that the faster domestic investment spending proceeds, the larger will be the waste of money. The Iranian minister of planning has recently declared that investments are now proceeding so fast that feasibility studies cannot be undertaken! Many plans and projects will probably remain on paper—indeed, for the countries' own sake it may be hoped that this will be the case lest huge amounts be spent on white elephants with little or no benefits to anybody except the sellers and consultants in the Western world.

3. The future net surpluses of the OPEC countries are now predicted by international organizations [the Organization for Economic Cooperation and Development (OECD) and the World Bank] as well as the U.S. Treasury Department to shrink rapidly and probably even change into deficits from around 1985. By 1980 the cumulated financial reserves should reach amounts of the order of US$250 billion.

Considering the possibility of continued strong world inflation and the fact that even when the net surplus becomes zero some countries will still be accumulating financial funds, the gross accumulation by 1980 may perhaps reach some $300-400 billion, a figure with large margins of uncertainty. Even so, it represents a drastic reduction of the original prediction of the World Bank talking about accumulations of the order $1 trillion by 1980 and $1.5 trillion by 1985. Of the financial reserves by 1980 perhaps some $250 billion will belong to Arab oil exporters; but this figure as well is a highly uncertain conjecture.

To get some feel for the size of the amounts involved, we may compare them with accumulations of financial capital in the United States. This comparison is useful because the United States may become the major intermediary in the process of investing the Arab oil funds. Total United States financial assets amounted to $4.5 trillion at the end of 1971. Their value has approximately doubled every decade since 1950. Simple extrapolation leads us to a figure of about eight trillion in 1980; allowing for inflation we may easily reach ten trillion by 1980. The total financial capital of the Arab oil countries at that time should thus be about 3-4 percent of that of the United States. A comparison with total tangible wealth in the United States leads to similar results. The Arab oil funds will be large; but the United States is financially enormously larger.

A comparison with annual flows also dwarfs the oil-fund accumulations. The increase of the value of financial assets in the United States was $415 billion in 1971. Developments in the stock market may have slowed the increase substantially in 1974, but assuming the stock market to recover completely a figure of some $500-600 billion would have been normal for 1974. Gross private savings in the United States may be about $250 billion in 1974. The financial accumulations of the OPEC countries were about $60 billion in 1974; those of the Arab oil exporters about $40 billion. And while gross private savings in the United States are bound to increase, the OPEC and Arab current financial accumulations are falling.

There is no denying that the oil funds at present are increasing rapidly and are bound to become very large; but there is also no doubt that they could be accommodated completely in the American financial system without serious upheavals, assuming careful financial policies from the side of the federal authorities. This is, of course, so much the more true for the developed countries considered as a whole.

It is the comparison with the Eurodollar (Eurocurrency) market that makes the oil funds look so unmanageable. In May 1974 this market reached its peak with a gross size (in terms of loans outstanding) of $185 billion and the oil exporters accumulations would in 1974 amount to one-third of this—clearly sufficient to have a strong impact. There is no reason, however, why the oil-funds in the longer run should have to be accommodated by the Eurodollar market; indeed, it may be argued that policies should be directed towards cutting the Eurodollar market down to size and inducing the main flow of oil funds to the United States.

The Nature of the Problem

Although roles are continuously changing, the world has always been and will probably continue to be divided into surplus and deficit countries. Surpluses have to be invested abroad because it is in the nature of things that an excess of foreign sales over purchases of goods and services must be accompanied by an increase of net financial claims (including exchange reserves) on other countries. Similarly, national deficits have to be financed abroad; a foreign excess of purchases over sales of goods and services must be accompanied by an increase of the country's net IOUs to other countries. Since surpluses must equal deficits globally, it follows that for any period or at any point of time, claims acquired by surplus countries must always equal IOUs issued by deficit countries.

This simple algebra is sometimes taken to mean that when some countries run surpluses and others deficits, the latter do not really have any financing problems. The amounts of financing forthcoming from surplus countries must always equal the amounts required by the deficit countries. Hence, financing is no problem. To argue complacently like that would be a great mistake, however, for the following reasons.

First, the process and conditions through which borrowers and lenders find each other may have repercussions on effective demand, production, employment, and productive investments in both deficit and surplus countries cannot be dismissed *a priori* as being negligible. On the contrary, prices and returns of financial assets, and their changes, as well as accumulations of assets and debts, may have profound effects on both demand and supply of commodities and services. And when the financial amounts involved are large, real economic repercussions may be strong.

Second, persistent deficits and accumulations of debts mean increasing interest payments to other countries. From a standard of living point of view, this may be a minor consideration for rich, fast-growing countries, but for poor, slow-growing countries such interest payments may in the long term become an intolerable burden. This problem is already acute in many less developed countries. It will become seriously magnified through the deficits induced by the increased oil prices. And for any oil importer, running deficits, it is bound to present an increasing balance of payments problem.

Another complacent view of the problem has to be disposed of. During recent years, developed countries have increasingly depended upon flexible exchange rates as a means of solving foreign exchange inbalances. Advocates of freely floating exchange rates even argue that this is the best possible way of tackling, or, rather, avoiding, balance of payment problems; recent experience is mixed but has not been unfavorable to this view. It might appear natural, therefore, to argue that the solution of the balance of payments imabalances created by the oil price increases could also and should be left to the market forces via the exchange rates between the currencies of oil exporters and importers. This solution cannot be expected to work in this particular case, however. The point is that we are up against the policies of a world monopolist, or, rather, a group of governments acting as a cartel that—as long as it lasts—will not let itself be pushed around by market forces:

First, this solution would require that the governments of the oil exporting countries be willing to let their currencies float. So far, they have preferred to peg their currencies first to the United States dollar, more recently to the Special Drawing Rights (SDRs) and have, at most, undertaken only minor appreciations to compensate for the depreciation of the dollar during 1974 and the first half of 1975.

Second, the extremely low domestic resource costs of oil extraction make oil output highly insensitive to exchange rate changes. With oil prices fixed in terms of United States dollars and production subjected to OPEC and government decisions, the adjustment of the oil exporters' balances of payments (in terms of dollars) would have to take place exclusively through increased imports. But with spending out of oil revenues largely a matter of discrete government decision, little, if any, automatic response can be expected on the import side either. If it were their deliberate policy to accumulate financial reserves as an investment policy for securing incomes in the future when oil reserves are depleted, these governments should, indeed, keep an adequate surplus on current account and, hence, should take care not to let spending in terms of dollars be boosted excessively. Adopting floating exchange rates for the purpose of wiping out the surpluses would, therefore, be a meaningless policy from the viewpoint of the oil exporters themselves.

Exchange rate policies do, however, have a bearing upon the problem. Lest credit worthiness for individual oil importers raises its ugly head, it is important that the global deficit of the oil importers be distributed evenly among them. This should be taken to mean that the financially strongest countries should carry the largest burden. And it surely means that the United States should aim at a substantial deficit in its balance of current payments. It is for that reason urgent that a realignment of exchange rates amongst oil importers take place. It would on balance imply a revaluation of the dollar in relation to other oil-importers currencies.

It cannot be sufficiently emphasized also that a revaluation of the dollar would have beneficial effects on the basic problem itself. Oil prices are fixed in terms of dollars but are, to a large extent, paid to the producers (Iran, Kuwait, and Iraq, for instance) in sterling pounds. And a substantial part of the spendings out of oil revenues are in other currencies than dollars. Thus, no matter whether the oil exporters receive dollars or sterling, their earnings would increase in value as a consequence of a dollar revaluation. It should not be forgotten that when oil prices were increased in 1973, one of the arguments was precisely the dollar devaluations of 1971 and 1973. The argument has appeared several times in the deliberations of the OPEC and there has been thought about fixing oil prices in terms of SDRs. It appears that the recent improvement of the dollar did, in fact, exert a dampening influence on the oil-price increase of September 1975. A further dollar revaluation would, undoubtedly, give the oil importers leverage on their attempts to get oil prices down or, at least, prevent them from increasing further.

Initial Impact and Policies

Almost two years have passed since the big boost of the oil prices. Still the accumulated funds of the oil exporters are modest compared with expected future funds and the recession in combination with spending in anticipation of future revenues have unexpectedly brought some minor exporters in the red. The total financial surplus may already have reached its peak but the financial accumulation process is unfolding. For gauging future problems and designing policies, it is useful to survey the initial impact on the international financial markets and patterns of reaction on both sides.

Recall, first, that under the old international monetary system—with exchange rates pegged in terms of United States dollars—countries would (should) invariably meet minor surpluses and deficits in the basic balance of payments with corresponding changes in their exchange reserves. Larger imbalances would be countered by "stabilization policies," aiming at adjusting the balance of payments through demand management, credit market policy affecting longer term capital flows, and, perhaps, incomes policy, whereas large and persistent imbalances sooner or later (more often later than sooner) would lead to adjustment of exchange parities. Under a system of freely floating rates the balance of payments adjustment would take place through exchange rate changes brought about by the market forces, as conditioned by domestic fiscal and monetary policies and, in some cases, public foreign borrowing policy. During the last few years of "dirty float" and "joint float," a mixture of the two systems has been applied by most developed countries and some less developed countries. In addition, some developed countries (Italy and Denmark, for instance) preferred for years to cover persistent deficits through private and official short- and long-term borrowing abroad rather than let exchange rates adjust or cut down domestic absorption; this is also the method adopted by the majority of underdeveloped countries.

After the increase of the oil prices, the European deficit countries chose to borrow abroad rather than let their exchange reserves be depleted or let their currencies depreciate. Only recently has the United Kingdom embarked upon a depreciation policy. There was in most of these countries a tendency to cut down domestic absorption, but this policy was in most cases adopted for anti-inflationary purposes rather than as an attempt to cope with the specific balance of payments problems created by the oil price increases.

The borrowing of the European deficit countries has so far mainly taken the forms of Eurodollar loans and direct borrowing from the oil exporting countries. In addition, there have been some investments by the oil exporters in the private sectors of the oil importing countries and some arrangements for recycling through international organizations [European Economic Community (EEC), International Monetary Fund (IMF) and the World Bank].

Total publicized Eurocurrency credits indicate an enormous expansion of this market from 1972 to 1974, mainly through credits extended to developed countries. The total size of the Eurocurrency market, measured gross by the amounts of deposits existing or loans outstanding at any given point of time, is not exactly known, but is supposed to have been of the order of $100-120 billion at the end of 1971, and it is reported to 'have reached a peak level of about $185 billion by mid-1974. From the fall of 1974 the market stagnated and even shrunk somewhat related to the recession and increased freedom of American banks to fix deposit rates (relaxation of Regulation Q). The very fast expansion during 1973 and 1974 was partly related to oil exporters depositing nonspent oil revenues in these banks to benefit from the relatively high returns. During 1974, about half the surplus may have gone into Eurocurrency deposits in London and elsewhere. With the relative fall of American interest rates in 1975 a large part continues to be invested in Eurocurrencies.

A substantial part of the oil revenues accrue in pounds sterling, however; they are paid to oil exporters' sterling accounts in London and have, to some extent, remained in the United Kingdom as sterling deposits and other short investments, attracted partly by the high interest rates obtainable there, and partly by special favors extended to oil exporters (exchange rate guarantees in various forms, and the like), but also as a result of direct negotiations about loans to the British government from certain oil exporters (Kuwait and Iran, for instance). The full details of these arrangements are not known except that interest rates are variable and with a margin linked to the current Eurodollar rate. It is these circumstances that until recently strengthened the pound sterling in the foreign exchange markets despite an abominable British current account.

It remains to be seen how important direct investments in private business will be—such as Iran's purchases of Krupp stocks and Kuwait's real estate investments in London. It is clear, however, that what can be expected by way of grants and low interest loans to less developed countries or aid through international organizations does not suffice to cover the increased costs of oil for Less Developed Countries (LDC) oil importers. The amounts so far obtained by the IMF for its Facilities to Assist Members in Meeting the Initial Impact of the Increase of Oil Import Costs are small compared to the needs. On the other hand, the developed countries—in particular the United States—have little to blame the oil exporters in this regard. Were the oil exporters to follow the basic United Nations rule of allocating 0.7 percent of their national income as official aid, a rule which few developed countries are living up to, the annual amount of official aid from the oil exporters would amount to less than half a billion dollars, and that is very little compared with what Arab oil exporters already have lent to the IMF's special facility, for development purposes or have invested in various aid funds to the benefit of Arab and Moslem countries. Sadly enough, the oil exporters are, in fact, generous compared with the United States and Europe, not to mention Japan.

An increasing amount of the oil-exporters' financial funds, were in 1974 invested on short-term conditions in New York rather than in Euromarkets. The U.S. Treasury believes that about one-quarter were invested in the United States during 1974; this proportion appears to have fallen considerably in 1975. It appears to be sensitive to relative interest rates and may thus be expected to fluctuate substantially.

These initial developments call for several comments.

The Exchange Rates. That individual oil-importing deficit countries such as the United Kingdom, France, Italy, and others initially refrained from depreciating their currencies as a response to the change in their balance of payments positions stemmed partly from fears that depreciation might add fuel to the already exorbitant rates of inflation in these countries, partly and, in all probability, from the insight that as a whole the oil importers cannot expect to improve their joint balance of payments position vis-à-vis the oil exporters for reasons already explained. Some of the countries participate in the joint float of Common Market currencies, and their currencies have been supported by the Bundesbank; a discontinuation of this policy would have consequences for the Common Market.

The OECD adopted in 1974 a resolution formulating a code of behavior to prevent competitive depreciation and trade obstacle moves from the side of oil importers. For whereas the joint deficit of the oil importers probably only insignificantly would be affected by depreciation of the oil-importers' currencies vis-à-vis those of the oil exporters, the distribution of the total deficit among the oil importers is highly dependent upon the foreign exchange policies pursued by the latter. While beggar-my-neighbor policies of competitive depreciations certainly would lead to no good, there is, as already mentioned, much to be said in favor of an exchange rate alignment between the oil importers so as to distribute the joint deficit more evenly among the countries involved. The recent change in the Birtish exchange rate policy allowing sterling to slip as compared to other currencies should be viewed in this light. The United Kingdom has carried an unreasonably large share of the joint deficit. Other European countries such as France, Italy, and Denmark might do well to follow the British example. The United States, on the other hand, has carried too small a part. Germany and Japan have even continued running surpluses. The exchange rate alignments necessary to distribute the global petroleum deficit could, assuming appropriate governmental long-term borrowing abroad and interest policies to induce appropriate private capital flows, be brought about by freely floating market rates of exchange.

The predictions for 1975, referred to earlier, suggest that by groupings the major international imbalance during the next few years may be between the oil-exporters and other less developed countries, the former running a big joint surplus, the latter a joint deficit of approximately the same size; while the developed oil-importers may run only a modest joint deficit. It is possible, perhaps even likely, that part of the oil-consuming, less developed countries' big joint deficit could be shifted on to the developed oil-consumers through devaluations of the former against the latter. It is doubtful, however, whether this policy would work without detrimental effects on the development efforts of the less developed oil-consumers or without severe hardships being imposed upon the populations in the form of cutbacks of private consumption. Exchange rate policy is, therefore, hardly a feasible solution for these countries. Genuine aid is needed; it may come from the developed oil-importers or from the oil-exporters. It would only be fair if the oil-exporters handed back to the less developed oil-importers all that is now exacted from these nations.

Demand Management. That oil-importing deficit countries generally have refrained from pursuing contractive demand management policies to improve the balance of payments stems, of course, from the fact that improvements of the balance of payments of an individual country, brought about in this way, would have to take place mainly through curtailment of nonoil imports, and that a strong recession with substantial unemployment might be required to call forth the fall in imports. Moreover, such a policy would also become a beggar-my-neighbor policy, shifting the deficit onto other oil-importing countries. It could induce competitive policies from the side of other countries, reinforcing the general recessionary tendencies in the world economy. Warnings have been sounded (among others, from the OECD) that generally expansionary policies in the oil-importing countries would even be needed to compensate for the deflationary effects of the increased propensity to save out of world income following from the shift of world income distribution in favor of the oil exporters, or, to put it in another way, to compensate for the oil importers' increased propensity to import. But that is a doubtful proposition because there must have been a strong fall in savings in the deficit countries. There was until recently disagreement between the United States and Germany, on the one hand, and Britain, on the other, as to the appropriate demand management policy, the former emphasizing the necessity of coping with the concurrent inflation. It would probably be easier to reach consensus if the exchange rates were aligned so that the deficits were distributed more evenly. Such a policy would require appreciations above all in Germany, but also in the United States, with deflationary domestic effects; these two countries would then be more positive to expansionist domestic policies. Conversely, the depreciations required for the United Kingdom and other European countries would have expansionary effects there and make domestic contractionary policies more attractive.

Exchange Reserves. So far, deficit countries have preferred not to run down their reserves. The reason is probably the prospects of very large, persistent deficits that in any case could be met only for a limited time from existing exchange reserves, together with the uncertainty of the future of the international monetary system, which conceivably may return to some form of pegged rates that would necesitate the continued holding of exchange reserves.

Methods and Problems of Large-Scale Recycling of Oil Funds

Four ways of arranging for the financial flows from oil exporters to oil importers have thus emerged:

1. Direct loans from oil-exporter governments to deficit country governments;
2. Investments by oil-exporter governments in private sectors in oil-importer countries (corporate bonds, commercial papers, equity, real estate, C.'D.s and so forth);
3. Recycling with Eurodollar (Eurocurrency) and other banks as intermediaries;
4. Recycling with international organizations [IMF, International Bank for Reconstruction and Development (IBRD)] and/or national governments as intermediaries.

Combinations of these alternatives are, of course, conceivable, and perhaps even preferable, and some of them—particularly case (2)—cover a multitude of possibilities.

Government-to-Government Loans. Were each oil-importer government to arrange for loans directly from "its" oil-exporter governments, no specific international financial problems would emerge. Each country would, as it were, pay part of its oil bill by handing over government securities, with appropriate specifications, to the oil-exporter governments. Exchange reserves and money supply in the oil-importer countries would be unaffected by the balance of payments deficit in the case of both pegged and floating rates; the exchange rates would in any case be unchanged. We assume that domestic fiscal and monetary policies would be pursued aimed at keeping employment unchanged, despite an increased propensity to import and the deficits—for example, through investments aiming at energy self-sufficiency.

Under this alternative, financing would be negotiated bilaterally. If oil importers could shift freely to other exporters, both oil prices and loan conditions would tend to become uniform. The fact that the financial accumulations would largely be concentrated in the hands of a few oil exporters at the Persian Gulf might perhaps result in monopolistic loan policies from the side of the latter. The oil importers might then be flayed twice: first, when buying the oil, and then when borrowing to pay for the oil.

Oil Exporters Investing in Oil-Importers Private Sector. To fix ideas, assume that oil-exporter governments initially prefer to invest their surpluses financially in the United States. At pegged exchange rates, other oil-importers' exchange reserves, kept as deposits in the United States banks, would fall, while oil-exporter governments' deposits would increase by the sum of the fall in other oil-importers' deposits and the fall in deposits owned by United States residents in consequence of the United States current account deficit. Total money supply (M_2) in the United States would remain unchanged. The immediate effect on the United States credit market would depend upon possible changes in the composition of deposits. We shall assume that both the United States and other oil importers pursue such fiscal and monetary domestic policies that the levels of economic activity are kept unchanged everywhere. The deficits are defined on this assumption.

Assume, then, that the oil exporters shift their United States funds from deposits to private financial papers (equity, for instance). Total money supply in the United States would continue to be unchanged, but (with the usual reservation for changes in the composition of deposits) the credit market would generally tend to be easier. Real investment would tend to increase because the desired long-term real capital stocks tend to increase with lower interest rates.[a] With the increase in current real investments, the (flow) supply of private financial assets would increase correspondingly. With real investments running at a higher level, a continued inflow of oil-exporter funds might thus take place without further increase in the prices of financial assets. However, as real capital stock adjusts over time, real investments would tend to fall, and the flow of newly created private financial assets would decline. Their prices would increase further so that investments would remain at a level that leads to a flow supply of private assets equal to the inflow of oil funds. In this way, a continuous fall in interest rates and an increase in the stock of real capital in the United States would take place until the inflow of oil funds eventually ceases. It is conceivable that the increase in investments during this process might be so large that no expansionary policy from the side of the United States federal government would be needed to prevent unemployment from increasing with the emergence of the United States balance of payments deficit. Should the process come to a stop, the United States would have an unchanged stock of money, a larger stock of real capital, a larger stock of liabilities in the private sector, and an unchanged stock of financial assets kept by the private sector. The difference is kept by the

---

[a]It is assumed that the process unfolds at a concurrently balanced federal budget. If a deficit on the federal budget is needed to keep full employment, part of the new supply of bonds will consist of government securities and real capital formation will be correspondingly smaller.

oil exporters. Interest payments to the oil exporters would have increased, but with oil exporters consuming their interest income, exports from oil importers would automatically increase correspondingly; their distribution by countries might, however, require exchange rate adjustments.

However, the other oil importers cannot for any longer time continue to finance their deficits through running down their exchange reserves. Granted pegged exchange rates, they would borrow in the United States financial markets, induced by the lower interest rates there. And the lower American interest rates would induce both domestic American capital and oil funds to invest in the other oil-importer countries. Hence the outflow of capital corresponding to the fall in the other oil-importers' exchange reserves (deposits) would be replaced by another outflow. The United States interest rates would therefore only fall to the extent that the United States itself is running a deficit, but if that were the case, the process, with an increase in the stock of real capital would take place, as described in the last paragraph, albeit on a smaller scale.

We have, so far, assumed that the other oil importers peg their exchange rates vis-à-vis the United States dollar. Should they all prefer to float their currencies against the dollar (or, rather, against the dollar *and* the oil-exporters' currencies), the whole deficit, corresponding to the oil-exporters' surpluses, would show up as a deficit in the United States foreign current account. The other oil importers would not, under this assumption, suffer from any deflationary pressures related to deficits and would need no domestic expansionary policies to keep employment high. And they would not need to borrow abroad. There would, on the other hand, be a huge deficit on the United States current account (corresponding to some 4-5 percent of GNP), calling for stronger domestic expansionary policies to keep employment unchanged (*ceteris paribus*), as well as for a larger net capital inflow. The downward pressure on interest rates would be stronger than in the case with pegged rates. The desired stock of capital would be larger, and current investments would have to run at a higher level.

Summarizing, we find that had the oil exporters initially invested all funds in the United States and other oil importers kept *pegged exchange rates*, the annual increase in foreign demand for financial assets in the United States would amount to some $60 billion in 1974, probably falling to modest amounts in 1980. The foreign (flow) supply of securities to the United States markets from other oil importers would equal that amount *minus* the United States current account deficit. The difference, equal to the United States current account deficit, would be supplied from new United States financial assets, issued to finance new United States real investments (disregarding budget deficits). Interests would fall just sufficiently to induce that amount of real investments (minus, in principle, whatever other oil importers might feel induced to borrow beyond their oil deficits). By 1980 the stock of financial assets issued in the United States should have increased by $400-500 billion, the larger part of the increase being foreign securities. Albeit big amounts, both the additional flows and the stocks accumulated are, as already noticed, small compared with the size of the existing financial flows and stocks in the United States. The United States financial markets alone should be able to absorb and intermediate all the oil funds without particular technical difficulties. With *floating rates*, the dimensions of the financial problems would remain the same, with the difference that the whole increase in financial liabilities would stem from American real investments, and United States interest rates might become much lower. To the extent that American and foreign capital were induced to seek investment abroad by the lower American interest rates the dimensions of the problem would be scaled down correspondingly.

We note that in this case all profits from intermediation would accrue to the United States, more specifically to United States banks and credit institutions.

Recycling via Euro-Markets. The Eurodollar (Eurocurrency) market is a highly refined, experienced market for international financial intermediation on a rather large scale. It would, in a sense, be natural to expect this market to take care of the recycling of the oil funds. In fact it has taken care of a substantial part of the funds so far. Such intermediation is precisely its speciality. What, then, should prevent it from serving this purpose?

1. The sheer size of the funds to be handled: It has been maintained that with traditional capital-to-transactions ratios, the Euro-banks would not be able to handle these large funds and that, indeed, many of these banks have already reached their maximum size in this respect. The answer to this problem— assuming the traditional capital-transactions-ratios to be rational and inescapable—would seem to be an expansion of the capital of these and the establishment of new banks. With good profit prospects, and they are certainly very good, and with ample supply of capital from the oil exporters, it should not be difficult to raise the capital needed. Indeed, why should the oil exporters not finance the credit institutions that recycle their funds? Is it not time for the Saudis to become the partners of the Rothschilds?

2. The difference between the time structure of Euro-deposits and Euro-credits: While Euro-deposits usually are medium-length time deposits (three to six months) and oil exporters so far seem to have deposited very short, Euro-credits have tended during recent years to be asked for and given on longer and longer terms with repayment up to about ten years. To absorb all the oil funds by 1980, the Euro-markets would have to expand to double or triple its present size in terms of outstanding credits; it has been felt that difficulties might then arise from this difference in time structure. In a sense, however, the Euro-banks here encounter the problem that all commercial banks are facing and which they themselves in fact have faced without running into difficulties during the fifteen years of existence of this market; part of their *raison d'être* as intermediaries is exactly to transform short funds into longer ones. Commercial banks solve this problem by keeping probabilistically adequate reserves and by

letting bank loans and advances formally be short-term loans with variable interest, yet for all intents and purposes, renewable as long as debt service is prompt and the credit worthiness of the borrower in other respects is unimpaired. The introduction in the Euro-market of so-called roll-over loans with variable interest has gone some way to solve this problem. And the gap between deposit rates and loan rates has tended to widen. If depositors—particularly the oil exporters—insist on highly liquid financial investments, they have to accept relatively low returns; if borrowers insist on long loans, they have to accept relatively high loan costs. Moreover, as deposits and loans expand and the oil exporters gain experience, there is little reason why they should continue to insist on liquid investments. Their funds will be so large that they can safely keep the major part as long-term investments; exchange rate risks can be minimized simply by depositing in several Eurocurrencies simultaneously. Likewise, oil importers have little reason for insisting on formally long loans, provided that the loan market is always open to them and that depends, to some measure at least, upon their own behavior. We do, however, run into a third problem here.

3. The stability of the Euro-markets: The analogy with an ordinary national banking system tends to break down because the number of depositors and borrowers is relatively small and because both deposits and loans will become more and more dominated by a small number of clients, some of them very large. Moreover, big deposits tend to be concentrated in the biggest, best-known banks. (Note the difference to case (2): the American banking system and domestic financial markets are large in relation to even the largest oil exporter.) It might contribute to stability were the oil exporters encouraged to invest capital directly in Euro-bank equity. They would then presumably tend to deposit in their own banks and would, of course, be careful not to create troubles for themselves by moving funds erratically. On the loan side, the emergence of so-called consortium loans has helped somewhat to alleviate this problem but does not really dispose of it because it is the same relatively few borrowers that are distributed over the same lenders. The tendency on the other hand for Eurocurrency and other banks to serve more and more as mediators between oil exporters and borrowers without directly involving the bank does, in fact, dispense with the problem. An alignment of exchange rates so as to distribute the deficits more evenly over the oil importers would also help, but again does not really dispose of the problem either. Another way to overcome it is obviously the establishment of some kind of lender of last resort that can support Euro-banks in difficulties, due regard being taken for the peculiarities of this market.

Governments in the developed countries have slowly and reluctantly come around to a position that something has to be done about the Eurodollar market, not only in view of its most recent expansion but also because its unfettered expansion during the sixties, propelled by an entirely irresponsible behavior from the side of the central banks (including the Federal Reserve System), carries some responsibility for the present world inflation. Occasional bank crashes—that in fact have little directly to do with the Eurocurrency markets—seem to have played a role, too. The problem is, on the one hand, to create lenders of last resort for the Eurocurrency banks and, on the other hand, to curb the expansion of world credits and money supply. A meeting of the Group of Twenty in 1971 appears to have made an end to Central Banks investing exchange reserves in the Euro-market; this was a praxis that tended to make the Euro-markets work as a fractional reserve banking system and make it a source of world inflation. And at a recent meeting of Central Banks at the Bank of International Settlement (BIS), it was decided that individual central banks should begin to act as lenders of last resort for banks operating in foreign currency within their jurisdiction. There are several tricky problems involved here and how this agreement will work out in practice remains to be seen. In any case there is clearly much to be said against having the oil funds recycled by banks that are not firmly under control by the monetary authorities of the country in whose currency they operate.

Let it, finally, be emphasized that the Eurocurrency market to some measure has American interest rate regulations to thank for, if not its existence, then certainly part of its spectacular growth until 1974. With Regulation Q and similar regulations abrogated, funds that now seek the Eurodollar market would prefer investment as deposits in the United States and the Eurodollar market would be substantially curtailed. The softening of Regulation Q, which actually has taken place, has helped to stop the expansion of the Eurodollar market.

4. *Recycling via International Organizations.* With its two successive special Facilities, the IMF has made an honest effort to channel funds from the oil exporters to less developed countries. The World Bank has proposed the creation of large funds under its controls, to be financed through loans from oil exporters and to be used for loans to less developed deficit countries, with debt-service payments guaranteed by the rich, developed countries. The United Nations Food and Agriculture Organization (FAO) food conference has sketched a similar fund for financing food supplies to less developed countries. And a couple of other proposals of this kind have been aired. There is something to be said in favor of recycling the oil funds through international organizations: the burden would be taken off the Euro-markets and the national banking systems; and the bilateral agreements between individual oil importers and oil exporters (in which the latter too easily might get the upper hand) would be replaced by agreements between the international (hopefully noncompetitive) organization(s) and individual oil exporters.

The basic weakness of these proposals is, of course, that the oil exporters have no reason for participating with substantial amounts unless it offers them special advantages. These could be of a political nature, giving the oil exporters a decisive say in the administration of the funds. Or higher returns than could be obtained elsewhere might be offered. In either case the schemes would be doomed for obvious reasons. In addition, it is probably fair to say that any large-scale recycling scheme via international organizations to less developed countries soon would be faced with demands for lower interest rates, moratoria and so forth that would challenge the very principle upon which all these schemes are based: loans at commercial rates.

The 1975 Facility is further burdened with a novelty of doubtful virtue: subsidization of interest rates. While this will benefit LDCs, it will, on the other hand, also tend to increase lenders' rates. The United States did well in insisting upon limiting the Facility to $6 billion.

On the other hand, the fact that the oil-exporters' surplus increasingly appears to be matched by less developed oil-importers' deficits, makes arrangements like the Facilities, with a substantial grant-element, a necessity.

At this point Secretary of State Henry Kissinger's "safety-net" scheme should also be mentioned. It is essentially a mechanism for loans between developed oil consumers. It is difficult to take sides upon the scheme because it is as yet unknown how exactly it is going to operate if at all ratified by the participating governments. It appears to be small compared with the potential need for loans from particularly badly hit developed oil consumers: $25 billion over two years with the maximum of loans limited to half the fund makes $6 billion per year, that is less than the current deficit of the United Kingdom alone. Its effects will depend entirely upon how funds are going to be raised by the contributors, whether domestically or directly from oil exporters. The scheme thus leaves open the crucial problem of the financial relations between the United States government and the oil exporters.

5. A number of proposals for solving or, at least, alleviating and smoothening the process of recycling funds, have appeared. One of the more interesting is the so-called Foreign Affairs Proposal.

The Farmanfarmian committee proposed in an article in *Foreign Affairs* to set up a kind of international investment trusts, to be financed through sales of equity to oil exporters, negotiable only between these, and investing in equity in (mainly) developed countries. Various constraints should safeguard the interests of both sides, and the trusts should function as politically neutral, financial intermediaries without monopolistic powers. The proposal is ingenious, but' apparently presumes that nobody is interested in wielding power for its own sake. This kind of intermediation arrangements, although it may only contribute marginally, should be welcomed.

Communist Countries and the Oil Funds

Economically, it would probably be advantageous to everybody if oil funds on a large scale were to flow to Communist countries. Such funds would almost certainly be used as payments for food and capital goods imports from developed, non-Communist countries, the only suppliers on a large scale of grain and capital goods. Communist borrowing would thus shift a corresponding part of the deficits of the developed, non-Communist oil importers onto Communist countries, obviously alleviating the financial situation of the former through improved trade balances and, perhaps, terms of trade, and making possible the commodity inflows that the latter are so badly in need of. To be sure, serious political problems are involved but they are outside the scope of this chapter. Economically, loans from the oil exporters to Communist countries would be an ideal solution of the oil funds problem as far as it goes, agreeable to both East and West.

The Communist countries have no compunctions in dealing with capitalist high finance. The Soviet Union was involved in the emergence of the Euro-markets (withdrawing its dollar funds from the United States during the cold war (1953) and depositing on dollar accounts with London banks) and other Communist countries have always been customers in the Eurodollar markets. Even Fidel Castro is a client there. They are reputed to be extremely punctual and conservative in honoring (their own) financial contracts (much to the annoyance of their most important debtors, the less developed countries).

At the end of the fifties and the early sixties, the Soviet Union was a depositor in the Euro-markets but became slowly an important borrower. During the last year, however, it has again emerged as a depositor with surpluses of convertible currency (dollars). The reason is partly increased oil revenues from non-Communist countries (the Soviet Union is a net exporter and benefits substantially from the high oil prices); but it would also seem that oil funds have already flown to the Soviet Union on a large scale through weapons payments. The Arab oil exporters have most certainly paid cash for the replacement of Egyptian and Syrian military equipment after the 1973 war although they have not paid off old Egyptian and Syrian debts for deliveries of weapons. This situation, however, is a temporary one. The Soviet Union will most probably be short of convertible currencies soon again and the Eastern European Communist countries (hardly hit by the oil prices) are in deep need of convertible currency loans.

Conclusions and Recommendations

While the annual accumulations of financial capital of the oil exporters already now have passed their peak, the accumulated financial reserves of the oil exporters continue to increase rapidly and call for policy action. Two fundamentally different strategies are possible: with and without concerted action from the side of the oil importers.

The United States government has tried and is still trying to line up the oil importers in a united front against the oil exporters. If successful, concerted action might lead to a package deal involving both oil prices and production as well as financial arrangements and conditions. Such a package deal is bound to lead to better conditions for the oil importers as a whole than a development without concerted action. A natural element of such a package deal would be to make the oil exporters handing back what they are now exacting from less developed oil importers. However, there is a risk that a bilateral confrontation might lead to open conflict rather than agreements, with unpredictable consequences. It is clearly the risk of such outcomes that has tempted European oil importers and Japan to reject concerted action.

Without concerted action the oil importers will be at the disadvantage but still cooperation is necessary to make the best possible of a difficult situation. The United States should take the lead in such cooperation, not pursuing narrowly defined and myopic goals, alien to its real national interest.

A leading principle of cooperation among oil importers should be to induce oil-exporter investments to be spread out thinly over the whole range of investment possibilities following a time-honored economic principle that total costs are minimized when marginal costs are the same in all applications. Nothing should be done that prevents this from happening and cooperation should, indeed, aim at removing possible obstacle to this end. Some important consequences of this principle are:

1. A realignment of exchange rates should be undertaken in order to distribute the joint deficit vis-à-vis the oil exporters more evenly among oil importers. This measure would alleviate the problems of credit worthiness and the burden of growing debt service payments. It would require an appreciation of particularly the deutsch mark and the yen but also of the dollar and might help lower oil prices, or, at least, prevent them from increasing further. Exchange rate policy is, however, hardly a feasible policy solution for the less developed oil consumers. Some kind of aid is needed.

2. The idea of having the oil funds spread thinly applies not only to their distribution between countries but also within countries. It means, on the one hand, that individual countries should not set up unnecessary obstacles to oil-exporter investments and, indeed, should adjust financial institutional arrangements so as to facilitate such foreign financial investment. But it means also, on the other hand, that it may be necessary to institute regulations that prevent foreign investments from concentrating too heavily in special fields. Thus, while permitting foreigners freely to purchase equity in domestic corporate business it might, for instance, be necessary to prevent foreigners from holding effective majorities in such business.

3. Since small developed and all less developed deficit countries are likely to have a weak bargaining position vis-à-vis the oil exporters, they should presumably abstain from obtaining direct loans from the latter. This is a financing method that only countries with sufficient economic or political muscle should

embark upon. It is important, therefore, that sufficient intermediation facilities are available for small and poor countries. This consideration leads to points four to six.

4. The Eurocurrency market fulfills important functions as a financial intermediary but has to some extent represented an element of anarchy in the international monetary system. There is a need, on the one hand, to bring this market under the control of central banks and, on the other hand, to furnish it with lenders of last resort. This is a general international monetary problem but it has been strongly accentuated by the flows of oil funds. Much has already been done during the last year and a half by the way of solving these problems; yet, present arrangements do not appear sufficient to ensure adequate policies vis-à-vis the Euro-markets. From the United States point of view the most efficient measure might be further relaxation and even the complete removal of Regulation Q and similar ceilings on interest rates in the United States. This would help cut the Eurodollar market down to size and relocate a substantial part of its activities in the United States within the controls and support of the United States government. This policy would, incidentally also help shift funds from other currencies into the United States, thus strengthening the dollar and diminishing further incentives to oil-price increases.

5. Countries with big financial centers (New York, London, Paris, Tokyo) should promote the international intermediation activities of private financial institutions removing obstacles to both official inflows and outflows of capital. The governments of such countries might act as underwriters for small and poor countries, and might even act as intermediaries themselves, borrowing from oil exporters beyond the country's own needs and relending to other needy countries.

6. Intermediation through international organizations should be expanded.

7. There may be little that can be done from the side of Western countries, the United States particularly, to further Communist borrowing from oil exporters. But obstacles should not be put in the way of either such borrowing or the resultant trade.

While the great petrodollar scare already now belongs to the past, there is no reason to belittle the problems accompanying the future accumulation of financial reserves by the oil exporters. There is no simple trick to handle these problems. Financial markets have, fortunately, proved extremely flexible and innovative, but they do need the support of adequate government policies. Cooperation over a broad field is needed, lest weak countries be overwhelmed by financial difficulties. The outcome depends much upon the policies of the United States.

V Middle Eastern Leadership

Morroe Berger

The considerable effort since the Second World War to raise the income and the technological competence of the poor or less developed countries, including those of the Middle East, has produced a certain pessimism about man's capacity to plan and to direct social change. The study of these efforts, in turn, should have induced a genuine modesty about the capacity of social scientists and practitioners to understand how "modernization" takes place. Most international aid—public and private, successful or not—has proceeded without great reliance upon systematic study of the institutions of the countries that were aided. International assistance has been extended pragmatically to needy countries willing to accept it. In most regions, so much is needed that it has been easy to select a few domains for aid. What has been much more difficult is to measure the results of aid, because (1) the effects of a single line of activity can seldom be traced clearly, and (2) the assessment of results depends upon expectations and goals, which are not always made explicit, are often not measurable, and may not be the same for those who extend aid and those who receive it. Expectations, moreover, change. If international comparisons, rather than changes within a country, are emphasized, then there is usually dissatisfaction over the remaining gap between poor and rich countries. International aid can do little to make a nation contented. Development involves the endless stimulation of desire, whereas contentment is more often associated with the absence of desire.

The vast infusions (mainly from Russia and America) of capital, food, technology, and arms into most countries of the Middle East have not provided them with the means to handle the problems already posed, and those to come, by their achievements and aspirations. Effective political institutions, including leadership at several levels, have been lacking at a time when government has assigned itself the crucial task of coordinating the various elements of development. The recent increase in income from oil and even the prospect of a continued flow of foreign exchange cannot automatically produce the institutions and leadership needed to achieve the goals already advanced. Country after country, regardless of wealth, faces serious challenges. This is not to say that Middle Eastern countries have made no appreciable advances in income for some sectors of the population, or in education, agriculture and even public administration. Yet, especially in the Arab countries, there has not been the kind of dovetailing of public and private power and initiative that economic growth seems to require. It is precisely this role of governmental institutions and leadership, now so important, that does not inspire confidence in the future. The unprecedented oil income of the Arab lands on the Persian Gulf may prove this judgment too pessimistic, but only if means are found to use and share this income or its fruits in economically constructive ways.

Power and Leadership in the World Today

It is no special derogation of Middle Eastern leaders if we draw attention to the gap between their capacities and the tasks that face them, for there is a similar gap in the industrialized world. Modern technology, of course, makes nations and states more interdependent but it also places increasing powers in the hands of governments; this is true even in democracies, which have traditionally been able to limit governmental powers. Other large organizations have also enjoyed greater powers, including industry, communications media, educational systems, and certain professions. Peoples, moreover, continuing to look for guidance and even salvation, have created leaders from such human material as has been available. It would be interesting to learn, if we could, whether this process of creation of leaders from the available pool of those seeking power or the opportunity to serve has pushed up greater or lesser personalities in different eras including our own. The question grows in importance when we consider that, as has been frequently said in one way or another, the more we overcome the restrictions of nature the more we must submit to restrictions established by men.

The existence of problems in a society does not mean that leadership has failed. Failure comes when leaders are incapable of defining problems, dealing with them and obtaining the best advice. With good reason, several influential journals and observers in the West have recently spoken of a "collapse of leadership" under the burden of great issues demanding new approaches that are not forthcoming.[1] New technology, especially in the media of communication, has aroused expectation of rises in living standards among masses of people everywhere who formerly were almost mute. World leaders have responded more readily in encouraging and proclaiming such desires than in finding ways to fulfill them. As a wise observer of politics and society said a decade ago, "power and folly often go hand in hand."[2] Leaders have great advantages, such as the possession of considerable information about the realm and the ruled, and a virtual monopoly of the peaceful and violent instruments of persuasion. Yet they often wilfully ignore what they know in order to serve narrow interests (including their own power), seek even greater power or exaggerate the power they have, and lose judgment as a result of overconfidence. They have thus far been inadequate to the huge task of bringing about the necessary cooperation among nations more dependent upon one another than ever before. Cooperation among peoples through their governments is more difficult under modern conditions of intensive communication and publicity, for cooperation often implies that some nations must accept, at least for the present, a status of inferiority in power or social condition so obvious that they are less and less willing to abide it.

Leadership is always inadequate in one sense or another, regarding one problem or another, to one group or another, for the modern world poses issues that are changing quickly, require immediate attention and action, and are seen differently by many groups with varying interests. Leadership is bound to appear to someone to be autocratic or insensitive or demagogic, and that too is a problem for leaders. Leaders may be more competent than their predecessors but the demands upon them may be greater. More than two and a half centuries ago, Bernard Mandeville observed in *The Fable of the Bees* (Remark 0) that leaders have tastes for material comfort no less than those of ordinary people. "What virtue is it," he asked, "the exercise of which requires so much pomp and superfluity" as we see in men of power? Are all governments so precarious that rulers need such outward signs of "superiority" over the ruled? Does "impartial justice" really require the "gaudy show" of "scarlet gowns" and "gold chains"?

Between Mandeville's era and ours Nathaniel Hawthorne's narrator in *The House of the Seven Gables* (Chapter 1) said, regarding execution for witchcraft, that "the influential classes, and those who take upon themselves to be leaders of the people, are fully liable to all the passionate error that has ever characterized the maddest mob." There is all too much evidence of both of these weaknesses among political leaders in our own time.

Nor have leaders in domains other than the political shown much more ability (although their responsibility is not so great or direct). The Western business and financial community has thus far not distinguished itself in responding to the problems leading to and created by the rapid rise in oil prices. Like the governments, and following a strong business precedent, they have taken a narrow view of large issues. Many business leaders, moreover, are not content to pursue business interests pure and simple but tend to find virtues in regimes that have capital no matter what threats such regimes may pose even to ultimate business interests. This has been their predominant attitude to the Soviet Union and the People's Republic of China, for example, and more recently to some Middle East countries. Business leaders feel, of course, that the responsibility for taking the larger view rests upon governments. Yet governments, especially democratic ones, are also limited, as the recent oil situation has shown. Leaders in countries where public opinion is important in daily affairs cannot act resolutely without national consensus. In the United States the public did not respond to many warnings of oil shortage in the early 1970s, then was aroused to a fever pitch when the shortage hit in the winter of 1973-74, and again became apathetic when relief came in the spring. If our leaders warn of impending crises, we often ignore them or accuse them of demagogy. If they wait for the crisis to hit us, we complain they lack foresight. The public suspicion of leaders and our leaders' penchant for the easy way bode ill for the next decade of problems surrounding the changing oil situation.

Where are the leaders who can create a national consensus or bring nations together in their own interests? Western governments face constitutional or parliamentary crises to the point where stable majorities cannot be found. This is true even in Middle Eastern parliamentary regimes, such as Turkey and Israel. This public unwillingness to commit its interests decisively signalizes a disenchantment with leadership as well as perhaps a yearning for something better.

All this is not to say that leaders are entirely to blame for the unsatisfactory condition of the world or a country. They are somewhat dependent upon the character of the people they lead and upon the "elite" groups that are the necessary aides to leaders. For several decades social scientists have studied the relationship among leaders, elites and masses and even the Middle East has come in for a certain amount of such study. On one level the connection between rulers and their agents is simple. Agents are supposed to help rulers govern. But these elites, though dependent, are not always loyal. Even more than masses do, elites are quick to resent their dependence and to envy the rulers their power. Though often rewarded (perhaps beyond their worth), elites tend to regard themselves as exploited. So rulers distrust their aides as rivals at the same time that they must rely upon them. All this is especially true in the kind of authoritarian and dictatorial regimes so characteristic of the Middle East. As important as military force is in the internal affairs of many countries there, rulers must be wary of trusting such power even to officers of their own choosing. Those closest to the ultimate power are often the greatest threat to it.

Suspicion within the Middle East has been matched by the region's suspicion of Western leadership over the centuries. Despite political independence, Middle Eastern countries are still dependent upon or closely involved with the more developed and powerful states of the Western world and the Soviet Union. Foreign leadership thus continues to have a great impact there. Ironically, the region has come to full sovereignty at a time when that condition is nowhere what it used to be, although the term continues to play a great part in international rhetoric.

Power and Leadership in the Middle East

The present leadership in the Middle East continues to pursue goals of modernization (including increased power as well as popular education and a rise in the standard of living) already advanced a hundred or more years earlier by their predecessors who also faced Western influences and domestic inadequacies. Although the decades since then have brought new conditions and techniques, the basic relationship is still recognizable. Middle Eastern indigenous leaders trying to arouse their masses to the need for some accommodation to the influence exerted upon them from cultures outside their own.

In the nineteenth century the process of change and reform involved tension between the central power (chiefly Ottoman) and provincial leaders (many of them basing their power upon religious loyalty). Interested mainly in the defense of their realm, the central or imperial leaders sought to strengthen the provinces by introducing reforms, some of which took hold despite the apprehension of the more conservative local elites and indifferent masses. That era's tension between central power and local elite prevails in some form today, but the central power is now the nation-state instead of a transnational empire like the Ottoman, and the local elites function in much-weakened regions within the nation-state rather than in large and somewhat autonomous areas within the Ottoman Empire. The more numerous central governments of today are thus much more powerful as nation-states than was the central administration of the Ottoman Empire, yet it is not at all clear that they enjoy greater success in the constructive tasks of leadership.[3]

The impetus for social change has passed from Western power to indigenous Middle Eastern leaders influenced by the West and to their equally indigenous elites in the civil and military bureaucracies whose members owe even more to their Western education in the intricacies of GNP, industrialization, management, weaponry, and military tactics and strategy. Western institutions stimulated Middle Eastern imitation in science, technology, and education, in constitutional government (for greater liberty and individual fulfillment), and in nationalism (to mobilize masses for any purpose). Technology and limited government were difficult to achieve, nationalism rather easy. The pursuit of all these goals has put a premium on a modern, Western-style education whether it is achieved in the West itself or in Middle Eastern school systems aiming to impart that kind of learning. The technically based elites—in law, journalism, economics, social work, and other professions—perform their work in government offices; they depend upon the nation's rulers for their tasks and emoluments and, conveniently for their masters, neither enjoy nor often seek much opportunity to cultivate a popular following. They are technicians, not very different from their predecessors a century or more earlier.

The social sources of both the top political leadership and the next level of bureaucratic technicians are not dissimilar. In an earlier era, the rulers inherited power or came from the commercial and religious elite. More recently they and their administrators come from more various backgrounds, but almost all go through the homogenizing experience of a modern education in arts and sciences, law, and military affairs. Even the military academies, however, while still a source of leadership through coups, elections or wars of liberation, are losing ground; their graduates who ascend to rule may continue to rely on the barracks, but in mental set and policies they tend increasingly to resemble their counterparts emerging from the civilian educational system. The current ruling elite thus retains the older connection with the West. Although it is more determined than its predecessors to reduce direct Western influence, it continues to put a premium on Western-style technology. The new rulers, however, give more attention to the masses, seeking both to arouse and use them.

The emphasis upon education and the liberalization of the educational system have widened the sources of leadership, bringing to the fore people who are younger, from obscure families, and from provincial backgrounds, and who in the future are increasingly likely to be women. The influence of more educated women has already been felt in the labor force, the professions, family life, and in the texture of social life generally. In the next decade, we may expect this influence to extend into the bureaucracies but not at the highest levels except in an occasional token ministry headed by a woman. Where elections are held, women may acquire further influence upon policy, for their general political participation is growing. Whether the influence of women will affect the general capacity of Middle Eastern leadership is problematical, though it will certainly give some women a greater opportunity for autonomy and self-fulfillment and is sure also to widen the popular base of the political system as a whole.

Such an enlargement of the political base as has already taken place or is expected to occur in the Middle East should not be confused with radicalism or socialism in the Western sense of these terms. Political power is likely to remain dependent upon personal attachments to leaders on all levels, high and low, despite the partial displacement of kinship and religious loyalties by military rulers and radical ideologies since the Second World War.[4] Earlier tendencies toward parliaments and parties did not eliminate the personal element, nor has the military socialism of recent decades done so. The concept of "office" is still very much intertwined with the background and affiliations of the person who holds it. It was thought, by foreign observers in the 1960s, that military regimes introduced efficiency, austerity and honesty in leadership and the bureaucracy, but experience in Egypt, Syria, and Iraq has steadily shown the naïveté of this view and the disillusionment of the peoples of the Middle East with military rule.

In most countries where the military have come to power they have resorted to a small number of radical intellectuals for rhetoric. This alliance is a natural one. The military have needed some kind of ideology to back up or vindicate their use of force, and the radical ideologists, with no popular base, have needed force to put across their programs or at least to give them access to (or a virtual monopoly of) the media of communication to spread an ideology that is not congenial to the populace. This is not to say that military regimes have introduced no popular changes in socioeconomic affairs or that the ideologies do not find some popular support. It is merely to stress that both have had to operate on the basis of force and of suppression of other tendencies. Internal poverty, the challenge of Israel, and a residue of anti-Western feeling—all encouraged by the Soviet Union regardless of real or imagined détente with the United States—will always be enough to stimulate radicalism and enable it to find a popular echo. At the same time force will always be necessary to support military radicalism against the normal indifference or resistance to it among the Arabs, who now know it better and are too diverse in their interests to do the bidding of such regimes wholeheartedly and for long.

The introduction of parliaments and parties into the Middle East has had very limited success in controlling governments and spreading political power. Military regimes, nevertheless, while destroying these "corrupt" and "ineffi-cient" institutions, have imposed substitutes in the effort to create a facade of greater legitimacy. It is also just possible that recent antidemocratic regimes have given educated public opinion a new respect for the "empty forms" still remembered by older people and now familiar to the young who see the difference between democratic institutions elsewhere and their counterfeits at home.

Nationalism, distinct from radicalism yet connected to it at some points, is another persistent issue in Middle Eastern power and leadership. Arab nation-alism has certain traits not shared by nationalism in Israel, Iran or Turkey. In those three countries, nationalism is of course related to foreign influences and internal unity (or questions of national "identity"). In Israel, however, foreign influence or neoimperialism has virtually disappeared as an issue, and in Iran and Turkey leaders have likewise long ago found it unnecessary to refer much to earlier dependence upon the West. Nationalist issues in all three countries involve chiefly disputes with neighboring but not superior powers. Israel, Iran, and Turkey, moreover, do not now face issues of unity with other states, only questions of integrating some internal groups within a national life most of them want to join.

Arab nationalism, however, still confronts more difficult issues. Since the Second World War, the increasing number of Arab states has unsuccessfully sought a degree of unity beyond ideological agreement about Israel. This quest has absorbed leaders to the point of enervating and fruitless attempts to dominate or unify each other. As the concept of unity has become more sacred in their speeches, the reality has evaded them; the leaders have persisted in the effort to strengthen their separate states and regimes. Yet, the holiness of the goal has continued to induce leaders of individual states to come together and to find new grounds for difference whether they meet as members of the Arab

League or under other auspices. The impulse to unity and meddling at the same time leads to a peculiarly Arab process of "mediation." Leaders rotate as mediators and the objects of mediation by other leaders. Egyptians mediate a dispute between Lebanese and Palestinians. Saudi Arabia tries to mediate between Jordan and Syria. The Sudanese leader mediates between Egypt and Libya. Leaders have thus spent personal and national energies in an unclear and so far largely fruitless search that many of them have already abandoned in fact while still paying a price for their failure to adjust goals and rhetoric to the realities they themselves perceive.

Palestinian national feelings are of course real and unfulfilled. The longer they remain in this condition, the more difficult it is to accommodate Palestinian nationalism to the realities of at least Israeli and Jordanian power and national feeling. Here, too, leadership in the Arab world, including leadership among the Palestinians, has failed to adjust to realities or to create manageable new ones, for "unity" efforts have not enabled Palestinians to unite with other Arabs or with Jordan and certainly not with Israel in a manner that would improve the life and future of the masses of Palestinians, for whom there are many spokesmen but whose own preferences are not yet clear beyond a desire not to live in a Jewish state. Israel itself, while enjoying capable leadership in its early years of building the nation and the state, became less fortunate as its military successes increased. The leadership, relying too much on military considerations and advice after 1967, failed to see or encourage openings for peace, thus strengthening Arab Palestinian militancy and ultimately inviting the surprise counterattacks by Egypt and Syria in 1973. Although the result may yet be favorable to the settlement of Arab-Israel disputes, it surely involved more conflict and a weakening of the Israelis' own negotiating position.

Closely related to nationalism is the issue of national "identity," which all the countries of the Middle East face. North African Arab countries, pulling away from Arab unity, still question how far they want to be associated with each other and the Arab states to the east. Egypt, having led Arab nationalism for a couple of decades, is reverting in name and feeling to a sense of being Egyptian. Iran is beginning, under the Shah's impetus, to think of itself as "developed" and not merely "developing," responding to ancient Persian symbols as well as Islamic attachments. Turkey has for several decades faced the consequences of a Western course under Ataturk. Religious loyalties and impulses complicate all the others and compete with them now, whereas earlier religion underpinned the others. And more recently material wealth, through oil, has come to complicate identity, for the nations and rulers enjoying this sudden increase in wealth are still (save for Iran) accustomed to thinking of themselves as poor and exploited, in contrast to the way the rest of the world is beginning to see them.

Recent experience with nationalism, military rule, and parliamentary systems suggests that in much of the Middle East it has been easier to dominate the people than to lead them. Rulers and elites have not trusted the people they rule and have refused to permit them much autonomy. Only powerful individuals and groups can stand up to rulers and then only if opposition is institutionalized to protect dissidents. Increases in power and wealth seem to accrue chiefly to the government, leaving the people with no more autonomy than before, as we are witnessing now in the case of oil.[5] Leaders have so much power through control of the mass media, for example, that an entire nation such as Egypt was for nearly two decades under Nasser believed everywhere to be anti-American. In the 1950s and 1960s, moreover, many American officials did not realize that the Egyptian people, far from being anti-American, were skeptical of or positively disliked their own regime, which *was* anti-American and brought military and economic disaster to the country. All the while, U.S. policy was based on the mistaken notion that the regime was popular and its policies beneficial. Yet in a very brief time Nasser's successor, Sadat, was able through the same media (and perhaps even the same writers and broadcasters) to present the nation as very friendly to America within a few months after the United States openly gave huge military aid to Israel on the Sinai battlefields in 1973.

Middle Eastern rulers, succeeding the colonial powers, have in many ways had no more respect for the ruled than they are willing to attribute to their foreign predecessors. Thus, Nasser often spoke of the great courage Egyptians showed in ousting the British, yet in 1965 he boasted that his regime had granted the demands of workers even before they could present them. If he was trying to show that his leadership anticipated workers' needs, he also showed that his regime considered such gains a mere gift from those on top to those on bottom. Such an attitude fits in with the frequent claims of indigenous leaders (aping the colonial predecessors) that the masses are not yet ready for democratic procedures.

Part of the political malaise of many Middle Eastern countries is that just as the leaders entrust nothing to the populace, the populace prefers to entrust nothing to the leaders. Government has always meant and still means trouble to Middle Easterners. Thus the leaders and masses really do not permit the other to play their political role, which is to say that governments make endless claims which the masses seek to evade. This passive skepticism of the masses, however, is often accompanied by bursts of an excessive credulity, born of despair and hope, that encourages manipulation by their leaders. Such mutual suspicion, probably justified in the circumstances, means that government, as the coordinator of development efforts, cannot effectively carry out one of its major tasks in this respect: to release popular energy and talent for social welfare. For government fears that popular incentive and freedom of activity in some domains are likely to limit all authority, particularly its own. Especially in the Arab world, leaders are held in thrall by the shrill ideologies and emotions they help to spread. The gap between their private and public speech seems to be greater than in areas where leadership, being more legitimate, lends greater confidence to the elites. Cromer early in this century pointed out this fear on the part of one Egyptian elite group of another when he asserted that members of the legislative council hesitated to speak their minds in the face of the power and propensity of the press to attack. "To the European mind," he recognized, "it may seem a contradiction in terms to say that freedom of speech is checked by freedom of the press."[6] Anyone who knows the contemporary Middle East can recognize the perpetuation of this kind of discouragement of nascent parliamentarianism.

Middle Eastern Leadership in the Next Decade

Criticism of Middle Eastern leadership abounds even among sympathetic observers. An Egyptian economist assessing economic change in the Arab world since the Second World War concludes that the governments have not so much reduced poverty as "modernized" it. An Arab scholar says: "The struggle which the Arabs have waged for their unity has produced nothing, with the exception of the short-lived Syrian-Egyptian union, but invective, recrimination and the active intervention by some Arab states with the backing of one or more of the Great Powers to keep the Arab world divided. . . ." Of the Syrian-Egyptian union (1958-61) itself, a careful British observer called it "a monument of self-deception" for the leaders on both sides. An American scholar has found that Palestinian Arab leaders have only "compounded the structural sources of dissension" in the community they aspire to guide.[7]

Can Middle Eastern countries, in the next decade, enjoy or acquire leadership adequate to the tasks of maintaining order, encouraging development, and avoiding further wars and moving toward peace? The entire area—Arab states, Israel, Iran, and Turkey—has been embroiled in war and faces a potential for more wars. The likelihood is that limited wars will continue to break out but that they will continue to be halted early by big-power intervention. As for domestic affairs, the leadership of Turkey, Iran, and Israel appears to be in a better position than Egypt and the Arab states.

Despite many years of educational reform at home and the education of many of their youth in Western universities, there is a serious lack of trained high-level manpower in almost every Middle Eastern country. Even in Iran, Turkey, and Egypt, for example, where modernization has proceeded intensively and for a long time and where the very highest level of government is staffed by capable people, once one goes below that level there is still very little competence or initiative. This is true not only in government but also in factories, universities, mass media, and so on. Such weakness is not likely to be overcome in a decade. Among the Arab states the deficiency is greatest both in general understanding of modern society, in science and technology, and in the capacity to organize large-scale enterprises in industry or education. Many individual Arabs, especially Egyptians, do understand these matters but they either prefer to live in the West or if at home are not in positions of influence. Governmental competence is simply not to be found in the magnitude needed to accomplish modern self-government. Civil relationships are poorly managed when they go beyond kinship and creed. The failure of leadership on this level is more than matched by failure on the highest political level. A simple fact demonstrates the point: the states bordering Israel have not so far been able to devote even their meager talents of modern leadership to the goals they have set up, but are almost entirely absorbed in simply trying to recover from Israel lands they only recently held securely. They have been running not merely to stay in place but to avoid falling behind.

Two very recent events offer some evidence to the contrary: the limited success in the war against Israel in October 1973 and the rapid increase in wealth from oil. Neither, however, is yet convincing for the long range. Whether and how the Palestinian question will be settled—and for how long—is far from clear or assured and its continuation will undoubtedly strain the general capacity of the Arab states to attend to other matters. The new oil wealth will almost certainly improve the position of Iran in all respects, but it is quite possible that it will not enable the Arab world to overcome its deficiencies appreciably, since it is accruing to the most backward of them and it remains to be seen how it can even find its way to the more advanced ones, let alone be used constructively at home by its owners.

There are one or two important notes to encourage moderate optimism that some elements of Arab and other Middle Eastern leadership have learned from the experience of the region since the Second World War. One is the limited progress toward the end of fighting between Israel and its Arab neighbors. The other, not unrelated to the first, is the possible existence of an open or tacit alliance between the leaders of Egypt and Saudi Arabia, perhaps with encouragement from Iran, to introduce a different, more pragmatic approach to Arab amity and the conduct of internal affairs in many of the Arab states.

The existence of the "alliance" is only an hypothesis, on which there is conflicting evidence. The hypothesis suggests that President Sadat of Egypt and the late King Faisal of Saudi Arabia preferred to see a different Arab world and Middle East from the one that emerged after the creation of Israel, the advent of Nasser and other military-Socialist regimes, and the absorption with the Palestine question. Sadat halted the drift toward socialism in Egypt and reduced the country's dependence on the Soviet Union. Faisal, who never favored Egypt's policies under Nasser, welcomed this turn and was prepared to add his country's prestige and wealth to the power of a different sort of Egypt. His successors are following the same policy for the present.

A similar pragmatism appeared to be growing in North Africa, where even Algeria has moderated its approach to regional affairs, bringing it closer to that of Morocco and Tunisia; Libya, of course, stands apart. Jordan can be counted on for sympathy, and Lebanon too, though Syria less so and Iraq perhaps not at all. The new Arab states on the Persian Gulf, some with considerable oil resources and incomes, are already close to Saudi Arabia. Iran has a certain interest in going along with such tendencies. Socialist or radical movements within most of these countries are not seen to be a major problem. The one serious hurdle for the "alliance" has been the Israeli-Palestinian Arab struggle. To be in a position to exert a moderate influence on the political and economic structure of the Arab world, Sadat and Faisal needed a popular position on this most emotional and intractable issue of all. This position of strength and credibility in the Arab world the "alliance" achieved to a considerable degree by the Egyptian performance on the Suez Canal in the war of October 1973, supported by Saudi Arabian money and the Arab oil boycott. Following their military success (hailed in the Arab countries despite its limited character and near-disaster), Sadat and Faisal turned to the United States for further help in bringing about an Israeli withdrawal, however slight, from the Arab lands.

In this way, during 1973-74, the "alliance" demonstrated that the moderate powers, in association with the United States (but without overt hostility toward the Soviet Union), could achieve a considerable degree of Arab unity in the practical task of liberating Arab lands and indirectly at least in promoting the Palestinian Arab cause by weakening (and humiliating) Israel. Sadat and Faisal were thus able to show the Arab world that *their* way—not extremism, terrorism, Socialist policies and rhetoric, and pacts with Russia—could move Arabs toward the accomplishment of their highest and most emotion-laden goal. The two leaders had many reasons, of course, to advocate a vigorous policy against Israel. This hypothesis merely suggests that one of their intentions may have been to make more credible and acceptable their influence in seeking to change the political and economic drift of the region.

The tendency of this "alliance" is moderate, even conservative, and anti-ideological. Its presumed goals, toward which it is moving slowly and not in a straight line, are threefold. First, internally, it seeks economic and social development of the region through use of the increased oil income and help from the United States and other Western countries to offset the massive aid and influence of the Soviet Union. Second, in regional and international politics it seeks United States aid in forcing Israel to withdraw from Arab lands and thus remove this enervating struggle from the Arab agenda. Third, in Arab political affairs it seeks a settlement of that other enervating struggle, that of the Palestinians against some of the Arab states. To achieve these related goals the "alliance" must obtain Israeli withdrawal and must insure Palestinian Arabs a state of their own on terms acceptable to the moderate Arab states. The latter may be the harder task. The position of the "alliance" is difficult and delicate. It must satisfy the Palestinian Arabs by giving them a stake in the sort of political stability the "alliance" seeks, yet it must also check the left wing of the Palestinian movement, which sees itself as a revolutionary vanguard of all Arabs. The intention of the "alliance" is to see moderate Palestinians control the others in a Palestinian state that will not threaten the Arab world.

This hypothesis about such an "alliance" is of course not proven and not fully demonstrable. Describing it this way already gives it perhaps firmer shape than is warranted even if it exists. Yet some recent events are consistent with its presumed existence. If it does exist, it can easily founder on Palestinian Arab intransigeance, or on Egyptian-Saudi rivalry once immediate and limited goals are realized. The place of Iran is a complex factor. It has good relations with Egypt and Saudi Arabia, with whose leaders the Shah seems to agree concerning the need to change the recent drift of the Middle East toward radical ideologies. Iran, moreover, is building up its armed forces and seeking to protect the Arab states in the Persian Gulf with the tacit approval of Egypt and Saudi Arabia. At the same time, Iran has good, if quiet, relations with Israel, as well as sharing the "alliance's" position toward the two superpowers: friendship with the United States without hostility to the Soviet Union.

To the extent that the "alliance" exists, then, some important Middle Eastern leaders are both leading and trying to be powerful, prudent and realistic. They have learned something from the turbulence of the 1950s and 1960s. Since the "alliance" is favorable to Western interests in a number of significant matters, the West will have to learn to deal with a different set of friends in the light of the oil states' relentless capitalizing on the seller's market for their most valuable resource. The West has recently known a Middle East that *talks* against colonialism while cooperating *in fact* in economic affairs relating especially to oil. The West also knew, somewhat earlier, a Middle East that it could dominate. Now the West faces a somewhat different Middle East, which is friendly in general political approach to world questions but is tough on oil prices and profits. It is a lot clearer to deal with leaders who both talk and act against you in general than with leaders, such as those of this "alliance," who talk for you but on the hard question of money act to a certain extent against you.

That is one important implication for the West of this "alliance" and its oil wealth. The Middle East is moving toward a more secure and powerful form of "sovereignty" as great economic power supplements national independence. Another adjustment many Western nations may have to make in the next decade is to recover from long-standing and rigid positions "for" or "against" this or that Middle Eastern country or its leaders. If the "alliance," or some other force, is able to bring about a form of settlement between Israel and its Arab neighbors, even the most tentative approach of "normal" relations between them will shake old expectations and comfortable animosities. To be realistic, however, we should keep in mind that improvement is sure to be slow enough to permit adjustment by all but the most fanatical on every side.

Leadership and Elites in Selected Countries

Leaders and elites in the various countries of the Middle East confront in the next decade a number of problems already discussed in previous sections, such as peace and social development. In this section we shall examine specific problems in a number of countries, giving more attention to Turkey, Israel, and Iran since we have until now concentrated on the Arab states.

Our discussion of the military-Socialist compact has perhaps implied too sharp a distinction between the commonly regarded "conservative" and "radical" regimes. In any case, this distinction has applied less to the non-Arab countries than to the Arab, and even among the latter the distinction is becoming less sharp and significant as Algeria, Syria, and Iraq, for example, show signs inconsistent with the familiar "radicalism" of the 1960s, while Egypt has changed considerably with the death of Nasser and the advent of Sadat. It would be more correct, indeed, to distinguish now between the Arab countries that still adhere to the old "Afro-Asian" approach (backed by the Soviet Union and China) in the United Nations and those who have moved from it, or to speak of the Arab states that appear to be ready to contemplate a peaceful solution to the conflict with Israel and those still using the rhetoric of intransigeance.

Throughout the region, another issue has lately returned: the realization that religion still exerts great mass appeal after the considerable emphasis upon secularism, economic development and international politics. Turkey in the 1950s, moving toward democracy, began to feel the effect of what was regarded as a religious "revival" although it was more probably the open expression of impulses that had been discouraged by the heirs of Ataturk and ignored by most observers in Turkey and abroad. Similar "revivals" have been noticed in other countries, where the influence of popular religious feeling, as in Turkey, has been felt also in politics. Turkey and Israel, differing in many ways, have experienced the political power of religious parties in the 1970s. Leading left-of-center parties in both countries have had to make costly alliances with right-wing religious-based parties in order to be able to form a government. This was the case in Turkey even after the popular military victory in Cyprus in 1974.

This instability in the two leading parliamentary countries is exceeded by a deeper instability as well as a certain volatility of policy in the countries not burdened by genuine legislative bodies. "Conservative" and "radical" regimes, whether monarchical or "republican," react to the danger of coups by establishing extraordinary intelligence services, surveillance made as efficient as possible, outright prevention of political liberty or suppression of open opposition, and the unhesitating use of not only police power but also the military services. Where there are elections, leaders must constantly worry about the next one; where there are no elections, they must worry about plots and coups. In either case, a great deal more attention is paid to the preservation of power than to its beneficient use. Consider the following record of threats to regimes in the year beginning with the summer of 1970. The king of Morocco put down an attempted coup that appeared to be motivated by a desire to rule, with no ideological basis. The king of Jordan repressed the Palestinian guerrilas, who had set up a parallel and independent regime. The president of Egypt suppressed a leftist group he suspected of planning a coup. Turkish military leaders, imposing martial law to enable the government to maintain order, threatened to resort to force to oust the government if it failed to follow through resolutely. The Sudan government repressed a long-brewing Communist challenge.

Or consider the sort of volatility displayed by President Sadat of Egypt with regard to the massive Soviet aid to the preceding regime. When he succeeded Nasser in 1970, Sadat began to criticize Russia and indicate a desire for better relations with the West. A year of so later he signed a fifteen-year treaty with Russia providing for various kinds of aid and cooperation, including military. The following year, in the summer of 1972, he expelled all but a handful of Soviet military advisers. In October of 1973 he crossed the Suez Canal with vast military equipment and other aid from the Soviet Union. Following the war, Sadat based his policy on friendship with the United States to the point where the Soviet leaders openly and strongly criticized him.

Change of leadership is a problem Middle Eastern countries will continue to face in the next decade. Narrow parliamentary majorities, improvised among parties with negative rather than positive common goals, are likely in Turkey, Israel, and Lebanon. In the authoritarian regimes, including monarchies and republics, succession may create difficulties. Tunisia will have to find a way to replace Bourguiba. Many younger rulers such as the Shah of Iran, Qaddafi of Libya, King Hassan of Morocco, and King Hussein of Jordan are the objects of intensive if not widespread opposition; if elections do not affect their reign, more volatile methods of succession may. Egypt peacefully managed Sadat's succession on the death of Nasser, but the next change may have to be an electoral one when Sadat's term ends in October 1976, and that may be more difficult. Saudi Arabia was able to withstand the assassination of Faisal, a considerable challenge to the leadership. The rich Arab mini-states on the Persian Gulf are sure to experience succession problems in view of their weakness and wealth. Syria and Iraq are less dominated by individual rulers but have a history, since the 1950s, of coups and countercoups. An independent Palestinian state, if it came into existence, would also experience struggles for top leadership. It is not only rivalry for power that bedevils these countries; other factors working in the direction of instability are the role of the superpowers and the genuine desire, on the part of considerable numbers within most of the countries, for new approaches to domestic and regional affairs.

The national aspirations of the Palestinian Arabs will tax their leadership as well as that of the Israelis and the Arabs in general. The growing recognition of the Palestine Liberation Organization has recently changed matters so rapidly that predictions are especially hazardous. The long-range likelihood is that the Arab states, having for so long supported Palestinian aspirations as expressed by the Palestinian Liberation Organization (PLO) will continue this support through any rough times to come. Israel will undoubtedly have to find a way to negotiate with the PLO if there is to be further movement toward peace or nonbelligerence. Though often vexed by the whole issue, Arab leaders react to it as they do to the emotional and divisive appeals to "unity": they accept Palestinian aspirations even if they are doubtful about the means used by the PLO in pursuing their goals. Some Arab leaders may no longer seek the destruction of Israel, yet they will not renounce support for the PLO even if that continues to be its goal. These leaders simply find it easier politically, if not preferable emotionally, to acquiesce in Palestinian aspirations. They may regard the Palestinian Arabs as a threat to order, but they prefer to see that threat deflected toward Israel than to try very seriously to contain it. Palestinian Arabs have been expelled and suppressed by Jordan, barred by Egypt, become very unpopular in Lebanon, and controlled closely in Syria and the oil countries, yet their national goals are steadily supported by the leaders of these countries rhetorically and financially.

It is necessary for the United States to understand also the reasoning of Palestinian Arab leaders themselves who have risked criticism by adopting terrorism as a weapon on an international scale even to the point where some Arab leaders have felt impelled to criticize it openly or at least to refrain at times from endorsing it. Palestinian Arab leaders have found terrorism useful even if international public opinion is shocked by it. They see it as advantageous and effective because it (1) hurts Israel and those who support it actively or passively, (2) keeps their cause before a world that might otherwise be totally indifferent—unfavorable attention is considered better than total neglect, (3) promises gains in reaction to fear and disruption even if the justice of their cause is not recognized, (4) keeps the Palestinian Arabs strong and dangerous enough to warrant continued Arab financial support even if money is contributed reluctantly and only to avoid the application of terror to the donors if they falter in their generosity.

Terror by Palestinian Arab agencies and the oil policy of certain Arab states have given Arab leaders at the very least a "bad press" in the West. Though these policies may have drawbacks, the alternatives—less support for Palestinian aspirations as guided by the PLO and forbearance in taking advantage of the seller's market in oil—are less attractive. Some leaders, notably in Egypt and Saudi Arabia, have sought to improve the Arab "image" by moderate speech while maintaining their basic policies. There is, however, virtually no free domestic public opinion urging such moderation, and the reaction of the West, morally and economically, has been too weak and diffuse to encourage it.

Thus far we have been considering rulers and top political leaders. We must also consider the next level of leadership in governmental (and other) agencies, the bulk of the civil servants. Probably the chief characteristic of this level is that in its upper reaches there are many highly capable political thinkers, administrators and technologists. Below them there is a bureaucratic mass which is much less competent; most of them are also overly cautious and view their jobs as sinecures. The expansion of scholarly interest in the developing world since the

Second World War has produced many studies of governmental and other elites: members of parliament, civil servants, military officers, and so on. The Middle East has a small share of such studies, though unfortunately they hardly deal with nongovernmental elites; about governmental elites, moreover, these studies do not often enough deal with their competence, actions or attitudes but more often with their social background and employment experience. Another drawback is that studies do not permit comparisons among the various countries.[8]

In Turkey the governmental elite is shaped considerably by the influence of the armed services as the watchdog of the state, seeking to preserve at least the spirit and impetus given half a century ago by Kemal Ataturk and to extend the social reforms introduced in his time. The bureaucracy is imbued with Kemalism, which some younger members have stretched to mean a degree of Socialist radicalism of a more contemporary sort. Perhaps more than in the Arab countries, Turkish civil servants went into politics. Of all the deputies in parliament from 1920 to 1957, a third came from posts in government, where they were familiar with power. Military officers were, up to 1933, the largest single group of high government officials who entered parliament but as civil democracy advanced in the 1950s they declined considerably. At the same time, the military elite established itself as the caretaker of the country, wielding a veto power on all civilian regimes. Nongovernmental elites have a reputation for greater efficiency in the last quarter century, a period in which the private sector (aided by the state) enjoyed considerable growth.

The Israeli second-level elite, helping to govern a very small but united (if socially heterogeneous) population, has been closely knit and closely tied to the top leaders and the political parties. Lebanon, incidentally, resembles Israel in this respect probably more than it does Arab countries. The skepticism of Israelis about their top leaders since the 1973 war has probably penetrated to the working bureaucratic levels. Because of the close dependence of these levels upon the top leadership, the new attitude was bound to spread to them.

Iran, to an even greater degree than Turkey, has experienced growth of the private sector of the economy, with the similar consequence that the nongovernmental elites are regarded as more efficient and more highly motivated. The new sections of the governmental bureaucracy, notably the Plan and Budget Organization and the managers of oil-related agencies, also enjoy a good reputation for competence. The Shah's control reaches down to these levels of both types of bureaucracy, although the private sector, which in day-to-day affairs does not affect national interest very directly, has more autonomy. Because of foreign and domestic limitations on his power in the 1940s and 1950s, the Shah acted resolutely to bring the military, civil and religious elites, as well as the landowners, under his direct control. Economic expansion has made such control more palatable. One group, the intellectuals in and out of government, remain unreliable and are the objects of greater surveillance. The next generation of elites, the youth at home and many of those studying in Western universities, are also recalcitrant, demanding, if not a new regime, then greater sharing of power and more freedom of expression. As Iran's role in the Persian Gulf grows with the country's increasing oil income and the regime's intention to assume responsibility for the security of the region, there will be increasing demands for competence and loyalty placed upon the bureaucracy. The chances for success in this effort would probably be increased if the ambitions of the regime were carefully adjusted to its potential and the heavy lid on freedom of expression lifted somewhat.

For the entire period since the Second World War, the fairly good basis for governmental services in Syria has been overshadowed and undermined by two predominant themes in political life. The first is an insistence of the rulers on playing the leading role in Arab causes, especially that of the Palestinian Arabs and of Arab unity. The second is a combination of ethnic and military alliances that has given army officers with sectarian loyalties an increasingly strong grip over otherwise volatile tendencies. The civil bureaucracy has been easy to dominate and has, like the military bureaus above it, reflected sectarian competition for influence and benefits. Radical ideologies have been used by minority groups to appeal to a wider constituency. The outcome of all these forces has been to prevent, ever since Syria's independence in 1946, the development of the nation's potential for good administration inherent in its educational background and economic prospects.

Mainly because of substantial oil revenues, which stimulated modern technology and some degree of economic expertise, the governmental elite in Iraq showed some promise in the early 1950s of a growing capacity to deal with new tasks. Like the Syrian, however, the Iraqi bureaucracy was soon overwhelmed by long-standing military, ethnic, and sectarian rivalries for broader political control and by regional Arab power struggles. Military influence began well before the late 1950s, when it became dominant. Through varying forms of government and ideologies, the ruling elite has remained a small circle manipulating both the bureaucracy and broader social groups. The road to leadership since the 1960s has broadened somewhat to include more people from the provinces and with university education. Yet, the power has been increasingly concentrated among the military officers and a minority religious-ethnic group, thus continuing the traditional narrow rule behind a superficial coating of Socialist-democratic ideology and talk of modernization.

Saudi Arabia has to face a problem other Arab states with oil must also face: how to distribute wealth without sharing powers. This means a quick and considerable increase of the public and private bureaucracies in order to build up state agencies for education and medical care, for example, while encouraging a nascent entrepreneurial class. The country, until quite recently, had to depend mainly on American business and universities to train the leadership at various levels; modern higher technical and general education have only just begun there.

The royal family, allied to a few tribal leaders, no longer constitutes the entire government, which must learn to carry out more complicated tasks both centrally and in outlying districts. For a long time to come, Saudi Arabia will have to increase its reliance on Western and Egyptian (even Palestinian) technologists. As the bureaucracies grow in size and importance, the demand for the sharing of power will also grow, and the royal family will have to give increasing attention to representative institutions and media of mass communication, and to more advanced modes of social control. These developments will in turn, of course, swell the elites of the public and private sectors.

The Egyptian elites, shaped by the Ottoman Empire, French and British influences, and American education, are in a sense prototypical of the region, displaying its worst and best traits. There are islands of high-level talent, surrounded by oceans of incompetence. Egypt, before the revolution led by Nasser in the early 1950s, had a fairly good bureaucratic infrastructure in the private and public sectors. Excessive zeal to nationalize capital and employment opportunities reduced this administrative capacity by driving out not only resident foreigners but also many hard-working Egyptians who merely wanted a reasonable return for their talent and work. Now Egypt under Sadat has moved along a different course. Can the various elites rise to the demands created by the country's goal of rapid development? Is the planning apparatus up to the tasks it now faces? Are the ministries and state firms capable of using to full advantage the foreign and domestic capital Sadat hopes to provide? There is a vestige of the older elites whose independence and ability can be called upon; indeed, Sadat seems to have brought back to positions of authority a few people prominent in the 1950s among the technicians of the early Nasser regime and who, because of their independence, drifted into other posts abroad and at home. Can Sadat attract the hundreds of talented Egyptians who are now working very efficiently in Western countries and whose loss to Egypt in the last decade or two has been incalculable? It is too early to tell, although he certainly gives evidence that he understands the loss and Egypt's needs.

The French legacy in most of North Africa—Algeria, Tunisia, and Morocco—remains influential there, while unity with the Arab East, important in ideology and rhetoric as these countries became independent, has receded steadily to the point where it is no longer paid much lip service. Despite differences in development since independence, the bureaucracies are technocratic and tied to French culture and ways. Algeria, especially, with a large population, natural resources and resolute leadership, seeks rapid industrialization and therefore began building a new elite to construct a modern society when its leaders learned that the freedom fighters were not appropriate to the new tasks once independence was achieved. Tunisia lives still in the shadow of Bourguiba even so far as the lower levels of the public and private bureaucracies are concerned. Smaller and less grim than Algeria, Tunisian elites are also less impatient and ardent. The short-lived plan of early 1974 for union with Libya, had it been carried through, might have changed the Tunisian outlook over the next decade. It was, however, an uncharacteristic step and was soon canceled, to the satisfaction of the Tunisian elites of all types. Moroccan elites are firmly under King Hassan's control, more so than when he ascended to power in 1961. Questions of political power, succession to rule and the role of opposition groups so far overshadow questions of administration by the lower-level bureaucracies.

Libya remains apart from the rest of North Africa under its military regime headed by Qaddafi. Since the country became independent a quarter-century ago under United Nations auspices, it has acquired oil wealth and the beginnings of a modern bureaucracy. Until now it has far more of the first than the second. Political power is still the main issue. Qaddafi's arrested Arab nationalism of the 1950s, when as a boy he adulated Nasser, enables him to act without regard to public opinion in a small country with few educated people, with plenty of money in the official treasury, and hardly any public or private elites to challenge him. He rules through military power, of which he has an unquestioned monopoly, and oil wealth, which is produced for him by Western technicians present only on his sufferance. The civil bureaucracy is thus far hardly equal to the task of competent administration. Students abroad, who are increasing in number, are still quiescent though many are critical of the regime.

Leaders and Elites: The Weak Linchpin

Until recently, national poverty has been a severe test of leadership in most countries of the Middle East. Now national wealth may be an even more severe test for some of them. In the West we have looked at Middle Eastern oil wealth from our viewpoint; we speak of the problems it creates for us. We must also look at the way the leaders in the oil-exporting countries see this wealth. To the West they appear to be "arrogant" and insensitive. This is not surprising, considering that the West is unaccustomed to dealing with a Middle East in so strong an economic position. The oil exporters, at least the bigger ones such as Iran and Saudi Arabia, look forward to additional real power not only in the region but in world affairs generally. Though some of their leaders and representatives speak cautiously, Western observers detect in them a certain condescension as they push their weight around. Yet, is not this the way in international relations?

If we look at the petrodollars from the viewpoint of the countries that have them, we behold a different scene. Their mood is not merely "arrogant" if it is that at all. They have big problems even if they have a great deal of money to apply to their solutions. In the first place, if their wealth causes difficulties for the world's monetary system or threatens other countries, they themselves stand to suffer. The oil exporters depend upon world stability but their profits are viewed as promoting instability. This is a serious and perhaps unfair dilemma for them. In the second place, they fear the exhaustion of the oil or the reduction of its importance as their reserves decline and other sources of energy are resorted to in the industrialized West and Japan. The exporters' problem is thus to diversify their economies and modernize their societies before their supplies of oil and dollars dwindle. They are far from certain that they will be able to do so. "Arrogance" to the West looks more like apprehension in the Middle East.

The test in the Middle East will center upon the capacity of governmental institutions. Middle Eastern nations have not been able to create effective ones in modern times. Ruling individuals and classes have made large claims and acted repressively, but they have seldom been able to command genuine loyalty by facilitating the pursuit of group interests outside the circles of governmental power. In turn, Middle Eastern peoples have not thought of government as a positive force exercising power usefully and to be itself controlled by other agencies; instead, they have regarded government as something to be avoided or, if contact with it was necessary, as something to be exploited.

One is tempted to say that most Middle Easterners dislike government so much that they prefer one ruler to many. They seem to enjoy seeing their lower-level exploiters humiliated. Waste and corruption transcend differences in rhetoric and regime. There seems to be a will to redirect society but toward what end and by what means are not clear. Governments must be the instruments, through action and self-restraint, of such redirection, yet they are more concerned with preserving their own power and are still not trusted by the governed to conduct affairs in the public interest. Many governmental actions stem from their large claims and small capacities. One such action is nationalization justified by ideology to cover up an incapacity to regulate in the national interest. The rulers, in self-defense, blame the public bureaucracies, and this criticism finds a popular echo among people often frustrated by the bureaucratic levels they most often meet. It is nevertheless the top political level that is chiefly responsible for failures.

Among the most obvious symptoms of failure is the ever-expanding governmental budget, usually the first consequence of an announced interest in national development. Egypt is a prime example, still reflecting the legacy of the "revolution" of 1952. In 1975, an official agency reported, there were three million workers in the public sector, constituting about a half of all the 6.5 million workers in the private sector. Yet the total wage-bill for the public sector was double that for the private sector.[9] This huge public payroll is undoubtedly a drain on the whole society's productivity.

Is the Middle East on the threshold of a new advance in culture, power, and standard of living? Can indigenous talent, increased wealth from oil and the social changes of more than a century produce that industrial progress which David Hume, expressing a widely-held view in eighteenth century Europe, considered favorable to wealth, culture and liberty? Hume's conclusion is certainly true of the older great civilizations of the Middle East: "The same age which produces great philosophers and politicians, renowned generals and poets, usually abounds with skillful weavers, and ship-carpenters."[10]

Government nowadays in the Middle East is—for good or evil—the linchpin to the wheel of social life. Governmental institutions fitted closely to others and to human needs and proclivities can promote orderly growth and welfare by allowing popular talents to play a part. Pressing too heavily, as they usually do, governmental institutions can prevent movement. The problem in most of the Middle East today is not very different from what it has been in the past: government has taken increasing control of affairs through modern techniques before people have been able even moderately to control government.

Notes

1. *The New York Times*, editorials, May 11, 1974 and December 8, 1974. *The Times* (London), editorial, May 8, 1975. *Time*, "Leadership in America," Volume 104, No. 3, July 15, 1974. *The Economist* (London), "The Fading of America," April 5, 1974. *Commentary*, "America Now: A Failure of Nerve?" July 1975.

2. R.M. Mac Iver, *Power Transformed* (New York: Macmillan, 1964), p. 3.

3. On nineteenth century leadership see William R. Polk and Richard Chambers (eds.), *Beginnings of Modernization in the Middle East* (Chicago: University of Chicago Press, 1968), papers by Shimon Shamir (pp. 351, 378-81), Albert Hourani (pp. 48-49, 57, 63-64), Moshe Ma'oz (pp. 333-35), and Stanford Shaw (pp. 36-37).

4. See, for example, H.B. Sharabi, "Power and Leadership in the Arab World," *Orbis* 7 (1963): 583-95, at p. 591. Majid Khadduri offers a cogent full-length study of several leaders in this century in *Arab Contemporaries. The Role of Personalities in Politics* (Baltimore: Johns Hopkins University Press, 1973).

5. On the frequent failure of economic development to lead to the sharing of political and economic power see Irma Adelman and Cynthia Taft Morris, *Economic Growth and Social Equality in Developing Countries* (Stanford: Stanford University Press, 1973), especially the last chapter.

6. Lord Cromer, *Modern Egypt* (London: Macmillan, 1908), Volume 2, p. 278.

7. These observers are in the order quoted: Galad A. Amin, *The Modernization of Poverty. A Study in the Political Economy of Growth in Nine Arab Countries 1945-1970* (Leiden: Brill, 1974), pp. 110-11. A.R. Kelidar, "The Arabian Peninsula in Arab and Power Politics," in Derek Hopwood (ed.), *The Arabian Peninsula. Society and Politics* (London: Allen and Unwin, 1972), p. 145. Patrick Seale, *The Struggle for Syria* (London: Oxford University Press, 1965), pp. 323-24. William B. Quandt, *The Politics of Palestinian Nationalism* (Berkeley and Los Angeles: University of California Press, 1973), p. 79.

8. The literature on Middle Eastern elites has recently grown considerably. An earlier brief review may be found in William B. Quandt, *The Comparative Study of Elites* (Beverly Hills, California: Sage Professional Papers in Comparative Politics, 1970). Two studies which appeared too late for use in this paper are George Lenczowski (ed.), *Political Elites in the Middle East*, American Enterprise Institute· for Public Policy Research (Washington, D.C., 1975), with chapters on Iran, Turkey, Egypt, Iraq, Syria, Israel, and Lebanon; and R. Hrair Dekmejian, *Patterns of Political Leadership, Egypt, Israel, Lebanon* (Albany: State University of New York Press, 1975). Elites in a number of countries are treated well in Menahem Milson (ed.), *Society and Political Structure in the Arab World* (New York: Humanities Press, 1973). A review of several elite studies is given in I. William Zartman, "The Study of Elite Circulation," *Comparative Politics* 6 (1974), 465-88, and in 'The Elites of the Maghreb: A Review Article," *International Journal of Middle East Studies* 6 (1975): 495-504. Following are studies of particular countries and regions consulted for this chapter, given in the order of discussion. William B. Quandt et al., *The Politics of Palestinian Nationalism* (Berkeley and Los Angeles: The University of California Press, 1973), pp. 79-93. Frederick W. Frey, *The Turkish Political Elite* (Cambridge: Massachusetts Institute of Technology Press, 1965). Leslie L. and Noralou Roos, *Managers of Modernization. Organizations and Elites in Turkey (1950-1969)* (Cambridge, Massachusetts: Harvard University Press, 1971). Yuval Elitzur and Eliahu Salpeter, *Who Rules Israel?* (New York: Harper and Row, 1973). Marvin Zonis, *The Political Elite of Iran* (Princeton: Princeton University Press, 1971). Leonard Binder, "Iran's Potential as a Regional Power," Chapter 10 in Paul Y. Hammond and Sidney S. Alexander (eds), *Political Dynamics in the Middle East* (New York: American Elsevier, 1972). P.J. Vatikiotis, "The Politics of the Fertile Crescent," Chapter 7, ibid. R. Bayly Winder, "Syrian Deputies and Cabinet Ministers, 1919-1950," *Middle East Journal* 16 1962-63, 407-29; 17:35-54. David Pool, "The Politics of Patronage. Elites and Social Structure in Iraq," Ph.D. dissertation, Princeton University, 1972. Phebe Ann Marr, "Iraq's Leadership Dilemma: A Study in Leadership Trends, 1948-1968," *Middle East Journal* 24 (1970): 283-301. Ayad Al-Qazzaz, "Power Elite in Iraq, 1920-1958," *The Muslim World* 61 (1971): 267-82. Morroe Berger, *Bureaucracy and Society in Modern Egypt* (Princeton: Princeton University Press, 1957). Elbaki Hermassi, *Leadership and Development in North Africa* (Berkeley: University of California Press, 1972). A methodologically-oriented collection of essays, edited by I.W. Zartman, *The Study of Elites in the Middle East*, is forthcoming.

9. National Bank of Egypt, *Economic Bulletin* 27 (1974): 296.

10. David Hume, "Of Refinement in the Arts" (1752), in John W. Lenz (ed.), *Of the Standard of Taste and Other Essays*, (Indianapolis and New York: Bobbs-Merrill, 1965), p. 50.

VI Inter-Arab Relations

P.J. Vatikiotis

Many Arab states are the fragmented successors of the Ottoman Empire, and subsequently of the British and French dominions in the Middle East. As such, they are riddled with obsessive and violent nationalisms, and governed by unstable individuals or groups who invariably achieved power by force. Today, the survival of most of these rulers depends on perhaps three main factors: (1) a tight and ruthless internal control of the three essential structures of state power: the armed forces, the security apparatus, and the bureaucracy; (2) the maintenance of a client relationship with a superpower patron; and (3) a claim to satisfy perhaps unattainable national aspirations and popular expectations.

Even without the Arab-Israel conflict of the last twenty-seven years, the Arab Middle East would have been a conflict-ridden and conflict-generating area. The aspirations and pretensions of Arab nationalism, with its visions of Panarabism and Arab unity, would have clashed—as they did—with the interests of the several Arab states which, except for Egypt, were literally put together from the debris of the collapsed Ottoman Empire. The lid on that cauldron was kept down (if not tightly shut) by the presence of the new European hegemonies, Britain and France, for a quarter of a century (1920-1945). Their withdrawal or eviction—not without American encouragement incidentally[a]—ushered in a new era of unstable, conflict-ridden inter-Arab relations from that time on, and more specifically from 1955 to 1967. This condition was aggravated by the varied and different political evolution of the several Arab states, as well as by their disparate economic and social development.

[a]Here I refer to the tendency of U.S. policy after the last war to favor—and encourage—nationalist, anticolonial movements, the involvement in Egypt in the period 1949-53; the heyday of what I would call the American inclination to "fix" things. At that time Americans seemed to think that by "fixing" a big boy among the Arabs, he, in turn, would fix the rest. Foremost example was American enthusiasm for Nasser.

Several of these states, for instance, contain within their territories large ethnic, tribal, and sectarian minorities which are, in most cases, economically deprived and politically underprivileged. Frequently, these seek a greater share in wealth and power, often autonomy. Among them are the Kurds in Iraq, the tribes in South Arabia, the non-Muslim tribes in the southern Sudan. Until this year, there was for example, a Kurdish-Arab civil war in Iraq, a guerrilla war in Dhofar, supported by the radical regime in South Yemen against the ruler of Muscat and Oman who, in turn, is assisted by Saudi Arabia, Iran, and Britain.

As a result of this diversity and heterogeneity, Lebanon experienced a dreadful communal war in 1958, almost a hundred years after its first one. Yet another and even more terrible one is in progress while this is being written. Such civil strife in Lebanon also reflects the delicate and awkward relationship of that country to the rest of the Arab world. In addition, an attempt to undo an Arab state or regime in the name of Arab national revolution led to a bloody civil war in Jordan when the Jordanian army crushed the Palestine Resistance Movement's armed bands in 1970-71.

Iraq, for example, has harbored irredentist designs on neighboring Kuwait. Under a treaty provision, newly-independent Kuwait sought and received British military assistance in 1961 when it feared Iraq might invade its territory. A similar crisis could arise in the future, involving this time Saudi Arabia and Iran, as well as indirectly the Soviet Union, the current superpower patron of the Baath regime in Baghdad, which is also keen on achieving a position in influence in the Gulf. Potential crises, with both regional and international repercussions, can occur over irredentist claims and counterclaims between Saudi Arabia and the Union of Arab Emirates, especially oil-rich Abu Dhabi, that could also involve other local powers, in particular Iran. Similarly Saudi involvement in North Yemen against the radical regime of South Yemen would generate flashpoints of inter-Arab conflict which could attract, say, Egyptian involvement, as well as that of outside powers.

These prefatory remarks and cursory, random illustrations of variety, diversity, and sources of actual or potential conflict in inter-Arab relations suggest the absence of an Arab world monolith. That there can be instances of a convergence, or commonality, of interests among a number of Arab states over a particular issue and therefore a common policy cannot be denied. It is therefore important that outsiders who must respond to these instances be fully aware of their provenance, intricate, and complex motivation, and possible effect. They must be seen in their proper perspective, not as the manifestation of an ideological or other phantasmogoric monolith.

The ready articulation and official promotion of something called Arab nationalism or Arab socialism will remain a prominent activity of individual Arab states. But Panarabism and its variant of Arab unity are, for the time being, dead issues. This, in effect, has been the impact and consequence of the failure of Nasserism on inter-Arab relations since 1967. In partaking of a common

Islamic heritage (which, incidentally, remains at the heart and basis of Arab nationalism) with its universalist pretensions—and past confrontations with the non-Islamic world—Arab rulers and states, as well as individuals, will continue to perceive their collective interest in terms of the solidarity of the Community of the Believers and its struggle for power, prestige, and dignity vis-à-vis the outside world. The tensions they experience in their relations with the non-Muslim world and their feeling of alienation from it will continue to influence the Arabs' response to events. Stated more simply, they are committed to a different scale of values, virtues, and ethic, regardless of the imported secular rationalizations they may adumbrate for that commitment. This fundamental perception of a major confrontation between the Islamic and non-Islamic worlds aside, the Arab Middle East will continue to suffer the dissonance and conflict of local rivalries and differences between its several states, rulers, communities, and factions as much in the Maghreb as in the Fertile Crescent, the Arabian Peninsula, Egypt, and the Gulf.

Patterns of Inter-Arab Relations Since 1920

The dominant feature in the modern history of inter-Arab relations is the struggle for leadership in the name of Arab unity. Ideologically, that is, regional Arab politics have been concerned with the problem of Arab unity, the supreme, or ultimate, objective of Arab nationalism. Closely linked to this, since 1948, has been a collective position towards Israel. Theoretically, the two issues are interrelated, but practically quite separate. They, moreover, often obfuscate and gloss over the more practical problem of the relations between Arab states, governments or regimes and leaders. Since the mid-nineteen fifties, regional Arab politics and inter-Arab relations have also been concerned with the relationship of the Arab states to outside powers and their positions in the rivalry between the superpowers.

Having postulated Arab unity as a desirable end, its attainment in the last twenty or thirty years has been constrained by the power struggle between the major Arab protagonists: the Hashemites in Iraq and Jordan before 1958, the Egyptians both under their monarchy and republic, and the Saudis. Until 1958, or even later, the Arabs could argue that their efforts in the attainment of unity were thwarted by colonial powers in the region, i.e., Britain. But even after these departed from the area, the struggle for hegemony among some of the Arab protagonists has continued undiminished.

Before 1920, inter-Arab relations were confined to the Fertile Crescent area, where the victorious Entente Powers had defeated the Ottoman state and put an end to its dominion over those parts. Separatist Arab movements converged within the orbit of the Hashemite-led Arab Revolt out of the Hejaz to provide the first governing cadres in the new British and French mandated territories of Iraq, Syria, and Transjordan.

Until 1936, there were only two fully independent Arab states, Saudi Arabia and the Yemen. The others, including Egypt, enjoyed semi-independent status in some treaty or tutelage relationship with one or the other of the dominant European powers in the area. The independent ones were virtually isolated from Arab affairs, whereas the foreign power dominated ones sought a greater measure of independence.

The manifestations of rivalry in the struggle for leadership between them however can be traced back to this earlier period. The independent Arab Kingdom of the Hejaz under the Sherif Hussein, for example, was literally undone and integrated by the Saudis in 1924. Soon after that, in 1926, a political row, involving some use of force, over pilgrimage arrangements to the Holy Shrines in Mecca and Medina, broke out between Egypt and Saudi Arabia. The dispute, however, was linked to the issue of the Caliphate to which the Egyptian monarch aspired. The blatant aggrandizement of Saudi Arabia at the expense of the Hashemites was being countered by the other major contender for regional, or Arab, power, Egypt. The chosen arena for this struggle was the issue of Islamic solidarity, the Caliphate, and related matters.

There were, moreover, disputes between the Saudis and Iraqis over tribal activity which were not settled until 1936. The Iraqis for their part, after *formal* independence in 1932, sought a wider Arab role by improving their relations with Arabia, the Yemen, and Egypt. This was in part the inevitable response of a Hashemite ruler in Baghdad and his governing class of Sunnis who were and still are the politically dominant minority in Iraq over a politically underprivileged and suspect heterdox, Shia, majority.

The Arab far west, the Maghreb, was too far removed from the center of inter-Arab relations and politics in the Arab east, the Mashreq. Algeria, Tunisia, and Morocco were all under French control, whereas the buffer country of Libya was under Italian colonial rule. Yet even there an Islamic revivalist and reformist movement, influenced mainly by trends in the Arab east, made its appearance as a prelude, if not as the progenitor, of the later struggle for independence from French colonial rule.

On the whole, the presence of Britain and France restrained inter-Arab relations and rivalries. The Arab countries themselves were wholly occupied with the task of freeing themselves from the control of their European masters. Their foremost national priority was the attainment of complete independence.

By 1936, international conditions and other considerations prompted Britain and France to negotiate new treaty arrangements with their mandated and other client countries in the Arab Middle East, with a view to allowing them a greater measure of independence. In Iraq this had already been accomplished in 1930-32; Egypt, Lebanon, and Syria followed suit in 1936. But it was another issue altogether which brought these relatively weak Arab political entities into the wider arena of regional politics and inaugurated a new phase, or cycle, of the struggle for Arab leadership. This was the Palestine question, which until 1937, was more or less a local matter between the Arab and Jewish communities in Palestine and the British Mandate authority.

A Royal Commission, appointed in 1936 to look into the question of Palestine, recommended in 1937 the partition of the country into Arab and Jewish areas. Meanwhile, the local Arab rebellion, which began with a six-month general strike in April 1936, by October of that year had invited the mediation of at least Iraqi political leaders in its settlement. In the following year, a conference of leaders from the Arab countries at Bludan (Syria) marked the first "official" or formal involvement of those states in the Palestine question.

Egyptians, Saudis, and Yemenis may not have been equally deeply concerned over the fate or problems of the Palestinian Arabs. They were more interested in checking the influence of Iraqi, Transjordanian, and Syrian politicians in the affair. But the involvement of all these countries in the Palestine problem was given official recognition at the end of 1938 when the British government announced the convening of a conference to which would be invited not only representatives of the two rival communities in Palestine but also those of the Arab states. This unilateral act by HMG so to speak "regionalised" the issue, and rendered it prey to inter-Arab political rivalries. The latter were to surface more thunderously in the 1948 Palestine War. Furthermore, it limited the freedom of British action over Palestine, and granted the right of intervention by the Arab states in the conflict. From a local conflict, Palestine became a regional one, and Egyptian, Hashemite, and Saudi rivalries were injected into it.

Similarly, the exigencies and requirements of wartime policy prompted Britain to encourage greater Arab political cooperation and cohesiveness. In the face of the military dangers in 1941-42, HMG encouraged and inspired Hashemite-sponsored schemes of Fertile Crescent and Greater Syria unity. For instance, Abdullah's Greater Syria plan (Syria, Transjordan, Palestine) and Nuri's Fertile Crescent Union (Iraq, Syria, Transjordan) were opposed by both Egypt and Saudi Arabia since they would have meant the domination of an important Arab area by their rivals, the Hashemites. Eventually, Britain supported the less contentious scheme of a League of Arab States which was also preferred by Egypt and Arabia. In recognizing the sovereignty and independence of the member states, the League allowed for the containment of the struggle for power among the Arab states. But it also recognized the major protagonists for Arab leadership at the time as being Egypt, Iraq and Saudi Arabia. Until his assassination in 1951, King Abdullah of Jordan dominated the inter-Arab squabble over Palestine. But his own plans were thwarted in the end by Egypt and Saudi Arabia, using for that purpose the Palestinian followers of the Mufti, Haj Amin al-Husseini who, until 1959, resided in Egypt.

On the whole though, during this period, all the Arab states, especially the weaker ones, were interested mainly in the security of their territory and the maintenance of their independence regardless of how diluted this may have been. Saudi Arabia and the Yemen, one observes, for a long time preferred a state of near isolation from inter-Arab affairs so long as the more active among the Arab countries did not encroach upon their interests. It was a period of limited inter-Arab activity. What there was of it was confined to the Palestine question and inter-Arab relations arising from it, which mainly involved Iraqis, Syrians, and Transjordanians. Otherwise, the major interest of the Arab actors in the Middle East scene was still the attainment of complete independence or the ending of special relationships with an outside power.

The patterns of inter-Arab relations after the Second World War can be observed in four periods: 1948-1958; 1958-1967; 1967-1973; 1973- In considering these patterns or trends, one must bear in mind several major developments that are relevant: the increase in the number of independent Arab states (Libya, the Sudan, Kuwait, Tunisia, Morocco, Algeria, South Yemen, Bahrain, Qatar, and the Gulf States); the rise of military despotisms (i.e., the accession of soldiers to political power) in several of these states since 1949 (Syria, Egypt, Iraq, the Sudan, North Yemen, Algeria, and Libya); the so-called radicalization of regimes and the Arab nationalist movement under the impact of (a) military regimes; (b) parties, or movements, with ideological pretensions, e.g., the Baath in the Fertile Crescent area, and the Palestinians; (c) the use of single-party state organizations (which are not really parties, only agencies of state control) by military regimes, as in Egypt, Iraq, Syria, Algeria, and Libya; (d) the failure of western attempts at regional defense or other mutual security arrangements, and the reentry of the Soviet Union into the Middle East; and (e) the continuation of the conflict with Israel, involving three wars after the armistice agreements of 1949.[1]

The Period 1948-1965

Between 1948 and 1958, inter-Arab relations were dominated by the two traditional rival centers of Arab power, Egypt in the Nile Valley and Iraq in Mesopotamia. They struggled against each other either for the control of Syria and Jordan, or failing that, in order to prevent each other from exerting exclusive influence in those countries. Until 1952, the contest occurred within the framework of the Arab League. Syria, in particular, was an attractive arena for this struggle in view of the rapid succession of ephemeral military governments after March 1949. Yet until 1955 both contestants were constrained by the presence, however weak, of a foreign power, namely, Britain. The Palestine question was in abeyance, with Jordan having emerged as the major Arab beneficiary of the 1948-49 war.

By 1955, there were certain developments which tended to proliferate the protagonists for Arab leadership, and that led some of them to shift the ground of their respective roles in inter-Arab relations without, however changing the nature of the struggle. Once Egypt had resolved the question of its relation to

Britain (1954), it felt free to turn its attention to its role in the region. Almost simultaneously, the introduction of a Western-sponsored security or defense arrangement (the Baghdad Pact) supported by the Hashemites in Iraq elicited a sharp Egyptian reaction. Egypt interpreted this step as an attempt on the part of its erstwhile British occupiers to isolate Cairo in the Arab world, and deny it a position of leadership in favor of its arch-rival, Iraq. Positive neutralism, adopted by Nasser as a slogan if not a policy after Bandung in 1955, inaugurated a campaign of anticolonialism in the Arab world, aimed at the elimination of the remaining Western presence in the region from North Africa to the Gulf. It also served to attack and discredit Nasser's main rivals, the Iraqis, for Arab leadership. The "battlefield" was to be mainly the Fertile Crescent, particularly Syria and Jordan.

The emergence of the radical Arab Baath in Syria, Lebanon, and Jordan, vociferously opposed to the Hashemites and the West, facilitated Egypt's eventual, although temporary, triumph over its Iraqi adversary. Egypt succeeded in preventing Jordan from joining the Baghdad Pact, and pressed that nation to sever its special relationship with Britain. Syria then joined Egypt in an "organic" union to form the United Arab Republic, and Lebanon blew up in a bloody civil war. The opposing regime in Iraq was overthrown by a military coup, and so was the regime in the Sudan.

Despite Egypt's defeat in the Suez War of 1956, Nasser in the late fifties emerged triumphant in this contest to lead a movement of Arab unity whose primary objective was the eviction of imperialism (i.e., Western influence) from the Arab Middle East. Saudi Arabia, meanwhile, fearing either Iraqi control of Syria in the mid-fifties, or Syrian-Egyptian control over Jordan, reconciled its differences with Egypt, only to resume its more traditional opposition to Cairo two years later.

Although some of the protagonists in inter-Arab relations in 1958 were newcomers to the game (the Iraqi military rulers and the Syrian Baath), Egypt in the end could not overcome the traditional, strategic differences in state interest between them. A period of sharp conflict between Cairo and Baghdad, from 1959 to 1963 followed, despite their mutual commitment to Arab unity and opposition to imperialism and its agents among the conservative, or reactionary, Arab rulers in the Middle East. It involved the alleged Egyptian subversion in the Shawwaf Mosul uprising of February-March 1959, Egyptian accusations of Iraqi surrender to communism, and other less edifying mutual recriminations.

The vaunted ideological agreement between Nasser's Egypt and its Baathi clients and partners in Syria could not overcome the more serious differences between them in the UAR (1958-1961). These eventually brought about the secession of Syria from the union, leading first, to the widespread devaluation of the idea of Arab unity; second, to the loss of Egyptian prestige; and third, to a more active opposition to Egypt's policies by her foes in Arabia, Tunisia, and elsewhere in the Arab world. One of the difficulties arose from the fact that

Egypt, on one hand, was not in Syria strictly for ideological reasons, but also for the pursuit of its state interests in the Arab Middle East. On the other hand, neither the Baath nor the Syrians generally were prepared to forego their own pretensions or claims to Arab leadership, or their state.[2]

In the meantime, Egypt had forged a new relationship with the Soviet Union which, since 1955, allowed its leader, Nasser, to preside over a virulent anti-Western campaign and to improve his position in the struggle for Arab leadership over that of his adversaries, particularly those who were supported by the West. He managed to establish radical, revolutionary nationalism as the basis of Arab unity while, at the same time, using it to promote further Egypt's claim to leadership. He combined, that is, Arab revolutionism with Egyptian state interests. He grabbed and retained the initiative of Arab leadership for a decade (1955-1965) against the Baghdad Pact, the Eisenhower Doctrine, Iraq's so-called separatism under Qassem, Syria's secession from the UAR, and Saudi opposition and hostility in South Arabia. He succeeded, at least in his own eyes, in preventing the isolation of his country from the region.

The rejection of Egyptian leadership expressed in the Syrian secession, Iraqi insistence on independent opposition, and Saudi Arabia's and Jordan's quiet resistance constituted a defeat for Nasser's Arab policy. He retreated to his corner to brood and ponder over his next step. The result within a year was the proclamation of an Egyptian National Charter (1962), which was not as significant for Egypt as it was for the declaration of war on Egypt's enemies. In the face of Egypt's differences and quarrels with Syria and Iraq, Nasser scorned normal dealings with governments and regimes, and the kind of Arab unity that might result from a collaboration with them. Instead, he declared that Arab unity would be attained by a Socialist revolution throughout the Arab world. The declaration implied a call to Arabs in other countries to rise against their reactionary rulers, and suggested they could expect Egyptian help in their sedition and subversion. The polarization of the Arab world was now complete. What this also meant was that Egypt would resume its struggle for Arab leadership, armed with the new weapon of Arab national socialism, and backed by its new superpower patron, the Soviet Union.

The polarity was given a bloody expression in the Yemen War, the events in Aden and South Arabia in the period from 1962 to 1967. The focus of inter-Arab relations shifted to the Arabian Peninsula and the protagonists in the struggle for Arab hegemony now were Egypt and Saudi Arabia. Historically, of course, Egypt had been concerned with the protection of its eastern flank, especially the approaches to the Red Sea between South Arabia and Suez. While flaunting its ideological commitment to Arab revolution anywhere by its immediate support of the Sallal regime in Sanaa, Egypt was at the same time responding to a perception and consideration of its strategic needs and interests. Cairo's response to both these concerns, moreover, carried the prospect of discomfiting its rival in the Arab struggle, Saudi Arabia. The initiative in inter-Arab relations was somehow retrieved.

By 1963, however, inter-Arab relations generally had reached a low ebb. Egypt was at odds with Syria, Saudi Arabia, Jordan, Tunisia—even Iraq. Syria was at odds with Iraq; Algeria came to blows with Morocco over a border dispute; Tunisia and Morocco quarreled over the recognition of Mauretania.

Soon, though, the combination of the stalemate in the Yemen, changes in regimes in Damascus and Baghdad and the catalyst of Israel's challenge in diverting Jordan river waters imposed on inter-Arab relations and the main protagonists in them an interlude of reconciliation. Presidents of republics and fellow ideologues could agree to disagree; and monarchs were no longer monsters to be ostracized by the Arab community of nations. All this presaged a period of Arab summit meetings at which adversaries were temporarily reconciled in the face of the common danger.

But this was preceded by a last (?) attempt on the part of the so-called revolutionary Arab Socialist states of Syria and Iraq (both of them now, in 1963, under Baath control) to seek a union of sorts with Egypt. These efforts came to naught, not only because of the accumulated mutual distrust between the three parties involved, but also because Egypt was literally tired out. Its army was bogged down in the Yemen quagmire, its African policy had failed and backfired, and it preferred, in any case, to remain free to take the initiative of wider Arab leadership on its own at the propitious moment.

The outcome of the summit meetings in Cairo in January and September 1964 and in Casablanca in 1965 was a beginning in the settlement of the Yemen conflict between Egypt and Saudi Arabia, a reconciliation between Egypt and Jordan, and Egypt and Tunisia. But it also afforded Nasser the opportunity to reestablish Egypt's leadership in dealing with the Arab-Israel conflict in a way that suited its own purposes. The seeds of future conflict, however, were also sown in these summits. In order to deal with the matter of Israel without recourse to war, Egypt convinced its sister-Arab states to organize the Palestine Liberation Organization (PLO). This immediately worried King Hussein of Jordan and, as it turned out, not without good reason. As for the hoped for settlement of the Yemen War, it soon foundered on the rocks of indigenous Yemeni tribal factionalism which neither regional patron power of the local adversaries could easily manage or control.

A further radicalization of regime in Syria (February 1966), the activities of the PLO, Jordanian anxiety and unease, and the temporary campaign led by Nasser in his old firebrand style against West Germany over the recognition of Israel all seemed to erode the apparent achievements of the summits. By 1966, the era of Arab reconciliation was over. A realignment of conservative monarchs against radical regimes occurred. The old mutual abuse between Cairo and Riyadh was resumed, exacerbated further now by the new Saudi King Feisal's campaign to construct an Islamic bloc, to which King Hussein of Jordan immediately lent his support. Syria almost clashed with Iraq over a dispute about transport royalties from the Iraq Petroleum Company (IPC) oil pipeline which passes through Syrian territory. King Hussein was having his problems with Ahmad Shuqeiri and the PLO, who were now supported—and exploited—by his enemies, the Syrians. The struggle for power between Egypt and Saudi Arabia that year, moreover, presented the Syrians with a golden opportunity to seek the pivotal security of a rapprochement with Cairo, especially in view of their difficulties with neighboring Iraq, and the border tensions created by the activities of their Palestinian clients. It is, incidentally, a safe rule of thumb to assume that when Cairo and Riyadh are feuding, Damascus will seek an alignment with Egypt. The same is true of Cairo in these circumstances. In 1966, then, inter-Arab relations were characterized by a return to the 1958-61 alignments of Cairo-Damascus-Sanaa versus Riyadh and Amman.

In this atmosphere of Arab dissension and mutual recrimination Egypt had resumed the leadership of radical regimes. This time around, however, Cairo did not enjoy the same control over its even more radical Syrian junior partners (with whom Egypt had concluded a military alliance in November 1966) which she did back in the days of union. Thus, for their own purposes of embarrassing the Iraqi regime that had tried to improve its relations with Cairo in 1964, and in order to intimidate King Hussein, the Syrians encouraged Palestinian activities against Israel launched from East Jordan.

In these circumstances, Nasser felt obliged to prove his concern for the Palestinians and to assert his leadership of the Arab revolution, whatever that was. With his army stuck in the Yemen, his economic problems at home getting worse, and in the face of a virulent Saudi-led and financed campaign against him (which he incidentally suspected was inspired by the Americans), he believed the time had come for a showdown. The rest was all downhill towards the abyss of the June 1967 debacle.

Whether or not Nasser really intended to go to war in June 1967 is a question that falls outside the scope of this survey.[3] What is certain though, in relation to inter-Arab relations, is his determination to assert his leadership and control over the Arab political arena. When it was clear his brinkmanship would result in a third Arab-Israel war, King Hussein of Jordan, eager to protect and improve his standing in the inter-Arab political galaxy, abandoned his fellow-monarch Feisal and his conservative camp, and signed a military pact with his enemy of yesterday, Nasser.

A major consequence of the 1967 defeat for inter-Arab relations was its effect on the Cairo-Riyadh confrontation. The immediate question was that of a settlement with Israel. Nasser could not, of course, contemplate such a step without wider Arab support primarily because his prestige had been shattered. At this juncture Nasser's arch-rival King Feisal came forward at the Khartoum Conference with magnanimous (and devastatingly humiliating for Nasser) offers of generous financial support, on condition that Nasser carry on the implacable struggle against Israel. Feisal, in short, had brought Nasser to his knees. Not only was Egypt soon to exit from the Peninsula, but Saudi Arabia was to embark, thanks to its inordinate wealth, on the road to Arab pre-eminence.

After the Six-Day War

The 1967 War ended the sharp polarization of the Arab states between radical and conservative, and reconciled monarchies and republics in the agony of shame and defeat. But it also ended a decade of Egyptian primacy in Arab affairs under Nasser, and an era of inter-Arab subversion and war in the Yemen. It allowed countries like Jordan to rehabilitate their standing among the Arab states and to protect their independence. Most importantly, it allowed a weightier role, on the basis of wealth, for the more conservative rulers of Arabia in inter-Arab affairs. Equally significant, although in the short term less important, was the emergence of the Palestine Resistance Movement in a more radical form.

The conflicting interests of different Arab states, however, were not less apparent. Egypt and Jordan, and to a lesser degree Syria, were clearly anxious to recover some of their occupied territories. This common interest brought their two rulers, once bitter enemies, closer together. Both, in a way, became dependent on the financial assistance of a major rival in the struggle for Arab leadership, Saudi Arabia. One may view the willingness of rich oil-producing states in the Peninsula and the Gulf to aid Egypt, Syria, and the Palestinians since 1967 as a matter of paying protection money to troublemakers in the hope and expectation that they will behave. Oil-rich, but otherwise weak, states such as Saudi Arabia, Kuwait, and the Gulf Emirates have been, in effect, doing this since the early sixties. Kuwait's £150 million Fund for Arab Economic Development, for example, dates from 1962. The fact remains that King Feisal at least emerged as the most serious contender for Arab primacy. For the time being he had destroyed the prospects of another Egyptian thrust into the peninsula or its affairs.

Even though by 1969, Egypt, or really Nasser, had chosen to withdraw from the inter-Arab arena as a prelude to accepting the Rogers Plan, he nevertheless thought it necessary to forge a convenient relationship with the new maverick regime of Qadhafi in Libya, as an alternative axis for his Arab initiative and as a counterweight to the conservative rulers.[b,4] No Egyptian ruler in fact can allow the initiative in inter-Arab affairs to pass exclusively, or for too long, into the hands of a rival Arab leader.

The threat posed by the Palestinians to certain Arab regimes derived in part from the struggle between their several patrons: Syrians, Libyans, Iraqis, and the Sheikhs. But their most immediate, credible threat to Jordan was removed by forceful, bloody military action in 1970-71.

It was inevitable after Nasser's death, the impasse on the Canal, the deteriorating relations with the Soviet Union and the eventual rupture between Cairo and Moscow that Egypt should seek a working, profitable alliance, or accommodation, with a rich Arab state that would permit it greater freedom of

---

[b]Heikal, in *Road to Ramadan*, argues that Nasser considered Libya as providing the "defence depth" Egypt needed in a war with Israel, and that he began laying plans for another war on the morrow of the 1967 defeat.

action in the regional Arab and international arenas via the Middle East conflict. Once again, the interest of the state of Egypt (as distinguished from any ideological preferences or pretensions of the Egyptian regime) asserted itself in the policy of seeking to reclaim the initiative in the Middle East. The growing support of the Palestinians by Syria, Libya and Iraq could well produce certain unwelcomed changes in the Fertile Crescent area and thus a shift in the Arab balance of power. This was a dangerous prospect for Egypt which it could not tolerate. It is in this context that the forging of the Cairo-Riyadh axis before the October War must be viewed.

Aftermath of the October War

The October War did not lead to the abatement of the inter-Arab rivalry for leadership. It did, however, affect the form and level of the conflict, for it introduced a somewhat different pattern of Arab alliances and alignments, and somewhat changed perceptions of Arab capabilities and limitations as well as priorities. Inter-Arab relations are to a great extent dominated, or at least influenced, now by the availability of the so-called oil weapon. Some have argued that with this vital commodity and the fantastic revenues from it, the Arab states can hold the industrial world in their power, even to ransom. After all, the argument goes, a group of states belonging to a single cultural group have access to this seemingly perfect weapon. They can, for a variety of purposes, hold the industrial (primarily the Western) world responsible for the occupation of parts of their Arab national territory by Israel and, therefore, use it to press them to abandon it. Others may feel that with this weapon the Arab states acting in concert, or in a subregional constellation of power, can challenge a rival Western civilization over influence, power, and domination. They can possibly also challenge the hegemony of either or both of the superpowers.

One detects in recent Arabic writings, and particularly statements by Arab officials for home consumption, a resentment of all the past real and imagined ills and injustices visited by the West, from the Crusaders to the nineteenth century imperialists, upon Muslim Arab society. There is in these utterances a sharp tone of defiance and an allusion to revenge, which project the "Arab Restoration" at hand.

In terms of inter-Arab relations one can identify, among others, three fundamental changes wrought by, or at least ensuing from, the October War. First, the balance of political influence, if not power, among the Arab states has shifted from the radicals to the conservatives, and from the Fertile Crescent and Egypt to the Peninsula. An important corollary of this is the proposition that haphazard radicalism is unproductive both in terms of Arab advancement and of bringing about Israel's defeat. Second, an unholy alliance between two of the strongest contenders for Arab hegemony, Egypt and Saudi Arabia, has been forged. Third, a partial way out of the thorny issue of the Palestinians has been found.

In the November 1973 and October 1974 Arab Summits (Algiers and Rabat) a formula for the integration of the Palestinians into the "official" pattern and mainstream of inter-Arab relations was found, albeit at the expense of King Hussein of Jordan.[c] Briefly, the formula was as follows: The PLO agrees to abide by the leadership of the Cairo-Riyadh axis in return for its recognition as the sole legitimate representative of the Palestinian people and its inclusion as a party and essential ingredient to any Middle East peace settlement.

The question which remains is whether this formula heralds, or even envisages, the abandonment of the previous Arab position which held that peace with Israel is impossible. Needless to say, according to their declarations, this, as of this writing, remains the position of Libya, Iraq, even Algeria, and the extreme organizations within the PLO. The assumption, never publicly expressed, is that the leading contenders for Arab leadership, Egypt and Saudi Arabia, would accept peace with Israel if it can be reconciled with Palestinian rights, which rights, they go on to assert, can be defined only by the Palestinians themselves, not by other Arabs.

To what extent, however, these paymasters and current mentors of this political arrangement, or authors of this formula, can control their new Palestinian partners, is not certain. What is clear is that for the time being inter-Arab relations are marked by an Egyptian-Saudi axis, an Egyptian-Syrian rapprochement over the PLO, an implacable opposition to the new constellation of Arab power by Libya and Iraq, a split within the PLO between its presumed "establishment" and its more extreme members and the alienation of Jordan from the whole arrangement.

The perceptions of the October War and its achievements by the Arabs is an interesting, revealing, and relevant factor in inter-Arab relations. For the Egyptians it constituted a new departure that provides them room for maneuver both in regional Arab and international diplomacy. They believe that by crossing the Canal they broke the impasse in the Arab or, more accurately, Egyptian-Israel conflict, extricated themselves from total dependence on the Soviet Union, and, by extension, restored their relations with the United States. On the Arab front, they countered radical accusations of timidity and ineptitude, thus regaining their prestige and initiative in the struggle for Arab leadership. More typical is the perception of the *solidarity* achieved among some Arab states on the basis of a convergence of their interests in coordinating the use of financial, oil, and military resources in a common policy for the prosecution of the October War and its diplomatic aftermath. They believe that they achieved the

---

[c]Hussein's willingness to abandon the West bank to the PLO is, in my view, based on two factors: (a) he knows the Israelis will vigorously resist its falling under PLO control, in which case Arafat's prestige will suffer; (b) he has satisfied for the moment the demands of his own East Jordanian establishment to relinquish the West Bank.

diplomatic and political isolation of their enemy Israel; that is, they have attained the only condition in which they could fight against Israel with any hope of even partial success.

With Saudi backing, Egypt's option for gradual or piecemeal negotiations with Israel became more acceptable to other Arabs. More significant for inter-Arab relations, Saudi support permitted Sadat of Egypt a certain authoritative cogency in Arab councils and gave Cairo an opportunity to moderate Syrian and Palestinian attitudes. This was clearly shown particularly in the November 1973 Algiers Summit and in the eventual disengagement agreement between Syria and Israel on the Golan. Closer to home, it made it easier for Egypt to deal with the wild Colonel Qadhafi of Libya and, in many ways, isolate him from the mainstream of Arab affairs.

But the situation was fraught with dangers and uncertainties. The Rabat Summit of October 1974 stirred the undercurrents of inter-Arab conflict. Winning international public opinion to the side of the Palestinian or Arab cause in the Middle East conflict restricted Egyptian freedom of action and only precariously bridged the widening rift between Syrian and Egyptian interests, not to speak of the alienation of Hussein and the repercussions in Jordan that it caused. Syria's position in the Golan Heights seemed to limit Egypt's options in another round of disengagement negotiations with Israel over Sinai. Then Arafat's unexpectedly strident and uncompromising address in the UN General Assembly in November 1974 highlighted the differences in perception among the Arabs of a lasting settlement of the Middle East conflict. More dangerous to Sadat was the reaction at home to, and unease about, Egypt's overdependence on a conservative ally like Saudi Arabia and its impact on Egyptian society, as well as to the alacrity with which Sadat embraced the American diplomatic and economic *démarche* that jeopardized Egypt's military arrangements with Soviet Union.

The vital Cairo-Riyadh axis between the two major local Arab centers of power in the Middle East will probably hold so long as their respective interests relating to the Middle East conflict and the region as a whole are served. The Saudi regime is mainly interested in improving its chances for Arab leadership, and this is, in turn, linked to its ambitions in the Peninsula proper.

For Egypt, the axis gives its rulers time to retrench at home, and allows the recent successful isolation of Israel with its attendant difficulties to erode their adversary's power. Unlike Syria, a state that could be self-sufficient without having to play a wider role in the region, Egypt, *not for ideological reasons*, must view the conflict with Israel not simply as a territorial dispute, but as a long-term contest for the strategic and economic control of the core eastern area of the Arab Middle East. It is this *state* interest of Egypt which leads one to believe that regardless of its moderation ("Egypt is the least Arab of the Arab states") Cairo cannot—perhaps will not—under whatever ruler easily accept a permanent accommodation with its most obvious rival in the region, Israel, unless it is clearly to its advantage.

It was common after the Arab defeat in the Six-Day War of 1967 to argue a shift in Arab priorities. It was, for example, widely held that the Arabs had revised their policy in relation to Israel, from one of destruction to one of containment. Is one to assume that after the October War the priorities have given this policy its original order, from containment to destruction, not necessarily by war, but by economic pressure, political and diplomatic isolation, as well as by international pressure?

That the 1967 defeat had a profound impact on inter-Arab relations there is no doubt. The overwhelming, dominating presence of Nasser in these relations was permanently diminished and his role in them undermined. Smaller and weaker states secured their legitimacy and independence: they felt safer from the subversive effects of the struggle for Arab leadership. Whereas the emergence of the Palestine Resistance Movement tended to radicalize the region, threaten and mesmerise Arab regimes as well as the international community, established Arab states became more determined to resist its disruptive intrusions and defend their regimes. Egyptian regional influence however could not be exercised single-handedly, but only in collaboration with another—and alternative—credible Arab leader whose influence was based on wealth. Together they were able to push to the background the vaunted old style Arab nationalism of the radical variety and instead project Arab *solidarity* between independent Arab states that have the resources to pursue credible policies. Above all, the Cairo-Riyadh axis showed that less radical, even conservative, Arab rulers or regimes could successfully promote and defend Arab interests even when such rulers are associated with the "imperialist" United States. The central position of Egypt in Arab affairs since World War II was not ended; rather it acquired a partner, Saudi Arabia, a country that also aspires to regional power.

The October War and its aftermath put an end to the ideologically phoney but otherwise earnest inter-Arab contest inaugurated by Nasser in 1958 between monarchies and republics. In any case, ideological agreement between Arab radicals in the decade 1958-1967, or at any other time, did not and does not preclude serious conflict between them as states or regimes. This was the glaring case of Syria, Iraq, Yemen, and Libya in their relations with Egypt.

One must expect, though, efforts at subregional arrangements both by Egypt and Saudi Arabia in anticipation of future disagreements, even a rupture, between them. To this end Egyptian interest in Libya will remain keen. Saudi Arabia is already seeking to "organize" its lesser sisters in the Gulf in a common policy. Although the immediate thrust of these Saudi peninsular moves is directed against Iraq to the north and Iran to the east, any successful local groupings of oil-rich states (Kuwait, Bahrain, Qatar, Muscat, and Oman, the Gulf Emirates) under Saudi leadership will provide little comfort for the other aspirants to Arab leadership, whether in Egypt, Libya or the Fertile Crescent.

Qatar for all practical purposes is a Saudi "satellite," and its integration in the future is not a fanciful projection. In the Levant, a parallel prospect is the reduction of Lebanon to a Christian enclave, with part of the north going to

Syria, and part of the south to Israel—assuming the latter still exists. Jordan, on the other hand, might conceivably be dismembered, with its southern territories from Kerak to Aqaba going to Saudi Arabia and a small section of its northern part being grabbed by Syria. In view of the Iranian-Saudi Arabian antithesis in the Gulf, Iraq may manage no more than a "buffer state" role.

The present political map of the Arab Middle East may not be a permanent one, in view of the nature and main features of inter-Arab relations presented above. The sharp new differences perforce engendered between the very rich oil-producing Arab states and those less naturally endowed are a major factor in this instability or impermanence.

The Cairo-Riyadh axis and the outcome of the October War muted, for a while, the more shrill polarization in the Arab world that had been promoted by Nasser and his followers for over a decade. The apparent shift this brought about locally and regionally from "radicalism" to "moderation" and in the Arabs' external orientation away from the Soviet Union one feels is an ephemeral, transient by-product. Thus, the assassination of King Feisal, "the architect of Arab solidarity" and financier of the anti-Soviet push in the Arab world, was unexpected. The same impermanence, incidentally, attaches to another prominent, local architect of a "permanent future" in the Gulf, the Shah of Iran.

All UN member states (including some of the Arab ones) that clamored for the recognition of the PLO did so on the assumption and expectation that with such recognition the Palestinians would finally agree to negotiate with an Israeli state, however small in size. This, so far, has not been the case. The other assumption was that the Arab states that count in the region, e.g., Egypt, Saudi Arabia, Syria, even Jordan, were already willing to recognize an Israeli state, and they would therefore be able to cajole a politically and internationally respected PLO into coming to the conference table. This too, in my view, could be a mistaken assumption, perhaps a hopelessly fanciful one. There will always be a vast number of Arabs who will not accept an Israeli state in the Middle East, even if it were miniscule in size, because of their particular conception of Islam and the history of Arab-, or Muslim-, Jewish coexistence.

Regardless of the limited objective of Dr. Kissinger's efforts, namely, a further disengagement in the Sinai, its implicit long-term corollary has to be a peaceful accommodation between the two countries. This has been and remains mainly a Western (and, reluctantly, Soviet) objective. No Arab state, or ruler, has really accepted it *unequivocally*. The long-term objective of all the Arab states, including Egypt, which supports the declared objectives of the Palestinian movement, is for the region to be freed of a sovereign independent Jewish political entity—the State of Israel. And this, incidentally, is not necessarily synonymous with the physical extermination of that state's population, since the Arabs have historically accepted and do today accept coexistence with sectarian, ethnic, and other minorities so long as these do not lay claim or aspire to or attain a sovereign political existence.

It was suggested at the time that the breakdown in the negotiations of March 1975 occurred over the matter of further Israeli territorial concessions in Sinai. The Israelis, in turn, claimed that these could not be made without an Egyptian declaration of nonbelligerency which the Egyptians refused to offer as a counterconcession. Ostensibly, the justification for this Egyptian refusal was that nonbelligerency can be attained only after Israel has withdrawn from all Arab territories. Arab interpretations of what this entails abound: pre-1967, 1947 Partition boundaries, etc.

Sadat, in a closed session briefing of the Arab Socialist Union (ASU) Central Committee on July 18, 1972, justified his expulsion of Soviet personnel from Egypt in part on the following:

There is between us and the Soviet Union a fundamental disagreement on principle regarding Israel. . . . Despite the sincere Soviet stand in supporting the Arab states in their struggle against Israel, and specifically in their demand to remove the traces of aggression which occurred in 1967, the Soviet Union still recognizes Israel and believes in the importance of protecting her existence. The Soviet Union (unlike us) is not concerned with international legality and its violation when Israel was founded on Arab land in 1948.[5]

Moreover, after the October War, as far as can be gauged from public statements and published materials (October-December 1973), most Arabs were convinced of their long-term advantage in the fight against Israel.

In short, there still remain certain minimal entrenched positions on both sides of the conflict which are not negotiable: security for the Israelis; unwillingness to recognize a Jewish state for the Arabs, unless Israel withdraws from all Arab territories (*all* is as yet undefined), and satisfies the rights of the Palestinians (as yet undefined, nor agreed upon, by the Arabs).

At the same time, the Arabs have tended since the October War to use oil as a tactical weapon not simply to press Europe and the United States toward an anti-Israel policy—and to divide Europe from the United States over that policy (the so-called Euro-Arab dialogue)—but very much as one against Jews in the Middle East and elsewhere.

Dr. Kissinger's successful "shuttle diplomacy" in August-September 1975 generated further conditions of renewed inter-Arab conflict. The political implications of the second interim agreement over Sinai between Egypt and Israel are dangerous. The agreement has significantly introduced two important elements of regional conflict, one being the exposure of Egypt to Arab attack resulting in a sharper polarization of the Arab states, the other consisting of the more direct involvement of the United States as the patron power of two adversaries in the conflict, Egypt and Israel, and as a convenient target of attack by other Arabs and the Soviet Union. Upon the conclusion of the agreement, the United States was immediately accused by the Arabs opposed to separate agreements between Egypt and Israel as wishing to strengthen conservative Arab regimes in the Middle East; to isolate Egypt from the rest of the Arab world; to secure the existence of Israel by forging a closer alliance with it; and to deny the Palestinians their legitimate rights. On the other hand, the second Egyptian-Israeli interim agreement could attract the remaining two Arab "confrontation" states, Jordan and Syria, to a policy of actively seeking a similar accommodation with Israel.

Inter-Arab conflict, however, persists not so much over Israel (although tactical differences between certain Arab states over this issue and between them and the Palestinians have always been present) as over the resurgence since October 1973 of a pressing Islamic impatience with the careful tactics of the so-called moderates: thus Libya's impatience with Egyptian diplomacy in the Middle East conflict and the Palestinians' involvement in a fear-dominated confessional system in the Lebanon.

There is a renewed contest between the Arabs over "Islamicity," similar to the one over radicalism and socialism a few years ago. Sadat of Egypt and Feisal of Saudi Arabia helped suppress a Communist coup in Khartoum in July 1971, only two months after Sadat had suppressed his own Nasserite radicals at home. The lip-service paid by Arab leaders since the October War to the analogy between the struggle against Israel and that of their Muslim ancestors against the Crusaders eight and nine hundred years ago has encouraged extremist calls for holy wars and Islamic revivals, such as the one emanating from Qadhafi of Libya. In short, the Islamic euphoria and new psychology of confrontation with an alien world that has kept Arab genius down, provides still further sources of inter-Arab conflict.

It is clear that if Egypt has been and remains unable to control the Arab Middle East, neither can any other Arab state, however rich. Differences over local issues, fear between states and communities within them will persist for the foreseeable future and so mar and complicate domestic and inter-Arab politics. Internal explosions from time to time, such as the food riots in Egypt, communal conflict in the Lebanon, Syrian-Iraqi contests, tribal rivalries in Arabia and the Gulf, border and other disputes in the Maghreb, will occur. Those Arab states without revenue from oil, will remain dependent on outside economic aid and the diplomatic patronage of one or other of the great powers.

It is, in fact, the essentially Islamic-Arab rejection of an alien Jewish state in the area which enables Egypt, for instance, to remain the most influential state among them, by virtue of its dexterous manipulation of the Middle East conflict's local dynamism. The Arabs are divided over most issues. But the potency of a perception since October 1973, consisting of the destruction of the myth of Israeli invincibility, the recruitment of the United States and Europe (as a result of the oil weapon) as concession extractors from Israel, and the inevitable triumph of the combination of Arab numbers and money renders the belief in the superfluousness of a permanent peace with Israel irresistible.

Major Areas in Inter-Arab Relations

On the basis of the preceding brief survey of the patterns of and trends in inter-Arab relations, one may outline some of the major problem areas and main elements of potential conflict which could affect inter-Arab relations and impinge upon United States interests in the region.

Economic Considerations

The following conditions affect inter-Arab relations:

1. A division between rich oil-producing states, on one hand, (Saudi Arabia, Kuwait, some of the Gulf States, Iraq, Libya, and Algeria), and, on the other, those states not so naturally endowed (Egypt, Jordan, Lebanon, Morocco, the Sudan, Tunisia, and the two Yemens). Bahrain, which is also oil-producing, is, as an island, in a special position. The mixed composition of its population (Arab and Persian) and its location, as well as Iran's irredentist claims upon it, impose upon it a circumspect stand vis-à-vis its Arab neighbors. Muscat and Oman, moreover, also oil-producing, equally maintain a peripheral involvement for the time being. But its current domestic turmoil and its possible outcome may inevitably push it into the mainstream of Arab peninsular affairs.

2. In addition to the basic division (1), there is also the fact of the disparity in development between these two groups of Arab states. The richest among them are also, by and large, the least developed economically, socially, and politically. Many of them, such as Kuwait and the Gulf States, employ in their current programs of development vast numbers of expatriates from other Arab states, in particular Egypt (medical, engineering, and educational services) Palestinians, especially in Kuwait (educational and entrepreneurial projects), Iraq (mainly political refugees in administrative services), and the Lebanon (banking, financial, and contract enterprises). These constitute not a wholly comforting or reassuring intrusion for the Peninsula and Gulf States.[6]

3. Syria and Iraq can conceivably become economically self-sufficient states given the size of their populations and resources. Syria, however, will continue to depend, to some extent, on financial assistance from some of the oil-producing states (Saudi Arabia, Abu Dhabi) in the prosecution of the struggle against Israel. Lebanon, on the other hand, has an economy which rests largely on financial and related services, and is also dependent, to some extent, upon its ability to attract capital and contracts for these services from the richer Arab states, and upon its continued ability to extend these services throughout the region. Both Syria and Lebanon have oil-pipeline terminals on their coasts. They would be interested in maintaining the flow of income from them. (A glut of oil on the world market led to the closing down in 1975 of the pipeline terminal in

Lebanon.) Iraq and Saudi Arabia are also interested in the security and continued use of these pipelines. To this extent, the economics of overland oil transport is a factor in these inter-Arab relations. With the re-opening of the Suez Canal their importance may diminish.

4. Egypt and Jordan are the least favorably placed in the oil game. By virtue of the September 1975 interim agreement with Israel, Egypt has regained control of its oil wells in the Sinai, and Cairo may yet strike it rich with major oil finds in the Western Desert. For the time being, Egypt remains dependent on massive financial assistance from the oil-producing states, and Cairo is not sanguine about the prospects of capital investment for economic development in her own country from them. Inevitably, the current dependence constitutes a constraint upon Egypt's freedom of action in relation to Israel and the wider area of inter-Arab relations. The reopening of the Suez Canal may improve its economic situation, as it may also infuse some life into the Aden complex in southern Arabia. For the time being Egypt may have to make do with the economic palliative of the United States offer of some $800 million in economic aid as part of the September 1975 interim agreement "package" with Israel. Meanwhile, there are those who argue that the reopening of the Suez Canal may free Egypt from the "collective" Arab constraint regarding its policy towards the Middle East conflict. On the other hand, a future rehabilitation of the Egyptian relationship with the Soviet Union and the intensive use of the Canal by the Soviet Fleet may lead Egypt's rulers to adopt a more aggressive, intransigent, and strident position over the Arab-Israel conflict.

5. The structural differences in the economies of Arab states (state controlled, private enterprise, etc.) constitute a relevant factor in inter-Arab relations. It is not, therefore, only the disparities in resources, but also the different economies which must be considered.

6. Libya is perhaps heard of only because of its oil revenues. It has used and, under the present regime, will continue to use its income from oil to create for itself a role in inter-Arab relations out of all proportion to its other capabilities, which are almost nil. With a very small population, it can afford to do so. But this also suggests an inter-Arab "bribery" contest with regard to the Palestinians and in the pursuit of state rivalries, as, for example, between Libya on one side and the Peninsula on the other, or as between Libya and Egypt, or Libya and Morocco.

7. Generally then, the recent accumulation of astronomical money reserves from oil revenues affords some of the Arab states greater influence in inter-Arab relations than they would otherwise possess. Such influence, however, reflects vulnerable power. In most of the oil-rich Arab states this "economic" or financial power is not underpinned by the credible infrastructure one normally associates with powerful states. In the meantime, the division between the rich and poor Arab states (although some of them are more advanced in other respects) could initiate a new phase of inter-Arab conflict. Despite the existence

of the odd regional Arab economic institution, such as the Arab Development Fund and similar organizations, until now the full use of Arab resources for regional economic development has not occurred. Most of the capital flow from oil rich states into the Arab region so far has gone to finance the conflict with Israel, as well as "useful" political groups in several countries. Oil money has always been, in passing, a weapon of subversion in other Arab states, and the "oiler" of several propaganda campaigns in the press and other media.

8. If, however, the pattern of inter-Arab relations has been one of independent states resisting integration into subjugation under a wider Arab arrangement, led by one or another of the protagonists for hegemony in the region, their economic behavior may well continue to rest on that basis. A scramble for resources by those not possessing them when the opportunity arises is not unlikely. A case at hand is Morocco's claim to the Spanish Sahara that may develop into a first-class inter-Maghrebi row.

9. If by some good fortune the Arab-Israel conflict is peacefully settled or resolved, one can expect a deterioration in inter-Arab relations with economic overtones. So far, the rich Arab states, for their own purposes, can use their financial resources for the maintenance of the conflict at relatively little expense to themselves and, in the meantime, derive maximum benefit in the struggle for Arab leadership.

10. So far, only Egypt, among these states, really entertains hopes of a wider inter-Arab economic role by virtue of its relatively vast human (educational, technical, industrial) resources. The Syrians and Iraqis could conceivably compete. So far only the Lebanese have done so credibly. To this extent also, Egypt will maintain an interest in an integrative kind of Arab economic development as long as Cairo perceives a leading role for itself.

Political Considerations

Despite the appearances of Arab solidarity after the Rabat Summit of October 1974, the centrifugal tendencies and other tensions in inter-Arab relations remain, albeit muted for the time being. Strategic calculations may have changed since the October War. There has been a transformation of the balance of power in the core Arab Middle East. At least the Arabs perceive this to be the case and that is what counts in dealing with them, for it entails the matter of Arab "bargaining power" in the conflict with Israel and in their relations with outside powers. Having discredited Arab radicalism and its usefulness in the struggle against Israel, Egypt at least contends that the successful recruitment of the financial resources of the rich Arab states helped it perform a "miracle." The myth of Israeli superiority and invincibility, according to Cairo, was shattered. The quick "recruitment" of the United States first into extracting concessions from Israel and second, into a new economic relationship with Egypt and Saudi

Arabia was achieved. As for the Arabs generally, they believe that the combination of military action and economic pressure by virtue of the oil weapon did the trick in October 1973. The United States, according to Arab perceptions, has been committed to the role of concession-extractor from Israel as well as the provider of economic and other assistance to some of the Arab states. All this, the Arabs believe, was achieved in return for an Arab promise of continued energy supplies, new investment opportunities, etc. There have been, however, no known, clear, and unequivocal undertakings by the Arabs on the matter of the permanent acceptance of America's client, Israel, as a sovereign independent state in their midst. There are, indeed, many Arabs who believe the United States, in its new relationship with them, will help them achieve in relation to Israel what they themselves have not been able to achieve in the past twenty-six years, seventeen of them crowded with Soviet help. The ambivalence over this *ultimate* issue in the conflict will plague inter-Arab relations as well as relations between the Arabs and the outside world, particularly the United States and the USSR. It is the kind of gnawing uncertainty which breeds suspicion and distrust among Arabs, and between Arabs and outsiders.

Negotiations for the peaceful settlement of the Arab-Israel conflict have not, so far, progressed beyond the stage of disengagement agreements. In the meantime, a vastly accelerated rate in the importation of arms not only by the principal adversaries in the conflict, but also by those Arab states on its periphery could lead to the further escalation of the conflict and the outbreak of hostilities, as well as to serious domestic trouble in some of the Arab states. Then the American offer in 1974 of nuclear reactors to Egypt and Israel can trigger a chain reaction in other Middle Eastern states. It has already pushed Iran, on the periphery (also with India in mind), to follow suit by rumored negotiations with French suppliers. The Soviet Union may well offer nuclear arrangements to Iraq and/or Syria. Algeria may feel obliged to seek similar arrangements with France or the Soviet Union. What the impact of such developments on inter-Arab relations, let alone the Arab-Israel conflict, will be is difficult to say, but the prospect is daunting.

Arab insistence on the satisfaction of the "legitimate rights" of Palestinians and the continued clashes between Palestinian terrorist infiltrators and Israeli security forces sustains the tension in Arab-Israel relations. But it also exacerbates inter-Arab relations, depending on the perception of interest individual Arab states have in the crisis. If, for example, Israel and the PLO remain at odds, the tendency will be for an Arab regional realignment. The PLO will be inclined to blame the policy of the Cairo-Riyadh axis for failure to reach its objectives. The Libyan-Iraqi loose alliance will also attack the Egyptian-Saudi constellation. Meanwhile, the Jordanians, having abandoned the West Bank to the PLO, will move to split the Palestinians settled in East Jordan.[d] Together with the

---

[d]The recent proposals for constitutional amendments in Jordan indicate Hussein will ask those of Palestinian origin to choose between Jordanian citizenship and Palestinian status. If a majority of them opt for the former, a similar move by Lebanon is possible as regards its 300,000 Palestinian residents. This will seriously weaken the PLO.

probable failure of the PLO to regain the West Bank from Israel within a reasonable period of time, all these problems will lead to another cycle of inter-Arab differences—and disarray.

The tactical manipulation of the Palestinians both by the Soviet Union (for its own purposes) and the Arab states is bound to continue, hindering further peaceful negotiations. Until recently, one could not dismiss, for instance, the possibility that the Cairo-Riyadh policy of sponsoring the PLO regionally and internationally, and the threat of the further use of the oil weapon was one of procrastination in order to gain enough time during which Israel would collapse without recourse to another round of hostilities. Domestically though, Egypt, as it turned out, was unable to afford too long a hiatus between the first interim agreement with Israel in 1974 and the second in 1975. Nor, incidentally, was Cairo able to resist for too long the offer of sizable U.S. economic and financial aid. One cannot rule out the possibility, however, that in the future Egypt may abandon its Saudi paymaster and present ally in favor of a return to the old close relation with the Soviet Union, a development which will affect the pattern of inter-Arab relations, and influence the evolution of the Arab-Israel conflict. For the time being, Egypt has sought to strike a balance between an opening to the West in the hope of regaining Sinai, involving a guarded and cautious movement toward an accommodation with Israel on one hand, and a continued attachment to the general Arab position regarding a final settlement of the Middle East conflict, on the other.

Continuing Trends and Patterns in Inter-Arab Relations

The Arabian Peninsula and the Gulf

In addition to being the richest oil-producing area in the Arab Middle East, it is also, in contrast to the Fertile Crescent and the Maghreb, the center of traditional, conservative, tribal-dynastic states. The Arab side of the Gulf has only recently (1971) emerged as independent of a protecting power. It is, therefore, exposed to the momentum of local, or regional, powers that may seek to dominate and control it, as for example, Saudi Arabia and Iran. Saudi Arabia at the center of the Peninsula may seek to dominate the Union of Arab Emirates and South Arabia, i.e., both Yemens. In doing so, it may come into conflict with Iraq and Iran. It will, in the meantime, resist what appear even now to be Iranian "salami tactics" (to achieve immediate goods without revealing the long-term policy) in the lower Gulf (Muscat and Oman) in order to assert its own gradual domination. One must note in this connection the presence of sizable Iranian communities in Dubai and the other Gulf states, as well as in Kuwait and Bahrain.

Saudi activities in the Gulf, however, are not altogether welcome. One observes a form of resistance to them on the part of the Emirates, particularly when one considers the lavish use of funds by Abu Dhabi, especially in the support of the Palestinians, Syrians, and other so-called Arab causes; or in the now nearly indiscriminate distribution of largesse among propagandists in the West. All the same, on a broader front, Saudi Arabia with its vast wealth will continue to assist such rulers as Qabus of Muscat and Oman in resisting domestic sedition, and will also continue to manipulate the Arab-Israel conflict (as it has since the Khartoum Conference in 1967) to its advantage in the context of inter-Arab relations.

Such widespread inter-Arab activities based strictly on money, however, invite the mistrust of other Arabs. This remains the case especially in view of Saudi Arabia's relation to the United States. Nor is the ability to exercise such influence in inter-Arab affairs a permanent feature of Saudi Arabia's role in the region. The uncertainties that surround the future and fortune of the Saudi family and establishment after Feisal's assassination by his nephew are too great and the consequences too complex to permit any prognostication. For the moment, however, in the absence of a genuinely strong local or regional power (not merely rich), able to maintain stability, the Gulf at least remains a potential center of conflict that attracts the interference not only of the local contestants but also that of outside powers.

The Fertile Crescent

The problems that have historically plagued the relations between Syria, Iraq, Lebanon, and Jordan remain. In view of the developments discussed in an earlier section, Jordan may introduce a new factor in relations with the Palestinians which will affect Syria and Lebanon, too. Until the beginning of 1975 Iraq had been too busy with the Kurdish War to concern itself with Syria and Jordan, or even Kuwait. Despite the recent recognition of the PLO, Lebanon will continue to face difficulties in its relations with the Palestinians whose administrative, political, propaganda, and military headquarters remain in that country. The recent clashes between the Christian Phalangists and the Palestinians in Beirut in April-May 1975, are a grim reminder of these difficulties. Whereas in 1958 the civil war was in effect contained and the political crisis eventually sorted out, today the massive Palestinian factor intervenes to threaten the delicate and precarious Lebanese communal system. It adds tremendous weight to the existing Lebanese Muslim community. Moreover, if the Libyan inspired inflammatory articles in the Libyan-subvented Beirut paper, *al-Safir*, are any indication, the explosive situation in the Lebanon tends to attract the interference of the more extremist and less responsible Arab rulers. In addition, in the latest clashes, the Phalangist and Liberal Christian militia proved as well, if not better, armed and trained as their Palestinian adversaries. Then, suspicion between the two camps is deeper than ever before and, consequently, armed clashes could easily recur.

As long as Syria under Assad cooperates with the Cairo-Riyadh axis, Iran will counter it with a more intransigent stand associated with distant Libya. In view of the closer relations between Syria and Iraq with the Soviet Union, Cairo and Riyadh will seek to minimize their impact on inter-Arab relations. Until the spring of 1975, however, Iraq faced a separate problem with Iran on its eastern frontier in connection with the Kurds. Now that it has ostensibly composed its differences with Iran, it is assumed that it will play a more active role in inter-Arab affairs. If the recent dispute with Syria over Euphrates waters is any indication, it may not be too peaceful or constructive a role.

Typical of the volatile, unsettled inter-Arab relations in this connection has been the recent flare-up between the Damascus and Baghdad Baathis regimes. Reminiscent of their quarrel over pipeline oil transport nearly ten years ago, the dispute over the distribution, share-out, of Euphrates Dam waters was, incidentally, the epiphenomenal expression of deeper, more serious differences between them. The Iraqis had been, for some time, unhappy about arms supplies to the Kurdish *peshmerga* coming from across the Syrian border as late as February 1975. A complicating factor was the Iraqi suspicion that the Soviet Union may have been the source of these supplies, which increased Iraqi resentment already aroused by Soviet participation in the construction of the Euphrates Dam at Tabqa. The usual Iraqi inclination to attack any ruler in Damascus who had negotiated and accepted an accord, even a limited one of military disengagement, with Israel was a further point of friction. Meanwhile, President Assad's action in arresting several Iraqi Baathi political refugees in Damascus for allegedly passing to Baghdad versions of his secret deliberations with Dr. Kissinger leading to the May 1974 disengagement agreement with Israel on the Golan, increased the tension between the two regimes. Underlying all of these events was the long-standing suspicion and occasional feuding between Baghdad and Damascus dating from the nineteen twenties and particularly the nineteen fifties when the Baath, under whatever faction or military cabal, came to power.

A recent dimension of the Iraqi-Syrian "dispute" was provided by the rapprochement between Syria and Jordan, prompted by developments in the Arab-Israel conflict, namely, the second interim agreement between Egypt and Israel in Sinai. Iraq immediately expressed its hostility to the Syrian-Jordanian alignment. At the same time, Iraq, which is interested in greater revenue from its oil, has equally differed and disagreed with sister oil-producing Arab states over oil policy.

Generally, the Fertile Crescent will remain a contested area in the struggle for leadership not only between Iraq and Syria, but also between Egypt and Saudi Arabia. It might conceivably also become the center of confrontation, demarcating the boundaries of influence between the superpowers. With Syria, Jordan, and Lebanon contiguous to Israel, "the enemy of the Arabs," these states are exposed both to the vagaries of hostilities and the political gyrations of the "Arab policy" against Israel. They are relatively small countries. Consequently, wars can quickly reduce their respective size. In a way, they are seen by the major protagonists in the struggle for Arab leadership (Egypt and Saudi Arabia) as buffers between themselves and Israel. This is the meaning and true import of the appellation "confrontation states" used by the Arabs to denote the array of frontline states in the struggle with Israel. None of them enjoys the strategic depth and bulwark of a Sinai or Suez Canal.

The survival of the Fertile Crescent states so far has been due first, to the influence of foreign powers in the area, and second, to Arab factionalism in the struggle for leadership. Conversely, these states themselves, realizing that their survival depends on these extraneous forces played an appropriate role in both inter-Arab rivalry and the contest between the great powers.

The region will remain, for some time to come, a contested one among the Arabs, among indigenous movements for its unification, and between the powers. Israel for its part will seek to maintain its threat of an overwhelming military deterrent—and domination—over this immediate area.

Egypt

Although a part of the Arab east, Egypt in fact sits astride the two parts of the Arab world, the Arab east and Arab west. It must avoid isolation from either and must therefore be involved in the affairs of both. Its national state interests and security in fact dictate a regional role for Cairo in Arab politics. In the past, with a British connection, Egypt projected a leadership role in Arab affairs primarily through the Arab League. Later, with Soviet backing, Cairo was able to increase the intensity and widen the scope of its Arab role, albeit with indifferent, meager results.

In the east, Egypt has faced its rival, Saudi Arabia, both in the Fertile Crescent and South Arabia.[e] In the west, despite the so-called special relationship between Nasser and Algeria till the overthrow of Ben Bella in 1965, Egyptian interests require that it exert some influence over contiguous Libya, of failing that, prevent a powerful Maghrebi rival from exerting the same there. To this extent, Libya, under whatever regime, will be confined to a buffer role between the Maghreb and the Mushreq, and particularly in any rivalry between, say, Algeria and Egypt. Divided internally between east-oriented Cyrenaica and west-oriented Tripolitania and governed by a cabal of officers open to sedition, Libyan policy must balance itself on the tight rope linking the Arab west to the Arab east. This was, in fact, the case under the Sanussi monarchy, also. Neither Algeria nor Egypt would tolerate a Libya that is more than a buffer.

Unlike the Arab east, but like the Maghreb, Egypt must also consider its African periphery. This is especially relevant in relation to the Sudan, where an

---

[e]There are those who interpret the present Egyptian-Saudi alliance in part as one aimed against a possible Iraqi-Syrian constellation in the Fertile Crescent under Soviet influence.

Arabized political elite governs a vast country exposed to the dangers of separatist sedition by the non-Arab, non-Muslim south and its African hinterland.

Theoretically, Egyptian hegemony, at least over the eastern Arabs (e.g., the Fertile Crescent), and the attainment of primacy over the Arab region as a whole can be secured by an accommodation with Israel. One could argue that Egypt and Israel are the two states in that core area of the Middle East which might conceivably entertain "imperial" ambitions or designs. Without a permanent or final accommodation between them, one will always check and frustrate the other. As it is not possible, for the moment, for Egypt to proceed toward such an accommodation, it must be satisfied with an uneasy Saudi partnership in inter-Arab affairs. But this remains an insecure, shifting alliance. It has, moreover, engendered domestic political divisions in Egypt, between those in favor of the Saudi alliance (and by extension the American association), on one hand, and those against it, as well as the general resentment among Egyptians of oil-rich Arabs and their suspicion that the oil-rich Arab states are not forthcoming with the financial or economic assistance Egypt requires.

A dimension of this current split within Egypt is its exploitation by the weaker, though very rich, Libya. Colonel Qadhafi's Arab-Islamic ambitions aside, the steady deterioration of Egyptian-Libyan relations since 1973 is a result of this situation. The very recent irresponsible Soviet offer of arms and a nuclear reactor to Libya should also be viewed in this context. President Sadat's quick, vigorous attack on these developments underlines the tension between the two countries.

The dynamism of continuing local inter-Arab conflict has been, in fact, highlighted by the abrasive Libyan-Egyptian relationship. Mutual accusations and recriminations in the press of the two countries have not been elegant in thought or expression. Name-calling has been a common occurrence. Sadat was recently described in Libyan public print as the master, the one who thinks he is a twentieth century Caesar. Where is the money we have deposited in his banks? Can the Pasha face the people and tell them where he has hidden the money? He will not be able to do so because Cleopatra has spent it all on her dresses, on lavish wedding ceremonies for her daughters and on her trips to Europe. The Pasha then comes and accuses us of cutting off financial aid to Egypt. Of course we did, but only when we had become convinced that our money was going into special private pockets and into European bank accounts. The master should know that we know all about him and his kind and revealing the truth about their thefts and treacheries to the Arab masses we shut their mouths. Retorting in press interviews, Sadat referred to Qadhafi as a sick, unreliable man, possessed by the devil.

Meanwhile, in Egypt there has been a growing revulsion against other Arab states. This manifests itself both on the official, practical level and the popular, emotional one, and constitutes a new potential source of inter-Arab discord.

Thus, the parlous, depressing economic situation in the country is generating its own scapegoats and villains, from Nasser's disastrous promotion of a privileged "class" to the new rich Arabs of the Peninsula, the Gulf, and Libya. The Sadat regime appears to be trying to put the blame for its economic difficulties on the Nasser legacy. At the same time, members of the National Assembly, not without encouragement from the top, are arguing that whereas the October War raised the income of the Arab oil states from £15 billion to nearly £70 billion a year, over half of Arab investments have been going to the United Kingdom and the United States, another 45 percent to Western Europe and only a meager 5 percent to developing countries. They suspect oil-rich Arab states are reluctant to commit long-term investment in Egypt due to a combination of uncertainty about political conditions and fear of another war.

Among the general public, feelings of resentment against Saudi, Kuwaiti, Libyan, and other oil-rich visitors to their country run very high. Incidents reflecting this feeling occur daily in Egypt.

Inherent in the Arab alignments and realignments of the October War and its aftermath are the seeds of new, perhaps different, inter-Arab discord and conflict.

Generally, the economic needs of a populous, relatively advanced Egypt add to the urgency of its pursuit of a major role in inter-Arab relations. A popular view is that Egypt can, in fact, opt out of Arab affairs altogether. Theoretically, and on the face of it, this is a valid suggestion. Actually, events in 1975 seem to corroborate it. Validity, however, is not synonymous with practicality or the pressures of reality. Whether under the Pharoahs, one observes, or throughout the Muslim Fatimid, Mamluk or Albanian dynasty domination, Egypt has always had to engage from time to time in a regional policy.

Wider Considerations

I have already argued that since the October War the tendency in inter-Arab relations has been one of eschewing the old objective and ideology of Arab unity in favor of solidarity, based on the convergence of the interests of individual Arab states. This was manifested in the use of the oil weapon (the coordinated policies of Egypt, Saudi Arabia and Syria) against Israel, and against its European and American friends. Nevertheless, the most likely development in the immediate future will be one of the consolidation of several loci of Arab power, for example, Saudi Arabia in the Peninsula allied with Egypt for a while, Algeria in the Maghreb, and possibly Syria and/or Iraq in the Fertile Crescent. To this extent the whole area of inter-Arab relations and relations between Arab and non-Arab states in the Middle East, as well as with Europe and the superpowers, will remain dangerously problematic.

Relations between the Arab states will continue to carry the seeds of inter-Arab dissension and diversion over (1) the Arab-Israel conflict; (2) economic matters; (3) regional and subregional rivalries, and (4) relations with Europe and the superpowers. Equally critical will be the relations between Arab and non-Arab states in the Middle East. The controversy over oil prices, oil production, the confrontation between Iran and the Arab states in the Gulf, all of these matters constitute sources of tension and potential conflict. Recently, however, the dispute between Iran and Iraq over the Kurdish issue and other matters of difference between them have been at least formally—and temporarily—settled.

On March 6, 1975, Iran and Iraq signed an accord, which formally composed a number of long-standing differences between the two countries. The immediate effect of what soon came to be known as the Pact of Algiers was the collapse of the Kurdish insurgents once they lost their main source of support in Teheran. Thousands of hapless Kurdish refugees streamed across the border into Iran, or trekked further up into the wild heights of their mountain fastnesses.

For the Baath regime in Baghdad the advantages of the timely accord with Teheran were immediately visible and crucial. It freed their army from a costly endless struggle against a determined and tenacious adversary very much at home with irregular warfare. This alone was an attractive enough gain for the Iraqi regime to be willing to make several concessions to the Shah. But the Pact entails certain dangers that may still come to plague Baghdad in the future.

For many years, in addition to his support of the Kurdish irregulars, the Shah organized and financed several seditious elements, inside the Iraqi armed forces and among the vast numbers of the Shia community in Iraq. In the light of his policy in the Gulf, he has been concerned with military developments in Shatt al-Arab at the top of the Gulf. Meanwhile, he has been involved in Oman.

The Shah probably perceives the recent agreement with Iraq as helping him to accomplish several objectives. By sacrificing the Kurds, he believes he has acquired greater flexibility within Iraq through his sympathizers and "agents" among the Shia community. He may also feel that he is in a better position to curb, if not neutralize, Iraqi or Baath activities throughout the Gulf. While pressing the Iraqis, as well as embarrassing them, over the Soviet naval and air station facilities in Umm Qasr he can extract Iraqi recognition of an Iranian naval presence in Shatt al-Arab. Among the more concrete gains has been the agreement on interim steps in relation to some ten thousand former Iranian residents of Iraq who had been expelled. Even more significant has been the major concession the Shah extracted from Iraq by persuading that county to abandon its claim on the oil-rich province of Khuzistan, and so-called al-Ahwaz, in which lie the oil towns of Abadan and Ahwaz. There were some two million Arabs in the province when the British, after the Great War, attached it to Iran. Until then it had formed part of the Ottoman Empire and comprised parts of southwest Persia, south-east Iraq and a small part of Kuwait, and enjoyed "home rule" under Sheikh Khazaal's family. In 1960, the Iraqi ruler, Abdul Karim

Qasim, launched a campaign to liberate "Arabistan" as the Iraqis referred to the province, and formed the "Al Ahwaz National Popular Front." In 1969, Saddam Hussein, vice president of the Revolution Command Council, launched an active campaign of subversion in Khuzistan as the main thrust of Iraq's conflict with Iran. Nearly 6,000 Khuzistan Arabs were recruited and trained in Iraq. Financial help for the "freedom fighters" of Arabistan and Iraqi officers were infiltrated into the province. All of this was stopped by the Pact of Algiers.

Both Iran and Iraq believe that their accord frees them to better withstand the Soviet presence in Iraq and Syria. This is in line with the Shah's policy of closing the Gulf to the interference and/or presence of outside powers. Yet an indication of the attraction of this area for outside powers has been the alacrity with which the Shah of Iran followed up the Pact of Algiers by talks with the vice-prime minister of China, Li Hsien-nien. A joint declaration issued last April heavily tilted against the Soviet Union and the presence of all outside powers in the area.

The agreement between the two countries, however, is also a source of inter-Arab differences. Syria and Libya, for example, have been more sympathetic than other Arab states toward the Ahwaz National Popular Front and its solicitation of Arab support. That is, they have been critical of Iraq's accommodation with a non-Arab regional power that has clear ambitions in the Gulf and the region as a whole.

Israel and Iran might still find it convenient to combine in a common anti-Arab cause. Even though Iran has not extended even de facto recognition to Israel, the contacts and cooperation between them have been extensive, not to mention the oil supplies Israel received from Iran via tanker to Eilat. The Arabs, incidentally, already allude to this Iran-Israel collaboration, and have from time to time alleged the existence of a United States-Israel plan, in collusion with Iran, to frustrate Arab objectives.

Similarly, Israel enjoys formal relations with another non-Arab Middle Eastern state, Turkey. The confrontation between Greece and Turkey in the Eastern Mediterranean, whether over oil rights in the Aegean, or over Cyprus, so close to the Middle East conflict, is worrisome. The Greeks and Arab states have already bargained and horse-traded with each other over their respective conflicts. One cannot, therefore, rule out completely a greater involvement of Turkey and Iran in Arab regional affairs.

The United States and Inter-Arab Relations

Essentially, the United States seeks to:

1. prevent the Middle East from becoming the exclusive sphere of influence of its rival superpower, the Soviet Union; for that would immediately threaten its interests in the security of Europe (NATO), the Gulf, Africa and the Indian Ocean;

2. maintain an influence in the region which will

    a. guarantee the flow of oil to the West,
    b. guarantee the integrity and independence of all states in the area,
    c. provide an outlet for U.S. economic activity (development investment, trade and commerce),
    d. exercise via bilateral agreements with Middle Eastern states some control over the use and impact of their huge reserves on the international monetary system.

3. Maintain the strategic role of the U.S. Sixth Fleet in the Mediterranean which is still the main American deterrent in southern Europe and the Middle East.

The United States must pursue the above objectives and protect these interests for the next few years in the following context of inter-Arab relations:

1. The center of wealth, if not economic power strictly speaking, in the Arab Middle East has shifted from its core to the peripheries: Arabia and the Gulf in the East; Libya and Algeria in the West;

2. The fact that there has never been and there is not now a monolithic political entity called the "Arab Middle East," and the United States must not approach it as such. Rather the tendency is for the existence of several, competing loci of Arab power, and a preference among Arab states for bilateral arrangements with each other and with outside powers. Joint or collective Arab policies toward others is predicated on the convergence of the respective interests of the several states;

3. The more permanent, even constant, sources of inter-Arab conflict remain. There are, as indicated, different interests and perceptions which both historically and existentially separate, and divide, say, the Arab east from the Arab west, Saudi Arabia from Egypt or the Fertile Crescent. All of these factors remain important for the region's future evolution. Added to these today are agreements and disagreements among Arab states over, for instance, the role of the United States in their region and their relations to it. They are all reconciled to the fact that the United States will compete for influence in the Middle East against the Soviet Union, and that it will furthermore work to prevent Russian domination of it. The weaker among the Arab States, perhaps all these states, are not inimical to the American interest of safeguarding the independence and integrity of all states in the area. The disagreement arises both with the United States and among themselves over whether this principle should also apply to Israel. There is sharp disagreement between them over American economic activity in their region. This, however, flows partly from their disparate respective interests and varied relations with patron powers or superpowers. Considering the central position of Saudi-Egyptian collaboration to the area presently, American attention, in its political and economic manifestations, to these two countries seems for the moment wise.

4. Arrangements are still made with rulers and regimes open to sedition and coups. This condition in itself renders relations between Arab states, as well as between them and external powers, especially difficult. Because of it, too, Arab power remains vulnerable, though difficult to assess, and its potential effectiveness unpredictable. So far it has manifested and expressed itself through the use of the oil weapon in connection with the conflict with Israel. The Arabs, that is, succeeded in making America's major interest the guarantee of the flow of oil from the Middle East to the West contingent upon a reconsideration of her relations with the Arab states as opposed to Israel. The weaker West Europeans, heavily dependent on Middle East oil, appear to have bowed to Arab pressure.

5. In the event that Western dependence on Middle Eastern oil over the next five years is not appreciably reduced, and there is a resumption of Arab-Israeli hostilities, the Arabs may well use the oil weapon again. In those circumstances it is likely that Italy in Europe will collapse, and Britain could come close to the brink. If such an eventuality occurs, the United States may have to consider a role for itself other than that of peacemaker—not for the defense and preservation of Israel, but for the protection of the Western Alliance in Europe. In this connection, it is fair to suggest that any superpower deals with the Middle East not because of its intrinsic local value, but because of the superpower's concern with the defense of Europe, as well as its interests in the Indian Ocean.

6. The Arab-Israel conflict is only one of several conflicts and potential conflicts in the region. Developments in the Gulf may entail some conflict between Arabs locally, and regionally between Arabs and Iranians. These may attract some form and level of superpower intervention. The rebellious, unsettled regions of South Arabia already command the attention of China and the Soviet Union. Related to developments there is the prospect of conflict over the control of the Horn of Africa and the Indian Ocean.

In the Arab Middle East, inter-Arab relations themselves remain a labyrinth of intricate and often irreconcilable elements. In the past, as a rule, divisions, differences, and local conflicts were contained within and under an imperial arrangement. Today, in the absence of such an arrangement, local states which can dispose of wealth can generate more deadly conflict, dangerous not only to the region's stability but also to that of the rest of the world. Aware of the rivalry between the two superpowers, the Arab states today believe they can "win" because neither the United States nor the USSR can impose its will or *pax* over them. Is this, however, the case?

I believe that the resolution of the Arab-Israel conflict will not solve the Arab-Jewish antithesis and enmity in the Middle East. The Soviet Union, one is told, does not need Middle East oil; the West desperately does. How far is the Soviet Union prepared to risk an armed confrontation with the West merely in order to deny the latter access to oil it, itself, does not need?

In October 1973, the United States embarked upon the arduous and delicate role of peacemaker in the Middle East. It faces a monumental task of juggling all the dispárate and competing elements of the Arab and Middle Eastern reality. Its basic assumption, at least in dealing with the Arab-Israel conflict, is that at some point peace will be concluded between the Arab states and an independent sovereign Israel. I have tried in this chapter to emphasize the dubious validity of this assumption, and, therefore, the fragility of the whole enterprise. America's partners in détente may refuse to cooperate fully in the task of peace-making in the Middle East. Recently, they have loudly publicized their support for the PLO even after Arafat's uncompromising speech in the United Nations. Meanwhile, they seem, on the face of it at least, about to recover their "losses" in Egypt with a military presence of sorts in Libya. The old advantages of shore base facilities for the Soviet fleet in Mersa Matruh and Bernis may soon be reproduced in Libya. In addition, they continue to chip away relentlessly at the strategic corners and peripheries of Western defense arrangements in the Mediterranean basin. They procrastinate over the Geneva Conference, while they press, for instance, the Egyptians over their loan repayments.

Reported American economic arrangements with some Arab states alone, regardless of how ingenious, guarantee very little, if anything at all. The question therefore is, in view of these difficulties and possible complications in peace-making, what other options does America have and is prepared to take in defense of its interests in the Middle East?

Optimists today insist that the newly-acquired respectability of the PLO will breed eminent reasonableness in Yassir Arafat; that with the assistance of other Arab states he will prevail over his detractors and enemies—the "rejection" front—within the movement. They hope that all of this will eventually lead to his coming to terms with Israel, settling for a state of sorts somewhere on the West Bank and/or Jordan and the Gaza Strip. What is often overlooked is the fact that before any of this can take place, Jordanian action over the Palestinians will infuse new elements of inter-Arab conflict. Also, civil strife among Palestinians on the West Bank is already in evidence. There are, furthermore, too many loose gunmen about. Moderation and compromise on the part of Arafat may place him in what I would call an "Abdullah role" regarding the Palestine question. Immediately when that happens, his life will be exposed to the bullet.

Even if the Palestinians acquire a state on the West Bank and Gaza, it is perhaps, on present evidence, too much to hope that, because it is viable only on the basis of a close economic-political relationship with Israel and Jordan, it will live in peace with its Jewish neighbor. It could conceivably invite a Soviet presence in whatever guise in the hope of realizing its goal of a "secular democratic Palestinian state," i.e., one that will take the place of Israel.

One thing is certain in the immediate future. To settle or not to settle with Israel, and what kind of settlement it should be, will become a central issue of discord and dissension among the Arab states. The rumblings in Egypt already surveyed are only one indication of this. In April 1975, a leading Egyptian journalist, Muhammad Sid Ahmad, who is considered to be a Marxist, published a book, *After the Guns Have Been Silenced.*[7] In it, he makes the bold, extraordinary and, among the Arabs first and singular, proposal that the Arabs must now come to terms with Israel, and permit it a developmental role in the region, implying the Israelis with their knowledge, skills, and advanced technology can contribute greatly to the development of Arab societies. *Al-Hawadith* (issue of March 30, 1975), a Beirut weekly, probably subvented by the Kuwaitis and Saudis, published a scathing, blistering attack on the book and its author, rejecting his proposals and implying that they constitute treason.

President Sadat, on the other hand, has contended since the October War that that war proved finally and conclusively that the Arab-Israel conflict cannot be resolved by war. The reason is that the superpowers will not permit the local adversaries to settle their conflict by war. What President Sadat wishes to convey to the world is that his country is now committed to the search for peace. This may sound logical, but it cannot be taken as the reflection or expression of an everlasting reality. If, according to Sadat, Egyptian and Arab strategy is not to surrender "an inch of Arab land" and not to compromise over or negotiate away the rights of the Palestinians (as yet undefined), the tactics of peace-making, buying time, or whatever, about which Arabs can differ and quarrel with each other, relate only to current conditions. Conditions, alas, may change in the next five or ten years.

For the foreseeable future, inter-Arab differences and conflict will continue, whether over Israel, the piecemeal or the Geneva Conference approach to a settlement, over natural, economic, and financial resources, over Islamic or less native views of the world, over communal, sectarian, and ethnic matters. This is a feature of the area that will remain more or less a *constant.* The question of American choices or options in the future, therefore, is one that must first of all be resolved on the basis of this fundamental reality: inter-Arab relations cannot be placed on a spectrum of linear development, moving from hell to paradise or vice versa. Rather their course is partly cyclical, partly jerkily spiral, and always resting occasionally at some "grey" area. Secondly, American choices must be made on the assumption that what the Arabs want or desire is not always—if ever—what Americans desire; in fact, the two desires may be diametrically opposed and radically different. Finally, if the Arab Middle East is important to the United States for the security of Europe, NATO, and the Western Alliance, as a source of energy supplies and their transport, trade routes, and communications in the Mediterranean and Indian Ocean, then the only choice Americans can really have is to maintain their strategic (military and political) capability in the area. This capability, whatever its detractors say, was amply demonstrated in 1971 in connection with the Jordan-Syria clash. Alas, in a conflict-ridden area even a superpower as technologically advanced as the United States still needs to consider—and respect—some of the unfashionable strategic concepts and practices of the nineteenth century. Often, one has the distinct impression that America's rival superpower seems to consider them.

Notes

1. Here only an outline of these patterns and trends is presented. For a more detailed exposition of the events illustrating these trends, I refer the reader to my *Conflict in the Middle East* (George Allen & Unwin, 1971), in particular Chapters 2, 4, 5-6, and 8.

2. In explaining why Nasser broke with the Syrian Baath leadership during the Union (1958-1961), Muhammad Hasanein Heikal suggested, among other reasons, that Nasser could not very well allow a member of one of the minorities (i.e., Michel Aflaq, a Christian Arab) to govern a predominantly Muslim country like Syria. See Fuad Matar, *Bisaraha an Abdel Nasser: hiwar ma Muhammad Heikal* (Frankly Speaking about Abdel Nasser: a dialogue with Muhammad Heikal) Beirut, 1975.

3. See Mohamed Heikal, *The Road to Ramadan* (London, 1975) and General Salah el-Din al-Hadidi, *Shadid aba harb '67* (Witness to the war of '67) Beirut, 1974.

4. Ibid.

5. Organizational Directive of the ASU Secretariat, August 1972. Reproduced in Fuad Matar, *Nasserite Russia and Egyptian Egypt* (Arabic), Beirut 1972, pp. 196-201.

6. Generally on the shambles of economic development (planning, investment, savings, industrialization), see the devastating monograph by the Egyptian economist Galal A. Amin, *The Modernization of Poverty, The Political Economy of Nine Arab States, 1945-1970* (Leiden, Brill, 1974).

7. Muhammad Sid Ahmad, *After the Guns Have Been Silenced* (Beirut: Dar al-Qadaya, 1975).

VII Religion and Secular Nationalism in the Arab World

Elie Kedourie

In their overwhelming majority, the Arabs are Muslim. This, of course, is no more than a truism to which it would be superfluous to draw attention, but for the fact that its consequences in Arab society and politics, fundamental and far-reaching as they undoubtedly are, have been widely neglected, or even utterly forgotten in the West. It is interesting in the context of this chapter, to explain how this happened. It was during and after the First World War that the Arabs appeared once more on the stage of world politics. They appeared to do so as seceders from the Ottoman Empire. This empire was the last great Muslim state in the world. When its rulers joined the war on the side of the central powers, they appealed to and tried to make use of Islamic loyalties. Success here would have put a formidable weapon in their hands to use against the British and the French who, in India, Egypt, the Sudan and North Africa, and elsewhere, ruled over large numbers of Muslims. It was, therefore, to the interest of the allies to play down or to counteract the appeal to Islamic sentiments. One way of doing this was by encouraging dissidence and rebellion against the Ottomans by their own muslim subjects. By establishing contact with, and encouraging the Sharif of Mecca to rise against his Ottoman suzerains, the British succeeded—or so they thought—in dividing Muslim ranks and in neutralizing the Ottoman call to a holy war against the infidel. Thus the rising of Husayn, the Sharif of Mecca, was represented by himself, and even more so by his British patrons, as an Arab national movement, a wholesome assertion of the claims of Arab nationality against the reactionary pernicious and sinister attractions of Pan-Islamism.

The fear of Pan-Islamism on the part of Britain and France was nothing new. It dated, in fact, from the reign of Sultan Abd al-Hamid II (1876-1909). As the evidence shows, it was an idea widely and firmly held in Europe that Abd al-Hamid sat at the center of an intricate web of intrigue and conspiracy with tentacles all over the world of Islam. The evidence also shows that such a conspiracy did not exist. What did exist was a very deep feeling of Islamic solidarity, a vivid sense of the Muslim world as a world on its own, standing over against the non-Muslim world. This feeling manifested itself now and again, whenever Muslims were in distress, or their existence or way of life threatened by non-Muslims. Examples abound. The Italian attack on the Ottoman province of Tripoli in 1911 evoked a widespread and active feeling of sympathy by Muslims for their fellow-Muslims who were the latest subject of European-Christian aggression. Another manifestation of the same Muslim feeling of solidarity is not so well known, but perhaps even more significant. In the same year as the Italian attack on Tripoli, a group of Muslims from Setif in eastern Algeria, and another from Tlemcen in western Algeria decided, separately, that they could not bear to live under non-Muslim rule. They abandoned their homes and immigrated to the Ottoman Empire. The precise discontents which led to such a decision are not at issue here; what is remarkable is the character of the decision itself, namely that Muslims in difficulty sought a solution to their problems in taking up abode in the domain of Islam, however distant it was, and however uncertain their material prospects there.

This overriding feeling of Islamic solidarity somehow came increasingly to be depreciated and indeed forgotten during and after the First World War. Such oblivion, as has been said, suited the Allies. But there was more to it than a deliberate playing down of dangerous beliefs and attitudes. British officials in particular genuinely thought that Arab nationalism was opposed to, and would thus weaken, what they called Pan-Islamism. This was not the least reason for encouraging the Sharif's rebellion and spreading the gospel of a future independent Arab state. The notion that Arabism and Islam were opposites was spread by Arab nationalists. These, at the outset, were mostly officers who had deserted from the Ottoman army. Their training and education had Westernized them more or less profoundly; they were accustomed—like their young Turk fellow-officers—to the categories of contemporary European political discourse, and had adopted Western political ideals—first and foremost that of nationalism. In nationalism, as is well-known, the primordial value is the nation, and not, say, class or religion. The Arab nationalists therefore sincerely proclaimed that their aim was to establish an Arab nation-state in which Muslims, Christians, and Jews would enjoy equal citizenship. These nationalists were also aware that their Western patrons and protectors looked with fear and aversion on Islam as a political force, and they emphasized therefore all the more the opposition between Arabism and Islam.

It was between the wars that the theory of Arab nationalism was endowed with a body of theoretical literature, and began to make real headway in the schools and colleges from whence the official classes—whether civilian or military—were recruited. As propounded then by its most influential theoretician, Sati al-Husri, the doctrine of Arab nationalism clearly differentiated between loyalty to Arabism and loyalty to Islam, and it was in no doubt that the former ought to have the primacy over the latter. But this aspect of the doctrine did not occasion a great debate. The younger generations who were becoming enthusiastic Arab nationalists did not feel that there was anything in the circumstances of the Arab world which required a confrontation between Arabism and Islam: the struggle for Arab independence and unity—a struggle directed against European-Christian powers and against Zionism—was in no way weakened or harmed by Islam, or any Islamic figures or institutions. One can even go further and say that Islam actually gave great strength to Arab nationalism. This is because the Arab world is overwhelmingly Muslim, and Arab nationalist leaders, Muslims almost to a man, naturally attracted to themselves the powerful feelings of loyalty and solidarity towards their leaders which Islam has instilled in its followers. Whether these nationalist leaders practiced their religion, or were indifferent to it did not affect the issue. And the situation was the same all over the Arab world: in Iraq and the Levant as well as in the Maghrib.

On the level of practical politics, then, not only was there no opposition between Islam and Arabism, there was actual cooperation. But this cooperation was not formulated or incorporated in the doctrine of Arab nationalism until after the Second World War. This development may be seen as a dialectical one, arising out of the very doctrine of Arab nationalism as originally formulated. The doctrine insisted, as has been seen, on the primacy of Arabism, on there being a historic Arab nation, now dismembered and subject to alien rule, but entitled—and destined—to full independence and unity. It was therefore necessary for the doctrine to seek out and describe the lineaments of this nation; the doctrine, in other words, had to rely heavily—as other nationalist doctrines have commonly done—on a historical mode of argument. But to define the Arab nation in terms of its history is—sooner rather than later—to come upon the fact that Islam originated among the Arabs, was revealed in Arabic to an Arab prophet. Great significance must be attached to this tremendous fact. The ideologies of Arabism drew in the main two consequences which, in spite of their difference of emphasis, yet produced a new theoretical amalgam in which Islam and Arabism became inseparable.

Thus, Ba'thist doctrine, as articulated by its most influential exponent, the Damascene Greek Orthodox Dr. Michel Aflaq, held that Muhammad the Prophet of Islam was also *ipso facto* the founder of the Arab nation, and was to be venerated as such by every Arab nationalist, whether Muslim or not. Aflaq developed the views in a lecture of 1943, in which he declared that Islam "represented the ascent of Arabism towards unity, power, and progress." In such a perspective, we may say, Islam is seen as the product and expression of the Arab national genius. Another theorist, the Baghdadi Muslim Dr. Abd al-Rahman al-Bazzaz argued somewhat differently. In an influential not to say seminal lecture of 1952, Bazzaz categorically stated that the apparent contradiction between Islam and Arab nationalism which is still present in the minds of many people is due to misunderstanding, misrepresentation and misinterpretation. He eloquently showed how Islam appeared in an Arab environment, was revealed to an Arab, and embodied the best Arab values. Islam was certainly a universal religion, but it is the religion of the Arab *par excellence.* The position of the Arabs in Islam, he said, was like that of the Russians in the Communist world, i.e., it was a special and privileged position. There could in no way be a contradiction between Islam and Arabism: "the Muslim Arab, when he exalts his heroes, partakes of two emotions, that of the pious Muslim and that of the proud nationalist." We can even go further, and affirm that Islam and Arabism largely overlap; and where they do not, they are not in opposition. More, Arabism exalts the original Arab values which obtained at the time of Muhammad, and in doing so it purifies Islam which had become tainted with foreign corruption, and restores its true essence.

Thus the ideology of Arab nationalism which was fashioned during and immediately after the Second World War, and which holds the field today, in one way or another, affirms a fundamental unbreakable link between Islam and Arabism. In doing this, it articulates the unspoken assumptions of Muslim Arab nationalists, and chimes in with their feelings and practical experiences. This articulation and codification into a doctrine in turn fortifies such feelings and justifies experience, so to speak, by philosophy. But there are other reasons why Islam has come to the fore today in the politics and the political discourse of the Arab world.

We may first mention the influence of the Muslim Brethren. This organization began in 1928 in a small way in Isma'iliyya—on the Suez Canal—where its founder Hasan al-Banna was a schoolteacher. To start with, the Brethren were not concerned with politics. Banna conceived it as his mission to reclaim to Islam and a self-respecting mode of life those Muslim multitudes who had been banished to the margin of society and become spiritually disoriented through the ravages of Westernization and Western forms of economic enterprise. In a very short while, the Brethren gathered a large and devoted following. But they did not long persist in showing a lack of interest in politics. If, as they believed, the ills of Egyptian society all stemmed from the abandonment of Islam, the cure for these ills, it followed, lay in the reestablishment of the original pure Islamic order. The very dialectic of their doctrine thus led the Muslim Brethren to become a political enterprise dedicated to changing the political and constitutional arrangements which then obtained in Egypt. The Brethren had a following not only among the unsophisticated, unlettered masses, but also among students, officials, and junior officers, who were themselves highly discontented with the political corruption and maladministration which was rife in Egypt under the monarchy. It is significant that some of the Free Officers who carried out the *coup d'état* of 1952 were Muslim Brethren. Some ten years or so after its foundation, the movement was well on the way to becoming a formidable political power to be reckoned with in Egypt, and between 1945 and 1952 it is estimated that it had about half-a-million members and about another half-a-million sympathizers.

The doctrine of the Muslim Brethren was in principle applicable not only to Egypt or the Arab countries, but to all the world of Islam. If they contributed to what is now the prevailing consensus about the connection between Islam and Arabism, this came about as a result of their stand on the Palestine question. From the establishment of the British mandate in Palestine the strategy of the Palestine Arab leaders—who were of course Muslim in their great majority—was to denounce Zionism as a threat not only to Palestine, but to Arabism and Islam. By thus widening the conflict they hoped—quite rationally—to strengthen their own hands against the Zionists and their British sponsors. From the nineteen-thirties, in fact, Palestine and the Zionist threat to which it was subjected became a leading preoccupation of the Pan-Arab leaders in Iraq and the Levant. The threat was to Palestine as part of the Arab nation, but of course it was equally and simultaneously a threat to Palestine as part of the domain of Islam.

The Palestine issue did not, in the nineteen-thirties, engage very much the attention of the Egyptian political leaders. This was to come later, when the Arab league was established in Cairo under Egyptian leadership and King Faruq aspired to the leadership of the Arab world. Even so official Egypt remained cooler and less impassioned over Palestine than the Arab leaders of Iraq and the Levant, and in fact up to the very end of the British mandate in May 1948 Egypt kept on insisting that it would not intervene. The Muslim Brethren, on the contrary, were from the nineteen-thirties steadfast champions of the Arabs of Palestine, and it was their writings, processions, and speeches against the Zionist peril in 1945-1948 which awoke the Egyptian mass to the merits of this Arabo-Muslim cause and made them its fervent supporters. In addition it was the Muslim Brethren who took the initiative in organizing military help for the Palestinians, before the Egyptian army was ordered to intervene in the conflict. If Arabism became a popular cause in Egypt it was thus very much through the agency of the Brethren. In Egypt, therefore, Arabism and Islam were from the start very much associated with one another, both in theory and in practice: Palestine, which effectively involved Egypt in Arabism was simultaneously and inextricably both an Arab cause and a Muslim cause.

During Nasser's long dominance in Egypt the Brethren were generally under a cloud, because they came into conflict with the *Ra'is*, and because Nasser encouraged, for a variety of reasons, an official ideology of so-called Arab Socialism which deliberately eschewed appeal to Islamic sentiments, and the use of an Islamic vocabulary or Islamic concepts. But this official ideology remained merely official, something which everybody knew to emanate from the government, and which was dead, which did not have the power to touch the feelings or move people to act. During Nasser's eighteen years the Brethren were a proscribed body, but it is estimated that they had something like a quarter-of-a-million or three hundred thousand secret adherents. The figure seems by no means an exaggeration, for the Brethren appealed to that Islamic solidarity which is perhaps the most profound instinct of the people, and they thus constituted a hidden but powerful current.

Though the Brethren have still not been allowed to operate publicly as an organization, under Nasser's successor the Islamic theme in Egyptian public life has come very much to the surface. Sadat himself seems to have more religious fervor than his predecessor, and his regime seems to have no qualms about openly appealing to the traditional Islamic sentiments. Two apposite and striking examples may be given. In April 1972, Sadat gave an address in the mosque of Imam Husayn in Cairo on the anniversary of the Prophet's birthday. His theme was the fight against Israel, and the necessity to be patient and to stand fast against the enemy who will, inevitably, be defeated. Such a theme is by no means original. Arab leaders have devoted countless speeches to it over the years, but what is remarkable about Sadat's speech is that it is couched wholly in religious terms, and appeals entirely to the hallowed themes of Muhammad's life and career. America and Israel have forgotten, he says, that we are the bearers of Muhammad's message; they have forgotten that in spite of persecution Muhammad never surrendered; "he fought bravely, he stood fast and resisted until the message of truth, the message of faith, the message of Islam was realized, and its standard was raised aloft at the end of twenty-three years." Today "we are bearers of the same creed, we are the bearers and trustees of the message. . . . We believe that God, exalted be He, is with us, we believe that right is on our side." Sadat exhorted his listeners to be patient, as is enjoined on the believer, and when the time comes to vindicate their honor in battle: to liberate not only their land, but also Jerusalem, the first *qibla* (i.e., the place towards which the Muslim turns at prayer) and the third *haram* (Holy Place). About Jerusalem there can be no bargaining: "it is not the property of an individual, but the property of us all, of the Islamic *umma*." Jerusalem will be retrieved "from those of whom our Book has said that submissiveness and humility is their portion." With these people there can be no direct negotiation, since in their relations with the Prophet at Medina they showed themselves to be "vile, untrustworthy and treacherous."

Another document is even more significant than this speech in exhibiting the political vocabulary and arguments by means of which the present Egyptian regime seeks to establish a *rapport* with the people and involve them in its purposes. This is a small booklet entitled, *Our Religious Faith is our Path to Victory.* This booklet was printed in a million copies in the summer of 1973 and distributed to all Egyptian soldiers, obviously in preparation for the coming war. In itself a booklet of this kind is nothing out of the ordinary. All armies find it essential to indoctrinate their soldiers, teach them the virtues of discipline and obedience, and the necessity of surmounting fear on the battlefield, as well as the allurements of enemy propaganda. What is remarkable about this Egyptian booklet is the manner in which it seeks to attain this end. It does this exclusively by quotations from the Koran and the Traditions of the Prophet, by recalling Muhammad's record and the early Islamic conquests. There is hardly any reference to Arabism as such, or to the Zionist or Israeli enemies. The cause is Islam, the example is the Prophet and his Companions, and the Jews are the enemies, the very same Jews whom Muhammad had to fight. The relevant section here is entitled: "Good Tidings of Victory over our Enemies the Jews." The good tidings consist of citations from the Koran where the Jews are cursed for their transgression, denounced for their hostility to the believers and threatened with punishment here and hereafter. *Jihad* is recalled as a Muslim's duty the accomplishment of which is rewarded with Paradise, and the military virtues which *Jihad* necessitates are extolled as peculiarly Islamic virtues which the Arabs have learned in "the school of Islam." Islam, the booklet says "praises the believer who is strong, and considers him more useful and better in the sight of God than a believer who is [physically] weak." Islam, again, exhorts the Muslim to be prepared to encounter his enemy: the Prophet is quoted as saying that "Whoever learnt the Koran and then forgot it is not one of us, and whoever learnt shooting and forgot it is not one of us"; the Prophet, the booklet also recalls, approved the use of mosques as military training grounds.

In short, then, the cause for which the soldiers are to do battle is preeminently an Islamic cause, and the military virtues are preeminently Islamic virtues. The whole doctrine of the booklet may be summed up in the Koranic verse that God has made the Arabs as the best among nations (*umma wasatann*), which the booklet quotes and follows with the comment that God in his wisdom has designed Muhammad's *umma* to be an *umma* given to holy war, to be impregnable and not submissive or acquiescing in humiliation. Arabism and Islam are coeval or, rather, Islam is the soul of Arabism.

Such a view is now all the more influential because of a shift in the political center of gravity in the Arab world. In the last decade or so, the income derived from the oil of the Arabian peninsula has greatly increased the weight of Saudi Arabia, and even of Kuwait and the United Arab Emirates, in Arab politics. The rulers of these countries, much less exposed to European influences and modes of thought, take for granted the equation of Islam and Arabism: for them, and indeed for their subjects, one would be meaningless without the other; Islamic pride blends completely here with the feeling of Arab tribal superiority. This enhancement of the importance of the Arabian Peninsula could not but influence the tone of Arab nationalist ideology, and reinforce the tendencies manifested in the writings of Bazzaz, the propaganda of the Muslim Brethren, and the political rhetoric favored by the present Egyptian regime.

Yet other developments contribute to strengthen this current. One such is the character and influence of the Algerian regime. Owing to the circumstances in which Algeria attained independence in 1962, the regime enjoys particular prestige. Rightly or wrongly, the Algerian revolutionaries now in power are believed to have defeated France, a major military power, on the field of battle, and to have thus put an end to one hundred and thirty years of European colonization and settlement which, up to 1954, seemed utterly solid and unassailable. During the first three years of independent Algeria, under Ben Bella, the ideology of the regime was European in its vocabulary and categories, a mixture of Marxism and nationalism which the writings of Frantz Fanon best exemplify. A great change came with the assumption of power by Boumedienne who, besides overthrowing Ben Bella, effected a radical break with the ideology by which the National Liberation Front [Front Liberation National, (FLN)] had captured so many sympathies in France and elsewhere in the Western world.

Nothing indicates the change better than the fact that Fanon, more popular than ever in the West, has been allowed to fall into oblivion in Algeria. Boumedienne's regime appeals precisely to that amalgam of Arabism and Islam which we have seen so prevalent elsewhere in the Arab world, and which strikes a sympathetic chord in a Muslim population for whom the French settler was indeed a greedy and oppressive conqueror but, above all, the Christian enemy who had tried—and failed—to humiliate Islam, if not to destroy it. These Islamic loyalties and reflexes, thus given a new lease of life, will operate in such a way as to anchor in the popular mind a traditional interpretation of current conflicts: the anti-imperialist struggle becomes an extension of the centuries-old struggle against Christendom, and the war against Zionism and Israel a continuation of the Prophet's war against the Jews of Medina.

Besides Boumedienne's Algeria, another Arab country, Libya, has recently come to play a prominant part in inter-Arab politics, and its influence has weighted the balance further in favor of existing tendencies. The *coup d'état* of September 1969 brought to power, in Qadhafi and his fellow-officers, a group fervently imbued with the ideals of Pan-Arabism, the glamourous champion of which during their formative years had been Nasser. But unlike their hero, the present rulers of Libya very strongly emphasize the Islamic roots of Arabism, and the inseparable connection between the two. So emphatically has Qadhafi, in particular, expressed himself about this, that he has aroused general hilarity abroad. People have been amused by Qadhafi's intention to give what are generally considered outmoded and obscurantist Koranic prescriptions the force of law, by his seemingly naive admonitions to Jews and Christians to hearken to God's word as revealed to Muhammad, and by his impetuous, flamboyant, and apparently childish attempts to bring about instant Arab unity.

It is true, of course, that Koranic prescriptions are not exactly adapted to the needs of the modern world, that there is very little chance of Christians and Jews meekly accepting the status to which Islam destines them, and that popular marches from Tripoli to Cairo are no more than a stunt. But it would be a great mistake to conclude from all this that Quadhafi is, therefore, only a figure of fun and of no consequence in the Arab world. For, after all, should it be forgotten that it was the Libyan revolutionary regime which, together with Algeria, first decisively routed the Western oil companies, thus starting the process which led to the present turmoil in the international oil market? Again, the exact detail of Qadhafi's proposals and suggestions does not really much matter; what will impress a great multitude of his fellow-Muslims and fellow-Arabs is their insistence on the abiding validity—and indeed superiority—of Islam, and the claim that, as a prominent member of the regime, Bashir Hawadi, put it, "Arabism is a body and Islam is the living soul which moves this body."

This statement was made in the course of a popular meeting which took place in Tripoli in October 1972. The meeting was organized in order to expound what Qadhafi has called his Third Theory. The theory claims to provide an alternative to Marxism and liberalism or capitalism, which are declared to be equally bankrupt. On examination, the Third Theory turns out to be based on Islam and Arabism and, in spite of a lame attempt to assert its universal value, to be really addressed to the Arabs, whose allegiance to Islam is taken to be part of the natural order of things. Thus, in a speech of October 1971, Qadhafi declared:

The revolution of the Arab Libyan people represents something deep and well-rooted in the region. It is a new chapter in the evolution of the struggle of our Arab nation and of the Arab revolution. It affirms the established and individual character of the heritage of our nation, holds fast to Arabism and Islam, resurrects those values and principles which are most alive in them, and proclaims that the Arab nation is one nation having its place in the world and its role in the civilization of humanity.

At the meeting of October 1972, Hawadi affirmed: "In our belief, the Arab personality must be founded on a total commitment to belief in God and in Islamic values." And, at the same meeting Jallud, the prime minister ended his speech by saying that, "Arab unity, in so far as it constitutes a strength for the Arabs, is also a strength for Islam: this is something fundamental."

This insistence on the intimate connection between Arabism and Islam must be considered as the most prominent feature of Arab nationalist ideology today, one which may well prove lasting and tenacious. Its effect on the Arab world cannot but be far-reaching. In appealing to, and strengthening traditional Islamic sentiment, it will help reverse a trend which had been prominent in the Middle East since the nineteenth century, when Middle Eastern leaders like the Khedive Isma'il aspired that their countries should henceforth be part of European civilization—in their eyes the only civilization properly so called. This is scarcely now the case, and will be even less so when the effects of ideological indoctrination will have fully worked themselves through Arab society. A paradoxical situation will then arise. Though communication between the Arab world and the outside will be easier and speedier than ever, yet intellectual or spiritual intercourse will be more difficult, more hedged about with controls and restrictions than in the last one hundred and fifty years; the Arab and the non-Arab world ending up by becoming, once more, like medieval Islam and Christendom, opaque and unintelligible to one another.

Nor are the reasons for such isolation far to seek. They are the outcome of those technical innovations borrowed from the scientific and industrial civilization of the West. Today, the state in most of the Arab world exercises strict centralized control over education, publishing, and the press. Its hold over broadcasting and television is complete. It is, therefore, in a position to control what the young are taught and what citizens are told about public affairs in their own country and in the world at large. This comparatively new development has meant a prodigious reinforcement of the dominant political tradition in Islam, namely that of passive obedience to the ruler. But it does not follow from this, or from the undoubted fact—illustrated above—that Islam is, once again, politically to the fore both in theory and practice, that what we see is a simple reassertion of traditional values and attitudes. Tradition, rather, serves to clothe an ideology somewhat remote from the traditional worldview of the mass of Muslims. This ideology, which many Arab rulers obviously find attractive, has to do with "socialism," "social justice," and "democracy." Such notions are quite remote from, not to say alien to, the political tradition of Islam, as well as to the preoccupations of the mass of traditionally-minded Muslims. There is, thus, here a gap between the ideas and purposes of rulers and those of the ruled, which the traditional Islamic political vocabulary and rhetoric may possibly hide but cannot bridge.

The formulation of this ideology varies from regime to regime, but it may be conveniently summarized here by a sentence which occurs in the foreword of the work expounding Qadhafi's Third Theory, which has been recently published. "Our religion," the foreword asserts, "is the religion of democracy and social justice for which the noble Koran has called since the appearance of Islam." What meaning does such an assertion carry in the mind of Qadhafi and his associates? In the first place, it encapsulates a view of world history which—notwithstanding the claims for originality made on behalf of the Third Theory—has many points of similarity with the doctrines of the Tatar Sultan Galiev, the Chinese Li Ta-chao, and the Japanese Ikki Kita. Quoting the Algerian writer, the late Malek Bennabi, Qadhafi affirms that the true division in the world is not between East and West or communism and capitalism, but between North and South:

There is no East and West; there is rather North and South: the North extends from Washington to Peking, the South from Tangiers to Djakarta; so that East and West can be considered as the two great camps allied against a third camp which is underdeveloped, or subjected by force. The Moslem world constitutes the centre of gravity of this camp . . . . the important thing is the existence of this doctrinal division in the world, this ideological map of the world.

Qadhafi, it is clear, operates with an amalgam of Marxism and nationalism, in which the fundamental struggle takes place not between an industrial proletariat and the capitalists oppressing it, but between poor nations and the rich industrial nations who exploit them. It is this amalgam which justifies the universalist claim of the Third Theory. It is clear, furthermore, that the theory is activist in its thrust: struggle is emphasized, and political legitimacy is associated with successful struggle against the non-Muslim, capitalist or Communist exploiters. Thus, at the same meeting of October 1972, where Qadhafi explained the fundamental division of the world between North and South, another speaker affirmed that "*jihad* by the sword by all means for the sake of God: this is what ought to govern our relations with the other [i.e., outside] world in order to spread the message." The speaker went on to say that a limited truce might interrupt the *jihad* for a time, but it must be resumed whenever the Muslims become strong. The same speaker broached another activist, revolutionary theme when he said that he who raises the banner of Arab unity, and struggles for its sake, is the only legitimate *imam* or ruler, "and all the other *imams* are illegitimate."

Together with the identification of Islam with Arabism, this revolutionary activism is the most important characteristic of the dominant ideology in the Arab world today. The activism is obviously directed against the outside world: Qadhafi's opposition of North and South expresses eloquently this particular thrust of the doctrine. But the activism has also an inward direction which the claim that Islam represents democracy and social justice, quoted above, may make clear. Such a statement represents not so much a description as an aspiration. The aspiration is towards a society in which poverty would have disappeared, and traditional political and social hierarchies abolished. Clearly, such a vision has nothing to do with traditional Islam as understood by its adherents, and is entirely derived from a recent European model. This vision is not shared by the ruled and this constitutes the gap mentioned above: where rulers and ruled used to inhabit one common universe of discourse, they now inhabit two separate ones.

What are the implications for the future of Arab politics of this seemingly generous vision? The vision is a blueprint, but since it has almost no contact with existing realities, the blueprint becomes an abstract doctrine. Political discourse ceases to be a way of dealing with emergencies in a customary and familiar manner, and becomes a series of logical-seeming imperatives to which all citizens must, at all costs, be committed.

Political indoctrination is the concomitant of this style of politics, and it has to be forwarded by means of an ideological rhetoric which cannot but obscure, and thus make more intractable, existing political problems. The doctrine or blueprint here in question goes under the name "Arab Socialism" or "Islamic Socialism." These labels are meant to distinguish the doctrine from Marxism and similar European ideologies. The ground for the distinction is principally that the latter are founded on the idea of class struggle, whereas "Arab" or "Islamic" socialism is based on the solidarity and cooperation of all classes. But to make this cooperation and solidarity an actual fact requires large-scale intervention by governments in economic and social arrangements: property rights, business relations, intellectual activity must come under government control. This means a prodigious extension of that centralization and enhancement of power which is the most significant characteristic of the Middle-Eastern state in the nineteenth and twentieth centuries. Economic, social, and intellectual activities thus become gradually more politicized, and caught up in a tight mesh of administrative control and regulation. This state of affairs, while it certainly gives incomparably greater power to the rulers, by no means necessarily increases welfare, solidarity, or cooperation. On the contrary, bureaucratic regulation may actually increase social tension, decrease welfare, and make society at large altogether less prosperous and happy. In this way, the reality will contrast sharply with the claims and promises of the doctrine, and this may itself lead to political instability.

As has been said, the appeal to Islam will find a wide response among the traditionally-minded masses. The "socialism" which has somehow been yoked together with Islam and Arabism will not elicit from them the same response. Those who will be most attracted to it are the increasingly numerous products of the school and university systems who, by reason of their training, are recruited into the ruling institution, as its younger members who, albeit they are less powerful, will still have access to the levers of military and political power. They will see that the reality does not conform to the doctrine, and will ascribe this to the corruption and backsliding of their elders. As the gap between the doctrine and the reality widens, the attraction of the ideology, and its critique of existing conditions, will grow. The mixture of socialism, Arabism, and Islam is a powerful one, and so is its corollary, namely that justice and unity will not come about until Arab society is cleansed of reaction, privilege, capitalism, and godlessness.

In order to carry out the purification, the younger members of the ruling institution, *purs et durs* as they are, will be tempted to resort to precisely those revolutionary methods sanctioned alike by the ideology and by the practice of their elders. If they are successful in their enterprise, they will set the ships of state—for a time at any rate—on the rigid course which ideological rectitude demands. This vicious circle is not likely to disappear because of the large sums which are now flowing into the Arab world from oil royalties. So much wealth which is, in any case, unevenly distributed through the region, and completely under the control of governments, is likely to exacerbate discontent and make for political instability: Iraqi oil revenues in the nineteen fifties and Libyan prosperity in the sixties did not prevent, perhaps even hastened, revolutionary upheaval. The circle of ideological discontent leading to *coup d'état*, leading to further discontent, can no doubt be broken, but this requires an efficient police apparatus itself immune to subversion, treachery or demoralization.

It may also be asked what bearing the above analysis may have on the policymaker's preoccupations. The first consideration relates to prominence which Islam has acquired in Arab political discourse. If this tendency continues— and there is no reason to think otherwise—we must expect an increase in the impermeability of the Arab world to outside ideas, and increasing difficulty in communication. It may not be possible to show how this state of affairs will affect a specific negotiation, but its long-term indirect influence we might suspect to prove considerable. In the second place, the ideological style of politics, so rife in the Arab world, may give rise to illusions against which it is important to guard. Policymakers must be wary of ideology and its rhetoric. Its claim to be a report of present reality and a blueprint for future developments cannot be taken at face value. The caution ought to be superfluous, but recent experiences show that it is by no means so.

The attitude of U.S. policymakers to so-called Nasserism in the decade or so after the *coup d'état* of July 1952 is a case in point. There seems to have been then a dangerous readiness to believe that, as the "Free Officers" were saying, the ills of Egypt could be remedied only through a "revolution"; that this "revolution" would eventually create a new social structure which would promote economic development and prosperity, create a middle class, and hence establish democratic constitutional government; and that this would promote U.S. interests in this region. In retrospect, one may clearly see that each chain in this line of reasoning was so weak as to be utterly worthless. But hindsight is not necessary to reach such a judgment. Even at the time, it would have been quite possible to be sceptical about large claims of this kind.

Policymakers, then, ought to be wary of confusing the interests of a government—foremost among which is self-preservation—and the claims and demands of its ideology; they ought to ask themselves whether the aims of an ideology can possibly be fulfilled, and whether the very attempt to fulfil them may not itself make these impossible to attain. Over and above everything else, policy ought not to be tied to large speculative views about long-term changes in politics, economy, and society. British policy towards the Ottoman Empire between the eighteen thirties and nineteen fourteen started out by being based on the assumption that the preservation of the empire—which was a British interest—could be secured only through far-reaching "reforms." The "reforms" were successful neither in themselves, nor in removing Ottoman military weakness which, if anything, became relatively worse. Then, during Abd al-Hamid's long reign, British attitudes to the empire became gradually more hostile, and no small part of this hostility derived from the belief that the Sultan was against "reforms," and that he was a reactionary despot. After a brief burst of enthusiasm for the Young Turk *coup d'état*, British policymakers again dismissed the new rulers as hopelessly reactionary. There was a large element of misinformation and misunderstanding in these judgments but, even if there had not, they would still have been largely irrelevant to the issue whether British interests required or did not require a friendly Ottoman Empire. In this particular case, the misjudgment on an issue which was anyway irrelevant may be shown to have led to an atmosphere such that the British took for granted Ottoman hostility in 1914, and what they did to avert it was too little and too late.

There is another episode in British relations with the Middle East which carries a lesson to policymakers who have to deal with an ideological style of politics. This is the encouragement of Arab unity during and after the Second World War. Assuming that the current for Arab unity was powerful—which was by no means clear—it did not necessarily follow that to support it would automatically benefit British interests in the area—interests which were scattered and complex. The support which was, in fact, given led between, say, 1945 and 1952, to a new situation in which British interests were by no means safeguarded, but rather threatened in new and unexpected ways.

In sum, what is being argued for here is a crude empiricism in the belief that this is an area in which a long-term analysis of political trends would not, even if it were correct, yield any readily applicable policy prescriptions. The long-term prospect in these societies is one of intellectual isolation, if not downright hostility, while the ideological style of politics which has made such inroads makes for activism and instability. All that one may hope for is to exploit the instinct for survival of regimes which are narrowly based and insecure. This kind of policy can only be played by ear. Every morning one is dealt a new hand, and yesterday's match offers little guidance in today's challenge: agility is all. The conclusion is negative, but nonetheless of some value since, as the examples cited above show, its disregard has led in the past to disappointment and failure.

VIII The Arab-Israeli Conflict

Shimon Shamir

In analyzing and attempting to understand the pattern of conflict between Israel and the Arab states, it must be borne in mind that while the Arab-Israeli conflict is a salient cause of regional instability, it is definitely not the only conflict in the area which has led to armed confrontation in recent years. Other disputes that have evolved into sporadic wars include those between Arab and Kurd in Iraq, Greek and Turk in Cyprus, and Arab and black African in Sudan. Within the Arab world proper, civil wars of varying types have been fought in Lebanon, Yemen, and Dhofar. The Yemen civil war led to a massive Egyptian intervention which at one point threatened to involve Saudi Arabia and escalate into a regional confrontation. A Syrian invasion into Jordan was halted by a combination of Jordanian armor and United States-Israeli pressure, and only the dispatch of ·British and Arab League troops induced Iraq to reconsider its claim to Kuwait.

Nor has the Arab-Israeli dispute been the sole contributor to the eruption of the Arab-Israeli wars themselves. In addition to the factors pertaining to the Arab-Israeli conflict itself, escalation toward war has been initiated or accelerated by other factors which can be grouped into three categories: the domestic interests of the various Arab regimes, inter-Arab rivalries, and competition between the superpowers. Thus, the conflict should be conceived as a multi-dimensional complex, which combines ideology and power-struggle, interlocks local and global interests, and serves both as a means and an end.

The aim of this chapter is not to discuss all the aspects of the Arab-Israeli conflict but to analyze the fluctuations in its intensity as the function of different constellations of all these determinants. It seeks, first, to establish the principal factors that feed the conflict and contribute to its escalation, with reference to the period up to 1967, and to outline the various stages of Arab-Israeli relations in that period, as determined by these variables. Second, it seeks to analyze the constituents of the present phase of the conflict, which have been shaped by the consequences of the 1967 war, somewhat modified by the cease-fire of 1970 and significantly transformed by the 1973 war and its aftermath. Third, it seeks to project possible developments in the determinants of the conflict and to define the alternative levels of conflict they may produce.

Basic Factors, 1949-1967

At the foundation of the Arab-Israeli conflict lies the issue of Israel's existence. For the Arabs, the establishment of the State of Israel was an infringement upon the rights of the indigenous Arab population, the Palestinians; it dispossessed them of their land and created the refugee problem. For these reasons, the Zionist state must be liquidated. For the Israelis, the establishment of their state was the fulfilment of their historical rights in their ancient homeland. Hence their resolution to maintain it as a national Jewish state entitled to sovereignty, security, and recognition.

Thus, the conflict is not a symmetrical one. While Israel seeks to defend and consolidate an accomplished fact, the Arabs challenge its establishment and expect to wipe it out. The Israelis wish the area to be pacified and stabilized, the Arabs want to shatter the *status quo*. This distinction is not made here to express moral judgment but simply in order to indicate the fact that, historical circumstances being what they are, the aspirations of the former would be best served by termination of the conflict and those of the latter by its perpetuation. For this reason, any study of the dynamics of the conflict must deal more extensively with the factors which operate on the Arab side.

The Arabs

Arab Attitudes. The first group of factors comprise attitudes which exist in Arab society and nourish belligerency towards Israel. It is impossible to accurately measure how widespread and vigorous these attitudes are and the extent to which they affect the policies of Arab governments in practice, but they are frequently asserted both among the popular classes and, in a more articulate form, among the intelligentsia, and the interplay between these attitudes and political decision-making in the Arab states can often be observed. Four categories of such attitudes deserve to be mentioned.

Solidarity with Palestinians. In view of the meager material assistance the Arab states render to the Palestinian refugees, it is plausible that Arab solidarity with the Palestinians is by nature political, rather than humanitarian, but there is no reason to doubt its genuineness. In spite of a certain impatience with the Palestinians, which is on occasion to be heard in several Arab circles, identification with Palestinian aspirations is widespread. It is nurtured by the Arab media, by the political and intellectual leadership, and the Palestinian intelligentisia itself contributes extensively to its dissemination.

Islam. The Islamic conception of the Jews is one of a religious minority, tolerated and protected by the Muslim state, but with no role of its own to play in political and military affairs. Jewish statehood thus becomes a flagrant violation of the traditional order of things. The establishment of Israel is also seen as an incursion of a non-Muslim force into the heart of *dār al-Islām*, which has to be met with *jihād* (i.e., Holy War). The inclusion of Jerusalem within Israel exacerbates resentment toward the Jewish state. Although these attitudes do not cover the whole range of the Islamic view of Israel, they are those preached by Muslim *'ulamā'* and Islamic populist movements throughout the Arab world and beyond.

Arabism. A millenium of Arab decline, culminating in the humiliating political and cultural domination by the West in modern times, has generated a sense of trauma and deep crisis in Arab society. In response, a vision of Arab regeneration and future greatness has been produced. The encounter with Israel is viewed as a microcosm of the Arabs' historic confrontation with the West and a symbol of their efforts to assert themselves in the modern world. Israel is regarded as the spearhead of the great Western ("imperialistic") attack on the Arab world. The vigor with which this view is held had often been demonstrated by the effectiveness with which it serves political mobilization in the Arab states. It affects Arab attitudes towards Israel in two principal ways:

1. The ability of Israel to assert itself and inflict defeats on Arab armies not only humiliates the Arabs' pride but also casts a shadow on their self-image and the validity of the vision of their future. The desire, therefore, to recover Arab honor through victory over Israel is manifest in Arab life to an extent that goes far beyond the scope of the Palestinian problem proper.

2. The Arabs' march towards fulfilment of their national destiny is conceived as an inevitable historical process which is ensured by the Arabs' potentialities and vast resources. In the long run, they feel, Israel can hardly expect to compete with Arab assets—economically, geographically, and in terms of sheer manpower. Therefore, there is a tendency to draw the conclusion that compromise with Israel is simply not called for.

Radicalism. The diffusion of various radical revolutionary doctrines in Arab society, ranging from mild, nationalist pseudo-Marxism to Maoism, also feeds the inherently negative attitude towards Israel. All these doctrines represent Israel as a tool formed by Western imperialism to suppress national revolutionary movements. By its very nature, they argue, Israel is the enemy of the Arabs and the whole Third World. This view of Israel is elaborated upon mainly within doctrinaire leftist circles but in a popularized form it has been absorbed and disseminated by most Arab regimes.

Strategic Considerations of the "Confrontation States." All four "confrontation states"—i.e., Egypt, Jordan, Syria, and Lebanon—have specific strategic problems which have emanated, in the main, from their adjacence to the State of Israel. The deployment of their forces along the international frontiers and the armistice lines, which separate them from Israel, often brought about border incidents that were liable to rapidly get out of hand. The situation became particularly acute where there was a dispute over the demarcation of the borders, or where demilitarized areas, whose status was always controversial, separated the two adversaries. Every one of the "confrontation states" has been exposed to massive Israeli retaliatory strikes whenever it allowed its territories to be used as a base for operations against Israel, either by its own regular armies or by Fedayeen and other infiltrators. The implementation of Arab policies calling for increased pressure on Israel exposed these states to risks of escalation beyond the manageable level. Throughout the period under review, Israeli military superiority has been a major constraint on the behavior of all four "confrontation states."

There is, however, a basic difference between the strategic outlook of Jordan and Lebanon, on the one hand, and Egypt and Syria, on the other. For the former, occasionally threatened by their more powerful Arab neighbors, Israeli military supremacy helped to guarantee the perpetuation and viability of their political independence. For Egypt and Syria, however, both in possession of strong armies and with aspirations to regional influence, it has imposed restrictions on their efforts to achieve their policy goals. Therefore, it is mainly Egypt and Syria whose strategic interests should be considered in this context.

Egypt. As the biggest and most influential Arab state, Egypt strives to maintain a hegemony in the region. Israeli military superiority in itself thwarts Egypt, and thus its principal strategic interest has been to neutralize this hindrance. The State of Israel also severs Egypt geographically from the Arab states of the Fertile Crescent, which have been the main targets of the Egyptian desire for predominance in the region. It was the Israeli geographical barrier which handicapped the Egyptians in their attempt to crush the Syrian revolt in 1961 and restricted their pressure on Jordan at times when the Egyptians were interested in augmenting it. For this reason, Egyptian strategy has often focused on the Israeli Negev as an immediate or long-range target and on one occasion at least, in May 1967, it became an operational goal of Egyptian diplomatic and military maneuvers.

The Egyptian capacity to prevent Israeli shipping not only through the Suez Canal but potentially in the waterways leading to the Port of Elath as well, has been another factor which either placed Egypt under pressure from other Arab states to challenge Israel or tempted it to do so.

On land and along the Egyptian-Israeli lines, two sections attracted Egyptian strategic interest, at various periods. The first was the 'Awja-Nizana (formerly) demilitarized zone which contained the most important crossroad along the international border. Egypt was concerned about preventing an Israeli presence in that zone and, possibly, about imposing Egyptian control over it. The second, and much more important, was the Gaza Strip which projects deep into the area of former Palestine, to a distance of thirty-five miles from Tel Aviv. Egyptian interests centered on turning the Strip into a military base which would pose a serious threat to the vulnerable Israeli armistice lines and to use the local Palestinian population, as well as its own regular units, to constantly harass Israel by infiltration, commando raids, and other types of border incidents.

Syria. The strategic concern of Syria bears some similarity to that of Egypt but it operates on a lower level and its confines involve a more limited area. The concept of Greater Syria, which would include the territories of Syria, Lebanon, Jordan, and Israel (or Transjordan and Palestine), has been clearly asserted at times and left implicit at others, but it has always remained at the basis of the Syrian strategic outlook. Thus, for the Syrians too, Israeli military superiority has been the main obstacle which has prevented them from realizing their long-range goals in the area.

The fact that one of the major sources of the Jordan waters is situated in Syria and any Arab diversion project had to be carried out mainly from within Syrian territory, created either an opportunity or a political necessity to challenge Israel on this issue. In addition, the superior Syrian positions on the Golan Heights could easily be used to harass the Israeli settlements in the Huleh-Kineret valley below, either by allowing Palestinian Fedayeen to operate from behind the Syrian lines or by directly employing Syrian troops. The status of the many demilitarized zones, interspersed along the Syrian-Israeli armistice lines, was disputed by the Syrians and these zones became the foci of numerous incidents aimed at the dislodgement of the Israelis.

Domestic Interests of Individual Regimes. The need of Arab ruling elites to consolidate their power has been another factor which has served, on occasion, to nourish belligerency towards Israel. In most Arab states, government has been in the hands of military officers, or former military officers, who seized power and/or held it by force. Two of the most acute needs of such regimes are legitimization and mass mobilization. Upgrading the conflict with Israel can justify the primacy of the military, the monopolization of power, the mobilization of national resources, and the slow progress of economic and social development.

An interesting case in point is that of the Ba'th regime in Syria, where a military junta, mainly 'Alawite in origin and radical in political outlook, seeks to compensate for its low level of popular support by maintaining a militant posture in foreign affairs. This is one of the factors which has contributed to making the Syrian regime the most extreme of all the "confrontation states" vis-à-vis Israel. Considerations of a similar nature have also affected—at certain periods and to a more limited extent—the policies of Egypt. The requisites of charismatic leadership, which is most effective at times of great national struggle, moved President Nasser more than once to direct his energies to the Arab-Israeli struggle, thereby escalating the conflict.

Inter-Arab Factors. Polarization and Palestinization are two inter-Arab factors in the Arab-Israeli conflict.

Polarization. The polarization of the Arab world into rival blocs—what Professor M. Kerr called "the Arab cold war"—has usually induced one or both blocs to assert its leadership and loyalty to the Arab cause by adopting a more militant posture towards Israel. This has been evidenced in all the major rivalries which split the Arab world in the past: the contest between the Baghdad Pact and the Nasserite forces in the mid-'50s, the Nasser-Qassem competition in the late '50s and early '60s, which was to be followed by the Nasser-Ba'th rift, and finally the struggle between the "progressive" and "reactionary" blocs on the eve of the Six-Day War. In all these instances, one of the contestants or both sought to mobilize support for themselves and concomitantly to embarrass their adversaries by escalating the conflict so as to demonstrate their commitment to the struggle against Israel.

Palestinization. Another means of displaying commitment has been through political or operational assistance offered to the Palestinian movement. The issue of the "Palestinian Entity" emerged in the context of the Nasser-Qassem rivalry in the late '50s. The Palestinian Liberation Organization and the Palestinian Liberation Army were established in 1964 by the first Arab summit conference which had been originated by Egypt in an endeavor to recapture the initiative in inter-Arab affairs. The radicalization of the Syrian regime in its offensive against the conservative regimes in the mid-'60s was coupled with an agreement with the Fath Fedayeen organization, allowing it to operate from Syria. The dynamics of inter-Arab relations have tended to strengthen the commitment of the Arab states to the Palestinian organization which held the most uncompromising attitudes towards Israel, and therewith has had the effect of radicalizing the attitudes of these states themselves.

Extra-Regional Factors. The superimposition of great power contests over the regional conflicts of the Middle East has usually accelerated the escalation processes. Though it is generally true that the two superpowers have been apprehensive of the outbreak of war in the region, the dynamics of their competition, by its very nature, could only increase polarization—either between rival Arab blocs, thus contributing indirectly (as seen above) to the upgrading of the Arab-Israeli conflict, or directly between Arabs and Israelis.

This holds true of the Middle Eastern rivalry between great powers in general (which, at certain periods, included competition between the Western powers themselves—the United States, France, and Britain). However, throughout the period, there has been a basic difference between the policies of the two principal superpowers: while the United States was essentially interested in maintaining stability in the area, the Soviet Union was engaged in a major offensive which sought to extend its influence and to establish Soviet predominance in this region. In pursuit of this objective the Soviet Union has been prepared to go to great lengths to espouse the causes of its local clients, offering them extensive support and escalating the conflicts of the subordinate system to the brink of full-scale confrontation. The Soviets have encouraged Arab belligerency towards Israel by a great variety of methods, ranging from verbal support in international forums to active assistance in the planning of anti-Israeli strategy of Arab armies. The most decisive factor was, perhaps, the almost unrestrained supply of weapons which helped to precipitate the arms race in the region—in terms both of the quantity and quality of weapons—and which accelerated the drift towards war.

Israel

Strategic Considerations. As shown above, there is no symmetry in the motives, policies, and objectives of the two adversaries in the Arab-Israeli conflict. Israel's basic interest has been in maintaining the *status quo* and deescalating the conflict. However, it initiated actions when it felt that its strategic position in the area, and hence its security, were in serious jeopardy.

Israel tended to launch a preventive or preemptive strike in the following circumstances:

1. The emergence of an Arab alliance, which threatened to encircle Israel by a unified Arab front, usually accompanied by the deployment of other Arab forces in Jordan (Egypt-Jordan-Syria, both in 1956 and 1967);
2. The acceleration of arms supplies to Arab states, which carried the threat of Arab supremacy in the arms race (Soviet-Egyptian arms deal, prior to the 1956 war);
3. The build-up of Arab forces along the Israeli borders, which created an almost intolerable situation for Israel's army, largely manned by reserves (Sinai, 1967).

Several issues have been regarded as grounds for war or at least massive military strikes:

1. Border incidents. Arab military pressure on the armistice lines, especially in the demilitarized zones (along the Egyptian frontiers, prior to the 1956 war, and along the Syrian frontier, mainly prior to the 1967 war), led to the inevitable Israeli reprisal raids, and twice escalated into all-out war.
2. Raids by Palestinians. Both in 1956 and 1967, infiltration by hostile Palestinians (from the Gaza Strip and the West Bank, mainly prior to 1956), and raids by Palestinian guerrillas (the Egyptian-controlled Fedayeen units in Gaza prior to 1956, and the Syrian sponsored Fath prior to 1967) triggered large-scale Israeli reaction.
3. Blockade. The Egyptian closure of the Tiran Straits to Israeli shipping was a major precipitating element in the 1956 and 1967 wars. The issue of free navigation in the Suez Canal acted as a contributory factor to escalation in 1954-56.
4. Diversion of water resources. Israel's partial diversion of the Jordan River waters was accompanied by Arab threats of a resumption of hostilities to prevent this (from 1963 onwards). Subsequently the Arab counter-project to divert the Jordan's headwaters was met by an Israeli military response (which, in neither case, evolved into a full military confrontation).

Stages of the Conflict

The examination of the various stages of the conflict—during the period discussed in this section (1949-1967)—leads to several conclusions. First, it shows that the level of belligerency has been greatly uneven, ranging from sporadic all-out war to periods of coexistence in practice if not in name. Second, it confirms the proposition that the conflict is a multidimensional one and the level to which it is activated is determined by *combinations* of factors of differing types. Third, it indicates that while the factors pertaining to the local conflict itself were responsible for the persistence and vigor of basic attitudes, those emanating from external circumstances usually regulated the level of its activation. This can be shown by the following schematic synopsis of the factors which had shaped the conflict's principal stages.

1949-1953. The period which followed the 1948 war and the signing of the four armistice agreements was one of relative calm. This can be attributed to the following factors.

1. Although the *ancien régime* collapsed in the two key-states, Syria and Egypt, during this period no new radical-nationalist doctrines and movements had yet emerged.

2. Hostilities along the Israeli armistice lines were almost exclusively confined to infiltration by nonorganized Palestinians (from the West Bank and the Gaza Strip in the main). These infiltrations were carried out without involving the regular armies to any major degree. (The notable exception: the brief clashes with the Syrian army in 1951, which mark the beginning of the dispute over the Jordan waters and the DMZ.)

3. The military *juntas* which seized power in Syria from 1949 onwards and in Egypt in 1952, were preoccupied with internal struggles to bolster their new regimes, and with the basic issues of political transformation.

4. King 'Abdallah, whose concern was to establish Jordanian rule in the West Bank, wanted to consolidate the *status quo* and, at one point, even considered a peace settlement with Israel. (In the second half of the period, Jordan was preoccupied with the problems of succession.)

5. Lebanon established its nonactive posture in the conflict.

6. Although two central forces competed in the Arab League—the Hashemite and the Egyptian—the pattern of inter-Arab rivalries remained fluid and the polarity did not predominate.

7. Great power competition in the Middle East was confined to the Western bloc and had only limited impact on the Arab-Israeli conflict. The Tripartite Declaration of 1950 served as a moderating factor.

8. The Soviet Union had not as yet launched its penetration offensive into the region.

1954-1956. The second period witnessed an escalation process which culminated in the Sinai-Suez War of 1956. The principal factors were the following:

1. Nasserism had emerged as a messianic movement committed to the vision of the reemergence of the Arabs as a world power "from the Gulf to the Ocean," and to an unyielding struggle against "the imperialists and their agents." This inflamed the political climate in all Arab states.

2. The growing rate of infiltration and border incidents created an escalating cycle of hostile Arab action and Israeli retaliatory strikes, which gradually grew in magnitude and frequency.

3. In the course of this process, and within the context of inter-Arab and superpower rivalries mentioned below, Egypt assumed an active posture in the conflict. Egypt activated its troops to increase pressure on the Israeli borders and from 1955, Fedayeen groups, under Egyptian direction, made deep raids into Israel.

4. Within Egypt, Abdel Nasser had completed the concentration of all power in his hands. He initiated a mobilization campaign for the struggle against the historic enemies of the nation, among whom Israel loomed larger and larger.

5. The efforts of Nuri Sa'id to assert Iraqi leadership in the Arab world through the signing of the Baghdad Pact, and the fierce counteroffensive launched, in turn, by Abdel Nasser polarized the Arab world for the first time

into two well-defined camps. The Arab public throughout the Middle East felt the repercussions of the contest, and tension was raised to new heights. One of Nasser's tactics in this struggle was to identify the Baghdad Pact camp with Western imperialism and the latter with Israel and thus to label his adversaries as betrayers of the Arab cause. Conversely, the loyalty of his own camp had to be made demonstratively evident by adopting an active role in the struggle against Israel. The influence of the Nasserite camp began to increase, bringing Syria into it, and slowly bending Jordan to its will.

6. With the entry of the Soviet Union into the area, the pattern of the Middle Eastern Soviet-American competition emerged, conforming to the rivalry patterns of the subordinate system and increasing its intensity. The anti-Nasserite camp thus found itself on the defensive on two counts.

7. The Nasserite camp aligned itself with the emerging Third World bloc, thus drawing support from that source for its campaigns, which included the campaign against Israel.

8. The Soviet Union formulated a strategy for increasing its influence in the Arab world, which was based, to a large extent, on supporting the anti-Israeli posture of the Nasserites. In 1955, the Soviets began building up the Egyptian arsenal through an unprecedentedly extensive arms deal. Similar deals with other Arab states followed.

9. Nasser's campaign to eliminate the last positions still held by the former Western rulers of the Middle East—the British and the French—culminated in the nationalization of the Suez Canal. This created the opportunity for Israel to align itself with these European powers in an endeavor to break what Israel regarded as the stranglehold tightening around her borders.

1957-1963. The third period was once again one of relative calm, until tension gradually increased again towards the mid-sixties. The following were the formative factors.

1. Nasserite Arabism, having reached its peak in 1958, suffered a series of setbacks and began to lose its credibility and thus its capacity to mobilize the masses of the Arab world.

2. The war of 1956 had increased Israel's deterrent power. It led to the stationing of UN troops in Sinai and the Gaza Strip. Accordingly, the Israeli-Egyptian border warfare was terminated.

3. Between 1958 and 1961, the years of the union with Syria, Nasser's main concern was to consolidate his rule in Damascus. After the collapse of the union, Nasser turned his attention to the implementation of Arab Socialism inside Egypt, and to the struggle against the "reactionary forces" upon whom he laid the blame for the failure of the union. Similarly, in Syria, the ruling elite was preoccupied with the internal struggle that ensued from the termination of the union.

4. Nasser's campaign to impose his hegemony on the Arab world was checked

in 1958, when the new revolutionary regime in Iraq refused to join the Nasserite bloc and the Nasserite forces were suppressed both in Jordan (with British help) and in Lebanon (with American help). The collapse of the union with Syria in 1961 was followed two years later by the failure of the projected tripartite federation with Iraq and Syria.

5. The Soviet Union suffered a series of setbacks in the Arab world with the suppression of the communists in Iraq and Syria, which led to a major crisis in Soviet-Egyptian relations (but dependence on Soviet arms even increased).

6. The United States abandoned attempts to form a pro-Western Middle Eastern alliance, thus removing one of the causes of regional unrest. Instead, it adopted the Eisenhower Doctrine, and sought to stabilize the *status quo* in the Middle East. Towards the end of the period the global cold war subsided.

7. Israel managed to establish relations of practical collaboration on matters of defense with Western states, including Germany, France, and the United States, and this in turn added to the effectiveness of its deterrence.

1964-1967. In the fourth period, a combination of several factors reactivated the Arab-Israeli conflict. Their emergence was gradual but by 1966 a full-fledged escalation process could be perceived. In the following year it led to the Six-Day War.

1. The Arab world witnessed a trend of radicalization. This was reflected in the Ba'th regimes established in Iraq and Syria in 1963 and particularly in the neo-Ba'th regime which seized power in Syria in 1966. This radicalization was also reflected in the emergence of various clandestine leftist revolutionary movements in the Arabian Peninsula, in Palestinian circles, and elsewhere in the Arab world.

2. The failure of the attempts to reach an agreement on the allocation of the Jordan River waters, and the unilateral completion of the Israeli irrigation scheme produced an inter-Arab resolution to divert the headwaters of the Jordan. Syrian attempts to implement the resolution resulted in sporadic conflagrations along the Syrian-Israeli lines. At the same time, the number and magnitude of border incidents, focusing on the demilitarized zones along those lines, increased.

3. The new Ba'th regime in Syria, controlled by a leftist 'Alawite clique of military officers and encountering the resentment of the traditional Sunnite majority of Syrian society, adopted a militant posture—unprecedented in its extremism towards Israel.

4. The same regime endorsed, for the first time, a Palestinian Fedayeen organization—the Fath. In 1965, the Fath began operating against Israel from Syrian territory with the support of Syrian regular forces.

5. In an endeavor to recapture the initiative in inter-Arab politics, Nasser convened the first Arab summit meeting in 1964. The same motivation played a part in the establishment, at that summit conference, of the Palestine Liberation

Organization and Palestine Liberation Army, thus reintroducing a separate Palestinian element into the Arab-Israeli conflict.

6. After the third Arab summit meeting, in 1965, the bloc of "progressive" Arab states—comprising Egypt, Syria, Iraq, Algeria, and Yemen—launched a political offensive against the conservative Arab regimes. The offensive grew in intensity, with increasing repercussions upon the Arab-Israeli conflict.

7. The Soviet Union, which had reached a rapprochement with Egypt in 1964, was the driving power behind this offensive. It sought to polarize the Middle Eastern political spectrum and encouraged the "progressive" states to adopt an aggressive posture toward the pro-Western forces in the area, including the State of Israel. In May 1967, the Soviets triggered the remilitarization of Sinai by Egyptian forces.

8. Throughout the period the arms race had been intensified. Speculations on the possible introduction of nuclear weapons into the area were also increasing.

9. The failure of the UN peace-keeping system to prevent the remilitarization of Sinai encouraged Nasser—at that time profoundly frustrated by the decline of his Pan-Arab movement and the seemingly endless war in the Yemen—to impose a blockade on the Tiran Straits and mass his troops in Sinai, thus posing a direct threat to the Israeli borders. When Jordan joined the Syrian-Egyptian alliance, once again Israel's security doctrine called for a preventive strike.

The Present Phase

The Six-Day War of June 1967 opened a new phase in the Arab-Israeli conflict. The level of conflict was regulated in this phase, as in the previous period, by the five categories of factors outlined above. What is typical of this phase is the fact that they affected the conflict in two diametrically opposite ways. On the one hand, a number of factors conducive to a settlement emerged at various points in the period since June 1967, and on the other, the elements nourishing the conflict have increased and reached a level of such intensity that the cycle of military confrontations has drastically been accelerated. Thus, while the period of 1949-1967 was a period of relative calm with long intervals between wars (eight and eleven years), the period after 1967 can be described as one of either active or impending war: The Six-Day War of 1967 was followed by the 1969-1970 War of Attrition; these wars were followed by a period of Arab threats to substantiate the "military option" culminating in the Three-weeks Yom Kippur War of 1973: and in the aftermath of the war the threat of a yet another conflagration still looms on the horizon.

This phase has been one of rapid fluctuations, with the principal changes usually surfacing after each round of fighting. Thus, the constituents of this phase would best be discussed as they appeared at three points: after the cease-fire of June 1967, after the cease-fire of August 1970 and after the cease-fire of October 1973.

Cease-Fire, June 1967

The immediate results of the Israeli victory in the Six-Day War created several conditions which were favorable for a settlement. For the first time since 1949, Israel held territories which could be used as bargaining counters in negotiations for a peace settlement. Among Arabs, the shock of defeat generated doubts concerning the ability of their society to modernize, even under the dynamic revolutionary regimes, and raised the question whether time was really working in their favor. Following the war, the Arabs tended to see Israel as a formidable regional power which they could not expect to overwhelm by force of arms. A heavy blow had been inflicted to Soviet prestige in the Middle East and it made the Soviets and their Arab clients more amenable to some sort of political settlement.

The degree of convergence attained, as a result of these developments, aroused hopes of an imminent settlement and produced Resolution 242 calling for mutual recognition and the establishment of "a just and lasting peace." It was accepted, albeit with different interpretations, by both the superpowers and the local adversaries (eventually by Syria as well).

Yet, the war also created counteracting factors the weight became increasingly overwhelming. It had deepened the agonizing humiliation felt by Arabs and fostered their determination to vindicate their honor. Their pride as Muslims had been wounded particularly by the loss of Jerusalem and its holy places. By the same token, the capture of old Jerusalem aroused in Israel the latent attachment to the city as the focal point of the Zionist vision and made this issue all but nonnegotiable.

The Arab "confrontation states" had lost parts of their own sovereign territories in the Six-Day War—a fact which invested their conflict with Israel with an entirely new dimension. Their firm determination to regain these territories in full clashed with the Israeli conviction that Arab threats to their security, as demonstrated in the 1967 war, justified and necessitated changes in the Fourth-of-June borders so as to make them more defensible. The gap between these two positions became a formidable obstacle to settlement.

The PLO began to emerge, on the Arab side, as an independent factor. This was due to several developments: the Fedayeen guerrilla doctrine and warfare offered a "substitute" to the defeated war-machines and strategies of the established Arab states; identification with the Fedayeen served as an emotional outlet to the mortified Arab society; and the occupation of the whole of Palestine by Israel enabled the PLO to focus attention on the grievances of the Palestinians and gain worldwide attention. Thus, the Arab states tended increasingly to commit themselves to a political force which rejected any compromise settlement with Israel.

Finally, the Soviet Union, in order to improve its position in the area, acted vigorously to rehabilitate Arab armies and lend support to militant Arab policies (including, with some reservations, the PLO), in order to impose a settlement which would force the withdrawal of Israel without necessarily terminating the conflict.

These factors intensified the Arab determination to prevent the consolidation of the Israeli victory into substantial assets that might compel the Arabs to compromise their basic position in the conflict. President Nasser—who had a direct responsibility for the 1967 catastrophe and, consequently, a persona: motivation for upholding this determination—formulated a policy which called for the "liquidation of the consequences of the 1967 aggression," while leaving open the option of dealing with "the 1948 aggression" at a later stage. Arab consensus on this matter found expression in the four "No's" adopted by the Khartoum summit conference: no peace with Israel; no recognition of Israel; no negotiations with Israel; and no compromise over Palestinian rights.

The operational implementation of this position meant resumption of hostilities. In 1968, as soon as the rehabilitation of his forces reached an adequate level, Nasser renewed hostilities along the cease-fire lines and in March 1969 escalated them to a full-scale War of Attrition. The basic concept of his strategy was to exert continuous and growing pressure on Israel, through concerted military operations along all Arab fronts, in combination with Fedayeen warfare and international political coercion—all with Soviet support. The aim was to erode Israel's position to the point where it would be forced to withdraw from the occupied territories in return for certain military and political arrangements which would fall short of a binding bilateral peace treaty.

Nevertheless, Israel's military superiority and the disarray in the Arab military alignment ruled out for all practical purposes the likelihood of an all-out conflagration at that stage, and kept hostilities at a level of immobile war.

Cease-Fire, August 1970

The acceptance of the cease-fire in August 1970 marked the failure of Nasser's strategy. The War of Attrition had caused greater damage to Nasser's regime than to Israel's position; the operational involvement of Soviet troops in the fighting had created a concern on the part of both superpowers to terminate that war; and an international consensus had not emerged to support the Arab position with sufficient effectiveness.

The stalemate which prevailed after the cease-fire appeared to have improved prospects for a settlement. In the Arab world, belief in the "military solution" reached an unprecedented low and in some circles, such as the Egyptian intellectual elite, voices were heard that the Arabs should seek a compromise settlement with Israel in order to free themselves from an onerous and purposeless struggle. The Fedayeen, unable to register any substantial gains to their credit, lost much of their appeal in Arab society and, after September 1970, they were suppressed in Jordan, where Hussein deprived them of their main base of operations.

The Soviet Union, although continuing its efforts to create an effective military option for its Arab clients, wanted to discourage them from indulging in what it considered to be a premature military venture. The United States remained firm in its insistence on a compromise peace settlement and, after Secretary Rogers' abortive mediation attempts, appeared to have tacitly endorsed the *status quo* and resolved "to sit it out" until a peace settlement became feasible. With the emergence of détente, there were speculations that it would apply to the Middle East as well, thus ruling out the Arab military option and leaving a compromise settlement by peaceful means as the only avenue acceptable to the superpowers.

However, there had been a strengthening of counteracting factors as well. Whatever moderate trends existed in the Arab world, they did not pervade the leadership of the power structure. King Faisal, motivated by militant Islamic sentiments, President Assad, adhering to the radical anti-Israeli doctrine of his regime, and President Sadat, pursuing in this conflict the basic Nasserite goals (even if the methods he chose for attaining them were different), tended to resort to force. Sadat, vexed by the intolerable situation created for Egypt both in the international arena and in the domestic front by the state of "no-peace no-war," and alarmed by the emergence of what he considered a *status quo*-enforcing détente between the superpowers, chose the military option, at least as a means to break the deadlock. The Soviets had their apprehensions about the risks of another military confrontation but they continued to pour arms into the Arab arsenals and could be relied upon to render the Arabs effective support once war was imminent. What is more, towards 1973, the situation in the energy market brought about conditions in which the employment of the oil weapon, in coordination with a military offensive, promised to be both profitable to the producers and effective for the "confrontation states." And, finally, throughout that period, both Israel and the United States were inadequately aware of the pressures building up in the Arab camp for a military offensive and did little to initiate moves to break the stalemate by peaceful means. Within the Israeli political structure, pressure against extensive concessions to the Arabs had increased to the point of becoming a considerable constraint on Israeli foreign policy.

Thus, the apparent tranquility along the Arab-Israeli lines and the absence of any active hostilities did not reflect the real level of the conflict at that stage. The situation was, perhaps, *potentially* conducive to a settlement but in fact it led to escalation. The same Israeli advantages which aroused the hope that they could be exchanged for a peaceful settlement actually developed into a factor intensifying the conflict. The principal Arab decisionmakers remained adherent, as mentioned above, to the basic principle of Arab post-1967 policy, i.e., to prevent the solidification of Israeli gains into a historical reconciliation between the Arabs and Israel, while the Israeli government was generally unwilling to exchange them for anything less than that. Unlike the Israelis, the Arabs did not regard the *status quo* as a starting point for a regional settlement and resolved that before seeking a political arrangement, the existing balance of power would first have to be changed. It was precisely this aim that the Arabs set out to achieve in the Yom Kippur War.

Cease-Fire, October 1973

The cease-fire of October 1973 was designed to save the Arab armies from total collapse, but yet the Arabs had not lost the war. The overall Arab offensive achieved several important objectives: it restored Arab self-confidence and dignity, it improved the Arabs' position in the regional balance of power, it placed a heavy drain on Israeli manpower and economic resources, it achieved a high level of inter-Arab collaboration, it demonstrated the significance of the oil weapon, it broke the deadlock and induced the United States to resume an active role in seeking an Israeli withdrawal, it further isolated Israel in the international arena, and it led subsequently to the restoration of the Suez Canal's east bank to Egypt and the town of Quneitra to Syria.

The constellation of factors which emerged after the war once again affected the conflict in two opposing and contradictory ways. The restoration of the pride and dignity of the Arabs has allowed them latitude in dealing with Israel and enabled their leadership to pursue the diplomatic course to achieve their targets. The contest was now regarded as more balanced and the Arab leaders could not be accused anymore of negotiating from a position of weakness. In Egypt, the aftermath of the war has focused attention on the ever-increasing domestic problems, particularly in the economy. The *rapprochement* with the United States, led by President Sadat, allowed American diplomacy to play an active role, on both sides of the fence, in mediating a settlement. The Soviet Union, whose position had weakened as the result of it, chose to refrain from interfering directly in this process.

In the wake of the October War, the Israeli government showed greater readiness to probe new formulae of agreements and undertake greater risks for advancing the prospects of a settlement. The United States's assistance to Israel—in the form of the dramatic airlift during the war, and the substantial financial aid and arms supplies after it—increased the Israeli preparedness to collaborate with the American peace-making efforts, partly by contributing to Israeli self-assurance (having ensured Israeli military superiority and conveyed to the Arabs the extent of U.S. commitment to the defense of Israel) and partly by demonstrating Israel's dependence on the United States.

The Arab military defeats, at the end of the war, led to the acceptance of Resolution 338 which called for negotiations "between the parties," thus nullifying the Arab allegation that Resolution 242 was self-implementing and had to be imposed on Israel. Subsequently, the Geneva Conference was created as a universally accepted framework for negotiations which could be convened at appropriate times and utilized for averting the threat of war. And, finally, the disengagement agreements on the Israeli-Egyptian and Israeli-Syrian fronts defused, at least temporarily, the main danger spots.

These developments created the setting for the United States sponsored "step-by-step" diplomacy and produced the most dramatic attempt, since 1949-50, to reach an Arab-Israeli accommodation.

The factors hindering such progress, in addition to those mentioned above, were the following. Arab achievements in the war and the drain on Israeli resources boosted Arab self-confidence and nourished the Arabs' conviction that time was on their side and therefore a compromise with Israel was not called for. The emergence of Arab oil power and financial influence affected attitudes in a similar way. The massive arms supplies to the Arab armies, particularly from the Soviet bloc to Syria, increased the Arabs' expectations for achievement through military pressure on Israel. There emerged a coalition of Palestinian Fedayeen and Arab radicals known as the "rejection front," which opposed any diplomatic efforts to achieve agreement with Israel, and although it remained in the minority, it nevertheless acted as a constraint on the states engaged in these efforts. Of particular importance is the fact that the Soviets strengthened their ties with members of this radical front, thus extending their capacity to veto United States-sponsored agreements.

This militant mood, and the group dynamics of Arab summitry, led the Arab leaders to institutionalize the role of the Palestinian Liberation Organization (PLO) (at the Algiers Conference) as indispensable to any future negotiations with Israel and substituted it for Jordan (at the Rabat Conference) as the sole representative of the Palestinian territories occupied by Israel. The whole Arab world thus committed itself to a political factor which does not accept the framework of the postwar diplomatic efforts (Resolutions 242 and 338) and categorically rejects the right of Israel to exist.

These developments, in turn, affected Israeli attitudes and increased apprehension of extensive withdrawals, particularly from the West Bank.

It remains an open question how all these factors affected the level of the conflict at that stage. The post-1973 situation has sharpened the polarity between factors of escalation and factors of pacification to such an extent that both paths remain reasonably probable. This period witnessed the conclusion of the first Arab-Israeli agreements since the 1949 armistice, and the first peace conference in the history of the conflict. At the same time, it has also seen the growth of the anxieties and euphoria which fan the flames of war. The situation has remained constantly on the brink of an eruption, particularly since its evolvement has been regulated by a timetable of recurrent "crucial dates." Thus, this stage, more than any previous one, is a phase of transition which bears the seeds of a wide range of possibilities.

Possible Developments

What are, therefore, the alternative developments which may ensue from this situation? Before attempting to indicate some of them, a word of caution would be pertinent. The projection of future developments, which is always a complex and uncertain undertaking and which no established methodology can render systematic or infallible, is even more difficult in the present case. The factors involved in the Middle Eastern conflict are so numerous that the future interrelationship among them can form endless combinations. Thus, for example, Israel is likely to have differing relations with the various neighboring Arab states. One can think of at least five basic levels of armed conflict, from sporadic border incidents to all-out war, which may exist between Israel and each of these states, at any given moment. There is an even larger number of basic types of coexistence, from cease-fire to political settlement, which could be taken into account. It would, therefore, be pointless to speculate about the probabilities of the numerous combinations.

Similarly, the range of global developments which may have a bearing on the Middle Eastern situation is extremely wide. The extent of the uncertainty is particularly large considering the gravity of the global crises which are projected as possible within the foreseeable future—such as an aggravation of the energy and minerals crises, economic and political decline in Europe, food shortages in the Third World, and a serious disruption of the world financial order. Furthermore, with the evolvement of such crises, other danger spots may acquire primacy over the Arab-Israeli arena. Some possible conflagrations would be an Iranian-Arab conflict in the Gulf area, civil wars in the Arabian Peninsula, and possibly in Eastern Africa as well, Soviet encroachment on any part of the Middle East, Western-inspired military operations in the oil fields regions, and the collapse of the equilibrium and the *status quo* in Europe. Such conflagrations carry the threat of global confrontation and it would be futile to speculate whether this would downgrade or escalate the Arab-Israeli conflict.

Therefore, what can be attempted here is no more than a broad outline of major scenarios for a medium time range of probably five and possibly ten years. They are based on the following assumptions, which definitely do not cover the whole range of possible situations: that the United States-Soviet relationship remains basically that of controlled competition without deteriorating into a major conflagration or turning into a comprehensive settlement of their differences; that neither of the two superpowers completely disengages itself from the Middle East, nor manages to establish full hegemony over it; that neither China nor any other power enters the area in a capacity similar to that of the two superpowers; that in spite of the decline of Europe, possible setbacks for the West in other world regions, and a superior Soviet arsenal, the United States manages to maintain a reasonable degree of strategic equilibrium with the Soviet Union in the Middle East; that Arab wealth and Arab dependence on the industrialized world (food, technology, etc.) counterbalance each other so that the Arabs neither become a world power nor encounter such difficulties as to neutralize their involvement in the conflict with Israel; that in the Arab world, in spite of possible *coups d'état* and bilateral clashes, the present division into states and types of regimes remains in force; that the international position of the oil-producing states improves continuously but the "confrontation states" remain the most significant militarily; that no such new technologies or such new weapons, conventional or unconventional, are introduced into the Arab-Israeli arena that the balance of power may be drastically altered.

Within these limits, the following appear to be the major possibilities to be considered.

Step-by-Step Progress towards a Settlement

The step-by-step concept envisages a series of interim agreements between Israel and the various Arab parties to the conflict, leading gradually towards a peaceful settlement. The implementation of this concept requires such a protracted process that it can be regarded not merely as a method of conflict resolution but actually as a basic scenario for Arab-Israeli interaction in the foreseeable future.

The principal premises of the step-by-step diplomacy, as moulded by its American architects, are too well known to require more than a brief enumeration. "Step-by-step" is basically an exercise in the art of the possible. It seeks to identify at each stage the parties and the issues that are most amenable to an interim agreement, leaving the more difficult ones to a later stage. In each agreement the intent is to define the most vital needs and demands of each party and try to work out an exchange which would reasonably satisfy what is vital at the expense of what is relatively expendable. It seeks to separate the normative from the practical, and affect the *realities* of the situation rather than the formal or ideological positions. Time and movement are the essential factors: the process of negotiating agreements and the progress from one agreement to the other are expected, by themselves, to avert the danger of war, to deescalate the conflict and transform the political climate in the Middle Eastern arena. The inner logic of this "momentum of peace" is the assumption that each stage of agreements would create new realities which would make the next stage feasible. Thus, for example, partial withdrawals and the creation of buffer zones might reduce the motivation to fight and the danger of conflagration and this, in turn, would allow a political compromise based on more substantial withdrawals at a later stage.

Whatever the merits and prospects of this political course, it may be worth pointing out that it is, so far, the only one to have been adopted by the parties to the conflict and sustained for a considerable period of time. The step-by-step diplomacy was sharply attacked by the Syrian and the Soviet governments, among others, and it has been severely criticized even within the United States, Egypt, and Israel, but nevertheless all these parties have collaborated, actively or tacitly, in advancing it. Furthermore, because of its pragmatism and flexibility, it stands a good chance of withstanding crises and to reappear as a feasible option after the miscarriage of one of its phases, or even after another conflagration.

The factors which made the recourse to this concept possible, after the October War, have been described in the previous chapter. These factors have indeed kept the momentum alive for about two years, yet the long-range prospects of the step-by-step diplomacy are uncertain.

The diplomacy yielded, in the first year after the war, two disengagement agreements, those of January and May 1974, although it may be argued that they should be seen in a separate category. The two agreements were *military* by nature and were meant, above all, to solve the immediate problems of the two sides: for the Arabs—to relieve the encircled Third Army and drive the Israelis back from their newly-occupied positions at distances of some sixty miles from Cairo and twenty miles from Damascus; and for the Israelis—to allow their reserve forces to demobilize. The step-by-step diplomacy faced its first severe test in efforts made in 1975 to reach an interim agreement in the Sinai and, at the time of writing, these efforts have drawn close to a successful conclusion. However, the prospects of a similar agreement in the Golan, where the political and geographical conditions allow a much narrower scope for maneuver, are somewhat more limited. When it comes to the West Bank, where the Israelis feel that the very defensibility of their state is involved and where even the identity of the legitimate Arab contender is disputed, the obstacles appear now to be all but insurmountable. Yet, without progress in these sections of the Israeli-Arab confrontation lines there is hardly any chance for further progress in the Egyptian section, all the more so since there seems to exist now a near-consensus that the next step will have to be a comprehensive settlement. Moreover, if no agreement is reached between Israel and at least one additional Arab party, even the durability of the interim agreement concluded with Egypt will become questionable.

Some of the factors which hinder the step-by-step scenario—such as Arab mood and basic attitude, the Arab commitment to the PLO, which rejects the radical front premises of the diplomatic process, interference from Soviet ambiguity and Israeli domestic constraints—were mentioned above; others have emerged in the process of negotiations. While the Egyptians voiced the suspicion that Israel was not well-disposed to any further progress (i.e., withdrawals) beyond that of the 1975 interim agreement, the Israelis began to question the intentions of the Egyptians with regard to that agreement itself. For the Israelis, the fiercely hostile statements being made by the Egyptian leaders, and Egypt's firm objection to any meaningful change in its *political* relations with Israel, throw doubts on their readiness for any agreement based on genuine compromise. Accordingly, the Egyptians were seen in Israel as trying either to impose on it, through the United States, what is tantamount to a dictate or, should Israel resist, to drive a wedge between it and the United States.

The Israelis are deeply aware of the fact that in the step-by-step process they are required to yield substantial "real estate" in return for what are basically verbal commitments. And since in spite of all their external and internal difficulties their susceptibility to pressure, as the experience of the first half of 1975 has shown, is not unlimited, it becomes vital for the step-by-step process that Israel's confidence in the worthiness of the deal, at least as a reasonably reliable substitute to war, is gained. Therefore, the rigidity of the Egyptian stand on military questions, such as deployment of forces, inspection systems, and demilitarization, has been detrimental to the credibility of this process for it left the Israelies with the heavy suspicion that the aim of Egyptian diplomacy was, after all, none but the utilization of the time needed to prepare, militarily and politically, another war against Israel for advancing their forces as deep into Sinai as possible and dislodging the Israelis from any strategically advantageous defense lines. This factor, which naturally looms large in Israel's decision-making process and its domestic politics, could impede the pursuance of the step-by-step scenario.

The negotiations of 1974-75 have also brought out some of the shortcomings of the mediation role performed by the United States. Although it is quite obvious that without the good services of the United States the step-by-step process could never have taken off, it appears that some aspects of these services are not entirely compatible with the cause of a substantial and durable accommodation between Israelis and Arabs. Since the United States does not have the same leverage over Israel and over the Arabs, it can hardly perform its mediation role in a symmetrical way. Thus, instead of seeking genuine compromises between the parties it appears sometimes to be trading with the Arabs in Israeli concessions.

Furthermore, Israeli assets are offered to the Arabs admittedly not solely for obtaining Arab reciprocal concessions for Israel but also, and not the least, for promoting American interests in the Arab world. Since the United States cannot offer the Arabs much more beyond its Israeli connection, and in view of the discouraging consequences of the attempts made by superpowers in the past to establish influence in Arab states, the durability of agreements mediated this way between the Arabs and Israelis, and of the assets acquired for the United States through this process, seems to be rather shaky. Given the domestic and global constraints on American diplomacy, which more than once in recent years have induced the U.S. administration to opt for immediate gains at the expense of long-range consequences, it is not inconceivable that American mediation was in fact undermining Israeli—and American—bargaining position in return for temporary achievements which would not promote real progress towards a settlement.

Whatever is the case, American mediation has definitely eroded the Israeli demand for direct negotiations—which are indispensable for mutual recognition and genuine accommodation—in spite of the fact that this demand was met, at the end of the October War, by Resolution 338. Moreover, the negotiated agreements themselves have been losing their bilateral nature, for an Arab-American consensus has emerged to the effect that it is the United States which must carry most of the burden of giving a *quid per quo* to the Israelis, and the latter, hard pressed for American assistance, have reconciled themselves to this procedure.

Thus the validity of the step-by-step's conceptual framework comes under question: instead of encouraging Arab moderation it might nourish Arab intransigence; instead of preparing the grounds for coping with more subtle and substantial problems at a later stage it might waste the best bargaining assets at the initial phase; instead of creating concrete obstacles to block the "military option" it might increase the temptation to launch a new offensive.

What leaves the step-by-step process, in spite of all this, within the range of possible options is the fact that the other options, as shown below, are not much more probable or palatable for the parties concerned. In spite of all its shortcomings, it *does* narrow the gap between the adversaries and *may* carry the seed of a serious accommodation in the future.

Comprehensive Settlement

A comprehensive settlement is not necessarily identical with a historical termination of the Arab-Israeli dispute and a complete normalization of relations between the two societies—for those can be achieved only through a protracted process which a diplomatic act is more apt to initiate than to conclude. However, for a settlement to be comprehensive it must deal with the basic issues of the conflict, produce compromise solutions and express them in a contractually binding peace agreement. An agreement of this kind would necessarily be reinforced by such internationally sponsored devices as guarantees and buffer zones (discussed in the following section), but what sets it apart from other options is its reliance primarily on the quality of the solution it offers to the *issues* of the conflict.

Among observers it is almost a matter of universal consensus that a comprehensive settlement of the Arab-Israeli conflict, in the present context, could not mean anything but an implementation, in some form, of Resolution 242—probably with some additions to accommodate the Palestinians. Accordingly, beside offering at least partial solutions to such problems as refugees, demilitarization and freedom of navigation, the settlement would commit the Arabs to some formula of recognition of the State of Israel and peaceful coexistence with it and make the Israelis—according to this view—withdraw to lines which would not be considerably different from those of 1967.

Theoretically, such a comprehensive settlement could constitute the ultimate phase of the step-by-step process. However, given all the obstacles discussed above, the probability of such a development is quite low.

Another channel to a comprehensive settlement, which is often advocated by critics of the step-by-step approach, is the peace conference—either in the Geneva framework or in any other forum. Such a peace conference would be expected to produce, through a process of collective bargaining, a multilateral agreement covering the principal issues of the conflict.

A more sophisticated version of this concept envisages a step-by-step process in reverse. First the broad principles of a comprehensive settlement would be formulated by the participants of the peace conference, and then the details would be worked out, step-by-step, through a series of bilateral agreements. Implementation would be gradual and phased out, so as to allow the time factor to establish a system of assurances and a measure of mutual confidence.

The merits of the comprehensive approach are obvious. For the Arabs, it would remove the suspicion that Israel's overriding goal is territorial expansion. For the Israelis, it would eliminate the high strategic risks involved in partial withdrawals without reciprocal concessions. Instead of wasting the best Israeli bargaining cards piecemeal for second-rate and transitional gains, they would be used in concentration for achieving a clear and definite commitment to peace. Instead of leaving the Soviets, Palestinians, and other Arabs as uncommitted bystanders who can undermine at will every interim agreement by pressure from the outside, the comprehensive process would bind them to the terms of the agreement. The implementation of this approach would constitute a gradual progress towards a predetermined objective and not a journey into an unknown land—as it is the case with the step-by-step diplomacy.

Yet, with all the attractions of the comprehensive method it should be recognized that its course is strewn with pitfalls no less, and probably more, than that of the step-by-step process. First of all there is the immediate problem of the lack of sufficient support among the principal parties, at present, for the comprehensive approach. The Americans clearly prefer the step-by-step approach for considerations which are at least partly shared by the Egyptians. The Israelis, doubtful of their chances to elicit an equitable compromise from a Geneva-type forum, are apprehensive of the comprehensive method. Even the Soviets, who are considered its greatest protagonists, have had second thoughts about it and do not stand in the way of the step-by-step diplomacy; and some of their considerations are shared by the Syrians. *All* these parties fear, at the present stage, that a premature attempt to implement the comprehensive approach might soon break down, creating an inexpedient and dangerous vacuum.

On the level of basic issues, there is a wide gap separating the ways in which the Israelis and the Arabs conceive the nature of a peace settlement. For Israel, the essence of a comprehensive settlement is bilateral reconciliation and peace, identical in nature to other settlements which have resolved in modern diplomatic history conflicts between nations. For the Arab states, including the most moderate ones, the settlement in question is no more than an international arrangement, which may become expedient in view of the prevailing circumstances, but would not involve any reconciliation with Israel or any acceptance of it (beyond the recognition of an existing fact) and would not preclude the possibility of the liquidation of the Jewish state at some unspecified time in the future. While the step-by-step approach seeks to outflank this question, the comprehensive approach will have to tackle it directly, and with uncertain consequences.

The achievement of a comprehensive settlement would be further hampered by the fact that in this framework Israel would deal not with each Arab state separately but with a heterogeneous and predominantly militant Arab world. This would include radicals who adhere to the "rejection front," conservative Muslims for whom animosity to Israel is an article of faith, oil tycoons whose power and prestige in the Arab camp are best served by the perpetuation of the conflict; all these groups are not affected by the constraints which compel a "confrontation state" like Egypt to seek an arrangement with Israel.

Egypt, of course, can be expected to play a central role in negotiations, and Egypt does have some interest in deescalating the conflict in order to be able to turn its energies to internal problems, and possibly also to maintain its independence from the Soviet Union. However, the practical import of this consideration has often been exaggerated: while it has not yet been established that it overrides the motivation to pursue the struggle against Israel, it has definitely been demonstrated that in inter-Arab forums Egypt tends to subscribe to the prevailing militant trends at the expense of narrower Egyptian interests. As experience shows, the group dynamics of inter-Arab relations ultimately leads to the adoption of extreme positions as an Arab consensus. The more the Arabs witness external pressures being applied on Israel, the more their conviction that time is on their side grows and the influence of pragmatic and relatively moderate trends among them diminishes.

Moreover, the Soviet Union, which in a framework of a comprehensive settlement would enjoy a wider scope for political action, can hardly be expected to commit itself to the support of the relatively moderate (and United States-oriented) Egyptians, instead of the more militant Syrians, the PLO, and the radical Arabs.

The full burden of these difficulties will bear upon the negotiators when they reach the specific, and the more subtle, issues of the conflict, which in the comprehensive framework cannot be evaded or postponed. The following are probably the most salient.

Borders. The Arabs adhere to the principle that "every inch" of the occupied territories must be restored, and they enjoy widespread support for their position. Israel would find it difficult to challenge the international consensus that the 1967 borders should serve as a basis for working out an agreement. However, the genuineness of the Israelis' apprehensions that a return to the 1967 borders, especially in the West Bank, could render their state defenseless and would be tantamount to suicide, should not be minimized. (The whole of Israeli aviation can be paralyzed by a handful of terrorists operating from some points in the vicinity of the former "green" line.) A comprehensive settlement will, therefore, have to delineate borders that would bridge the gap between the Arab maximalist principle and Israel's need for modifications in the 1967 lines.

Palestinians. The Arabs are committed to the restoration of the "legitimate rights of the Palestinians" and to the PLO as the sole body authorized to define those rights and represent them, and there is an increasing international support for this position. At the present, the PLO owes allegiance to the Fedayeen organizations alone and adheres to the "Palestinian Charter" which not only insists on the destruction of the State of Israel but also implies the expulsion of a considerable part of its Jewish population. Israel has recognized the need to grant the Palestinians self-expression but it is against the detaching of this problem from that of Jordan and it cannot find any common ground for negotiations with the PLO. Thus, in order to be included in a comprehensive settlement, the Palestinians will have to produce a representation that would recognize Israel's right to exist, be approved by the Arab states, coordinated with Jordan and acceptable to Israel.

Refugees. Given the vast resources and spacious territories of the Arabs, the economic and humanitarian aspects of the refugee problem can be solved without great difficulties. For the Arabs, however, the symbolic and political aspects of the issue have always been of decisive importance and therefore they undoubtedly would insist that Israel accepts and rehabilitates a substantial number of refugees. The settlement will have, therefore, to bridge the gap between this demand and Israel's inability to absorb a considerable number of refugees without upsetting its internal cohesion.

Jerusalem. In spite of the great sensitivity and complexity of this issue, considerable accord appears to exist with regard to several principles, e.g., that the city should not be remilitarized and dismembered, and that all religions should have access to their holy places. However, the question of sovereignty remains the main stumbling block. A comprehensive settlement will have to elaborate a sophisticated political and jurisdictional arrangement to overcome this difficulty.

It thus emerges that the obstacles to a comprehensive settlement are so numerous and formidable that even a favorable constellation of the factors regulating the level of conflict (such as the constellation outlined in the following section) would not suffice to produce it. Therefore, in order to make this comprehensive scenario feasible, a *qualitative* change in the constituents of the conflict will have to take place.

Deescalation to a Lower Level of Conflict

The evolvement of a series of interim agreements concluded between Israel and individual Arab "confrontation states" may stop at a point from which progress towards a comprehensive settlement would become impossible because of the wide gap separating the basic positions of the parties. Nevertheless, the level of the continuing conflict would be brought closer to the level which existed during the period 1949-1967 (see above) than to that of the post-1967 phase. Such a development would not eliminate the possibility of more hostilities but may decrease the probability of their outbreak.

In order to deescalate the conflict to that level, the interim agreements would have to accomplish two things. First, they would have to reduce Arab motivation to upset the existing state of affairs by force. This cannot be achieved without coping with some of the issues of the conflict. Thus, the agreement would have to provide, in return for appropriate consideration, for the restoration of substantial parts of the occupied territories as well as some satisfaction to the Palestinians.

Second, the agreements would have to create obstacles to a military conflagration so that the initiation of a military offensive would put the initiating side at a great disadvantage, strategically as well as politically. For this purpose a system of demilitarized areas, effective inspection, mutual deterrence, and international guarantees would have to be worked out.

The realization of these two conditions is far from a simple matter. As seen above, the Arab governments have committed themselves to the restoration of "every inch" of the lost territories and to the representation of the Palestinian case by a maximalist political body. It thus may very well be that a "partial satisfaction" of Arab goals simply does not exist.

There are also open questions regarding the effectiveness of preventive measures designed to check the outbreak of hostilities. The demilitarization of substantial areas could reduce the chances of an accidental war or a surprise attack, handicap the offensive side and put it in an unfavorable political condition. But demilitarization is not panacea and cannot be applied equally to all sections of the Arab-Israeli front. In the Golan Heights the area in question is so narrow that it could hardly form a meaningful demilitarized buffer zone. In the West Bank demilitarization could be more effective but its durability would depend on the political status of the area.

The area most suitable for demilitarization is Sinai, which could be made into a formidable buffer zone (and which did, in fact, partially fulfill that role before

1967). Yet, even here many difficulties would have to be overcome. So far the Egyptians have rejected the notion that this should be the future role of the Sinai desert and, indeed, the principle of demilitarization had already been considerably eroded in the Egyptian-Israeli agreements which emerged after the Yom Kippur War. If the creation of a meaningful buffer zone is earnestly desired, the agreements concluded in the future will have to rule out the deployment of Egyptian troops and weapons in territories evacuated by Isaael, to stipulate that no military installations and logistic infrastructure are set up in Sinai, to design and apply an effective inspection system, and to spell out clearly what would be considered a violation of the demilitarization agreements and how such violations would be dealt with.

Of these problems perhaps the least severe is that of inspection, which can be solved to a large extent by modern technology. Direct supervision of demilitarization and other security arrangements can be performed, ideally, by joint Israeli-Arab units. In the absence of Arab consent to such collaboration, alternative arrangements can be made utilizing the good services of third parties who enjoy the confidence of both sides (such as the United States in the case of Israeli-Egyptian agreements in Sinai).

The stationing of UN troops as a barrier between the Israeli and the Arab forces has proven to be of limited value. The lessons of the hasty and disastrous withdrawal of the UN troops in 1967 have been learned, but no adequate alternative solutions have yet been produced to ensure that the same situation would not recur. The basic problems have remained unchanged: the United Nations, in which pro-Arab Afro-Asians and Communists have an overwhelming majority, is not neutral in the Middle Eastern conflict and in a time of crisis its troops can hardly be relied on to act effectively and impartially to check the outbreak of hostilities. In all likelihood, UN troops would be withdrawn precisely at the moment when their presence was needed most. As a matter of fact, the record of the UN troops stationed in the area after the Yom Kippur War shows that even without any crisis, governments which have despatched contingents to the Middle East tend to withdraw them prematurely, for reasons of their own, and replacements cannot be easily found. It seems, therefore, that in order for an international force to be effective, it would have to embody a higher level of superpower involvement based on a mutual understanding between the United States and the Soviet Union and established and controlled either directly or through the Security Council.

Similarly, international guarantees could contribute to deescalation only if they emanate from the superpowers. Only the United States and the Soviet Union have sufficient presence in the Middle East, leverage over the local adversaries and motivation to assert themselves in the area to give their guarantees a measure of credibility. However, no guarantees have ever outlived the international situation and the specific interests which were originally their *raison d'être*. Guarantees given jointly by the two competing superpowers would probably reflect a desire on their part to reduce the friction between them, but with the resumption of competition, the validity of their guarantees would almost certainly diminish proportionately.

In recent history guarantees given to each party in a conflict by *one* great power have proven to be of greater effectiveness, but in the nuclear age it has become less likely for a superpower to risk a global confrontation even when the terms of guarantees it has given call for it. In the case of the United States, there are additional factors which lower the reliability of its guarantees: the American political system restricts the effectiveness and durability of commitments made by the administration; the geographical distance limits the capability of the United States to intervene in the Middle Eastern arena; and it is improbable that the United States would employ force against an Arab state in order to honor its commitment to Israel. The potential contribution to Middle eastern stability of a possible Soviet guarantee is restricted by other factors, such as the Soviet's basic interest in penetrating the area and maintaining there a certain level of tension to serve that purpose. Guarantees, therefore, could not be expected to accomplish more than to provide supplementary reinforcement to a more extensive and elaborate regional arrangement.

Perhaps the most essential element in such an arrangement is mutual deterrence. Deterrence would be needed on two levels: for checking partial violations of the regional arrangement and for preventing the outbreak of full-scale wars. Mutual deterrence can be maintained only if the flow of weapons to the area is regulated in such a way that Arab quantitative superiority is not abruptly augmented by massive arms supplies and the introduction of superior weapons, or that Israel's defensive capability is not diminished by denying it the quantities and types of weapons it needs to compensate for its numerical weakness.

In the past, deterrence has not managed to accomplish any of the above-mentioned aims, but it is possible that with the rapid increase in the strategic destruction capabilities of the adversaries and the rising costs of military confrontations, mutual deterrence could become more substantial. It is a fact that mutual deterrence prevented Israel and Egypt from hitting each other's heartlands in the Yom Kippur War, and it has evidently occupied a central place in their political considerations following that war. Economic considerations have never played a decisive role in determining the course of the conflict, but the fact that the economies of both countries are becoming increasingly vulnerable to damage by war could add in the future to the effectiveness of mutual deterrence.

The main factor that could be conducive to deescalation is a realization (particularly on the Arab side) that in the Arab-Israeli conflict it is not only difficult to make peace but also increasingly unfeasible to make war. Accordingly, the two parties might regard as the lesser evil a *modus vivendi* which, though not fulfilling their aspirations entirely, would satisfy at least their most immediate interests and would not oblige them to make concessions on sensitive political issues where they are constrained by the more militant elements of their respective publics.

However, given all the factors feeding Arab-Israeli tension and the limitations of the instrumentalities which could be used to check processes of reescalation, it is difficult to envisage the stabilization of the conflict at a low level without some changes in the positions of states involved in it. Thus, for example, the Soviets and Arab militants who at present have an interest in the perpetuation of a certain level of tension in the Middle East, would have to reconsider their positions, possibly as the result of a new awareness of the risks and costs of hostilities.

Some of the factors regulating the level of conflict outlined in the first section of this chapter, would have to realign in a more favorable constellation in order to stabilize the Arab-Israeli relationship at the level described in this scenario. Such a combination of factors would include, among others: a deradicalization of the political life of the Arab states and a growing stress there on economic and social progress; in inter-Arab relations, neither sharp polarization into two rival camps nor unification under a militant leadership; and, on the global level, a higher level of United States-Soviet coordination. Development in these directions is possible, but so are developments in the opposite directions. The prospects of this scenario thus cannot be better than those of the conditions and developments which are its prerequisites.

Imposed Non-Belligerency

The cycle of recurring Arab-Israeli wars may be broken by concerted action on the part of the two superpowers to neutralize the capacity of the local belligerents to resume hostilities, thus imposing a *de facto* state of "non-belligerency" in the area. This would be non-belligerency only in a limited and negative sense, for the differences between the local adversaries would remain unsettled; only their ability to resort to force would be restricted. Unlike the previous scenario, which evolves from the attainment of a level of mutual agreement, this scenario would be produced by intervention and imposition from the outside.

However, this would not necessarily tend to freeze the *status quo*, for joint United States-Soviet action would, in all probability, seek to implement the degree of congruence existing between their respective concepts of a solution to the Middle Eastern crisis, and this congruence is incompatible with the *status quo*. Furthermore, although this type of superpower intervention is based on pressure or even coercion, it is quite likely that the powers would also seek ways to defuse the most explosive issues and to make the imposed non-belligerency as tolerable as possible to the local adversaries. Thus, an imposed arrangement of this kind would include substantial Israeli withdrawals from the occupied territories—possibly with the integration of a Palestinian element into the arrangement—and some guarantees and arms controls to reduce the threats to Israel's security.

The readiness of the two superpowers to collaborate for the implementation of such a scenario could theoretically evolve from a process of growing détente and increasing harmony between their global policies but, given the basic differences between them, and particularly the far-reaching aspirations of the Soviet Union in the Middle East, the chances for such a thawing process are very low indeed. There is a greater likelihood of the emergence of a United States-Soviet agreement to impose a joint policy in the Middle East as the result of an acute crisis—in the region itself, or possibly even in other regions—which would involve great risks for the superpowers and shake the confidence of their decisionmakers to the point where they would be ready to abandon some of the traditional features of their respective policies. Such a scenario might lead to United States-Soviet co-management of the Middle East or to its agreed division into two spheres of influence.

The ability of the two superpowers to neutralize the local belligerents may be questioned, but a convincing case might be put to affirm it. It is true that in the past Arab-Israeli wars broke out in spite of the declared objections of the two superpowers, but in each case the objection of one of the powers to its client launching a military offensive was half-hearted or verbal only (United States-Israel, 1967; Soviet Union-Egypt/Syria, 1973). When the two superpowers acted with genuine accord and determination they managed effectively to impose the termination of hostilities (Suez-Sinai evacuation, 1956-57; cease-fire, 1973). The local belligerents' demands for weapons in growing quantities and of increasing sophistication upgrades the leverage of the superpowers. The dependence of the Arabs on the Soviet Union to safeguard their "red lines" in the face of Israeli military superiority, and the dependence of the Israelis on the United States in view of their limited resources, also contribute to this leverage.

Given the present state of the international system, the possibility that the United States and the Soviet Union would utilize their combined assets for joint action in the Middle East remains quite remote, and only an international crisis of the highest magnitude could precipitate it. Even if a superpower arrangement were successfully imposed, it certainly would not solve the Arab-Israeli conflict. The arrangement itself would endure only as long as the superpower accord were in force, and it might very well be quite short-lived.

Recurring Military Confrontations

The failure of all other alternatives may leave as the only possibility a cycle of recurring large-scale hostilities. According to this scenario, the intervals between outbursts of hostilities would probably remain of the same duration as throughout the post-1967 period, i.e., approximately three years, but the level of military operations would be upgraded. This would be the result of the growing sophistication of weapons, continued expansion and improvement of the opposing armies and more desperate attempts on their part to achieve a decisive victory. The types of hostilities might alternate between various forms of limited warfare (attrition, blockade, single operations) and all-out wars. The great powers would be instrumental in imposing and maintaining the nonviolent intervals—which, in any case, the belligerents would need for their own purposes—but would not act to terminate hostilities altogether.

The conclusion of interim agreements does not necessarily preclude this scenario. Such agreements might collapse from the outset or "expire" without being followed by further agreements. A state like Egypt might break its agreement with Israel as the result of pressure from other Arab states or a change in its government. In addition, there is always the possibility that its manifested interest in an interim agreement was purely tactical from the outset and aimed solely at improving its strategic positions towards the next military confrontation.

There is one aspect of the post-1967 dynamics of the Arab-Israeli conflict which almost enforces this scenario on the course of developments. As is seen in the previous section of this paper, the parties to Arab-Israeli conflict have been caught, since 1967, in a vicious spiral. This process may be described schematically in the following terms. The 1967 war convinced the Israelis that as long as the Arab world challenges the right of Israel to exist they need more defensible borders for their security and physical survival. The Arabs, who have lost parts of the territories of their own states, are equally resolved that no sacrifice ought to be spared for the restoration of these territories and exclude the option of an historical reconciliation with the Jewish state. Such a resolution generates, mainly in Egypt and Syria, a process of national mobilization and military build-up to an unprecedented degree. The arms race, in terms of both the quantity and sophistication of weapons, is accelerated. The growing threat to Israel's security only hardens its determination to maintain the strategic advantages the administered territories provide. The Arabs, convinced that "what was taken by force can be regained only by force," increase the operability and efficiency of their war machines and apply military pressure on Israel. The War of Attrition is followed by the Yom Kippur War which poses a serious challenge to Israel's military superiority. At this stage, the size of military forces in the arena, and the capacity and range of the weapons they operate, reach such proportions that for the hard-pressed Israelis the risks involved in territorial withdrawals, particularly in the Golan and the West Bank, grow even greater. This leads to intensive preparations for another, more devastating, round of fighting. The partial agreements which the diplomatic search for a peaceful settlement may possibly produce could somewhat narrow the territorial issue but the vicious spiral would persist: Arab military build-up generating Israeli need for defensible borders, countered by Arab insistence on full withdrawal without real peace, producing a military build-up and so on.

In the final analysis, the basic factor which tends to generate the scenarios recurring confrontations is the Arabs' rejection of the legitimacy of the State of Israel and their growing conviction that at some point in the future they will be able to liquidate it—and the more wars Israel has to fight the nearer they will be to that point.

Several future developments could enhance the factors which are conducive to this scenario: radicalization in domestic Arab politics and lower priority to internal development; ascendancy of the right-wing in the Israeli political structure; predominance of militant Arab regimes in inter-Arab relations; greater involvement of the PLO in all-Arab decision-making; continued Fedayeen warfare; escalating arms races and strategic threats; and increasing superpower competition, with the Soviet Union seeking unilateral advantages through the perpetuation of the conflict.

The scenario of recurring confrontations would constitute, to some extent, a gain for the Arab side, for it would bring to bear upon the conflict Arab quantitative superiority in manpower and economic resources. Could Israel endure such a contest? The answer to this question would probably be determined by several factors, the most important of which are Israel's ability to sustain its military superiority and to ensure an adequate level of U.S. backing.

The balance of power between belligerents can never be measured with absolute certainty for it depends in part on intangible and unmeasurable components. But, judging by criteria based on the cumulative experience, it is reasonable to assume that within the range of this projection Israel will retain its military superiority over the Arabs.

In recent years, and particularly after the October War, the strength of the Arabs has definitely been increasing. In spite of the differences with the Soviets, the latter have continued their arms supplies to a number of Arab states, augmenting their arsenals with such sophisticated weapons as Mig-23's and Mig-25's, and Scud and Frog missiles. Arab petrodollars are being used for arms purchases from more diversified sources and in increasing quantities. The level of inter-Arab collaboration has risen, including possibly the activation of the "Eastern Command" in future confrontation. Arab strategic planning has improved and Arab commanders manifest today a greater degree of self-assurance. Finally, the Arabs have now the capacity to back their military efforts with the full weight of the oil weapon and their newly acquired international influence and prestige.

Yet, Israel's power has also been growing. Weapons and military equipment, provided by the United States since the Yom Kippur War on an unprecedented level, both qualitatively and quantitatively, are extending Israel's military capabilities in a very substantial way. The Israelis have also been making efforts to utilize their technological advantages for increasing the effectiveness of their war equipment. Their military superiority has been maintained, thus far, even with a ratio of roughly 3 to 1 in favor of the Arabs, in terms of troops, tanks, aircraft, and other weapons. With a more economic utilization of its manpower, and considering also such factors as efficiency, mobility, fire-power and ordinance delivery capacity, it is highly probable that within the range of this projection Israel will be able to retain superiority. As a matter of fact, military observers agree that the strength of the Israeli army in proportion to the combined force of Syria and Egypt has considerably grown in the period since the October War (all the more so since Soviet supplies to Egypt have sharply decreased).

The internal crisis in Israel after the Yom Kippur War was certainly detrimental to Israel's rehabilitation efforts, but it was grossly exaggerated and misread in the neighboring states. Hardships and danger, as recent studies show, intensify and do not depreciate the identification of most Israelis with their state. Whatever the intensity of Arab animosity to the Jewish state, it can hardly compete with the determination of a people defending its existence.

The second condition necessary for Israel to be able to sustain the pressure of frequent conflagrations is the ability to secure a certain level of American assistance. The Israelis cannot take U.S. support for granted, yet a significant feature of U.S. assistance to Israel in recent years has been its decreasing dependence on sympathetic attitudes and domestic pressures and its clearer integration into the self-interest strategies and policies of the United States.

The association of the United States with Israel has frequently been described as detrimental to American relations with the Arabs, but recent developments make this rule highly questionable. It is, after all, the special relations between Washington and Jerusalem which allows the United States to gain influence in Cairo (and perhaps improve its relations with Damascus) at a time when the Soviets, who had committed themselves to the Arabs and severed their relations with Israel, must sit back and watch.

The case for the continuation of U.S. assistance to Israel can be summarized, in simplified form, as follows. The two principal Israeli requests from the United States are, first, to provide Israel with the arms needed to match Soviet supplies to the Arabs and to render it the financial assistance necessary for defense; and second, to neutralize potential Soviet intervention in support of the Arab side.

If a positive response on the first point can enable Israel to take care of its own defense then, it is argued, it would be a low price to pay for avoiding the dilemma of whether or not to commit U.S. troops to the Middle East arena in circumstances of an acute crisis. Maintaining the existing balance of power is, perhaps, the most significant contribution to regional stability: it reduces the chances of both Arab offensives and Israeli preemptive strikes, and it enables Israel to undertake the risks involved in the regional arrangements promoted by the United States.

The response to the second request involves direct U.S. interests. It is obvious that the toleration of a unilateral Soviet intervention in the Middle East would bring about the collapse of the pro-Western regimes and the whole Western deployment in the area, and allow the Soviet Union to assume control in an area vital to the Western world.

As seen above, the scenario of recurring hostilities is one of steady escalation, in scope and intensity, of the military confrontation. As none of the adversaries stands a good chance of winning a decisive victory in this process, and the losses and costs imposed by continued warfare become increasingly onerous, any of them might be tempted to go nuclear or resort to other nonconventional weapons of mass destruction.

It is plausible that the proliferation of atomic weapons is an inevitable process which therefore, sooner or later, is bound to reach the Middle Eastern arena as well, and that the escalation of the Arab-Israeli conflict, and particularly the dynamics of mutual suspicion, may even accelerate the process. On the Arab side, the diversity of political regimes and the concentration of vast financial resources, often in the hands of the least responsible leaders, may open a door to the acquisition of nonconventional weapons. On the Israeli side, the fact that superiority in conventional warfare is bound to be limited in time may produce the same result.

However, within the range of the foreseeable future, both adversaries have good reasons to oppose this trend. With all the risks and costs of a protracted conflict with Israel, the physical existence of the Arab peoples has never been threatened; with the introduction of nonconventional weapons it will be. Most Arab states are vulnerable to a nuclear strike, particularly Egypt when the whole population is concentrated in the narrow Nile Valley, and a good part of it in a two megalopolises. In addition, most Arabs fear that a balance of terror would neutralize their superiority in manpower and resources.

Israel clearly prefers a conventional *superiority* to a nuclear *equilibrium*. The narrow geographical space of Israel makes it extremely vulnerable to mass destruction weapons. It would be quite difficult for Israel to develop, and convincingly demonstrate, a second strike capability and thus the deterrence value of its nuclear weapons is limited. With the diversity of Arab regular and irregular forces, the unpredictability of the Arab regimes' level of responsibility, and the uncertainties concerning the timing, direction and forms of nuclear retaliation, the ability of a nuclear threat to prevent conventional attacks becomes questionable.

The scenario of escalating confrontation leads inevitably to disastrous consequences for all parties concerned. On the conventional level, it may devastate both Israel and the Arab "confrontation states." On the nuclear level, it may result in mutual destruction. On both levels it may involve the superpowers, spill over to other danger spots and end in a global confrontation.

It is precisely the magnitude of the perils involved in this scenario that reduces its probability. In spite of occasional appearances to the contrary, the political behavior of Middle Eastern states has been basically rational, in terms of their own self-interest and lists of priorities. It is thus not inconceivable that in light of the catastrophic consequences of this scenario they would find ways to avoid it. By the same token, it is plausible that the superpowers, which several times in the past have engaged in brinkmanship in this region, would make a concerted effort, in the face of the growing risks, to defuse the Middle Eastern powder keg. If the positions of the parties concerned indeed take this turn, they may do so either in the initial stages of the scenario or in the wake of one or more conflagrations, but in both cases this fact would probably lead to one of the previously described scenarios.

Conclusions

The Arab-Israeli dispute is perhaps the most difficult conflict of this generation, in terms of the polarization of the positions of the adversaries and the complexity and variety of factors intensifying it. A complete solution to this conflict within the foreseeable future is inconceivable.

However, taking the long-range view, the possibility that the sources and tributaries of the conflict may dry up should not be precluded. With modernization, development and secularization, the role of ideologies may decline, making mutual understanding and acceptance more feasible. Radicalism may diminish, giving way to pragmatism and moderation. Inter-Arab rivalries may subside, leading to a greater stress on the particular interest of each Arab state rather than on Pan-Arab issues. The superpowers may develop new modes of collaboration and thus act in accord to contain and settle local conflicts.

In the same perspective, there is no reason why the respective demands of the adversaries could not be satisfied to a reasonable extent. Israel's security can be ensured within a satisfactory regional and international arrangement. The Palestinians can be allowed self-expression in a political body which may be federated with Jordan and could maintain special links with Israel. The acknowledgement of Israel as "an established fact" can develop gradually into a genuine recognition. Subtle problems, like those of the refugees and Jerusalem, can be solved by multilateral cooperation and some political ingenuity.

However, there is no assurance that future developments will take this course, and a no less convincing case can be put for a projection of the opposite. Thus, for example, failure of economic and social development schemes in the Arab world may intensify frustration and generate a spirit of militant radicalism. Similarly, the emergence of Soviet military superiority may produce a bolder Soviet strategy in the region leading to sharper superpower competition. Such developments would result in a protracted conflict rather than in a settlement.

Taking a "worst case" view of the future developments, the following appear to be some of the critical problems that may ensue for the world community and particularly for the United States: A concentrated Soviet effort to establish firm control in parts of the Middle East; the emergence of a superpower confrontation from a local conflict; the proliferation of nuclear and other nonconventional weapons; interference with the flow of oil from the Middle East to the industrialized states; disruption of the international economy by Arab financial maneuvers; inter-Arab conflicts upsetting the status quo in the region; the collapse of pro-Western Arab regimes such as those of Jordan and Lebanon; an increase in the volume and effectiveness of terrorism (possibly with the development of more mobile and sophisticated weaponry); an accelerated arms race, which may put Western suppliers at a disadvantage; economic crisis and shortages in countries which possess limited resources, necessitating substantial economic aid; and perhaps even subversion and other interference by Communist China.

Beyond all this, it may be worthwhile to point out that the possibility that future developments would not be determined by any of the factors, options and scenarios mentioned above, but by what is today unpredictable, looms very large.

IX   The Arab Response to the Challenge of Israel

Boutros Boutros-Ghali

To establish a coherent explanation of the pattern of Arab attitudes toward the Zionist challenge, one may begin by defining the factors which colored Arab reactions before the October 1973 war and which continue to play an important role in determining their actions. The first of these was the Balkanization of the Middle East immediately after World War I. This promoted a widespread anticolonial attitude which crystallized public sentiment regarding the stance of the Western powers and the growing Zionist presence in Palestine. There is a very strong case indeed for considering this particularly anticolonial attitude as the basis for Arab policies in international affairs to the present day. The second factor was the disparity in rates of social, political, and economic development among the countries in the area. Although this disparity caused variety in attitudes primarily towards the outside world, it produced tensions and realignment within the Arab world itself. Recently, moreover, the disparity has been accentuated by the consequences of the sudden increase of already vast oil revenues in some of the countries. We must emphasize, as a third factor, the involvement of the Middle East in the cold war. This inevitably led to both direct and indirect influence of the two superpowers in the affairs of the region. Finally we must mention the growing and unpredictable importance of oil as a factor in international politics. This may involve the Arab world in a set of positions and attitudes which cannot be foreseen at the moment with absolute certainty.

So much for constant factors rooted in the past. Today we are witnessing a radical change in the self-image of Arabs resulting from the impact of the October war of 1973. It is unnecessary to list the factors of change since that historical event, for they have been discussed publicly at great length. There are, however, a number of observations about new Arab attitudes that are worth mentioning because they have far-reaching implications. By presenting to the world what is, for all intents and purposes, a common front, the Arabs are certainly experiencing a stage of increasing political unity. In addition, their morale has been considerably uplifted by a sudden awareness of their remarkable competence in the use of highly sophisticated weaponry. Their awareness has been especially heightened, following a period of distress and self-doubt due to the disastrous blow suffered in 1967. Furthermore, as if by common consent and concerted planning, the Arabs have demonstrated their effective use of the oil weapon at the international level. A sobering thrust in October 1973 certainly lent credibility to later threats to use the oil weapon again, should it prove necessary. To the Arabs this credibility assumed larger strategic importance as Western statesmen alluded to the possibility of reversion to the gunboat and airborne brigade as tools of international negotiation.

A new element to be taken into account is the recent formation of a combination of Arab approaches including an increased determination to curb Israeli expansion and a readiness to recognize the existence of Israel as a sovereign state for an interim period, pending her peaceful integration with the Palestinians into a secular state or a confederation.

The conduct of the October war had significant effects on the Arab self-image. In spite of the partial success of the Israeli counteroffensives on the African side of the Suez Canal and on the Golan Heights, there was no diminution of the Arab image. This was due, in large measure, to several factors. Both inside and outside the Arab world, the initial military victories made a greater impact on the imagination of the public than did the later setbacks, which were, naturally, not so highly publicized. In addition, while the Israeli counteroffensives on the African side of the Suez Canal and on the Golan Heights were successful, they did not bring about an ultimate victory. This left the military outcome of hostilities inconclusive. This in turn was due, of course, to the convenient compromise of the cease-fire, which provided a welcome face-saver for all the parties. While the war news was, on the whole, very well reported, the Arab mass media certainly understated the importance of the Israeli thrust west of the Suez Canal. On the other hand, the "war of attrition" on the Golan Heights clearly demonstrated Syrian ability and determination to maintain pressure on the Israeli forces in the region.

Prospects for the future are equally enhancing to the Arab self-image. This has already found expression in the Arabs' decision to begin major rearmament programs in order to realize their increased military potential. A rhythm can be observed in the increase of the Arab arms supply. In terms of manpower, financial resources and diplomatic alliances, the Arabs have established a sort of counterpoint to that rhythm. This surely signifies their overwhelming superiority. In appraising the new balance of power, Israel finds itself in a position where it must weigh the possibilities not only of the "front-line" states, but of a vast, hostile, and united hinterland consisting of Saudi Arabia, Libya, Algeria, Morocco, Sudan, Somalia, and the two Yemens, as well. Consequently, new theaters of operations have now made their appearance in areas quite remote from the immediate borders of Israel-namely, such strategic areas as the Straits of Bab al-Mandab, Hormuz, and even Gibraltar.

Finally, we must candidly admit that from a military point of view the Arabs cannot be said to have won the October war with any degree of decisiveness. The economic and political effects of the oil embargo, however, have been to isolate Israel, making that nation totally dependent on the United States for its survival as a military force. It has also become abundantly clear to the Arabs that Britain, France, the Soviet Union, and the United States would all be unhesitantly well-disposed toward the conclusion of multimillion dollar arms deals with the Arab governments in exchange for cash payments and/or oil supplies. This certainly is a new element in the situation, and all parties concerned are well aware of it. Regarding any lesson in strategy which the protagonists may have learned from the October war, it is the Arabs who are more likely to have acquired new knowledge from their experience, whereas the Israelis had already achieved a very high level of military efficiency when war broke out. As a result of the improvement in their military performance the Arabs are quite likely to win a fifth war, should it occur, but it is certainly a foregone conclusion that civilian and military casualties are bound to be higher for them than they were in 1973. This fact alone might cause some of the governments concerned to pause and think. Yet, the trauma resulting from losses in human lives and material wealth would probably have even more far-reaching consequences in Israel than in the Arab countries.

In view of what has been suggested so far, it might be useful to divide the rest of our comments into several themes in order to grasp the rapidly changing situation. First, we shall consider the balance of power within the Arab world before and after the October war. Then it will be useful to consider three other topics related to each other: the oil weapon and the new balance of power, the impact of the war on Israel as it is understood by the Arabs, and, finally, the impact of the Zionist challenge on the spectrum of Arab policies.

The Balance of Power Within the Arab World Before and After the October War

Between 1945 and 1956 the Arab world was dominated by two opposing groups of monarchical states: Egypt, Saudi Arabia, and the Yemen, on the one hand, and the Hashimite states of Iraq and Jordan, on the other. The balance of power was achieved by the maneuvers of Syria and Lebanon, which vacillated between the two groups, supporting now the one and now the other. The year 1958 was pivotal, for the union between Egypt and Syria in February, when the United

Arab Republic came into being, had the effect of creating a "radical" group of states, while the July 14 revolution in Baghdad, which marked the end of the Hashimite ascendancy in Iraq, strengthened the predominance of the radicals in the struggle for power in the Arab world.

A rapid survey of the political chronology of the ensuing years shows important developments. The admission of Morocco and Tunisia to the Arab League in September 1956 contributed to a definite shift of the center of gravity in the Arab world toward the countries of the Maghrib, which lent a more clearly African character to Arab political activity. It also added importance to the voices of those moderate states, which came to include Saudi Arabia, Jordan, Tunisia, and Morocco. Almost overnight they became a power to be reckoned with. On the other hand, the abortive coup of the pro-Nasser officers in Iraq (March 1959) split the Arab radical front into two incompatible wings: Egypt and Syria on the one side against Iraq on the other. After its secession from the United Arab Republic (U.A.R.) in September 1961, Syria joined the Iraqi camp. The moderate wing, however, was further reinforced not only by the admission of Kuwait into the Arab League (July 1961), but also by the growing evidence of Kuwait's financial importance in the Arab community of nations as well as on the stage of international finance and politics. With the admission of Algeria into the Arab League (August 1962) and its decision to cooperate closely with Egypt, Cairo was able to see its way out of isolation and into a new phase which afforded the opportunity of creating a new group of radical states. In due course it became possible to distinguish between the radical and Socialist states, comprised of Egypt, Algeria, Syria, Iraq, and Yemen, on the one hand, and the reformist but nonetheless traditionalist states—namely Saudi Arabia, Jordan, Morocco and Kuwait—on the other.

The power struggle between these two groups of states, indeed between these two ideological positions, lost much of its bitterness following the disastrous outcome of the June 1967 war. Subsequently, the death of Gamal Abdel Nasser and the outbreak of hostilities in October 1973 were to play an important role in bringing about a new alignment and coalition of forces in the Arab world. The nerve center or, one might say, the nucleus of this new coalition consisted of three countries, Egypt, Saudi Arabia, and Algeria, with Syria, as it were, on the periphery. The ideological basis of these countries' common policy, largely the result of pragmatic approaches to recent experience, included several principles. First, the idea of achieving Arab unity through revolution was superseded by the concepts of political coexistence and the imperatives of practical economic and cultural cooperation. If one may be permitted to adapt General de Gaulle's terse phrase to an Arab context, they were now calling for "*l'Arabisme des patries.*" Second, the new coalition was clearly disposed to work towards a political solution of the Palestine problem which would include implicitly the recognition of the existence of Israel. Last, a permanent or at least durable settlement in the Middle East would have to take into account the Palestinians' right of self-determination. In the light of this basic decision the Palestine Liberation Organization was unanimously recognized at the Rabat summit conference of November 1974 as the sole representative of the Palestinian people.

The net result of this evolution of Arab political stances was a shift in the emphasis of the declared positions of the various Arab countries. Having no common frontiers with Palestine, the so-called new radicals, Iraq, Libya, and South Yemen, became more strident, giving expression to their new radicalism secure from any perilous military consequences. In spite of what appears to have been a common philosophy on some points, they were, apparently, unable to reach a community of views sufficient to form a coalition or alliance. The reasons for this inability are not difficult to discern. On one hand, their lack of participation in the October war has considerably discredited their opposition to the main stream of Arab thinking. On the other hand, in terms of strict *realpolitik*, the new coalition of Egypt, Saudi Arabia, and Algeria has almost completely prevailed in the counsels of the Arab community.

It is now clear that there is a common attitude among the majority of Arabs with regard to a political solution of the Palestine problem. This position can be characterized as a careful balance or neat discrimination between two aims (depending on policy and opportunity): a genuine disposition, bordering on determination, to ensure a continuous flow of oil to the industrialized nations of the West, and the containment of Soviet influence in the region. Containment of the Russians is both ideological and a matter of expediency. (The aim is not to eliminate the Soviet presence completely, which would be difficult even in the best of times, for some measure of Soviet presence and influence is an essential prerequisite or ballast for the policy of nonalignment.) A further target is to ensure firmly, but discreetly, that the influence of the radical group of Arab states be diminished and, ultimately, neutralized. Finally, there is the quite definite desire to overcome recalcitrance in arriving at a *modus vivendi* with the State of Israel within its recognized borders.

The Oil Weapon and the New Balance of Power

On October 17, 1973, ten days after the outbreak of the fourth Arab-Israeli War, the Arab oil ministers met in Kuwait with the declared purpose of deciding how best to deploy the oil weapon in support of the military war of liberation undertaken by Egypt and Syria. They agreed to cut oil production by at least 5 percent monthly until Israel's evacuation of all Arab territory occupied during the June 1967 war and the achievement of the rights of Arab Palestinians, or until further cuts would be detrimental to the national and Arab policies of the producing countries.

The Arab oil ministers also reserved the right to deny oil to any country they considered unfriendly. In fact, they actually imposed oil embargoes on the

Netherlands because of that country's overt support for the Israeli cause. The use of Arab oil was by no means a policy without precedent, for prior to the October 1973 war there had been two important attempts by the Arabs to use their oil as an instrument of political pressure. The first of these took place following the Anglo-French-Israeli aggression on Egypt in 1956. The flow of oil was partially interrupted as a result of the blowing up of the pump stations along the pipelines in Syria. The second attempt took place when several Arab oil-producing countries imposed an embargo on oil supplies to the United States, Great Britain, and West Germany, following the Israeli aggression on Egypt in June 1967. This embargo, however, was not successful, and an analysis of the reasons for its failure may provide a clue regarding subsequent policies.

First, one should bear in mind the fact that the Arab states were in open disagreement before the war and unlikely to be in any frame of mind for consenting to sacrifices for one another soon after the Arab defeat. The main polarization of opinion was between Saudi Arabia and Egypt, for along with a profound political discord between the two countries there was a very clear personality clash between President Nasser and King Faisal. Besides, the embargo followed a disastrous military defeat and was not sustained by any common political front. The division was widened when the Arab countries concerned became unable to agree on any precise political target which would allow them to lift the embargo either individually or collectively. Furthermore, there was the unmistakable bitterness in the realization that the Arabs lacked sufficient political maturity, and certainly the monetary reserves, required to withstand the political and economic effects of the oil embargo which they were expected to impose on the powerful industrial countries of the West.

Some six years later, however, the Arab position had changed in a number of ways. First, a genuine alliance was formed between President Sadat of Egypt and King Faisal of Saudi Arabia, an alliance which has been maintained and strengthened even after King Faisal's untimely death. Second, the unanimous approval of all the Arab states ceased to be essential to the deployment of the oil weapon with effective results because the combined production of Saudi Arabia, Kuwait, and Abu Dhabi alone amounted to more than 60 percent of the total Arab production of oil. Third, the military success of the Arab armies in the October war created the necessary political and moral pressures on the noncombatant Arab states to exert their utmost in the total deployment of their own oil weapon. Fourth, the Arab oil exporting countries had achieved a position of such economic and financial strength and security that they were able to cut back oil production without damaging their own developing economies in any way.

On the other hand, there was the increasing dependence of the United States (a main target of the Arab oil embargo) on Arab supplies, not to mention the near-total dependence of Western Europe and Japan on Arab oil. Finally, two factors which might have had an adverse effect on the Arabs' use of the oil weapon were neutralized by the course of events. The first was Iraq's dissociation from the measures decided in Kuwait in October 1973, stemming from its preference for the nationalization of oil and of other interests held by hostile powers in the Arab world, rather than an embargo. The other factor was that the Libyans had also disassociated themselves from the decisions made in Kuwait, on the grounds that the October war had not been a genuine war of liberation. These attitudes provided a sort of diversionary polemic for some time, but they were unable, in any detectable way, to undermine the effectiveness of the Arab oil weapon.

Learning from past experience, the Arabs will almost surely bear in mind certain elements of policy: the credibility, beyond any shadow of a doubt, of the oil weapon, and its enhanced effectiveness as a deterrent; the fact that only selective embargoes backed by overall cutbacks in production can be effective, although some moderation in the use of restrictive oil measures, such as the easing of the deadline for the implementation of political objectives, may be necessary and desirable during the period of the embargo. In other words, the oil weapon will have to be used according to a strategy of "flexible response" rather than a policy of "massive retaliation." It should always be remembered that the real strength of the weapon lies in its function as a deterrent rather than as an instrument of coercion. It has also been recognized that there is a need to devise and implement a system of mutual aid among the Arab states, as the oil weapon is bound to impose unequal burdens on the various Arab economies.

From the point of view of Arab military strategy, the oil weapon will continue to be employed as an adjunct to any Arab military action rather than as an independent striking force, because it represents the effective contribution of the Arab oil producing states to the common war effort. Any coalition, in order to be successful, must involve the active participation of all.

Should the industrialized world, however, decide on military intervention in the future, a plan of massive retaliation by the Arabs has been formulated and adopted. This will take the form of the systematic destruction of those oil installations which might become the target of foreign military intervention or occupation. This drastic measure would immediately cut the oil flow, with disastrous consequences for the West and, almost certainly, for the Arab states themselves. The so-called Masada complex is by no means confined to Israel. This final element of the plan, however, should sound a helpful note of warning: the Arab countries have not yet reached so advanced a stage of economic development that they would suffer equally with developed countries from an economic collapse of the magnitude that destruction of oil facilities would entail. They would surely be able to weather the rough consequences better than the West.

Arab Views of the Impact of the War on Israel

One of the most important results of the October war has been a psychological break-through for the Arabs, who had been smarting in the bitterness of previous defeat. The widely accepted image (reaching almost mythological proportions) of Israel as an invincible military power suffered heavily. The eye-opening experience of one of the most terrible desert battles of all time was a lesson which was lost neither on Israel's supporters nor on the Arabs. Within the space of two weeks Israel abandoned on the battlefield no less than half its armored force and a quarter of its military aircraft. This led to a rapid loss of Israeli self-confidence on all fronts within a matter of days. Consequently, the strategic role of Israel as a guardian of American and Western European interests in the Middle East came under serious reconsideration in the United States and Europe. It became evident that henceforth both the United States and Western Europe would be obliged to step up their cooperation with the Arab states at the expense of their alignment with Israel.

The new political imperative became more than a matter of expediency: it almost reached the proportions of a strategy for sheer survival. Furthermore, the morality of the case came under much closer scrutiny as the colonialist and expansionist policy of Israel was given maximum publicity by Arab diplomacy. Beyond the rhetoric of inflammatory discourse certain unmistakable Israeli acts of aggression and atrocities spoke for themselves. The facts broke into the conscience of the world with great force as it learned the full extent of the violence involved in the human tragedy. The world learned of the massive expulsion of Palestinians participating in Arab political leadership in occupied Palestine, of the massive and collective dispossession of countless Arabs from their own homes, based on the shifting justifications of specious policies which first denied the right of return to half a million Palestinian peasants who had fled from the combat areas to the East bank of the Jordan during the June war of 1967, and then reduced the native population to the status of wandering refugees or camp-inmates within areas now under Israeli domination. There were massive land expropriations in rural and urban areas in order to establish Jewish settlements in their place, together with the indiscriminate use of large-scale administrative detention by the military authorities in occupied territories.

An international reaction was bound to come. World opinion came to view the Israeli cause with rapidly mounting suspicion. Israel was finding itself in an advancing state of diplomatic isolation. The overwhelming majority of African, Asian, Socialist, and nonaligned countries broke off diplomatic relations with Israel. The international community was no less forthright in its condemnation. The United Nations and many international agencies voiced their horror at Israeli violation of human rights and its inexplicable intransigence, which could render that nation nothing but disservice in the long run. Within Israel there was widespread shock among the population, to such an extent that the war was widely referred to as an "earthquake" by the mass media. The feeling grew that the Israelis had been let down by their own leaders. There was a crisis of confidence in the military leadership and an unmistakable sense of doubt as to the wisdom of the political guidelines of the Zionist establishment. The Left and even mildly progressive or liberal opinion in Israel began to call into question the very viability of the Zionist idea and movement as such.

One of the interesting side-results of this collective reappraisal of ideals and strategies was the emergence of the first signs of a possible political alliance between progressive Israeli Jews and left-wing Palestinian Arabs. It is in the light of this possibility and this new soul-searching that one must assess the significance of the prosecution of Israeli Jews on various charges, such as the attempt to establish a joint Israeli-Jewish and Palestinian-Arab armed underground movement and membership in anti-Zionist organizations. Similarly, there were increased political contacts made with Arabs, which frequently led to the failure to inform Israeli police authorities of what might be considered illegal subversive activities.

This was only one aspect of Israeli reactions as seen by the Arabs. Another was more difficult and potentially dangerous: the revival of the "Masada complex" and the ever-increasing possibility of an Israeli preemptive strike against the Arabs. This impression was confirmed by widespread Israeli discussions which illustrated the extent to which Israelis are aware of the basic insecurity of the Israeli identity and all that it includes in the way of fears concerning the future. The Israelis have suddenly been brought to the harsh realization that time is on the side of the Arabs.

The Impact of the Zionist Challenge on Various Arab Policies and Attitudes

Our concern here is not the individual attitudes adopted by various Arab states towards the Zionist challenge, as this is largely a spectrum of overlapping and similar policies. More specifically, our purpose here is to examine the three principal currents of opinion which have prevailed in the Arab world in the face of the Zionist presence, namely rejection, isolationism, and compromise, which have been exacerbated by the conclusion of the Sinai agreement of September 1975.

The Rejectionists

The "rejectionists" constitute a body of opinion which holds that in order to face the Zionist challenge there can only be a general revolution which will begin with the liberation of those Arab states which are governed by their own reactionary military or decadent regimes which are the "objective allies" of the Zionist state. It is the very existence of these regimes, the argument goes, which constitutes the prime reason for the series of Arab defeats. The bulk of the rejectionists can be found among the Palestinian radicals who, for the most part, come from the ranks of the refugees of the first Palestinian diaspora. These are the Palestinians who used to live in those parts of Palestinian territory which were handed over to the state of Israel according to the 1947 partition plan. They believe that the boundaries of Palestine should include a combination of what has been the State of Israel for more than twenty-five years, the territories acquired by Jordan and the Gaza strip. In other words, nothing less than the whole of pre-1948 Palestine is acceptable to them. This political position comprises a complex pattern of arguments holding that the acceptance of a political settlement based on the surrender of the fundamental rights of the Arab Palestinians after half a century of struggle constitutes a total defeat not only for the Palestinians but for the entire Arab world as well. The argument continues with the point that none of the strategic goals of the Palestinian revolution has been reached, as organized popular resistance has not been fully realized in the occupied territories.

Should negotiations take place under present conditions, then the Palestinians would consider themselves to be in an extremely weak bargaining position. Furthermore, the new trends in highly effective small-weapons technology have altered the basic tactics of modern warfare. A well-trained guerrilla group with modern weaponry can direct a significant thrust at the very infrastructure of the enemy state, putting its entire oil industry, for example, out of action. In addition, by the judicious use of modern war technology, the Straits of Hormuz and Bab el-Mandeb could easily be blocked for long periods of time, which would have catastrophic implications for both Israel and the lifelines of the world powers, which would then be forced to respond seriously.

Now that the Arabs have entered upon a new era of military and political power, it would be unwise to jeopardize the fundamental rights of the Palestinians in order to move toward short-run gains. Consequently, while expressing itself in favor of a democratic, secular state for Muslims, Christians, and Jews, within the borders of pre-1948 Palestine, the Palestine Liberation Organization has refrained from explaining how this objective can be reconciled with the short-term aim of constituting a West Bank-Gaza ministate. It would indeed be short-sighted to believe it possible to achieve this minimal objective without formal recognition of Israel and the conclusion of a lasting peace with its leaders.

This argument has been taken up as well by the radical Arab states Iraq, Libya, and South Yemen, who are uncompromising in their demand for those territories occupied by Israel during the June 1967 war as well as for the liberation of the whole of pre-1948 Palestinian territory. They are particularly outspoken in their criticism of the leadership of the Palestinian Liberation Organization (PLO), Egypt, and Saudi Arabia for what seems clearly to them their capitulation to Zionist demands by virtue of the acceptance of the restitution of not more than 15 or 20 percent of original Palestine. These radical states regard themselves as "front-line" states at war with the Zionists, although they do not have any common frontiers with the Zionist state. They have not accepted Resolution 242 adopted by the Security Council in 1967, for that would imply recognition of Israel.

One should, however, point out that the elements of the situation in this regard have undergone considerable change, since Iraq did agree to attend the last summit meeting in Rabat in November 1974. This was but to usher in a definite Iraq-Iranian rapprochement, that is, a conciliatory move towards a country well-known for its "moderate" positions, as well as to heal that running sore, the civil war with the Kurds in Iraq. All this was bound to make Iraqi diplomatic policy flexible and more amenable to influence by the new elements which would come into play with regard to the Zionist challenge.

The role of Syria should be emphasized among the rejectionist states, for it occupies a special position in this pattern of argument. Until 1917 Palestine was an integral part of the province of Syria under the Ottoman regime. Moreover, Syria, with some justification, regards itself in a very special way as the standard-bearer of Arabism. Syria has succeeded in integrating into her own institutions the military and ideological structure of one of the Palestinian resistance movements. One of the consequences of this integration has been the mutual strengthening of Syrian and Palestinian radicalism. Although circumstances have led Syrian policy to soft-pedal some of its major theses with regard to the Zionist challenge, it remains nonetheless true that Damascus is profoundly convinced of its inescapable role as one of the most uncompromising advocates of a policy of rejection. It should be observed, however, that rejectionism is not the monopoly of certain radical states and elements in the Palestinian resistance movement. It is a philosophy which animates countless political parties and factions throughout the Arab world, varying from extreme left-wing to extreme right-wing positions.

The Arab Left and Marxism

For a considerable section of the Arab Left, Israel is clearly the watchdog of American imperialism in the Middle East. This belief postulates that the Palestinian revolution will create the opportunity for the anti-Zionist Israeli left to seize power and thereby contribute to the salvation of all the peoples of the area.

The Palestinian revolutionary movement will, it is believed, bring about the collapse of the decadent and bourgeois regimes in the area. The revolutionary forces will then find their rightful place as allies in the larger movement of the world proletarian revolution. In the short term, however, a series of new Arab-Israeli wars will weaken the bourgeois regimes and speed up the socialization of the Arab world.

Clearly, this line of argument has minor variants in the varying contexts of the Arab world. For example, in Arab North Africa this left-wing outlook is colored by memories of the Algerian war of liberation and by its points of resemblance to the Palestinian war of liberation. Parallels are drawn between the colonialism of the French in Algeria and the colonialism of Zionist settlers. In both cases settlers seized the land and drove the native inhabitants towards the desert. Parallels are also drawn between the way in which the French *metropole* gave its support to the French *colons* and the way in which America provides the lifeline for the Zionist settlers. There are also similarities between international conspiracy of silence on both issues. The nonrecognition of an Algerian nation is echoed in the nonrecognition of the people of Palestine. Similarly, the two liberation movements appear to have undergone the same type of internal split.

For the Somalis and the Sudanese, *apartheid* is mirrored in Israeli discrimination against the non-Jew. This has become a point of their condemnation of any form of Zionism on the grounds that it is merely a form of colonialism. They reject it as profoundly incompatible with the philosophy of a liberation movement.

The bloody civil disturbances which continue to tear Lebanon apart provide a typical example of the alliance which exists between the Arab Left and the Palestinian rejectionists. The Left is convinced of the need to get rid of the desectarian structure of the state institutions and the capitalist nature of its economy, while the Palestinians regarded themselves as committed to blocking U.S. Secretary of State Kissinger's mediation, which was adjudged an attempt to isolate Egypt from the rest of the Arab world. It goes without saying, however, that the confrontation between the Lebanese Phalangists and the Palestinian resistance had a number of other causes, such as Arabism, sectarianism, anti-Zionism, and the class struggle, all of which constitute a complex set of motivations. It is nevertheless undeniable that the situation is dominated by the activities of the Arab Left.

It must be borne in mind at this point that whatever shades of opinion might divide the variety of Arab left-wing groups, one principle dominates the thinking of all: the revolution that they have in mind should take place both in the Arab states and in the Zionist state. Another principle in their thinking is that this comprehensive revolution will constitute, in the last analysis, the only common denominator between Arabs and Israelis, the only hope for a platform of reconciliation between the two.

The Arab Right and Islam

The extreme Right in the Arab world is mainly represented by the Muslim Brotherhood and a number of lesser politico-religious groups. Their common ideology is a militant Islam committed to saving the Islamic-Arab world from Zionism as well as from colonialism and communism.

Islamic theologians have, in fact, elaborated a doctrine which governs the coexistence between the three great monotheistic religions of Islam, Judaism, and Christianity. They are convinced that a return to the religious doctrines of these faiths should be sufficient to resolve all the differences which may have developed in the Islamic-Arab world. Another point is that the frontiers imposed by Western colonialism are fundamentally alien to the idea of the Abode of Islam (Dar al-Islam). Ultimately, after liberation, Palestine is bound to transcend its frontiers and become part of a much larger entity. A Muslim commonwealth, according to theologians, must have priority over any merely nationalist policy and over any non-Muslim entity.

While the Arab extreme Left bases its arguments on Marxist dialectic in order to explain the historical determinism which is bound to bring about the liquidation of the Zionist colonial phenomenon, the Arab extreme Right bases its arguments on history, pointing out with incontrovertible logic that the Christian kingdoms of the Levant set up by the Crusaders were not impervious to erosion by Islam.

Finally, the possibility of a tactical alliance between the Arab extreme Left and Right is not to be dismissed. The profound faith which animates these opposing movements and the shared sense that history is on their side provide their ideologies with a proselytizing force which should not be underestimated. Naturally, the Balkanization of the Arab world into a score of sovereign states has made contacts and exchanges between these movements difficult. This situation does not enhance their potential for concerted action. Yet, although these various movements appeal mainly to minorities, they certainly are capable of causing serious complications for the advocates of compromise towards a peaceful settlement of the Middle East crisis.

The Isolationists

The isolationists are committed, in general, to the proposition that the local interests of each Arab state should be allowed to prevail over the idea of Pan-Arab solidarity. They advocate a unilateral disengagement by each state, an opting-out of the Middle East crisis consonant with the dictates of local interest. This movement of ideas is sustained by the exaltation of a form of local particularism that is concomitant with the development of micronationalism. It sometimes disguises itself as an outspoken radicalism or a de facto isolationism, but the basic ideas which animate it have found some understanding among many sections of Arab public opinion.

The Zionist challenge, the argument proceeds, should be taken up by the Palestinians alone, and the whole dispute should remain, in the last resort, a purely Palestinian affair, since the Arab commonwealth does not enjoy the privileges of a common will. Furthermore, Arab intervention against a background of clashing interests can only add fire to an already explosive situation. In Egypt, for example, it is mainly a body of opinion with a marked nostalgia for the *ancien régime* which supports the thesis of "Egypt first." Their contention is that the country has already contributed sufficiently to the Arab cause and that the results have been negative. They argue that in the years between the two world wars, when Egypt kept aloof from any special relationship with the Arab or the Muslim states, Egyptian policy was on the right track, as it corresponded to Egyptian realities. For them Egyptian Arabism is only an ephemeral accident of history, associated directly with the regime of the late President Nasser and condemned to disappear with the disappearance of its leader and principal ideologist. On the other hand, they still regard the unity of the Nile Valley as the cornerstone of their political outlook. This means that they would look with favor upon an association of Egypt and the Sudan in some sort of association based on a community of interests, for this, they feel, is the natural formula for both countries, the one which responds most meaningfully to the true nature of their realities.

There is also another group of ideas which finds expression in isolationism. This is the aggregate of ideas which depict Egypt as linked with Europe, indeed as in the process of becoming part of Europe, realizing Khedive Ismail's nineteenth century dream for his country. This attitude is one which definitely considers an outward-looking policy, turned towards Europe, as far more rewarding in the long run, and far wiser, than military adventures in Palestine. The isolationists point out that thirty years of Egyptian Arabism have not borne much fruit in the fields of political and economic development. They argue that this policy has been the cause of an uninterrupted series of setbacks. Disengagement from the affairs of the Arab world is what they suggest as more likely to achieve the peaceful recovery of the Sinai, giving the country a chance to devote its attention to the host of pressing domestic problems.

When all is said and done, surely it would be in Egypt's interest to renounce its dynamic foreign policy, for which there is clearly no warrant in economic or political terms. There would be much to say for a marked reduction of Cairo's activism in the Arab world, in Africa and, even farther afield, throughout the Third World, in favor of the wiser course suggested by the idea of cultivating one's own garden. Would not the misery of the Egyptian fellah be much alleviated if so much energy were not devoted exclusively to the international arena of politics? Substantially, these are the main guidelines of isolationist thinking in Egypt.

The isolationist thesis is greatly weakened, however, by an array of contrary elements. In the first place, Egypt is endowed with a history in which it is too involved to be able to withdraw so cozily from the world. Throughout the centuries it has taken upon itself the burden of so much that one can hardly expect it not to reach out in solidarity with the disinherited countries of the Third World. Besides, Cairo is much too directly threatened by Zionism for it to be able to think in such terms of her own well-being. Moreover, Arabism, not unlike Italian and German movements of the nineteenth century, is a federalist movement. It has become so important with the passage of time that the isolationist position would immediately be regarded as an expression of betrayal should it hazard public circulation. In any case, the isolationists have never really constituted a coherent school of thought, nor have they ever had the possibility of obtaining a sympathetic audience for their point of view.

This is not the case in Lebanon where, in 1958 and again in 1975, an entire section of the population expressed its opposition to a policy which was quickly becoming too Pan-Arab. An important group among the Christians, the Phalangists, continue to believe that Lebanon should remain neutral and disengaged from the rest of the Arab world by practicing a policy of noninvolvement in the Arab-Israeli conflict. Their positions are justified on the grounds that any policy of Pan-Arab integration would almost certainly mean that the denominational equilibrium inside Lebanon (which gives the Lebanese Christians a certain number of privileges) could no longer be maintained. In addition, there are more than three hundred thousand Palestinian refugees in Lebanon, and they are predominantly Muslim. It is no secret that the ultimate integration of these refugees into the country would seriously jeopardize the denominational equilibrium which the Lebanese are striving so hard to maintain. The task is not easy, however, for these diehard Christian nationalists. The Palestinians are armed and enjoy a wide degree of autonomy in their camps. Their allies are woven into the very fabric of Lebanese society, where they find a sympathetic audience among the Muslims and the left-wing movements. Yet, all this is nothing compared to the extremely pressing influence of the interstate Arab community. Although the Phalangists are finding it almost impossible to implement their own policies, they have enough power, nevertheless, to prevent the implementation of any Pan-Arab Lebanese policy at an official level.

One should also mention a number of isolationist currents of opinion in Saudi Arabia and some of the Gulf emirates. The isolationist argument in these countries takes this form—although the countries of the Arabian Peninsula are extremely rich in oil deposits they are, nonetheless, among the most underdeveloped countries in the Arab world. Their wealth has also made them the target of covetous designs on the part of many and diverse interests in the world. They feel that they must protect their new-found wealth and guard it jealously, strengthening their independence by means of an accelerated rate of development which, of necessity, can be achieved only with a certain amount of noninvolvement. On the other hand, a more subtle consideration is that the pursuit of the Arab-Israeli war carries with it a certain assurance of nonintervention in the interior affairs of the Gulf states by the stronger Arab "superpowers."

One must realize, however, that this isolationist tendency, represented by no more than a minority, is counterbalanced by considerations of an entirely different order of magnitude. Clearly, the majority of the leadership in these states, together with the bulk of their populations, regard Arab solidarity as the best guarantee of safety and protection for the Arab oilfields. This is strengthened by the presence of an important and active Palestinian community in their midst, with its skills now part of the very structure of the state. They have enjoyed a long residence there, going back to the first diaspora. This serves as a safeguard against any inclinations toward isolationism and disengagement from the struggle for the liberation of Palestine.

We may, therefore, draw the conclusion that isolationism is not a public attitude. It is a discreetly expressed current of opinion, guarded from publicity. It is interesting that even the Lebanese Phalangists constantly reiterate in general terms their solidarity with the cause of the Palestinian Arabs. Consequently, there has never been a proper institutionalization of the isolationist position, nor has it been adopted openly by any political organization. The retirement of an opinion into the status of an undercurrent makes it necessarily marginal and quite without effect on official policy-making in the Arab world.

The Compromisers

Any attempt to describe the kind of compromise solution which the Arabs are prepared to accept as a first condition for peace in the Middle East not only requires political and historical insight, but demands as yet undeveloped skills in predicting the future. It is, nevertheless, enlightening to examine the point of view of the Palestinians and of the Arab states, as presently formulated, regarding conditions to be set for a peaceful settlement of the Arab-Israeli confrontation.

The Palestinians. The only alternative to total liberation which the PLO would accept, by all accounts, is an independent Palestinian state on the West Bank of the Jordan, in the Gaza Strip and the Arab parts of Jerusalem. Gaza would be linked to the West Bank by a highway which would cut across Israeli territory. The highway would constitute a corridor under complete Palestinian sovereignty, and would provide the new state of Palestine with access to the sea. The actual territory of the projected state would, however, be too small to make possible the absorption of the whole Arab Palestinian diaspora. Thus, Palestinian pockets would continue to exist in Jordan, Lebanon, the Gulf states, and Israel. Those Palestinians who continue to live outside the borders of the new state would be entitled to Palestinian nationality. The possibility of instituting dual nationality for the Palestinians of the diaspora must be envisaged. The relationship between the Palestinians in the projected ministate of Palestine and the Palestinians of the diaspora would be an important factor in giving shape and consistency to the new state, which could choose a form of government suited to its own conditions.

The first possibility is that of a liberal and capitalistic country open to investment by Arab capital—in fact, a new Lebanon. Money would pour in from the rich Arab countries in the form of aid and investments, and rich Palestinian nationals would feel compelled to participate in the development of this new Monaco. It could well become the financial, cultural and touristic center of the Arab world. The second possibility is that of a militant, Socialist people's democracy. There is reason to believe, however, that the vested interests in Jordan, Saudi Arabia and the Gulf states might run counter to such a possibility. The third suggestion is that Palestine become a state with a mixed economy, satisfying the various tendencies represented in the leadership of the PLO. This compromise formula would bring the state into alignment with present-day Syria, where the private and public sectors have managed to coexist.

This brings us to the question of the relations between the new state of Arab Palestine and the neighboring Arab states. This question would probably be decided later on, when the new state might act in the light of its development requirements. Here again, a number of different solutions can be foreseen: association with Jordan or Syria, or with both at once. This is not to say that such a formula of subregionalism in the Arab world is not fraught with danger. It is most likely that it would arouse hostility from a number of quarters and, not least of all, from Israel. We are convinced, nevertheless, that such a regional formula is the best guarantee of stabilization in the Middle East. It would allow for the absorption of the Palestinian diaspora into the Arab East (the Mashrek) by means of the new Palestinian state and would provide impetus and security for the integration of the Palestinians into the Arab states. Of course, relations between the new state and Israel would have to be governed by a set of well-designed special rules such as mutual recognition, international safeguards and demilitarized zones. In this respect the agreements which have governed the relations between West and East Germany could serve as a useful precedent (though the specific nature of the Arab-Israeli problem should not be lost from view).

One thing is certain, however, and that is that the new state of Palestine will have to be closely linked with its Arab neighbors (Lebanon, Syria and Jordan). Moreover, this careful dovetailing of the state into its Arab context will have to be actively nurtured so that the micronationalism encouraged by the emergence of a new ministate can be transcended by macronationalism, which is alone able to eliminate the contradictions within the Arab world stemming from the Israeli presence, and, possibly, to achieve a durable peace.

The "Front-line States. These states bordering Israel have agreed to demand, in the very first place, a total withdrawal of the Israeli troops from the territories which they occupied after June 5, 1967. This demand is not open to debate for the Arabs. It is unfortunate that international public opinion does not seem to be aware of the extent to which the principle of territorial integrity is beyond discussion for all the front-line states. In their eyes, not even the most trivial territorial modifications can be the subject of negotiation. They are prepared, however, to entertain the idea of a possible neutralization or demilitarization of certain portions of the occupied territories with the presence of United Nations troops.

In any case, the front-line states may in the near future accept a de jure recognition of Israel, but not the possibility of instituting diplomatic, commercial or cultural relations with it. This is not to say that such relations are inconceivable in the more distant future. It will remain for the State of Israel to prove to the interstate community of the Arab world that it wishes to and is able to integrate itself into the region. This willingness on Israel's part would have to include a vast program of Arabization in which Arabic would become a language of Israel on equal footing with Hebrew. This would involve an active process of cultural and social decolonization, in which the policies of both immigration and emigration would be calculated to encourage the integration into the Israeli population only of elements that could adapt to this profound change in the nature of Israeli society. The author does not underestimate the difficulties that would be created in Israeli society by this sort of change. Sooner or later, however, it will have to be realized that only a change of this nature can incur the passage of the front-line states from a stage of confrontation to one of coexistence, and, from there, to a level of active cooperation without which there can be no real or durable peace in the area.

The Non-"Front-Line" States. It is undeniable that it will be difficult to obtain the consent of the non-front-line Arab states to a compromise solution. As we have mentioned before, their distance from frontiers with Israel has allowed some of them to adopt more stiffly radical attitudes. This has also led them to be more and more inclined towards the policies of the rejectionists. It must also be admitted that although they have no common frontiers with Israel, their consent will have to be obtained in any attempt at the establishment of a durable peace in the region. This is essential for a number of reasons. Most important is the fact that these states are mostly members of the rich oil-producing group. Having escaped the consequences of war, they seem to be more ready to take the risks that would be involved in an outbreak of further hostilities.

The support of the non-front-line states is essential for the front-line states to be able to overcome their own inhibitions about negotiating directly with Israel and thus recognizing its existence. Surely the Arab League presents the institutional form most likely to succeed in obtaining an Arab consensus within the framework of all the previous Arab summit conferences.

The following remarks about the role of the Arab League in the past and present will serve to justify the suggestion that hope lies in its direction. The League has often served as a front behind which the Arab states have attempted to hide their weakness while they openly criticize the League for its own inadequacies and failures. The League will, however, continue to maintain its prestige and value as long as there is no other institution to replace it, and as long as the Arab states require a comprehensive framework for their consultations. In addition, the new dominant coalition in the Arab world, consisting of Egypt, Saudi Arabia, and Algeria, is favorable to the Arab League and to the idea of actively cooperating within the framework of its institutions.

The League also provides a common ground for debate among those Arab states which have a direct stake in the conflict and those which do not. This has had a moderating effect on the various shifts in the balance of power between moderates and radicals. It should be borne in mind that ever since its creation in 1945, the League has had Palestinian representation, which has steadily used it to assert the Palestinian presence within the Arab community. Furthermore, the massive revenues now flowing to the Arabs will enable the Arab League to carry out more ambitious programs designed to promote Arab integration. Finally, it should be observed that the Arab-European dialogue, as well as the Arab-African dialogue, have been initiated within the framework of the League, and that any institutions formed as a result of these dialogues will almost certainly fall under its aegis.

Conclusion

The main tenor of our discussion has emphasized the importance of several general points.

First, no formula for peace is of the slightest value if it is not sanctioned by the community of Arab states. Any attempt, therefore, to obtain interim agreements through bilateral arrangements made with separate Arab states can do nothing more than serve the aspirations of certain American or Israeli circles. In reality, such an attempt has no chance of success, for no Arab state can possibly allow itself to betray its own sense of being Arab.

Second, the Arabs attach the highest priority to the solution of the Palestine problem. The projected state of Palestine (or the state of the West Bank and Gaza) can provide only a first stage towards the establishment of a just peace in the region. Yet, the integration of this new state into a federation of the states of the Arab East (in other words, a revival of the Greater Syria project) would achieve a second stage towards peace, for it would provide for the absorption of the Arab Palestinian diaspora, which cannot be entirely absorbed within the frontiers of the new state. Consequently, it is only by means of an integration and association of the various subregions in the Arab world, such as that of the *Mashrek* and the *Maghrib*, that the Arabs would be ready to take up the problems of underdevelopment. The wisest policy for great powers is to encourage such integration rather than to resist it as they have so continuously done in the past decades.

Finally, I should conclude that there is no doubt that it is the population explosion which will dominate all future Arab policies throughout the remaining quarter of the century. There can be no doubt that it is the population explosion, with its great force, which will sweep aside any formulas for peace, however carefully prepared, unless the State of Israel finally decides to become an integral part of the area, willing without hesitation to take on an Arab character. In the last analysis, it is the population explosion in the refugee camps, on the banks of the Nile, and on the flanks of the Atlas range which will ultimately give shape, meaning, and direction to the Arab response to the challenge of Zionism.

X

The Middle East, the United States, the USSR, and Europe

Walter Laqueur

Throughout most of known history the Middle East has been an area of conflict, involving both indigenous powers (whenever existent) and outside forces. This has not changed in recent decades, and while there has been at times an exaggerated tendency to regard the Middle East as the most dangerous area to world peace ("No other crisis area of the world has greater importance or higher priority for the United States in the second term of my Administration"[1]), it is perfectly true that it will remain, in the foreseeable future, internal conflicts quite apart, one of the major bones of contention between the United States and the Soviet Union.

There has been remarkable continuity in American policy towards the Middle East since the end of the Second World War. Two illustrations should suffice: President Kennedy, in a letter to King Hussein of Jordan dated May 11, 1961, stated that the United States will, to the best of its ability, lend every appropriate assistance to all Middle East states that are determined to control their own destiny, to enhance the prosperity of their people, and to allow their neighbors to pursue the same fundamental aims. As a statement of intent this could have hardly been bettered, and every president and secretary of state before and after Kennedy has said the same in similar words.

To provide another illustration: briefing the Senate Foreign Affairs Committee on May 31, 1974, Secretary of State Kissinger said (according to Senator Frank Church) that three obstacles remained in the way of permanent peace in the Middle East—the rectification of frontiers, the problem of the Palestinian refugees, and the question of Jerusalem. Almost twenty years earlier, addressing the Council of Foreign Relations in New York (August 26, 1955) Secretary of State Dulles had listed what he regarded as the three principal problems of the

Middle East: the problem of refugees, the lack of permanent boundaries and the issue of fear of aggression on both sides. Two decades and three wars later, Dr. Kissinger, probably unknowingly, repeated almost verbatim the assessment of another secretary of state. If there has been such continuity in the objectives of American foreign policy, it has never been quite clear how its objectives could be attained. It is the contention of this chapter that America's appraisal of the Middle East scene has been correct as far as it went, but that it has been deficient in perspective since it has been almost totally preoccupied with the problems at hand and the most immediate contingencies.

The United States has seldom looked beyond the Arab-Israeli dispute, ignoring other sources of unrest in the area, emanating from the domestic situation in the Arab countries, Iran and Turkey, and from conflicts between these countries.

There has never been full clarity as to whether American interests in the Middle East are compatible with those of the other superpower, the Soviet Union. Since the Soviet Union has been playing an increasingly important role in the Middle East since the middle fifties, this is, needless to say, a question of cardinal importance, inasmuch as the future of the whole area is involved.

This concentration on the Arab-Israeli dispute, at the expense of other aspects of the Middle Eastern crisis, can be easily explained. Foreign ministries and diplomats are usually not interested in crises that might happen at some future date; they are fully preoccupied dealing with those at hand. And it is of course perfectly obvious that the Arab-Israeli conflict has been the most acute manifestation of unrest in the area. It is equally true that this fixation on the Arab-Israeli conflict leads to a distortion in our thinking about the future of the Middle East. It is the contention of the present chapter that the importance of the Arab-Israeli conflict will probably decrease in the near future, not necessarily because it will be solved but because it will be just one of several international crises of equal, or perhaps even greater acuteness. Even within the Middle Eastern context the Persian Gulf is likely to emerge as a trouble zone of at least equal importance.

Second, in view of the many other latent conflicts in the area, political and social tension inside the region, the confrontation between "radicals" and "moderates," friction about disputed territories and the unequally divided mineral wealth (oil), it is unrealistic to expect peace and stability in the Middle East even if a solution is found to the Arab-Israeli conflict. Some of these conflicts were submerged while the Arab-Israeli conflict figured so prominently, but they are likely to surface again in the future, especially if the Arab-Israeli dispute should lose some of its sharpness and acuteness.

Lastly, there is no sound reason to assume that American and Soviet interests in the area will coincide in the future anymore than they did in the past; on the contrary the Middle East will remain in all likelihood one of the main battle fields of détente. What Philipp II said about another emperor ("My cousin and I are in full agreement, both of us want Milan") applies *mutatis mutandis*, to the interests of the superpowers in the Middle East. It is a basic Soviet aim to include the Middle East in its sphere of interest; it is in America's interest that this should not happen.

To give a precise definition of America's interests in the Middle East is difficult and not only because there is no consensus about "national interest" except in the broadest outline. The geopolitical importance of the Middle East is no longer what it was in past periods.

While it is true that the interests of major powers converge in this region, they also converge in many other parts of the world, and in the age of planes and missiles, it is somewhat anachronistic to think of the Middle East as a "bridge" between East and West, between North and South. Military bases in the Middle East are not a necessity for the United States nor are political alliances; even its economy would not collapse if the flow of Middle Eastern oil were interrupted. (There would of course be considerable temporary problems, but these difficulties have to be considered in the wider context of long term energy supplies.) On the other hand, there is no denying that the interruption of the flow of oil would have the gravest consequences for Western Europe and Japan, and if the Soviet Union were to dominate the Middle East this would constitute a basic shift in the global balance of power to the detriment of the West. To put it differently: if the Soviet Union were not interested in the Middle East and if it would not engage in activity to strengthen its position in the area, there would be no need for constant American involvement, or a high level of activity by the United States.

There has been a recurring pattern in American policy in the Middle East since the end of the Second World War: immediate American interests in Turkey and Iran were few and far between in 1945-47, but Soviet pressure on these countries and on Greece resulted in the Truman Doctrine. American aims in the Middle East have been, for obvious reasons, far more restricted than Soviet aims: the United States is a distant country whereas Russia is nearby; there are no "American" parties inside the Middle East, but there are "Russian" ones; America could not dominate the Middle East even if it so desired. American policy has been to provide a counterweight to Soviet initiatives in the area. The pattern could change if the Middle East acquired the capability necessary to resist any outside domination through its own strength; but this seems virtually impossible. It could change, at least temporarily, if the United States and the Soviet Union were to reach agreement about the division of the Middle East into spheres of influence similar to an agreement concerning Persia before the First World War. But these practices, however effective, have gone out of fashion in the second half of the twentieth century. Finally, the pattern could change if the Middle East were no longer of such crucial importance; this is almost certainly bound to happen, but not within the next decade, and probably not for an even longer time.

There is only one Middle Eastern country—Turkey—tied to the United States by specific alliance commitments, through its membership in NATO. (At one stage, in the nineteen fifties, an attempt was made to establish a Middle East Defense Organization, but the results were disappointing.) But aside from the recent deterioration in United States-Turkish relations, which resulted in the closing of American bases, there has been a shift towards neutralism in Turkish public opinion. There has been no overt Soviet pressure on Ankara for two decades, and while the threat from the North is not discounted, it is no longer considered acute. At the same time there is apprehension that precisely because Soviet military power has grown so much in the Mediterranean, Turkey has to be careful not to antagonize its powerful neighbor by allying itself too closely with the United States.

The situation is further complicated by the domestic polarization in Turkey, the vanishing national consensus, and the growing internal instability. Not so long ago, it was widely assumed that given a decade of sustained economic development Turkey would emerge as a medium power which would be able to play a role of some importance in the regional context. But the results have fallen short of these expectations, the internal friction has further weakened the country, and according to all indications Turkey will face a prolonged period of unrest and will be largely preoccupied with domestic affairs.

Iran, starting on a considerably lower level of general development has made far more impressive gains than Turkey, mainly of course as the result of the great increase in oil revenues. There has been stable, if not exactly democratic government, and militarily the country has increased its strength. Thus, Iran is a power to be reckoned with insofar as the future of the Persian Gulf is concerned.

However, the base of the present regime is narrow, and sudden, dramatic changes cannot be ruled out. Iran's policy towards the United States is shaped above all by its perception of a latent Soviet danger. While relations between Tehran and Moscow have been outwardly friendly, there is uneasiness about long-term Soviet intentions. The Shah realizes more acutely than the Turkish political leadership—not to mention the Arab ruling groups—that in order to survive and to maintain national independence in the close vicinity of a superpower, the help of the other superpower is necessary. No profound study of political philosophy is needed to understand such a home truth. If some Middle Eastern countries, nevertheless, failed to realize this, it was because they were sidetracked by their internal disputes. Iran's exposed position is made more vulnerable precisely because it has become so much richer. At the same time Iran's relations with the United States are governed, as in the case of Turkey, by great caution, in order not to give offense to the Soviet Union: there is no defense treaty and there are no bases.

United States relations with Israel have been traditionally close, but support for Israel has never been uncritical and inside each administration there has been a fairly strong anti-Israel group. The Truman administration long wavered before it decided to support the division of Palestine; after the Suez War (1956), the Eisenhower administration insisted on immediate Israeli withdrawal, and after the Six-Day War the United States was among the signatories of UN Resolution 242 stressing the inadmissibility of acquiring territory by war and the need to work for a just and lasting peace in which every state in the area can live securely. U.S. spokesmen have stressed time and time again that the United States follows a balanced policy in the Middle East. "We do not support expansionism," said Secretary of State Rogers, in 1969. Yet, beyond these sentiments there was, according to Nixon, an understanding of the "elements of intractability" of the conflict; there was not just "a powerful legacy of mutual fear and mistrust," there was a suspicion that the legitimate concerns of both sides were perhaps incompatible.

Between the Six-Day War and the Yom Kippur War, U.S. policymakers were extremely active (the Four Power talks, the Rogers Plan, negotiations with the USSR) and this despite the fact that the Vietnam War overshadowed the Middle East conflict during much of the time. Underlying this was the correct assumption that a protracted period of "no war and no peace" with recurrent violence would lead sooner or later to a new war which would involve outside powers. While the tenor of U.S. speeches was that "peace cannot be imposed from the outside," U.S. policymakers who talked to Soviet leaders about an Arab-Israeli settlement were encouraged by occasional hints of compromise, such as Brezhnev's remark in 1972: "The possibilities here are quite broad." Such remarks seemed to call for superpower restraint and, above all, for an accommodation between Egypt and Israel.

These negotiations failed, but the search for a peace settlement continued; a fresh initiative was envisaged just as the Yom Kippur War broke out. With all the sympathy for Israel, there was no symmetry between U.S. support for Israel and Soviet aid to the Arab states. U.S. policy was to control and to scale down the arms race in the Middle East; the Soviet Union had no such intention. The Soviet Union, quite correctly, regarded massive arms supply to the Arab countries as its main political lever in the Middle East; without arms deliveries, Moslem's position in the area would have been infinitely weaker. Thus, the United States was reluctantly drawn into the arms race. Whenever it seemed that the military balance would be radically upset following some massive Soviet supplies to Egypt, Syria, and other Arab countries, U.S. deliveries were made to Israel to restore the balance. But the United States was unhappy about this mounting spiral, and the failure of arms control in the Middle East; America continued, albeit unsuccessfully, to look for a way out of the impasse. The United States was committed to the survival of Israel, but it also had other interests in the Middle East and felt concern about the fact that the Arab countries considered U.S. policy one-sided, harmful, and antagonistic, and regarded America as the main supporter of Israel. There was a genuine desire to improve relations with the Arab world. The occasion came, temporarily at any rate, after the Yom

Kippur War and it became possible, paradoxically, only because the United States was closely identified with Israel in Arab eyes.

The relationship between the United States and the Arab world reached its nadir after the Six-Day War when six Arab countries broke off diplomatic relations with Washington. The Arab-Israeli conflict was not, of course, the only factor which led to the estrangement; in radical regimes all over the globe there was a considerable amount of ill-will against the West and "neo-imperialism." There was a residue of mistakes and misunderstanding (such as the U.S. refusal to collaborate in the Aswän Dam project in 1956 after having initially promised its help).

However, the United States had always possessed certain important advantages over the Soviet Union and its ability to attract the Arab countries was greater than appeared on the surface. Irrespective of their ideological orientation, most Arab governments realized, however dimly, that undue dependence on the Soviet Union not only limited their freedom to maneuver on the international scene; it jeopardized, in the long run, their national independence. From their point of view it would have been far more advantageous to have normal relations with both East and West, playing one against the other whenever possible. Furthermore, precisely because the Soviet Union had become so closely involved in the Arab world, especially after the Six-Day War, there was bound to be friction on many levels between the Russians and the Arabs, partly because there was a fear of growing political interference, partly because of the identification of the Soviet Union with native Communist forces, and partly because however much the Soviet Union helped, it could not possibly live up to all Arab expectations. Arab governments realized that while the Soviet Union would supply a great deal of arms, they could hope for little else. Soviet arms were thought to be not quite up to Western standards, and they had to be paid for. The scope for developing trade and obtaining economic aid from the Eastern bloc was narrow; the real markets for the Arab world were in the West—and likely to remain there for a long time to come. Lastly, it dawned upon most Arab governments that even with regard to the conflict with Israel only America was in a position to bring enough real pressure on the Jewish state to force a retreat from the territories occupied in the Six-Day War. Thus behind the anti-American speeches, there was the willingness to normalize relations with the United States; it was generally realized that the decision to break off relations in 1967 had been a mistake.

The preceding analysis is true mainly of Egypt and Algeria. In the case of Lebanon and the "conservative" countries such as Jordan and Saudi Arabia, dependence on American good will had been known all along. If South Yemen joined the radical, anti-American camp, North Yemen was the first Arab League country to resume diplomatic ties with the United States after the 1967 war. Attitudes towards the United States reflected to a large extent the internal political lineup inside the Arab world. Events after the Yom Kippur War, the seemingly sudden swing from the extreme hostility (oil embargo) to the acceptance of American mediation, and the renewal of diplomatic ties, can be understood only in connection with the struggle between "radicals" and "moderates" and, of course, also in the context of the traditional rivalries between the Arab countries.

The retreat of Europe from the Middle East was the direct result of the Second World War. There still exist substantial economic interests in the area, but there is no longer a "European presence" in the Middle East. If Britain and France were still signatories of the Tripartite Declaration of May 1950 guaranteeing Middle East borders, the European position collapsed following the ill-starred Anglo-French landing in Egypt in 1956. While Europe's political and military influence rapidly dwindled, its dependence on Middle Eastern and North African oil grew by leaps and bounds to its present 85 percent.

On the other hand the Middle East continues to buy more from Europe than from all other parts of the world. Under de Gaulle and Pompidou, France became the first European country to try to establish a special relationship with the Arab world. France provided military assistance to the Arab war effort, political and diplomatic support in the United Nations, and it sponsored various European-Arab meetings. Following France, Britain and other European countries also adjusted their position in the Arab-Israeli conflict in accordance with their growing dependence on Arab oil. At the same time, efforts were made to establish closer relations with Iran. France reaped a certain amount of goodwill from this policy, but few tangible benefits: the Arab oil producers choose to invest their money elsewhere.

On closer examination the idea of a European-Arab bloc had not that much to recommend it. A weak and divided Europe was of no great help to the Arabs either politically or militarily; a strong and united Europe, on the other hand, was a potential danger to the Arabs for it would be in a position to assert forcefully its interests in the Eastern Mediterranean and the Persian Gulf. This did not, of course, rule out close cooperation on a bilateral basis, mainly in the economic field, but politically the options were limited. Pressure on Europe could have a certain effect by influencing the United States, but too much pressure was bound to weaken Europe, which was not of ultimate interest to the Arabs.

The increase in the oil price was bound to cause grave difficulties in most European countries. Since there was reluctance among the oil producers to make massive investments precisely in those countries which were most affected, because of the economic and political risks and uncertainties, the prospects for close collaboration were further limited. While there are certain common interests between Europe and the Middle East, close collaboration is also impeded by the fact that both these blocs lack unity and political will; they constitute many countries with diverging interests. There is, in brief, neither a European nor an Arab foreign policy, except on an *ad hoc* basis and with very limited targets. This is unlikely to change in the foreseeable future.

It would be premature to write off Europe altogether as a political factor in Middle Eastern politics in the coming decade, but it certainly will not be a major factor.

Russian interest in the Middle East predates the revolution of 1917 by almost two centuries. The extension of Russian influence in the "general direction of the Persian Gulf" (to quote Molotov's famous phrase of 1940) has been one of the constant factors in Russian foreign policy. During the immediate post-war period (1945-48) Soviet interest (and pressure) was mainly focused on Turkey and Iran; since the middle fifties Russia has become increasingly involved in the Arab world. These developments are well known and need not be reiterated in the present context. Soviet policy aimed at the neutralization of Turkey and Iran and at the installation in the Arab world of regimes on which it could rely for close collaboration on the pattern established in its relationship with President Nasser. The general assumption behind this policy was that power in the Arab countries was bound to pass gradually into the hands of people closely identified with Soviet policies. It was, of course, generally expected that there would be ups and downs in this process and occasional setbacks. But regarding the general trend of the development there was little doubt in Moscow.

There is no denying that events in Egypt, Syria, Iraq, Algeria, and other countries in the 1960s seemed to bear out Soviet expectations. There was a progressive radicalization in domestic affairs in these countries, as well as growing identification with Soviet policies: factories and banks were national-ized, and important sections of the state apparatus were revamped according to the Soviet model. If the local Communist parties made only modest progress, Communist ministers were appointed in several Arab countries and, more importantly, "Russian parties" came into being, consisting of politicians, military men, and intellectuals, who, while not Communists, advocated close cooperation with the Soviet Union. Nevertheless, beyond certain limits, the Soviet Union has so far failed to expand from within its positions inside the Arab countries. The deeper reasons for this failure are of importance because the obstacles inhibiting the growth of Soviet influence will probably not disappear in the years to come.

In some respects Soviet expectations were simply unrealistic. This refers to the belief that the stormy break up of the colonial (or semi-colonial) system would lead the Middle East, if not to the Communist, then to the non-capitalist road of development. It was thought that the impossibility of solving the basic problems of the developing countries—in the Middle East and the Third World in general—would inevitably compel the leaders of the new states to choose Soviet style socialism for their future. The anti-imperialist and anti-capitalist slogans of the new leaders strengthened these illusions.

The process of disenchantment began around 1965 with the overthrow of Third World leaders such as Qassem, Ben Bella, Sukarno, Nkrumah—almost without struggle. Furthermore, in their analysis of the situation the Soviet leaders had underrated the powerful appeal of nationalism; they regarded it as a transitory phenomenon—an assumption which may be correct *sub specia aeternatis*, but which was of little help in assessing concrete situations in the contemporary Middle East. While it is perfectly true that radical nationalism can turn "right" and "left" and lead equally to a pro-Soviet or anti-Soviet orientation in foreign policy, it is also true that nationalism frequently creates a negative attitude towards communism, and not only in view of the strong religious admixture in nationalism.

Soviet observers furthermore tended to misjudge the role of the military elites in the Arab world and in the Third World in general. Power in most Arab countries passed into the hands of military leaders and the Soviet commentators after some initial hesitation persuaded themselves that this was a "progressive" development. Unlike the West, there was in the Middle East close connections between the military leaders and the "common people"; above all, there was a great deal of affinity between the officers and the radical intelligentsia. Soviet observers assumed that the suppression of Communist parties was a temporary phenomenon. Since purely military regimes could not last in the contemporary world, the new leaders would have to mobilize the masses and for this purpose they would need an avant-garde political party. Thus, the logic of events would lead them into cooperation with the Communists.

Soviet observers were mistaken insofar as they attributed to the military leaders political motives and an orientation which simply did not exist. More often than not military leaders are inspired by the desire to seize power and to keep it. But even when dealing with military leaders with radical political ideas, Soviet observers erred in assuming that this trend was irreversible (as in the case of Nasser).

At the same time the Russians overrated the influence and the political attraction of the Communist movement. While there was a general trend towards the Left, and all kinds of Marxist, or quasi-Marxist ideologies especially among the intelligentsia, the Soviet model had no monopoly among these circles. Organizationally, the Communist parties were weakened by internal splits; the Maoists, the Trotskyites and various other left-wing nationalist groups provided effective competition. This conjured up yet another specter—the installation of a Communist regime not necessarily friendly towards the Soviet Union. The Soviet leaders continued to believe that in the long run the non-Communist elites would be unable to solve their domestic problems and that, as a result, they would in the end have to accept Communist guidance and leadership. But they had not counted on the economic upsurge and the new prosperity in the oil producing countries.

Thus, in the final analysis, the revolutionary process in the Middle East seems to be much slower than in certain European or Asian countries. If the Soviet position in the Middle East should grow stronger in the years to come it is more likely to be the result of its increased military might and a shift in the overall balance of power, which would enable the Soviet Union to exert greater and more direct pressure.

This is not to deny that certain circumstances still favor Soviet policy in the area. The political and military weakness of the Middle East has greatly facilitated Soviet progress, as have the internal divisions and conflicts. In the eyes of many Arab leaders, Israel is a greater danger than Russia, despite the fact that Israel is a small country with limited resources. The image of the Soviet Union, on the other hand, throughout much of the fifties and the sixties was that of a benevolent, distant, and disinterested power which, in contrast to Israel and the Western imperialists, had no desire to interfere in Arab affairs. This image was severely damaged as the Soviet Union itself became involved in the Middle East. Moscow had to take sides and thus was bound to make enemies. The existence of Communist parties and pro-Russian factions was a further source of irritation and conflict.

The Soviet Union is not just a superpower but also heads the world Communist movement, or, at any rate, the main faction in this no-longer-monolithic movement. It cannot opt out entirely from its commitments to its local followers without causing fatal damage to the legitimacy of its claim to leadership, a problem which is complicated by the fact that its authority as the leader of the camp is contested anyway. It can advise the Communist parties to keep a low profile, not to antagonize the "progressive" rulers, but it cannot dissociate itself from the local Communists altogether. While the Communist parties are small and uninfluential the problem can be sidestepped, but the moment their influence grows the dilemma is bound to reappear with a vengeance.

Whereas in Europe the existence of a Communist party is perfectly legitimate within the framework of parliamentary democracy, this is not the case in the military dictatorships and authoritarian regimes of the Middle East. Soviet policymakers are reconciled to the fact that political power in the Arab world will remain for a long time to come in the hands of military rulers rather than political parties supporting Moscow. This, seen from Moscow, is not *per se* a major disaster. Since the Communist movement lost its monolithic character, the Soviet Union can no longer count on the automatic support of other Communist parties. Albania is Communist and Finland and Afghanistan are not, but there is little doubt that Soviet leaders vastly prefer the governments in Helsinki and Kabul to that in Tirana.

To provide another example: many Communist parties dissented from the Soviet invasion of Czechoslovakia in 1968, whereas the military governments of Egypt, Syria, and Algeria supported it without reservation. The Soviet leaders know that in a critical situation they can rely on clients; they can no longer count on the automatic support of Communist parties. The advantages of having to deal with non-Communist rulers are obvious: considerations of "proletarian internationalism" and of "Socialist humanism" are irrelevant; the clients support

Soviet policy, not because they believe in Soviet ideology but because they need Soviet help.

But Soviet help is needed only in some respects, and for specific purposes, and this creates new problems. The Arab-Israeli dispute provides an excellent illustration. It undoubtedly facilitated the Soviet advance in the Middle East even though it was, of course, not the only factor. At the same time it also pointed to the limits of Soviet progress. For the Arab Communists the conflict is certainly a mixed blessing for while it lasts it narrowly circumscribes the scope of their activities. The Arab Communists cannot afford to ignore the appeals for national solidarity and for a truce both inside the Arab countries and between the "radical" and the "conservative" regimes. The conflict cannot possibly be transformed into a "revolutionary war"; all other considerations apart, the state of anarchy resulting from such a war would benefit the pro-Chinese rather than the pro-Soviet elements in the Arab world. The struggle against Israel acts as a stabilizing factor, it provides virtual immunity for the "conservative" regimes against attack from the "left," which, of course, is not desirable from the Soviet point of view.

There is furthermore a real danger of an Arab Brezhnev doctrine in reverse, i.e., a "reactionary" alliance preventing revolutionary uprisings. The Soviet Union could ally itself with certain Arab countries against others (for instance with Iraq against Saudi Arabia, with Libya against Egypt, etc.). But by taking sides in inter-Arab conflicts, the Soviet Union ceases to be the disinterested friend of the whole Arab world, it risks its past gains and it will drive some Arab countries into an alliance with the West.

More important still, by tying its political initiatives in the Middle East mainly to the Arab-Israeli conflict, Soviet policy has severely restricted its options. It should have been clear from the beginning that in the case of an Arab defeat by Israel, the Soviet Union would be blamed for providing insufficient support to its allies, for not standing up to the United States, for not supporting wars of national liberation in violation of its promises, etc. If the Soviet Union counseled a policy of wait-and-see it was also bound to be blamed. If, on the other hand, it did provide full support to the Arab countries and if these succeeded in their objective of defeating Israel, there was a real danger that in the future Soviet help would no longer be needed. The recent history of the Middle East, in particular the inconclusive war of 1973, its prehistory and aftermath, has shown that these were not imaginary dangers.

From the Soviet point of view the ideal policy was, and still is, to perpetuate the conflict, the continuation of "controlled tension" and the prevention of any conclusive outcome, either through a military victory or by means of a political settlement. But since, unlike in Eastern Europe, the Soviet Union is not in full control as far as the course of events is concerned, there always remains a considerable element of uncertainty. The regional conflict might get out of hand, some of the key Arab countries may come to resent their dependence on the Soviet Union, the road to success is narrow and complicated and at every corner and turning a major mishap may occur.

The long-term aim of the Soviet Union is to turn the Middle East into a sphere of influence from which other powers are excluded. This target is to be achieved by consolidating and strengthening past gains, by the replacement of the present rulers by others more closely identified with Soviet policies, and ultimately by the transformation of these regimes into political coalitions dominated by the Communists or other trustworthy elements.

But since these aims are not likely to be attained in the near future, Soviet tactics have to be adjusted accordingly. This means, in practical terms, gaining official recognition as a Middle Eastern power which has to participate in all important decisions concerning the future of the region. It also means supporting the forces that share the Soviet interest in perpetuating the Arab-Israeli conflict (Iraq, Libya, the Palestinians). This has been Soviet policy for quite a while, and if one were to draw up a balance sheet, it would appear that it has worked well up to a point. The Soviet Union has made a breakthrough, it has become a Middle Eastern power. It has gained political influence and military bases; economically, it has not benefited much for it has had to invest a great deal of money in the area, mainly by means of arms deliveries which were only partially paid for.

The policy has not worked too well inasfar as Egypt is concerned, which in Soviet eyes is still the key to the Arab world. There is, of course, always the hope that Egypt's difficult economic problems and its dependence on outside help will sooner or later drive the country once again into a more pro-Soviet orientation. But these are uncertainties and the Soviet Union will have to look for alternative policies in the Middle East.

In historical perspective, the Arab-Israeli conflict provided the opening needed by the Soviet Union to make a breakthrough in the Middle East; traditionally Soviet interests were directed more towards Turkey, Iran, and the Persian Gulf. These regions were neglected after 1950, but it is quite likely that Soviet interest will again shift to this area during the years to come.

The openings for Soviet policy created by the Arab-Israeli conflict have been more or less exhausted. The "Northern tier," on the other hand, especially the Persian Gulf, now offers opportunities which did not exist before. The Persian Gulf oil fields have assumed an importance which was not even remotely foreseen in the fifties. Turkey is internally divided, the anti-Soviet national consensus no longer exists; economically, the country faces an uphill struggle. Iran has made a great deal of economic progress, but politically, power still rests on an exceedingly narrow base. Industrialization creates prosperity but also growing political and social strains and stresses. Above all, immensely rich ministates have emerged in the Persian Gulf with virtually no defense capabilities.

While a nineteenth century style takeover is unlikely in the present world situation, there may be other ways and means to achieve the same end. Lenin's dictum about the road to Paris and London leading via Calcutta has not been borne out by subsequent events. It is not impossible on the other hand that the road to Kuwait and Abu Dhabi might lead through Baghdad and Damascus, and whoever rules the oilfields will be courted (and obeyed) by Europe and Japan for many years to come.

So far as world politics are concerned, it is not a matter of vital importance who rules Sinai or the Golan, whereas domination of the oil fields is a different proposition altogether. It could be argued that the Soviet Union has been sidetracked to a certain extent from its real aims in the Middle East. But what does "domination" mean in practical terms in a world in which gunboat diplomacy has become the exception rather than the rule? Has it not been the experience of the postwar period that even very small countries can successfully resist pressure on the part of superpowers? If Finland as a result of the Second World War found its freedom of maneuver in foreign politics strictly limited, Albania has defied the Soviet Union for many years, despite the fact that it is located in what is generally considered to be the Soviet sphere of influence. If Egypt demanded from one day to the next the withdrawal of 20,000 Soviet military advisers, and if the Soviet Union complied with this demand, does this not mean that "domination" and "sphere of influence" become meaningless terms? For the restraints imposed (or self-imposed) by the superpowers are such as to make direct military intervention at present virtually impossible. Even the victory of Communist forces inside a certain country provides no guarantee from the Soviet point of view as past experience has shown; a secure base can be established only as the result of direct, military intervention. But even if the Soviet Union had militarily intervened in the Arab-Israeli War of 1973 such intervention would have been, in all probability, temporary in character. With the end of the war the Soviet divisions would have been withdrawn.

A secure base involves the permanent stationing of Soviet forces in a foreign country. Since Soviet manpower and resources are already heavily engaged in Eastern Europe it would appear that the danger of Soviet expansion in the Middle East is negligible. If certain Middle Eastern countries (Iran, Israel) were to acquire a more than token nuclear arsenal and the means of delivery, this would constitute a further complication as far as military intervention is concerned. At first sight, the Middle East seems to provide a near-perfect illustration of the thesis that military power can no longer be translated into political influence—at least as far as the superpowers are concerned.

But this assumption rests on premises that are transient in character. Soviet restraint derives not from the belief that the application of violence in international relations is morally wrong; the restraint was imposed by a certain international constellation in the postwar era, the global balance of power. If the balance should change, if the West should grow progressively weaker (as according to Soviet predictions it will), if the Soviet Union should no longer be threatened by China, either as the consequence of a preemptive military strike or as the result of a reconciliation between the two Communist powers, the Soviet Union would have a much freer hand to take military action in the Middle East, provided it reached the conclusion that such action were in its own best interest.

The risks involved would be negligible. Neither NATO nor, of course, the Middle Eastern countries would be in a position to offer effective resistance; there would be no danger that such action might lead to a wider conflagration. But military action may not at all be necessary, for as the result of a decisive shift in the global balance of power, Soviet influence in the Middle East would become predominant without the application of military force. Since in a changed world situation military resistance would be senseless, the countries concerned would have to give in to Soviet demands.

One could go even further: if it should become obvious that the Soviet Union has gained full ascendancy and is no longer restrained in its freedom of action, specific Soviet threats would not be necessary. The countries in the area would adjust their policy more or less automatically to Soviet wishes. In these circumstances military occupation would not be needed either, for power would pass into the hands of leaders trusted by the Soviets, and there would be every inducement for the countries concerned to cooperate closely with Moscow. Thus the thesis that military power does not translate itself easily into political influence is valid only in a very specific constellation, namely the one prevailing at present. It would no longer be valid if there should be a substantial change in the balance of power. Any such change would affect first and foremost the Middle East, in view of its geographical proximity to the Soviet Union and the fact that it has a great deal to offer the Soviet Union, while it is at the same time, militarily weak and internally divided.

Even a less-than-dramatic change in the balance of power could have direct repercussions on the Middle East, such as, for instance, the political consequences of a major economic depression which would lead to political upheavals in various parts of the globe. The postwar period, with its rigid confrontation between two camps, provided a measure of stability which is gradually disappearing, not because of the emergence of a new ("multi-polar") world order, but because of the absence of such an order and of America's withdrawal from some of its previous commitments.

As a result of this trend, but also as a consequence of technological progress in the military field, conventional wars and war-like conflicts are becoming more, not less, likely in various parts of the world, and while the superpowers will still have an overriding interest not to be drawn into a military confrontation, the chances that they will be on collision course are much greater. The "rules of the game" will no longer be certain; there will be various sets of rules for different parts of the globe, which will emerge by trial and error.

On the abstract level, a clash between the superpowers could be prevented if they would agree on the division of spheres of influence in various parts of the world, such as the Middle East. But such action would be totally out of tune with the spirit of the post-imperialist period as far as the United States is concerned; the Soviet Union might find it a little easier to adjust itself *de facto*, but not *de jure*. A division of the Middle East into spheres of interest seems conceivable only in an extreme situation; following, for instance, a dangerous crisis which led to the brink of war.

The initiative in the Middle East in a long-term perspective will be largely with the Soviet Union and it will almost certainly lead to friction between the two superpowers. To provide, at random, a possible scenario: if at a time of general turbulence in world affairs there should be an upheaval in Iran leading to a civil war, there would be strong temptation for the Soviet Union to intervene directly or, more likely, indirectly. Such intervention, as past experience has shown, can take many forms and various degrees.

The decision as to how far the Soviet Union would be willing to go would depend entirely on the likely American reaction. This refers primarily to the overall effect of such action on East-West relations. If the Soviet leadership should reach the conclusion that the likely gain (the Persian oil fields, the general strengthening of its position vis-a-vis the Middle East and Europe) would be greater than the dangers involved, they might be willing to accept the risk of a breakdown in détente and a strengthening of the Atlantic Alliance. Thus, the question "how far is the Soviet Union likely to go in the Middle East" can be answered only in the general context of East-West relations and the overall balance of power. Should there be a substantial shift in the balance of power in favor of the Soviet Union, this will be the end of détente as interpreted by the West at present. In this case America will no longer have to concern itself with the future of the Middle East, for it will be part of a Soviet co-prosperity sphere and the West will no longer be in a position to influence events in this part of the world.

The observations which follow are based on the assumption that the overall balance will remain, *grosso modo*, as it is at present, or that it will change only slightly in Russia's favor.

The starting position of the United States in the Middle East is in essential respects advantageous for the simple reason that the countries of the region will have a vital interest in the preservation of the balance of power—America as a counterweight to the Soviet Union. (For obvious reasons they will not be able to play out China against the Soviet Union for many years to come.) This refers to "moderate" and "radical" regimes alike, for the latter also want to preserve their national independence. This basic self-interest has been beclouded by the Arab-Israeli conflict; the major danger was overshadowed by an issue which is, in the final analysis, not a matter of national survival. For this reason the United States has an obvious interest at least in the reduction of tension between Israel and the Arab countries (since a final peace settlement seems highly unlikely in the foreseeable future).

The Soviet Union, on the other hand, will support, openly or surreptitiously, the extremist forces aiming at the perpetuation of the conflict within the limits of Soviet interests. While the United States will have to cooperate with the Soviet Union in trying to achieve an interim solution, it cannot count on Soviet goodwill because the interests of the superpowers diverge. The Soviet Union may lose interest in the conflict if there should be more rewarding openings elsewhere in the area (the Persian Gulf).

In the Arab-Israeli conflict, American policy should concentrate on a settlement between Israel and Egypt even though Egypt's freedom of action may be limited; there are no irreconcilable differences between these two countries. Such a settlement would not constitute a guarantee against a renewal of hostilities but it would substantially reduce the risk. The other aspects of the Arab-Israeli conflict seem soluble only in the more distant future. The absence of a Palestinian Arab state is a permanent cause of tension, but the establishment of such a state might cause a further escalation of the conflict. It would create a situation on the pattern of Ulster, and it would not remove the danger of outside intervention.

Two other dangers are likely to loom even more prominently in the years to come. A short-sighted policy on the part of the oil producers, based on the desire to maximize their profits, will cause great harm to the economies both of industrially developed and underdeveloped countries and thus undermine the global balance on which the security of the Middle East is based. While some of the leaders of the oil producing countries will be more moderate than others it would be unrealistic to expect them to act with statesmanlike vision. The element of short-term interest and egotism will probably prevail; furthermore, there is always the possibility that the present regimes in Saudi Arabia, Kuwait, etc., will be overthrown. United States policymakers will face an uphill struggle in warning the oil producers against the likely effects of their actions. Their warnings may fall on deaf ears until serious, perhaps irreparable, damage has been done. There is a tendency in the oil producing countries to ignore their own military weakness. They are not aware of the vulnerability of their position. The purchase of vast quantities of modern arms will not change this basic fact; on the contrary, it may hasten the overthrow of their regimes. The smaller the oil producing country, the greater the danger that it will act irresponsibly and irrationally and the greater also the danger of a takeover.

The United States will not be in a position to influence domestic political trends in the area decisively. It will have to deal almost exclusively with monarchs and military dictators in the hope that these rulers will be mainly interested in prosperity and national independence. Whether these regimes will be "Socialist" in character or leave room for private enterprise is not really material, as far as the future of the Middle East is concerned. A dangerous situation could arise if an oil-rich country should decide to use its wealth for furthering an expansionist policy; the purchase of nuclear devices (from India for instance) is a possibility that cannot be ruled out. The Soviet Union and the United States share an interest in preventing the spread of nuclear weapons, but in view of their competition in almost all other fields, concerted action seems unlikely—at least until a catastrophe has occurred in some part of the globe.

While the military strength of countries such as Iran, Israel, Egypt, and Syria in conventional arms now exceeds that of most West European countries, the Middle East will remain a power vacuum in world politics. The assumption frequently voiced that the oil crisis constituted a "decisive shift" in the global balance of power which will deepen with the transfer of so many billion dollars is patently untrue. Or to be precise, it would prove to be correct in a roundabout way inasmuch as the Soviet Union might benefit in a long-term perspective from the Western crisis; Saudi Arabia, Kuwait, and Iran will not. Europe's weakness existed well before 1973, the oil crisis only made it manifest. The transfer of great sums of money does not constitute a real shift in power, unless the recipient is in a position to use the income for strengthening his political-military base. This is not the case in the Middle East; even the limits set to Iranian influence are fairly narrow. Far from being a source of strength the influx of enormous wealth makes the oil producing countries more vulnerable to internal subversion and external aggression.

In the short run, no solution is in sight for the Arab-Israel conflict; a separate peace between one or more Arab countries and Israel is possible, but unlikely. It is equally unlikely that Israel will negotiate with the Palestine Liberation Organization (PLO) unless the Palestinians accept the existence of the State of Israel and give up the demand for its dismemberment. This is likely to happen in the long run, perhaps after some more fighting. Should the existence of Israel be in danger in a coming war, nuclear weapons are likely to be used. At the same time Arab governments will try to acquire nuclear devices. It is possible that this will have a stabilizing effect, but the prospects are not as good as in other parts of the world.

The suggestion that peace in the Middle East should be based on United States—Soviet cooperation should be explored, so that there will be no myth about opportunities that were missed, but the chances for success are very remote. Lasting collaboration can only be based on a community of interests which does not at present exist. To act as a bona fide guarantor of a Middle East settlement restoring real peace to the area would create many difficulties for Soviet policy in that area and no tangible benefit. This does not, of course, preclude *ad hoc* United States-Soviet cooperation in the field of crisis management.

Perhaps the most disconcerting aspect of Arab-Israeli relations is, as already mentioned, that it is only the tip of the Middle Eastern iceberg (to use a farfetched simile) of tension and conflict. Even if this conflict were solved, it would not restore peace and stability to the area. It would probably release and intensify various other conflicts at present submerged as the result of the

Arab-Israeli conflict. The danger of a military confrontation between the superpowers in the Middle East, be it as a result of the Arab-Israeli conflict or the oil crisis, seems distant. There is the understanding between the superpowers that conflicts in the region have to be contained. The threat of Western military intervention in the Persian Gulf or other oil producing regions will be credible only if oil supplies should be cut off. The industrial nations of the West would have to pay a price, namely the division of the Middle East into spheres of influence. But this seems a very distant possibility, for the oil producing countries will, no doubt, show willingness to compromise if their security will be threatened.

Note

1. Richard Nixon, (Wash., D.C.: U.S. Government Printing Office *United States Foreign Policy for the 1970s*, 1973).

XI

Lebanon, Syria, Jordan, and Iraq

Albert H. Hourani

I

The four states with which this chapter deals all formed part of the Ottoman Empire for several centuries. What is now Iraq was divided into a number of Ottoman provinces, the capitals of which lay in or near the valley of the Tigris and thus were amenable to some kind of central control. This control did not, however, spread far into the rural hinterland, the mountains or the steppe. The population was divided on ethnic and religious lines: Kurds and Arabs, Sunni and Shii Muslims. The regions now included in Syria, Jordan, Lebanon, and Israel were also divided among a number of Ottoman provinces, but had a broad social unity: most of the inhabitants were Arabic-speaking, and the majority were Sunni Muslims, although there were other Muslim groups and a considerable number of Christians and Jews. Ottoman control extended down the great roads to Aleppo and Damascus and a wide rural hinterland, but the steppe in the east and the mountains in the west were not directly ruled, and one mountain district, Lebanon, had a political structure of its own.

In the century before the Empire collapsed in 1918, it had begun to change in more than one way. The commercial and technical revolution had given the European powers, and in particular England and France, positions of strength inside the Empire: merchants established direct contact with producers; missionaries with eastern Christian communities, ambassadors and consuls with groups of political clients. Encouraged by those European states which wished the Empire to survive, the government tried to create a more modern legal and administrative system, more closely controlled from Istanbul because of new means of communication. This led to an extended domination of the cities over

269

the countryside and the growth of a new class of landowners. In Lebanon with its mainly Christian population, however, European intervention led to the creation of a special regime, that of the organic law of 1861.

After World War I Ottoman was replaced by European authority under the supervision of the League of Nations (the "Mandate" system), and new political frontiers were created. Great Britain held the Mandate for Iraq, Palestine (with an obligation to encourage the creation of a Jewish National Home while safeguarding the position of the existing population), and Transjordan; France had those for Syria and Lebanon. The mandatory governments took over the task of creating a new administrative framework within which modern societies could develop, but in circumstances which in some respects were unfavorable. They had to build political structures within units which were artificial and of recent creation, and they tried to do so in different ways. In Lebanon there was something to build on: the organic law could serve as the basis of a republican constitution. But in Syria the French created a republic out of nothing; in Iraq and Transjordan the British imported ruling families; in Palestine, the conflict of interest and national aspirations between Jews and Arabs made it impossible to build a political structure at all.

The process of creating a political society, difficult in any circumstances for a foreign ruler, was made more so by the growth of nationalist movements. They were primarily movements of urban elites, but able at times of crisis to draw on wider support. They aimed not only at limiting or ending European control, but also at removing the frontiers this control had created. Among Christians in Lebanon and Jews in Palestine a territorially limited nationalism did indeed emerge, but among Arabs in Palestine and Muslims in Lebanon, and in Syria and Iraq, the dominant idea was that of an Arab nation united within broad frontiers.

Even after the final withdrawal of British and French forces (from Syria and Lebanon in 1946; from Palestine in 1948, leading to the creation of Israel in part of it, and the addition of most of the other part to Transjordan to form' Jordan; from Iraq in 1955; from Jordan in 1957), the Arab nationalist movement continued to aim at some form of unity and the removal of what was left in the Arab countries of direct or indirect foreign power. In the years between 1955 and 1967, such hopes were symbolized by the magical figure of President Nasser. In these years, too, the idea of Arab unity became linked with certain others: that of a position of neutrality and balance between the two great power-blocs, and that of a state-controlled economy.

To some extent, the three problems of unity, foreign orientation, and economic organization continue to be linked with each other. But in the last few years the ways in which they are posed and answered have changed. The Middle East, like the rest of the world, has crossed some frontier into another phase of history: an invisible frontier which suddenly became visible in October 1973.

A number of interrelated factors have contributed to this change. The most obvious perhaps is a change in the way in which the various states of the Arab world regard themselves and each other. Political units which were artificial creations of foreign rulers have to some extent taken on a life of their own. Since independence, governments have acquired enough life and power to make control of them worth winning and maintaining, and they have acquired also a certain legitimacy, as feelings of solidarity, previously focused on smaller units or on some large and visionary ideal, have come to relate themselves more to what actually exists. At the same time, Arab governments (with some exceptions) are more willing than before to accept each others' existence, and not to appeal over each others' heads to public opinion.

The increase in oil production, the rise in prices and profits, and the accumulation of resources have also worked in the same direction. The loans and gifts made by richer Arab countries to poorer ones, and the activities of the various funds for development have created a network of shared economic interests such that no Arab state would wish to weaken it without necessity; shared economic interests lead to a closer coordination of policy. Moreover, the fact that most of the Arab states which have money to lend or invest belong to that group which would, a few years ago, have been called "traditional" or "conservative" means that the sharp division of that time between "traditional" and "progressive" states has been half forgotten.

Such political changes are linked in more than one way with rapid economic and social changes. These are too complicated to describe in full, but they include such changes as the following. There is a general increase in population because of a decline in mortality rates, in particular child mortality, which poses acute economic problems in countries where population threatens to outrun existing resources; everywhere it brings about changes in age structure and affects family relations and patterns of authority and obedience. The surplus population of the countryside flows into the towns, and in particular to capital cities; this causes a change in the nature of cities, where an urban way of life is engulfed in a sea of rural immigrants. In city and countryside alike, rapid economic development may create, in its first phase, a growing gap between different sections of the society. If uncontrolled by the government, certain classes are in a position to profit rapidly from economic growth: landowners with the knowledge and influence to make use of access to credit facilities and to introduce new methods of cultivation; merchants and industrialists in the private sector, the managerial class in the public; and those with a high professional or technical training. The masses, both urban and rural, may also profit, but slowly and to a lesser extent.

In due course however two intermediate groups tend to emerge from them; those who, although of humble origin, have managed to acquire a higher education and the technical skills necessary to administer a modern society (those of the officer, bureaucrat, economist or engineer); and the industrial workers, possessing certain essential skills and the power to organize themselves.

Both groups can play a part in the making of decisions, and their power or influence will tend to be used in the direction of greater state control over economic processes, for the sake of national strength or social equality. In town and countryside alike, the spread of literacy and education leads to a widening of the sphere of radiation of government and political leadership, and to a growing demand for political participation and reluctance to accept existing patterns of social subordination. An important aspect of such changes is the participation of women in them: in higher education and entry into the professions, the growth of a class of skilled wage-earning workers, and the spread of literacy.

Changes in society and the emergence of new social groups express themselves in political ideologies different in emphasis from the Arab nationalism of the former elites. Some of them appeal explicitly to Islam, which may be interpreted in terms of order, restraint and tradition or of fundamentalism and revolution. Others are Marxist, and here too there may be more than one version: Russian, Chinese or national. Between these two there has emerged a wide consensus in favor of a cautious, mixed, empirical type of policy less exposed to the winds of ideology; secularist without a radical break with religion, Arab but not to the extent of sacrificing sovereignty or local interests, but rather aiming at a balance between private enterprise and public control of the economy, and giving high priority to popular education and technical training. There is a broad spectrum of political forms as of political ideas: the absolute rule of dynasties, constitutional government, a partnership of military politicians and technocrats, the absolute rule of ideologically motivated parties. As education advances and economic development affects the nature of society, it may be that political life will tend towards an alternation between the second and third of these: the desire of socially powerful groups to participate in government and the need to reconcile interests in an increasingly complex society will lead in the direction of constitutional government. On the other hand, the need to carry out economic and social development rapidly and by direct intervention of the state, and the concentration of effective force in the hands of the army, will tend towards the formation of governments of military politicians assisted by technocrats, which at least hold out the promise of creating a strong executive power.

A combination of all such factors is bringing about a change in the relations of Arab states not only with each other, but also with the outside world. Recent changes in the relationships of the great powers, and the increased bargaining power of those states which control the world's supply of oil, have made it possible for the Middle Eastern states to formulate the problem of their foreign relations in a new way. No longer compelled to make the same hard choices as before, even if circumstances compel a state to incline towards one or other of the great powers, it will still try to preserve a certain freedom of action by maintaining relations with others: those formerly classified as "pro-Western" now for the most part have closer relations with Russia; most of those regarded as "pro-Russian" are now more open to American influence; all try to create and maintain a close and independent relationship with Western Europe. Within the Middle East, lines of division between Arab and non-Arab states are less sharp: Iran has closer relations than earlier, even with the Arab states of Iraq and Egypt from which it was most sharply divided; Turkey is less distant from its Middle Eastern neighbors than it was.

One basic line of division, that between Israel and the Arab states, still exists, but it too may be softened in the next phase. The present situation is clearly an unstable one: Israeli military superiority is more or less counterbalanced by Arab economic power and diplomatic influence. But in the longer run the Arabs are increasingly confident of their ability to impose, without too long a delay although possibly after one or more further wars, the kind of settlement which they believe to be just. This confidence rests not simply on a half-victory as in the war of 1973 (although that was the symbolic moment of change), but on other factors already mentioned: the firmer diplomatic unity of the Arab states, which springs partly from the mutual acceptance of each others' existence and regimes, and partly from the new financial relations between them; the changes in the international situation which have made it possible to create friendships across the frontiers of what were hostile camps; and the new wealth of the Arab states, which has enabled them to buy military technology on a scale hitherto beyond their resources and to exercise pressure (within limits which have not yet become clear) on states most likely to be favorable to Israel.

At the same time, the kind of settlement which the Arab states would regard as just is being defined more clearly than before and, to some extent, in different terms. It would involve a return to frontiers close to those of 1967, with some provision for demilitarized zones and international forces or guarantees; the creation of some kind of Palestinian entity, in a form acceptable to a large part of the Palestinians; and, on these conditions, a de facto acceptance of the existence of Israel. This changed view of a settlement is itself a product of the same factors. It is clearly in the common interest of the Arab states to seek a settlement which does not upset their relations with each other or the outside world and gravely retard or distort the process of development. In their new position in the world, moreover, Israel no longer appears to them to present the same danger as before: that of semi-permanent military domination, or of an advanced industrial state controlling a backward rural hinterland. It is in the Arab states' interest, too, to bring about a partial settlement as soon as possible, before Israeli control of the occupied territories produces results which would be difficult to eradicate.

II

Lebanon differs from the other three countries with which this chapter deals in that its institutions were not created by the mandatory government but by further development of a system which already existed. In the mountain valleys there had grown up over the centuries a number of small-scale rural societies clustered around their leading families and differentiated by religious allegiance: Maronite Christians in the north, Shii Muslims in the east and extreme south, Druzes (an offshoot of Shiism) interspersed with Christians in the south. Under Ottoman sovereignty there evolved a framework within which different groups could live together. There were two stages in this process. In the first, a hereditary "prince," recognized by the Ottoman government as chief tax collector, ruled through a hierarchy of families both Druze and Christian; in the second, under the organic law of 1861, a Christian governor drawn from outside Lebanon ruled with the help of an administrative council in which the main religious communities. were represented. The constitution of 1926, and the system of political conventions which grew up around it, developed this system further. There was an elected president, a council of ministers, a Chamber of Deputies, and a civil service in which once more the various communities were represented.

This constitution has now survived for half a century, during which it has been exposed to pressures which have brought about changes in the way in which it works. From time to time, adjustments have been made in the distribution of offices, so as to satisfy the demands of different communities. Under the French mandate the main problem was that of the Sunni Muslims of Beirut and other coastal towns, incorporated into Lebanon by the French in 1920. Formal satisfaction was given them by a convention which came into force in 1937: the president should be a Maronite Christian; the prime minister should be a Sunni Muslim. At much the same time, the system faced a minor but important test: the need to absorb the Armenian community. The Armenians were, for the most part, recent immigrants and were the only group not linked to the others by the Arabic language. A third claim was that of the Shii Muslims, numerous, but mainly rural, scarcely represented in the capital and educationally backward. In 1943 the convention was adopted that the third office of state, that of president of the chamber, should go to a Shii, but growth in numbers and progress in education have led to a further assertion of their separate existence and claims in recent years.

The relations between communities have at times been affected by strains arising from issues of foreign policy. The final orientation of most of the Christian population has always been towards "the West" (whether France or the United States is regarded as its prime embodiment); that of the greater part of the Muslim population is towards the Arab world (whether Cairo or Damascus is regarded as its center). The tension between these attitudes was formally resolved by the "National Pact" of 1943, an unwritten agreement that the Muslims of Lebanon, and by extension of Arab states, would accept the separate existence of Lebanon so long as it followed a policy in general conformity with that of the other Arab states. The efficacy of this agreement depended on

Lebanon being able to avoid a position where it had to choose between alternatives, and where such a choice would expose it not only to foreign pressure or intervention but to internal conflicts.

The difficulty of avoiding such a position was all the greater because Lebanon is a small state with a population of some two and a half millions, living among more powerful neighbors. Two moments of choice and crisis have in fact occurred. The first came in the years between 1955 and 1958, because of the rise of an Arab nationalism which seemed to aim at the formation of a large Arab state or bloc which would tend to absorb Lebanon, and because of strained relations between that nationalism and the dominant Western powers. The result was the civil war of 1958, which ended, however, in a kind of reassertion of the "national pact."

The second moment was that which began a few years ago and is still not ended. Once more there is a combination of internal and external factors: the presence in Lebanon of roughly a quarter of a million Palestinians, who in some ways have become a separate Lebanese community, but one which aims at the creation of its own Palestinian state rather than at full incorporation into the Lebanese system; and great pressure from the neighboring state of Israel, with the purpose of obliging Lebanon to suppress Palestinian nationalist activity. Once more Lebanon has found itself before a choice which would lead to deep division. The natural desire for peace and stability (among Muslim and Christian villagers and townspeople alike) inclines it in one direction; but general sympathy with the Palestinian people, fear of Israel, and the links of political leaders with the Palestinian masses in another. The result has been a series of local clashes, ending in temporary agreements, which have continued from 1969 to 1975.

The most significant challenge to the system, however, may be that which arises from certain changes in the nature of Lebanese society. It was formerly a society of mountain villages and small market towns, but it is now dominated by Beirut, a great commercial city, which provides services (banks, airlines, schools, summer resorts) for a vast Middle Eastern hinterland, and houses a large part of the population and gives work to many more. This city, moreover, is changing the nature of its activities: while services account for two-thirds of the gross domestic product, industry now accounts for almost 20 percent. It employs a similar proportion of the labor force, and a larger proportion than is employed in agriculture; this tendency is likely to be carried further under the present and future development plans.

Such changes have important political implications. The nature of political activity in a large city differs essentially from that of the countryside. The interests and loyalties of the individual can no longer be contained within a single community or focused on hereditary local leaders, city life creates links with members of other communities, exposes men to direct pressures from the government, and brings them nearer to the process of political discussion and decision. Since Lebanon is nearer to complete literacy than most Middle Eastern countries (some 90 percent of those over fourteen years of age), and the highly educated elite is large, the desire for effective political participation is comparatively great. Moreover, although the extremes of wealth and poverty are not as great as in some other Middle Eastern countries, and the intermediate class of the moderately rich is larger, the poverty of the city is harder to bear than that of the countryside, and the possibility of action to change it may appear to be greater.

But political activity aiming at social change is difficult to absorb within the existing framework of the country. This is partly to be explained by the existence of a certain link between socioeconomic and communal differences. On the whole, urban wealth is in Christian hands, and movements of the poorer groups, who tend to be Shiis or Palestinians, can threaten to disturb the delicate communal balance, and so arouse a strong reaction. There is also a kind of immobility inherent in the system. The concentration of power in the hands of the president creates around him a political "family" which shares in the profits of office; the way in which deputies are elected, and their role as guardians of local interests, cause government to be carried on by a continuous process of delicate adjustment of the balance between individuals and blocs; and the domination of the country by Beirut gives rise to close links between politicians and merchants or financiers, who want a government which cannot control them. There are some political parties based on different principles, but they have not been able to shake the system. The difficulty of changing the system in such a way as to take account of shifts in the balance of social and political power, and to deal effectively with the problems posed by the presence of a large and well-organized Palestinian community, led in 1975 to serious clashes which involved Christians and Muslims, Lebanese and Palestinians, "right" and "left" wings, and provided an opening for external influences.

III

In Syria, the legacy of the Ottoman period was not a system of political institutions but an urban elite which could serve as the nucleus of a political society. In each of the great provincial capitals, Aleppo and Damascus, there was a group of large landowners and merchants who possessed economic power and social prestige, and who played a subordinate but important role in the Ottoman administrative system as intermediaries between government and urban population, ultimately loyal to the government, but keeping a certain distance from it and acting as spokesmen of urban aspirations.

World War I overturned the delicate balance by seeming to hold out prospects of Syrian or Arab independence. The end of the war brought the urban elite briefly to power, but soon placed them in a position of more radical opposition to government than before, when the French imposed their control in 1920. In spite of several attempts, the French government and the urban politicians were never able to reach more than momentary agreement, until a combination of circumstances during World War II compelled the French to withdraw completely and gave power to the urban nationalist elite. They had gained something from the French presence and policy: the prestige of national leadership ending in victory, and the establishment of good working relations between different sections of the elite in the two cities, within the framework not so much of an organized party as of a loose coalition of families and groups. On the other hand, they had not had the experience of daily administration of constitutional life; the constitution drawn up in 1930 had been suspended soon after. The mode of political action which they had inherited, one based on relations of alliance and patronage, was not conducive to the smooth working of a parliamentary system, and the sphere of radiation of their influence did not spread over the whole country. Besides Aleppo and Damascus with their hinterlands, the Syrian state included two mountainous areas inhabited by separate Muslim communities, the Alawis in the west and Druzes in the southeast, and the Jazirah district in the northeast, which was just being opened up to settlement and attracting a population of mixed origin. These districts had scarcely been under Ottoman control; under the French they had separate regimes which insulated them from political processes in the two large cities.

In the first twelve years or so after the French withdrawal in 1946, the political elite found itself faced with problems which it was in no position to solve. The end of the struggle against the French weakened the coalition of leaders and split them into rival groups. Between the elite and the population as a whole, even in the cities, there did not exist the active unity necessary to mobilize national strength, and this became clear during the first Palestine war in 1948. Among elite and masses alike, political feeling was not focused on the idea of Syria as a separate entity. Syria, as the French had created it, was too large to be the object of primordial feeling which was still attached to the city or district, too small and artificial to satisfy the aspirations of those who hoped for an Arab or at least a larger Syrian state. The desire for a larger political entity had an important political result: it caused different political groups to look for external support and gave external powers the opportunity to fight their battles through the medium of Syrian political conflicts. In the first phase, it was the rivalry of Hashimis and Saudis which was reflected in Syrian politics; later, it was the struggle between "pro-Western" and "Nasserite" wings of the Arab movement, with Great Britain and the United States giving support to the one and Russia to the other.

In the end, the older political groups proved powerless in the face of a triple attack. Nationalists accused them of perpetuating divisions and failing to mobilize national strength; those concerned with social and economic development wanted reform of land-ownership, nationalization of industry, and the construction of large-scale public works—all measures which might affect the bourgeois interests with which the older leaders were linked. The rural population, basically hostile to the urban elite and hitherto outside the sphere of urban politics was being drawn into it because of better communications, the drift into the cities, and the growth of a new professional class of village or small town origin, in particular the army officers trained in the military academy.

The attack on the older political groups was led by the Baath party, which for a time was able to bring together a combination of forces: Socialists, radical nationalists, and army officers using the language of the Baath and affiliated with various groups within it. In the end the old political elite virtually disappeared: it was weakened during the years 1958-61, when Syria was joined to Egypt in the United Arab Republic, and then, after a brief return when the union broke up, was eliminated when the Baath came to power in 1963. Since then, certain radical changes have taken place in Syrian society. Economic development has been rationally planned since the beginning of the 1970s, and has been aided by loans, first from Eastern Europe and in the last few years from the Arab countries of the Gulf. Agriculture has expanded, in the cotton-growing regions of the Jasirah and in the Orontes valley; the Euphrates dam, of which the first stage is completed, will double the area of irrigated land. Oil wells have been exploited and there is now a small but appreciable export surplus. Some modern industries have been created: cement, oil-refining, phosphates, textiles. The resources of the country are more than adequate of its population of some seven millions.

In the course of this development, a Socialist society has been created in which large estates have been confiscated and redistributed, large industries and foreign trade nationalized, and a considerable part of the bourgeoisie has moved across the frontier into Lebanon. Foreign policy has been reoriented towards a Russian alliance which has guaranteed a supply of modern arms and diplomatic support as well as economic aid. A broader political society has come into existence, which includes the peripheral rural areas as well as the larger cities; and immigration from the former into the latter has drawn them closer together. Damascus, with almost a million inhabitants, now has a large rural element.

But within this political society political fragmentation has taken place much as it did in the old. The political coalition which brought about the changes has split into political "families" expressing their rivalries in terms of disagreement about various issues of policy. Groups of officers and politicians, all speaking the political language of the Baath, have been engaged in a struggle for power. Between 1963 and 1966 the civilian and military wings of the party governed in uneasy partnership; from 1966 the military groups were in power but were themselves split; in 1970 one group, that led by Haffez Assad, came to the top, and since then there has been comparative stability. Drawn largely from villages in and near the Alawi district, the dominant group of military politicians has followed an empirical policy: a mixed economy, with state control of large industries and public works, but encouragement of foreign investment and private enterprise; wider scope for the new managerial and technical class in those areas of policy which do not affect the security of the regime; an opening to the West in foreign affairs, as long as it does not endanger the supply of arms. Arab unity is now thought of more in terms of agreement between states and less in those of absorption into a larger unit, after a series of unsuccessful attempts such as union with Egypt during 1958-61; unity talks with Egypt and Iraq in 1961; the attempt to wage a "people's war" in 1967; and federation with Egypt and Libya in 1971. A growing sense of national difference, and the close financial links with Kuwait, Saudi Arabia, and the United Arab Emirates have both contributed to this.

These changes have not yet been institutionalized. Although the new rulers come from outside the former elite, they exercise power in much the same way, making alliances, doing favors for clients, balancing interests, and in the end using force to maintain themselves. In spite of the introduction of a constitution in 1973, the methods of political life have changed less than its scale, and so long as this is true it seems likely that there will be an alternation of groups roughly similar to that which is now in power, none of them solidly based and competing with each other in the name of certain great issues: that of Palestine, that of socialism, and perhaps that of religion. (The fact that some of the present leaders are of Alawi origin permits opposition to them to express itself in Islamic terms.) At some point in the not very distant future, however, there may emerge a solid basis for regimes of a different kind. Education, in particular scientific and technical, is being extended very quickly, the openings for private enterprise are being widened, and the number of skilled industrial workers is growing. The educated urban population may soon be large and strongly entrenched enough to secure wider participation in the government.

IV

Jordan differed from both Lebanon and Syria in the way in which it came into existence. It began neither with a political inheritance of institutions nor with the social inheritance of a great city and its hinterland. The land east of the Jordan, which formed Transjordan before 1948, had been part of the Ottoman province of Damascus and was a region of small market-towns with limited areas of agriculture, surrounded by larger areas of pastoral steppe. The land west of the Jordan, added after the partition of Palestine in 1948, was mainly agricultural, with no really large cities, and with its political and administrative framework shattered.

The British mandatory administration established in Transjordan a ruling family, a branch of the Hashimis of the Hejaz, with enough of an appeal to Arab feeling to be able to serve as a focus of loyalty, but without the independent strength to obstruct British policy in Palestine or elsewhere in the Middle East. In spite of various challenges the regime has proved to be reasonably stable, but has changed its nature in course of time. In the earlier phase, power lay in the hands of a dynastic ruler, limited by pressure from outside but not subject to great pressure from within, ruling through court politicians and surrounded by a dependent elite of tribal chiefs and notables of small towns. Something of this has continued until the present, but it has been changed by two processes. The first is the incorporation after 1948, and again after 1967, of a large Palestinian population, or rather of two, the mass of refugees in the camps, and the commercial and professional bourgeoisie of the towns. (The present population of the East Bank is approximately 1.8 million that of the West Bank, 700,000. All those on the West Bank, and perhaps half of those on the East, are Palestinians.)

The second process is that of economic development. Under a succession of plans, and with aid both from Western and Arab sources, an efficient infrastructure has been built: communications, power, and transportation. Irrigation works, in particular the East Ghor canal, have made possible an extension of the area of cultivation; industries, mainly for consumption goods, have been created in the region between Amman and Zarqa; and in recent years the export of phosphates, mainly to countries further east, has made a considerable difference to the balance of payments.

In this new and more complex society, the monarchy still has ultimate power, both because of a certain inherited prestige and because of the army, in which the tribal and non-Palestinian element is still dominant. But its power is mediated in a new way, through a bureaucracy in which the Palestinian element is strong, and is exercised within an environment in which certain interests must be taken into account: those of the bourgeoisie of Amman and other towns (Amman has a population of some 400,000), and those of the masses, both urban and rural, and the refugees. The interests of the former have been served by an economic policy which leaves economic enterprise mainly to the private sector. To some extent, an attempt has been made to meet the needs of the masses by rapid agricultural development and the extension of rural education, but there has been no reconciliation between the political aspirations of the Palestinian element, towards the recovery of Palestine and the establishment of a Jordanian regime which will help actively in it, and the desire of the monarchy to maintain a stable regime against pressures from inside and outside.

The loss of the West Bank in 1967 temporarily checked the evolution from the first phase to the second, and when it resumed it did so in circumstances which seemed to strengthen the position of the monarchy: the main centers of potential opposition in the West Bank cities had been removed, and both U.S. aid and Israeli pressure tended to maintain the status quo. When the regime was challenged by the Palestinians in 1970, it was able to defeat them and reimpose its authority. But in the long run its nature seems certain to change. The growing prosperity and solidity of the urban middle class and the expansion of the educated elite increase the stability of the regime up to a point.

Acceptance of the separate existence of Jordan has probably increased in the last decade or so, as what was artificial has become natural. But there may be a demand for the limitation of monarchical power and the establishment of an effective constitutional system, although, as in Syria, social and educational advance may not for some years reach the point where the demand is irresistible. Moreover, the increasing dependence of the regime on Arab financial support limits its freedom of action in regard to the Palestinian element in the population.

All this would be likely to happen even if events on the West Bank had no impact on the East, but of course they do, and in thinking about the future of Jordan we must speculate about what might happen in Palestine. Before October 1973, it was possible for Israel and its supporters to act on the assumption that there need be no change on the West Bank for years, and that when it came it would be a change willed by the Israelis. Even for a few months after the 1973 war it seemed that there were several different forms which change might take. But more recently the range of alternatives has narrowed. It seems unlikely that there can be a restoration of Hashimite sovereignty on the West Bank, or an autonomous Palestine under Israeli protection. The only alternatives (short of a change in the whole Middle East, and therefore in the whole world, so cataclysmic that it is useless to speculate about it) are those which are compatible with the emergence of a Palestinian state including the West Bank, Gaza, and (subject to some special arrangement) the Arab part of Jerusalem. This may not come into existence soon, or without at least one more round of fighting, but, given the present structure of the Middle East and the world, it is difficult to think of any other basis for a stable settlement.

It would be no more than a basis, however, and the kind of Palestinian state which emerges, and its relations with Jordan, will depend on a number of factors. Some of them are economic. It seems likely that a Palestinian government would be able to draw on enough money (from Arab or other sources) and enough technical knowledge (from the thousands of highly educated Palestinians in the outer world) to make possible development on such a scale as to attract at least some of the Palestinians now outside the West Bank and Gaza: some of the educated class now in Jordan, Lebanon and the Gulf, and some of the refugee masses on the East Bank (in particular those who left in 1967). But the land and resources of the new state might be too small to make possible the absorption of all Palestinians in the outside world, should they wish to return, and the state would therefore be in the position of having a large group of people who identified themselves with it but who lived in the surrounding countries: Jordan, Syria, Lebanon, and Israel. This might work in either direction: the state might use them to bring pressure on other governments; but consideration for their welfare and future might make it more cautious in dealing with its neighbors.

There are also political factors to be taken into account. In the early years of its existence, there is likely to be a tension within the state between those who, having at last secured something of their own, are not anxious to jeopardize it by following a policy which would arouse Israeli opposition and lead to foreign pressure, and those who think of the state as a stepping stone towards the creation of a secular, multinational state in the whole of Palestine. This tension might be linked with another one: between those who had played an active part in the Palestine Liberation Organization (PLO) outside Palestine, and the urban notables and educated class of the West Bank, whose support and participation will be necessary. Such internal tensions would create openings through which external influences might come. Israel, the Arab states, the European states, and the USSR and the United States would all be concerned over what was happening, and this might affect their attitude not only towards Palestine but also towards other states where Palestinians live—Jordan in particular.

If we take such factors into account, there seem to be three possible relationships between Jordan and Palestine. The first would be a formal or virtual absorption of Jordan into the Palestinian state. The force of Palestinian feeling on the East as well as the West Bank, strengthened by the creation of a state, might work in this direction. On the other hand, the vested interests bound up in the existence of Jordan (interests shared by many of the East Bank Palestinians) would run counter to it; so too would the influence of the great powers, and perhaps that of the other Arab states, which might well be reluctant to return to a situation in which existing frontiers were questioned and governments appealed over each others' heads to public opinion.

The second possibility would be that of an equal association with Jordan. This might take one of two forms: a very loose relationship in which each party retained its sovereignty but goods, money, and persons moved freely and there was consultation on matters of policy; or a closer and more organic one, with a single federal head (either permanent or by alternation), a common parliament, and a government administering some common services. The first form of unity would be likely either to lead on to the second or else to dissolve in course of time. The second form, if it could be achieved, might be stable. It would have in its favor the fact that the majority of the Jordanian population is of Palestinian origin and connections and have a strong common interest in using limited resources and resisting Israeli pressure. The basic problem would be that posed by the deep mutual suspicions left behind by the events of 1970.

The third possibility is that of some kind of association of both Jordan and Palestine with Syria. Here again there are shared feelings and human links, within a geographical area which has always had an economic and cultural unity, even if it has never found a lasting political embodiment. There are common interests, both political and economic, and the relationship of Hashimites and Palestinians might be easier within a broader framework. Recent developments in the relationship of Syria with the Palestinians and with Jordan indicate that the

Syrian regime is interested in the possibility of such an arrangement. On the other hand, the union of three sovereign states would pose more complicated problems than that of the second possibility: not only technical problems of framing a constitution, but political problems both internal (mutual suspicions and vested interests of three different political systems) and external (hostility of Israel and its supporters towards a strong eastern neighbor).

V

In Iraq once more we find a different social and political structure inherited from the past. In the northeast, as in Lebanon, the mountains gave birth to small-scale rural communities clustered around local ruling families; but the families were destroyed when Ottoman control was extended in the nineteenth century, and there survived nothing similar to the unified political system of Lebanon. In the river-valleys, and particularly in the great alluvial plain of the south, there has always been the possibility of the existence of large cities controlling fertile hinterlands, but this has depended on the maintenance of large and complicated irrigation works, and Iraq entered the modern age after a long period during which the irrigation system had broken down, the social control of cities over hinterland had been weakened, the balance between pastoralism and cultivation had shifted in favor of the former, and authority had been fragmented by the rise of chiefly families in the countryside. Both social and political unity were lacking. The territories incorporated into the modern state of Iraq had formed part of several different Ottoman provinces, and their population was deeply divided: ethnically, they were Arabs or Kurds (with some smaller groups); in religion, Sunni or Shii Muslims (again with some smaller groups). Of a total population of some ten millions today, roughly 55 percent are Shiis, 20 percent Arab Sunnis, and 20 percent Kurdish Sunnis. But Arab Sunnis are dominant in the cities of the river-valleys which were the centers of Ottoman rule.

As in Transjordan, the mandatory government had to create a local authority strong enough to serve as a focus of unity but not so strong as to challenge British power or policy. Here, too, it did so by bringing in a ruling family, another branch of the Hashimites, with an inherited position of such a kind that Sunnis and Shiis, Arabs and Kurds, might be able to identify themselves with it. Around the throne there grew up a ruling group drawn partly from the notable families of the Sunni cities of the river valleys, partly from the former Ottoman military and administrative elite; to this a younger educated element was added in due course. This system of government was just able, by the time of effective British withdrawal in 1945, to rule most of the country through a blend of expanding bureaucratic control and political manipulation. By the late 1940s direct control had been extended to the point where rural disturbances could no longer be used by urban politicians as a means of political action. Political manipulation was mainly in the hands of the Palace, which had built up a clientele of court politicians and rural chiefs such that no politician, however strong, and no nationalist or left-wing movement, could successfully challenge it.

The power even of the dominant group, however, was limited: it was working within a framework which in a sense was artificial, as it included far less than the whole country. The active political society was that of the main Sunni cities, Baghdad, Basra, and Mosul, together with a handful of Shii, Kurdish, and tribal leaders who were able to work within an urban environment. Political life scarcely touched the masses, whose alienation from the ruling group was more dangerous after 1945, because of the rapid growth in the population of the large cities, and of a development plan financed by oil royalties which emphasized large-scale irrigation works, the benefit of which would only be felt by the masses in the long run. Even within the educated class, active support for the ruling elite was less than it might have been because in the 1950s it was pursuing a pro-Western foreign policy which ran counter to public opinion.

In 1958, the opposition was given a strength it would not otherwise have had by the action of part of the army, which overthrew the monarchical regime. For a time the revolution gave an outlet to the violent expression of popular feeling, and in the longer run it caused change at more than one level. It opened the field for the formation of new political "families": groups of ambitious politicians linked to a certain extent by the kind of ties which gave them a certain trust in each other—ties of kinship or local origin or education. The conflicts of these groups expressed themselves in terms of new ideologies which had implications over the whole range of policy: Arab nationalist, Baathist, Socialist, and Communist. These conflicts passed through two main phases. In the first, stretching from 1958 to 1968, power was in the hands of a military group led by Qasim, and then (after a brief interlude) of another led by the 'Arif brothers. Conflicts of policy centered largely around two questions: that of the relationship to be established with other Arab states, and particularly with Nasser's Egypt; and the extent and nature of state control of economic life—economic issues centered upon whether land-reform should mean the creation of small holdings or of state-farms, and in the cities, whether industry, trade, and banking should be owned and managed by the government.

The second phase began with a Baathist revolution in 1968 and this led, after some years of confusion, to the ascendance of a group of Baathist army officers, that of Bakr and Sadam Husain. This group has followed a fairly consistent policy. Economic development has been resumed after the period of stagnation which followed the revolution of 1958, and on a larger scale than before because of the vast increase in revenues from oil (some $7 billions in 1974). Large-scale irrigation works have made it possible to extend the area of agriculture; small holdings and collective farms have been established, both under bureaucratic control. Until 1971 the main emphasis was upon industry: some oil fields have been taken over from the concessionary company, the Iraq Petroleum Company, and exploited with Russian or French help by the Iraq National Oil Company; in addition to oil-refining and petrochemicals, textile and other factories have been built. National education has been expanded quickly at every level. The foreign policy of the government has been keenly Arab nationalist, supporting Palestinian and other revolutionary movements, and oriented mainly towards Soviet Union, the chief supplier of arms.

Although the government seems more firmly in control of society than any previous one, political life still exists within a space narrower than that of Iraq as a whole. There is still more than one sense in which Iraq is not yet a unified political society. Political activity is mainly concentrated in the towns of the Tigris valley. If the rural force which once played an important part in political life, that of the tribesmen of southern and middle Iraq, has virtually ceased to exist, another force, that of Kurdish nationalism in the northeastern mountains, has now taken a form which threatens the fragile unity of the country. The Kurdish revolts of a past generation were of limited importance; they were movements of particular tribal or local groups, inspired not so much by national feeling as by reluctance to accept the rule of Baghdad, and to achieve limited concessions in education or administration. But in the 1960s and 1970s, there has emerged an explicitly nationalist movement, supported by the growing Kurdish population in the towns, and receiving help from outside the country—first from the Soviet Union and then from Iran, which had bad relations with Iraq for a number of reasons from 1969 until the agreement of 1975. Even at the height of their success, the aim of the Kurdish nationalists probably stopped short of complete independence, but went beyond the concessions which the Iraqi government was willing to offer. Now that Iranian support has been withdrawn, the Iraqi government may be in a position to impose a settlement more in accord with its own ideas, and some Kurdish nationalists may accept it, at least for a time.

Even within the cities, the consensus which supports the government is limited and weak. Power tends to lie, as in Syria, in the hands of new men from smaller provincial towns who have come up through the main channel of social mobility, the army; in the present regime, in those of a group from the northern Tigris town of Tikrit. They rule in uneasy partnership with technocrats, civilian ministers, and officials of high education and special qualifications, but with no independent basis of political power. The educated class of the cities does not provide such a basis nor, until now, do the urban masses, although their part in political life may increase as industry develops and the cities grow. (Baghdad now has roughly two million inhabitants, or one-fifth of the population of the country.) At the same time, pressures from outside are not so great as to compel the government to change its nature or direction: pressure from Iran has relaxed since the agreement of 1975, that from the other Baathist regime in Syria is limited, and Iraq's wealth from oil gives it a relative freedom of action.

But there are signs of a change. Economic development brings greater self-confidence and generates a need for the import of capital goods and high technology. In such circumstances, the voice of the educated class may be heard more effectively than in the past. But, given the present state of Iraqi society, it is unlikely that any basic institutional change will take place for some time; in the immediate future, such change as takes place is likely to be from an ideologically motivated coalition of officers and technocrats to one which follows a more empirical policy.

VI

The preceding sections have tried to describe some of the important features of the framework within which political decisions have to be made. This section indicates briefly the kind of matters on which the United States may have to make decisions. Certain assumptions will be made. First, it will be assumed that the détente between the United States and the USSR is likely to continue, at least at the level which it has now reached; that is to say, while each nation will pursue its own interests in various countries of the Middle East, it will do so within limits set by its acceptance that the other also has interests which have to be taken into account. Second, it will be assumed that the position of the United States has changed in the last year or two. In some ways it is weaker: the détente and the virtual end of the cold war mean that the United States can no longer act as leader of a solid bloc of states with an overriding common interest, and the Western European states will pursue their own policy in the Middle East; the financial power of some Middle Eastern countries makes them less vulnerable to pressure and capable of exercising it themselves.

On the other hand, the United States still possesses the military power which would make it possible, in case of absolute need, to impose its will over a large part of the world; and it has the largest supply of the high technology, military, industrial, and agricultural which embattled or developing nations want. In spite of the détente, the United States and Russia will still have differing interests and a certain rivalry; states strongly opposed to the USSR or its Middle Eastern allies will tend to look for support to America, and even those whose main inclination is towards Russia will wish to have as close a relationship with the United States as circumstances allow. What is perhaps most important in the short run, the United States alone has the power to put pressure on Israel (within limits which cannot by their nature be clear) if its ideas about what is necessary for peace differ from Israel's. (This is a wasting asset however. If the United States does not succeed in putting pressure on Israel, the fact that it could have done so and did not will be a handicap in dealing with other Middle Eastern countries; if it does so successfully, this will be taken for granted and soon forgotten.)

Thus, an active involvement of the United States in the Middle East is possible, and if it is possible, it is unavoidable; to have power and not use it is as much an act of policy as to use it. In what follows, an attempt will be made to suggest the kinds of problems to which the use of U.S. power is relevant. No attempt will be made to say what the United States is likely to do, or ought to do; this would involve considerations of American policy going far beyond the limits of the chapter and the writer's competence.

In the urgent political problem, that of Palestine and Israel, U.S. involvement is patent and inescapable. But, just as the alternatives for Israel are more limited than they were, so are those for the United States. An indefinite continuation of the Israeli presence on the West Bank, and a semi-autonomous Palestinian entity under Israeli protection seem to have become impossible; so does a return of Jordanian rule on the West Bank, although Jordan may well play an active part in whatever negotiations take place.

Even if it wished, the United States could probably not prevent the establishment of an independent Palestinian state in the fairly near future. Nevertheless, the United States can still have some influence on the way in which it comes into existence and the form it takes. It may come into existence after another round of fighting or without it, and through discussions at Geneva or elsewhere; and the precise balance of American policy, between giving Israel assurances for its survival and putting pressure on it to negotiate with the Palestinians, is clearly a question of the utmost delicacy, the answer to which might be one of the factors preventing or causing another war.

When negotiations take place—at Geneva or elsewhere, without or after another war—the United States may not be able to avoid taking up a position on the precise territorial arrangements to be made: major or minor changes in the frontiers of 1967; the nature of the link between the West Bank and Gaza; special arrangements for control of the Old City of Jerusalem and access to it; and, most important of all, the form of international guarantee of the frontiers which emerge from the negotiations, whether by means of demilitarized zones, limitation of armaments and forces, international forces or supervision.

Once the Palestinian state comes into existence, the United States will have a number of choices to make about the extent of economic or technical assistance to give it, and these choices of course will have political implications. They will help to determine the general orientation of the state, the extent to which it will be able to absorb Palestinians from other countries, and the extent also to which it will become a "satisfied" state, having something of its own to preserve and therefore less likely to follow a policy of confrontation with Israel. In the long run, no doubt, the new state could secure the financial help it needed from other Arab states, but the settlement of refugees would be an urgent problem which would need help, both financial and technical, from the United States and Western Europe.

There will also be consequential decisions to be made in regard to the countries surrounding Palestine. This chapter does not deal with Israel. So far as

Jordan is concerned, an earlier section of the chapter has tried to define the alternatives: virtual absorption of Jordan into Palestine, more or less equal union of Jordan and Palestine, association of both of them with Syria. The military and economic support which the United States gives to Jordan will probably enable it to play a large part in deciding which of these three possibilities comes into existence. This will involve a prior decision about the extent to which American interests demand the preservation of the present regime or something similar to it in Jordan.

The United States would of course be in a stronger position to influence the choice between the three possibilities if it had close relations not only with Israel and Jordan but with the Palestinians and Syria as well. In Syria, too, the alternatives seem more limited than they might have appeared to be a few months ago. As long as it seemed possible for Israel to move towards peace by a series of separate negotiations with its neighbors, it also seemed possible that at some stage in the process Israel would reach mutually advantageous agreements with Egypt and Jordan and be able to continue occupying part of Syria without effective resistance from Syria itself or from other Arab states. In the international situation which has emerged since 1973, no agreement on any front is likely to be effective unless there is substantial Israeli withdrawal from the occpuied parts of Syria. Once more, U.S. policy can have some influence on the timing and circumstances of withdrawal, on whether it takes place without further fighting and what form of international guarantees can be given for the frontiers which emerge.

The establishment of a Palestinian state will certainly have far-reaching effects inside Lebanon. It is unlikely to lead in the first instance to a large-scale migration of Palestinians from Lebanon to the West Bank: a large proportion of them come originally not from areas which might form part of the new state but from those lying inside Israel. On the other hand, it will continue to be difficult for the mass of Palestinians in the camps to be absorbed more fully into the Lebanese economy than they have already been. In these circumstances, whatever opposition there is from uncompromising Palestinian groups to the establishment of a limited state on the West Bank is likely to draw much of its support from Palestinians in Lebanon, encouraged perhaps by one or two of the Arab governments. If so, something like the present situation may continue to exist: Israel will retaliate against Lebanese as well as Palestinian targets in order to put pressure on the Lebanese government to follow a different policy, and tension between Palestinian and Lebanese activists will lead to civil strife from time to time. The position of the Lebanese government will, however, be somewhat different: the Palestinians in Lebanon may be regarded as citizens of the new Palestinian state and therefore as foreigners in Lebanon, and a closer control of them may be possible. But on the other hand, the political considerations which make it difficult for any Lebanese government to take strong measures against the Palestinians will still exist, to an extent difficult to estimate.

Here, too, the United States may have to make a number of decisions closely linked with each other. The basic decision may be one about Lebanon itself: To what extent is it in the interests of the United States that the present constitional system or something like it should continue to exist? In the light of this, other decisions might have to be made: To what extent can or should the United States exert pressure on Israel to limit its retaliation, or on Lebanon to follow a different policy towards the Palestinians, and how far can or should it give financial and technical help to the new state to absorb the Palestinians of Lebanon, or to Lebanon itself to absorb them?

In the longer run there will be certain continuing demands on the United States, posing problems, not of the kind which can be disposed of, but of the kind which recur and provide the continuing matter of international relations. One large subject—that of arms supply to Middle Eastern countries—will be left out of this account, since it involves considerations which go far beyond the limits of this chapter. But two other kinds of recurrent problems must be touched on.

The first is the problem of degrees and kinds of aid to development. In spite of new possibilities of raising loans and attracting investment from the richer Arab countries, it seems likely that the economic needs of some of the countries we are dealing with will be large and urgent enough to lead them to ask for aid from the United States and other industrial countries. This is probably not true of Iraq, with its large oil resources and a regime which does not encourage foreign investment. But Syria, with its considerable natural resources, its relatively large supply of managerial and technical skills, its favorable balance between population and resources, and its need to make up for the damage incurred in and after the 1973 war, seems capable of rapid and diversified economic development and may well be able to attract the capital it needs, either from Arab or other sources, under normal conditions of international borrowing or investment. The economy of Jordan seems likely to rest, as now, on two bases, agriculture for internal consumption and production of phosphates for export; whether many of its Palestinian refugees leave or not, it will need considerable aid for agricultural expansion. The development of Palestine and the absorption of Palestinians in Lebanon seem likely to need international help on a large scale.

Apart from financial aid and development, there will be a need for technical advice and assistance, and for the training of local technocrats, either in Europe and America or in the Middle East itself; it is clear that, after a long period in which education was regarded as aiming primarily at the production of lawyers, doctors, and government officials, the importance of technical and vocational training of every kind has been understood. Governments of the technically advanced nations like the United States, and private foundations and other institutions, will find themselves faced with continual problems of priorities; even the largest reservoir of skill has its limits, and it will never be easy to decide between the needs of the Middle East and those of other parts of the world.

Closely connected with this is the problem of the kind of regimes which the United States is likely to find in the Middle Eastern countries, and its attitude towards them. In our survey we have come upon a whole spectrum of regimes: more or less unrestricted monarchy; ideologically motivated rule by military politicians; more empirical rule by a balance between military politicians and technocrats; more or less stable constitutional democracy. Of the four actual and one potential state we have studied, only one, Lebanon, seems more or less firmly fixed at one point on the spectrum, that of constitutional democracy. Iraq lies at present at the second point, but as development proceeds it may move towards the third. Syria is at the third, with the possibility that in time it may move to a point midway between third and fourth, where (as in parts of Latin America) periods of constitutional rule alternate with those of military-technocratic rule. Jordan is at the first but seems likely to move away from it, probably—given its level of development—towards the third or fourth. About a future Palestinian state it is difficult to say anything; but its unusual social structure, with a large educated class in a position of national leadership, and a relative absence of strong urban or rural vested interests, makes it at least possible that it will move in the direction of constitutional democracy.

Here as elsewhere in the world where types of regime change fast, the United States may find itself face-to-face with continual problems. On the one hand, the need for rapid economic development may make it incline in favor of strong military-technocratic or monarchic governments which seem likely to act quickly and efficiently; on the other, its own traditions and common convictions would incline it towards democratic institutions. The belief that democratic institutions cannot work in countries of a certain kind, for example in Muslim countries, may appear to offer a way of avoiding this dilemma. But this is an illusory solution, and the demand for some kind of institutional restraints on the exercise of power, and some participation in it, is likely to grow stronger rather than weaker. Moreover, regimes which seem efficient may only be so in the short run; they accumulate round themselves the vested interests of a new possessing class, and may in the end precipitate violent popular explosions which will bring to power regimes of a very different kind. A great power actively engaged in the life of countries in process of rapid change must walk delicately, supporting regimes whose interests seem to conform with its own, but keeping its distance from them.

XII Egypt: The Wages of Dependency

John Waterbury

Egypt is the prisoner of its economy and the structure of its human and material resources. The Nile Valley, in the pre-industrial, pre-petroleum era, was the golden goose of the Middle East, a cornucopia of agricultural produce relative to the rest of the area, and a resource base for a myriad of dynasts, exclusively non-Egyptian, who sought to extend their control throughout the Middle East. The long struggle to give Egypt back to the Egyptians, launched by a non-Egyptian, Mohammed Ali (1805-1849), initially emphasized the inseparability of economic development and political sovereignty. But Egyptian mastery of its economic fate was substantially eroded through the actions of the European powers in 1841 and then destroyed when the British occupied Egypt in 1882. From then on economics and national sovereignty tended to drift apart analytically, as the bulk of Egyptian politicians, nationalists, and intellectuals turned their attention to the quest for political independence and ridding the Nile Valley of the presence of British troops.

There were, of course, scholars and politicians who explored in great depth the economic rationale of British imperialism, variously interpreting the themes of the terms of trade between Egypt's single export crop of cotton and the textile mills of Lancashire, European banks that thrived on the Egyptian debt, and the vast comprador class of intermediaries that emerged to serve European economic interests in the country. Yet, as in many other countries under foreign domination, economic questions were held in abeyance as all efforts were given over to the struggle for national independence.

When independence was achieved in stages between 1936 and 1954, the realities of Egypt's economic situation had changed so drastically that the golden goose of the Nile Valley had become an albatross. The rich, labor-intensive peasant cultivation of the Nile Valley, unique in its continuity and sophistication in the Middle East, had, in the nineteenth and the first half of the twentieth centuries, bred a monster. The Egyptian population grew steadily throughout this period without any major disruptions resulting from epidemics, natural disasters, or wars. The result has been that Egypt was at least a generation in advance of the other countries of the area in attaining a self-sustaining rapid rate of population growth. These countries will certainly have their day of reckoning, but many—Syria, Iraq, Sudan, Algeria—have a good chance to develop their economies in anticipation of what is to come.

Egypt, on the other hand, entered its phase of effective political independence shackled to an outsized population within the narrow confines of the Nile Valley. Nasser and various of his colleagues and advisors wished to reestablish the equation of economic development and national sovereignty as first set down by Mohammed Ali. But the basic problem over the last twenty-five years has been that the Egyptian regime was forced to deal with the cumulative defects of the economy as it had developed over the period 1882-1952. Rather than looking forward, economic planners found themselves absorbed in an incessant effort to deal with the errors and distortions of the past. Egyptian economic strategies have been retrospective rather than prospective.

Even though the Nasser regime once more clearly enunciated the interrelationship between economics and sovereignty, Nasser and his colleagues were by inclination drawn to other spheres of activity at the expense of developing a coherent economic strategy. The order of their priorities seemed based on the twin assumption that their "revolution" was inherently threatening to the imperialist powers and that no economic experiment could be attempted unless and until Egypt established its primacy in the area. In other words, a propitious environment, necessarily Arab in character, had to be created in order to permit some measure of "Egypt-firstism." This assumption, and the perceptions underlying it have, it seems to me, considerable merit. Nonetheless, from 1955 on Egypt's regional and international policies began, superficially, to determine economic policy.

In terms of man-hours invested by Egyptian leaders in policy-planning, it was the international arena that stole the show. Indeed, the atmosphere of the cold war, the balance of power-cum-arms level concerns of Washington and Moscow, the attentions of the international press were all skewed in the same direction. What was meaningful in international and Egyptian eyes were "events" such as the Czech arms deal, the nationalization of the Suez Canal, Nasser's skirmishes with the Baghdad Pact, and so forth. During the 1960s attention was paid to issues that bore upon fundamental economic choices, but these issues were normally couched in noneconomic terms. The suspension of U.S. wheat deliveries in 1965-66 was wrapped in the international machinations over the fate of the Congo rather than in terms of the Egyptian balance of payments. The High Aswan Dam became at once a subject of excessive abuse and overzealous apologia because it also became a Soviet project, was intimately connected to Egypt's decision to nationalize the Suez Canal in 1956, and to the alleged ambition of Nasser to build a latter-day equivalent of a pyramid. Few commentators looked closely at the merits of the dam in terms of the basic dilemma of resource allocation in Egypt.

Despite the fact that observer and observed alike laid primary stress upon the politico-international determinants of economic options, the lines of causality so implied are superficial and misleading. It is in times of economic crisis that the real priorities emerge, and that political options are adopted in light of economic considerations. The conduct of the first Five Year Plan (1960-1965), the balance-of-payments crisis of 1965-66, and the economic dislocations resulting from the 1967 military defeat all served to force the issue of fundamental economic options and, derivatively, of new regional and international alignments.

In the two decades of Nasser's regime, many critical choices were avoided while the challenge of distributing limited resources to a growing population took on awesome proportions. Those choices that were made generally were prompted by crisis situations of arms supplies, food imports, or balance-of-payments deficits and, as such, represented selecting among lesser evils. Policies so adopted, particularly in the 1960s, were at best palliatives and scarcely affected the growing polarization in the kinds of economic strategies open to Egypt. President Sadat has had to bite the bullet. He has had to make choices. But any choice he might have made could no longer be middle-of-the-road. The economic problems of which Egypt is prisoner are of a nature that only a revolution— Socialist or capitalist—could deal with. The primacy of economics has become undisputed in the Egypt of 1975, and the regional arena has become an essential but somewhat annoying constraint.

The above remarks are fairly bold assertions for which I think there is ample empiric evidence. The assertions, however, unsubstantiated they may appear, will have to be taken to some extent on faith. It is in light of these assertions that the focus of this essay has been chosen. Egypt's critical choices over the last quarter century and in the quarter that remains, whether they have impinged upon the international and regional arenas or upon the domestic political system, have been consistently modulated, if not determined, by the state of the Egyptian economy.

Egypt is not alone in this kind of determinism. The kinds of political and economic policy options that Egypt has considered in the past few decades are a litany of those faced by most developing countries. In other words, Egypt is not a unique case; at most it displays unique variations on a common theme. The characteristics that it shares with the bulk of humanity can be briefly summarized. Egypt is still fundamentally an agricultural country with over half its population dependent upon farming for its livelihood. The country is overpopulated and the agricultural carrying capacity of the Nile Valley is being stretched to its outer limits. In relation to its population Egypt is not notably rich in mineral and other natural resources. Even the waters of the Nile must now be considered as a scarce resource. In this sense Egypt does not enjoy the same prospects as other currently poor agricultural economies, such as Algeria or Iraq, which may overcome their backwardness through the investment of their oil and natural gas earnings. Nor has Egypt yet developed a large expatriate work force that remits a large amount of its hard currency savings on a regular basis. Such work forces have been essential to the solvency of the Spanish, Turkish, and Algerian economies, among others.

Deprived of the capacity to earn substantial amounts of hard currency through the exportation of a valuable natural or human resource, Egypt has faced chronic balance-of-payments deficits since the late 1950s. These have stemmed from three principal sources: rising imports of foodstuffs to meet the consumption needs of a growing population; capital goods and raw materials imports to nourish a nascent industrial sector that is Egypt's best hope to break loose from an overburdened agricultural sector; and massive arms purchases, particularly since 1967. It will certainly come as no revelation that the size and nature of the external debt constitutes the Achilles heel of national sovereignty. For Egypt, and several other countries, there is no choice but to maintain a very large debt in proportion to GNP with heavy servicing obligations. The basic strategic choice becomes not so much how to reduce the debt and hence one's reliance on outside sources of funding, but rather how to distribute one's dependency and thereby leave some room for maneuver.

A final characteristic that Egypt shares with many Third World countries is its growing dependency on outside sources of food grains. Egypt has long been a net importer of food grains, and, short of converting all of the country's six million feddans (1 feddan = 1.038 acres) to wheat production, import needs are likely to grow enormously throughout this century. Egypt already ranks along with Bangladesh and India as one of those countries that will yearly absorb a large proportion of the annual world grain harvest that finds its way into the export market.

On this very broad and, I believe, determinant level of population and resource structure, Egypt is just one among several countries that represent about 60 percent of humanity that can no longer afford their traditional agricultural bases, but at the same time cannot find the wherewithal to pay for their own modernization. Having insisted then upon the common plight that Egypt shares with the rest of the developing world, it is important to take note of those respects in which Egypt is different, if not unique.

The major factor in this vein is Egypt's peculiar geopolitical situation. The country's geographic location inevitably elicits a flow of clichés that are nonetheless true. It is a crossroads, a vital link in east-west trade and communications, a fate to which it has been condemned particularly since the construction of the Suez Canal. Indeed, the canal brought Egypt so thoroughly into the trade nexus of Western Europe that it could never again enjoy the luxury of its own geographic isolation. Mohammed Ali and his successor, Abbas I (1849-1854), both seized the international portent of the canal, fearing that it would create for Egypt a second Bosphorous that would inevitably stimulate the "greed" of the great powers. These fears were laid to rest by the Khedives Said and Ismail who backed Ferdinand de Lesseps' scheme. As a direct result of the construction of the canal and the crucial place that it then occupied in imperial communications, Egypt was occupied by the British in 1882.[1] Over the last century, the feeling has grown among Egyptian thinkers and statesmen that one of the choices they do not have is to decide freely how best to organize their political and economic life. The widespread impression is that any experiment in the Nile Valley will arouse the concern, and perhaps stimulate the direct intervention of the "great powers" in Egyptian affairs. There is ample historical evidence to substantiate these apprehensions. To achieve some minimal room for maneuver in terms of internal development, Egypt must try to promote a stand-off between and among great power ambitions.

Egypt is also distinct in that its population is so much larger than that of any of its neighbors: over twice that of the Sudan, five times that of Saudi Arabia, twelve times Israel's, and eighteen times Libya's. When the contributions of oil production are excluded from other countries' accounts, Egypt has the largest GNP in the area, with the most advanced industrial sector and the greatest abundance of highly-trained professional personnel. With a standing army of some 300,000, that can be expanded to 900,000 during periods of mobilization (viz. October 1973), Egypt is the preponderant military force among the Arab states. Despite its poverty, Egypt is the only country which all other Arab states must, to some degree, fear, and almost always court.

Finally, precisely because of the factors mentioned above, Egypt is the linchpin of the Arab-Israeli conflict. It has, since 1948, carried the main burden of military confrontation with Israel and, for the foreseeable future, it will be the determinant weight in any new round of fighting. This strength is simultaneously an oppressive burden, for the Arabs look to Egypt to uphold their end of the struggle and demand of Egypt sacrifices that they themselves have been reluctant to make. Egypt, then, stands alone in its size, its geographic location, and the military burden it has been obliged to shoulder.

One can draw a few virtually self-evident conclusions from the foregoing analysis. While Egyptian leaders and probably the Egyptian masses aspire to national independence and the degree of mastery over their resources that would allow them to determine their own development strategy, that mastery has in fact been involuntarily shared with non-Egyptian powers or swept aside by the movement of prices in world markets. Egypt constitutes a national "system" in only the most relative sense. It can be said that the Egyptian political elite can and does make decisions affecting all the resources utilized within the system, but it is also the case that other decision-making centers outside Egypt can and frequently do take measures that significantly influence Egyptian resource utilization, sometimes intentionally and sometimes inadvertently. Although we shall return to both instances, one may cite by way of illustration the suspension of Food for Peace shipments to Egypt in 1965-66, an act of political retribution, and the United States-Soviet wheat deal of 1972; the latter's impact upon world grain prices was so devastating that Egypt, and other grain-deficit countries, found themselves faced with a hard-currency grain bill three to four times larger than the previous year's. In such circumstances where does the system end and its environment begin?

Egypt's critical problems can best be analyzed within three highly-interlocking policy domains: economic strategy and resource allocation; the organization of political life; the orientation of foreign and regional policy. The basic dilemma facing Egyptian policymakers is to find that balance among the policy domains that assures the greatest diversification of dependency within what are considered to be the tolerable limits of change. The definition and redefinition of those limits are in themselves a fourth domain, that of ideology, providing an explicit, generally *post hoc*, rationale for actions taken within the other three.

Population and Resources

One hundred and fifty years ago, the population of Egypt was probably no more than four million, sustained by a cultivated area of some three million feddans. By the end of the century the population approached ten million, having grown at the rate of 1.7 percent per annum. Although this rate is modest by twentieth century standards (several developing countries have maintained population growth rates in excess of 3 percent per annum), it does not detract from the fact that during the nineteenth century Egypt underwent a population explosion—perhaps the first of its kind in the Middle East. Over this same period, however, the cultivated area of the country nearly doubled, reaching 5.4 million feddans, while the introduction of perennial irrigation led to the effective expansion of the cropped area (i.e., through double-cropping the same feddan in any one year) to 7.6 million feddans. From then until the present time, person-land ratios have deteriorated without interruption. The Egyptian population of 1974 is estimated to exceed thirty-seven million people, perhaps ten times that of 1820. By contrast total cultivated acreage in 1974 stood at only 5.9 million feddans, while the cropped area, through the generalization of perennial irrigation, stood at about 9.5 million feddans. Since the turn of the century per capita shares of cultivated and cropped areas dropped from 0.53 and 0.71 feddans (1897) to 0.18 and 0.33 feddans in 1970[2] (see Table XII-1).

During the two decades following World War II the population growth rate accelerated to 2.6 percent a year as the full impact of public health measures and improved nutrition was finally felt. Accompanying this surge was a vast

Table XII-1
Growth of Population, Cultivated and Cropped Land, Egypt, 1821-1970*

Year	Population (in millions)	Cultivated Area '000 Feddans	Per. Cap. Cultiv. Area	Cropped Area '000 Feddans	Per. Cap. Cropped Area
1821	4,230	3,053	.73	3,053	.73
1846	5,290	3,764	.71	–	–
1882	7,930	4,758	.60	5,754	.72
1897	9,717	4,943	.53	6,725	.71
1907	11,190	5,374	.48	7,595	.67
1917	12,718	5,309	.41	7,729	.60
1927	14,178	5,544	.39	8,522	.61
1937	15,921	5,312	.33	8,302	.53
1947	18,967	5,761	.31	9,133	.48
1960	26,085	5,900	.23	10,200	.39
1966	30,075	6,000	.20	10,400	.34
1970	33,200	6,000	.18	10,900	.33
1975 (est.)	38,000	5,900	.15	10,800	.28

*The cropped area of Egypt measures that surface that is cultivated more than once each year. As a rule of thumb, for every feddan (1.038 acres) of cultivated land under perennial irrigation there are 1.6-1.7 feddans of cropped land. The sources for this table are varied and not always in total accord. See Gabriel Baer, "The Beginnings of Urbanization," in his *Studies in the Social History of Modern Egypt* (Chicago University Press, 1969), pp. 133-148. The population *estimates* 1821-1882 are drawn from his table, p. 136. They do not correspond to a more prevalent estimate for 1821 of between 2,158,580 (for example, Helen Rivlin, *The Agricultural Policy of Mohammed Ali in Egypt* [Harvard University Press, 1961], p. 256), and 2,536,400, which Baer himself advances in order to refute it. He sets forth his reasons, which I will not reproduce here, for assuming that the 1821 population was grossly underestimated. The cultivated and cropped surface figures were taken from Patrick O'Brien, *The Revolution in Egypt's Economic System* (Oxford University Press, 1966), p. 5, up to 1947. O'Brien, like Rivlin, uses a population figure of 2,514,000 for 1821. More recent figures on land and population have been taken from Central Agency for Public Mobilization and Statistics (CAPMAS), *Population and Development* (Cairo, 1973), p. 172, and CAPMAS, *Statistical Yearbook* (1952-1971), July 1972. Figures for 1975 are the author's estimates.

movement of rural population to the cities where the crude birthrates over this same period clearly surpassed those of the countryside, even allowing for a greater incidence of underreporting in rural areas.[3] Then, coinciding with the June War of 1967, the situation began to change. A combination of factors has led to a perceptive, albeit unspectacular, decline in crude birthrates so that over the period 1970-1974 the annual growth rate has been about 2 percent per annum. Without attributing relative significance to any one factor, one may note that fertility rates in Egypt have typically been depressed during times of international crises in which Egypt has been involved (1914-1918, 1940-1945, 1956-57, 1967-?). This may reflect a certain fear of the future as well as the fact that a substantial segment of the male population is under arms or at least away from home. At the same time the urban environment appears to have begun to produce its "normal" effect in lowering fertility rates, and Egypt is now about 40 percent urban. Economic privation, posponed marriages, the greater availability of contraceptive materials distributed through the public family planning program (instituted in 1966), and perhaps a slight increase in the crude death rate (about 16 per 1,000) have also contributed to slowing the population's growth.

At this point in time (1975), it is too early to tell if the slight easing of regional tensions following the October War of 1973, along with some steps toward demobilization, will lead to a sustained baby boom. However that may be, the shape of Egypt's population growth for the remainder of this century can only be drawn in terms of relative gloom. The projections presented in Table XII-2 are based on three hypothetical patterns for population growth, and even under the most favorable of these patterns Egypt would wind up with a population of 54,771,000. In other words, there is no way to avoid further rapid population growth in Egypt, given the current age structure of the population and particularly the present and future sizes of its childbearing cohorts. The question is simply how to minimize the damage.

While the sheer size of the population is of obvious importance, its age structure is in many ways of greater significance. In 1970, 43 percent of the population was fifteen years old or younger (i.e., 14,480,000 of 34,000,000). This dependent population puts a severe drain upon private savings and public

Table XII-2
Estimates of the Total Population of the UAR According to Three Hypotheses
(In '000)

	1960	1985	1990	1995	2000
Hypothesis I*	26,180	45,583	48,761	51,585	54,771
Index	100	174.1	186.3	197	209.2
Hypothesis II	26,180	50,368	55,057	58,797	62,551
Index	100	192.3	210.3	224.6	238.9
Hypothesis III	26,180	53,820	60,500	65,965	70,759
Index	100	205.6	231.1	252.0	270.3

*Hypothesis I assumes that the growth rate will fall to 1.87 percent per annum in 1970-1975, and then stabilize at 1.4 percent until 2000. Hypothesis II assumes a rate of 2.34 percent between 1970-1975, 1.87 percent 1975-1980, and 1.4 percent thereafter. Hypothesis III assumes a rate of 2.6 percent until 1975, 2.34 percent 1975-1980, 1.87 percent 1980-1985, and 1.4 percent thereafter.

Source: Adapted from Nabil Azzat Kharzati, "Population Trends in the UAR by Age Groups and Sex to the Year 2000," Memo No. 642, Series 26, Institute of National Planning (Oct. 1968), in Arabic, p. 14.

resources. It must be fed, clothed, and educated, and then absorbed, in ever larger cohorts, into the work force. There are many facets to this problem, but let us concentrate on one, mass education.

Egypt's stated objective since 1952 has been to extend primary education to all children between the ages of six and fourteen. In absolute numerical terms impressive progress has been made: enrollment at this level rose from 1.5 million in 1952-53 to 3.7 million in 1970-71. But because the eligible age cohorts were growing in size, the goal of universal schooling has constantly receded. The number of eligible children not accommodated by the school system stood at 1.8 million in 1960 and had risen to 2.06 million a decade later. If current trends are not reversed the deficit may rise to 4.3 million by 1985. Even for those who enter primary school, the dropout rate is impressive: on the average for every 1,000 males that enter the six-year primary cycle, 318 drop out before completing it. For girls the dropout rate is 458 per 1,000, and they constitute only 38 percent of primary school enrollments to begin with.

In other words, so fundamental a problem as mass illiteracy is not really being dealt with by the present educational system. Nor have governmental outlays on education kept pace with population increase. In 1964-65, educational expenditures represented 2.3 percent of national income, and that amount had slumped off to 2 percent by 1969-70. The prospect is then that the ranks of the illiterate and the unskilled will be replenished as rapidly as the ranks of dependent youth unless there is a major reallocation of national resources to education with potentially negative short-term repercussions upon the economy.

What has been the response of Egyptian policymakers to this demographic situation? First, they have, since 1962, openly acknowledged its gravity and have endorsed the notion of reducing fertility. Second, at the risk of an oversimplified generalization, policymakers have placed little faith (and even less money) in the conventional family planning program. In constituting a new government in October 1974, President Sadat announced that one of its main priorities would be to cope with population growth. But the remedy seemingly lies in rapid economic development and social change. This was the line followed by Egypt at the World Population Conference at Bucharest (August 1974) and it represents official thinking on the matter. In this view, the family planning program, in the absence of a significant rise in the standard of living, would prove a waste of time and energy. The horse of this equation must be economic growth and the cart, voluntary fertility control.[4]

This conclusion is faithful to the philosophy practiced, with scant success, throughout the Nasserist period. It was concluded, rightly, that agriculture over the long haul could not continue to be the source of livelihood for most Egyptians—*unless* one was prepared to accept a lowering of the standard of living at the same time. Land and water were seen to be the limiting factors, and while some new land could be brought under cultivation and yields on old lands increased through more modern cultivation methods, these measures would at best serve to slow the rate of decline of per capita agricultural resources. The way out clearly lay in industrialization. Egypt's advantages in this respect lay (and lie) in its large domestic market, its relatively abundant supply of engineers, managers, and other professionals, the nucleus of a skilled work force, and its privileged geographic location with access to Arab, Black African, Asian, and European markets. One of the principal bottlenecks in moving towards industrialization consisted in finding a cheap and abundant energy source.

Egypt is an oil-poor country, at least so far.[a] Thus, the possibility of generating large amounts of thermal energy was not open to it. However, the Nile waters could be put to double-duty, and therein lay the attractiveness of the High Aswan Dam project. The High Dam was to store water in a basin (i.e., Lake Nasser) so large that it could accommodate several floods at a time. Not only would this minimize the substantial fluctuations in the discharge of the Nile, thereby reducing the harmful effects of floods and drought,[b] but it would create a regular, seasonably-adjusted supply of water which would facilitate land reclamation and allow more extensive cultivation of summer rice. Simultaneously, the great head of water lying behind the dam was to be released through turbines in order to generate some 10 billion kwh of power each year. In sum, the dam would help Egypt draw maximum returns from a faltering agricultural sector and provide the energy to push the country towards its industrial salvation.

Neither hope has been fulfilled, and it is now clear that it will take a great deal more than the High Dam to remedy the situation. This does not mean that the dam was a mistake but merely that too much was asked of it. Moreover, the planning of the utilization of its benefits has been deficient. It is admittedly unfair to summarize rapidly what has gone wrong, for much has gone right, but the situation is such that what has gone right constitutes a palliative against the resource-population conundrum which will lose all significance in the next fifteen years, while what has gone wrong has forced some very hard and expensive choices upon Egyptian planners.

One of the most sobering facts to emerge in the 1970s is that the dam has not provided a net addition to Egypt's cultivated land. Land reclamation has proceeded far more slowly than anticipated and at a far higher cost. Reclamation has been begun on some 900,000 feddans, but only about half that number have actually been brought up to the marginal level of productivity. With the

[a]Despite the loss of the Abu Rudeis fields in Sinai after the June War, Egypt's production of crude oil reached nine million tons in 1974 and is likely to rise to twelve million in 1975-76. The return of the Abu Rudeis fields as a result of the second Egypto-Israeli disengagement agreement in September 1975 could raise total production to seventeen millions in 1976-77. Over thirty companies are currently involved in oil exploration in Egypt and its territorial waters, and the Ministry of Petroleum is optimistic that production will rise to fifty million tons by 1980.

[b]Over the last hundred years the annual discharge of the Nile at Aswan has averaged 84 billion cubic meters, but the standard deviation has been 20 billion cubic meters.

additional water currently available from the High Dam (7.5 billion M^3 per year) only about one million feddans, net of buildings and roads, are likely to be added to Egypt's cultivated surface. It is of course possible that with more economical use of irrigation water, the introduction of covered irrigation canals to minimize evaporation, tile drainage to reduce the area given over to field drains, sprinkler and drip irrigation, and the reutilization of drainage water, the existing water supply could be stretched a good deal further. A reasonable estimate is that under the best of circumstances Egypt could bring no more than 1.5 million new feddans (including the 450-500,000 already being farmed) under cultivation by the year 2000. In the meantime the state is losing about £E10 million a year on its investments in the new lands.

To make matters worse, as reclamation has proceeded, the old cultivated areas of the Nile Valley have been losing, on the average, 60,000 feddans a year to urban and village expansion, roads, factories, and military installations. The land going out of cultivation has easily offset that being reclaimed in surface area. The net loss over the period 1963-1973 was on the order of 200,000 feddans. Moreover, the soils of the new lands are distinctly inferior to those of the Valley proper and are not likely ever to achieve the levels of production of the older cultivated soils.[5]

Given the inevitability of continued population growth, the person-land ratio and available per capita agricultural resources can only decline over the next twenty-five years. Indeed, the director of the Arab Organization for Agricultural Development, Dr. Kemal Ramzi Stino, predicted that Egypt's cultivated area in the year 2000 would be no more than four million feddans, that is, only a quarter again as big as the area in 1820, while the population may well have grown twenty times over in the same period.[6]

One immediate and momentous consequence of this situation is that Egypt is condemned to rely on outside sources to meet its basic food needs. Any illusions of self-sufficiency, if they have not already disappeared, will soon have to be abandoned. Per capita grain production has increased almost imperceptibly in the last twenty-five years. In 1950-1954 Egyptians produced, on the average, 202 kilos of grain per capita per year. In 1971 the figure was 221 and may have declined subsequently.[7] Per capita consumption, however, is considerably higher. For instance, in 1975 it was estimated that four million tons of wheat and flour (108 kilos per capita) would be consumed in Egypt. Only about 1.6 million tons would be grown locally while the rest, 3.4 million tons, would be imported at a cost of £E400 million. The value of all food imports in 1967-68 stood at £E120 million. By 1975 that figure would stand at £E700 million, virtually all of it involving hard currency payments.[8]

It is illuminating, although hazardous, to project present trends to the end of the century, but the exercise is probably necessary at least to establish some order of magnitude of future food needs. It has been assumed that current levels of *consumption* include, on a per capita basis, 190 kilos of locally-produced grains and 60 kilos of imported grains for a total of 250 kilos per annum. Without any change in that level and assuming a population in the year 2000 of sixty million, total grain requirements would be fifteen million tons. Barring any increase in acreage under cultivation, and assuming a 30 percent increase in wheat production, 20 percent in maize, current levels of rice production and slight increases in barley and millet, local grain production might reach 8.5 million tons. Egypt would be faced with a gargantuan deficit of 6.5 million tons. This would not include imports of food oils, meat, poultry, and sugar, which are growing each year.[c] All that the Aswan Dam has done to alleviate this situation in any direct way has been to permit the spectacular extension of rice cultivation in Egypt (from 373,000 feddans in 1952 to 1,143,000 in 1972) and the annual export of some 200,000 tons.

It is conceivable that Egyptian agricultural exports of rice, cotton, onions, fresh vegetables, and citrus fruit may some day be sufficient to pay for grain imports that seem to be increasing at an exponential rate. Still it does not seem likely, and even if it was, Egypt would still have to choose, if any choice is possible, the sources of annual grain imports. At present there is little room for maneuver; the United States, Canada, Australia, and to a lesser extent western Europe and Argentina are the only likely providers. It is also the case that in the years to come these countries will not have large exportable surpluses. Other importers, such as India, Indonesia, and Bangladesh may generate aggregate demand well beyond the capacity of world markets. Egypt's dependency in this vein is twofold: who will sell to Egypt, and will they have enough to sell? It is with this consideration in mind that Egyptian planners have turned with increasing urgency to promoting the expansion of food production in other parts of the Arab world. The Sudan and Iraq appear to be especially propitious targets.

Given the magnitude of Egypt's agricultural problems, the effort to industrialize has become all the more crucial. Yet, here, too, while the High Dam has performed nobly, it will leave Egyptian industry and other sectors far short of the power they will need over the next quarter century. The figure of ten billion kwh annually of electrical power generated at the Aswan power station had become graven in stone, but it was never more than a theoretical figure representing maximum power generation of installed capacity in optimal circumstances. The operational maximum level of power generation has so far been about 7.5 billion kwh, and that level is not likely to be surpassed in the coming years. Two major factors have brought about this situation. First, there is a lack of mesh between the water requirements of agriculture and land reclamation and the power needs of industry. In the winter months (January-

---

[c]It would also not include the importation of agricultural production inputs whose costs are rising spectacularly: fertilizers, pesticides, herbicides, farm machinery, etc. Egypt uses about 3.6 million tons of all kinds of fertilizer per annum, of which, in the mid-1970s, about two million tons have to be imported.

February), there is a slack agricultural period in which water requirements are low and during which irrigation and drainage networks are cleaned. Agriculture has so far prevailed in seeing to it that, during this period, water is not simply allowed to flow into the sea. Instead it is stored so that it can be drawn upon in the peak summer months. For industry this has meant that power generation drops off sharply in the winter and must be compensated for by new thermal generating capacity.

The second factor is that Lake Nasser has not filled to its maximum level of about 180 meters. It is at this level that the head of water behind the dam is sufficient to make the turbines work at their maximum. Due to low or moderate floods between 1964 and 1974, the lake has so far risen to 173 meters, which means the turbines are functioning below capacity. Moreover, many experts believe that the lake should not be allowed to rise to 180 meters, because at that level surface evaporation of water might become exorbitant.

Looking to the future, even were the dam to provide the maximum power of its installed capacity, Egypt's power needs would be far in excess of the dam's supply. As Egypt moves into iron and steel, aluminum smelting, petrochemicals, and large-scale fertilizer production, energy needs will soar—or if they do not, it will simply mean that the industrialization drive has proved unsuccessful. One must add to industrial needs the ambitious plans to bring electricity to all Egypt's villages, to redevelop the Suez Canal zone, and to develop the northwestern extension of the Delta and the Mediterranean coast. In light of these plans, energy consumption in 1980 has been estimated at 20.7 billion kwh, in 1990 at 47 billion kwh, and in 2000, at 85.3 billion kwh. The Aswan Dam could only provide a tenth of this.[9]

If these projections are reasonable, new sources of energy msut be developed. Some small proportion may be generated through the substantial natural gas fields that Egypt is developing in the northern Delta. Oil is not scheduled to enter into the picture and will be used instead either as an input in the petrochemical industry or for export. That leaves three other sources: Aswan, the Qattara Depression, and nuclear energy. The Qattara Depression project is currently undergoing feasibility studies. It would consist of allowing Mediterranean sea water to flow into the depression at a rate, when the depression is full, that would equal the rate of surface evaporation. The inflow would be used to generate as much as ten billion kwh annually by the year 2000, assuming that the power plant could be installed by 1985. At £E500 million, the project would be far more costly than the High Dam. Construction could not start before 1977. Still, even if this project were successfully executed, Egypt would be facing an energy deficit of some sixty billion kwh in 2000. That enormous gap must be filled by nuclear energy. Here again Egypt's only choice is to choose its kind of dependency by buying, or wooing, the most desirable technology available. It may turn out to be Westinghouse, United States—subject to congressional approval—versus Westinghouse, France. Whatever the choice, it will be a far cry, in terms of national sovereignty, from harnessing the waters of the Nile.

To maintain present agricultural production, let alone increase it, and to lay the ground for industrial development will require enormous investments. Where will they come from? Who will pay? Whose technology is to be used? These questions shape not only the economic domain but the domains of domestic politics and international relations as well. Does one barter for Soviet technology on relatively soft terms but then perhaps forego Western export markets and Western technology? Or does one accept stiff Western terms for credits and loans and hope to recoup by raising the quality of Egyptian exports? How much choice is there when one may have to import six million tons of wheat from Anglo-Saxon sources?

Beyond these questions there are others that boggle the author's mind, but which seemingly leave Egyptians unfazed. Egypt is going to be a Third World pioneer, and the kind of pioneering it will be called upon to undertake would best have been avoided. The Nile hydraulic system is simplicity itself. It is a river flowing through a desert with a delta at its head. There are no forests, prairies, steppe lands, or mountains. It is a homogeneous zone. It should, logically, remain an agricultural system, but rapid population growth has precluded that possibility. Egypt's need to pioneer stems from this fact. In order to intensify agricultural production, Egypt will have to be at the forefront of perennial irrigation systems, and an innovator in the use of chemical fertilizers, pesticides, and herbicides. It will be exploring, unhappily, soil salinity (resulting from perennial irrigation). It will be a leader in scholarly studies on the impact upon water quality of increasingly massive runoffs of saline drainage water containing large amounts of chemical residues. It will be looking closely at the rising levels of salinity and chemical pollution in its large brackish coastal lakes and the influence of these factors upon fishing. Egypt will be, finally, in the company of Japan in learning the effects of industrial waste upon intensive agricultural systems.

Simultaneously, the effort to cope with the inevitable degradation of the Nile Valley will require integrated planning of a level so sophisticated that it must result in a kind of cybernetic model of the functioning of the Nile ecosystem. Rationalized crop-rotation, fertilizer imports, mechanization, agricultural supplies to processing industries, shipping and marketing abroad, planning water and power needs in such a manner that the agricultural and industrial sectors will draw maximum advantage,[d] are but a few of the factors that Egyptian planners must build into any dynamic model of the country's economy. The official credo of Egypt endorses centralized planning and decentralized execution. To

---

[d]Energy allocation can be very complex even within sectors: for instance, the Kima fertilizer plant at Aswan was first established in the late '50s with four different lines of production in order to accommodate seasonal fluctuations in power supply from the old Aswan Dam.

date there has been little planning and what has been executed has been centrally-determined. The fact that .60,000 feddans of good land are annually lost to production is indicative of the failure of the present system to cope with the basic challenges facing the Egyptian economy.

Economic Change and Social Stratification

It is unnecessary to trace in detail the development of the Egyptian economy in the last three decades because there are several excellent studies that meet this need.[10] What shall be attempted in the following two sections is to highlight the alternatives open to Egypt in financing its development and how these alternatives interact with policy in the domestic and international arenas.

Since the inception of the revolution, Egypt's leaders have had no perceptible commitment to any particular economic ideology. What seems to have informed Nasser's economic preferences was a concern with bringing Egyptian resources under Egyptian control, strengthening the Egyptian economy so that it bolstered independence, bringing about a certain degree of distributive justice, and protecting the "revolution" (a term that came to be synonymous with the regime) from regional and great power machinations. Nasser did, it is true, maintain an abiding suspicion of the Egyptian bourgeoisie of the *ancien régime*, and in a general sense he was apprehensive of any groups that appeared able to accumulate wealth and derivatively political leverage. Many of the nationalizations that accompanied the overtly "Socialist" phase of the revolution can be seen as simple preemptive maneuvers to destroy potentially dangerous sources of material wealth.

There were groups that sincerely and fervently advocated ideological and programmatic solutions to Egypt's problems, and they continue to do so today. Muslim Brethren, Left Wafdists, the remanants of Misr al-Fatat or the National Socialist party, unattached "liberals," and Marxists have all been consulted at one time or another in the elaboration or justification of policy.[11] The Free Officers who came to power in 1952 were sprung from the urban and rural *petite bourgeoisie.* Their image of the Egypt of the future was one of a powerful state, prosperous, without class antagonisms, and internally cohesive and disciplined. They rejected liberalism without rejecting capitalism and their models came from the political experiments of the 1930s: Attaturk, Mussolini, with favorable references to Mohammed Ali.[12]

Prosperity consistently eluded the new regime. A liberal foreign investment code in the early 1950s failed to attract any capital investment except in oil exploration and secondarily in tourism. The regime inched its way towards bolstering the public sector of the economy as it planned for the Aswan Dam, the Helwan Iron and Steel plant, Kima Fertilizers, and so forth. The nationalization of British and French assets following the Suez War of 1956 committed

Egypt to a path it had already begun, hesitantly, to follow. Before 1956, government holdings in mixed enterprises amounted to only £E17 millions. By 1957 paid up public capital in mixed and entirely public enterprises rose to £E59 million.[13] From then on the state moved inexorably towards the consolidation of its grip on all major establishments in manufacturing, banking, insurance, cotton, and foreign trade, and transportation. Two processes were at work; the state was creating new industrial and manufacturing units under public ownership and, at the same time, nationalizing or taking controlling interests in existing private enterprises. The takeover of Abboud Pasha's companies and the effective nationalization of Bank/Misr and derivatively the companies in the Misr Group (principally spinning and weaving at Mehalla al-Kubra) were the first steps toward the massive nationalizations of July 1961.

The measures can be seen as the counterpart of the land reforms of 1952, 1961, and 1969. The first of these was aimed primarily at destroying a landed class of a few thousand families which had dominated Egyptian politics in the twentieth century and which the new regime regarded as the natural allies of the British and of foreign interests. Redistribution of agricultural resources was an important, but secondary consideration.[e] So too after the elimination of British, French, and Belgian interests between 1956 and 1960, came the turn of the Levantine and Egyptian bourgeoisie. The Socialist Decrees of 1961 were probably inspired by three basic motives: first, to cut the grass from under the feet of any "counterrevolutionary" force that might oppose the growing importance of the state sector of the economy; second, to acquire new assets that would help finance the First Five Year Plan (1960-1965); and third, to put at the disposal of the regime the industrial capacity and financial institutions of the country in order to underwrite Egypt's increasingly dynamic role in the Arab world. The fact that the private sector, in the first year of the Five Year Plan, failed to live up to the investment levels expected of it by the government, and the fact that it had been distributing about two-thirds of all profits as dividends to shareholders, were the ostensible but perhaps not the dominant causes of the nationalizations. The process of politico-economic consolidation was continued after the secession of Syria from the United Arab Republic in September 1961, as several hundred families suspected of complicity in the secession had their assets sequestered. Other sequestrations followed in 1964 and again in 1966. The upshot was that by the early 1970s the state dominated the nonagricultural sectors of the economy. By 1974, capital invested in the public sector totalled £E4 billion, exclusive of agriculture, and that of the private sector, £E400 million.

The right of private ownership was never attacked, rather systems of

---

[e]All three land reforms had resulted, by 1971, in the distribution of 850 feddans to 410,000 small-holders or landless peasants: i.e., about 14 percent of the cultivable surface was redistributed to about 10 percent of rural families. In other words, 85 percent of the rural poor did not benefit from this aspect of land reform.

exploitation, and "feudalism" were to be destroyed. Either evil could of course be defined in many ways. The inverse of the exploitationists and feudalists were the "national capitalists" who invested their capital, treated their workers well and served national interests. The line between exploiter and national capitalist was politically determined and tended to vary over time.

Despite these momentous changes the private sector continued to thrive and flourish. Most of Egypt's cultivable land is still privately owned. Seventy percent of all commercial operations are still in private hands. Over 25 percent of all industrial production still comes from the private sector, which may employ about 40 percent of the industrial work force.

Somewhere around 1969 the distributive revolution came to a halt. In that year individual holdings of land were limited to fifty feddans, but Nasser announced that there would be no further reductions. The so-called kulak class of the Egyptian countryside was still intact: 5.2 percent of all landowners (168,000), owning between five and fifty feddans, possessed 32 percent of all cultivable land (i.e., 1.9 million feddans).[14] As we shall see, the economic options open to Egypt had begun to polarize dramatically in Egypt by 1969. The choices were to intensify the revolution through more land reform, nationalization of commercial activities, and rigorous efforts to collect taxes and force savings, or to open the economy to a combination of private Egyptian and foreign capital investment. Nasser never fully committed himself, although he was clearly leaning away from the intensification route.

As these options crystalized, two new middle classes or, perhaps more accurately, strata, emerged in Egypt. The first consists of the state technocracy and managerial personnel that grew with the public sector itself. Good trend data are not at present available, but Table XII-3 gives some idea of the size of the technico-managerial strata in both the public and private sectors.

The first two entries in Table XII-3 indicate a managerial-professional strata of 473,000 persons, mostly employed by the state. This is the most privileged segment of a far larger mass of public employees: some 1.5 millions in various ministries and agencies and over one million (including labor) in public sector companies and organizations. At the pinnacle of the public sector are some 2,000 Egyptians who make up the boards of directors of public companies.[15]

This group has diverse origins and it is hazardous to make many generalizations about it, but some claim to technical or managerial competence has been a requisite for entry into it. Army officers and engineers, civilian technocrats, university professors, technically competent offspring of the old bourgeoisie (of whom there are many), and a part of the mass of university students graduated since 1952 are all represented in it.[16] While base salaries for public sector managers are modest, they are still superior to those of civil servants at equivalent grades and can be doubled with housing and transport benefits, production bonuses, representational allowances, etc. Like all public employees, the managers cannot avoid income tax, forced savings, social security payments,

Table XII-3

Distribution of Egyptian Work Force by Sectors and Sex, 1967-68

Category	Male	Female	Total
Technical and Professional	247,500	80,700	328,200
Directors and Managers	137,800	7,100	144,900
Clerks	376,500	49,200	425,700
Sales and Commerce	454,700	49,600	504,300
Agriculture	3,757,800	245,700	4,003,500
Mining, Quarrying	9,000	–	9,000
Transport, Communications	266,000	1,800	268,400
Industrial Labor	1,350,700	71,000	1,421,700
Services	510,400	121,800	632,200
Other	89,300	15,400	104,700
Indeterminate	6,600	3,300	9,900
Total	7,206,900	645,600	7,852,500

Source: Adapted from Central Agency for Public Mobilization and Statistics, *Sample Survey of the Work Force in the UAR: Results of the May 1968 Round*, Reference No. 1-222 (Oct. 1970) (in Arabic). The figures for services appear to be substantially underestimated, although the problem may be one of definition. More recent figures, which unfortunately give no breakdown by level of skill, estimate employment in services for 1972 at 1,713,400. See Price Planning Agency, "Distribution of Industrial Income," Memo. No. 18 (Jan. 1973) (in Arabic).

and special levies—all of which are deducted at the source—but they are well placed to feather their own nests through contract kickbacks, investments in rural or urban real estate, and black market activities. Indeed, since 1960 and the beginning of the First Five Year Plan, the managers have entered into an increasingly intensive symbiotic relationship with a new private bourgeoisie.

The new bourgeoisie are a curious phenomenon. They do not have the social prominence or the colossal wealth of the illustrious prerevolutionary elite. They are more likely to summer at Ras al-Barr than in Europe; they do not give sumptuous dinners nor mix with the diplomatic set. They are somewhat "sha'abi"—of the people—and caricaturists inevitably depict them in *gallabia*, waistband, potbelly, and handlebar moustaches. Their origins are diverse: middle range, rural landowners who have made licit profits in vegetables and citrus fruits and illicit killings in black market dealings in food grains, fertilizers, and pesticides; urban and provincial wholesalers who have become the cogs of growing black market operations in scarce goods, as well as the movement of gold and hashish; small factory owners, scrap metal merchants, taxi and truck fleet owners; labor and building contractors.

They are the center of gravity of the new bourgeoisie and they come into contact with the public sector through two main avenues: subcontracting and black market operations. Ironically, they began to accumulate wealth at the same time the state began to concentrate more and more economic activities in its own hands. The elimination of the Levantine and a part of the Egyptian business community left the way open for them, and the administration of investments during the First Five Year Plan played directly into their hands. It has been estimated that about 40 percent of all investments in that plan (or about £E660 million was channeled through private contractors, who in turn recycled some part of those funds through subcontracts.[17]

As a result of the Socialist laws of 1961, it was difficult for this new stratum to find outlets for productive investment. It constituted the only discernible group that could lay claim to the title "national capitalists" (i.e., the nonexploitative bourgeoisie), but nationalized banks, low interest rates, and long-term bonds could not attract its savings. Heavy profits tax proved a disincentive to investment in manufacturing, although not an insuperable one, for investment has taken place and also, presumably, widespread tax evasion. Accumulated savings went instead into housing, farm land, retail trade, transportation, and, inevitably, black market activities. Between 1960 and 1970, the private sector invested £E180 million in middle income and luxury housing in urban areas, and in recent years private investment in housing has been outrunning public investment five to one. With the opening up of the housing sector to Arab capital, it is expected that in 1975 Egyptian investers, in partnership with Arab businessmen, may place £E60 million of their own savings in housing. This sum, it is interesting to note, is roughly equivalent to all annual treasury receipts of taxes on wealth.[18]

In housing and other spheres the new bourgeoisie has been joined by state employees, university professors, lawyers, doctors, and officials in Egypt's only authorized political organization, the Arab Socialist Union. One of the other spheres concerns goods administered by the public sector, sold at subsidized prices, always in short supply, and that find their way into private hands. Let us mention a few items just to give some idea of the scope of the problem: cement, window frames, steel reenforcing bars, copper, copper cable, scrap iron, fertilizers and pesticides, spare parts of all kinds, Kastor cloth (sold at fixed prices to the masses), cooking oil, sugar, flour, rice, tea, school books, school smocks, bottled gas cans, etc. All of these items are either imported by the state, or manufactured by state enterprises, and in either case the state is supposed to control sales prices. The goods are simply allowed to "slip" into private hands and are sold at market value. Public servants and private entrepreneurs make a killing, and the poor, whom the price subsidization policies are designed to serve, are the victims.

Earnings from these kinds of operations may then be channeled into acquisition of contraband goods or put into housing or rural real estate. If urban housing is the target, then rent control laws will be violated. There is no way a private contractor can make a profit on middle or upper income housing and at the same time abide by Egypt's rent control laws. Key money, rent advances, or the sale of apartments have become absolutely standard, even for cooperative and publicly-owned housing. The investor might, on the other hand, acquire agricultural land. If he plants crops that are outside the scope of compulsory purchase laws (i.e., *not* wheat, sugar cane, rice, cotton), such as fruits, vegetables, berseem (clover), lentils, etc., he stands to make handsome profits. Land taxes are based on the rental value of the land, not its income. Thus for as lowly a crop as berseem, earnings net of taxes might be as much as £E150 per feddan and for vegetables and fruits earnings would be several times that amount. It should not be forgotten that any given feddan (except for those under orchards, sugar cane, or fallow) is likely to produce two crops a year. Thus, despite a certain stagnation in gross agricultural production in recent years, there is money to be made for middle-range landowners and urban absentees.

In short Egypt's drive toward socialism (perhaps Atatürk's phrase of "état-ism" is more appropriate) in the 1960s, with all its attendant laws and decrees that aimed at a massive redistribution of income, failed, on the one hand, to raise real per capita income for the great mass of Egyptians, and, on the other, it did not prevent the accumulation of wealth in the hands of a new bourgeoisie. It is important to try to develop some image of how income is distributed in Egypt, not only for its relevance to the performance of the economy but its relationship to the actual and potential interests which must be considered as economic policy is devised. To put the matter more vividly, the present situation as it has emerged since 1965 is increasingly fraught with the possibility of class conflict. At the same time, it is practically impossible to measure income distribution with any tolerable degree of precision. This is so for a number of reasons. First, it is a question of some embarrassment for Egyptian officials who would like to show greater results for the efforts of the last twenty-five years. Second, some great but unknown proportion of higher incomes are earned illicitly, are not reported, or, perhaps, are not legally subject to taxation. (This is the case, for instance, for members of parliament who receive £E1200 per annum, tax free.) Third, at the other end of the income scale, subsistence agriculture, real income can only be guessed at.

Nonetheless, we do have some clues as to the general evolution of incomes. Since the beginning of the century per capita income has stagnated. In 1913 per capita income (1954 prices) stood at £E36. It declined to £E28 in 1945 and began to climb again, reaching £E32.5 in 1957, and £E53.2 in 1970.[19] However, in the course of wide-ranging debates on the state of the economy, coming in the wake of the October War, more pessimistic estimates were produced. Utilizing 1973 prices, Dr. Ahmed Morshidy of the Ministry of Planning calculated that per capita national income was £E112 in 1960, that it rose to £E121 by the end of the First Five Year Plan, and that it has declined, in absolute terms, to a level between £E100-112 in 1974.[20] It seems certain that the combination of rapid population growth, increasingly high rates of inflation, and, at best, modest rates of economic growth have contributed to a real decline in the standard of living for most Egyptians. At the same time, it should not be overlooked that the vast expansion in educational and public health facilities, however deficient their quality, plus occasionally successful attempts to hold down the prices of basic goods, have softened the impact of declining real income.

The oft-declared objective of the First Five Year Plan was to serve as the first leg in doubling national income in ten years. That obviously did not come to pass for reasons that we shall examine further one. Nor did the Socialist laws of that period mitigate the enormous disparities in income that characterized Egypt's system of social stratification. On paper Egypt has a fiercely progressive income tax schedule: gross incomes of over £E10,000 are to be taxed at 90 percent. Save for public employees and salaried personnel, the tax rates have never been systematically applied. In 1973 land and property tax receipts were estimated at £E22 million, business and profits taxes £E126 million; and personal income tax at £E28.5 million. This represents only 30 percent of all government revenues from direct taxation and even then reveals nothing about actual receipts. Cumulative tax arrears in 1973 amounted to £E200 million.[21] The fact that tax evasion is widespread is tacitly acknowledged in an official report that also gives us some idea of total income distribution.

The entries in Table XII-4 are presumably informed guesstimates, but what they show is that at least 2,000 families are enjoying incomes vastly superior to the £E10,000 that was to have been the outer limit of the rich. The gap between the richest and the poorest members of Egyptian society is enormous, while that between the richest and the middle strata, earning £E350 per family, is only somewhat less so. Even within the public sector and government, where salaries can be controlled by public authorities, the ratio of the highest annual salaries

Table XII-4
Average Income Per Family: 1972*

No. of Families	Individuals	Average Per Family Income
2,000	15,000	£E33,000
10,000	81,000	4,340
400,000	2,226,000	1,318
5,500,000	28,000,000	350
1,000,000	5,000,000	61
91,000	400,000	17

*Adapted from figures presented in *Ruz al-Yussef*, No. 2420 (Oct. 28, 1974), p. 12, apparently referring to the report or studies of the Price Stabilization Agency. For comparative purposes it is worth consulting the earlier study of Cérès Wissa Wassef, "Le prolétariat et le sous-prolétariat industriel et agricole en Republique Arabe Unie," *Orient*, 3-4e Trimestre, Vol. 13, No. 51 (1969): 87-112.

(£E1900-2000) to the lowest (£E60-84) is 26:1. When representational allowances are added in, the ratio becomes 40:1.[22]

It is clearly excessive to attribute class consciousness to the upper strata. Their origins are too diverse, ranging from rural and urban petty bourgeoisie, to renaissant elements of the old bourgeoisie that have been allowed to resurface since 1971. They do have self-appointed spokesmen, in the parliament, various chambers of commerce, the Federation of Industries, some of the professional syndicates, and, since October 1973, in the press. And while they may not be aware of them in any collective sense, they do have shared interests, which, since 1966, have been increasingly catered to: liberalization of private export; new laws easing the importation of cars,[23] appliances, and other luxury goods; the creation of the "parallel money market; exemption of all owners of three feddans or less, *including orchards*, from agricultural taxes; making literacy a requirement for membership on agricultural boards; the lenient regulations for importing taxi cabs, the restitution or compensation to individuals whose property was sequestrated in 1964; etc. Their spokesmen have become more vocal in urging further "liberalization" measures: repealing the guaranteed 50 percent representation of workers and peasants in all elected bodies, raising the theoretic limit of licit incomes beyond £E10,000, easing profits and business taxes, and allowing private Egyptian investors to play a more active role in import-export, and perhaps raising the ceiling on land ownership.

It is frequently argued that the Nasserist regime represented the petite bourgeoisie, but this is too facile a judgment. There has been no coherent set of objectives to represent. There have been loose strands of an ideology, anti-Socialist, ferociously anti-Marxist, occasionally pious Islamic, advocating a greater role for Egyptian private capital, but ambivalent about foreign capital, seeking to contain but not destroy the public sector. But the strands are inconsistent, for the public sector managers want to assure the expansion of the public sector and keep the private bourgeoisie as convenient outlets for individual operations. Likewise stalwart liberals and cosmopolitan technocrats want a resurgence of the private sector without any concessions to Muslim conservativism. The ideal would be the maintenance of the public sector as the major channel for disbursing public investment, the possibility of the private sector to pursue freely its symbiotic relationship with the public sector and, now, with foreign private capital and, to the extent the regime is intent upon maintaining its price subsidies, continued expansion of black market ventures.

It is not a figment of leftist imagination to refer to this concatenation of economic interests as parasitic: what has so far been denied them is the possibility to enter into the role of compradors, but that may not be far off. As a whole these groups are reluctant to save and invest, and they lead the way in reducing voluntary savings and hence the mobilization of domestic resources. In fairness, it should be noted that there were few incentives or opportunities offered during the 1960s for what one might call enlightened capitalist activities.

Nasser's colleagues had links with these groups that became particularly intense during the 1960s. Hakim Amer did little to conceal his affinities, while Ali Sabri attacked the groups with whom he, on occasion, connived. Under Sadat the image of the bourgeoisie has been refurbished. He has married his offspring into it through the Marei and Abdulghaffar families and made the man who best symbolizes the Nassarist symbiosis, the building and construction contractor, Osman Ahmed Osman, the Minister for Reconstruction and Housing. The consolidation of the position of the new elite of "affairistes" has produced delicate political problems that revolve about the fundamental question of who is to bear the burden of development. Nasser hoped that he could raise up the masses without goring the middle classes. He could not. Sadat is faced with the same dilemma and is experimenting with his own formula. Rather than trying to serve both constituencies, Sadat's approach is to bank on the assumption that the prosperity of the middle classes will lead eventually to the prosperity of the masses. It is an assumption laden with political risk as the masses will be asked to wait their turn.

Financing Development

In the late 1950s Nasser apparently became convinced that Egypt's economic development could be brought about without pain. But for the politically dangerous, the better-off would not have to pay excessively, nor, on the other hand, would the workers and peasants be sweated. The late president somehow hoped to combine welfare socialism and forced-draft development. At the outset of the First Five Year Plan this reckoning did not appear absurd.

Total gross investments in the plan were £E1.6 billion. Prior to 1960 rates of domestic investment had been low: 12-13 percent of GNP for most years. The objective of the regime was to raise this to 20 percent of GNP during the plan period by *transferring* to public ownership agricultural and business assets whose revenues would accrue directly to the state and thus be available for reinvestment. This is what happened through the land reform and socialist decrees of 1961. The total capital of the companies nationalized at that time was £E258 million or two-thirds of all registered capital.[24] The second approach to financing was to enlist foreign assistance on a massive scale. The USSR had already shown its willingness to advance credit for large-scale infrastructural and industrial projects, such as the High Aswan Dam and the Helwan Iron and Steel Complex, on easy terms, while the United States began to sell large amounts of wheat to Egypt under the Food for Peace program, paid for in local currency. Table XII-5 shows the proportions of domestic and foreign sources in gross investment for the decade 1960-1970.

The first Five Year Plan was in large measure dependent on foreign sources of financing, particularly for the importation of requisite capital goods. Moreover

Table XII-5

Aggregate National Investment and Sources of Financing: 1960-1970*

Year	Total Investment		Local Savings		Foreign Financing	
	Mill. of £E	% of NI	Mill. of £E	% of NI	Mill. of £E	% of NI
1960-61	225.6	15.5	210.1	93.1	15.5	6.9
1961-62	251.1	16.6	164.7	65.6	86.4	34.4
1962-63	299.6	17.8	195.6	65.3	104.3	34.7
1963-64	372.4	19.7	236.8	63.6	135.6	36.4
1964-65	381.7	17.4	307.2	80.5	74.5	19.5
1965-66	446.2	18.7	309.6	69.4	136.6	30.6
1966-67	385.6	15.7	370.7	96.1	14.9	3.9
1967-68	342.2	13.6	288.2	84.2	54.0*	15.8
1968-69	318.2	12.0	341.0	107.2	−22.8*	7.2
1969-70	416.1	14.2	395.0	94.9	21.1*	5.1

*From Dr. Mohammed Sultan Abu Ali, "A Test of the Domar Model as a Model for Economic Growth with Reference to Egypt," *Egypte Contempraire* 64, 352 (April 1973): 104 (in Arabic). The entries for 1968-1970 do not include the (about) £E110 million in subsidies paid to Egypt following the June War by Saudi Arabia, Libya, and Kuwait.

Egypt's chronic food deficit was being met through surplus U.S. wheat deliveries under Public Law 480 (presumably not included in Table XII-5) which amounted to £E286.5 million throughout the plan period.[25] At the time this was judged an acceptable and temporary level of dependency. This judgment evidently grew out of the belief that the plan would be both import-substituting and export-generating. At the outset it was predicted that by the last year of the plan, the value of imports in 1959 prices would have dropped from £E229.2 millions to £E214.9, and that in the last year of the plan the economy would register a balance of payments surplus of £E40 million.[26] Both objectives proved illusory. Imports in 1966 were valued in current prices at £E405.8 millions, and there was a balance of payments deficit of £E142.2 million.

It is an irony of this plan that it was able to generate an admirable rate of growth in GNP (6.5 percent a year)[27] and an unprecedented rate of capital investment (16-19 percent per annum) and yet failed in the crucial respect of generating exports and hard currency earnings. Exports rose substantially at the beginning of the plan, but a good part of the increase is not real, having resulted from the devaluation of the Egyptian pound from $2.87 to $2.30 in June 1962.

In the final analysis what this meant for the Nasserist regime was that it approached a major watershed in 1965-66, one in which it was obliged to work out a strategy to cope with Egypt's growing external debt and to figure out who would pay for the Second Five Year Plan. Before looking more closely at the Nasserist response to this dilemma, it is important to note several other factors that had aggravated Egypt's balance of payments and foreign indebtedness.

Table XII-6
Commercial Balance of the A.R.E. 1951-1972
(£E millions)

Year	Imports	Exports	Commercial Balance
1951	283.2	205.0	−78.2
1952	227.7	150.2	−77.5
1957	182.6	171.6	−11.0
1958	240.2	166.3	−73.9
1959	222.2	170.4	−61.8
1960	232.5	197.8	−34.7
1961	243.8	168.9	−74.9
1962	300.9	158.3	−142.6
1963	398.4	226.8	−171.6
1964	414.4	234.4	−180.0
1965	405.8	263.1	−142.2
1966	465.4	263.1	−202.3
1967	344.3	246.1	−98.2
1968	289.6	270.3	−19.3
1969	277.3	324.0	+46.7
1970	342.1	331.2	−10.8
1971	400.0	343.2	−56.8
1972	390.8	358.8	−32.0
1973	632.3 (est.)	382.5 (est.)	−249.8
1974	1,266.0 (est.)	596.0 (est.)	−670.0
1975	2,178.0 (est.)	680.0 (est.)	−1,498.0

Source: Adapted from Federation of Egyptian Industries, *Yearbook, 1973* (Cairo, 1973), p. 42. There are some discrepancies between these figures and those used by Robert Mabro, *The Egyptian Economy: 1952-1972* (Oxford Press, 1974), and Karim Nashashibi, "Foreign Trade and Economic Development in the UAR: A Case Study," in Lee Preston, *Trade Patterns in the Middle East* (Washington, D.C.: American Enterprise Inst., 1970), p. 75, but the margin of error is quite small and the order of magnitude unchanged. These accounts do not include arms purchases. The figures cited are presumably and unfortunately current prices. The estimates of the last three rows have been taken from official sources as reported in the local press.

In chronological order, the first events that enter into the equation are the nationalizations of July 1961, resulting in some disruption of production and a drop-off in exports, plus the loss of about a third of the cotton crop to leaf worm and hence another cut in export earnings.

In September 1962 Egyptian armed forces became ensnared in the Yemeni civil war from which they were unable to extricate themselves before June 1967. What the Egyptian involvement cost the Egyptian economy has never been revealed. But in the period of recriminations and direct attack upon the Nasserist legacy since 1973, figures of "£E1 million a day," or "a war that cost the nation

4 billion" have been bandied about without reference to their source. Suffice it to say that expenses were high and a substantial proportion of them disbursed in hard currency.

Directly related to Egypt's presence in the Yemen was the decision to suspend PL 480 wheat deliveries to Egypt in 1966. This meant that Egypt would henceforth have to dip into its virtually nonexistent hard currency reserves to cover its growing annual food deficit. Imports of grains, oils, tea, and tobacco accounted for 35 percent of all Egypt's imports in 1967-68.

The Five Year Plan may have been Egypt's best hope to forge its own economic future since the experiment of Mohammed Ali. It failed essentially because it neither could systematize the mobilization of domestic savings (short of nationalization) nor generate sufficient exports to pay for subsequent stages of growth. These two factors were aggravated by Nasser's so-called regional adventures. It is unwarranted to accuse Nasser of impetuousness in this respect. The break-up of the United Arab Republic (UAR) in 1961 seemed to be part of a patent effort on the part of conservative Arab regimes (viz. Saudi Arabia) backed by the United States to bring the Egyptian experiment to an end. The Egyptian involvement in the Yemen was, in part, an effort to recapture the initiative in regional politics. However, with the death of John Kennedy and the advent of Lyndon Johnson to the presidency, the Yemeni campaign aroused the fears of the Pentagon, the White House, and the oil lobby about Nasser's intentions. Increasingly it became a confrontation between Saudi and Egyptian military forces, with respective U.S. and Soviet armaments, with the oil wealth of the peninsula and the gulf seemingly at stake. Whether or not Egyptians thought in these grandiose terms, the Saudis and perhaps the Johnson administration certainly did. Many Egyptians are prepared to believe, and it is hard to deny them their analogy, that the June War was the United States' response to a latter-day Mohammed Ali, Nasser's Navarino, and the deliberate abortion of Egypt's efforts to liberate its economy.[28]

Even before the defeat of 1967 hard choices had to be made. The first was whether or not to maintain the high level of imports of capital goods in order to sustain the growth of public sector industry. Given the lack of hard currency reserves, imports could only be financed through credits. Relations with the United States and West Germany were poor and with France and Japan, distant. Only the Soviet Union was likely to respond to Nasser's needs, but at the cost of making the Egyptian economy almost totally dependent on Soviet capital, technology, and markets. Still, no Western country could match Soviet terms.[f] To have pursued this course, one fundamentally distasteful to Nasser and most of his associates, would have required keeping a "pro-Moscow" team at the head of the government that would simultaneously advocate an intensification of the

---

[f]Soviet loans were repayable over twelve years at 2 1/2 percent interest one year after a project had been completed with an option to purchase any unmarketed produce. Only U.S. AID for foodstuffs or IDA could match these terms, and in 1965-66 neither were interested.

revolution at home: more land reform, creation of state farms on reclaimed land, increased state control over wholesale and retail trade, more diligence in applying tax laws, nationalization of contracting firms, etc. With Soviet aid and the mobilization of domestic savings the country could proceed with the second plan without restricting investment.[g]

Nasser hesitated, and then began to take steps in the opposite direction. In 1966 he dismissed Ali Sabry as prime minister and brought in the more economically-conventional Zakaria Muhy al-Din. He acceded to the advice of the International Monetary Fund (IMF) and introduced a policy of retrenchment (*inkimāsh*), which meant the abandonment of the Second Five Year Plan. It is said that even the Soviet Union supported this policy.[29] Nasser thus refused, even had he been inclined, to accept greater dependence on the Soviet Union or the idea of bleeding the Egyptian middle classes in the development effort. Whether or not retrenchment was a realistic response to the situation we shall never really know for the June War made folly of any attempts at redressing the economy.

Let us try to summarize the major economic repercussions of the June War. The most obvious consequence was that retrenchment was no longer a matter of choice but of absolute necessity. Imports fell off precipitously, and the Egyptian public sector began to be plagued by idle capacities that soon ranged upwards of 30 percent of full production. Import restrictions affected the supply of raw materials, replacement goods, and capital goods for new projects. Exports grew, but the rate of inflation, which has been consistently underestimated in Egypt, probably reduced the real growth. Overshadowing the commercial balance were the costs of rebuilding the Egyptian armed forces and purchasing Soviet weaponry—the average annual cost for military preparedness from 1968-1973, according to President Sadat, was £E700 million or about one-fifth of national income. Finally, the importation of food stuffs grew rapidly and at a time when world grain prices began to soar. The tripling and quadrupling of world wheat prices following the Soviet-U.S. wheat deal in 1972 left Egypt with an import bill of around £E250 million. Estimates for 1975 are that Egypt will pay £E750 million for all its food imports.

A second consequence of the June War was that Egypt had to accept the aid of its erstwhile conservative adversaries: Kuwait, Saudi Arabia, and Libya. At the Khartoum Conference of August 1967, it was agreed that these countries would pay Egypt an annual subsidy of £E110 million to compensate for the country's war damage and loss of oil, tourist, and Suez Canal revenues.[30] Navarino certainly seems an apt analogy: with his army and economy in shambles, Nasser accepted the contributions of his rivals and the curtailment of his own regional ambition.

---

[g]Advocates of this approach need by no means have been Marxists: Aziz Sidqi, the Minister of Industry, Ali Sabry, in 1965 the prime minister, and other non-ideologues close to Nasser may have urged variants of this approach.

The subsidies were not sufficient to prevent the continued growth of Egypt's external debt. Because it is a sensitive piece of information, speculations as to its size vary rather spectacularly, even among "authoritative Egyptian sources." For instance the nonmilitary debt—disbursed and undisbursed, but not including short-term facilities—at the end of 1974 was estimated between £E1.7 billion and £E2.5 billion.[31] Even if we accept the lower figure, it still represents over one-third of national income, and whatever the level, the debt and the annual amounts of debt servicing have grown at an accelerating rate.

In 1965, the debt had reached about £E600 million, or a little under one-third of national income. Debt servicing at that time amounted to only £E15 million, i.e., only about 2.5 percent of the net debt.[32] By 1969, according to the International Bank for Reconstruction and Development (IBRD) sources, the debt reached about £E720 million (not including the value of Soviet arms deliveries), but, more significantly, servicing had risen to £E87 million or over 20 percent of the value of all Egyptian exports. The situation has deteriorated since. The total debt has more than doubled in the last six years, fueled by growing food and capital goods imports. But the real burden now lies in servicing the debts. Debts accumulated in the late 1950s and early 1960s began to fall due in the early 1970s. Theoretically 55 percent of the debt was to have been paid off by 1974 and 87 percent by 1980. Debt servicing rose to £E140-170 million by the early 1970s.[33] In 1974 alone the value of servicing may have approached 40 percent of the value of Egyptian exports which in that year were on the order of £E590 million.[34]

The debt has four components whose relative magnitudes are not precisely known. Estimates of nonmilitary debts to Socialist countries seem to converge around the figure of £E1 billion. That owed "Western" or hard currency countries and institutions such as the IMF are on the order of £E1.5 to 2 billion (both figures include undisbursed debt). A second source of debt consists of medium- and long-term deposits placed by Arab oil-exporting states in Egyptian banks. Despite Libya's withdrawal of such funds in late 1974, these deposits have grown substantially. In the spring of 1975, President Sadat negotiated directly with Iran, Kuwait, and Saudi Arabia for an additional $1 billion in two- and three-year deposits. These funds relate directly to a third source of debt arising from massive short-term borrowing to finance imports. In 1974 Egypt utilized £E900 million in short-term (three-month) credits with servicing running up to 14 percent of principle. The Arab bank deposits at relatively low interest rates were designed to offset the short-term burden. Finally, there is Egypt's military debt to the USSR, so far kept secret, but quite conceivably as much as £E3 billion. Indicative of the cumulative impact of all four sources of debt was Sadat's trip to oil-rich states seeking emergency funds, as well as that of his minister of finance to Moscow in the summer of 1975 in a futile effort to persuade the Soviet Union to reschedule all Egypt's obligations.

It is an appealing but false notion that the greater one's debt, the greater one's leverage over the creditor. Egypt learned once, the hard way, that such is not the case when the British and French in 1879 set up a debt commission in Egypt to impound revenues to meet the country's external obligations. Chronic debt situations leave a country in a thoroughly defensive position, constantly guessing as to whether creditor nations will sweat political docility out of their wards. With varying degrees of success and at different points in time, the United States, Saudi Arabia, and the Soviet Union have done just that.

Egypt must buy abroad to survive, and while it is unlikely that the world community would allow it to go under, certain nations might not be unduly concerned to see Egypt limp along, living from hand to mouth. This in fact has been the situation for Egypt since 1967. Economic planning during this period was tantamount to administering the foreign currency budget frequently on a three-month basis. Even if assured hard currency sources become available to Egypt (exports, tourism, foreign remittances, Arab credits) and it becomes possible to plan the debt on a long-term basis, the debt, in roughly its current proportions, will be with Egypt throughout this century. From an economic point of view this may be a 'healthy' situation, but it can scarcely be so regarded politically.

The Line of Least Popular Dissatisfaction

From June 1967 on, Egypt entered the economically devastating phase of "no war, no peace." Facing up to hard economic choices was not only distasteful but impossible. Retrenchment had to be adhered to by the force of circumstances, but there was little possibility of encouraging local private or foreign investment as long as peace seemed distant. On the other hand, the need to rebuild and rearm the Egyptian armed forces left no option but to emphasize cooperation with the Soviet Union. The regime, in these circumstances, tried to give a little to everyone: keeping the public sector functioning, talking of free zones at Port Said to attract foreign investment (this motion was first proposed in 1966), liberalizing export activities, contracting military obligations amounting to £E700,000, and, in 1969 and 1970, fighting a war of attrition.

Obviously not all these interests could be equally served nor all these objectives reconciled. The result, for domestic policy, was the institutionalization of what Bent Hansen has felicitously called the principle of "the line of least popular dissatisfaction."[35]

The problem in 1960 had been to find a way to pay for development while minimizing and diffusing the level of sacrifice Egyptian society was called upon to sustain. After 1967 the problem was to find a way to mask the sacrifices inherent in a state of "no war, no peace," massive arm expenditures, increasing inflation, and economic stagnation. What one finds is a quasi-unpatterned, opportunistic ebb and flow of belt-tightening and political largesse.

On one side of the ledger we find various forms of forced or obligatory savings that apply to most salaried personnel in the public and private sectors, accounting for about 85 percent of all national saving.[h] These have included since 1966 the deduction of one day's salary per month from the pay of public sector employees. The peasantry was called upon throughout the 1960s to pay, in some measure, the price of industrialization. The government's means of leverage consisted in setting the prices of the main crops below world market levels, while selling in-puts (fertilizers, seed grain, pesticides, etc.) above world market prices. This constituted an effective means of indirect taxation of the peasantry.[36] It should be noted that since 1972, while the same policy still pertains, it gains for the state are more ambiguous. The rise in the world-market value of basic inputs has, particularly in the case of fertilizers, been more rapid than the rise in the prices of foodstuffs. For the Egyptian fertilizer industry, it would be more profitable to export abroad than to sell to the Egyptian peasantry.

The middle and upper classes were hedged in by a series of laws that limited their incomes, profits, the rents they could charge, the goods they could import, and their ability to travel abroad. No matter how poorly applied these measures may have been, they had some impact in restraining middle class consumption.

All the above measures were of the belt-tightening variety, but when the breeze seemed to carry the feeling that the tolerable limits of sacrifice were being approached, the authorities would habitually try to placate whatever constituency appeared most vocal or most dangerous. Thus, on the other side of the ledger we find the politically motivated give-aways.

The work force has been given periodic wage increases, first in the public but then in the private sector, without any discernible relation to production increases. Since 1967 wages in public sector industries have increased 13 percent per annum, the public sector work force has grown by 6.6 percent a year, while production in current prices has increased at a rate of 5 percent a year.[37] One of the most notable wage increases followed the widespread student-worker demonstrations in the winter of 1968 and, as such, were totally unrelated to productivity. President Sadat has sponsored various similar measures: tax relief for various artisans and professional groups, raising the minimum public sector wage from nine to twelve pounds a month (May 1974), doubling social security

[h]Principal sources of saving 1971-1973 were as follows, in millions of £E:

	1971-72 (actual)	1973 (estimated)	
Personnel Insurance and Pensions	84.2	101.3	involuntary
Social Security	102.5	127.4	
Receipts from Bond Sales	7.2	8.7	
Investment Certificates	18.0	25.0	voluntary
Postal Savings	3.6	4.3	
Total	215.9	266.7	

Figures from the Budget for 1973, *al-Ahram al-Igtisadi*, Jan. 1, 1973.

benefits, and, in the wake of scattered worker protests against the rise in the cost of living, giving a month's advance at the beginning of the school year in 1974, out of the monthly salary deductions.

Similar measures were extended to the rural world even before 1967. In 1961 the interest on loans advanced by state cooperatives was abolished, and in 1964 interest on the payments owed by beneficiaries of the land reform was suspended. Interest on cooperative loans, however, was reinstated after 1967 at a rate of 4.5 percent a year. At the same time, in the face of growing peasant complaints, the prices of the main crops have been raised just enough to take the edge off the cultivators' bitterness. Egyptian peasants know what a bale of cotton or a ton of rice sell for abroad. They tend to overlook what a ton of fertilizer sells for abroad, but because of local shortages they must pay the equivalent in the black market. In 1973, prior to the October War, President Sadat backed legislation that exempted from the land tax any peasant owning three feddans or less. The overwhelming majority of all Egyptian peasants fall within this category.

A third aspect of treading the line of least popular dissatisfaction has involved the administration of price subsidies. The black market has prevented many of these measures from alleviating the plight of the masses, but the state's investment in them has been enormous. For example, it has been estimated that the state will invest in 1975 £E600 million (about one-seventh of national income) in price subsidies in 1975. The breakdown is indicative of Egypt's economic malaise.[38]

Foodstuffs:	£E464.4 million
Cloth and Clothing:	£E23.0 million
Fertilizer:	£E95.0 million
Pesticides:	£E11.5 million
Agric.-Production Subsidies:	£E25.5 million
uncollected interest:	£E5.4 million

We come finally to the privileged classes, those best placed to complain about the discomforts of the post-1967 situation and to advocate their own remedies. They were placated by a relatively free rein in pursuing their interests in urban real estate, commercial farming, taxi-fleets, and the export trade.[39] The real plum was the black market which, by all accounts, blossomed spectacularly after 1967.

The line of least popular dissatisfaction was followed also with regard to the civil service and the bureaucracy. The political problem here stems from Egypt's potential intellectual proletariat. Since the early 1950s all stages of education have become nominally free (there are many indirect costs) and graduation from secondary school has virtually assured entrance into a university. At the same time, all university graduates have been guaranteed a civil service or public sector job, supposedly consistent with their training, if they so desire. The result has been that the mass of university students and civil servants has grown in lockstep. Efforts in 1968 to hold down new admissions to the universities to 35,000 a year have been abandoned, and by 1973, 60,000 students a year were being admitted. After four years of study, although military service may lengthen this period, the university graduates invade public employment. They occasionally burden the administration of public sector companies or are inserted into an already overstaffed bureaucracy.[40]

Employment and wages in the bureaucracy have risen at a rate well above those of national employment and wages. Between 1962-63 and 1971-72 the civil service grew from 770,000 to 1,291,000, or by 70 percent. Total national employment over the same period grew by only 20 percent. It is significant that senior civil service posts were increased by 98 percent during these nine years. Total outlays on the bureaucracy grew by 120 percent in the 1960s while national income grew, by the most favorable reckonings, by 63 percent.[41]

Within the public sector, as already noted, another facet of the politics of placation has been the growing level and apparent tolerance of theft, absentee-ism, misappropriation of funds, trading in influence, and black market activities. Figures are available on all of these operations, and it is generally conceded that they represent only the tip of the iceberg. All such practices have, it is universally agreed, taken on imposing proportions since 1967. Whatever their impact upon economic performance, they have made life somewhat comfort-able, or perhaps just less monotonous, for the middle and lower-middle classes of Egypt.

The Opening

The line of least popular dissatisfaction could not be adhered to indefinitely so long as the country was on a war footing, its economy stagnant, and unable to pay for its imports. Sadat had to make the hard decisions about war, peace, and economic strategy about which Nasser had so long temporized. Limited war and economic liberalization were selected by Sadat as the keys to a new era. With startling candor, Sadat emphasized, perhaps inadvertently, the primacy of economics in all fields of policy. Speaking to Egyptian student leaders in August 1974, he said:

I will not hide from you, my sons, that before the decision to go to war we had reached a very difficult economic situation, for without economic resistance there could be no military resistance. Our economic situation, six days before the battle, was so critical that I called a meeting of the National Security Council and told them that we had reached zero. My calculation was simple. The army cost us £E100 million a month, and all our tax receipts were worth [in one year] £E200 million, just two months' expenses for the armed forces. There was nothing left for us but to enter the battle whatever happened. We were in a situation such that if nothing had changed before 1974 we would have been hard-put to provide a supply of bread (raghif al-'aish). . . . After the 6th of October War we received 500 million dollars which saved our economy and gave us new life. . . .[42]

New life has meant new economic policies, and therein lies Sadat's choice of strategy and his major gamble. Assuming, at least for the moment, that some semblance of lasting peace (absence of hostilities) may be established between Israel and the Arab states, Egypt's economic future will then lie in attracting massive infusions of foreign investment. President Sadat and two prime ministers, Abdelaziz Hegazi and Mamduh Salem, have put together a package of programs to attract this investment, and these programs are known collectively as the economic open-door policy (al-infitāh al-iqtisādi).

None of the ideas of the "opening" are new: they were integral parts of Egyptian economic thinking until 1959 and had already begun to reemerge in 1966. With Sadat's accession to the presidency in 1970, they received a new impetus. The notion was simple but politically delicate. The National Charter of 1962, a kind of authoritative definition of principles, had been interpreted to mean that the public sector of the economy must not only lead but dominate all other economic activities. The private sector could follow this lead, and foreign investors could dabble in tourism or oil exploration, but strategic industries (iron, steel, power, most textiles, cement, fertilizers, metallurgy, petrochemicals, etc.), financial institutions (banks and insurance companies), and services (transportation for the most part) must be publicly owned. The new look consisted in changing the orthodox interpretation of the 1962 charter.

It was correctly pointed out that Nasser himself had stated that the charter could not be considered in immutable document, and that within a decade or so it should be reviewed and revised. Under the umbrella of that writ, talk of revisions began in 1973, several months before the war. The basic proposition was that the nature of the international arena, particularly the relations between the major powers, had changed so radically that smaller countries such as Egypt had no choice but to adjust accordingly. Détente had led to a normalization of relations between China and the United States and the beginnings of same between North and South Korea and East and West Germany. The same process had led to a major increase in the level of economic and technological interchange between the Soviet Union and the United States.

Two conclusions were drawn from this. The first, which could not be stated explicitly, was that small states would lose their leverage in bargaining or playing off the great powers if the latter had tacitly agreed not to exploit or allow themselves to be dragged into local disputes. For the Egyptians, dependent on Soviet military assistance, this meant that the USSR might have agreed to freeze the Arab-Israeli conflict with the Arabs in a position of military inferiority. If this were true, then the United States, Israel's major military backer, held the keys to a comprehensive settlement of the regional conflict. Nasser's acceptance of the Rogers Plan and the cease-fire in July 1970 is, I think, clear evidence of this growing realization. In this light, economic orthodoxy of the IMF variety might help bring the United States around to a more favorable view of the Egyptian side in the dispute. The second conclusion, that could be stated openly, was that détente proved that Socialist countries could accept exchange and investments with capitalist countries without selling out their revolutions. Yugoslavia[i] and the Soviet Union were the examples cited most frequently in this view.

The logic of the open-door policy becomes clear when it is realized that the option of intensifying the revolution and plunging deeper into credits, commodity imports, and technology from Socialist countries was rejected by Sadat and by those he selected as his advisors. Petrodollars, Western technology and markets, foreign private investments, the renaissance of the Egyptian private sector, and a gradual military reconversion appeared to offer the liberal way out. There is good reason to support the logic for the choice, but it is one that will accentuate economic and political cleavage within Egypt.

Internal pressures towards liberalization had been building since 1965. Indeed, as Fuad Mursi has argued, the substantial capital that had accumulated in the hands of private sector entrepreneurs and what he calls "bureaucratic capitalists," required an outlet.[43] "The natural result was the integration of the State, represented by the bureaucratic elite, with parasitic private capital . . . leading to the concentration of capital. At that point, the second phase began, consisting in the necessity to employ the accumulated capital without any restraints on the part of the State." Mursi adds that talk thus began of the importance of private sector investment, the encouragement of private capital, and the return of the public sector to private ownership. "Moreover, the alliance of the bureaucracy with parasitic capital was completed by the call for close cooperation with foreign investment."[44]

There were, as well, external pressures toward the same policies. These were expressed by some of Egypt's major creditors, such as Saudi Arabia and Kuwait, as well as other economically conservative regimes, like Abu Dhabi. It was said throughout the period of "no war, no peace" that various Arab emissaries bore messages from Washington to the effect that an economic opening to western capital and IMF—orthodoxy would make easier any future role for the United States in bringing its weight to bear in the search for peace.

None of these pressures, however, need have brought about any policy reorientation had it not been for the fact that President Sadat's own views on proper economic policy coincided with the advice he was receiving.

[i]Some Egyptian economists pointed out that Yugoslavia's success in this respect was modest. In the period 1967-1974, Yugoslavia concluded fifty agreements for foreign investment, worth only $100 million.

It is too early to judge the success of the experiment, but we may at least consider what it hopes to achieve. The first set of objectives interrelate: Egypt wishes to lessen its dependence on credits and technology from socialist countries; it wants to overhaul the public sector and stimulate the private sector by importing Western technology and improving the quality of Egyptian products. Only in this way can Egypt hope to find export markets in hard currency areas and thus earn the wherewithal to pay for growing imports, especially food grains. In recent years about 60 percent of all Egypt's exports have been to Socialist countries, while these same countries have provided only 25 percent of Egypt's imports. Of the estimated import bill for 1974 of £E1.26 billion, £E911 million would have to be paid for in hard currency.

As one member of the Egyptian parliament grandiloquently declared, "Like the Japanese, we must adopt the motto 'Export or die!'." While the formula will not be entirely abandoned, the Nasserist hope that a policy of import-substitution and export-maximization could be equally served will give way to greater stress on export-maximization. Markets will be sought in Western Europe,[45] Japan, black Africa, and the Arab world. In recent years, for instance, only 7-8 percent of Egypt's exports have gone to other Arab countries. The search for markets has only just begun and success in developing them will depend on at least three factors: peace; capital investment and the updating of technology in private and public manufacturing; greater attention to markets for fruits and vegetables abroad.

The first requirement is capital, be it in the form of investment, gifts, loans, or credits. How much is necessary? Hamid Sayyih, the chairman of the National Bank, calculated the order of the magnitude. If the goal is a 7 percent annual growth in GNP, and if the capital-output ratio is assumed to be 3:1, then £E650 million must be invested annually in the next few years. Local savings will not provide more than £E400 million, therefore upwards of £E250 million in foreign support will be required.[46]

One may speculate as to what will attract foreign capital to Egypt.[j] At the outset of the open-door policy there were great hopes that foreign private investment would be eager to come into Egypt. A liberal investment code was drawn up (Law No. 43, 1974), providing for tax holidays, duty-free importation of raw materials and capital goods, liberal profits repatriation regulations, and guarantees against nationalization. It was frequently pointed out that Egypt had a large domestic market, that its work force was both relatively skilled and relatively cheap, and that existing legislation on worker representation in management boards and profit-sharing need not be strictly applied in new projects. While all "strategic" industries were to remain under public ownership,

---

[j]The disincentives for private investment may be overcome but they are manifold: past experience of nationalization and arbitrary fiscal policy; the complex problem of the convertibility of the pound; price and wage management policies of the State; chronic underestimates of the rate of inflation; bureaucratic red-tape; poor communications (mail, telephone, telex); poor banking infrastructure; the absence of peace.

there was virtually no sector that was declared to be off limits to foreign investors. Finally, it was announced that "free zones" would be established at Port Said and elsewhere, where foreign investors could establish factories, using local labor and supplies, and taking advantage of Egypt's prime geographic location, to export manufactured goods to other countries.

At the same time the economic new look was aimed at existing communities of Egyptians resident abroad and potential migrants. Unlike Algeria or Turkey, Egypt has so far been unable to tap the earnings of Egyptians working in foreign countries. Their numbers are not precisely known, but may range between 300,000-500,000 including dependents. In 1971 Egypt instituted a "parallel" money market, offering incentive rates for hard currency purchases of Egyptian pounds. The goal is to attract the savings of Egyptians abroad for investment in the country and to bring in hard currency. In 1972 £E25 million were converted and in 1973 that sum had risen to £E100 million. The counterpart of this policy is that private Egyptian entrepreneurs may purchase hard currency through this market at official rates in order to pay for their imports.

Despite this package of enticements, there are legitimate fears that the private capital that comes in will be directed into urban housing, real estate speculation and tourism. Arab investors have moved precisely in this direction with the result that land values and the cost of housing have risen so meteorically that Egyptian private investors are being priced out of the market.

The kind of capital sources Egypt is likely to tap in the coming five to ten years will be in the form of bilateral credits, most of them advanced for political reasons. Egypt in the past has not been able to utilize its credits fully, especially those from the socialist countries, and what is used adds, of course, to the external debt. Iran, Saudi Arabia, West Germany, Japan, and the USSR all agreed to long-term credits following the October War. Also, because these accords are arranged between governments, most of the credits will be channeled through Egypt's public sector. The public sector that was to have been trimmed down, reorganized, and made fiercely competitive may find that it can afford its inefficiency. If that is the case, even if the quality of Egyptian products increases, they will still be produced at high cost.

Another of the major objectives of the opening is to bring Egypt up to date in terms of technology, production and management techniques. It is hoped that all public sector enterprises, from banks to state farms, will modernize themselves in competition with the domestic private sector and foreign investors. It seems more likely, however, that the acquisition of technology will come about, if at all, in a different manner. During the energy crisis Western industrial nations will be facing severe balance of payments problems of their own. There will be little incentive for Western investors to acquire equity in Egypt, but considerable incentive to sell technology and expertise through tied credits or in triangular arrangements in which the oil-rich states finance projects built under Western management. Projects of this kind are already beginning to accumulate: the

Suez-Mediterranean pipeline, a sponge iron plant at Alexandria, the plans for acquiring nuclear reactors, a projected aircraft industry.

In all likelihood the public sector will be the major beneficiary of the open-door policy, and this is ironic indeed for so many have placed the blame for Egypt's lackluster economic performance on its shoulders. There is no authoritative means for assessing the productivity and profitability of given enterprises. The handicaps that these enterprises have been forced to accept may be in fairly even balance with their privileges.

The handicaps consist largely in the fact that public sector companies are sometimes obliged to pad their payrolls with unneeded personnel, i.e., new university graduates. They are also the victims of wage increases, unrelated to production, decided at the political level. If they produce basic goods, their accounts carry the burden of price subsidies. Some industries must bear the cost of developing infrastructure: the Helwan Iron and Steel Company bore the expenses of opening up the Wahat Bahriya iron mines and the construction of a railroad to Helwan. Many companies have been unable to procure necessary raw materials, spare parts, and replacement equipment and are thus operating far under capacity. When they do receive imported raw materials and equipment, they must pay normal duties on them.

At the same time the public sector enjoys a counterbalancing set of privileges. These include substantial customs protection and quasi-monopolies in internal markets. The government, in the system of administered prices, has always allowed the companies to set their prices according to costs plus a "fair profit." There has thus been little incentive to try to hold down production costs. Some industries, such as Kima Fertilizer, may have more impressive accounts than is really the case because they receive inputs, such as electricity, at minimal charge. Export of public sector goods has apparently allowed many companies to improve their profitability artificially. In projects arranged with Socialist countries there has been a tendency to overvalue the capital goods imported from the creditor nation, but then, in paying in kind for the credit, an offsetting tendency to overvalue the produce of Egyptian industries is apparent.

Debate has been acrimonious over public sector performance with one group of defenders, who represent the mainstream, arguing that idle capacities due to hard currency shortages have been the major cause of low productivity and low profitability. Capital infusions and technological overhaul are held to be the required solutions. This is the orthodox view even among the major sponsors of the open-door policy: retrenchment (*inkimāsh*) is a dirty word, and the emphasis is on massive investments—at least £E800 million a year beginning in 1975. Still, on the fringes, there is a growing demand for meaningful cost accounting. One critic estimates that the net return (£E39.7 million in 1973) on capital invested in the public sector (about £E2 billion in the period 1960-72) is less than 2 percent.[47]

How the public sector will be held accountable in the period of liberalization is one of the most momentous questions facing Egyptian politicians in the mid-1970s. No particularly convincing approaches have been suggested. The public sector will not be liquidated. It is undeniable, despite all its shortcomings, that only state-guided public investment could have built up the basic infrastructure and heavy industrial establishments which are now among Egypt's assets. It is highly unlikely that any source of foreign investment could meet the same needs. The question is how to organize the public sector. How much autonomy should individual units have?. How are salary levels to be determined? What pricing systems should be instituted? Are certain industries, such as iron and steel, to be measured by criteria other than those of cost-benefit? Can the public sector hold its relatively reduced supply of competent managerial expertise in the face of the high salaries offered by foreign investors? Can or should the administrative *laisser aller*, including misappropriations of funds, black market operations, and the like, be brought under control? Although it will take some time, these questions must be answered.

In the meantime I am willing to hazard a few predictions about the short-term impact of the open-door policy. First the public sector may be allowed to lumber on, given new life by foreign credits, but without any determined efforts to hold it to account. The public sector is too big a plum for anyone to seek its destruction or even strict governance. Its own managers will in all likelihood try to strike up the same bargain with foreign investors that they have made with the Egyptian private sector. The latter have done too well through subcontracting and black market operations to advocate the erosion of their beneficiary, and for foreign capitalist credit sources, especially Saudi Arabia, Kuwait, Iran, Abu Dhabi, is there any reason to be alarmed that their credits are not being used to build the viability of Egypt's public industries?

The short-term impact of the open-door policy will be politically explosive. Inflation has increased and will continue to increase as foreign communities of investors, consultants, fixers, speculators, and salesmen build up. In combination with real estate speculation and black market operations, and new foreign presence means growing gaps in wealth, and accentuated feelings of relative deprivation. Albert Hirschman's "tunnel effect" is appropriate in this respect. If one can conceive of Egyptian society as two lanes of traffic stalled in a tunnel but moving in the same direction, then we have one lane, the new bourgeoisie and the bureaucratic capitalists, beginning to move. For a while those in the stationary lane are happy, for they think their turn will come next. But if they fail to move—and they have not since 1965—what will happen? As Hirschman suggests, a point in time will come when those who have remained behind will be "ready to correct manifest injustice by taking direct action."[48]

Politics and Ideology

Scattered fairly densely through the preceding pages have been references to "politics" in the conventional sense of the word. It is now appropriate to group these references systematically in terms of political constituencies and the ideological elaboration of the rules of political conduct.

It should be clear from what has gone on in other developing countries that there really is nothing peculiar about the so-called Nasserist system or Nasserism. The late president was, rather, a pioneer in programmatic terms, pursuing pragmatically, and often in an ad hoc manner, policies designed to cope with a set of problems of economic growth and decolonization that scores of other new nations have also faced. In this light, the difference between Sadat and Nasser is one of style, although this difference in the long run may produce systemic changes. Still Sadat's problems are the same as Nasser's, only bigger, and political liberalization, if that is Sadat's goal, cannot be carried out in a vacuum.

Nasser and his officer colleagues had an image of Egyptian society that emphasized the importance of social cohesion, national purpose, mass consensus, and discipline. It is not particularly relevant whether or not such an image emerged from the career conditioning of military minds. The important point is that theories and systems that place great stress on the legitimacy, if not the desirability, of the interplay of conflicting interests and forces were viewed by the Egyptian officers as divisive and threatening. Liberal democracy with its notion of the open arena for the expression of political interests was judged, on the basis of Egypt's own experience, to play directly into the hands of foreign powers who could "buy in" to Egyptian politics, as well as exploit the masses who, because of their poverty and illiteracy, could be no more than pawns in a pseudo-democratic charade.

Marxist theories of class conflict were no more appealing and were a good deal more threatening because the officers seemed to realize how great the potential for this kind of conflict was and is. The dialectic of class struggle was consistently and determinedly rejected. Egypt was to be a mass democracy under the dictatorship of no one, not even the proletariat. Fundamental contradictions in economic interests were acknowledged to exist, but resolving them through conflict could only prove destructive to the national fiber of Egypt. The correct way to deal with these contradictions is through the "melting of class differences" (*tadhwīb fawāriq bayn al-tabaqāt*). If this has any operational meaning, it is that the poor are to get richer while the rich get a little poorer or stay about the same. It is the ideological label for the economic policies that have been characterized above as development without pain.

The image of the correct organization of political life in Egypt that the officers gradually elaborated was distinctly corporatist. The image, although not reality, has been founded on the notion of the "alliance of working forces" (*tahalluf al-quwwa al-ʿāmila*) consisting of workers, peasants, national capitalists (*al-rasal-mal al-watani*), intellectuals (*muthaqifūn*), and soldiers (*junūd*). The vehicle for the expression of these corporatist interests became the Arab Socialist Union (ASU), founded in 1962 in the early years of the First Five Year Plan, a year after the Socialist Decrees and the dissolution of the UAR, and at a moment when Nasser's economic and political outlook had become more radical.[49] Perhaps most representative of the new mood was the guaranteed 50 percent representation of workers and peasants in all elected positions in the ASU, the parliament (Maglis al-Umma until 1971, and since known as the Maglis al-Sha'ab), agricultural coop boards, and management boards in industry and services.

During the 1960s Nasser pursued two political goals, and because they were contradictory, neither was fully achieved. On the one hand, he sought the order and discipline that seemed inherent in a corporatist order.[50] Organization along occupational lines tended to cut across class lines. According to Nasser's own definition:

The peasant is he who possesses no more than ten feddans and whose revenues derive from the land and who lives in the countryside. The worker is he who exercises a manual or intellectual activity, constituting his sole source of revenue, and who does not have the right to belong to a professional or managerial union, be it agricultural, industrial or commercial.

In June 1968 these became the legal definitions of workers and peasants. In this view a worker could range from a municipal street sweeper to a university graduate. The peasantry included strata as distant from one another as the owner of half a feddan and the owner of ten. Vast categories of the Egyptian work force—day laborers, the unemployed, street vendors, some craftsmen, tenants, the landless, migrant laborers—are for the most part left outside this framework. At the same time, all adult citizens had the right to belong to the Arab Socialist Union (ASU) and it was this openness that was to distinguish the ASU from a "single party," a term associated with class dictatorship.

In the context of Egypt's confrontation with Israel, skirmishes with American imperialism, and surviving great power rivalries, Nasser succeeded in "nationalizing the class struggle," suppressing any energetic expression of social conflict as tantamount to sabotaging the home front.[51] The regimentation implicit in this view was never effectively instituted. But the distance between the "working forces" and their passivity in the face of state policies was accentuated, and this was at odds with Nasser's second objective in the 1960s, to mobilize the masses. How could one control the expression of diverse interests while encouraging spontaneity, enthusiasm and sacrifice in the pursuit of national goals? There may have been a solution to this dilemma, but Nasser never found it.

His approach was partially borrowed from Yugoslav experience based on an alliance of Socialist forces within which a small, militant vanguard party would serve as a catalyst to political mobilization, ideological awareness, and *encadrement*. Thus after 1964 the ASU was endowed with a secret organization known as the Vanguard Organization (*at-tanzīm at-Tali'i*). Rather than encouraging ideological awareness, the Vanguard Organization was transformed into a congeries of personal cliques, each headed by a colleague of Nasser. These became networks for influence-trading, patronage, countering rivals, spying, and dirty tricks in a game that increasingly came to revolve not around ideology but a cult of the leader. In a general sense not only the Vanguard Organization but all leadership positions within the ASU were so heavily dominated by appointees or statutory members from the executive branch of government that one commentator suggested that the organization's name should simply have been the Ministry of Political Affairs.

Without gainsaying Nasser's sincerity in advocating socialism, which for him meant essentially "the eradication of man's exploitation by man,"[52] his own political inclinations gave rise to a new form of exploitation. "The revolution's fear of itself," as Louis Awad has put it, "limited it greatly in achieving its declared objectives."[53] Less anonymously, it was Nasser's fear of the masses, or at least the fear of the implications of their spontaneous participation in the affairs of the nation, that led him deeper into bureaucratic and "police" authoritarianism.

During the 1960s most of Nasser's military colleagues were eased out of power, and their places were filled by professionals from military and internal intelligence. The list is long but the most illustrious or notoroius names among them were Sami Sharaf, Salah Nasr, and Sha'rawi Goma'a. The only conventional military figure of importance left in the regime was Field Marshall Abdelhakim Amer, who committed suicide in the wake of the defeat of June 1967.

For the masses, in the 1960s, Egypt became the creature of its bureaucracy, while for the elite political life boiled down to a directionless pursuit of advantage and survival in which the in-fighting turned on controlling access to the president, feeding him selective information, and questioning the loyalty of others. This may seem an overly harsh judgment, but in the growing debate over the ASU and over the future of political organization in Egypt that has developed since 1973, a great deal has been revealed that would lend credence to this portrayal.

For the broad mass of Egyptians the alliance of working forces never became an operational vehicle for any kind of direct participation or the expression of their views. A combination of bureaucrats in the ministries of irrigation, agriculture and agrarian reform, along with local ASU officials and medium-range landowners held the peasantry as much in thrall as the former "feudalists." The purchase of inputs, obtaining credit, and marketing crops, constituted vital processes that local bureaucratic and private interests could manipulate to their own advantage. There were many honest, if not devoted, civil servants and political leaders, but the point is that, good or bad, their conduct could not be controlled by the masses short of violence, sabotage, or bribery.

For workers the situation was somewhat different. They indeed received many material benefits from the revolution in terms of job stability, working hours, medical and health insurance, paid vacations, and so forth. But these benefits were poorly distributed among them and hence tended to reduce the coincidence of interests among their ranks. A new public sector workforce, organized in the most influential unions, became a sort of proletarian elite in the midst of a much larger, poorly organized and poorly protected workforce scattered through the small, occasionally artisanal enterprises of the private sector. Both groups have been in a position of competition with rural migrants, the unemployed, the day-laborers, and the catch-as-catch-can drifters and scavengers who have no representation. The contextual vulnerability of organized labor has insured, with occasional lapses, its political docility and its subordination to the state apparatus. For instance there is no right to strike in Egypt, and while workers are entitled to 50 percent of all elected seats on management boards, only four out of the nine board positions are elective.

For all Egyptians the basic requirements of housing, food, clothing, transportation, education, and health have been brought under varying degrees of state control. Those who administer the system, who work in the coop stores, in the clinics, teach in the schools, issue ration cards, drive buses, process pay checks, issue work permits, etc., are all poorly paid bureaucrats, promoted on the basis of length of service. They have little incentive to "serve" the hoards of people who swamp their offices, and a great deal of incentive to take advantage of their modicum of power to sell services or misappropriate goods and funds. The civil servants themselves, now a couple of million strong, are as victimized in their out-of-office dealings with other bureaucrats as any citizen. Bureaucratic neglect and malfunctioning are the source of constant laments in the press, case studies, and periodic announcements that reform is on its way.[54]

Yet the bureaucratic apparatus has become so large, entrenched, and comfortable in its ways that reform seems a distant prospect. The regime's technique for getting around its own creation has been to create new bureaucracies, such as the Suez Canal Authority, or the High Dam Authority. In 1974, there was even the ephemeral institution of a Ministry for Administrative Reform which, without creating too many additional bureaus, was scrapped in April 1975.

Honeycombing the bureaucratic apparatus are virtual fiefdoms whose anonymous heads are not the least hesitant in failing to apply or to reject as "illegal," regulations, orders, and laws from higher authorities including the president himself. Customs is a state within a state and if the army and customs were to have a head-on clash on some importation issue, good money would be bet on customs to get its way. In these instances, executive orders are simply lost without trace in administrative sludge. And customs is merely *primus inter pares*.

Moving to a somewhat higher level of the interaction of the state apparatus with the Egyptian citizenry, we come to the question of effective interest representation. It has been a constant charge of the Egyptian Left, and one of considerable validity, that the alliance of working forces has been confiscated by the petite bourgeoisie—kulaks, bureaucrats, and entrepreneurs. Salah Jahin's caricatures of middle class Egyptians searching frantically through their closets to find their *gallabiyas* so as to be able to go to the parliament to represent the peasantry sum up a situation that has become commonly recognized. While these groups manipulated or lived off public funds and the advantages derived from public office, they also controlled the ASU locally and to some extent nationally and thus were able to ensure that it would never play a truly militant, revolutionary role in exposing profiteering and abuse of power. For the Egyptian Left, which cooperated closely with the ASU after 1964,[k] the hardest pill to swallow has been that socialism was applied by groups that had no affinity to Socialist goals, and whose errors and failings were attributed to the alleged fallacies of socialist doctrines.

At the elite level, sometime in the middle 1960s ideological coherence began to collapse along with the objectives of the First Five Year Plan. All pretensions to an integrated set of economic and political goals began to dissolve, and elite politics came to be dominated by the machinations of rival networks and cronyism (shillaliya) with the most prominent cronies coming from the police and intelligence apparatus. This was the era of the "centers of power" (marakiz al-quwwa) so abundantly denounced in post-Nasseriar Egypt. The making and breaking of presidential cronies was determined by a number of idiosyncratic factors, the settling of personal accounts, and shifts in Egypt's foreign policy stances. Who was minister of agriculture or industry, head of the ASU, or prime minister might be determined on the basis of how best to signal the United States or the USSR of a modification or a new look in Egyptian policy. The replacement of Ali Sabry by Zacharia Muhy al-Din as prime minister in 1966 was only the most ostentatious among several such changes. Right and Left in Egypt are equally persuaded that whatever Ali Sabry's leftist tendencies, his basic instinct was for maintaining his prominence within the Nasserist inner circle, and for that purpose playing the Soviet card had through most of the 1960s been a winner. Even an alleged rightist like Abdelhakim Amer played the same card successfully in military procurements.

In retrospect the power centers of the 1960s consisted of several disparate followings, and some of them rivaled others at given points in time. Sabry was most closely associated with the ASU, but his major attribute was, after 1967, his role as chief armaments procurer from the Soviet Union. He was paralleled by Sami Sharaf, the president's chef de cabinet and head of his own intelligence network, and Sha'rawi Goma'a who, as minister of the interior, controlled his own intelligence network and the Republican Guard.

Under the aegis of Hakim Amer the armed forces certainly constituted a power center, one which had escaped Nasser's control from 1963 on. But while Amer and his energetic subordinate, Shams Badran, had built his clientage network among the officers' corps, the armed forces had grown to such proportions that it could no longer be viewed as a single constituency. This was

---

[k]Egyptian Communists were released after five years of imprisonment in 1964. They had decided to dissolve their parties and to join the ASU on an individual basis. They were used to train cadres and give some content to the organization's ideology.

already the case before 1967, but the military build-up after 1967, and the overhaul of the officers corps after Amer's death, reenforced the trend.

There is, last but not least, Mohammed Hassanein Heikal. In 1974 he was relieved as editor of *al-Ahram* because he had turned this newspaper into a "power center." Heikal had been a close collaborator of Nasser, perhaps unique in that he advised Nasser and exchanged views with him. He had a vast range of Egyptian and international acquaintances, and, like some others, Nasser encouraged him to act as a clearing house for information and contacts. The networks he established, not to mention the formidable instrument of publicity he controlled through *al-Ahram*, added up, in Sadat's view, to a rival center of power for the manipulation of information and policy.

Like the economy the political system came irreparably unstuck after 1967; from the neatness of the corporatist model the system degenerated into cronyism and *sauve qui peut*. Just as Nasser had bequeathed an economic system in crisis, so too he left his successor a political system that needed either a real vanguard party (appropriate to an economic policy in which the distributive revolution would be intensified along with closer links with the USSR) or greater liberalization. Sadat, consistent with himself, chose the latter course. Even Sadat's critics are more than ready to acknowledge that among all of Nasser's colleagues, Sadat was the only politician, the only one sure enough of his own political instincts not to be frightened by the expression of diverse interests within Egyptian society.

A State of Institutions and the Rule of Law

It is apparent only in retrospect that from the outset of his presidency (November 1970) Sadat was already determined to move in the direction of economic liberalization, rapprochement with the United States and the conservative oil-producing states, and the reform of the political system. He also quite clearly set himself a deadline for breaking out of the state of "no peace, no war," failing which all other changes would become meaningless. His movements in these directions did not seem coherent. Policies that were launched would hang fire for months until everyone forgot about them, but Sadat always picked them up again.

In May 1971 Sadat eliminated one set of power centers that had momentarily coalesced in a cloudy plot to isolate or perhaps remove Sadat from the presidency; Sabry, Sharaf, Goma'a and the minister of war, General Fawzy, were all purged and imprisoned. In the wake of this housecleaning, Sadat announced the launching of the "Revolution of Correction" (*thawra at-tashīh*) that was to adjust some of the shortcomings of the previous system. There would be no more room for power centers or for the abuse of power, for Egypt was to become a "state of institutions" under the "rule of law."

As it has worked itself out over the intervening years this has meant the increasing advocacy of separation of powers, the establishment of a free judiciary, the abolition of press censorship as regards nonmilitary matters, the strengthening of parliament, and the reformation of the ASU.

Sadat has pursued these policy lines piecemeal and over a long period of time. He has done so by stimulating at different times debates on specific problems, and held in different arenas. Some of the more important issues that have been given considerable attention are: foreign and Arab investment in Egypt, freedom of the press, desequestration of individuals whose assets had been seized for political reasons in the 1960s, personal status law and the rights of women, restructuring the ASU (debated since 1972 when Sadat appointed Sayyid Marei as secretary), public sector accounts, and corruption.

In 1973 and 1974, these debates were amalgamated into a far-reaching discussion of the overhaul of the system at the national level. Sadat outlined his own ideas in a document known as the October Paper (approved by national referendum in April 1974) and in a paper presented in August 1974 under the title "The Evolution of the Arab Socialist Union." The emphasis in both papers was on continuity with the past with equal stress upon the necessity to correct past shortcomings and to adjust to new international realities. In an age of détente and growing international interdependency, the argument goes, it is only natural that Egypt should seek foreign capital and the technology and expertise that go with it in order to salvage an economy bled dry by the costs of war. This does not mean the liquidation of diminution of the public sector but rather its strengthening as it gains access to new capital sources and new possibilities of interaction with the Egyptian private sector. But to attract capital Egypt must open itself to the world, simplify its trade, banking, investment, and taxing procedures, and provide incentives to foreign and local investors. However, the president emphasizes that the public sector will still be the leading force in the economy, with foreign investment acting as a strategic supplement. This line of reasoning is fully in keeping with the directions Nasser was hesitantly pursuing after 1966. But the debate itself has been free-wheeling, and various voices have been raised advocating the liquidation of certain public sector enterprises; abolition of the 50 percent worker-peasant representation clause, denationalizing foreign trade, etc. Indeed, in 1975 it was decided to allow private interests to acquire shares in certain public enterprises.

Likewise, the debate on the future of the ASU has been lively and frequently acrimonious. It is under this rubric that what is undeniably an anti-Nasserist campaign has been launched.[1] The existence of power centers and the gross abuse of police powers has been attributed to the monolithic structure of the ASU and the concentration of power in the hands of Nasser's henchmen.

[1]The return of Mustapha and Ali Amin to *Akhbar* and *Akhbar al-Yom* have given these voices an important forum; as has *al-Musawwar* under the editorship of Fikri Abaza and Salah Jawdat.

Increasingly it is suggested that Nasser was fully aware of what his "people" were up to. The only way out, some liberals and rightists argue, is a return to a multiparty system with a strong parliament. The Right is joined to some extent by the Marxist Left on this score. The Left has always criticized the ASU for refusing the possibility of the working masses within the "alliance of working forces" to develop any coherent organizational structure, popularly-selected leadership, or means of expression. The alliance was no alliance at all for it had no constituent parts. A multiparty system would allow the working masses to organize, and, implicit in thie view, the class struggle would be denationalized.

Sadat has remained somewhat aloof from all this. He has warned that if there were abuses in the past, he was at least partially responsible for them. There would be no disavowal of Nasser. Second, the principle of the alliance of working forces is sacred. The ASU may be overhauled but the alliance must remain. What the future may bring Sadat refuses to predict, but over the next few years all that he felt was needed was to allow several forums to develop within the alliance for the expression of diverse views (the so-called multiplicity of minbars: *ta'ddud al-manabir*). In private he has allowed that he would like to see three political poles form: a Left grouping the Marxists, Socialists and Left Nasserists, a Center that might stand for all that was positive in the revolution, and a Right grouping liberal, capitalist, and perhaps Muslim fundamentalist opinions. Each tendency would have its own press outlet, and already many see the spectrum as *Ruz al-Yussef* (Left), *al-Ahram* (Center), *Akhbar* and *al-Musawwar* (Right).

Thus, in Sadat's view a multiparty system is not called for—yet—but he is perfectly willing to have the notion widely debated. What is called for are some institutional changes. Freedom of the press has been strengthened by the lifting of censorship although self-censorship is still practiced. The parliament, whose new speaker is Sayyid Marei, the major force in Egyptian agricultural policy since 1952 and a civilian whose son is married to Sadat's daughter, has been given new legitimacy and autonomy,[m] particularly now that the legitimacy of the ASU has been called into question. With the appointment of Abdelaziz Higazi as prime minister (October 1974) and his successor Mamduh Salem (April 1975) Sadat delegated responsibility for handling governmental affairs to someone else. The judiciary has been assured of its independence, and political detention and arrests without charges have been ended (although there have been repeated lapses into former practices). Although the president had initially suggested that the executive branch be strictly separated from the ASU, in the summer of 1975 he was reconfirmed as its head. Moreover, persistent rumors that he might relinquish the presidency in 1976 were dispelled when he accepted

---

[m]Indicative of this is the fact that upon the president's instructions a special parliamentary committee was to be constituted in 1975 to investigate the causes of the 1967 military defeat and another the effects of the High Dam. Sadat himself was for many years speaker of the parliament.

the ASU's unanimous resolution that he run again. This is of more than passing significance in that it may indicate the president's determination to remain in authority until after the United States elections in 1976 when a third and perhaps final Israeli disengagement could take place and the basis for an overall settlement established.

The result of all these debates to date has been an economy that is still overwhelmingly dominated by the public sector in nonagricultural activities and by the state bureaucracy in all spheres of activity. The open-door policy has made itself felt initially by increased inflation and expanded black market operations. Long-term investments are either not forthcoming or cannot be felt by the average Egyptian. The reconstruction of the canal zone cities and the resettlement of their evacuees is a major exception to this judgment, but it cannot proceed any faster than concrete steps toward a peace settlement.

While Egypt may become a state of institutions, it is not one yet. The ASU is in limbo and no new political organizations have come along to replace it. There are no institutional checks and balances that have emerged, but it is possible for a multiplicity of interests to be expressed in the press and the parliament. The groups that seem to be benefiting most from the situation are the same combination of the new entrepreneurs, speculators, and their allies in the public sector who are maneuvering for advantage in the application of the open-door policy. Not enough money has yet come in to salvage the economy, but there has been more than enough to bolster the fortunes of this stratum.

In this context political liberalization, in the absence of fairly immediate, tangible material benefits for the great mass of Egyptians, may have destabilizing effects. The open debate on national policy has laid bare momentous cumulative problems in all spheres of the nation's life. People now hear frequently about state corruption, the deterioration of public education, the failings of the Aswan Dam, black marketeers, chronic food shortages, polluted drinking water, and structurally-unsound housing. And the conclusion is evident that given the present distribution of domestic resources, very little can or will be done to deal with these problems. It is logical that resentment will build in the lower strata of society, and that the identification of class interests will be sharpened.

If economic liberalization pays for itself by promoting rapid economic growth, then this latent crisis may be avoided. But it is doubtful that Egypt has more than five years to test the wisdom of these policies. If an economic miracle is not wrought, Sadat or his successor will have to consider closing down the liberal economic and political arenas and returning to the centralist corporatism of the middle 1960s. Or elements of the military may intervene in some moment of acute economic crisis and social breakdown to redress the situation. That after all was what happened in 1952.

Of course the Egyptian armed forces of 1975 in no way resemble the police force that Nasser led to power twenty-three years earlier. They have become so large and internally diversified that they probably represent in microcosm all the political trends that one finds in Egyptian society as a whole. It would be very difficult for any group of officers to speak for any major segment of society, no less make them move.[n]

Moreover, the army has gradually receded from direct roles in Egyptian politics. Egypt was a military regime throughout the 1950s with the members of the Revolutionary Command Council (RCC) responsible for most facets of national policy. However, during the 1960s, as the needs of the state for technical, managerial, and planning personnel grew, the weight of the military was lessened. The prominence in the 1960s of Aziz Sidqi, a civilian engineer and minister of industry, was indicative of the shift. It was also in the 1960s that most of Nasser's closest associates from the RCC broke with him and left public life. Many officers did, it is true, invade the new and lucrative public sector jobs opening up, but even they have been gradually eased out and those that remain are likely to downplay their military past.

Counterbalancing these trends was, as mentioned previously, Abdelhakim Amer, who built a loyal following among the officers corps and thereby made the army his creature. Nasser could not remove him nor get around him. The stunning defeat of June 1967, however, destroyed Amer's reputation, as well as that of the armed forces as a whole. There was a strong popular feeling that the army had dabbled long enough in politics and the economy, and that it had forgotten what fighting was about.

After 1967 the senior officers corps was systematically overhauled and field commanders promoted. The Soviet Union furnished military training missions which went about their jobs seriously. The Egyptian army became once again a conventional fighting force. Military figures in leading civilian positions became increasingly rare: the minister of war, the minister of military production, occasionally the minister of supply, and the president himself were the only prominent officials with military backgrounds or active careers represented in the cabinet. The Egyptian vice president has been selected from the military since 1952, and even though it was thought that the civilian Sayyid Marei might step into that role, it was Husni Mubarrek, former commander of the air force and one of the heroes of the October War, whom Sadat chose in the spring of 1975 to replace vice president Hussein Shafa'i, the last member of the RCC other than Sadat himself to remain in power. The appointment reflected the general view that a military man must be at the helm as long as Egypt remained in a state of war with Israel, and quite likely, a feeling among the senior officers that a representative of the new generation of military leaders be close to the presidency. The appointments of Minister of War Gamassy and Vice President Mubarrek underscored Sadat's sensitivity to these feelings.

[n]General Sadoq, who was relieved as minister of war in November 1972, had tried to rally the armed forces by a campaign denigrating Soviet arms and training and calling for a reduction in the Soviet military presence in Egypt. He may have wished to exploit this theme in hopes of engineering a coup. However Sadat took care of the grievance by expelling the Soviet military missions in July 1972 and then took care of General Sadoq a few months later.

The relative success of the Egyptian army in the October War of 1973 symbolized the efficacy of the back-to-the-barracks movement. Professional military men who had never had any role in politics scored Egypt's first military success against Israel. Thus the army became another institution in its lawful place within Sadat's state. But the army is in no way isolated from Egyptian society and elements within it are aware of mass grievances and have their own remedies for them. The Egyptian army has been contained, but in times of severe internal crisis it, or parts of it, will inevitably become the final arbitor.

Foreign and Regional Policy

One of the chimerical objectives of Western, particularly United States, policy toward Egypt in the last twenty-five years has been to stimulate an "Egypt-first" policy. There were many Egyptians at the beginning of the Nasserist period, perhaps Nasser himself, who felt that Egypt would do best to tend to its own garden, or, at most, pursue unity of the Nile Valley. Arabism in the 1950s was a political option; Egypt could take it or leave it. Nasser chose to take it.

He did so because he was convinced that Egypt could not conduct its experiment, wherever it might lead, in isolation from its neighbors and the protection they might offer from nonregional forces. He acted out of a sense of Egypt's vulnerability and the inevitable pressures that he align his country with Western economic and cold war interests. Having refused this kind of dependency, he energetically set about reducing the influence of any Arab states (Iraq, Jordan, Saudi Arabia) that had aligned themselves with the same interests. To avoid total isolation, as well as to procure arms, he had to develop ties with the Soviet Union and thereby initiate a new kind of dependency. In 1955 Egypt entered the era of positive neutralism.

In these same years it may have become evident to Nasser that Egypt's economic problems were of such magnitude that they could only be solved through tapping regional resources. Oil, oil revenues, and unused land were the principal attractions. There was considerable talk of moving vast numbers of Egyptian peasants to the Sudan, Iraq, and Syria. Despite the political and psychological costs, added to the basic expenses of relocation, such talk periodically resurfaces, but few Egyptian planners believe that major population transfers are feasible.

On the other hand, the oil wealth of the Arabs has remained a constant attraction to the Egyptians. For years it seemed, with reason, that this enormous treasure was being wasted in palace expenses of various sheikdoms on terms set by the Western cartels. The teeming Nile Valley, that had set itself on a determined course towards economic development, was deprived of any benefit from these wasted revenues. Nasser's approach to this "scandal" was to try to coerce or subvert the oil-rich states into a sharing mood. The culmination of these policies was played out in the Yemeni civil war. Nasser came out the loser as a result of the Egyptian defeat in the June War, and King Faisal of Saudi Arabia emerged as one of the most powerful leaders of the Arab world. President Sadat, no less interested in the wealth of the Arabian peninsula, adopted a different approach. He worked for rapprochement with the oil-rich, and this meant attracting their wealth by more conventional economic policies. Egypt could trade in its regional militancy for regional docility and earn some return on the switch.

With regard to the superpowers, Nasser tried to protect Egypt's independence through his policies of positive neutralism. Throughout the period 1952-1967, he learned that in a bipolar world both the United States and the USSR would be vitally concerned about the levels of each other's influence in Egypt. The long and oft-repeated tale of the Baghdad Pact, the Czech arms deal, nationalization of the Suez Canal, the Soviet offer to help build the High Dam, the Eisenhower Doctrine, and the problems of arms supplies need not be recounted here. It is sufficient to note that Nasser tried to draw maximum economic and political advantage from a bipolar world without selling Egypt to either power. For some time—1955-1966—he succeeded. His army was equipped with Soviet weapons and his people fed with American wheat. Socialist countries advanced massive credits for the development of Egypt's infrastructure and industry, while American oil companies explored Egypt for new sources of oil.

The defeat of 1967, however, destroyed the foundations of Nasser's strategy. The rebuilding of the Egyptian army could only be brought about with the massive assistance of the Soviet Union; no other power could or would help Egypt to avoid capitulation. For that was Nasser's choice: capitulation in the face of Israel's overwhelming military superiority or accentuated reliance upon the USSR. In either case Egypt would become the plaything of outside forces. Choosing the lesser evil, and sincerely acting to preserve Egypt's dignity, Nasser accepted increased Soviet influence. A curious inversion of great power influence in Egypt resulted from this. Seen from one vantage point, Nasser's and Egypt's influence in the Arab world was greatly reduced and that of the conservative oil-rich states commensurately strengthened. Taken together with Israel's new territorial and military gains, the net benefits of the June War to U.S. policy objectives were enormous. Yet, while Soviet arms had proven unequal to the task and Soviet support during the fighting had remained verbal, the result of the war was a vast diminution of U.S. leverage in the so-called radical states (Algeria, Egypt, Syria, Iraq) and commensurate advances for the USSR.

Egypt's accentuated dependence upon the Soviet Union coincided in time with the first steps toward détente and the breakdown of cold war bipolarism.[o] It appeared that the United States might tolerate the Soviet presence in Egypt as

---

[o]It may be objected that multipolarity had begun to emerge in the early 1960s. That is of course true as China and Western Europe cut loose from their patrons. But for the Arab world, great power intervention was monopolized—and still is to a considerable degree—by the Soviet Union and the United States.

long as Egypt remained regionally docile and militarily shackled in undertaking any further hostilities with Israel. In other words, Nasser in the last months of his life and Sadat ever since became convinced that the United States-USSR détente would lead to the freezing of the situation in the Arab-Israeli conflict with the Israelis in a clearly superior situation. Egypt would then have to capitulate to Israeli terms for peace or further ruin its economy by holding out for some incalculable period of time. Only by bringing about a change in U.S. policy towards Israel, especially the delivery of arms, could Egypt restore some semblance of balance in their mutual bargaining positions.

It was left to Sadat to find the formula for effecting this shift in U.S. policy. The move towards the economic open-door policy and economic orthodoxy, and the expulsion of the Soviet military missions in the summer of 1972 were positive inducements.[55] Gradually moving major Arab oil producers toward the utilization of oil as a policy weapon, emphasizing among the European members of the North Atlantic Treaty Organization (NATO) that, precisely on the question of oil supply, their strategic interests were not coincident with those of the United States, and finally resorting to limited war to unfreeze the situation were the negative inducements. Whether the desired shift in U.S. policy will manifest itself to the degree the Egyptians would like remains to be seen. It is worth noting, however, that the October War put Egypt and the Arab world at the forefront of a set of cleavages and rivalries, of a nongeographic nature, which will dominate questions of national sovereignty and dependency throughout this century. These cleavages will develop around questions of world distribution of resources of which energy and food are the most outstanding examples.

Egypt's major problem for the next decades will be the distribution and level of its external dependency. Several aspects of this problem have been presented, but some of the major points bear repeating. Egypt needs massive amounts of capital investment to stimulate economic growth. It would like that capital to be Arab and Western, but if it is insufficient or not directed towards long-term infrastructure investment,[p] Egypt will have to continue its reliance on Socialist credits, Socialist technology, and Socialist markets. Whatever happens, Egypt will for some time have to rely on Western sources for food grains. Some deliveries may come on soft terms, others will have to be paid for in hard currency. To the extent the latter prevail, Egypt must increase its exports to Western markets in order to earn the necessary foreign exchange.

It is likely that a good part of the investments, aid, and credits Egypt receives will be politically motivated. King Faisal, the shah, the United States and the USSR are all willing to invest in Egypt's subordination. The fundamental question is can Egypt use this money to bring about real development? For

---

[p]A test case may lie in the very large phosphate deposits at Abu Tartur. These could make Egypt one of the world's largest exporters, but a mining city, a new port, roads, and railroads will have to be built before the first rock is extracted. It will be important to see who accepts to develop this resource.

instance, it can be legitimately questioned whether or not the basic objective of U.S. aid programs has been to promote development or to promote continued dependency. It can be argued circumstantially that the food for peace program, green revolution technology, and family planning support have been designed largely to make poverty tolerable in large areas of the world but not to overcome it. States that have to worry every few months about the next shipment of wheat, the delivery of spare parts or dwindling foreign currency reserves cannot pose many problems for the wealthy. To the extent that they are producers of raw materials and primary goods they will have to sell them on the world market to cover current deficits. Western policy planners may conclude that the economic vitality of the Third World is not necessarily in the interests of the industrialized nations (including the Soviet Union) in the growing competition for scarce resources. In this light Egypt risks being strung along.

From the point of view of the conservative oil-producing states it is moot whether or not it is in their interests to see Egypt prosperous. With its enormous population, industrial base, and large army an economically strong Egypt could conceivably menace the regimes of all its neighbors, as it did in the 1960s. King Faisal and his successor King Khalid may be content to invest just enough in Egypt to prevent economic breakdown, but not enough to break the links of dependency. It is conceivable that, given Egypt's disproportionate weight in the Arab world, the radical oil-producers (Algeria, Iraq, and Libya) would also invest in Egypt in order to counter Saudi influence. Indeed Egypt's stormy affair with Libya briefly allowed Sadat to flirt profitably with both Qadhafi and Faisal. However, Algeria and Iraq have capital requirements of their own which may prevent them from using their oil revenues to extend their influence abroad.

Whatever the level of capital investment, Egypt cannot forego the Arab world. It must be more regionally-oriented than ever before and this, leaving aside the vital question of capital investment, in four principal ways. First, there can be no separate lasting peace with Israel. The terms of any settlement must represent some sort of regional consensus; Egypt would risk isolation if it were to break away from the dispute before that consensus emerged. Egypt fully recognizes its special obligations as the Arab world's single largest military power, but many Egyptians, wearied by that role, have called for an Arab "Marshall Plan" to compensate Egypt for the losses it has sustained in the Arab cause since 1948.

Second, Egypt needs access to Arab labor markets. It must continue to send abroad teachers, doctors, managers, skilled workers, etc., who are theoretically vital to the Egyptian economy but who cannot be effectively absorbed in its present state.

A third factor is the need for markets for manufactured goods. If Egyptian industry revives, it will have to export in order to avoid another financing crisis as occurred in 1965-66. Growing, proximate markets are to be found in the Arabian peninsula, the Sudan, and Libya. If Egyptian industry does not revive, then Egypt will become the region's Bangladesh.

Finally, Egypt will need the Arab world as a further source of food grains and meat. It is now the technocrats, rather than the politicians, who are the most fervent advocates of Arab unity and economic integration. The vast and poorly-developed expanses of the Sudan, Iraq, parts of Syria, and Morocco must be modernized and turned into surplus areas of grain, oil-seed, and sugar cane. All of the above with the addition of Somalia must modernize animal husbandry and upgrade pasturage to provide the rest of the region with animal protein. The technical expertise, the capital, and the raw materials are all present in the Arab world to bring this about. The Egyptians would like to be the catalysts to this kind of integration. Egypt-firstism is now equivalent to increased regionalism.

So far we have examined various facets of the distribution of dependency. A few remarks are in order on Egypt's choices regarding levels of dependency. What is at stake here is the mix between domestic and foreign resources needed for development, which is another way of stating the problem cited earlier of determining the level and distribution of sacrifice demanded of the Egyptian poeple. One path is to intensify the revolution, level income differentials, restrict consumption and nonessential imports, expand forced savings, all, presumably, within a more resolute central-planning framework legitimized by a militant Socialist ideology. This would not do away with the need for external support, for raw materials and capital goods would still have to be imported. But it might minimize imports, curtail wastage of foreign currency, and raise the level of productive investment. Obviously, a militant Socialist regime would scare off Western capital sources to some extent, but depending on the style with which business is conducted (Algeria is a prominent example here) that risk can be minimized.

The second path, which is being followed now, is to satisfy the consumerism of the middle classes and rely upon them for political support. This inevitably leads savings away from productive investment and inflates the import bill with nonessential items. It accentuates not only economic dependency but political dependency as well. In Egypt, as in most other developing states, a new class has developed which in life-style and standard of living has adopted the same criteria as their counterparts in the industrialized west. While members of these classes may be at ideological odds with their Western counterparts, their life-styles, and not their beliefs, determine their position *vis-à-vis* the masses of their own societies. They are privileged, disproportionately wealthy and hence increasingly visible and vulnerable as economic conditions deteriorate. To preserve their own way of life they are prepared to increase their country's indebtedness. The fact that so many developing countries go to enormous lengths to produce private automobiles locally is representative of the consumerist needs of these classes. Such elites then become a bult-in element making for the continual regeneration of lines of external dependency and political docility.

It is not at all clear what set of incentives, or what "ethic" could move the bureaucratic, professional and entrepreneurial middle stratum to less self-serving behavior. But as long as its capacity for sacrifice is low, it is impossible for the regime to demand any kind of selfless effort on the part of the masses. For as long as the economic situation will permit, the regime will continue to pamper the well-off and seek the line of least popular dissatisfaction among the less fortunate.

U.S. Policy Options

It will be contended here that U.S. policy towards Egypt in the coming decades will be established on essentially the same lines as that towards other developing countries with chronic food deficits and balance of payments problems. The United States faces some momentous choices in this context, and they stem from the gross inequities in the distribution and utilization of raw materials and food resources between the rich and the poor nations.

To examine this challenge with respect to Egypt we must make a few assumptions which may well turn out to be utterly false. First, it will be assumed that something resembling peace will be established between Israel and the Arab states. Second, it will be assumed that the West will accommodate itself to high oil prices short of trade war with the producers or military occupation of some oil-producing areas. Third, and derivatively, it will be assumed that the United States will not be drawn into military confrontation with the Soviet Union over Israel, or oil, or both. If any or all of these assumptions prove false, then the range of possible scenarios that could develop is so vast that prediction becomes a hopeless task. I am not prepared to guess what would be the consequences of U.S. military occupation of Kuwait, local war with the Soviet Union, the military defeat of Israel, an Israeli nuclear strike against Egypt, a new oil embargo, or the destruction of the oil fields.

Short of these potential apocalypses, policy choices are difficult enough. The fundamental dilemma of U.S. policy is to decide whether or not it wants to see most of the Third World develop to the extent that its constituent nations control most of their own resources. Underlying U.S. policy since the Second World War has been a general awareness of the short-term benefits to be drawn from international poverty in terms of political leverage and with disregard for the cumulative long-term effects of pauperization. For the rest of the twentieth century the United States, as *primus inter pares* in the industrial world, has the chance to redress inequities in resource distribution. But to move beyond the short-term convenience of present policies will necessarily entail changes in American and Western styles of life. These have been occurring anyway as a result of the energy crisis.

One choice will involve United States reactions to the efforts of producers of primary products to form cartels and drive up the world market prices of their goods. Rather than fighting these cartels, accommodations with them will lead to a redistribution of wealth that would render most bilateral aid programs insignificant. After petrodollars there is no reason why there should not be copper-dollars, bauxite-dollars, phosphate-dollars, sugar-dollars, and coffee-dollars. Along these same lines the United States must decide whether it will encourage the recycling of funds earned by primary-produce exporters to Western capital markets or back to the developing countries themselves. The industrialized West, the upper class of world society, is being or will be taxed by the primary-produce exporters. However it is the upper class that controls the mechanisms and expertise needed to employ the tax revenues. Can this expertise and these mechanisms orient themselves to pump surplus funds to where they are most needed?

A second choice involves the international division of labor. Egypt, and other countries, will never be capable of producing all their own food needs, and only industrialization can provide them any kind of economic viability. Is it inconceivable that the United States, at the government level, might take the lead in actively encouraging the transfer of industrial technology to such nations and in opening Western markets to Third World industrial goods? The Soviet Union has already done this with undeniable benefits accruing to Egypt and other developing countries. At the same time the United States, Canada, Western Europe, and Australia may be wise in adopting a policy of maximizing their grain production for the main purpose of meeting the growing deficits in foodstuffs faced by countries like Egypt. There would thus be an inversion of roles to some extent: the primary producers would be encouraged to become manufacturers of middle-range goods, while the advanced industrial nations would play a willing role in providing food to the Third World. Egyptians have long eaten American wheat, but could not an American farmer drive an Egyptian tractor, or an American teenager listen to an Egyptian radio?

For this kind of inversion to occur, it would require that Western nations be committed to its success. Technology would not simply be sold, but supervised with all the worker and managerial training in the recipient country which that would entail. Efficiency and quality would become vital concerns for the advanced nations for they would be committed to absorbing Third World manufactured products in their own markets. At the same time, for the duration of the energy crisis, this inversion could help to ease Western balance of payments problems through the export of technology, expertise, and food grains paid for by the wealthy among the primary producers.

Ultimately, a major shift in Western styles of living seems inevitable. It is curious to see Maoist Chinese and capitalist Americans join in the view that man's ingenuity and technological expertise will find a solution to the problem of growing human and diminishing natural resources. This view seems fundamentally illogical and self-serving. It is a gimmick for postponing critical decisions in an increasingly zero-sum world. For Egypt, and the tens of other states like it, to ever become prosperous in even the most modest sense will require a reduction in Western consumerism and conspicuous waste. American children may have to select among something less than three hundred breakfast foods so that the Egyptian peasant can eat bread everyday and chicken once a month.

If Middle Eastern oil, phosphates, vegétables, minerals, citrus fruits, natural gas, and so forth were all processed locally, and partially consumed locally, the economic viability of the region would have been established. Its dependency on the advanced nations would, by the same token, have been considerably reduced. There would be, instead, interdependence and a felt need among the advanced and the advancing that both have vested interests in the economic health of the other. Egypt will merely be one among several test cases in the painful emergence of this realization.

Notes

1. See Anouar Abdel-Malek, *Idéologie et renaissance nationale: l'Egypte Moderne* (Paris: Editions Anthropos, 1969), pp. 38-39.

2. See on this subject Gabriel Baer, "The Beginnings of Urbanization," in his *Studies in the Social History of Modern Egypt* (Chicago Univ. Press, 1969), pp. 133-148; Helen Rivlin, *The Agricultural Policy of Mohammed Ali in Egypt* (Harvard Univ. Press. 1961), pp. 256-270; Patrick O'Brien, *The Revolution in Egypt's Economic System* (Oxford Univ. Press, 1966), p. 5; John Waterbury, "The Balance of People, Land and Water in Modern Egypt," *American Universities Field Staff Report*, Northeast Africa Series, Vol. 19, No. 1 (January 1974).

3. See Janet Abu Lughod, "Urban-rural differences as a Function of the Demographic Transition: Egyptian Data and an Analytic Model," *American Journal of Sociology* 69 (1963-64): 477-490.

4. See John Waterbury, "Egypt: Elite Perceptions of Population Problems," in Harrison Brown et al., *Population: Perspective 1973* (San Francisco: Freeman, Cooper and Co., 1973), pp. 195-215. See also President Sadat's speech to Parliament, *al-Ahram*, Oct. 24, 1974.

5. See "For whom are the new lands," *al-Talia* 10, 8 (Aúg. 1974): 11-61, summarizing the findings and debates of the Agriculture and Irrigation Committee of the Parliament. Also Waterbury, "The Balance of People," p. 22.

6. Remarks of Dr. Al-Stino reported in *al-Ahram*, Sept. 4, 1974.

7. See, for general background, Galal Amin, *Food Supply and Economic Development: with Special Reference to Egypt* (London: Frank Cass, 1966); and Central Agency for Public Mobilization and Statistics, *Population and Development* (Cairo, June 1973), p. 245.

8. See Karim Nashashibi, "Foreign Trade and Economic Development in the UAR: A Case Study," in Lee Preston, *Trade Patterns in the Middle East* (Washington, D.C.: American Enterprise Inst., 1970), pp. 73-93, and *al-Ahram*, Oct. 13, 1974 citing Prime Minister Abdelaziz Hegazi.

9. See the statements of Ahmad Sultan, minister of electricity, published in *Akhbar al-Yom*, July 27, 1974 and a memorandum from the same ministry: *Concerning the Lack of Electrical Power which Egypt will Face as from the end of the Year 1975:* April 1974.

10. The best sources are Charles Issawi, *Egypt in Revolution* (Oxford, 1961); Dr. Ali al-Gritli, *Population and Economic Resources in Egypt* (Matba' Masr, 1962), (in Arabic), and *The Economic History of the Revolution: 1952-1966* (in Arabic), (Cairo: Dar al-Maaref, 1974); B. Hansen and G. Marzouk, *Development and Economic Policy in the UAR* (Amsterdam, 1965); B. Hansen, "Economic Development in Egypt," in C.A. Cooper and S.S. Alexander (eds.), *Economic Development and Population Growth in the Middle East* (New York: American Elsevier Pub. Co., 1972), pp. 22-91; Patrick O'Brien, *The Revolution in Egypt's Economic System* (Oxford Press, 1966); K.M. Barbour, *The Growth, Location, and Structure of Industry in Egypt* (Praeger, 1972); Donald Mead, *Growth and Structural Change in the Egyptian Economy* (Homewood, Ill.: Richard D. Irwin, Inc. For the most part these studies reflect economic performance at the time of the first Five Year Plan, 1960-1965, a period that has not been typical of Egyptian growth. A solid study taking into account the long downward spiral of the economy since 1965 is that of Robert Mabro, *The Egyptian Economy: 1952-1972* (Oxford Press, 1974). Dealing with the same period are Essam Montasser, "Egypt's Pattern of Trade and Development: A Model of Import Substitution Growth," *Egypte Contemporaine* 65, 356 (April 1974): 5-109; and Samir Radwan, *Capital Formation in Egyptian Industry and Agriculture, 1882-1967* (London: Ithaca Press, 1974). Two studies emphasizing the political economy of modern Egypt are Hassan Riad, *L'Egypte Nasserien* (Paris, 1962), and Anouar Abdelmalek, *Egypt: Military Society* (N.Y.: Random House, 1968).

11. The post-World War II program of Ahmad Hussein's Socialist party contains most of the programmatic ideas eventually espoused by the Free Officers. See Tariq al-Bishri, *The Political Movement in Egypt: 1945-1952* (Egyptian General Book Org., 1972), pp. 389-415 (in Arabic).

12. See the incisive analysis of Salah 'Isa, "The Future of Democracy in Egypt," *Al-Katib* 14, 162 (Sept. 1974): pp. 9-28 (in Arabic).

13. Mabro, *The Egyptian Economy*, p. 127.

14. See Waterbury, "The Balance of People," p. 6, and "Special Study on Land Use," *Al-Talia* 8, 10 (Oct. 1972), (in Arabic). See also Price Planning Agency, "Distribution of Individual Income," Memo No. 18, Jan. 1973, which claims that 2 percent of all landowners own 29 percent of all cultivated land and earn 30.4 percent of all agricultural rents (p. 6). In contrast to this rural bourgeoisie is the growing class of subsistence, subsustenance, and landless peasants which must now be well over four million families.

15. See *Guide to Organizations and Companies 1972-1973*, Arab World Agency for Publicity (Cairo, 1973), (in Arabic).

16. For an interesting perspective on the technocrats, see Clement Henry

Moore, "The New Egyptian Technocracy: Engineers at the Interstices of Power," *International Journal of Middle Eastern Studies.* Also R. Hrair Dekmejian, *Egypt Under Nasser* (Albany: SUNY Press, 1971).

17. See engineer Fawzi Habashi, "The Extent of Parasitic Incomes in the Contracting Sector," *al-Talia* 9, 7 (July 1973): 27-31.

18. See *al-Ahram*, July 23, 1972, and John Waterbury, "Cairo; Third World Metropolis: Housing and Shelter," *American Universities Field Staff Report*, Northeast Africa Series, Vol. 18, No. 8 (Sept. 1973).

19. See al-Gritli, *Population and Economic Resources*, p. 197; Hansen and Marzouk, *Development and Economic Policy*, pp. 2-3; and CAPMAS, "Population and Development," p. 243.

20. His remarks are reproduced in "Seminar on the Investment of Arab and Foreign Capital," *al-Talia* 10, 7 (July 1974): esp. pp. 24-25 (in Arabic).

21. See the remarks of the Deputy Speaker of the Parliament, Gamal Uteify, published in *al-Ahram*, June 28, 1973, and the proposed budget for 1973: supplement to *al-Ahram al-Iqtisadi* Jan. 1, 1973.

22. Figures presented in Galal Amin's excellent article, "Income Distribution and Economic Development in the Arab World," *L'Egypte Contemporaine* 64, 352 (April 1973): pp. 5-37, esp. p. 18. Since May 1974 the minimum public sector wage was raised from £E9 to £E12 per month, or, on the assumption of full-time employment, £E144 per year; so Amin's ratios would now have to be reduced somewhat.

23. Before liberalization of car importation, in 1966-67, only 1,377 cars were imported at £E891,000. With liberalization, 15,191 cars were imported at a cost of £E9.5 million. Both cost figures are before customs which could double the purchase price. See Lutfi Abd al-Azim, "Forbid the importation of automobiles and establish a 'free market' for them?", *al-Ahram al-Iqtisadi*, No. 426 (May 15, 1973): 6-8. In 1974 18,177 automobiles were imported, and it is estimated that 25,000 will come in in 1975.

24. See O'Brien, *Revolution in Egypt's Economic System*, p. 153.

25. Nashashibi, "Foreign Trade," p. 75.

26. Mabro, *The Egyptian Economy*, p. 123.

27. Mabro has rightly pointed out that some of this growth is really fictitious, representing the expansion of the service sector and government employment. Mabro, *The Egyptian Economy*, p. 171.

28. See for instance Mohammed Hassanein Heikal, "The Golden Chain," *al-Ahram*, Aug. 17, 1973; and the interview of Yussef Idriss with P.M. Abdelaziz Higazi, *al-Ahram*, Oct. 25, 1974.

29. See Elizabeth Valkenier, "New Soviet Views on Economic Aid," *Survey*, No. 76 (Summer 1970): 17-29.

30. While there may be a little rug-selling involved, the cumulative losses of petroleum revenues for the Sinai fields and the Suez Canal tolls were estimated at £E750 million and £E1.2 billion respectively. See *al-Ahram*, Feb. 10, 1974.

31. The latter figure is attributed to Ahmad Morshidy of the Ministry of Planning, "Seminar on the Investment of Foreign Capital."

32. See Hansen, "Economic Development of Egypt," p. 25, and Hansen and Marzouk, *Development and Economic Policy*, pp. 178-210.

33. Gamal Nazir, "The Problem of Foreign Debts for Developing Countries," *L'Egypte Contemporaine* 64, 354 (Oct. 1973): 51 (in Arabic).

34. See "Seminar on the Investment of Foreign Capital," p. 35, and the remarks of Hamid Sayyih, chairman of the National Bank, in *Akhbar al-Yom*, May 25, 1974.

35. Hansen, "The Economic Development of Egypt," p. 73.

36. See Mabro, *The Egyptian Economy*, p. 78, and Hansen, "Economic Development of Egypt," p. 83.

37. These calculations are my own based on Ministry of Industry figures published in *al-Ahram*, Oct. 4, 1974.

38. *Al-Ahram*, Oct. 23, 1974. The first entry includes price subsidies for flour, bread, cooking oil, sugar, rice, etc.

39. On this latter point, see Mabro, *The Egyptian Economy*, pp. 178-180.

40. Despite the great influx of university graduates, the bureaucracy is not overeducated. Prime Minister Higazi cited the following figures from the Central Agency for Public Mobilization and Statistics: 85 percent of all government employees had less than a university degree, and over *half* were either illiterate or knew only how to read and write. *Al-Ahram*, July 9, 1974.

41. Figures from Muhammad Sabhy al-Atribi, "Bureaucratic Growth During the Last Ten Years," *al-Talia* 8, 10 (Oct. 1972): 72-75.

42. From *al-Ahram*, Aug. 27, 1974. President Sadat made the same point on other occasions. See for instance his interview with *Usbu'a al-Arabi* reprinted in *al-Ahram*, Oct. 9, 1974, where he also revealed Egypt lost 6,000 dead in the October War. The $500 million was from Arab oil-exporting states.

43. Fuad Mursi, "The Public Sector and Private Investment," *al-Talia* 10, 2 (Feb. 1974): 16-23. Dr. Mursi was Minister of Supply, 1971-1973.

44. Ibid., p. 21.

45. In 1972 Egypt concluded an agreement with the EEC that included a 45 percent tariff reduction on industrial goods, and reductions ranging from 20-60 percent on various kinds of agricultural produce. *The Times*, May 3, 1972.

46. Hamid Sayyih, cited in "Seminar on Foreign Investment," p. 19. For 1975, a planned investment of over one billion pounds has been planned. How it will be paid for is a matter of some mystery.

47. See Ahmad Abu Ismail, "The Proposed Budget for 1973: Presentation and Analysis," *L'Egypte Contemporaine* 64, 352 (April 1973): 117-154, esp. p. 141. Dr. Abu Ismail former chairman of the Dept. of Economics at Cairo University and head of the Budget Committee in the Parliament, was made minister of finance in April 1975.

48. Albert O. Hirschmann, "The Changing Tolerance for Income Inequality in

the Course of Economic Development," *Quarterly Journal of Economics* 87, 4 (Nov. 1973): 544-565, citation p. 545.

49. An abundant literature has now accumulated dealing with Egyptian political organization. See *Inter alia*, Fauzi Najjar, "Islam and Socialism in the United Arab Republic," *Journal of Contemporary History* 3, 3 (July 1968): 183-199; C.H. Moore, "Authoritarian Politics in Unincorporated Society," *Comparative Politics* 6, 2 (Jan. 1974): 193-218; Ilya Harik, "The Single Party as a Subordinate Movement," *World Politics* 26, 1 (Oct. 1973): 80-105; Leonard Binder, "Political Recruitment and Participation in Egypt," in La Palombara and Weiner (eds.), *Political Parties and Political Development* (Princeton Univ. Press, 1966), pp. 217-240; James B. Nayfield, *Rural Politics in Nasser's Egypt* (Austin: Texas Univ. Press, 1971); H. Dekmejian, *Egypt Under Nasser passim*; Robert Springborg, "Patterns of Association in the Egyptian Political Elite," in George Lenczowski (ed.), *Political Elites in the Middle East* (Washington, D.C.: American Enterprise Institute, 1975), pp. 83-102.

50. Nasser would probably have endorsed Phillippe Schmitter's definition of corporatism while rejecting the label. Indeed I have seen no example of the use of the word in official ideological statements. "Corporatism can be defined as a system of interest representation in which the constituent units are organized into a limited number of singular, compulsory, non-competitive, hierarchically ordered and functionally differentiated categories, recognized or licensed (if not created) by the state and granted deliberate representation monopoly within their respective categories in exchange for observing certain controls on their selection of leaders and articulation of demands and supports." (pp. 93-94). In another passage well worth citing, because of its relevance to the Nasserist experience, Schmitter writes "As for the abrupt demise of incipient pluralism and its dramatic and forceful replacement by state corporatism, this seems closely associated with the necessity to enforce "social peace," not by co-opting and incorporating, but by repressing and excluding the autonomous articulation of subordinate class demands in a situation where the bourgeoisie is too weak, internally divided, externally dependent and/or short of resources to respond effectively and legitimately to these demands within the framework of the liberal democratic state." Both citations in Phillippe Schmitter, "Still the Century of Corporatism?," *The Review of Politics* 36, 1 (Jan. 1974): 85-132.

51. This phrase and the concept underlying it has been developed by Mohammed Sid Ahmad of *al-Ahram* in several articles. Outbursts of course occurred, especially after 1967. Student-worker demonstrations occurred in the winter and fall of 1968 on such a scale that the regime had to placate rather than supress them. Incidents of less magnitude have been treated more harshly. A taxi strike in 1971, the Sadat era, was broken by massive arrests. The minister of interior suggested the strike was potentially treasonous as it had disrupted "vital communications in time of war." The grievance of the strikers was that they had not been allowed to raise their base fares since 1952.

52. Nasser cited by Najjar, "Islam and Socialism," p. 188.

53. Louis Awad, "Egypt or Egypt," *al-Ahram*, Oct. 11, 1974.

54. See, among others, Malak Guirguis, *Egyptian Personal Psychology and Obstacles to Development* (Cairo: Ruz al-Yussef Press, 1974), (in Arabic).

55. I find farfetched the arguments frequently advanced that Egypt could not have removed these missions had the USSR not decided to remove them anyway. They may have so decided but there is little evidence of it. The real question is what could the USSR have done had they been ordered out against their will? Occupy Egypt? Cut off all military and economic aid? Break relations? None of these would have been feasible. Egypt is a Third World country, nonaligned, a member of no military pacts, fighting for a cause the USSR has endorsed as just and is so viewed by most other Third World states. To have played the straight imperial "heavy" in Egypt would have caused a major setback to Soviet policy in the developing world. It would also have burdened the USSR with a nasty colonial situation. In this respect trying to compare Soviet policy in Czechoslovakia and in Egypt is totally misleading. See Uri Ra'anan, "The USSR and the Middle East: Some Reflections on the Soviet Decision-Making Process," *Orbis* 17, 3 (Fall 1973): 946-977.

XIII

The Social Structure of Israeli Politics

Ben Halpern

I

The viability of the Israeli social and political system has been continually doubted, from its obscure origins about a century ago to the present day. In its early days, the Jewish settlement in Palestine was viewed as a test-tube experiment which could hardly survive exposure to the trials of reality. After being tried by every conceivable extremity, including the unending wars that marked its brief quarter of a century as a state, Israel's existence still remains under question today.

The Yom Kippur War of October 1973 brought into sharp focus the extraordinary imbalance of forces against which Israel must struggle in order to survive.[1] Not only did a nation of three million have to fight a two-front war against enemies outnumbering it fourteen-to-one in population; the Soviet-armed and Soviet-advised Arab armies were backed by the economic power of Arab oil producers, whose pressure threatened to paralyze the entire economy of the West. Israel's enemies enjoyed at least the passive support of virtually the whole United Nations community, including the North Atlantic Treaty Organization (NATO) allies who hampered Israel's access to vitally needed American resupply and a massive UN voting bloc ready to endorse, actively or by abstention, almost any Arab-initiated proposition condemning Israeli or approving Arab policies.

Against this, Israel had the support of the United States. In earlier encounters with Arab states, it had the temporary support of France and Britain or of the Soviet Union. Such an oddly assorted and fluctuating series of near-allies makes it obvious that no paramount strategic connection but largely the chance concurrence of short-run interests explains Israel's past ability to obtain vital diplomatic support and military supplies from one source or another.

The longest-lasting friendly attitude toward Israel has perhaps been that of the United States, although it has hardly been the most consistent.[2] Rather it has been frequently reluctant, halting in its development, and continuously inhibited by powerful countervailing interests, which won repeated victories, only to lose in the long run, in the struggle over American policy towards the Jewish state. American support for Israel is broadly based on general sympathy for a much-persecuted people, and it is strongly promoted by the effective consensus of American Jews, a significant economic and political force. Partisan sympathy for the Arab cause is fostered by a small but extremely influential lobby of ministers, academics, and officials immediately responsible for policy, not to speak of powerful industrial interests which, in the context of current global rivalries, give primary consideration to the overwhelming strategic importance of the oil resources, critical location, and immense numerical and political preponderance of the Arab states in the Middle East.

Against this material force, Israel counterposes the strength of its own solid social structure. Small as the 600,000-man Jewish National Home was in 1947, it represented enough social, political, economic and, above all, military power to make impossible any attempted solution of the Palestine problem which excluded an area of Jewish sovereignty. This was the fundamental reason behind the international community's support of the Palestine partition plan.[3] Since 1947, Israel has been strong enough to protect its interests. To attack a fully-mobilized Israel today requires forces of major dimensions; it has been a society constantly mobilized, to a point hardly conceivable elsewhere; it constitutes an intractable problem complicating the strategies of everyone concerned in the area. The consequences for the policy of the two superpowers represent an oddly unbalanced, antagonistic parallelism.

The simplest solution for its particular interests would be for each superpower to consolidate its influence among the Arabs, who are dominant in the area. In view of the radical character of Arab hostility toward Zionism, this would mean eliminating Israel. Israel's stubbornly defended existence contributes to unrest, and thus it is a handicap for an American strategy which requires stability; equally, Israel's existence is an advantage for a Russian strategy, which requires instability. It would follow that American interests would dictate eliminating, and Soviet interests preserving, Israel. But the forceful elimination of Israel is not a credible policy for a democratic America; while, in spite of the advantage the USSR gains from Israel's existence as a flashpoint of conflict, support for attempts to eliminate Israel forcibly has been a thoroughly credible policy for the Soviet proletarian dictatorship. This imbalance was manifestly one of the reasons for the past growth of Soviet influence in the Arab area at the expense of that of the Western powers. It is also responsible for the undercurrent of hostility that has continuously abraded official American friendship toward Israel.[4]

Another set of circumstances, based on a revised American strategy reflecting among other factors the Vietnam War, led to more positive official evaluations of Israel's role. This view gained acceptance in the 1960s.[5] In the limited conflicts that are determined by the global nuclear stalemate, either superpower simply exhausts its own strength if it becomes directly involved beyond those strategic borders where its dominance is conceded by the other side. A successful policy for either side depends on finding reliable local allies capable of maintaining, or extending, their interests with minimal support from a super-patron. In the Middle East, after 1958, American strategy increasingly relied on Israel's strength; especially as, under the existing local conditions, this could often be done while simultaneously building up other connections, including the extension of friendship among the Arab states.

After the Yom Kippur War, the United States' acknowledged relationship with Israel helped turn Egypt and other Arab states towards America, since the Soviet military-political relationship had failed to achieve Arab objectives. Thus, the Soviet Union found its influence sharply diminished, in the aftermath of a war which Arabs could regard as a victory largely because of unstinted Soviet input, and increasingly direct Soviet involvement, on their side. Some Arabs today clearly calculate that they may attain their objectives vis-à-vis Israel peacefully through the United States, rather than militarily through Russia.

A new, delicately poised and very precarious balance now obtains, as peace prospects are explored in a series of cautious maneuvers, even while preparations for the next war are pushed on all sides. Russia, continuing to count on regional instability, remains committed to Arab extremism, while making certain, largely symbolic, gestures toward moderation even toward Israel in order to safeguard global détente and protect its future position in the event of regional stabilization. American policy seeks to advance a peace settlement and, at the same time,. extend the United States' influence among the Arabs by judiciously pressing Israel for maximum concessions; and its leverage for this purpose has been hugely enlarged owing to the quantum-leap in Israeli dependence on American economic aid and military assistance since the war.

An American policy of gaining Arab friends because the United States supports Israel is obviously fraught with internal contradictions, but is at present deceptively realistic. Indeed, it offers such a wide range of possibilities that hardly any of the old issues are decisively resolved. To help destroy Israel in war, for example, may not be an American option; but it could well be an option for America today to reduce Israel to such a state of dependency, and place such strains on its consensus and powers of resistance that conceivably it might submit passively, like Czechoslavakia after Munich, to the status Arabs design for it. On the other hand, to permit Israel not only to defeat, but to conquer existing Arab states, in the hope of ending the indefinitely continuing war, has been repeatedly ruled out as an American policy; but to maintain a convincing level of Israeli strength as a means of inducing Arabs to seek security in stabilized regional relations, including full peace with Israel, could well be an American policy.

The actual policy is, of course, a flexible if not erratic, combination of both approaches. The Arab turn to America may be predicated on our ties to Israel and our presumed ability to influence policy there; but it is clear that what Arabs hope, as an ultimate objective, is still to wipe out Israel's independent existence.[a] To rely on American help for this purpose is to expect the United States to weaken and ultimately break Israel's power of resistance. The weaker Israel in fact appears, not only externally but above all internally, the more often support develops in U.S. policy planning circles for precisely such an approach. Given Israel's persistent will to survive, the inevitable end of such a policy is war. If, however, the American aim is to build upon signals of Arab peaceful intentions in order to stabilize relations between existing states in the area and work toward true peace, then confidence in the continuing independent strength of Israel is a primary prerequisite for such a policy.

Considering the extreme difficulty of Israel's external circumstances, such confidence implies that, after the Yom Kippur War, Israel will still be capable of the same extraordinary level of social mobilization which it has hitherto successfully demonstrated. American policy regarding Israel has long relied on the assumption that, by continuing use of virtually all its resources—manpower, land, water, skills, human endurance—and not merely the normal maximum proportion used by other states when fully mobilized for war, the Jewish state could defend its existence against all foreseeable odds. The scale and consequences of the last war sharply revised the odds; the United States has committed itself to a new, unprecedented level of support in order to keep Israel at what America (and possibly the Israelis) can regard as a tolerable level of preparedness. But any such calculation still relies on a correct estimate of the capacity of the Israelis, their army, their civilian economy and, above all, their governmental policy, to survive under a continuous strain the United States would never dare to impose on itself even temporarily.

II

Beginning with its first government, Israel's political system developed as a direct carry-over of the personnel, rules, and practices of earlier Zionist bodies. The National Council which proclaimed the sovereign Jewish state, and later served as its provisional government until the first elections, was constituted by the members, all Zionist leaders, of the Vaad Leumi (national executive committee)

---

[a]Any contrary interpretation must discount not only the evidence of past actions but of present statements. Bourgiba and Cecil Hourani, who have come closest to proposing outright peace with Israel of any recognized Arab spokesmen, argue that Israel would be peacefully absorbed and submerged by their method. In Arafat's reluctant acceptance of the idea of a West Bank Palestinian state, he openly proposes to set it up as a base for further attack. That does not alter the fact that resort to such formulas tacitly recognize the dysfunctional effects and discouraging prospects of all-out hostilities for the Arabs at this moment.

of the Palestine Jewish community organization and the Jerusalem Executive of the World Zionist Organization (WZO), with added members from parties not represented on those bodies. That generation of Zionist leaders continued to dominate Israeli politics for decades, and the present leadership was largely trained under its direct influence. The electoral laws, party system, parliamentary procedures, and top-level executive processes of Israel today continue to be channeled by the conventions established in the relatively long political history of the Zionist movement, its Congress and executive organs.

The functions of the Zionist political system in Palestine under the British Mandate were far more extensive than those of a normal nationalist lobby, or even liberation movement, but also more restricted than those of a state.[6] The Vaad Leumi and WZO Jerusalem Executive, apart from their nationalist political activity in relation to the British, the Arabs, and the outer world, administered numerous functions and services for the growing Jewish community in Palestine. Land purchase, land settlement as well as training, immigration, and absorption of Jewish farm labor were primary responsibilities of the World Zionist Organization (WZO) Executive and its affiliated bodies. Jewish communal and welfare services, as well as the education of Jewish children, were primary Vaad Leumi responsibilities, with little involvement of the Palestine government itself. The Chief Rabbinate, as a functional section of the community organization, had legal jurisdiction over marriage, divorce, and other matters of personal status for registered members of the community. The semilegal, paramilitary defense organization, the *Haganah*, was a concern of both the Vaad Leumi and the WZO Executive.

However, neither body's competence remotely approached that which, after May 15, 1948, devolved upon the government of the new Jewish state. The Zionist political system dealt *only partially* (within limits set by the Palestine government's authority) with the affairs of *only part* of the Jews settled in Palestine up to 1948; not all, or even most of the Zionist settlers came under its primary aegis. The Palestine Jewish community was a voluntary organization, in spite of its public law status, and Orthodox, anti-Zionist groups which refused to join it were exempt from the authority of both the Chief Rabbinate and the Vaad Leumi. The Jewish municipalities and local councils, immediately governing the majority of Palestine Jews, were staffed largely by Zionist notables, but they too were under no effective Vaad Leumi control.[7]

Similarly, the WZO Executive exercised authority over only a minor segment of the Jewish community and of its Zionist components. The immigration of labor settlers, which the WZO managed, was only part of the total Jewish immigration, and at all times, not the greater part. National land purchase and settlement, while fundamental to Zionist political objectives, were by no means the dominant component of Jewish economic development and settlement in Palestine under the mandate. The larger part of the Jewish community, settled in Palestine as private persons and were not subject to the policy of the Zionist political system, nor were they substantially aided by it. But with the founding of Israel, they, as well as the Arab population and the old anti-Zionist orthodox Jewish community, became fully subject to the post-Zionist political system.

From the start those most deeply involved in the system's routine operations were the religious Zionists, organized in the Mizrachi party, and the several labor Zionist parties combined in the Histadrut (the General Federation of Jewish Workers in Eretz-Israel). The whole range of religious activities under the jurisdiction of the Chief Rabbinate and Vaad Leumi control was virtually monopolized by Mizrachi; they ran schools and cultural activities, under the aegis of the Vaad Leumi, parallel to those of secular "trends" in the communal organization. The labor parties were the main instrument for achieving the most critical immediate Zionist goals and the cardinal strategic means toward its ultimate end. They recruited, trained, and organized the farm laborers who settled on land acquired by the Jewish National Fund and who formed the economic base, staked out the future boundaries, and established the primary political facts which, according to the ruling Zionist theory, were prerequisite to the creation of the Jewish state.[8]

All voluntary constituents of the Zionist political system were ideologically committed to its long-range goals. As a result, their support of its operations was of a different order and quality from that which could be expected from those elements of the population who involuntarily became part of the system when Israel was created. The registered Zionists all supported the policies of the Zionist leadership either by affirmative vote or, if in opposition, by voluntarily submitting to the majority and regularly renewing their membership within the system. A more substantial and specific commitment was that of Zionist radicals, particularly the labor Zionists, who in the 1930s began their domination of the political system, and in different ways, the Orthodox Mizrachi and right-wing Revisionist Zionists. Whether in control or in opposition, or even, as in the case of the Revisionists from 1935 to 1942, in a state of secession, these radicals accepted ideological obligations affecting their private lives. They were personally committed to performances essentially related to the fundamental Zionist goals, as they saw them: in the case of Mizrachi, this meant the extension of traditional norms to the new situation of the Zionist Restoration; in the case of the Revisionists, this was interpreted to mean the organization of Zionist militancy; and in the case of the labor Zionists, the building, on Socialist lines, of the social and economic foundations of the future Jewish state.

Theodore Herzl organized the WZO on a principle of strong presidential management,[9] which was carried over into the party organization of center (general Zionist) and right-wing (Revisionist) Zionists. But in the radical Revisionist organization, control by the leader extended beyond the general conduct of party policy. Members, particularly in the paramilitary organizations, considered themselves soldiers in the ranks under the leader's command. So, too, for Mizrachi adherents the authority of official rabbis extended into various matters of general policy. In any case, Mizrachi members held themselves bound personally to live by and for the religious tradition.[10]

The most fully developed, extensive, and operational system of personal commitment, and the most effective nexus of solidarity between leaders and members, was that of the several labor Zionist parties.[11] These groups, in which several ideological variants competed vigorously with each other within a framework of comparative unity against other Zionists, all had a common pattern of organization. They combined principles of democratic centralism with intimate bonds of fellowship, actively cultivated from childhood, between movement spokesmen and rank-and-file activists. Policies were constantly attuned to the consensus, at the risk of a break nòt only in the ranks but in the very self-identities of the members; policies were carried out not only by executive action at the top, but at every point by a committed rank-and-file of individual activists. These volunteers took up the tasks of pioneering and strategic risk-taking not only as a matter of duty but with a clear purpose to impose their ideological stamp on Zionist policy.

III

Participation in the most critical Zionist activities in the field gave the farmer-laborers of the collective and cooperative settlements unusual opportunities and power to affect Zionist policy at the administrative level. But with no more than 5 to 10 percent of the Palestine Jewish community in their ranks, the raw voting strength of the elite labor Zionist cadres could hardly have prevailed in the Vaad Leumi, let alone the WZO Executive, in which the votes of Diaspora Zionists as well were counted. However, their influence was hugely enhanced by the fact that over half of the entire Jewish working class in Palestine in the 1930s had been trained in the Diaspora, brought in as immigrants, and lived at least for a time as working members of settlements in one or another ideologically defined collectivist movement.[12] Another segment, native to Palestine, received equivalent indoctrination in the local labor Zionist youth movements. Moreover, the Histadrut, organized by these men as a centralized, general-purpose workers' organization (comprising trade unions, producers' and consumers' cooperatives, rural settlement federations, health, welfare, and cultural services, and labor-controlled corporations) covered well over 80 percent of all Jewish workers in Palestine.[13]

From the 1930s to this day, this "labor camp" provided the largest solid block, or coalition, of Jewish voters, running from a third to two-fifths of the total electorate. During this period the Labor coalition was able to dominate the Zionist political system, owing to an historically-rooted, interrelated set of political conventions.

1. Election to all major political bodies has been strictly based on propor-

tional representation.[14] The combination of a high rate of voter participation and universal adult suffrage have guaranteed representation in Israel's legislative bodies to every minimally organized interest or opinion in the country, and have made coalition government a necessity throughout Israel's history.

2. One relatively large section of voters, averaging nearly 15 percent, was divided among the several religious (Orthodox Jewish) parties.[15] These organizations proved to be mainly concerned with one specific issue, the status of Jewish traditional (Torah) laws in the legal system that was to govern Israel. To the extent that the religious parties were neutral on the cardinal issues dividing Labor and its opponents, they reduced the ideologically motivated opposition to Labor by some 15 percent and increased the weight of the Labor plurality in the remaining 85 percent of the vote. Also, insofar as Labor could consider the specific Orthodox demands as neutral, concessions needed to gain part, or all, of the Orthodox parliamentary votes seemed a relatively reasonable price for a strong coalition—especially if the bargaining strength and potential veto power of the religious parties were counterbalanced by other congenial coalition partners to the government. This alliance relied on certain long-sustained, and unusual affinities which counteracted the tendency for clerical parties to seek conservative allies and Socialists to join anticlerical allies.[16] The Orthodox, like other Zionists, recognized the pioneering Zionist, national role performed by the Socialist workers, and a good part of the religious camp, long the dominant faction in Mizrachi, was composed of workers and religious Socialists. For their part, the Socialists, like other Zionists, generally acknowledged the unquestionable religious roots of Jewish culture; most of them understood only one historic version of Judaism—Orthodoxy. Also, in Mapai, the major labor grouping, religious workers were a significant part of the party members, particularly among those of Asian-African origin. The Labor-Mizrachi alliance therefore reflected to some degree a tacit mutual acknowledgement of legitimate claims.

3. A third element which contributed to Labor's dominance was its central position on major political issues that divided the Israeli electorate.[17] With a third or more of the votes committed to Mapai, with the religious parties neutral, and with the remaining votes divided among minor parties, none of which until recently reached half Labor's strength, and which opposed each other and were to left or right of Mapai's central position, no coalition was possible without Mapai's participation, and Mapai was able permanently to dominate any possible coalition. The same situation prevailed in the WZO, in the Histadrut, where Mapai drew a clear majority of the votes, and to a great extent in Israeli municipalities after the founding of the state, since municipal coalition administrations were formed in close connection with national coalition agreements.

The normal left-right issues of modern economic and social policy were complicated in Israel by the special character of its Socialist parties.[18] Their ideology committed them to certain tasks of Zionist construction—particularly rural settlement and self-generated employment and investment—beyond the normal trade union and political scope of Socialist party doctrine in Europe. One result was to inhibit the doctrinaire vigor with which conservative Zionists might normally have combated Zionist socialism. Another result was to displace normally expected political positions; thus, the anti-Labor right wing favored nationalization, and Labor opposed it in cases where the Histadrut itself controlled services or enterprises. Thus, commonly accepted labor demands, such as a minimum wage or unemployment insurance, were only reluctantly adopted by Mapai, owing to the primacy granted to the tasks of making work and training and settling workers. On other usual left-right issues, such as questions of international political alignment, the major labor grouping, Mapai, represented a center view, and was outflanked on the Left by minor, doctrinaire Marxist factions. Thus, in the early years of Israel's political history, Mapai-led coalitions excluded the Communists as a matter of fixed principle and the left-wing Mapam party as a matter of tactical preference.[19]

Mapai's options were further increased by its broad and flexible, and hence central, position on the hawk-dove dimension defined by degrees of nationalist militantism.[20] Both on the left wing (Mapam) and the right wing (Herut and the bourgeois Zionists), Mapai's opponents were internally divided on the pertinent nationalist issues—such as territorial demands and other aspects of national strategy and tactics toward the Arabs—so that a dovish faction on the Right or a hawkish faction on the Left often found itself more drawn to the centrist Mapai coalition than to Herut militants or the pro-Soviet faction in Mapam. For a long time, Mapai was thus able to exclude Herut on principle, in the same way as the Communists, from any possible coalition, thus increasing its advantage over all remaining, eligible coalition partners.

IV

Under the given combination of circumstances, the dominance of a center-left Labor party in Israel was guaranteed as long as Mapai could consolidate a cohesive group of supporters constituting a majority of Israel's workers. Until 1948, this condition was assured because of the tight social bonds between the leading cadres of the movement, identified particularly with the collective settlements, and the broad mass of Histadrut members. There was, at the same time, abundant evidence of strains arising from the "internal contradictions" of a system which sought to organize masses on an essentially voluntary principle of personal commitment.

The organization of ideological cadres under tight discipline in terms of total commitment—that is, the combination of revolutionary professionalism and democratic centralism in a voluntary ideological movement—has everywhere, under conditions of freedom, tended to produce ideological splintering and sectarianism. In the social context of an Israeli commune, or kibbutz, where not only the specifically political activity of members but their whole lives are invested in a common, collectively evolving ideology, these tendencies were enhanced. The·history of the Palestine Jewish labor movement is shot through with splits and secessions over ideological niceties, in which the crucial line of fracture began with a division in the kibbutz federations. Hence, it is not surprising that the unification of the three Socialist Zionist federations of collectives was a perennial, and perhaps the most critical concern of the Histadrut leadership until 1948.[21]

While unable to unite the kibbutz federations, Mapai was able to build a structure, always including one or more of the three Socialist kibbutz federations, which extended collectivist principles of mutual responsibility and personal commitment to the scale of mass organization. Sectarianism, which served to cement the internal cohesion of collectivist small groups, was not functional, and was certainly not encouraged in a popular mass party. Instead, a broadly defined ideological consensus, harmonizing subordinate ideological and interest groups at various stages of unification, ranging from coalition to coalescence, was characteristic of Mapai and its historical predecessors from the beginning. But the doctrines of total mutuality and personal commitment, the principles of democratic centralism and revolutionary professionalism, remained the recognized ideal of Mapai organization and retained considerable effectiveness in practice. This was possible in good part because of Mapai's continuing bond with kibbutzim and the role of kibbutz members in its leadership.

It was, of course, impossible to duplicate the complete kibbutz system of mutualism and commitment among the mass of Histadrut workers settled in the cities and in the private sector of the agricultural economy. Nevertheless, the Mapai-led Histadrut supplied its members with services, including employment, over so broad a range that their identification with the labor movement was a political rather than narrowly economic one. For that mass of members who had been recruited, trained and initially absorbed as labor immigrants by Mapai-affiliated kibbutzim, it was also a profoundly personal bond of comradeship.

The Mapai bloc was sustained by a cohesive majority of the Jewish workers, not only enjoyed the inherent advantages of a dominant centrist group in the Zionist political system. In addition, its opponents on the left and on the right accepted, in varying degrees and in different respects, some of the fundamental aims and activities of the ruling party such as the construction of a farmer-worker base for the future Jewish state and the settlement of its future borders. Mapai's approach was in full harmony with the basic WZO policy, under Chaim Weizmann's presidency, which favored gradual Zionist development, in cooperation with the British, under the terms of the mandate. As long as this policy prevailed, Mapai opponents within the Zionist political system confined themselves to specific, largely internal issues: rightists fought against WZO support for labor Zionist "social experiments," and leftists criticized the Histadrut's nationalist methods in the organization of Arab workers.

Such acceptance of Mapai hegemony, before 1948, was limited to registered Zionists and, even for them, applied only within the legitimate range of functions controlled by the Zionist political system. Preferential employment of Jewish workers in Jewish citrus plantations could not be exorted from Zionist private farmers by nationalist propaganda and union pressure; only anti-Jewish violence and the boycott of the Jewish economy by Arab peasant-workers in 1936 enabled Mapai temporarily to achieve this aim. In the Jewish municipalities, government-supported restrictions on the franchise, among other measures, kept control safely in the hands of the Zionist bourgeoisie in the face of generally fruitless Labor challenges.[22] A more radical right-wing, ultra-Zionist opposition, involving separatist organization for paramilitary as well as political action, was that of the Zionist-Revisionists, parent movement of the present-day Herut faction. Their demand that the WZO force a clear British decision to make Palestine (including Transjordan) a Jewish state, was radically opposed to Weizmann's policy, and they seceded from the WZO in 1935 when he returned to leadership.[23]

A few years after the Revisionist secession, the Arab rebellion and the deteriorating international situation caused Britain to begin considering the possibility of an independent Arab Palestine state, or of independent Arab and Jewish states in a partitioned Palestine. To raise this issue was to threaten the existing consensus not only in the WZO but in the Histadrut. One left-wing labor faction, Hashomer Hatzair, centered in a kibbutz federation, developed a line of increasingly independent political activity in the 1930s, leaning toward Marxist solidarity with the USSR and favoring a binational, Jewish-Arab, integral Palestine, west of the Jordan. In the 1940s another leftist kibbutz federation, Hakibbutz Hameuhad, was split by internal debates concerning a variety of issues but precipitated, basically, by apparent Mapai leanings toward speedy independence through the necessity of accepting a Palestine partition. The majority group of this split kibbutz federation left Mapai after the war to found Ahdut Avoda, an independent party combining Marxism with nationalist militancy, which later joined Hashomer Hatzair for a time in forming Mapam. The trend of Mapai policy towards immediate independence, even if at the price of partition, served on the other hand to pave the way for Mapai's old foes, the Revisionists, to return to the Zionist political system.[24]

The initial target of Revisionist hostility had been Weizmann's policy of accommodation towards the British. Owing to Mapai's developing entente with Weizmann in the 1920s, the labor leadership also became a primary Revisionist foe and, in consequence, hostility was steadily extended from the major political issue to a broader field. The Revisionists organized a minor rival labor organization and sometimes allied themselves with employers in labor conflicts with the openly proclaimed purpose of "breaking" the Histadrut. The labor Zionists regarded the Revisionists as fascists and, beginning with street brawls, hostilities escalated to a level sometimes threatening civil war. The independence of Israel achieved the main purpose of the militant nationalist underground, it also enabled a Mapai-led government to suppress all dissident paramilitary organization. Owing to these developments, some of the disbanded Revisionist-oriented guerrillas, who were primarily concerned with independence, found their way into a variety of existing political organizations, including Mapai as well as groups of the far left. However, the main body was converted into a civilian right wing party, Herut.[25]

Apart from those Zionists or ultra-Zionists who rejected Mapai hegemony in whole or in part before 1948, there were considerable sections of the Palestine Jewish community who stood more or less outside the Zionist political system, whether because of their principled opposition to it of because it was irrelevant to their daily lives. Roughly speaking, this category consisted of the traditionalist Jewish community of both European and Asian-African or native Palestinian origin, whose social institutions had been established in Palestine long before Zionism appeared and who were still a major part of the Jewish population at the inception of the mandate.

The most resolute opposition to the Zionists came from ultra-Orthodox Ashkenazim from Central and Eastern Europe, a group which had fought all modernizing and secularist trends in the Jewish community since early in the nineteenth century. Since 1912 they were organized increasingly in the anti-Zionist Agudat Israel, which conducted a determined campaign against the idea of a Jewish National Home. This faction and its allies left the organized Jewish community recognized by the mandate government, rejected the authority of the Chief Rabbinate, and sought recognition as a separate community. They no doubt regarded the Labor Zionists as notable examples of the impiety and wickedness of the general Zionist community, but had no specific antipathy to them. When Agudat Israel reached an agreement with the Zionists during the Second World War and subsequently participated in the political institutions of the Jewish state, they were able to adapt to Labor rule with full flexibility, and, in the case of their own labor faction, with some sympathy.[26]

Pious traditionalists of Asian-African descent had less extreme and more varied attitudes than did the Ashkenazi ultra-Orthodox towards the Zionists and their institutions.[27] The Sephardim, resident in the Ottoman Empire for many centuries were integrated in the Muslim social and legal system and the local economy; they dominated the authority structure of the autonomous Jewish community recognized by the Ottoman government. They were disturbed less by the modernizing trends imported by Zionists and others from Europe than by their pretensions to dominance. The Sephardim participated in Zionist political institutions but sought to secure representation at a fixed level as a distinct communal party, especially in the Vaad Leumi. In terms of their economic interests they tended to align themselves with the bourgeois right-wing parties.

On the other hand, the Yemenites, who arrived from Southern Arabia in numbers comparable to the Labor Zionist immigration and who, like them, settled on the land as workers in appreciable numbers, developed close ties with

Socialist workers. They were an object of special attention and concern on the part of both the WZO and Histadrut leadership, and generally held in high regard as an industrious, devoted, and deeply Jewish proletariat. This did not prevent the rise of specific grievances which set them apart as a special, disadvantaged element in the Zionist political system.

A third factor in the political composition of the Asian-African sectors of Palestine Jewry were younger people in the cities, who experienced the usual difficulties of undereducated groups in a modernizing society dominated by an unfamiliar culture. The WZO had little or nothing to do with them and the Histadrut, in spite of the efforts of its trade unions and Working Youth organization, was unable to integrate a considerable part of them into the society. Such elements expressed their maladjustment not only through delinquency, which became a noticeable problem rather late, but also through political activity. The Revisionists, who drew on disaffected Zionists in Poland for their main cadres, recruited Asian-African youngsters in Tel-Aviv or Jerusalem as their shock troops for anti-Histadrut street demonstrations in the 1920s and 1930s. Later these young men and women contributed in large part to those dissident Zionist underground forces who first proclaimed a policy of reprisals against Arab terror and of revolt against Britain, in defiance of the current Labor-led establishment policy.[28]

V

The creation of the state of Israel fundamentally altered the terms and conditions of Mapai domination, or of any effective government, of the political system inherited from Zionism. Not only did a liberation movement assume all functions of government, a problem common to all new nations emerging from a colonial status, but Israel had also to absorb into its traditional patterns a mass of immigrants of diverse backgrounds.[29] Within the twenty-five years following Israel's declaration of independence, the country's population increased fourfold. About three-fifths of the Jewish increase was the result of immigration. The immigrants sharply altered the composition of the Jewish community from a five-to-one dominance of 393,000 European-American over 70,000 Asian-African immigrants in 1948, to a near-equal representation of 704,000 European-American and 675,000 Asian-African immigrants by 1970. The political weight of those of Asian-African background was further increased because native Israeli Jews, a category that rose from roughly a third to nearly half the Jewish population, were by a five-to-four majority the children of Asian-African over European-American fathers, and differential birthrates in the two sectors were increasing this margin. (Native sons of native Israeli fathers still represented no more than one-tenth of the Jewish population in 1970.)

As a consequence of this influx of immigrants, the number who voted in Israeli national elections rose as follows:

1949	440,000
1951	695,000
1955	876,000
1959	994,000
1961	1,037,000
1965	1,245,000
1969	1,428,000

Notwithstanding this explosive growth, and the radically changing backgrounds of the new voters, the patterns of relative party strength and consequently of party dominance, remained substantially unchanged from those of the old Zionist political system. Mapai's share of the votes moved within a narrow range of from 32 to 38 percent of the valid ballots in the first five elections, a level roughly maintained by Mapai's successor, the Labor Alignment in 1965, and rose to 46 percent when Mapam joined in the Labor Alignment for the election of 1969. The several religious parties received a combined vote ranging from 12.5 to 15.4 percent over the same period. The right-wing and bourgeois parties (not including, except in 1961, the 3 to 4 percent in the progressive liberal faction that regularly joined in Mapai-led governments) received from 16.7 to 27.2 percent (in 1961) through the first seven elections, roughly the same proportions as in the 1930s and 1940s. The consequence, a coalition government regularly dominated by Labor, which had characterized the old Zionist political system, continued unchanged in spite of the radically changing electorate.[30]

There is no real mystery about the process that produced such a remarkable absorption into the establishment. A "party key," roughly proportioning each party's strength at the Zionist Congress, was used in determining the distribution of immigration quotas granted by the British, as well as for allocating funds donated by Zionist contributors. Experience in performing one or another recognized Zionist function, as demonstrated by Mizrachi's religious school system and Labor's immigrant training centers and service institutions, was another criterion used in allocating new immigrants to the care of party-controlled organizations. Since these principles continued to govern the access of party institutions to the new immigrants—especially when the bulk of immigrants were without private means and the massive investments needed to absorb them flowed in primarily through government and Zionist channels—the political attachment of new immigrants was initially conditioned by the terms of established arrangements among the old parties.[31]

By such an arrangement, the Histadrut's medical services and insurance fund, Kupat Holim, took care of all immigrants in WZO absorption centers. This service was made available after leaving those centers only on condition of Histadrut membership, which placed a clear premium upon belonging to the Mapai-dominated institutional network. The Chief Rabbinate's jurisdiction over personal status matters, which covered only voluntarily registered adult members of the Jewish community during the mandate (the Muslim clergy had compulsory jurisdiction over all Muslims), was extended in the Jewish state to cover all Jews. The Mizrachi school system was granted responsibility, during the initial period in WZO immigrant absorption centers, for all Yemenites and other communities where a traditional religious orientation was unquestionably universal. This monopoly (not made effective without conflict and powerful resistance) did not extend, to be sure, to settled Israeli citizens, who, as parents, had the right to choose their children's school. Nonetheless, the percentage of Jewish pupils enrolled in state-supported religious schools rose in the 1950s and 1960s to a third or more of the total, from less than a fifth of the total in Vaad Leumi schools in 1944-45.[32] The effectiveness of such factors in producing political integration into the old party networks was primarily demonstrated in those cases where, as nearly as possible, the entire life of an immigrant group was given continuous support and orientation. Thus, the religious parties not only organized schools but built housing developments and provided varied services in those villages (usually grouped close together), small towns, and urban quarters where their adherents were established. The Histadrut, and its component subparties, were even more thoroughly involved as headquarters for such services including, in their case, medical care, trade unions, corporate investment, purchasing, and sales' cooperatives, and other economic and technical facilities.

Parties providing such comprehensive services developed much more than a patron-client relationship with individual constituents. The range and type of service required headquarters planning on a broad political scale, not merely a narrow professional expertise, and it also required on the clients' side the organization of a parallel, locally rooted political structure to mediate the headquarters' services to the public. Wherever such a relationship was established, it produced a strong, flexibly articulated attachment to the sponsoring party, based on a sensitive two-way communications network between central and local organizations.

In the case of minor factions, like the religious parties or Hashomer Hatzair, the bonds of a shared personal belief system, well defined and elaborated, together with strong personal ties between the settlers in segregated, homogeneous villages or neighborhoods, strengthened the local commitment to a party. But such blocs of solid support for minor parties were scattered in small clusters in the national electorate.[33] Mapai's service network, on the other hand, not only dominated the new cooperative villages and development towns where the bulk of immigrants were first settled, it extended through the whole range of the Jewish population, old and new, including the organized workers in the major cities.

This wide-ranging control, however, was won at the cost of both a looser general ideological position and an increasingly impersonal relation between leaders and followers in the party. The consequences of this change in Mapai's internal relationships were far-reaching. Within the Histadrut camp, Mapai's ideological softening provoked sectarian splits in opposition. Outside, opposition was in any case encouraged by the absorption of non-Zionist Israeli citizens into the political system. Arabs who participated in the system, or even cooperated with the ruling party, certainly did so on no real basis of ideological consensus or social attachment, but usually upon calculations of group interest. Outside opposition among Jews rose or fell with the fortunes of bourgeois, of private sector interests, and of the disadvantaged poor who were not integrated into the network of Histadrut-centered relationships.

VI

By 1970, Israelis were, for the most part, a Middle Eastern people, similar in background to the people of the Muslim Arab countries surrounding Israel from which so many of them had recently immigrated. In the surrounding area, attempts to modernize Middle Eastern countries had resulted in politics that were, with few exceptions, authoritarian or dominated by the military. In terms of literacy and technical progress, these modernizing efforts produced comparatively meager results.[34] In Israel, people from this same milieu rose rapidly toward a European standard of literacy, technical skill, and income, while the country as a whole maintained a free, industrializing economy with a growth rate among the highest in the world. Israel's ability to accomplish this, in spite of the heterogeneity and newness of its population and the meagerness of its natural resources, evoked as much early admiration as did its military successes.[35]

Once these accomplishments lost the edge of novelty, Israel's unsolved problems, its stresses and strains engendered by rapid development, drew increasing attention. In spite of the apparently smooth functioning of Israeli democracy, scholarly observers continued to detect possible symptoms of internal collapse. The growth of communal self-consciousness among the Afro-Asians in Israel, spurred by their sharply increased level of expectations and their lower status compared with the better educated, better paid European or American settlers, was often read as an incipient revolt of underprivileged, ethnically segregated masses, of the same kind as was threatening the shaky American social consensus. Israel's galloping inflation, its continual relapse into huge trade deficits that depleted its exchange reserves and threatened its solvency, combined with severe swings in its economic cycles, made the impressively rising GNP, productivity, and per capita income levels seem artificial and precarious as well as entirely dependent on unreliable outside sources of voluntary support. These were omens of domestic tensions that were closely watched by outsiders engaged in calculating the shifting odds in the ongoing Arab-Israeli confrontation.[36]

While these problems, parallel to similar difficulties currently experienced elsewhere, were noted by outsiders, other stresses, specific to the local situation, profoundly concerned Israeli intellectuals and increasingly affected the political behavior of the public. These were in the main the result of deviations from the original ideological and structural principles of the Zionist political system under pressure of the new conditions encountered after independence.

At the very beginning, the leaders and the public had to recognize that the old ideological cadres, particularly the kibbutzim, could no longer channel and control the new immigrants as they had the old. The newcomers were no longer individually recruited, trained, and selected by the kibbutzim in the Diaspora and very few new citizens chose kibbutzim as a method of settlement. The Asian-African communities, which were transferred *en masse*, could not accept a new life style based on detaching young men and women from their extended families; and the European refugees from concentration camps and Russian *kolkhoz* or labor centers were not attracted by what seemed another form of barracks existence.

Instead, the mass of uprooted immigrants in the Zionist-administered tempo-rary camps, apart from those who made their way individually to their relatives or the cities, were resettled in new smallholders' cooperative villages (*moshavim*) or development towns, generally under Histadrut auspices. But to accomplish this task new methods were required which made the new Histadrut settlements differ considerably from their old models and tended to alter the traditional principles and structures of the Histadrut itself.

The old Histadrut settlements had rigorous principles of voluntary, individual commitment to cooperation and collectivism, economic self-management and self-employment, arising out of their own rebellion against the bureaucratic administrative regime that patrons tried to impose on them in their early years as settlers.[37] While the immigrants in the new Histadrut settlements willingly accepted outside instructors and managers and a bureaucratic regime, they also rejected, by a kind of immune reaction, the breakdown of old, traditional bonds, which was the implicit precondition for recomposing an ideologically committed cooperative or collective group by the free, unencumbered choice of individual volunteers.

Thus, the new Histadrut settlements started as administered organizations, in relation to the outside, and retained, internally, traditional social structures, like the *hamula*, or clan organization, as well as their traditional authority figures.[38] Subject to certain adjustments to the new conditions, such as the displacement of old by younger leaders, a traditional leadership mediated the relations between individual settlers and outside agencies like the Histadrut and the WZO, the political parties, and in many respects, the government as well. As a result, the increased personnel needed to handle the newcomers considerably expanded bureaucratic and political career opportunities for the older settlers; in the immigrant-communities a new set of potential party leaders, chosen by tradition-al and not ideological criteria, injected their group and personal claims into the political system.

The policy of the government, WZO, and Histadrut agencies in the new settlements had as its primary aim the integration of immigrant families from different Diaspora backgrounds into an emergent Israeli Jewish community. Outpost settlements founded on this principle soon began to fall apart because of the radically different backgrounds and expectations of the mixed settlers. As a result the agencies fell back on a pattern of a relatively homogeneous settlement, preserving the coherence of immigrant groups by combining them with others in compact clusters. This de facto segregation on quasi-ethnic grounds, reluctantly adopted in bureaucratically-managed settlements and spontaneously developed in the cities, produced the usual gap between educationally and economically disadvantaged immigrants and educationally and economically advantaged old settlers, together with others socially and culturally well-integrated in the more prosperous neighborhoods. A line of division was drawn between Asian-African and European-American Jews, with potentially significant political consequences.[39]

While both Sephardim and Yemenites had conducted quasi-ethnic policies in the old Zionist political system, the specific weight of the Asian-African voters became far greater in Israeli politics than it had been earlier. The attempt to integrate them into the Histadrut network could no longer succeed merely by enrolling individuals in youth movements and trade unions. There was, nonetheless, sufficiently effective integration so that, to this day, attempts by separatist quasi-ethnic Jewish parties to make an impact in the national elections have regularly failed. In good part, the Labor party held these voters; but in order to achieve this, special efforts were necessary to give the Asian-African leadership representation at all levels of the party leadership.[40]

As noted earlier, native-born Israelis of the Asian-African communities were an important source of anti-Labor political sentiment, especially in the cities, where many failed to be integrated into the institutional structure of Histadrut. The great, continuing increase of this segment of the population meant a steady rise in the potential opposition to Labor. The proportions of Labor's plurality have, indeed, decreased owing to such demographic factors. However, the political effect of the erosion has been counterbalanced by changes in the distribution of these opposition votes. Before 1948, the militant right-wing was the main beneficiary of disaffection among the unintegrated. There is now a growing tendency for such voters to express their resentment by supporting leftist opposition factions as well as Herut. This gradual shift reflects the generally widening inequality quotient in Israel's economy, which is perceived by Asian-African militants as a matter of ethnic social discrimination.[41]

The radical changes swiftly proceeding in Israel's economy ever since independence produced additional politically significant effects, directly affecting the ruling party as well as the whole political system. Israel has managed not only to absorb immigrants at an astounding rate, but to secure the impressive level of capital import needed to achieve this, and to invest it with a degree of effectiveness reflected in a notable rise of its productivity as well as its growth rates. But all this involved an emphasis on economic rationality and material incentives which, like the ensuing rise in income inequalities, clashed with certain traditional labor Zionist attitudes in a disturbing and politically consequential way.

Originally, Histadrut unionism was not, like most craft or industrial unions, concerned with the wages and conditions of specific occupational groups as its primary and almost exclusive function.[42] In its classical period, the Histadrut conceived itself as an organized community dedicated to the construction of a Socialist society and a Jewish state; it regarded its members as freely available for all tasks necessary in achieving those aims. Its wage struggles were concerned not so much with the highest possible return for one or another occupational group as with employment opportunities and wage levels that would enable Jews to be workers in Palestine. This meant a virtual denial of autonomy to most craft unions, which were under tight centralized control: it produced a high degree of egalitarianism as well as far-reaching mutual responsibility. The primary attachment of the members was to the organization and objectives of the Histadrut as a whole rather than to the particular group interests represented within it.

After 1948, normal trade union functions grew rapidly in importance. By its firm control of the labor market, the Histadrut protected the established workers from the pressures of mass immigration and also enabled them to accept and gradually absorb the newcomers with unexampled openness.

At the same time, the heightened importance of ordinary trade unionism in the post-1948 Histadrut sharply altered the structures and attitudes which predominated in the organization and the Labor community. Trade unions not only became increasingly detached from central Histadrut control; to the extent that they sought to subordinate particular craft interests to the general economic policy of the Labor government, they sacrificed their influence among workers and sometimes lost control to local, spontaneously organized strike committees. If they succeeded, nevertheless, in their tasks of maintaining and extending the general organization, it was by an elaborate, linked set of agreements, establishing a comprehensive set of differential standards of wages and benefits, craft by craft, and grade by grade of recognized skills.[43] The centralism, egalitarianism, and pioneering voluntarism of the Histadrut community, if not the scope of mutual responsibility within it, were sharply abridged as a consequence.

Only in this way, perhaps, was Israel able to maintain in its population a tolerable level of acceptance for an inflationary pressure that would have been catastrophic in any other country. But the result was to transform the ideological brotherhood which had sustained the old labor Zionists into more nearly a pragmatic coalition of allied interests. The Labor party thus lost, for a considerable period, the adherence of the greater part of the kibbutz movement, which became left-oppositionist. It also lost the general legitimacy which it had enjoyed among right-wing Zionist opponents as a band of pioneers committed to basic Zionist tasks. The attacks from this side, which had never been lacking, were now based on widely supported assumptions that the need for Labor pioneering was a thing of the past, and that the Labor partisans now represented no more than special interest groups, who got far more than their due from the state owing to their well-entrenched political domination.

VII

A series of political reversals following the Yom Kippur War of October 1973 are generally regarded as marking a new era in Israeli politics. What happened, however, was less radical a change than it appeared; it came as the summation of changes foreshadowed by numerous moments of crisis, tracing a long development over Israel's first quarter century.

The basic structural problem of the Israeli political system from the beginning was how to combine a fundamentally elitist, voluntaristic principle of social mobilization with the needs of a mass society and sovereign government. Zionism had achieved remarkable success in recruiting and organizing a relatively large mass under conditions of voluntarism and a high level of commitment, but there were obvious difficulties in imposing this technique all at once on the whole population of a state and an immense, unselected, and unindoctrinated influx of immigrants. The most natural method to adopt was to adjust the old principles to the needs of new areas as far as they could be stretched, while protecting, at least in their original setting, the kibbutz federations and Histadrut network from any fundamental alteration. Another method, which Ben-Gurion insistently advocated, would have been to apply the old principles and employ the old institutions in the emerging new tasks with near-total flexibility, to the point of considering them expendable. The dynamic interplay of these opposed tendencies in the labor movement has been a basic ground theme of Israeli politics.

Ben-Gurion's position has been summed up in the slogan "mamlakhtiyut": that is, "statism," or the transfer to the state of all those functions of social mobilization and all those sentiments of commitment which, in the old Zionist political system, had been vested in the various Zionist parties, the kibbutz federations, and the labor movement.[44] To this end, Ben-Gurion not only forced through the liquidation of partisan military and paramilitary forces and the centralization of all Israeli defense activities in the hands of the government; he also sought as far as possible to retain for the Israel Defense Force an effective relationship to individual Israelis similar to the activist, voluntaristic commitment of the youth movements. "Statism" was to be not only a defensive measure against the potentially fatal divisiveness of pluralism in military organization; it was to appropriate to the state the entire emotional freightage and personal meaning which had, until then, been committed to partisan youth movements and the paramilitary underground.

To carry out a conception like Ben-Gurion's changes in Israel's inherited political procedures were obviously necessary. Whatever intervened between the citizens and the chosen central leadership was a hindrance to his aims. Ben-Gurion pressed persistently and hard, but without success, for an electoral reform that would replace proportional representation by majority elections and eliminate countrywide elections based on indivisible party lists by dividing the country into constituencies directly selecting representatives. Within the hampering restrictions of the traditional system, he sought every available means to secure a wide range of discretion and the possibility of decisive action for the executive leadership. In particular, he fought, with considerable if not unfailing success, for the domination of defense and security services over foreign policy, and for personal control of this area, as prime minister and defense minister, free from tight supervision by his own or coalition party leaders.

Ben-Gurion's design required a direct tie of mutual reliance between the chief executive and the electorate and between the chief executive and the bureaucratic elite; in both cases, by shortcutting the traditional connection through the parties. At one point, during his first retirement from the Cabinet in 1954, he was strongly attracted by the notion of a national party, which would run him as a candidate or the people as a whole, rather than by a party machine.[45] While this idea was abandoned, Ben-Gurion was able to attach to himself a distinct faction of young army commanders, professional managers, and young leaders of the Asian-African communities more or less outside the standard, traditional cadres of party leadership or disaffected from them. The drive of Ben-Gurion's leadership and conceptions energized this group in a number of political rebellions which they attempted against the establishment, while remaining within it. These efforts culminated in the creation of the Rafi party in 1965, which significantly changed the odds and shifted the balance-point of the political game in Israel.[46] While the Rafi defection, together with the demand for majority elections, went down to defeat, the major parties were themselves realigning in a way that reduced the leverage of minor parties.

One issue that had provoked Ben-Gurion to create Rafi, eroding Mapai on the right, had been the decision to enlarge the Labor coalition for the 1965 elections by an agreement for union with the kibbutz-centered Ahdut Avodah on the left. In advance of the same elections, two right-wing parties, Herut and the Liberals, formed a similar joint list, Gahal. Like the Labor merger, this right-wing joining of forces produced a split of its own. The Independent Progressives opted out of the union with right-wing bourgeois Zionists in the Liberal party, which they had maintained from 1961 to 1965. This trend continued in later years. In 1968, the Labor party was extended to include a reunited Rafi, with the loss of a right-wing minority in that party who, with Ben-Gurion, persisted in opposition. In advance of the 1969 elections, Mapam joined in the Labor Alignment, with comparable losses on the left. Gahal also experienced continued growth by joining outside factions, at the marginal cost of some of its own, in a right-wing alignment, the Likud. The net result in the elections of 1973 was that the vote was divided between the two major groupings; the left-wing coalition now outnumbered the right-wing alternative party by no more than five to four.

The consolidation of major alternatives in Israeli politics thus, to some degree, carried out an element of Ben-Gurion's design, but hardly in the utopian form he had envisioned. His ideal of a direct bond between citizens and state, and a direct, charismatic, representative relation between the leader and his people implied the detachment of their loyalties from such intermediary bodies as the political parties and movements. Indeed certain trends in Israel's development favored the growth of independent voting. The rapid expansion of the civil service into areas and functions foreign to the old Zionist political system, as well as the expanded importance of economic considerations in both public and private sectors of society, called into being a crop of young Western-educated and American-oriented Israeli experts who were estranged from Israel's East European Socialist traditions. A majority of this group grew up within the Labor party and Histadrut network, but outside the traditional party channels of political advancement. Others belonged to a growing segment of the public not institutionally committed to any party, but who were essentially independent in social and economic terms. Such voters were neither numerous enough to build a ruling party for Ben-Gurion, nor were they united in this purpose. Instead, the pressures they exerted were absorbed by the system, though only through changes within each major party and in the relationships between the parties.

Gahal (not to mention the Likud) is far from being the old Herut. The impeccably militant activist party which attracted the disadvantaged and disaffected whom the establishment had failed to integrate is now joined with moderate, even dovish, and well-established bourgeois Liberals. The disadvantaged and disaffected now divide their votes between Herut and their own relatively leftist ethnic factions, as well as other left-leaning anti-establishment parties. The floating independent voters, too, continue to distribute their support among a variety of parties, but the margin by which they shifted to the right, under the exceptionally favorable circumstances of the 1973 election, was not sufficient to displace Labor from its dominance or make Gahal the nucleus for an alternative governing coalition.[b]

The growing pressure of disaffection and political independence has been effective in other ways in recent Israeli politics. Mass action by *ad hoc* pressure groups—for example, protest demonstrations by ethnic or religious militants, or wildcat strikes in defiance of the Histadrut—have become a recognized institution in Israeli life, and a proven method for extracting desired adjustments of policy from the establishment. On two major occasions, when a major collapse of public confidence coincided with internal pressures for a change in leadership in the establishment itself, popular pressure produced significant structural changes on the political scene.

---

[b]Pending the availability of a full analysis, conclusions regarding the 1973 election reflect impressions drawn from the raw data of results.

In the two weeks before the Six-Day War of 1967, public concern and apprehension about the situation became so acute, and the confidence in Prime Minister Eshkol among Mapai leaders was so low, that emergency measures fundamentally altering the pattern of politics were taken. Moshe Dayan came in as defense minister as the choice of the people, not the Labor establishment, and a national government was hastily assembled, in which for the first time Herut was acknowledged as a possible coalition partner.[47]

Following the Yom Kippur War, the public mood sank to depths of anxiety and frustration comparable to those of the two weeks of waiting in May-June 1967, and sharply contrasting with the confident mood that preceded the Arab surprise attack.[48] Yet, in the election which followed shortly after the war, the losses of Labor were so limited, and so distributed, that again a Labor-led coalition was the only possibility, other than a national union government. The voters continued to support the system, however disaffected they were with its leaders. That disaffection, however, spurred by the release of the first Agranat Committee report on Israeli prewar planning and intelligence, compelled the resignation of almost the entire old Mapai leadership in the Cabinet, as well as of Moshe Dayan. Other parties were subject to similar quakes and tremors, even though, as opposition parties without governmental responsibility, they were not compelled to yield full satisfaction to the pressures of discontent.

The Rabin government was constituted after the war and the elections on a knife-edge of insecure political superiority. Its precarious tenure of power was not radically remedied by an agreement that brought in Mizrachi's ten votes at the cost of minor defections of independent coalition partners. The war, and the inconclusive situation that ended it, left Israel with a still larger per capita debt than its immense prewar burden; with a rate of inflation and mounting economic pressure upon the public barely conceivable in other functioning societies; with a military budget taking a share of GNP matched only in Egypt; and with personal obligations for extended military service rising well beyond a prewar level of demands on the citizenry which hardly any other country would dare to imagine.

These conditions unquestionably kept Israelis under acute, sustained tension. The strain was expressed politically by mass protests against withdrawal from defensive positions prior to a formal peace agreement or, at least, an Arab declaration of nonbelligerency. Some opponents of the government vigorously resisted any retreat from areas considered part of the Jewish state in antiquity.

Yet the known terms for a final settlement announced by the Labor party and the Rabin government, as well as the government itself, enjoyed a reasonable level of support. A majority of the public, according to opinion polls taken in the spring of 1974, was prepared to yield some territory for peace, believed that Egypt was interested in peace, supported the government's separation of forces agreement with Syria—even while the population did not believe that Syria wanted peace, or that Arabs generally were interested in the kind of "real" peace that Israel could accept, and were increasingly convinced of the imminence of renewed warfare. The government enjoyed its greatest popularity in March 1975, when it defied Secretary of State Henry Kissinger; only such a demonstration of firmness, rather than the heavy-handed American reaction which followed, gave the Rabin government the needed support to retreat to new lines of military and diplomatic defense in September.

These responses strongly suggest that public support for the government extends only to the limited elasticity of its officially proclaimed policy, but not to any major retreat from it under American pressure. The prospects of future Israeli political development, therefore, depend critically on decisions that will be made by outside powers, and particularly America. Fear of another war, accompanied by a renewed oil boycott and confrontation with the Soviets, are the considerations said to dictate the current American policy of "evenhandedly" tilting toward the Arabs. The very same fear places evident limits upon such a policy, for war with all its consequences would be the easily predictable result of overstraining the Israeli public's extraordinary endurance.

The parameters of the specific equations for war or peace between Israel and the Arabs have been clearly established ever since the 1967 war. Israel can have "peace" from the Arabs, according to the Khartoum resolutions essentially reiterated at Rabat, only by ceasing to exist. The nonbelligerency which the Arab states might negotiate (but not with Israel directly) in return for Israeli withdrawal to its 1967 borders, would leave a Palestine guerrilla state with general Arab support, free and committed to carry out the ultimate "de-Zionization" (i.e., liquidation) of the Jewish state. As for the peace Israel offers to the Arabs, it depends on negotiations prior to an Israeli withdrawal to secure and recognized boundaries, to be defined in a formal peace treaty.

These mutually incompatible positions implicitly define the conditions under which war has occurred in the past and under which in the future, *rebus sie stantibus*, it will predictably break out. An Arab-initiated war might occur when continued suspension of hostilities makes the goal of de-Zionizing Israel by stages begin to seem unattainable. An Israeli-initiated war might occur in circumstances which are perceived as an imminent threat to the basic security of the state.

The sole common denominator of the opposed positions is that a perception of Israeli weakness is needed to trigger a war; and the single reliable safeguard against renewed hostilities, under existing conditions, is that both Arabs and Israelis should see Israel as relatively strong. While this may preserve the truce, barring a fundamental change, the fundamental position makes war at all times the most likely ultimate outcome. Only Israel's collapse or a true acceptance of Israel by the Arabs, on the same terms as they accept other non-Arab states, could eliminate or, given Israel's survival, reduce the chances of war to those normal between neighboring states. In anticipation of these developments, the Arabs live in fear of Israel's increased strength and consolidation and in hope of the moment of Israel's relative weakness or inner demoralization. On the other hand, the Israelis live in fear of diminished security and in hope of a basic change of Arab attitudes, leading to unconditional negotiations and a peace without reservations.

After the 1967 war, the Johnson administration (having witnessed the collapse of the Eisenhower-Dulles-engineered UN arrangements for Israeli withdrawal, without being able to make good the U.S. guarantees to Israel that accompanied it) adopted the position that a formal, negotiated peace establishing secure and recognized borders should be the condition for Israeli withdrawal. The Nixon administration swung to what was called an "evenhanded" policy and, after a few false starts, achieved a cease-fire in the renewed artillery and air war across the Suez Canal. The embarrassing disclosure of the Soviet and Arab emplacement of missiles in violation of the agreement discouraged further pressure on Israel. After the 1972 election, Dr. Kissinger became secretary of state, and began to work cautiously toward "proximity talks," if not direct negotiations, between Israel and Egypt in the hope of starting some movement, perhaps by interim agreements for limited Israeli withdrawal and Egyptian reopening of the Suez Canal.

This procedure was a concession to the Israeli viewpoint which aroused sharp apprehension in Egypt; having carefully prepared a comprehensive political and military plan for achieving local superiority and tactical surprise, President Sadat and his allies launched the Yom Kippur War. The shock of this unforeseen event, and the extensive damage to inter-NATO relationships and Western economies which it brought about, prompted Kissinger to return to "evenhandedness."

It is now too late for any real peace agreement to emerge directly from the 1973 Arab-Israeli War. The precondition for such a peace, or any serious approach to it, is that the Arabs, rather than Israelis, believe that they need it. The situation immediately before the war and even more at its close, with Israelis and Egyptian forces perilously intertwined and with Damascus under Israeli guns, was such that Arabs as well as Jews needed a formally negotiated settlement—that is, the kind of meeting which both Arabs and Israelis perceived as at least an approach to peace. But the course of the fighting, the diplomatic encirclement of Israel, and the oil embargo which accompanied it, as well as the Arab-American rapprochement that followed, sharply inflated confidence in Arab countries, not least of all in Egypt. The kinds of disengagements that were arranged remove any pressure forcing Arabs to negotiate on the basis of recognizing Israel.

The calculation underlying current American policy is that war must be prevented by allaying Arab fears of a stalemate through exerting pressure on Israel for continual, more or less unilateral, concessions. To make this palatable to Israel and also to forestall Arab anticipations of a significant decline in Israel's relative strength, American resupply, military and economic aid, and, in the last resort, guarantees would offer compensation for the surrender, without significant political gains, of territorial defensive positions. It is a by-product of such a policy, but by no means an unintended consequence, not only that Israel becomes more dependent and hence presumably more manageable, but that Egypt shift significantly away from the USSR and toward the United States.

The assumption that rationalizes the policy for Americans in terms of its bearing on peace, which is a goal deliberately set aside as an immediate objective, is that interim agreements presented by Arabs as purely military in character will slowly reduce the war fever in the Middle East and accustom the area to *de facto* peacefulness. Neither the Arabs nor the Israelis believe that this is really what is happening. The Arab rationalization is that continuing American pressure on Israel and their own increasing strength, considerably enhanced by the American connection, will bring Israel to its knees, whether by reducing it to military inferiority or, more likely, (especially because of the nuclear capability the Arabs believe Israel to possess) through the corroding effects of inner deterioration. The Israeli rationalization is that, given the latest change in American policy, peace is not immediately attainable and Israeli security depends on keeping closely enough in harmony with the Americans to obtain vitally needed military equipment and economic assistance.

To manage this complicated relationship is a problem of extreme delicacy and difficulty for all parties, but especially so for America and Israel. It is not enough that war is an ultimate calamity that all three parties, together with a good part of the rest of the world, seek to avoid. Egypt still counts on Israel's weakness. The Americans and Israelis alike can hope for a sustained truce, let alone an ultimate peace, only if Israel's strength remains adequate to all the extraordinary demands made upon it. But Americans, especially diplomatic and military experts who are fatally attracted by submissiveness and malleability in client states, do not appreciate, as the Israelis do, the crucial importance of a sense of self-reliance and independence in the compound that makes up Israeli strength. To understand this is vital if mistakes of the gravest consequence are to be avoided.

Not only sympathy, which America has in abundance, but deep understanding, which has often been sadly lacking, are needed for effective policy in relation to a state in the extraordinary position of Israel. The American failure in this regard has been painfully evident in numerous unpleasant and unnecessary clashes in the past. In view of the critical nature of the current situation, State Department expertise in Arab culture and politics ought to be balanced by something other than superficial acquaintance with Israel, and its relation to the long, troubled history of the Jews.

Notes

1. Unlike the 1956 and 1967 Arab-Israeli hostilities, which were followed by an immediate outpouring of books, the 1973 outbreak evoked few full-scale

instant analyses. Apart from Walter Laqueur's *Confrontation: the Middle East and World Politics* (New York: Bantam, 1974) the collective account by the London *Times'* "Insight" team, and Bernard and Marvin Kalbs' *Kissinger* (Boston: Little Brown, 1974), the analyses were mainly official, like the Agranat Commission's reports in Israel, or were current reports on specific postwar issues, such as the strategic alert of late October 1973 or the postwar balance of military forces.

2. Of the survey literature on the pre 1948 period, Frank E. Manuel, *The Realities of American-Palestine Relations* (Washington: Public Affairs Press, 1949) is uneven but most comprehensive, and J.C. Hurewitz, *The Struggle for Palestine* (New York, Norton, 1950) remains reliable in its coverage of the period of the Palestine Mandate. Solid studies of special topics in this period produced more recently include: John A. De Novo, *American Interests and Policies in the Middle East, 1900-1939* (Minneapolis: University of Minnesota Press, 1963); Joseph Schechtman, *The United States and the Jewish State Movement; the Crucial Decade: 1939-1949* (New York: Herzl Press, 1966); Joseph L. Grabill, *Protestant Diplomacy in the Near East* (Minneapolis: University of Minnesota Press, 1971); and Hertzel Fishman, *American Protestantism and a Jewish State* (Detroit: Wayne State University Press, 1973); John Snetsinger, *Truman, the Jewish Vote and the Creation of Israel* (Stanford: Hoover Institution Press, 1974); and a 1974 Brandeis dissertation by Zvi Ganin, *The Diplomacy of the Weak: American Zionist Leadership in the Truman Era.*

American-Israeli relations have not been covered comprehensively in a reliable source, but special topics like the Sinai-Suez war of 1956 and the Six-Day War of 1967, and American policy in each, have been treated in a voluminous literature. For general coverage, see the pertinent sections of John C. Campbell, *Defense of the Middle East* (New York: Harper, 1958); J.C. Hurewitz (ed.), *Soviet-American Rivalry in the Middle East* (New York: Praeger, 1969); and Nadav Safran, *From War to War: the Arab-Israeli Confrontation, 1948-1967* (New York: Pegasus, 1969).

3. The best discussion is in Ganin, *Diplomacy of the Weak.* See also Ben Halpern, *The Idea of the Jewish State* (Cambridge, Mass.: Harvard University Press, 1961), pp. 360-375, and Nadav Safran, *The United States and Israel* (Cambridge, Mass.: Harvard University Press, 1963), pp. 35-46.

4. Cf. Richard Nolte, "United States Policy and the Middle East," in the American Assembly (Georgiana G. Stevens, ed.), *The United States and the Middle East* (Englewood Cliffs, N.J.: Prentice-Hall, 1964), pp. 151-161.

5. For a concise and characteristic statement, see Lincoln P. Bloomfield and Amelia C. Leiss, "Arms Transfer and Arms Control," in J.C. Hurewitz (ed.), *Soviet-American Rivalry*, p. 45.

6. See Esco Foundation for Palestine, Inc., *Palestine: A Study of Jewish, Arab, and British Policies* (New Haven: Yale University Press, 1947), I, 334-366, for a concisely comprehensive description; see also Ben Halpern, "The Anti-Zionist Phobia: Legal Style," *Midstream* (June 1965).

7. Moshe Burstein, *Self-Government of the Jews in Palestine since 1900* (Tel Aviv: Bloch, 1934) remains the only comprehensive study of the Jewish community organization under the mandate.

8. The only full-scale scholarly study of an Israeli party is Peter Y. Medding, *Mapai in Israel: Political Organization and Government in a New Society* (Cambridge: Cambridge University Press, 1972). A related study of Israeli religious parties, Gary S. Schiff, *Tradition and Politics*, presently awaits publication. Official, textbook histories of other parties are Peretz Merhav, *The Israeli Left* (available in Several European languages, awaiting English publication), and Joseph B. Schechtman and Yehuda Benari, *History of the Revisionist Movement*, Vol. I, 1925-1930 (Tel Aviv: Hadar, 1970).

9. No complete study of these subjects is available, but see Joseph Adler, *The Herzl Paradox* (New York: Hadrian Press, 1962), pp. 36-60, and Joseph B. Schechtman, *Fighter and Prophet*, Vol. II (New York: T. Yoseloff, 1961), pp. 139-183.

10. Cf. Norman L. Zucker, *The Coming Crisis in Israel* (Cambridge, Mass.: MIT Press, 1973), pp. 153 ff.

11. The literature on this subject is large and rather diffuse. For reliable representative accounts at various stages of a rather long history, see, e.g., Arthur Ruppin, *Three Decades of Palestine* (Tel Aviv: Schocken, 1936), pp. 26 ff., 35 ff.; Alex Bein, *The Return to the Soil* (Jerusalem: Youth and Hechalutz Department, 1952); Ferdynand Zweig, *The Israeli Worker* (New York: Herzl Press, 1959); and Alan Arian, *Ideological Change in Israel* (Cleveland: Press of Case Western Reserve University, 1968).

12. Ben Halpern, "Hekhalutz," *Jewish Frontier* 12, 2 (February 1975), pp. 24-28.

13. See, in addition to references in note 11, Walter Preuss, *Die Juedische Arbeiterbewegung in Palastina* (Vienna: Fiba Verlag, 1936); G. Muenzner, *Jewish Labour Economy in Palestine* (Tel Aviv: Jewish Agency for Palestine, 1943); and Haim Barkai, "The Public, Histadrut, and Private Sectors in the Israeli Economy," in the Falk Project for Economic Research in Israel, *Sixth Report, 1961-1963* (Jerusalem: Falk Foundation, 1964).

14. Marver Bernstein, *The Politics of Israel* (Princeton: Princeton University Press, 1957), pp. 80-92.

15. For the most careful analysis of Israeli voting patterns, see Alan Arian (ed.), *The Elections in Israel, 1969* (Jerusalem: Jerusalem Academic Press, 1972).

16. Cf., Amitai Etzioni, " 'Kulturkampf' ou Coalition: le Cas d'Israel," *Revue Francaise de Science Politique* 8, no. 2 (June 1958), 311-335.

17. The attempts to classify Israeli parties on a left-right spectrum, using a small number of crucial issues, are surveyed in Arian, *Ideological Change*, pp. 29 ff. One would have to question Arian's classification of Ahdut Avoda as nonactivist.

18. For a brief account, see Medding, *Mapai*, pp. 6-13.

19. See Leonard J. Fein, *Politics in Israel* (Boston, Little, Brown, 1967), pp. 173 ff.

20. See Amos Perlmutter, *Military and Politics in Israel* (New York: Praeger, 1969) for a comprehensive and informed, while occasionally over-colored, account; also V.D. Segre, *Israel, a Society in Transition* (New York: Oxford University Press, 1971).

21. See Walter Laqueur, *A History of Zionism* (New York: Holt, Rhinehart and Winston, 1972), Ch. 6; also Medding, *Mapai*, pp. 22 ff.; and Arian, *Ideological Change*, pp. 58-91 ff.

22. For a brief contemporary account, see Abraham Revusky, *Jews in Palestine* (New York: Vanguard, 1945), pp. 196-198.

23. Ben Halpern, *Idea of the Jewish State*, pp. 31-45.

24. For very partial coverage of these developments, see Laqueur, *History* Ch. 6; J.C. Hurewitz, *The Struggle for Palestine* (New York: Norton, 1950), pp. 156 ff., 195 ff.; and Esco Foundation, *Palestine*, II, 1098 ff.

25. Laqueur, *History* Ch. 8. I am unable to suggest a reasonably satisfactory reference in English, or another European language, for more recent developments.

26. See Gary S. Schiff, *Tradition and Politics*; also Halpern, *Idea of the Jewish State*, pp. 84-86.

27. See Burstein, *Self-Government*; also Halpern, *Idea of the Jewish State*, pp. 114 ff.

28. For the continuation of the trend in later years, see Moshe Lissak, "Continuity and Change in the Voting Patterns of Oriental Jews," in Arian, *Elections in Israel*, pp. 264 ff.

29. For an analysis of demographic influences on Israeli politics, see Judah Matras, *Social Change in Israel* (Chicago, Aldine, 1965).

30. Herbert Smith, "Analysis of Voting," in Arian, *Elections in Israel*, pp. 63 ff.

31. See Benjamin Akzin, "The Role of Parties in Israeli Democracy," in S.N. Eisenstadt, Rivkah Bar Yosef, and Chaim Adler (eds.), *Integration and Development in Israel*, (Jerusalem: Israel Universities Press, 1970), pp. 9-46.

32. See Zucker, *The Coming Crisis*, Chs. 1, 3, 4, 7-10; also, Aharon F. Kleinberger, *Society, Schools and Progress in Israel* (Oxford: Pergamon Press, 1969), Ch. 3; and Great Britain, Colonial Office, *The System of Education of the Jewish Community in Palestine* (London, 1946), p. 103.

33. As Gary S. Schiff, *Tradition and Politics*, points out, the clustering is particularly marked among Mizrachi and Aguda voters. Supporters of Hapoel Hamizrahi, the religious workers, are more widely spread, and the organization exercises functions more or less parallel to those of Mapai and other Labor parties.

34. See Manfred Halpern, *The Politics of Social Change in the Middle East*

and North Africa (Princeton: Princeton University Press, 1963); Daniel Lerner, *The Passing of Traditional Society* (Glencoe, Illinois: Free Press, 1958); and J.C. Hurewitz, *Middle East Politics: the Military Dimension* (New York: Praeger, 1969).

35. See Howard Pack, *Structural Change and Economic Policy in Israel* (New Haven, Yale University Press, 1971), Ch. 8.

36. Georges Friedmann, *The End of the Jewish People?* (New York: Doubleday, 1967), pp. 131 ff., 146 ff., 272 ff.

37. See D. Weintraub, M. Lissak, and Y. Azmon, *Moshava, Kibbutz and Moshav* (Ithaca: Cornell University Press, 1969), and Murray Weingarten, *Life in a Kibbutz* (New York: Reconstructionist Press, 1955).

38. Albert Meister, *Principes et tendances de la planification rurale en Israel* (Paris: Mouton, 1962); Alex Weingrod, *Reluctant Pioneers* (Ithaca: Cornell University Press, 1966); and Dorothy Willner, *Nation-Building and Community in Israel* (Princeton: Princeton University Press, 1969).

39. See Carl Frankenstein (ed.), *Between Past and Future* (Jerusalem: Henrietta Szold Foundation for Child and Youth Welfare, 1953); the section on "Cultural Assimilation and Tensions in Israel," *International Social Science Bulletin* 8, 1 (1956); Giora Hanoch, "Income Differentials in Israel," in Falk Project *Fifth Report*, 1959-61 (Jerusalem: Falk Foundation, 1961); and Irving Howe and Carl Gershman (eds.), *Israel, the Arabs, and the Middle East* (New York: Bantam Books, 1972), pp. 45 ff., 125 ff.

40. Medding, *Mapai*, pp. 37-39, 68-72.

41. The careful analysis of the 1969 elections by Moshe Lissak, in "Continuity and Change in the Voting Patterns of Oriental Jews," in Arian, *The Elections in Israel*, pp. 264-277, will have to be revised to take account of stronger leftist tendencies apparent in the as yet unanalyzed returns of the 1973 elections.

42. See Ben Halpern, "The Problems of Israeli Socialism," in Howe and Gershman, *Israel, the Arabs, and the Middle East*, pp. 45-68.

43. See Sweig, *The Israeli Worker*, pp. 132-182, and Alex Rubner, *The Economy of Israel* (London: Cass, 1960), pp. 40 ff., 52 ff.

44. See Avraham Avi-hai, *Ben Gurion, State Builder* (Jerusalem: Israel Universities Press, 1974), and Perlmutter, *Military and Politics*.

45. On this and related matters, see the diaries of Moshe Sharett, excerpts published serially in the weekend edition of the Israeli newspaper *Maariv* during the spring and summer 1974.

46. Medding, *Mapai*, pp. 275-298.

47. See David Kimche and Dan Bawley, *The Six-Day War* (New York: Stein and Day, 1971), pp. 134 ff.

48. See Louis Guttman and Shlomit Levy, "The Home Front and the Yom Kippur War," in the 1974 *Yearbook of the Encyclopedia Judaica*.

XIV Political and Economic Trends in North Africa

Malcolm H. Kerr

Contrary to fashion, for purposes of the analysis of public affairs I have concluded that North Africa is little more than a geographical expression. To be sure, Morocco, Algeria, Tunisia, and Libya all share a common Arabo-Islamic history and culture; the first three of them share a French colonial legacy; and a number of general problems are common to all four. Yet each of them has a highly distinctive personality, geography, economy, social structure, political system, and place in the world. Their interactions are surprisingly slight: they trade little with each other, and it would probably be fair to say that politically as well as commercially, they are each usually moe preoccupied with their relations with Europe and the great powers than with each other. There has been frequent talk about Maghrib unity, and yet, with one brief exception, at no time has there been any serious prospect that in practice this would extend beyond piecemeal cooperation in selected nonpolitical fields, and a general display of good neighborliness.

In the light of these realities, I have generally avoided discussion of North African problems on an areawide basis, or even on a consistently comparative one, apart from some brief remarks in the conclusion. The bulk of this study is devoted to a country-by-country analysis of salient recent events and prospects in the political and economic fields. Some comments on the relevance of North African problems to the United States and its international policies are also offered in the conclusion.

Morocco

Among the four North African states Morocco possesses the most complex society and the most difficult set of internal political, economic, and social problems. Its population of seventeen million (in 1975), the largest in the area, includes a Berber minority of about 40 percent and is also divided between nomadic and settled, mountain and plain, rural and urban, as well as between regional particularisms and between rival traditional political leaderships. Since gaining independence in 1956 from France and Spain, Morocco has experienced a continuing atmosphere of political crisis and a stagnating economy; only in the last few years has the latter shown signs of modest upturn.

*Historical Background: Evolution of
Monarchical Dominance*

Several brief observations may be made about the significance of the period of the French protectorate of 1912-1956 (accompanied by a Spanish protectorate over the northern coastal strip). This was a much briefer period of colonial rule than that experienced by Algeria and Tunisia, and it was superimposed over an indigenous political system that had ancient roots and which the French encouraged and manipulated for purposes of their own. This indigenous system was presided over by the Sultan, heir to the Alawite dynasty dating from 1666 which had (unlike its other North African counterparts) been untroubled by the Ottoman Empire and maintained its own full sovereignty. However, the Sultan had traditionally governed not through an undisputed central control, but by juggling quasi-feudal interests, suppressing provincial dissidents, and relying on his considerable religious prestige to exercise a patrimonial arbitration among various segments of his society.

The French themselves capitalized on the divisions within the society, pacifying the rural areas by military means and then seeking to placate provincial clans and leaders by offering them renewed status under French patronage. The traditional royal court and the vizierial cabinet (*makhzen*) of the sultan were left intact, with the sultan as a useful national figurehead acquiescing in French rule, while the major responsibilities of government such as internal security, defense, finance, and economic affairs were taken over by the French under the authority of their governor general. An important modern commercial and agricultural sector sprang up in the hands of French settlers, who by 1956 numbered some 350,000.

Unlike the situation in Algeria, Moroccan political and social institutions were preserved, which meant that traditionally privileged classes remained intact, notably the commercially and culturally dominant Arab bourgeoisie of the cities of Fez and Rabat and the Berber tribal notables of the countryside. Unlike the Tunisian case, however, internal social evolution was very slight and social elites were neither infused with fresh blood by upwardly mobile lower groups nor did many of them receive modern French education or gain access to modern administrative and professional careers. Government employment came to be overwhelmingly French; in 1945 Moroccans occupied only 26 percent of 20,492 administrative jobs, mostly at the bottom of the scale. Similarly, between 1912 and 1955 only about 1,000 Moroccans completed modern secondary schools and obtained the French baccalauréat.[1] Furthermore, among those who did receive French education, urban Arabs in the great majority of cases attended one set of schools in Fez and Rabat, while the sons of Berber notables attended another, thus deepening previous social cleavages. A number of sons of rural families, mainly Berber, attended the French military academy at Meknès and were to remain markedly loyal to France until the moment of independence.

The urban Arab educated elements, both the beneficiaries of French education and those continuing to attend traditional Islamic schools such as the Qarawiyin mosque-university in Fez, combined to form the backbone of the national independence movement in the 1940s and 1950s, the Istiqlal ("Independence") party. By the 1950s they found increasing encouragement from Sultan Mohammed V, a process which culminated in the French authorities deposing and exiling the sultan with the help of a number of provincial Berber lords. When the French found themselves constrained to bring back the sultan in 1955 and grant independence in 1956, the sultan (henceforth retitled king) found himself a national martyr with unprecedented prestige.

Mohammed V sought for a number of years to share his authority in newly independent Morocco with both the Istiqlal and other leaders, but, unprepared as he was to see his monarchical role reduced to that of a constitutional figurehead and unwilling as the Istiqlal leaders were to accept a tame role as royal viziers in modern guise, an impasse developed. In 1959 the Istiqlali prime minister, Abdullah Ibrahim, joined a group of young secularly minded intellectuals and trade union leaders to break away from the Istiqlal and form the Union Nationale des Forces Populaires (UNFP), charging the rump Istiqlal (largely the more traditionally minded elements) with excessive caution, compliance with the Palace, and disinterest in social reform.

Political Evolution Under Hassan II

King Mohammed V's death in 1961 brought to the throne his French-educated son Hassan II, who was to seek in succeeding years more vigorously than his father to strengthen and consolidate the grip of the monarch over national affairs in the face of party competition, though without the advantage enjoyed by his father as a nationalist hero.

In this effort Hassan has succeeded remarkably well, and he has confounded repeated predictions that the demise of his regime was at hand. He has effectively neutralized the political parties, while building up an elite class of individuals who are unaffiliated to party or ideology but dependent on the throne for their livelihood, to staff the ministries. His main instruments of rule have included patronage, repression, diversionary gestures, and, until 1971, the army.

The Patronage System. The king sits at the apex of a vast system of clientelism, services and rewards, enticements, and manipulations, which has deep roots in Moroccan political and social traditions, yet which he has elaborated as a special monument to his own reign.[2] By occasionally dangling the prospect of participation in government, or at least a share in the material spoils, in the face of individual leaders of political parties, the king is able to blunt much of the potential opposition to the system that the parties would otherwise represent. Cooptation of prominent Istiqlal members by appointing them to ambassadorships, diversion to others of privileged business opportunities, etc., are also familiar instances of this strategy. It goes without saying that government by patronage in Morocco effectively precludes sustained attachment to programs of reform and development.

Repression. Again acting within established tradition, Hassan has not hesitated to balance carrots with sticks and, more particularly, to deal severely with perpetrators of disorder and challengers of the system. The brutal treatment by the police of student rioters in 1965, with several hundred casualties; the kidnapping and murder of UNFP leader Mahdi Ben Barka by the security service in the same year; their use of torture against political dissidents; the summary imprisonment of labor leader Ben Siddiq in 1967 for criticizing the government; the waves of arrests, mass treason trials, executions, and imprisonments meted out to UNFP members and others in the 1970s, have taught many Morroccans that opposition politics are a dangerous business.

Diversionary Gestures. King Hassan has established himself as a master tactician in his ability to gain political mileage out of public relations gambits in foreign and domestic affairs. Recent examples include the dispatch of Moroccan troops to Syria, where they were on hand to fight against Israel in the 1973 war, and the hosting of the Organization of the African Unity summit conference in 1972 and that of the Arab League in 1974, all of which greatly strengthened his reputation for statesmanship and averted the thought from potentially rebellious minds that in the wake of the 1971 and 1972 coup attempts against him, he was isolated, friendless, and unappreciated among the leaders of Africa and the Arab world. Again, in 1974-75 he exhibited his skill as a tactician, and bought himself valuable time and credit, by his abortive promise of parliamentary elections. Simultaneously, he displayed his nationalist militancy in pressing Morocco's claim of sovereignty over the sparsely populated but phosphate-rich Spanish Sahara, a cause on which all political groupings from right to left had no choice but to fall in line loyally behind him: the Communist leader Ali Yata even allowed himself to serve as the king's personal representative to the Eastern

European states to argue Morocco's claim to the Sahara there. Meanwhile, the Saharan question served King Hassan as a pretext for postponing the elections: national unity had to be preserved until the crisis was resolved in Morrocco's favor.

At the same time, Hassan sidestepped a military confrontation with Spain and pursued an adroit diplomatic strategy. First, he demanded an advisory opinion from the International Court of Justice as to whether the Sahara had been under Moroccan sovereignty before the advent of Spanish colonial rule in 1884. When the Court issued a ruling in October 1975 that fell short of sustaining Moroccan claims, Hassan's next move was to organize a march of tens of thousands of unarmed Moroccan civilians across the border—and then, as the price of their recall, to extract a favoráble diplomatic settlement from Spain. This bargain, reached in Madrid on November 14 amidst much secrecy, provided for Spanish abandonment of the Sahara and the staging of a referendum in conditions that seemed calculated to assure a vote in favor of dividing the territory between Morocco and Mauritania, in exchange for various Moroccan diplomatic and economic favors to Spain. King Hassan had been shrewd enough to display nationalist militancy and, at the same time, negotiate an excellent deal without firing a shot, taking advantage of the Spanish government's apparent desire to strengthen the hand of conservative Morocco against the rival demand of revolutionary Algeria that the Saharan population be granted self-determination. It was a masterly stroke of policy, consolidating the king's domestic position and gaining what promised to be a notable triumph for the country in foreign policy—provided only that the Algerians could somehow be induced to accept the fait accompli. At the end of November 1975, the issue still remained in doubt.

Military Support. Until 1971 it was generally taken for granted that whatever the disillusionment of many Moroccans with the prevalence of corruption in the regime and its failure to enact real reforms, the king retained the loyal support of the top echelons of the army. There were various reasons for this. He had himself served as commander in chief when he was crown prince, and had hand-picked key officers for promotion; after he became king, these officers were generously treated and effectively integrated into the network of Palace favors and emoluments, some of them becoming wealthy men. Again, almost all of the senior officers—colonels and generals—were Berbers who had served loyally in the French armed forces before 1956, who came from provincial and sometimes austere backgrounds, and who had little incentive to lend their support to the urban Arab intellectuals and commercial elite who formed the Istiqlal and UNFP opposition. Characteristically, both Mohammed V and Hassan II used these army officers as provincial governors, internal security officials, and royal advisers—the most prominent cases being those of General Mohammed Oufkir, long-time minister of interior, and now, since 1972, a much younger man, Colonel Ahmad Dlimi. Whatever the disaffections of some civilian groups of Moroccans and whatever the failures of the regime, there seemed no reason to doubt the reliability of the armed forces.

However, in July 1971 a bizarre attempt was made against the king when a group of military cadets attacked the summer palace on the occasion of the king's birthday celebration, massacring ninety-eight guests; the king survived, regained control with the help of General Oufkir, summarily executed ten high-ranking officers, and purged others. A year later, in August 1972, a second attempt followed: air force units attempted to shoot down a place on which King Hassan was returning from a trip abroad. This time none other than General Oufkir himself was implicated and either committed suicide or was shot; an additional eleven officers were subsequently executed.[3]

These two spectacular coup attempts shook the royal regime to its foundations. Much information about the motives and plans of the chief conspirators accompanied them to the grave, but it seems clear that these were not instances of radical young nationalist officers acting in the name of Arab nationalism, social revolution, etc. in the pattern of Nasser or Qadhafi. The Moroccan generals and colonels, conservative and apolitical professionals, were beneficiaries themselves of the system of royal patronage and spoils, and yet the perception of the extent reached by corruption in the royal entourage, and of the king's disinclination to do anything about it, were apparently too much for them to tolerate. (A few men, such as Oufkir and Chelouati, who themselves had reputations of notorious corruption, may have opted for the rebel side in order to protect themselves from their peers.)

In any event, the events of 1971 and 1972 virtually wiped out the class of senior officers inherited from the pre-1956 French army, on whom the king had placed such heavy reliance; for in addition to those executed, numerous others, whether rebel or loyalist, had died in the fighting. The group of officers now inheriting seniority in the army are a different breed: notably, some two hundred fifty members of the so-called "Mohammed V Class," the first crop of officers trained and commissioned immediately after independence, significantly better educated than their predecessors (a secondary certificate was required for admission to the Meknès military academy from 1956 on), with a considerable Arab and urban representation for the first time. Especially considering the political climate in the Arab world in the 1950s as these men were coming of age—the advent of Moroccan independence, the Algerian war, the rise of Nasser, the Suez war—it seems reasonable to ascribe to them a much higher degree of politicization and receptivity to radical ideas than their elders had had.

The king, openly declaring after the 1972 attempt that he could no longer trust anyone, resorted to the novel device of abolishing the ministry of defense as a unified agency and officially entrusting coordination of the various military bureaus to his cousin, Moulay Hafidh al-Alaw, an aged and infirm man widely regarded as unusually incompetent and corrupt. At the same time, real authority over the armed forces passed to General Oufkir's old adjunct Colonel Dlimi, chief of the king's aides de camp and head of the Bureau of Studies and Documentation, the principal intelligence service, and under Dlimi, the secretary of state for interior, Driss Basri. With their watchful assistance, units of the army have come under close monitoring from above; indeed, fear of putting too much firepower or authority to mobilize in the hands of the army may serve as an effective deterrent to King Hassan from becoming overly involved in the conflict with Spain over the Sahara.

After 1972 it became essential for the king to take some remedial action, and he did respond by arresting a number of notoriously corrupt individuals, introducing an ambitious five-year development plan, decreeing the long-overdue Moroccanization of foreign lands and businesses, and entering into negotiations with the opposition parties for the reorganization of the government and the holding of elections. All these actions were palliatives, designed to buy time. When it became apparent that the opposition politicians insisted on a real share of power and the implementation of real reforms, negotiations were called off and the king named his brother-in-law. Ahmad Osman, as prime minister.

In September 1974 the king made a fresh approach to the parties by promising to hold elections within a year at the same time that he held out the prospect of inviting representatives of the parties into the cabinet to supervise the electoral campaign. He was thus able for a time to entice leaders of the Istiqlal, the UNFP, the labor movement, and others into a posture of quasi-clienthood, whereby they were more or less rivals for his favor, and this added an extra stimulus to the split within the UNFP that had been building up for the previous two years. In September 1974 the Rabat section formally broke away from that of Casablanca to form a new party, the Union Socialiste des Forces Populaires (USFP). But once the ploy of promising elections had served its purpose of normalizing the domestic political atmosphere and dividing the opposition, in March 1975 the king abruptly cancelled his promise, declaring that the Sahara conflict required national solidarity and that elections must wait. Privately, and more aptly, he dismissed the electoral game as a "strip-tease." It was characteristic of Hassan's habit of manipulating his opponents with carrots and sticks to keep them off balance that almost simultaneously with the cancellation of elections, thirty USFP members who had been in jail for the past two years were released, while Mohammed Benjelloun, a prominent member of the Istiqlal, was arrested.

What is the future of this intricate relationship between the king, his clients, and his critics? Can he indefinitely perpetuate the meaningless minuet of party activity, in the name of legitimacy and pluralism, while undercutting the process every time it threatens to lead to a positive conclusion? Can he always count on the availability of individuals from the opposition for cooptation as courtiers and technocrats? Will the younger army officers, the university students and young graduates, and the urban and rural dispossessed patiently wait for reformist party politicians to arrive in power through some miracle?

The parties appear each to have evolved roles of their own which they can play within the monarchical system and within the present treadmill of powerlessness, while clinging to the myth that they will one day become real contenders and even rise up by democratic means to rescue the country. But the Istiqlal and the Berber-dominated and rural-oriented parties are emasculated by the personal ties of their aging leadership to the Palace, their long absence from power, and their failure to propose anything in the way of significant social reform. Moreover, the death in 1974 of Allal al-Fassi deprived the Istiqlal of a leader with forceful and magnetic qualities. The rump of the UNFP, under Abdallah Ibrahim and in tandem with Ben Siddiq and the Casablanca trade unions, can achieve little, whatever its attachment to the theoretical values of liberal bread-and-butter union democracy, in an underdeveloped nation full of underemployed people.

The USFP, led by radical intellectuals such as Abderrahim Bouabid and Mohamed Lahbabi, with a considerable following among the younger secularly-minded generation of professional men, appears to have no prospects for political power except, perhaps, as minority members of some temporary ministerial coalition, for it lacks any real power base other than the force of its own ideas. It would easily be outmaneuvered or simply swept aside by rival revolutionaries—Communists, army officers—in the aftermath of a coup. In the meantime, it does play the significant role of including uncorrupted idealists in a society dominated by corruption, posing their well-articulated criticisms of the system and proposals for change as long as the regime finds it inconvenient to silence them.

While the USFP and other radical critics present more of an annoyance than a threat to the king and his system, his tolerance of them undoubtedly reflects a certain realism: he recognizes that the traditional pluralism of the national society which he seeks to maintain in order to assure his own role as patrimonial arbiter necessarily carries with it some emerging modern elements of pluralism as well. An excessively systematic repression of organized labor, for instance, or of the membership of the UNFP and USFP would threaten to make waves successively unsettling other groups to which they have direct or indirect links—the Istiqlal, the urban middle and privileged classes and eventually public figures on whose loyal cooperation the king depends and whom he needs to counterbalance rural elites, military officers, etc.

Economic and Social Developments

The political stalemate in which Morocco has been caught since independence, and the preoccupation of the monarch with establishing his own predominance among competing political and social elites, has made it difficult for the government to develop the sense of priorities and enact the kind of reforms necessary for serious social and economic progress. In Algeria after 1962 there were no strongly entrenched indigenous privileged groups, and it took only Boumédienne's eventual consolidation of power to open the way to a massive technocratically led development program. In Tunisia the predominance of the Neo-Destour, from its beginnings a strongly reformist movement, assured an important (if moderate) momentum for directed social change after 1956. In Morocco, by contrast, the thrust of reformist commitment has been largely limited to the Istiqlal and its offshoot the UNFP, which posed too much of a challenge to the jealously guarded authority of a traditional monarch to receive an open mandate. Even the termination of the privileged position of French commercial and agricultural interests implied the threat that a momentum for further reform would be unleashed, excessively to the credit of the nationalist parties, since programs would have to be mounted not only to dismantel French interests but perhaps also to reorganize them as the nucleus of a Moroccan state sector.

Thus, for example, by the late 1960s half of the former French agricultural properties were still in French hands, the other half having largely found its way into the possession of a few privileged Moroccans. Thus also, between agricultural and commercial and industrial income, it was estimated in the 1960s that one-third of the income of foreigners was being transferred abroad, under Morocco's very liberal financial regulations, vastly outweighing the flow of investment capital into the country.[4] Meanwhile, in roughly the same period it was estimated that although agriculture contributed 30 percent of national income, only 2.6 percent of total taxes were collected from this source.[5] During that decade the proportion of investment to GNP languished between 11 percent and 15 percent (compared, for instance, to 26 percent in Tunisia and over 30 percent in Japan), and even this low rate reflected an inordinate dependence on public works.[6]

Morocco's stagnant agricultural sector has been among its most fundamental problems since independence. This sector has suffered from many handicaps, but above all from the failure of the government to reform the landholding system and provide improvements and services calculated to stimulate incentives in the countryside. There has been no lack of plans drawn up by bright young progressive-minded technicians in the ministries in Rabat, and some of these have been tentatively introduced here and there, but have always run up against the hard realities of entrenched social privilege and political manipulation.

Thus as early as 1962, a program of irrigation and reform encountered the resistance of local government officials suspicious of reforming initiatives outside their own control.[7] Dams have been built and irrigation works extended, but according to widespread report have largely redounded to the benefit of large landowners, who in turn are not investment minded, prefer to rent out their land in small portions, and fail to irrigate their properties fully. To be sure, those who succeeded in obtaining the highly developed farms of the French *colons* acquired with them an incentive to maintain their productivity, but not to translate this into any particular social benefit for the peasantry employed to work on it.

A decree enacted in March 1973 provided for the transfer of all remaining foreign-owned farmland to a state agrarian reform agency, for subsequent redistribution to poor farmers as part of a general program of rural improvements. By 1975, once again the real primary beneficiaries appear to have been those favored individuals to whom title was somehow smuggled, perhaps including members of the royal family. Only a few thousand hectares were redistributed to peasants, and for the time being—and perhaps the indefinite future—the bulk of the properties were retained in the hands of the state agency, which suffered from a severe shortage of qualified personnel with which to maintain production.

The stagnation of agriculture has meant a continuing depression of living standards for the rural majority of Morocco's population, and an urban migration with which the cities in their turn are unprepared to cope. It has also contributed to a worsening problem of maldistribution of wealth.[8] More serious than that, from the standpoint of national economic progress, is the incapacity of the agricultural sector to contribute capital, raw materials, or purchasing power to the development of industry and commerce, nor tax revenues to the state.

These compounding problems became evident in 1973 and 1974 when drought brought severe losses to Moroccan grain production and necessitated the importation of eight to nine hundred thousand tons of cereals in each of these two years—shocking figures in a predominantly agricultural country—at record-breaking prices. According to a report by the Banque Nationale du Développement Economique (September 24, 1974), overall agricultural income fell in 1973 by 11 percent; GNP rose by only 1.4 percent; the wholesale price index shot up by an alarming 36 to 38 percent. Thanks in large part to her agricultural failures, Morocco was importing severe inflation and consuming foreign currency badly needed for her 1973-77 development plan.

The precariousness of a traditional agricultural economy has thus asserted itself at the very time that windfalls in other sectors seemed to promise the means of national progress. One of these was tourism; yet has proved vulnerable to inflation, and 1974 was a disappointing year. Another consisted of the remittances from some 300,000 migrant workers in Europe; yet with the recession in the European economy, their future was in doubt.

The third windfall, and far and away the most important, was the quintupling of the world market price from 1973 to 1975 of phosphate rock, a material of which Morocco is the world's third largest producer and largest exporter. While Morocco's phosphates are by no means the bonanza that oil and gas are for Libya and Algeria, the revenue is still of great significance: the hard-currency earnings of the Office Chérifien des Phosphates increased in 1974 from a previous level of about $200 million to $1.1 billion with prospects of again doubling or tripling in future years with expanded production and with the development of local capacity for producing finished fertilizers.

Thanks to phosphates and despite problems of drought and inflation, GNP rose by 9 percent in 1974, and the government more than doubled its outlays for the 1973-77 development plan—though at the cost of a mounting budgetary deficit and the prospect of still more inflation.[9] The government will have to go in search of foreign credit, from the oil-rich Persian Gulf countries and in the West.

Much must depend in the future on the government's ability to keep up a high level of investment, given the poor record and prospects of investment in the private sector. It is still early to assess the full significance of the Moroccanization program in commerce and industry, decreed along with the Moroccanization of farmland in March 1973, which required at least 50 percent Moroccan ownership of establishments within deadlines of one to two years. Concurrently, the government issued other regulations governing taxation and profit repatriation designed to preserve a reasonably attractive climate for additional foreign investment.

Moroccanization in commerce and industry has its justifications in terms of economic development, as a means of stemming the flight of capital and encouraging Moroccans to invest their accumulated savings. The increase of foreign currency reserves since 1968 now enable the country for the first time to buy out foreign interests on a substantial scale, with the aid of loans of up to 90 percent at low interest from state banks. While perhaps 90 percent of the 2,000-odd enterprises subject to Morocannization were small businesses, attractive to Moroccan proprietors of similar establishments or to modest investors who would then rent them out to the former owners to operate,[10] the remaining 10 percent, which were the largest and most modern establishments, became choice targets of opportunity for wealthy and well-connected Moroccans who knew how to secure the lion's share of available loans of up to 90 percent at low interest from state banks. (Such loans were to be limited to customers possessing less than 500,000 Dinars ($125,000) of capital, but this restriction was predictably impossible to enforce.)

Thus this particular component of Morocco's campaign for economic independence has served, in the first instance, to further the concentration of wealth in the country, while stealing the reformist thunder of the opposition. At the same time, it has clearly added to the opportunities of the king, his courtiers, and his ministers for patronage: they can steer their clients into favorable arrangements with foreign partners, facilitate their access to bank loans, smooth their relations with government tax and regulatory authorities, and, in return, discreetly receive the usual rewards. This new element of corruption fits easily into a highly developed network of protection and payoff which is not merely a by-product but indeed a foundation of the monarch's manipulative method of ruling the country. Yet at the same time it does not bode well for the productivity of private enterprise, since it tends to reinforce an already existing tendency for the nation's economic priorities to be dictated by special interests, and for available capital to be diverted from productive investment to protective payoff.[11]

Notwithstanding these problems, one would like to hope that with the passage of time, the consolidation of the king's authority, the advent of a group of younger and better-educated men to high office, the increase in national revenues, and the new programs of investment and development promised in the 1973-77 plan, Morocco may have turned a corner and entered a path of continuing progress.

A comparison with the case of Iran over the last dozen years may suggest at least the possibility that a royal regime, embedded in a great network of special interests and corruption, uncertain of its authority and faced with deepening hostility from traditional nationalists and the newly educated sector of society, may somehow succeed in finding the path to fundamental reforms, and in the process to altering and expanding the base of its political support.

Unfortunately, such hopes for Morocco are probably misplaced, for the shah of Iran has enjoyed several crucial advantages over his Moroccan counterpart. One is the much higher level of education in Iran, which, despite the defection abroad of many university graduates and the political disaffection of others, has provided the government with the elements of a technocracy and a sizable army of lower-echelon administrative personnel, which Morocco does not possess in any comparable numbers. More particularly, even before the jump in world oil prices, Iranian oil revenues were substantial enough to provide capital for an ambitious long-run development program, absorbing the career aspirations of many people and creating major sources of wealth and power in society to counteract the traditionally entrenched privileges and prestige of the landowning class.

In the Moroccan case, it remains to be seen what King Hassan will find in the way of new financial and social support for his regime, even if he rises above his old preoccupation with the game of political manipulation and genuinely commits himself to a "revolution from above." Until now, as the critics complain, not only the king but his cabinet officers appear to be short on plans, perspectives, and solid ideas. Characterized by a Moroccan journalist as "a government of minor bureaucrats, not real politicians, functioning like members of a permanent caretaker regime and never acting on their own responsibility,"[12] the Council of Ministers leaves the king in an unchallenged yet sterile role. In the absence of a greater sense of direction and assurance of resources, the king's commitment seems implausible and his own conspicuous position of privilege must continue to stand as an anomaly, and thus an invitation to ongoing disaffection, within Moroccan society.

Algeria

Algeria is unquestionably the most dynamic, promising, challenging, important country in North Africa. With a population almost as large as Morocco's, oil and gas reserves comparable to Libya's, and a political and managerial leadership vastly more dedicated to the sober tasks of development than either, it faces very hopeful prospects for the coming several decades, in comparison to the other three North African states and much of the rest of the Third World. This nation has the promise of becoming a major African industrial power, a prosperous and active international trader, and a politically stable society.

None of this is automatically assured, however. Algeria's industrial progress risks falling afoul of too much haste, and even if it succeeds, the majority of the population may remain untouched by it, the growing class of educated people may not be forever content to leave political decisions to a secretive, increasingly autocratic president. Externally, it remains to be seen where Algeria's militant posture on the Third World's terms of trade with industrialized countries, and other issues, will lead it.

Historical Background: the Colonial Legacy and the Ben Bella Regime

One hundred and thirty-two years of French colonial rule and eight years of revolutionary war left Algeria with major problems. The economic, cultural, and political life of the country had been heavily dominated by the European population, and as they fled the country in 1962 they left Algeria with a glaring lack of government administrative personnel, managerial cadres in industry, commerce, and agriculture, skilled workers, teachers, and professionals in all fields. The country suffered several years of heavy loss in agricultural and industrial production, drastically curtailed commercial activity, and administrative chaos.

Moreover, the economic structure of French Algeria had reflected its dependence on the French metropolis: a low level of investment and growth, a low level of industrialization, concentration of modern agriculture on the production of wine for the French market, and an inordinately large commercial sector. Modern industry, agriculture, and commerce had been almost exclusively in French hands.

A few facts will illustrate the magnitude of the problem of putting newly independent Algeria on its feet, in the wake of the vacuum created by the flight of the French. Among the nine million Muslim Algerians, some 75 percent depended on agriculture. Among these, perhaps 25,000 families owned large farms, and some 100,000 workers held steady employment on French farms; thus approximately one million rural Algerians (including dependents) could be classified as tolerably well off. This left close to six million in rural deprivation. Already by 1954 some 400,000 Algerians, refugees from rural poverty, worked at low-skilled jobs in France. The urban population was largely confined to menial employment in French administration, industry and commerce, and to traditional crafts and small commerce, again with heavy unemployment. Illiteracy among Muslim Algerians was estimated in 1954 at 94 percent for men and 98 percent for women. A few thousand had received French university education.

Much of the potential leadership class of Algeria was eliminated during and just after the war of independence (1954-62). Many died during the struggle, while their survivors broke into severe factional rivalry immediately after independence.[13] By September 1962 power was established in the Hands of Ahmed Ben Bella, one of the original nine "historic chiefs" of the revolution who, however, had spent most of the war in French prisons. Ben Bella quickly eliminated the bulk of the Gouvernment Provisoire de la Republique Algerienne (GPRA) membership from power, but the rump coalition over which he presided was a shaky one, and his three years in office were marked by a series of rivalries, challenges, and purges. In June 1965 the army chief, Colonel Houari Boumédiênne, removed Ben Bella in a coup d'état.

The Boumédienne Regime: the Push for Industrialization

Boumédienne's advent to the presidency marked the final elimination from the regime of men who had played leading roles in the revolutionary war prior to its final year. After 1965 he settled down to govern Algeria through an elite which consisted chiefly of two new elements: (1) a few men who like himself, had been officers in the National Liberation Army (ALN) during the war, the so-called Oujda Group; these have remained loyal to him since then and have cemented his grip on the post-independence Algerian army; and (2) a class of young technocrats, who, for the most part, had been in school during the revolution.

Boumédienne has been highly successful in instilling stability into the country's politics through authoritarian means. Algeria's sole political party, the Front de Libération Nationale (FLN), already under Ben Bella a shadow of the prestigious movement it had been during the war, became a bureaucratically organized holding operation under Boumédienne, designed in reality to monopolize formal political life on behalf of the regime and forestall potentially dissident political activity rather than to serve its nominal purpose of giving policy direction to the government's operations. Boumédienne installed his most loyal "oujda" colleagues in key positions: Ahmed Kaid at the head of the FLN, Ahmed Medeghri as minister of interior, Abdelaziz Bouteflika as foreign minister, Cherif Belkacem in various posts. The last instances of political violence in Algeria were a rebellion in 1967 led by an old revolutionary commander, Colonel Zbiri, which was promptly quashed, and an attempt on Boumédienne's life in 1968.

Since July 1970, when seven cabinet ministries were reshuffled, there have been no major shakeups in the membership of the regime, yet three of Boumédienne's four principal Oujda aides have disappeared from the scene in 1974-75, Medeghri by death, Kaid and Belkacem by dismissal. This left Boumédienne seemingly more autocratically in control, yet also more dependent on his technocrats and, perhaps, his army officers.

The primary concern of the Boumédienne regime over the past decade has been that of economic development, and within this field the government has made a consistent and unmistakable choice of priorities in favor of the rapid development of oil and gas production, heavy industrialization as well as urban-based programs of higher education and technical training needed to support an industrializing economy.

This option has, of course, been a natural one. The oil industry, begun mainly by French companies before Algerian independence and continued by them thereafter, progressively came under greater Algerian control with agreements negotiated in 1965 and 1971; by the latter year Algeria acquired a majority interest in the production, refining, and transportation of its oil and a monopoly on internal distribution. Meanwhile the foreign exchange it derived from oil exports, which in 1969 stood at only $250 million, reached $4 billion in 1974, thanks to the great worldwide price increase of 1973. While its proven reserves are limited, and in 1971 it was estimated that they would suffice for only another thirty years' production at current rates, [14] the current and prospective income has already dramatically revolutionized the country's opportunities for investment in general national economic growth. Thus already in 1973, before most of the impact of that year's price rise had been felt, the petroleum sector accounted for over 75 percent of Algeria's exports, 68 percent of its foreign exchange earnings, and 35 percent of the government's budget revenues. Gross domestic product, which had risen by 10 percent per year from 1969 to 1972, and over 18 percent in 1973 alone, reached $6 billion in the latter year. [15]

This great spurt in capital accumulation has enabled Algerian planners to step up their investment projects correspondingly. While the 1970-73 plan was budgeted at about $6 billion, that of 1974-77 is budgeted for no less than $27.5 billion, and is scheduled to lead to a GDP figure of $12 billion by the latter year. This will be faciliated not only by oil revenues but by those from natural gas as well, an industry that is still in its infancy. Algeria has approximately 10 percent of the world's proven reserves of natural gas and is expected to develop massive long-term sales to Europe and the United States, eventually petroleum will be displaced by gas as the mainspring of Algeria's development financing. [16]

The program of industrialization, already well under way, centers naturally in

the first instance around projects related to oil and gas: refining, gas liquification, pipelines, port facilities, tankers, petrochemicals, fertilizer, synthetic
rubber, artificial fibers, plastics. Three refineries are in current operation; a
fourth and much larger one is planned at Skikda. Gas liquification plants at
Arzew and Skikda will be supplemented by others; these and related facilities
will cost at least $6 billion in the next five to ten years. A gas pipeline, at a cost
of over $1 billion, if planned to run from the Saharan gas fields across Tunisia,
the Mediterranean, and Sicily to northern Italy. An iron and steel complex near
Annaba, built with Soviet assistance, is in operation and due to expand rapidly,
capitalizing on substantial iron-ore deposits at Ouenza in the northeast; in
addition a very large deposit or ore, estimated at two billion tons, is located at
Tindouf near the Moroccan and Mauritanian borders, but will not go into
production until the late 1970s.

All told, the 1974-77 development plan encompasses over five hundred
projects (two hundred of which were already under way by the end of 1974) of
heavy industry and 800 light industrial projects, altogether consuming $12
billion or 43.5 percent of the total budget. In addition to oil- and gas-related
projects, the most notable areas of projected industrial expenditure include iron
and steel, chemicals and fertilizer, electric and mechanical construction, and
construction materials.

In addition, the plan provides for the investment of $3 billion in agricultural
improvement; $1.15 billion in dams and irrigation; $2.5 billion in education;
$3.88 billion in economic infrastructure (transport, communications, etc.);
$3.65 billion in housing, health, and other social services. In all, it envisages the
creation of 456,000 new jobs, outside of the agricultural sector, in addition to
the 480,000 created in the period 1966-73.

These are all impressive figures, but they are not the whole story: to translate
them into concrete achievements is a difficult business. First of all, the plan
assumes a higher volume of oil income than may prove available: declining prices
and production would already reduce the level in 1975 to $3.5 billion, down
from $4 billion in 1974, as the minister of finance acknowledged when he
presented the 1975 ordinary budget. Furthermore, inflation would eat heavily
into resources. Thanks to the insufficiency of Algerian agriculture, the 1975
budget of $5.5 billion would include $820 million for the subsidization of
imported food prices, half of it, or $25 per capita, just for sugar. Revenues from
public-sector corporations were down 25 percent; the cost of imports increased;
the balance of payments would require Algeria to continue borrowing money
abroad.[17]

Moreover, many of the industrial projects entail rapidly rising costs, and the
prospective efficiency of each can only be guessed at, especially in view of the
heavy dependence of the country on foreign contractors to construct them, the
paucity of qualified Algerians to operate them, and the inevitable bottlenecks
and unforeseen technical problems involved in attempting to implement such a

large number of projects at once. Foreign firms urgently hired to do jobs and give technical advice are not always competent, lacking as they frequently are in the slightest acculturation to local conditions. United States government sources have privately reported that the International Bank recommended to the Algerian government that investment be more diversified, concentrating less on industry and more on agriculture, and that the rate of investment be reduced for the sake of some increase in the heretofore austere level of consumption. As this would not only slow down industrial progress but require more expenditure on unproductive commodity imports, the government naturally is reluctant to take such advice.

Perhaps the most serious area of concern in evaluating Algeria's development program is the problem of unemployment, especially in the countryside. The 456,000 new jobs envisaged by the plan will approximately absorb the 140,000 expected new arrivals onto the labor market for each of the four years, but will not greatly reduce the existing level of unemployment. In the agricultural sector, out of a total rural active population of 1,270,000, only 450,000 are regularly employed, and 820,000 only seasonally. The development plan only forecasts the creation of 85,000 new agricultural jobs, a negligible quantity.

The problems in the countryside cannot be easy for any Algerian government to solve. Most of the cultivated land in the country is only marginally productive, the best lands having been appropriated long ago by French *colons* who employed a limited number of Algerian laborers. After independence, local workers seized French farmland and claimed title to it, thus forming the nucleus of the much-touted program of "auto-gestion" (self-management); as the new Algerian government found its feet, however, they fell progressively under state regulatory control, while other former French lands were reorganized as state farms.

The 2.5 million hectares of formerly French lands, comprising the post-1962 public sector of agriculture, represented overwhelmingly the richest agricultural property in the country. They had generated some 55 percent of total agricultural income before independence although they comprised only 18 percent of the arable land. On the other hand, these lands supported only about 11 percent of the overall rural population (150,000 workers plus their families, i.e., about one million inhabitants by the mid-1960s). An additional 11.5 million hectares of privately owned land remained to support another eight million Algerians with the proceeds of only 45 percent of total production. These figures give a summary idea of what is a social problem of tragic proportions, one which neither Ben Bella nor, at least until very recently, Boumédienne has seriously grappled with—Ben Bella because he could not, during the confusion that reigned during his regime, and Boumédienne because his government has placed its priorities elsewhere. The problem, of course, long predated Algerian independence: rural poverty and overpopulation was the direct consequence of French actions in the nineteenth century that had progressively deprived the indigenous population of choice farmland and pushed it into the marginally productive mountains and steppes of the interior, undermining in the process the social structure.

Added to these pressures were those of the 1954-62 war, when an estimated two million rural Algerians became victims of the French military device of "regroupement" and were forced off their land into Algerian equivalents of what were later to become known as "strategic hamlets." Coupled with the migration of another two million rural Algerians to the cities between 1959 and 1965, most of whom remained no more than marginally employed, there was a nucleus of one-third of the population of the country by the mid-1960s forming a destitute subproletariat, alongside a roughly equal number in the countryside whose agricultural livelihood was scarcely more affluent. Much of the sting of these harsh circumstances has been removed only by virtue of a growth in the migration of Algerian unskilled labor to France, now estimated at around 800,000.

Algerian planners and spokesmen are quick to deny the charge that they have neglected agriculture and the rural poor, and it is true that the $3 billion allocated in the current plan vastly exceeds anything devoted to the agricultural sector previously. Manpower authorities in Algeria claim that the unemployment program will have been essentially solved by 1980, though it is difficult to imagine how this will be done.

It remains to be seen how much of the rural investment will find its way into the improvement of the poorest sections of the countryside, as opposed to the state and self-managed farms, and more particularly how much success the authorities will have in coping with what are after all very intractable problems in transforming the conditions of rural life. For what is needed is not simply (or perhaps even primarily) money but qualified personnel, education, and effective means of inducing social and cultural changes in the ways of the population.

It may be, as the government obviously hopes, that in course of time industrialization will lead to the creation of new jobs on a large scale, but in the short run—that is, for the next decade or two—employment generated by the new capital-intensive industries cannot more than very marginally alleviate the problem, especially in the context of a population growth rate of over three percent, among the world's highest.

In the words of one authority:

The planners show a total disregard for the problem of unemployment. One of them argues, "It is better to have an immediate elite of 300,000 skilled workers in strategic sectors than to lose our money making hammers and spoons." An another claims, "With the $70 million that this ammonia plant has cost us, we could have employed thousands of idle men, but what would be the real benefit for our country and its agriculture?" There is little doubt that these options are realistic in the long run, because synthetic ammonia cannot be manufactured by enthusiastic peasants.[18]

Industrialization, with the promise of an enormous leap forward in overall national productivity, will doubtless continue to absorb much of Algeria's energy and attention in coming decades. Several important implications are clear. On the domestic level, one can foresee a steady growth and consolidation of Algeria's new privileged classes. Initially these could be identified as the groups who moved in to assume the functions or inherit the career opportunities left behind by the departing French, a constituency calculated by one economist to represent, with their dependents, approximately one-third of the population.[19] Since then, of course, these numbers have grown significantly with the expansion of education and the economy, and important new groups have begun to take shape: skilled industrial workers; army officers; university-trained managers and professionals. Around these groups have grown the infrastructures of government bureaucracy (still today abysmally cumbersome), the administration of state-owned enterprises (in some cases impressively efficient and well led), a modern army, and a rapidly growing system of education. Despite everything that may be said of the hardships suffered by the majority of the population, it appears that Algeria is in the process of evolving a modern sector of society that is large enough, prosperous enough, educated enough, progressive enough, and secure and optimistic enough to more than offset the unsettling potential of the disadvantaged rural and urban masses and to afford the government the basic preconditions of social and political stability.

For the next decade or more, this prospect is not encouraging from the standpoint of social conscience. It does suggest, however, that the social discontent of the mass is unlikely to find effective outlets through accompanying discontent among the more privileged. At the same time it is worth considering that even if, as one author insists, [20] social inequality among Algerians is today much greater than before independence, and perhaps comparable to what existed between Algerians and Europeans, today's privileged do not belong to an alien and hostile culture, do not represent inherited privileges, and are by no means inaccessible through the accrual of education and social reforms. In the longer term, the Algerian planners may be right in assuming that an industrialized society will eventually find natural means of drawing vastly larger numbers into education and employment.

Another projection is less optimistic than the above. The progress of the top third of Algerian society may provide the preconditions for political stability, but it can hardly assure it. One wonders whether a political base of support consisting of army loyalty and an administrative infrastructure of technocrats can suffice forever to preclude political conflict. As an educated class emerges, as the army matures under a continuously replenished officer corps, as differentiated interests take shape within a newly industrialized society, and as a succession of foreign and domestic policy questions present themselves for decision, it would not be surprising for political factions to arise, producing new dissidents and challengers with their own priorities and ideologies. What may be a small foretaste of such emergent conflicts was supplied by violent clashes in May 1975 between two factions of university students in Algiers, those pursuing French- and Arabic-language curricula respectively—the two languages reflecting not only alternative cultural traditions and values, but relatively privileged and disadvantaged social origins and career prospects, respectively.[21]

Foreign Policy

Algeria's foreign policy priorities must be distinguished from those of Morocco and Tunisia. The latter two states have generally aimed at cultivating close relations with France and the United States, maintaining good trading relations with Western Europe keeping polite relations with the Communist states, and having a reputation for orthodoxy on nationalist causes among their fellow African and Arab states. These countries hope that by these means they will be aided and protected by the rich and the powerful, and left in peace by all the others.

The Algerians are determined to play an active rather than passive role in international affairs and to establish themselves as pace-setters in Africa, the Middle East, and the Third World generally, even at the cost of considerable conflict. There are two main issues which particularly concern Algeria. In the first place, since the days of Ben Bella Algeria has never ceased to make militant gestures and statements in behalf of Third World liberation movements everywhere: Palestine, Angola, Cuba, Vietnam, Chile, et al. As is often pointed out, these displays are highly symbolic in character, and they do not interfere with the businesslike, if hard-driving, manner in which Algeria pursues its commercial relations around the world.[22]

The other issue impinges directly on those relations. Algeria strives to play a leading role in the campaign to restructure the terms of trade between the former colonial world and the industrialized nations. During the first decade of independence this mainly took the form of liquidating vestiges of French economic privilege in Algeria: nationalization of French lands and businesses, renegotiation of French oil company contracts, and finally, in 1971, nationalization of a majority share in these and other foreign operations.

Especially since the dramatic rise in oil prices after the 1973 war and the enhanced power of the Organization of Petroleum Exporting Countries (OPEC), there has been a much more consistent and generalized thesis reiterated by the Algerian government at every opportunity: not simply that the new oil prices were justified and necessary, but that they represented a whole revolution in commercial relations by which exploitation of the exporters of raw materials by the industrial nations would be ended.

Thus the first UN conference on raw materials, in April 1974, was held in response to Algeria's call, and the Algerians were in the forefront of such subsequent activities as the "Declaration on the Establishment of a New Economic Order" at the United Nations, the Dakar Declaration on Raw Materials in February 1975, and the Lima Declaration on industrial development in March. President Boumédienne, in a letter to Secretary General Waldheim on October 2, 1974, demanded revision of the world economic order to protect raw materials producers against the exportation of inflation from the industrial states. With India, in November 1974, Algeria issued a call for the formation of an iron ore exporters' organization.

In opposition to the United States and most of its industrial partners, who sought to form a united front through creation of the International Energy Agency (IEA) to bargain for lower oil prices, Algeria supported the French proposal for a conference organized on a global scale among oil-exporting, industrial, and non-oil Third World countries to debate the general terms of trade. Its press denounced the IEA as an "obviously hostile coalition against the oil-producing countries" and an "aggressive mechanism of confrontation."[23] Algeria declared on February 21, 1975 that it would not attend the proposed Paris conference unless the agenda included all aspects of world trade and raw materials exports, rather than only oil, which would permit the oil-producing countries to be made into scapegoats.[24] Eventually Algeria and others yielded on this issue, but as Algeria and other OPEC members continued to insist on the principle of indexing the prices of industrial goods as a basis for oil prices, the preliminary negotiations for the Paris conference broke down and the conference was cancelled. Yet the Algerians had made their mark and served notice that their position went beyond mere rhetoric: they would continue to insist emphatically that OPEC should use all its collective power to maintain oil prices, they would encourage other raw materials producers to band together in similar fashion, and they would drive hard bargains in all bilateral commercial dealings with the Western world, the markets, capital, technology, and industrial products which they continue to need.

In its relations with fellow Arab states, Algeria has shown a somewhat similar mixture of militancy and accommodation. It has always taken rather uncompromising positions verbally on the Arab-Israeli conflict, espousing the cause of the Palestinian resistance, deploring the notion of compromise with Israel, breaking relations with the United States in 1967 and advocating the use of oil as a political weapon; yet it has been careful not to obstruct Egyptian and Syrian efforts since 1973 to negotiate partial settlements through American mediation, and it restored its relations with Washington late in 1974.

In his growing role of OPEC statesman, President Boumédienne demonstrated his ability to rise above ideology by mediating personally between the shah of Iran and Vice President Saddam Hussein, the strong man of Iraq, in the spring of 1975 to bring a negotiated end to the long-standing conflict between those countries. Subsequently, Boumédienne reportedly aspired to mediate Iraq's strained relations with Syria, Saudi Arabia, and Kuwait as well, but was obliged to renounce those efforts.[25]

Despite stark differences with Morocco in regimes and ideologies, and lingering memories of their brief border war of 1963, Algeria under Boumédienne has dealt with the Moroccan monarchy prudently and correctly, even to the point of sending congratulations to King Hassan on his narrow escape from the abortive Skhirrat coup of 1971. A dispute over jurisdiction over the iron-rich region of Tindouf was peacefully negotiated: the territory belonged to Algeria, but the two countries would collaborate in mining operations.

A more serious problem since 1974 has been the question of the Spanish Sahara, in which Algeria has dissented from the Moroccan-Mauritanian claims—endorsed by several other Arab states—and has championed "self-determination" for the sparsely populated territory. While denying any territorial claim of Algeria's own, Foreign Minister Bouteflika declared that the Sahara did not belong to Morocco either;[26] and when the case was put before the International Court of Justice for an advisory opinion, Algeria asserted to the court that it was an interested party.[27] Algeria meanwhile lent its support to an armed liberation group in the Sahara known as the Polisario, which had vowed to resist a Moroccan takeover by force.

The Algerians had a number of reasons to challenge Morocco's ambitions in the Sahara. There were the rich phosphate deposits in the territory; there was the prospect of shipping Algerian iron ore from Tindouf out to the Atlantic across a friendly, perhaps subservient, independent Sahara instead of across rival Morocco. Then there was a matter of ideological conviction: Algeria had consistently supported the principle of self-determination in ex-colonial territories, and had no reason to stop doing so in the face of a right-wing monarchy's ambitions, especially when success for the latter would seem to strengthen its prestige as a West African power.

Algeria and Tunisia, again, have divergent ideological positions, have experienced some strains in the past, have in some instances given asylum to each other's political refugees, and have developed rather slender economic ties, apart from the shipment of Algerian oil by pipeline to a terminal near Gabès in southern Tunisia. Yet they have evolved an unruffled diplomatic relationship, aided by mutual visits between Presidents Boumédienne and Bourguiba.

Tunisia

Among the North African countries, Tunisia possesses the most modest natural resources and the second smallest population (about six million in 1975) and causes the smallest ripples in the outside world. Yet, since its independence in 1956, Tunisia has enjoyed unique advantages. It has been the most geographically compact, culturally advanced, socially homogeneous, efficiently governed, politically stable, and tranquil in its foreign relations with the nations in the area. Its colonial legacy was the most benign. Its president, Habib Bourguiba, has been in office the longest and is justly counted among the outstanding figures of Third World nationalism in modern times. Its ruling Destourian Socialist party, founded by Bourguiba in 1934, is the oldest in Africa and has been exceptionally effective in its institutional vitality, broad roots in the society, and contribution to orderly government and progress. While not altogether democratic in its political processes, Tunisia has enjoyed a significant measure of openness, tolerance, and consensus, and has better prospects than its neighbors for political democratization in the future. Alone in North Africa, Tunisia is satisfied to possess only a very small and modestly equipped army. Its economy, based only on limited natural resources, has experienced ups and downs but is currently undergoing rather impressive growth.

Despite all these positive features, however, serious questions must be raised about the prospects for orderly political succession, which make Tunisia's generally favorable prospects rather precarious.

Historical Background: The Evolution of the Bourguiba Regime

Unlike Algeria, where French colonialism had the effect of destroying local social structure, culture, leadership, and institutions, French rule in Tunisia under the Protectorate established in 1881 tended to respect and, in some ways, even strengthen these societal attitudes. The local government of the Ottoman Bey, modernized and reinvigorated shortly before the French arrival by a reformist prime minister, already possessed a respectable administrative infrastructure through which it maintained effective control of the country. The French chose to rule by discreet and indirect means through the medium of the Bey, assisted by French *contrôleurs civils*. There was little French military presence in the country, let alone in the administration, that characterized Algeria and Morocco. French settlers, though eventually significant in number—they were to reach 7 percent of the population before independence—acquired only a portion of the best farmland and never penetrated some important areas of the country such as the fertile and commercially prosperous Sahel belt along the central eastern coast. Modern education had begun prior to French rule, and under a dual Arabic and French educational system (actively discouraged in Algeria and never well developed in France's relatively brief period in Morocco), a sizable bilingually educated Tunisian elite grew up, including several thousands who received university degrees in France well before independence. The attendant cultural and social progress was eventually to produce a new middle class of men combining the petit-bourgeois provincial background of the Sahel (such as Bourguiba himself) and the conservative, sometimes aristocratic families of Tunis.[28]

The Neo-Destour party was founded in 1934 by Bourguiba and others of this social vintage and was dedicated not only to militant insistence on national independence, but also to societal modernization and mobilization through extensive grass-roots organization and political education. Despite intermittent French repression, this effort proved successful enough to ensure that in 1955, when France granted internal autonomy, and in 1956, when Paris granted full independence, the Neo-Destour as a body was unchallenged within Tunisia in its claim to national leadership. At the same time it demonstrated that the party possessed the organization and manpower to take effective administrative control of affairs; it also meant that the challenge to Bourguiba's leadership raised in 1955 by his ex-associate Salah Ben Youssef, in the name of more uncompromising militancy and pan-Arabism, could be defeated, thanks to the consensual belief in the rationality and effectiveness of Bourguiba and the majority of the party.

With independence, the departure of French civil servants, farmers, and businessmen was not a headlong and panicky affair as in Algeria; under Bourguiba, the Neo-Destour proceeded in a deliberate manner to establish a new constitution and administration and pressed successfully for the expansion and modernization of education, the creation of public-works projects to relieve unemployment, the emancipation of women, and the inculcation of secular notions of progress.

Domestic Politics and Economic Policy

Bourguiba's struggle with Ben Youssef in 1955-56 appears to have convinced him of the unacceptability of allowing any of his associates in the party to gain an autonomous following of their own. This, combined with a limitless capacity for vanity and didacticism, led Bourguiba over the years to purge a succession of prominent figures, although occasionally rehabilitating them afterward. Thus Ahmed Ben Salah was eased out of his post as general secretary of the Labor Federation (UGTT) in 1956, only to be brought back five years later as minister of planning; in 1969 he was again dropped from office, and this time tried for treason and jailed. Ahmed Tlili was also introduced to, then dismissed from, the leadership of the UGTT; Habib Achour was elected, dismissed and disgraced, then again returned. Mohammed Masmoudi was dropped from the Political Bureau of the party in 1958 for having encouraged press criticism of the government, readmitted, dropped again in 1961, appointed foreign minister in 1970, then ousted in 1974 and drummed out of the party in disgrace. Bahi Ladgham was removed from the prime ministry at the height of his popularity in 1970 and purged from the Political Bureau the following year; Ahmed Mestiri was ousted from the Cabinet in 1970 and from the party in 1971. Six men, including four former ministers, were expelled from the party in 1974 for criticizing Bourguiba's manipulation of the party Congress.

Bourguiba was able to engineer these successive purges, and maintain his patrimonial authority over party and government, partly because of his own enormous prestige, partly because of his skill as a political tactician—always eliminating his potential challengers one at a time while maintaining the support of others—and partly because of the continuing availability of highly talented men to take control of governmental affairs. In addition to the excellent service he was able to obtain from most of those whom he purged before moving against them, he has enjoyed the support of such a talented succession of others as Mongi Slim, onetime foreign minister; Mahmoud Messadi, onetime minister of education; Taieb Mehiri, minister of interior until his death in 1965; and Hedi Nouira, the current prime minister. For a small and newly independent state, Tunisia has enjoyed a truly impressive supply of Founding Fathers.

The most significant challenge Bourguiba has faced since the Ben Youssef affair has sprung from the Socialist-oriented economic program directed by Ahmed Ben Salah in the 1960s. Appointed in 1961 to multiple cabinet ministries with extraordinary powers, Ben Salah proceeded to draw up an ambitious ten year plan of economic development and reform based heavily on state control and initiative in industry and agriculture. The program was formally adopted by the party at its 1964 Congress, at which time the name of the party was officially changed to the "Parti Socialiste Destourien" (PSD). At the heart of Ben Salah's plans was a program to develop a system of agricultural cooperatives, centered initially on the large nationalized French estates in the north of the country but including the participation of Tunisian smallholders as well. Hastily conceived and overly centralized, the plan met with widespread resistance in the countryside from small landowners and landless peasants alike, who found their desires ignored and their needs misunderstood. When Ben Salah's reforming activities reached beyond the former French-dominated regions into the Sahel and threatened the status of larger Tunisian landowners, many of whom had personal ties to Tunis and the government, opposition to Ben Salah became more directly political. His mismanagement, which resulted in large subsidies having to be pumped into increasingly unproductive agriculture, as well as the failure of other portions of the development plan, led in time to Ben Salah's dismissal and imprisonment and consequently, to an abandonment of most of the Socialist orientation he had introduced to the nation's economic policy-making.

Undoubtedly the failures were not entirely Ben Salah's fault, and it was more convenient than justifiable for Bourguiba to lay the blame at his feet, on the pretext that Ben Salah had falsified figures and deceived him about developments in the economy. The fact was, however, that with the failure of the development program, the Tunisian economy stagnated throughout the 1960s. National income barely kept pace with the rise in population, increases in imports and in the civil service payroll swelled out of all proportion to exports and to domestic savings, and only a mounting volume of French and American aid kept the country above water. (American aid, for example rose from about $35 million to over $100 million from 1960 to 1967; but during the same period, the proportion of debt servicing costs to export receipts climbed from 12 percent to 57 percent.[29]

A period of austerity and retrenchment followed Ben Salah's departure, particularly after the conservative and cautious Hedi Nouira assumed the premiership in 1970. With an exceptional harvest in 1972, an influx of tourists, and sudden rises in the world prices of oil and phosphate, both of which Tunisia exports on a modest scale, recovery was under way and the Tunisian economy began to grow significantly. The GNP shot upward by 17.6 percent in 1972[30] and after a year of poor harvests, by 10.9 percent in 1974, with a rate of inflation in the latter year of only 4.5 percent.[31] A 9 percent annual growth rate was forecast for the Four Year Plan begun in 1973.[32] With a law passed in April 1972, the government opened the door to foreign investment in Tunisian industry, offering exemption from taxation and other incentives.

The Tunisians must be wary of congratulating themselves for this economic upturn, which has led for the first time to a favorable trade balance and an increase in foreign exchange reserves to an unprecedented level near $400 million, and allowed the country to reduce its dependence on foreign investment, according to the prime minister, from 40 percent of total investment to only 12 percent (1974 figure).[33] The rise in oil and phosphate income has been the result of fortuitous price increases rather than from increased production; the exportation of approximately 3.3 million tons of oil netted approximately $460 million in 1974, compared with $130 million in 1973, and phosphates netted $160 million in 1974, more than three times the 1973 total.[34]

The cash is welcome but the payoff in domestic productivity remains uncertain, although more mineral exploration and production is expected. Agricultural ups and downs in recent years have followed the weather, but while employing more than half the nation's work force, agriculture has only accounted for 15 to 17 percent of GDP, and is not expected to improve markedly. As Premier Nouira acknowledged publicly on September 13, 1974, 40 percent of the population remains "on the threshhold of poverty" (clearly a euphemism for "deep in poverty," as conditions in the slums of Tunis or in remote villages in the hinterland would suggest).[35] To maintain unemployment at its present officially estimated level of 15 percent, some 50,000 new jobs a year were needed; in 1974 42,000 had been created. But the need inexorably will grow: 65 percent of the population is under the age of twenty-five, and the rate of population increase is given at 2.8 percent.[36]

The future of economic growth is of particular political relevance in conjuncture with the question of the eventual succession to Bourguiba, since renewed economic difficulties would undoubtedly deepen the differences among rival contenders for power. Bourguiba, who was born in 1903, has been in shaky health since 1970 and was obliged to spend five months in a Geneva clinic in

1971, leading many to speculate that his political grip was destined to falter. He has confounded the speculators on various occasions since then, but not definitively. At Monastir in the fall of 1971 the party Congress, acting on the premise of a speech he had given the year before urging liberalization and democratization within the regime, passed a number of resolutions amending party procedures in a democratic direction. For example, these provided for the election by the Congress of the Political Bureau, a step which Bourguiba succeeded in avoiding. Two recently dismissed cabinet ministers, Ladgham and Mestiri, were elected by especially large majorities to the Central Committee. Taking this as a challenge, Bourguiba had Mestiri dismissed from the party.

At the 1974 Congress, Bourguiba reasserted his control. He stated that in 1971 "the ideas of a large proportion of those present were based on the assumption that I was about to die and that the presidency would be vacant. I have now come back in full strength and in very good health to be at the helm of this Congress which is to adopt resolutions to put matters in order."[37] The Congress obliged him: it revoked the provision for election of the Bureau, called for a constitutional amendment enabling the prime minister to inherit a full unexpired presidential term in case of vacancy (thus endorsing Bourguiba's implicit designation of Nouira as heir apparent) and reelected Bourguiba to the presidency of the party for life. The proceedings of the Congress, including the selection of delegates and the election of the new Central Committee, were heavily orchestrated, causing six absent party members to protest and thus to be dismissed from membership. In October the Tunisian Parliament formally reelected Bourguiba as president of the Republic, and in March 1975 it extended his term for life. It also ratified the above constitutional amendment.

These developments leave Bourguiba and Nouira very much in charge for the time being. Outside the confines of the party and government, which have acquired a distinctly establishmentarian ethos, and the silent majority in the country which presumably continues to accept the existing regime without much question, the atmosphere is less complacent. Among the politicians there is now a rather sizable band of former cabinet ministers ostracized in recent years: Ben Salah, Ladgham, Mestiri, Ben Ammar, Sebsi, Mualla, Boulares, Masmoudi, etc. These are energetic, capable, ambitious men, who will not necessarily be impotent under the circumstances of the future.

In addition, it must be noted that the party is conspicuous in the growing absence of youth from its ranks, and that university students and young intellectuals have shown significant indications of disaffection in recent years, including a series of university strikes and other disturbances leading in some instances to mass arrests and imprisonment on charges of sedition, communism, etc. Under Tunisia's ambitious and well-financed educational program, university enrollments have grown very rapidly, passing 10,000 by 1970, and have been stimulated by the distribution of generous—by Tunisian standards even lavish—scholarships. (Thus in 1971 60 percent of all university students held scholarships, which ranged between 350 and 450 dinars $700 to $900, i.e., two to three times the national per capita income.)[38] Much of the student unrest has seemingly been attributable to malaise over career prospects in a stagnant economy; some of it also is the result of the growing perceptions among students of the regime as a reflection of self-satisfied, stand-pat interests in the society. The question today is thus whether the economic upswing can be maintained, and translated into an expanding employment market for graduates as has been the case in Algeria; or whether the PSD and the government, at least after Bourguiba's departure, can recapture its old aura of reformist vigor; or both.

Foreign Policy

In foreign affairs in the years following independence Bourguiba was able to walk a tightrope. He gave strong support to the Algerian independence struggle, prompted a bloody confrontation with France in 1961 over the continued operation of the Bizerte naval base, nationalized French landed properties in 1963, yet for the most part kept the diplomatic door open to Paris and maintained a flow of French economic and technical assistance which Tunisia vitally needed.

Bourguiba maintained close relations with the United States, which had the effect of moderating the French response to his challenges and of providing an important secondary source of foreign aid. He refused to accept Nasser's leadership and Egyptian hegemony within the Arab League, and angered several radical Arab governments with his call, in 1965, for a negotiated settlement with Israel, but he rode out the storm and managed by the 1970s to acquire a positive, if belated, reputation for fundamental loyalty to Arab national causes, including Palestine. Meanwhile he managed to maintain smooth relations with both Algeria and Libya, two revolutionary neighbors which could have proved immensely troublesome.

Bourguiba's success was due in part to the failures of his old enemy Nasser, in part to the internal preoccupations and more pragmatic attitudes of the Algerians after the Boumédienne coup in 1965, and in part to the strength of his own domestic position within Tunisia. His steadfast pro-Americanism and his predominantly friendly relations with France, not to mention his moderate and rationalistic approach to the question of Israel, were not particularly popular in the Arab world at large nor perhaps even within Tunisia, but they eventually won acceptance.

Beginning with the appointment of Mohammed Masmoudi as foreign minister in 1970, Tunisian foreign policy took on a new coloration that provided extra insurance. Masmoudi conducted a vigorous campaign of fence-mending with the more leftist-oriented Arab and African states and with the Communist countries, without sacrificing good relations with the French, the Americans, or most of the Arab and African conservatives. This campaign took the form of a constant round of diplomatic visits and the negotiation of commercial and cultural agreements, plus symbolic pronouncements on behalf of the Palestinians, national liberation movements, etc. Bourguiba went out of his way in 1973 to suggest that King Hussein of Jordan should step aside in favor of the Palestine Liberation Organization, prompting Jordan to break diplomatic relations (later restored). Also in 1972 Tunisia voted in favor of the ouster of Nationalist China from the United Nations in favor of Peking, thereby inviting the official displeasure of the United States, though without sacrificing the aid program. Continuing this pattern, Premier Nouira paid successive visits in the spring of 1975 to China and the United States, returning home in time for Soviet Premier Kosygin's visit to Tunisia.

Masmoudi's campaign came to a head in a bizarre episode of the Tunisian-Libyan unity agreement of February 1974, which the ailing Bourguiba signed with the encouragement of Masmoudi at a hastily organized meeting with President Qadhafi. Premier Nouira hastily returned from a visit abroad and persuaded Bourguiba to dismiss Masmoudi and allow the unity pact to lapse; Masmoudi wound up exiled and disgraced, claiming that he had been punished for an excess of pan-Arab loyalty and for a critical attitude toward the United States. Bourguiba returned for a time to his clinic in Geneva.

The Libyan venture was clearly an aberration on Bourguiba's part, and was explained away in succeeding months. Qadhafi kept pressing: he proposed a referendum; he made the provision of financial credit conditional on the execution of various cooperative programs; he rejected Tunisia's proposal for arbitration of the disputed boundary of territorial waters, thought to be rich in petroleum, between the two countries on the pretext that they had already agreed in principle to unite; in March 1975 he caused a stir by inviting himself to attend a religious ceremony in the Tunisian city of Kairouan. But the Tunisians held him at arm's length, and Foreign Minister Chatti openly described relations with Libya as "frozen."[39]

There seems to be little likelihood that in the foreseeable future, this or any other unity agreement will regain Tunisian interest, even under a very different regime, for Tunisia is too distinctive from its neighbors in its history, economy, and society to make unity an easy proposition. Still, much will depend on economic circumstances. One attraction that union with Libya would undeniably present would be an open market for Tunisian labor. According to a Tunisian source, 40,000 Tunisians are present in Libya;[40] the elimination of controls would no doubt increase this figure significantly. The idea that Tunisian manpower and Libyan capital are natural partners would certainly gain impetus if Tunisia's own economic prospects were to take a turn for the worse.

Meanwhile Tunisia's economic relations with its other Maghrib neighbors have remained insignificant, despite excellent political relations, for there is little complementarity. The ministerial economic council which was to work toward the creation of a common market had not met in four years, Chatti noted in December 1974.[41]

Libya

Though a contiguous Arabic-speaking North African state, in several important ways Libya stands apart from Tunisia, Algeria, and Morocco. Its population is much smaller—roughly two million, compared to Tunisia's six million, Algeria's fifteen million, and Morocco's sixteen million; its cities are smaller; its agricultural base is comparatively negligible. On the other hand its oil income—conservatively estimated at 4.5 billion for 1974—vastly outstrips its absorptive capacity, so that it can easily take care of primary consumption needs whether it progresses or not. Libya's colonial experience was mainly Italian rather than French and left a more transient legacy. Its international posture since the 1969 revolution has been strident and disruptive even by Algeria's fairly militant standards.

Until 1969, Libya ranked among the quietest, most obscure Middle Eastern states, taken for granted by all concerned as a conservative monarchy whose only functions were to supply one-third of Western Europe's oil consumption, provide military bases to Britain and the United States, and give employment to skilled workers and professionals from other Arab countries. With a backward and isolated society ruled over by an aging and ineffectual monarch, Libya could not be taken seriously. This perspective was to change with the coup d'état of Colonel Mu'ammar Qadhafi and his group of officers on September 1, 1969.

Domestic and Foreign Politics

Libya's revolutionary regime under Qadhafi may be compared in some ways to the Egyptian regime created by Gamal Abdel Nasser, the man Qadhafi so much admired. Both regimes arose from the seizure of power by young, obscure officers from a discredited monarchy. Both Qadhafi and Nasser prospered politically by closing Western military bases, rejecting British and American influence, and adopting the cause of pan-Arabism. In both countries the soldiers perpetuated their control of society by highly authoritarian means, behind a facade of mainly civilian administration and a single-party apparatus which, despite the official verbiage, seemed designed more to preempt mass politics than to encourage genuine popular participation.

The parallels do not carry very far, however, for Libya is not Egypt and Qadhafi is not Nasser. The Egyptian Free Officers, men in their early thirties, had grown up before the 1952 coup in a relatively cosmopolitan and sophisticated society; many of them were well educated; they inherited a rather highly developed (if inefficient) civil service and national economic infrastructure. The Libyan officers in 1969 were only in their mid-twenties (though Qadhafi himself was variously reported to be between twenty-six and thirty-one), and many of them were from truly deprived provincial backgrounds even by the standards of an impoverished and isolated Libya. Qadhafi himself was born in a Bedouin tent in Sirte and attended school in the desert oasis of Sebha in the Fezzan; Prime Minister Jalloud is also of Fezzani nomadic background.

Whereas Nasser was an essentially secular-minded man with a broad familiarity with world events, Qadhafi is a religious puritan and fundamentalist who proclaims the conviction that Koranic scripture should serve as the basis for national and international policy and denounces foreign cultural influences on Libyan life as poisonous. It would be difficult to imagine Nasser or any of his colleagues promulgating the likes of Colonel Qadhafi's "cultural revolution" launched in April 1973, in which he enunciated the following agenda:

1. The repeal of all existing laws, in favor of revolutionary decrees.
2. The elimination of "feeble" minds, perverts, and deviationists" from society.
3. An administrative revolution against "bourgeois" and "bureaucratic" tendencies.
4. The creation of popular committees to seize power for the people from bureaucrats and opportunists.
5. A cultural revolution against imported ideas.[42]

In practice, nothing of significance emerged from this confused verbiage. Qadhafi was evidently inspired at least superficially in his "cultural revolution" by the example of Mao Tse-tung, whom he is known to admire. He also had a "Green Book" of his own sayings issued and may have vaguely been influenced by the "Long March" of the Chinese Communists when in July 1973 he dispatched a convoy of several thousand Libyan citizens across the border into Egypt to demand union between the two countries.

But whatever the outward gestures of populism, fundamentally Qadhafi and his fellow-officers followed the Nasserite practice of keeping all political life under tight central control. From the beginning, independent organization and activity, even in support of the new regime, were discouraged; all political party activity (other than that of the officially sponsored Arab Socialist Union, a carbon copy of its Egyptian counterpart) was prohibited; even the "popular committees" of the cultural revolution were carefully supervised from above and were prudently kept away from government ministries altogether. The trade-union movement, potentially a focal point of political participation at the popular level and of organized autonomy from the government, was sternly admonished by Qadhafi to keep away from all politics and even from bread-and-butter bargaining.[43]

In the early stages, the attitude of the regime toward autonomous political parties and other popular institutions was frankly hostile, and bespoke a belief—not unlike that enunciated more recently by General Saraiva de Carvalho in Portugal—that the army itself represented the only valid popular political movement. When asked by a French journalist a few weeks after the coup why the military monopolized the revolution, Qadhafi replied:

Frankly speaking, the officers have the conscience to recognise the people's claims better than others. This depends on our origin which is characterised by humbleness. We are not rich people; the parents of the majority of us are living in tents. My parents are still living in a tent near Sirte. The interests we represent are genuinely those of the Libyan people.[44]

As time passed, the expressions and institutional formulae became more subtle, though the underlying perspective did not. In April 1975, for example, Qadhafi announced the creation of a new organ of popular representation, the National General Congress, within a new system which would "turn the whole people into an instrument of rule." Members would be drawn in part from local committees, which in turn would be chosen by meetings attended by all citizens; other members would be sent by syndical bodies. But whatever the method of selection, it would not be by election, for according to Qadhafi, "election is not a democratic method."[45]

Despite periodic abortive announcements of his decision to resign from the government and rumors of rifts within the Revolutionary Command Council, Qadhafi has continued to dominate Libyan affairs consistently since the 1969 coup. In 1972 he turned over the prime ministry to Major Abdel Salam Jalloud, and in April 1974 the RCC announced that it had relieved Qadhafi of his administrative duties at his own request, to enable him to devote his attention to ideological questions. But, despite these formalities and some apparent differences in temperament between him and Jalloud, it became evident thereafter that Qadhafi was still very much in charge.

In foreign affairs, Qadhafi's Libya has become an international byword for reckless adventurism in the service of a zealous commitment to pan-Arabism. Arms and money have been sent to revolutionary movements that have caught Qadhafi's fancy as far afield as the Irish Republican Army and to Muslim dissidents in the Philippines. Closer to home, Libya has been deeply involved in the affairs of Malta, Chad, Uganda, the Palestinian liberation movement including its terrorist branches, and virtually every fellow-Arab state, in several cases loudly preaching the overthrow of established regimes.

Among the great powers Libya has walked a somewhat more cautious path: although its leaders have expressed a good measure of harsh opinions from time to time about Britain, France, the Soviet Union and particularly the United States, correct diplomatic relations and normal commerce have been preserved. In fact, of Qadhafi's first gestures was to buy *Mirage* aircraft from France. In

May 1975, soon after the British government turned down Libya's application to buy large quantities of weapons, Soviet Premier Kosygin visited Tripoli and concluded a major arms deal with the Libyan government, conservatively estimated at $800 million.[46] Several years' coolness to the Soviets on grounds of Qadhafi's fundamentalist religious ideology was evidently overcome.

The most consistently dominant concern in Libya's external relations since 1969 (and in some ways even before) has been Egypt. This has been only natural, in view of Egypt's proximity, its role as supplier of skilled manpower to Libya, and its predominant role in Arab affairs. Qadhafi's admiration of Nasser, his attachment to Arab unity, his fervent commitment to the confrontation with Israel, and Egypt's need for transfusions of Libyan money lent extra impetus to Libyan-Egyptian collaboration.

In April 1971 Egypt, Libya, and Syria agreed to form a loose confederation, the Union of Arab Republics. Qadhafi pressed subsequently for a full union between Libya and Egypt, finally inducing Sadat to agree in August 1972 that this would take place by September of the following year. As the deadline approached, it became evident that the Egyptian government had no intention of going through with the merger and preferred a mere continuation of close cooperation and the flow of much-needed Libyan subsidies and investments. Qadhafi had to settle for a vaguely worded joint declaration with Sadar of future intentions of union.

The Egyptian-Syrian war against Israel in October 1973, in which Sadat turned his back on Qadhafi and prepared the ground for negotiations with Israel and the United States, completely wrecked the Tripoli-Cairo axis and caused Qadhafi to denounce what he considered the Egyptian "sellout." By mid-1975, relations had settled into a pattern of continuous recrimination. Meanwhile, Qadhafi had turned in January 1974 to his neighbor Bourguiba, president of Tunisia, and signed an agreement for union; but the Tunisians soon thought better of it and hastily backed away. Whatever the attractions of Libya's wealth, neither of her poorer and more populous neighbors thought it worthwhile to be dragged into a permanent embrace with the difficult Qadhafi.

Oil and the Economy

Libya is among the world's most fabulous examples of a poor country suddenly acquiring great wealth as a result of the discovery of oil. Libyan oil first entered the international market in a trickle in 1960; within five years production reached a million barrels a day, a climb of unmatched rapidity elsewhere. By the time of the 1969 coup, the figure was over three million, and the government's oil revenues had reached around $800 million per year.

Unlike other Middle East countries, the Libyan oil fields in the 1960s were exploited by a host of different companies operating under a national Petroleum

Law calculated to diversify concessions. By 1969, some thirty-eight companies—mostly American, but also British, French, German, Spanish—operated a total of one-hundred and thirty-six concessions. The Qadhafi regime after its seizure of power initially showed great circumspection toward the companies, but once its position was consolidated it set out with great vigor and skill to transform its relations with them. First, in 1970, it successfully demanded an increase in the posted price of crude oil; then, in 1971 when the Teheran agreement on price increases was reached between the major oil companies and the major producing countries of the Gulf, Libya rejected the terms and successfully insisted on an additional premium for its oil, on the grounds of proximity to the European market and its higher quality. Later in 1971 and again in 1973, along with other OPEC members Libya secured further increases to compensate for the devaluation of the dollar; and of course it shared in the general quadrupling of prices engineered by OPEC after the October 1973 war.

Beginning in December 1971, the Libyan government also carried out an extensive series of nationalizations of concessionary companies and, under threat of unilateral nationalization, negotiated 51 percent participation agreements with others. As in the case of price increases, the Libyan strategy was to confront foreign companies one at a time; some capitulated readily, others held out for a time but eventually bowed to the inevitable and accepted the modest book-value compensation offered them. By the time of the last capitulation—that of Royal Dutch-Shell, which was fully nationalized in March 1974 and accepted terms in June—the share of the Libyan National Oil Company (LINOCO) in total production had risen from virtually zero in 1971 to 61.53 percent.[47]

The significance of the aggressive oil strategy of the Qadhafi regime cannot yet be fully assessed. If measured in terms of negotiating success, it has been not only brilliant in itself but a dramatic example for other OPEC members, whose boldness after the October War surely owed something to Libya's earlier determination and ability to force its own terms on the companies. Libya has also set an example, at least for other surplus revenue earners like Kuwait and Abu Dhabi, in deliberately reducing production for the sake of conservation: with estimated reserves of 26.6 billion barrels, production at the rate reached in the peak year of 1970 (3.3 million barrels a day) would have meant exhausting the supply in twenty-two years. The daily production rate was cut to 2.2 million in 1972. Subsequently, however, production dropped further as a result of the lack of demand, falling to about one million barrels a day in the first months of 1975. In June 1975 it was reported that Libya had cut the price of its direct-sale and buy-back crude by twenty to thirty-six cents in an effort to increase production, and the oil minister, Izzeddin Mabruk, expressed his hope that production would return to a level of 1.7 million barrels a day.[48] Evidently the Libyans were finding that price and production levels were not as readily manipulable, under conditions of a declining world demand, as they had hoped.

As for the significance of nationalization and participation, it remains to be seen whether Libya will manage to turn the new formulas of ownership into something more than merely advantageous financial arrangements with the foreign companies, which continue as before to produce, ship, and market the oil while buying the Libyan share of the production from LINOCO.[a] Such "buy-back" arrangements, which have now become familiar throughout the Middle East, are no doubt more in keeping with the prevailing ideological climate of post-colonial nationalism than the old system of royalty payments by Concessionnaires, but the substantive difference is not very great, and the term "participation" is misleading: a more apt term, commonly used by one noted authority, is pseudo-participation."[49]

Certainly Libya would like to move beyond psuedo-participation to the point where its oil industry could genuinely be operated and controlled by Libyan personnel and made to serve as the basis of a broader program of industrialization and economic expansion along the lines being followed by the Algerians. However, Libya lacks several important advantages possessed at least in part by Algeria: a pool of trained manpower, a local market, an agricultural base and a commercial network.

Despite the spectacular growth of oil revenues, Libya has made only modest progress in the development of its economy and its future prospects for economic development are not very good. Translating an abundant supply of public funds into a substantial harnessing of latent productive capacities, and thus into a sustained affluence for the mass of the population, is not an easy matter. It is probably true to say that too much available money is one of Libya's handicaps, since it tends to remove important incentives.

Several other handicaps are evident. Natural resources other than oil are negligible. Only 2 percent of Libya's 680,000 square miles is arable, although there are some prospects of finding and developing additional sources of water. The population numbers only two million, almost half of it nomadic, and is widely dispersed, largely unskilled and uneducated. The Italian colonizers left the Libyans with little to build upon in the way of communications, industry, or a system of public administration, health and educational services, etc. Moreover, like the French in Algeria, the Italians had tended to monopolize crafts and commercial trades and the small modern agricultural sector, leaving behind great gaps in expertise when they departed. When Libya became independent in 1951, it was habitually cited by economists as among the world's most unpromising nations. With a per capita income estimated in 1945 at $25, its resources exhausted, and capital accumulation zero or even negative, it seemed more accurate to describe Libya as overdeveloped than underdeveloped.[50]

Despite the obvious benefits, the advent of the oil industry created enormous

---

[a]To be sure, Libya and other producing states are moving rapidly into the refining business into which they feed their own oil, and to some extent into direct bulk sales to foreign governments.

distortions in the Libyan economy. Among the main problems one may cite inflation; stagnation of agriculture; heavy urban migration; heavy unemployment and underemployment in the unskilled labor sector combined with serious shortages of skilled labor; a great influx of non-Libyan workers and managers to compensate for the shortage; a burgeoning and incapable bureaucracy and a haphazard, wasteful, ineffective process of planning for economic development. These problems were full-blown by the time of the 1969 revolution and, despite important political changes, they have largely remained.

The basis of these problems lies in the nature of the oil industry itself; it is a capital-intensive, high technology enterprise run by foreigners, and employing only a handful of Libyans.[51] While the industry is integrated into the international industrial economy, it is almost completely insulated from the backward local one. Yet it pours money into the hands of an ill-equipped government that must search for ways to dispose of it but lacks incentive to invest it in the most productive channels.

The greatest needs, from the standpoint of economic health and social welfare alike, are the improvement of agriculture and animal husbandry, training of skilled manpower, and the restraining of a rampant inflation which impoverishes the mass of the population. Two-thirds of Libya's population live on the land and one-third of its work force is engaged there, yet, in 1970, agriculture's share of the gross domestic product had fallen to less than 3 percent.[52] Meanwhile the rapid migration to urban centers and the influx of foreigners stimulated a dramatic increase in food consumption, all of it imported; importation was an easy alternative to the development of domestic agriculture, a field which the farmers themselves were fleeing and which offered no attraction to investors and speculators.

The revolutionary government has shown a notably greater interest in agriculture, allocating first 14 percent and later 22 percent of the budget of the 1972-75 development plan to it, but it has also exhibited a deplorable fascination for high-technology, fundamentally irrelevant and wasteful schemes such as the Kufra project, which it inherited from the monarchy, in which livestock are raised on a patch of remote desert land reclaimed at great cost with deep-drilled underground water. In the words of one critic, Kufra is like "shooting pigeons with rockets. . . . Like the oil industry, Kufra will be a slice of technology inserted into a backward economy and, like oil, run by foreigners. . . . It is a combination of the extravagant spending momentum of the oil economy together with the army cult of management and technology."[53]

The solution of Libya's manpower problems is also deflected by easy money. Well before the revolution, the monarchical regime made the fateful error of establishing civil service salary rates higher than those available in the commercial economy, including the oil industry itself; the military regime has perpetuated this policy, meanwhile guaranteeing government employment to the swelling numbers of secondary school and university graduates. As a result, by

1972 the Civil Service Department reported a government payroll of 134,560—over a quarter of the total national work force—not counting the armed forces and police. A high proportion of foreigners were employed in the top echelons, and one-third of such posts were actually vacant for lack of qualified candidates; with skilled employees being paid little more than unskilled ones, incentive for technical education is lacking. Meanwhile, skilled manpower for agriculture and industry cannot be developed.[54]

Moreover, an overcrowded and underqualified civil service, combined with a secretive, authoritarian, romantically inclined political leadership, cannot produce an orderly and rational selection of planning and investment priorities. There is no lack of reports, commissions, imported foreign expertise, and projects available for inspection at Cabinet level, in fact there are probably too many; but with a plethora of capital, every choice is always plausible and open to adoption on the basis of whim.

To be sure, despite misplaced priorities, some elements of progress seem inevitable. Schools, dwellings, roads, and hospitals are being built; Libyans are being educated, fed, and medically treated. In time, more of them will no doubt become qualified themselves to administer these services rather than leave them to foreigners. The course followed by national education in the future decades will be one of the keys to whether these benefits have any appreciable multiplier effect.[55] But even if they do, they may remain within a limited and privileged social stratum that grows up in the shadow of oil prosperity and passes for a middle class, leaving untouched a larger popular sector of rural and urban poor.

Future Prospects

In the future, Libya is likely to be both a source of international disruption and, as a wealthy but weak society, the object of its neighbor's designs.

Great powers and Arab and African neighbors alike will have to ponder the example Colonel Qadhafi has set. Oil wealth, plus energy and zeal, can provide immense possibilities for reckless adventure to an ambitious leader bored with the tasks and challenges at home. Were Qadhafi to disappear, his fellow-members of the Libyan military regime would probably develop a more accommodating international posture, yet the difference might not prove to be fundamental. Qadhafi's greatest limitations are not those of his own personality but those that must confront any regime in that backward country, especially a regime of soldiers with a provincial and authoritarian outlook. On the other hand, it seems natural that Qadhafi's international activism should be practiced at least to some degree by his successors as they search for a role in the world and an object to which to devote the surplus funds they control.

Meanwhile, one cannot discount the prospect that at some time in the coming decade some form of political and economic union between Libya and either

Tunisia or Egypt may come about, under circumstances that cannot now be specifically predicted. It is enough to recall that Libya came to the point of reaching a formal agreement for unity with Egypt in 1972, and again with Tunisia in 1974, and that in each case there were some influential men such as Mohammed Hasanein Haikal in Cairo and Mohammed Masmoudi in Tunis, who saw good reason to consummate the arrangement. Given the attractions of Libya's resources to its more populous and developed but poorer neighbors, it is not at all inconceivable that at some future time efforts will be made by one or the other to revive the idea of unification, even by the use of force or subversion, or even with the concurrence of a visionary Libyan leader like Colonel Qadhafi. In extreme circumstances in the course of a future international- al oil crisis, Libya could conceivably find itself threatened with military attack from Western Europe or the United States; and no matter how flatly and sincerely the latter countries may disclaim such intentions at present, this is an eventuality than any Libyan leader must give thought to. In comparison, such dangers make little sense under any imaginable circumstances in the three Maghrib countries to the west.

Internally, Libya's need is to use its revenues efficiently to develop agricul- ture, industry, and education so an economically viable base exists after the oil is depleted, as it may be within several decades. Given its current income, even under conditions of mismanagement, some measure of success seems assured, but it is not clear what class of people will emerge to lead the country and operate the economy or with what infrastructure available. Libya is certain to continue to be overshadowed in the production of high-level manpower by all its North African neighbors, especially Egypt; and it is likely that in the long run any Egyptian regime will seek ways to tap Libya's wealth, either by intimidation or cooperation.

Conclusion

Despite the differences in their societies and institutions, it should be clear from the foregoing analysis that the states of the Maghrib share some important problems with much of the underdeveloped world at large. Although all four have, in greatly varying degrees, experienced some significant increase in national income (thanks especially to windfall raises in oil and phosphate prices), none has yet been successful in developing its agricultural sector on which the livelihood of the majority of its population depends or in dealing with the grave problems of urban as well as rural unemployment. In each country, the advent of independence, the increase in disposable revenues, and the spread of education have stimulated the growth of large bureaucracies and these, to a considerable extent, provide the framework for the growing new middle classes. These classes employed by the state do not, by and large, contribute greatly to national productivity, but dependent as they are on their local regimes, they inevitably encourage the rulers' instincts, inherited from more traditional times, of authoritarianism and patronage by providing a ready clientele.

In each country, the problem of integrating the most modern sectors of the economy into the whole has not been solved. As we have seen, this is most pronounced in Libya, where a vast and sophisticated oil industry, closely geared to an international network of production and trade, is operated overwhelmingly by foreign experts, gives employment to very few Libyans, and results in very little transfer of usable technology to the local backward society. To some extent this problem is duplicated in the phosphate, oil, and gas industries of Tunisia, Morocco, and Algeria, as well as in a host of other enterprises which their governments promote in the name of development, from steel mills to telecommunications. In these countries, to be sure, many more local citizens are trained and employed at responsible levels, yet to the extent that they are, they are separated from the mass of their fellow citizens and form a privileged and insulated social and cultural corps of their own.

Thus industrialization, while it may be the salvation of ministries of finance in the North African countries, is unlikely to prove to be the salvation of the common man, as long as it remains unaccompanied by the modernization of agriculture and the effective mobilization of rural society. This is not a challenge that can be met by foreign technical experts, nor by national leaderships— whether "revolutionary" or conservative—preoccupied with status, prestige, and the acquisition of the latest technology. And yet in all likelihood it is these experts and leaderships that will remain on the scene in North Africa for decades to come, despite whatever changes in regime may take place, in the name of whatever radical ideology. As long as the state revenues and the elaborately drafted four-year plans are on hand, the impetus toward bureaucratic solutions to national problems will always be difficult to overcome. If that is the case, large pockets of poverty and backwardness may be expected to remain on the scene.

Of course, that is only one side of a complex picture. On another side, with equal assurance one can forecast some ongoing success in the development of modern industrial, commercial, and cultural sectors of North African society— more, perhaps, in Algeria and Tunisia than in Morocco or Libya, yet in all cases enough to justify at least a plausible claim of national progress, and at the same time to affect the social and political structure, and undermine the grip of each of the currently ruling regimes. And certainly it will make a difference what the pace and style of change in each case will be. Leaving aside Libya, the disposable revenues of which seem destined to continue to outstrip the wildest ambitions of its economic planners, one may at least say that in the other three countries the struggle for long-range economic viability as national entities on the world stage will face uncertain prospects and preoccupy each set of national elites for an indefinite time. Success and failure will come disjunctively, unevenly, and often unrecognizably. The ability of governments to maintain their authority will depend heavily on what sort of progress, for whose benefit and with what continuing prospects, key segments of the elite think is being made; but in any case, there will surely be no lack of difficulties available to lend credence to critics and challengers of the government of the day.

This is most obviously the case in Morocco, where the very institution of the monarchy is more and more an anomalous symbol in the contemporary world, and what a direct connection between the stagnation of the economy and the glaring corruption of the regime is there for all to see. It seems likely that there will be more violence in Morocco. In Tunisia the problem is more limited: Bourguiba has accomplished a great deal, but has remained in office too long. In so doing he has shut out too many politicians, alienated too many young people, and allowed too much entrenched privilege and self-satisfaction to set in. Moreover, in Tunisia as in Morocco, after the current leadership there will probably be room for a long time to come for left-right ideological conflict on economic policy, since advocates on both sides are available in large numbers and the experience of past years offers no clear basis for consensus.

In Algeria the prospects for political stability seem better, though not altogether unambiguous. This is less a judgment about Boumédienne personally— who, like strongmen elsewhere, is always in some danger of being suddenly ousted—than about the general system of authority and social and economic policies that he represents. Any successor must rule with the endorsement of the army and the participation of the technocracy and, for a host of reasons, is very unlikely to break with the established patterns of the Algerian state-dominated economy, with its emphasis on industrialization, education, and bureaucratic regulation. Struggles for power are unlikely to reflect basic conflicts over ideology and policy, nor among competing social interests except at a local level, for whatever the disabilities of several million rural Algerians, there is no one to speak for them and no very convincing argument, so long as investment capital and industrialization blueprints are available, that present priorities are seriously misplaced. By the same token, Algeria's foreign policy, which is so emphatically oriented toward the goal of optimizing the terms of trade with the industrialized world, is unlikely to be a bone of contention in its internal political life, although issues may arise over more specific aspects of it.

What interests of the United States, and what policy choices for this nation are at stake in the future of the North African countries? The interests are not negligible, but they are few and secondary in comparison to other parts of the world, including the Middle Eastern region adjacent to the Maghrib. American ties with Morocco and Tunisia have been friendly and cooperative since they each became independent in 1956, but there is not a great deal to cement them in the way of commerce, shared culture or the exchange of persons. Conversely, diplomatic relations with Algeria and, since 1969, with Libya have been cool at best, while commerce has thrived, although by American standards the volume cannot be considered of great significance. American air bases in Libya and Morocco, when they existed, were no doubt of some strategic importance, but this was already fast dwindling by the time the bases were given up years ago; the present American naval communications facilities in Morocco are not of vital importance.

There are three areas of American interest in North Africa, however, that ought not to be overlooked in any serious review of the affairs of the Maghrib countries. First, they have a close and continuous relationship with the rest of the Arab world. They are therefore involved in the Arab-Israeli conflict and capable in some ways of influencing the front-line Arab participants. Strong ties with the United States, or at least the maintenance of smooth diplomatic relations, must count for something in facilitating U.S. peace initiatives or in promoting Arab tolerance of American positions that are relatively favorable to Israel.

Second, there is the Mediterranean strategic arena. While the United States has no need and even less expectation of access to naval or air bases in the Maghrib states, it goes without saying that the establishment of Soviet bases there—and thus the strengthening of Soviet military capabilities in the Mediterranean—would be alarming, especially in the context of political crisis in one country after another all around the Mediterranean in recent years.[56] With Libya's purchase of Soviet arms in the spring of 1975 and its growing estrangement from Egypt, the prospects in the next several years for the Soviets' acquisition of some form of base rights in Libya cannot be dismissed, if indeed they have not already secretly obtained them. Reports have circulated that the Soviets concurrently communicated their interest in establishing bases to the Tunisian and Moroccan governments—a highly implausible proposition on the face of it, yet perhaps explainable as a Soviet move to anticipate changes in the regimes of those two countries. Paradoxically, it is Algeria, for many years the North African country in closest relations with the USSR and the only nation to rely mainly on Soviet weapons, that now seems the least likely in the next decade or so to grant special military rights to the Soviets—or to any one else.

These first two areas of interest for the United States present no particular clear-cut set of policy options. America will find North Africans available as friendly intermediaries in the Arab world, and resistant to Soviet requests for military privileges, pretty much to the extent that the United States takes care to cultivate good bilateral relations and to display respect for general Pan-Arab and Pan-African sensitivities, especially in relation to Israel and southern Africa respectively.

The third and last area of interest is different; it is more fundamental, more complicated, and poses a real policy dilemma for the United States and its industrial partners at large. I am referring, of course, to oil and gas and potentially to all the other primary materials exported by the Third World which the Algerians, particularly (seconded by the Libyans), would like to harness to their campaign for the transformation of world economic relations.

Materially speaking, it is obvious that neither Algeria nor Libya, with their limited oil reserves, is at the center of U.S. concerns (although imports of Algerian natural gas are prospectively important to the American consumer). Yet Algeria's role is important far beyond what the volume of its own exports may suggest, in view of its deadly serious determination to exert leadership among raw materials producers at large and to press for dramatic changes in the terms of trade. And it is highly unlikely that the Algerians will trade away this position for other gains, such as a change in American policy toward the Middle East conflict, nor that the replacement of Boumédienne by someone else would make a difference. The terms-of-trade issue has acquired the status of a fundamental priority in Algeria and appears destined to grow in importance in the outlook of other countries too—including Morocco, Tunisia, and a number of other Arab and African neighbors. Thus the only critical choice for Americans in North Africa is really no more than a part of a broader choice they face in restructuring their international trade relations with much of the developing world.

Notes

1. Elbaki Hermassi, *Leadership and National Development in North Africa* (Berkeley and Los Angeles: University of California Press, 1972), p. 102.

2. An extended analysis of the Moroccan patronage system and its clientele is contained in John Waterbury, *The Commander of the Faithful: the Moroccan Political Elite* (New York: Columbia University Press, 1970). *passim.*

3. The 1971 and 1972 coups are discussed in detail in two articles by John Waterbury: "The Coup Manqué," American Universities Field Staff, *Fieldstaff Reports: Africa* 15, 1 (July 1971); and "The Politics of the Seraglio," ibid., 16, 1 (September 1972). Information about the army presented here is also based on interviews in Rabat in January 1975.

4. Abdel Aziz Belal, *L'investissement au Maroc* (Paris: Mouton, 1968), pp. 314-316.

5. André Tiano, *LeMaghreb entre les mythes* (Paris: Presses Universitaires de France, 1967), p. 542.

6. Mohamed Lahbabi, *Les années 80 de notre jeunesse* (Casablanca: Editions Maghrébines, 1970), pp. 44-45.

7. Hermassi, *Leadership*, pp. 181-183.

8. See various statistics provided by Lahbabi, *Les années 80*, pp. 32-43.

9. Minister of Finance Abdel Kader Benslimane, press conference, December 30, 1974. *Arab Report & Record*, December 16-31, 1974, p. 584.

10. Information provided by Omar Benmansour, Chef de Cabinet, State Secretariat for Planning and Regional Development, interview, January 23, 1975.

11. I am indebted for these conclusions to John Waterbury, "Endemic and

Planned Corruption in a Monarchical Regime," *World Politics* 25, 4 (July 1973): 533-555.

12. Abdelkrim Ghallab, editor, *Al-Alam* newspaper, Rabat, interview, January 23, 1975.

13. See William B. Quandt, *Revolution and Political Leadership: Algeria, 1954-1968* (Cambridge: MIT Press, 1969), *passim*.

14. U.S. Department of Commerce, Overseas Business Reports 74-30: *Marketing in Algeria* (July 1974), p. 8.

15. Ibid., pp. 7-8.

16. Ibid., pp. 9-10.

17. Finance Minister Smail Mahroug, "Les Grandes lignes du budget 1975," *Algérie Actualité*, January 5-11, 1975, pp. 3-5.

18. Hermassi, p. 207.

19. Samir Amin, *The Maghreb in the Modern World* (London: Penguin, 1970), p. 138.

20. Ibid., *passim*.

21. See *Le Monde*, May 15 and 16, 1975.

22. See for example William B. Quandt, "Can We Do Business with Radical Nationalists: (1) Algeria: Yes," *Foreign Policy*, No. 7 (Summer 1972): 108-131.

23. *El Moujahid*, November 20, 1974.

24. *Arab Report & Record*, February 16-28, 1975, p. 130.

25. Ibid., May 1-15, 1975, p. 270.

26. *Le Monde*, April 29, 1975.

27. *Arab Report & Record*, May 1-15, 1975, p. 270.

28. See the interesting study of Henri Montety, "Enquête sur les vieilles familles et les nouvelles élites en Tunisie," mimeo, Paris, 1939 (translated in I.W. Zartman (ed.), *Man, State, and Society in the Contemporary Maghrib* [Praeger: New York, 1973], pp. 171-180).

29. Amin, *The Maghreb*, pp. 161-162.

30. U.S. Department of Commerce, *Economic Trends and Their Implications for the United States, ET 74-008: Tunisia* (January 1974), p. 4.

31. *The Guardian* (London), February 28, 1975.

32. *Le Monde*, September 15-16, 1974.

33. Ibid.; Associated Press dispatch, cited in *Arab Report & Record* (London), August 16-31, 1974, p. 356.

34. *Arab Report & Record, loc. cit.*

35. *Le Monde*, September 15-16, 1974.

36. *The Guardian*, February 28, 1975.

37. *Arab Report & Record*, September 1-15, 1974, p. 380.

38. For this and other data on higher education see Malcolm H. Kerr, "Tunisian Education: Seeds of Revolution?", *Middle East Forum* (Beirut) 47, 3-4 (Autumn-Winter 1971): pp. 83-92.

39. Speech of December 22, 1974, reported in *Arab Report & Record*, December 16-31, 1974, p. 589.

40. *L'Action* (Tunis), February 27, 1975.

41. *Arab Report & Record*, December 16-31, 1974, p. 589.

42. For an account of the cultural revolution, see Ruth First, *Libya: The Elusive Revolution* (Penguin, 1974), pp. 137-140.

43. Ibid., pp. 123,131.

44. Ibid., p. 121.

45. *Arab Report & Record*, April 16-30, 1975, p. 254.

46. This was the figure given out by the Soviets. The Cairo daily *Al-Ahram* on May 23, claimed that $4 billion in arms were being provided, with Libya providing the Soviets with military bases in return—an allegation vigorously denied by Libyan spokesmen. President Sadat told *The Los Angeles Times* (May 28) that the arms were worth $12 billion. It must be borne in mind that these Egyptian changes were made at a time when relations with the Libyan regime were bitterly hostile, and the Egyptians had every motive to exaggerate.

47. *Arab World File (Fiches du Monde Arabe)*, No. 66 September 4, 1974, "The Libyan Nationalisations."

48. *Middle East Economic Survey* (Beirut), June 14, 1975.

49. M.A. Adelman, "Is the Oil Shortage Real?", *Foreign Policy*, No. 9 (Winter 1972-73): 69-107.

50. See Galal Amin, *The Modernization of Poverty* (Leiden: E.J. Brill, 1974), pp. 4-5.

51. Figures released by the Libyan Census Department showed that in 1970 only 6,478 Libyans were employed by the oil companies themselves, and another 6,391 by companies providing services to the oil industry (cited in First, *Libya*, p. 175.) This represents 2.6 percent of a total labor force of 500,000.

52. First, *Libya*, p. 162.

53. Ibid., pp. 169-170. In 1975 Libya signed an agreement with the Soviet Union to build a nuclear reactor, apparently in hopes of using nuclear power to pump underground water for large agricultural projects. (*Arab Report & Record*, June 1-15, 1975, p. 339.)

54. First, *Libya* pp. 174-176.

55. Ragaei El Mallakh, "The Economics of Rapid Growth: Libya," *Middle East Journal*, XXIII, 3 (Summer 1969), p. 319, cites seemingly impressive statistics of educational progress under the monarchy: notably, an 85 percent rate of school attendance by 1968. But such figures even if accepted at face value, tell us little about the content, product, or social impact of education.

56. See John C. Campbell, "The Mediterranean Crisis," *Foreign Affairs* 53, 4 (July 1975): 605-624.

XV Saudi Arabia and the Gulf States

John B. Kelly

Introduction

Until the end of the Second World War Saudi Arabia and the Gulf states lived in comparative isolation from the outside world and even from the rest of the Middle East. In large measure this isolation was the product of geographical and economic circumstances but it also owed something to the presence of Great Britain as the protecting power in the region. British policy was primarily concerned to exclude outside powers from interfering in the Gulf's affairs and to restrain the ambitions of Saudi Arabia, Iran, and Iraq within the Gulf, especially those ambitions which bore upon the minor states which had special treaty relations with Great Britain: Kuwait, Bahrain, Qatar, the Trucial shaikhdoms, and Oman. The end of the Gulf's isolation came with the discovery and development of the vast oil resources lying along the shores and in the interior of Arabia and Iran. After the Second World War, the Gulf was transformed from one of the poorest areas of the world into one of the richest, a transformation which was attended, not surprisingly, by profound social and economic upheaval. Politically, the consequences were not so marked, and they did not begin to make themselves felt until the early 1960s, when the Gulf states began to be drawn, one by one, into the wider circle of Arab politics, and, after 1967, into the Arab-Israeli dispute and the orbit of great-power diplomacy.

The British withdrawal from the Gulf at the end of 1971 ended the era of protection, and since that time the Gulf states have remained in a condition of uneasy equilibrium, sustained by the prodigious wealth they derive from oil production and by the attention and deference of an anxious world. It is a lull which, given the record of the past and the inherent political instability of the Gulf, cannot last for long.

The examination which follows of the current situation in Saudi Arabia and the Gulf states, and of the elements in this situation which make for change and instability, is concerned, first, with social and economic conditions, second, with the internal politics of each state, and, third, with relations among these states. The final section examines United States and Western interests in the Gulf region.

Social and Economic Conditions

A generation ago the nature of society in Saudi Arabia and the Gulf states was very much what it had been for previous centuries. Its basis of organization was the tribe, and tribal customs and traditions, along with the prescriptions of Islam, constituted what might be called the common law. The population was divided in every state but Bahrain into sedentary and nomadic sections. The sedentary section was composed of cultivators, artisans, merchants, fishermen, seafarers, and others, while the nomadic consisted of tribes or segments of tribes which customarily wandered in search of pasture for their flocks and herds. There were also semi-nomadic tribesmen—cultivators or fishermen who grazed flocks in the vicinity of their settlements—and an amorphous group known as *huwailah*, detribalized and semi-Persianized Arabs who roamed the Gulf in search of employment. The layers of eastern Arabian society were traditionally composed of the ruling dynasties, the shaikhly families of the tribes, the *qadis* and *ulema*, the merchants and artisans, seafarers, nomads, cultivators, and slaves. Sunni Islam prevailed throughout the eastern Arabia, although there were substantial Shii minorities in Bahrain and Hasa (the eastern province of Saudi Arabia) and a large Ibadi community in Oman.

The balance which formerly existed in Arabian society—which outside the seaports was highly homogeneous—has in large measure been destroyed by the influx of immigrants in the last two decades. Detribalization has also gone on inexorably, so that nowadays it is only in the interior of Saudi Arabia and Oman that the tribal character of society is still marked. Bedu have virtually disappeared from the interior of Kuwait, Qatar, and parts of the United Arab Emirates; most of them have drifted to the coastal towns in search of work, or to live, like so many inhabitants of these towns who a few years ago were fishermen or seafarers, off the bounty of their rulers. These detribalized Bedu and other tribesmen are now a minority of the population in the coastal towns, most of which have been overrun of late by outsiders. Small colonies of Persians, Indians, and Baluchis have existed in the coastal states for generations, earning their living by trade or as artisans and laborers. Now they have been joined by many thousands more of their fellow-countrymen, and by several thousand "northern" Arabs (Palestinians, Egyptians, Jordanians, Lebanese, Syrians, and Iraqis), all of them attracted by the wealth from oil. Since the coastal shaikhdoms are, in effect, city states, this flood of immigrants has fundamentally altered their character, rendering it less distinctly Arabian and more conspicuously Levantine. Only in Saudi Arabia, outside the burgeoning cities of Riyad, Jeddah, and Dammam, and in Oman generally, has Arabian society preserved its familiar character more or less intact.

The distortion brought about by this large-scale immigration is most marked in Kuwait, and in Abu Dhabi and Dubai, the two principal states of the United Arab Emirates (UAE). Kuwait's population has grown from around 120,000 in 1950 to something in the vicinity of 900,000 today, of which over sixty percent are foreigners. The first census ever taken of the seven Trucial states which now compose the UAE was made in 1968, and it revealed a total population of about 180,000. An estimate made in 1972 put the figure at 320,000, the greater part of the increase was the result of immigration into Abu Dhabi and Dubai. Of Abu Dhabi's reputed population today of nearly 100,000, a good 60-70 percent is probably made up of foreigners. Much the same is true of Qatar, where possibly half the estimated population of 90,000 consists of foreigners. Only in Bahrain, Saudi Arabia, and Oman do the indigenous inhabitants predominate. In Bahrain there are approximately 37,000 foreigners in a population of 216,000.

Reliable figures for Oman and Saudi Arabia are virtually unobtainable. Oman's population of perhaps 600,000 has few foreign elements outside the long-established Indian and Pakistani communities in Muscat, Matrah, and other seaports. Saudi Arabia may have a population of as many as five million, although some estimates put it as low as three million. There are, in addition, at least 250,000 foreign laborers employed in the country (recent estimates put the figure as high as one million, although this seems an exaggeration), most of them Yemenis, along with a few thousand Omanis. How many "northern" Arabs and Pakistanis there may be it is impossible to say. The Saudi government welcomes Pakistanis and it also employs several thousand Egyptians, mostly as teachers. It is more cautious, however, in admitting Palestinians, Syrians or Iraqis in any numbers.

The occupations followed by most of these immigrants in the states where they are a majority or a substantial minority are determined as much by their origins as they are by their skills. Of the *émigré* "northern" Arabs, the Palestinians are employed mainly as government clerks, the Egyptians as teachers and doctors, the Lebanese as contractors and technicians, and the Syrians and Iraqis in a variety of nonmanual occupations. The Indians are mostly merchants and clerks in commercial companies, the Pakistanis are artisans and craftsmen, and the Persians, Baluchis, and Omanis are laborers. All are engaged in tasks which, by and large, the indigenous inhabitants either cannot or will not perform. Yet what they reap in the way of rewards all too often bears little relation to the value of the work they do, regardless of whether the comparison is made between the earnings of different groups of immigrants or between the earnings of the immigrants as a whole and those of the native Arab inhabitants.

These disparities of effort and reward have naturally created tensions within the ranks of the immigrants, and between them and the indigenous population, especially as the disparities are, as often as not, created by policies of discrimination practiced by the local governments.

To keep their subjects contented, the rulers of Kuwait, Qatar, Abu Dhabi, and Dubai have, from the time that oil revenues began to flow in abundance, distributed a considerable proportion of these revenues to their people in the form of employment, subsidized or free housing, education, health services, and straight grants of cash. These benefits have been, with a few minor exceptions, confined to the indigenous population, who have as a consequence become a privileged class of state pensioners. Priority is given to them in employment, regardless of the fact that the great majority of them are either illiterate or barely literate, as well as devoid of the skills needed for the jobs they are given. The result has been the growth of a system of dual appointments—of foreigners with the required skills and of natives without them. The exclusivism practiced in the disbursement of benefits also operates with respect to civil rights. The rulers of most of the Gulf states have made it extremely difficult for immigrants, whether Arab or non-Arab, to obtain local nationality. Kuwait is the most stringent in this respect: not only does it place almost insuperable obstacles in the way of obtaining Kuwaiti nationality and citizenship, but it also has a propensity, which is shared by some other states, for sudden and arbitrary deportations of foreigners whose presence has for one reason or another become unwelcome. It is little wonder, therefore, that the immigrant communities as a whole harbor feelings of resentment towards the governments and subjects of the states in which they dwell and to whose development their labor and skills have contributed so greatly. They have no civil rights, no legal standing, no customary recourse, even though in many cases their abilities are superior to those possessed by the natives who enjoy these rights by mere accident of birth.

Relations, then, between the immigrant and native communities, particularly in shaikhdoms like Kuwait and Abu Dhabi, where the *per capita* income from oil revenues is so great, are marked by mutual resentment and recrimination, suspicion and uneasiness. There are, of course, gradations of feeling among the several immigrant groups, and between them and the indigenous inhabitants, gradations which do not correspond necessarily to differences in financial reward or status. Persian and Baluchi laborers, who work the hardest and are paid the least, are not unduly troubled by the degree of wealth possessed by the ruling families and their circles, or by the discrimination practiced against them because they are non-Arab. Omani laborers fare a little better because they are Arab, but the improvement is hardly remarkable. The Indians and Pakistanis, who tend to live in close-knit communities, secure in their self-esteem, are mostly content with their roles as merchants, clerks, and craftsmen, making substantial profits and a comfortable living from the profligacy of others.

It is the *émigré* Arab community in each state which most exhibits discontent with its lot. Whatever the differences that divide them—Palestinian from Egyptian, Egyptian from Iraqi, Iraqi from Syrian—the "northern" Arabs are united in their conviction of the superiority of their attainments, intellectual, political, and social, over those of the Gulf Arabs. Being of such mind, it galls them that providence should have placed in the hands of untutored tribesmen riches beyond measure, which they more properly merit and could put to so much better use. Nevertheless they temper their irritation with a certain discretion, lest they jeopardize their livelihoods. The condescension displayed by the *émigré* Arabs has not gone unremarked by the local Arabs, or the irritation unreturned, with the consequence that relations between the two communities are characterized as much by tension and ill-feeling as they are by the outward show of brotherly amity.

Social and economic conditions in Bahrain, Oman, much of Saudi Arabia, and the poorer shaikhdoms of the United Arab Emirates differ in degree or in kind, and sometimes in both, from those in Kuwait, Qatar, Abu Dhabi, and Dubai. Bahrain has probably the most balanced economy of the Arab states of the Gulf. Its revenues from oil, while not insubstantial, do not bear comparison with those of Kuwait, Saudi Arabia, and Abu Dhabi. To a considerable extent Bahrain exists, as it has long existed, on its role as a trading depot and a supplier of services. Its population is stable, the proportion of foreigners, Arab and non-Arab, less than 20 percent, and the number of recent immigrants small. As education is no novelty in Bahrain, and as many Bahrainis have received an elementary or higher education, there is little disposition to feel inferior to the "northern" Arabs, who are in any case a small minority in the shaikhdom. On the contrary, Bahrainis are themselves disposed to regard other Gulf Arabs as inferior in knowledge, talents, and sophistication. There is no great show of wealth in Bahrain comparable with that in the richer oil states, so that any vivid contrast between gross opulence and grinding poverty is lacking. Discontent exists, to be sure, but it arises as much from political ambition as it does from economic causes.

Oman is a poor country by the standards of the Gulf today and the lives of its people have been little affected by the discovery and exploitation of oil in the country in the past ten years. In part this is the result of the comparative smallness of the oil reserves, in part to the expenditure of more than half those reserves upon armaments, mostly to suppress the revolt in Dhufar, and in part to the size and condition of the population. Omani society is still intensely tribal, its habits formed by centuries of internal feuding and isolation from the world outside. The vast majority of the people are illiterate, ravaged by endemic diseases, and inveterately suspicious of outsiders and innovations. Their lives are influenced more by religious sanctions and confessional loyalties than those of most of their neighbors in eastern Arabia. They live by agriculture, pastoralism, and fishing, producing little in the way of a surplus for export.

What economic development has taken place since the oil revenues commenced has been almost wholly confined to the capital, Muscat and its vicinity, and to the coastal strip to the north. It has taken the form common in the Gulf oil shaikhdoms of construction projects designed more to appease local yearnings for grandeur than to improve the basic economy of the country. A certain number of foreigners have been employed on these projects, but the inflow of immigrants, and especially of "northern" Arabs, has been meager compared with that into the Gulf states.

While most of the consequences of the access of oil wealth which have been felt in the Gulf oil shaikhdoms have also been experienced in Saudi Arabia, their impact, for a variety of reasons, has been felt less by the general population. One reason for this is that Saudi Arabia is a much larger country than any of the littoral states, and its population, although greater in number, is more scattered. For another, the expenditure of oil revenues within the country has been confined, by and large, to the towns of Hasa, the eastern province, to the capital, Riyad, and to Jeddah and other towns in the Hijaz. The principal beneficiaries have been the numerous members of the Al Saud dynasty and their adherents: the shaikhly families of the major tribes whose support for the regime has always depended to a great extent upon *douceurs* received; the religious establishment; the merchant class; the countless functionaries of the Saudi bureaucracy, and the officers of the armed forces.

Although the bulk of the population earns its living from agriculture or pastoralism, the Saudi government has so far made no sustained effort to improve methods of cultivation or animal husbandry. Millions of dollars have been expended upon luxuries for the Al Saud and their courtiers, and billions have been spent in the acquisition of armaments for which the Saudis have no real need and the more complicated of which they cannot operate or maintain. Yet further billions have been shuttled around the money markets of the world in a search for interest and influence. What has not been spent in this fashion, or for political purposes in other Arab countries, has been expended upon urban construction of an unproductive kind—palaces, hotels, office blocks, apartment buildings, etc.—while industrial investment has been limited to so-called "prestige" projects like petrochemical works and steel mills. The result is an economy with a highly complex petrochemical industry at one end of the scale, near-subsistence agriculture at the other, and virtually nothing in between.

Although the provision of education and medical services to the Saudi people has been much publicized, there are grounds for doubting whether these benefits are very substantial. According to the Saudi government there were some 360,000 pupils in primary schools in 1970 and another 40-50,000 in secondary schools. By 1975 the enrollment was said to have risen to 800,000. These figures are impressive, and for this very reason highly suspect. Little is known of the quality of the education these 800,000 pupils are receiving—if, in fact, they are receiving it. School accommodation is more often than not of a primitive nature, the curriculum is modeled upon traditional Koranic teaching, and the teachers are for the most part of limited ability. The dropout rate is high: nearly half the pupils do not complete their primary school education, and roughly the same proportion does not finish secondary school.

The regime's attitude to education is equivocal: the religious establishment, upon whose support the regime places much reliance, frowns upon secular education as upon most innovations, and the Al Saud themselves are less than wholeheartedly in favor of its spread lest it awaken the political consciousness of the younger generation. The latter for their part appear to value education less for its intrinsic worth than as a means of securing employment in the bureaucracy. They evince little interest in professional or technical training, still less in careers as veterinarians or agriculturalists. Of the 2,900 students at Riyad University in 1970, only 90 were studying agriculture, and the proportion has changed little since that time. The professional occupations for which Saudi students show preference are medicine and engineering (30 percent of Saudis educated abroad qualified in these fields), and even here they tend to end up within a short time in administrative posts in the bureaucracy. At the handful of institutions of higher education in the country a high percentage of students fail to graduate, but failure does not close the doors of the bureaucracy to those whose ambition it is to become government functionaries.

There is, in short, little urge among educated or semi-educated Saudis to engage in productive work requiring technical skills. The life of the bureaucratic *flâneur* is their ideal. Nor is the reluctance to engage in sustained effort confined to the multitudinous ranks of officialdom. The true Saudi cultivator of the soil, however mean his condition, shuns the more menial tasks. These were performed in the past by slaves (of whom there were from 500,000 to 750,000 in the country) and are today performed by emancipated slaves or by poverty-stricken Yemenis. The Bedu will not soil his hands with work he considers beneath him: he has little interest even in improving the health and care of his herds and flocks but would rather wander off to the towns or oil fields in search of diversion or money or both. All the hard manual work involved in the frenzy of construction which now grips the country is done by imported laborers, mostly Yemenis, while the architectural, technical and other required skills are supplied by Europeans, Americans, "northern" Arabs or Pakistanis. The schools are staffed by Egyptians and the oil industry is run by Americans.

To moralize about conditions in any Asian or African country nowadays is considered hopelessly unfashionable, yet it is difficult to contemplate what has happened to Saudi Arabia and the Gulf states in the last twenty-five years under the impact of oil wealth without experiencing some stirrings of regret and a sense of foreboding. That there should have been folly and extravagance was only to be expected, given the common constituents of human nature and the harshness of the lives led hitherto by the people of the Arabian shore. But folly and extravagance of the magnitude which Saudi Arabia and the Gulf oil states have indulged in exceed the bounds of understanding and give rise to some disturbing questions. There is more than a touch of megalomania about many of the grandiose constructions which abound in these petty states, whether palaces or airports or dry-docks. Yet it has become the custom among impressionable Western observers—indeed, it has acquired the quality of a ritual—to applaud the wisdom and far-sightedness of the governments of these states in soliciting the aid of eminent Western planning consultants in designing their contemporary Xanadus, and in pouring forth their treasure to furnish them in splendor. Viewed more skeptically, this alleged wisdom and far-sightedness appears nothing more than overweening vanity, a compulsion to impress the world with the wonders that have been wrought upon the desert sand, the dream of Ozymandias.

Politics in Saudi Arabia and the Gulf States

Saudi Arabia

Saudi Arabia's system of government is monarchical, with strong theocratic overtones. The origins of the kingdom lie in the Islamic revivalist movement of the eighteenth century known as Wahhabism, after the reformer who inspired it, Muhammad ibn Abdul Wahhab. Among the early adherents to his cause were the Al Saud clan of Diriya in central Najd, and it was their support which enabled him to carry his message of reform to the tribes of central Arabia. In turn the reformer's mission lent a patina of piety to the ambitions of the Al Saud, who by the close of the eighteenth century had welded the tribes of the Najd and Hasa into a religio-military confederacy under their leadership. Ever since that time the Saudi ruling house has been identified with the reformed faith, and every Saudi ruler down to the present day has assumed the office of *imam* of the Wahhabiya, that is to say, the spiritual as well as the temporal leader of his people. Religion, then, is the first pillar of the Saudi state, the *sharia* according to the Hanbali rite is the law of the land, and it is strictly enforced by the governmental authorities in concert with the religious establishment.

The second pillar of the state is the alliance between the house of Saud and the shaikhly families of the major tribes. These alliances were one of the principal means by which the late King Abdul Aziz ibn Saud extended and consolidated his kingdom between 1902 and 1932, and they have been preserved and cherished by his sons and successors. Some of the leading tribal families like the Sudairi and Jiluwi have been so long associated with the Al Saud that they are virtually an extension of the ruling house. (For example, the mother of both the present prime minister, Fahad ibn Abdul Aziz, and his brother, Sultan, the minister of defense, was a Sudairi.) Their allegiance, like that of the other tribal shaikhs, is maintained by preferential treatment in the form of financial subsidies, governmental appointments and social precedence. The third pillar of the state is, or was, the Arabian-American Oil Company (Aramco), which for thirty years provided the major portion of the state's revenues, supplied it with all manner of services and advice, and stoutly defended the regime's reputation abroad. Now that Aramco is on the verge of being expropriated, although it will continue to manage the major part of Saudi Arabia's oil industry in a contractual capacity, its loyalty to the regime may have lost some of its fervor. Doubtless, however it will continue to identify itself, and be identified by others, with the Saudi government and its interests.

Government in Saudi Arabia is highly centralized. All power resides in the royal house and in particular in the person of the king. Any matter of consequence is referred to Riyad for decision, and the governors of the provinces are all royal nominees, if not actual members of the royal house. The various ministries which have been established over the years have the sole function of carrying out the orders of the king, and the more important of them are headed by his brothers. There are no representative institutions of any kind in the country, and the first duty of the religious establishment is to support the authority of the *imam* and his house. In turn, the ruling house upholds the primacy of Islam in the state and gives heed to the pronouncements of the *ulema* where they do not intrude upon questions of high policy. Throughout the country, committees for the enforcement of morals toil diligently and ceaselessly to keep the Saudi populace faithful to the observance of their religious duties and obedient to the commands of their sovereign. Together with the myriad informers and spies who infest the country, they constitute a network of surveillance which is of inestimable value to the regime in detecting and suppressing discontent.

Methods of government in Saudi Arabia have always been severe, partly of necessity, given the turbulent nature of the tribesmen, partly from inclination, given the character of the Al Saud and the spirit of Wahhabism. Wealth has slightly tempered this disposition, at least as far as it affects the educated and semi-educated classes. They have been kept in check less by arbitrary and condign penalties than by the lure of the lucrative posts in the bureaucracy. So far as is known, there has been little expression of political discontent from these classes. They may lack the diversions available to their counterparts in the less puritanical societies of the minor oil states, but they show no conspicuous tendency to compensate for this lack by taking an active interest in politics, other than to engage in endless rhetoric about Islam, Arabism, imperialism, and Zionism.

To say this, however, is not to imply that discontent with the regime is entirely absent or that potential causes of political disruption do not exist. There would seem to have been a conspiracy, or perhaps two separate conspiracies, against the government in 1969, involving army and air force officers and men, government employees and members of some prominent Hijazi families. The conspirators, most or all of whom would appear to have been arrested, were not brought to trial until 1973, by which time the ringleaders had died in prison, reputedly as a result of torture. Of those tried in 1973, 135 were sentenced to death, 305 to life imprisonment, and 752 to terms of from ten to fifteen years. A few were released. The possibility of a military *coup d'état* against the ruling house seems remote. One reason is that the armed forces are not numerous, and Saudi Arabia is a large country. For another, it has been the regime's policy to preserve a balance of force in the kingdom through the agency of the national guard, which is recruited from tribes traditionally loyal to the Al Saud and is roughly comparable in strength to the regular army. Nor should the religious element in Saudi national life be overlooked; not only is Wahhabi Islam an essential, even the dominant, constituent of the system of government, but the Saudi dynasty itself is also an integral part of the system in its spiritual as well as its temporal aspects.

Several clandestine political organizations are said to have been established in recent years, mostly Baathists or Marxist-Leninist splinter groups of the Movement of Arab Nationalists, which a decade ago or so spawned the Popular Front for the Liberation of Palestine and the National Liberation Front in south Yemen. It has been suggested that the assassin of King Faisal ibn Abdul Aziz, his nephew Faisal ibn Musaid, subscribed to the radical political philosophy of the movement and that he frequented extremist political circles in Beirut. The absence of solid evidence makes it impossible to reach any conclusion as to whether he was part of a conspiracy, or the tool of conspirators, within Saudi Arabia or abroad. What is known of Faisal ibn Musaid indicates that he was an unbalanced and overindulged young man whose mind may have become further disturbed by his exposure to radical political ideas when a student in the United States or as an *habitué* of Beirut's political *demi-monde*. His motives for assassinating King Faisal may well have been simply personal vengeance.

At most the underground political organizations in Saudi Arabia have a potential nuisance value: it is difficult to visualize them as undermining the foundations of the kingdom. A more deep-seated source of instability is the resentment still felt in some regions of the country at the predominance of the Al Saud. It runs most deeply in the Hijaz, whose inhabitants tend to regard the tribes of Najd as barbarous Bedu. The Najdis, for their part, consider the Hijazis liars and hypocrites. A similar animosity, arising from comparable historical origins, exists in the Jabal Shammar, in the north of the country, and in the Asir, to the south of the Hijaz. Any upheaval in the central government, brought on, for instance, by a contest for the succession within the ruling house, might bring these regional discontents into the open, precipitating a civil war, and culminating ultimately in the disintegration of the kingdom. Further speculation along these lines would be idle: too little is known about the internal condition of Saudi Arabia for prognostications about its future to be of much value.

Kuwait

There is a basic political disunity in Kuwait which derives from the existence, already noted, of two virtually separate communities in the shaikhdom—the native inhabitants who number less than 40 percent of the population, and the immigrants who number over 60 percent. Only the native Kuwaitis, and a handful of foreigners who have been accorded Kuwaiti nationality, enjoy any political rights, and these are circumscribed by the authority retained by the ruling family, the Al Sabah. The Al Sabah have ruled Kuwait since its beginnings in the early eighteenth century. They are a merchant dynasty which earned its living before the discovery of oil in the shaikhdom from shipping, the pearl trade, and Kuwait's function as a clearing-house for the trade of northcentral Arabia and much of southern Iraq. Oil revenues began to flow in quantity from the late 1940s, and they were expended in a fashion which has made Kuwait's name a byword for ostentatious consumption.

For the first dozen years or so the Al Sabah kept both the oil revenues and political power firmly in their own hands, but in 1962, a year after the shaikhdom had terminated its special treaty relationship with Great Britain, the Al Sabah ruler promulgated a constitution which provided for the establishment of a national assembly of some fifty members and a council of ministers, the latter to be appointed by and responsible to the ruler. The franchise was restricted to adult, male, native-born Kuwaitis. The assembly, whose members are drawn from the ranks of urbanized tribesmen and the merchant class, is a tame body, with no power of the purse and only the right to approve legislation. It could hardly have been otherwise, for the constitution declares Kuwait to be an Islamic state with the *sharia* as the source of law, and the *sharia* imposes almost no limits on the power of the ruler but enjoins complete obedience to his commands.

The constitution enumerates all manner of fashionable contemporary rights and freedoms which are to be enjoyed by the citizens of the state. Although these rights and freedoms are, for the most part, illusory, the fact that they are reserved to Kuwaiti citizens rankles with the educated and technically skilled sections of the immigrant community, who believe themselves to be more politically sophisticated than the enfranchised Bedu of Kuwait. The sense of grievance, especially among the Palestinians, who have no home other than Kuwait, is an enduring source of political discontent.

Among the younger generation of educated or semi-educated Kuwaitis there are also signs of political unrest. Nurtured by the state, educated by the state, and now, as often as not, employed by the state, they are the true *jeunesse dorée* of the Gulf, with all the confidence and self-esteem that their privileged station confers. Naturally, they feel that their talents and abilities entitle them to a share—perhaps the preponderant share—in the government of the shaikhdom, even though they are not perhaps prepared to go so far as to jeopardize their financial security by proclaiming their feelings too openly. Some of them, after the fashion of radical-chic youth in the West, have dabbled in the shallows of revolutionary politics, Baathist or Marxist, often under Palestinian mentors. Whether they will ever attempt to translate theory into action it is impossible to say. More extreme influences have also been at work underground in Kuwait in the shape of Marxist-Leninist cells organized by south Yemenis, Dhufaris and

Omanis, deriving some support from Iraq and the People's Democratic Republic of Yemen (south Yemen), and directing their activities towards fomenting unrest among the immigrant laborers. So far they have not proved any real threat to the security of the state.

The Al Sabah's response to every actual or apprehended danger to their rule has been, as a general policy, to buy it off, either with money or by the adoption of fashionable political attitudes. Kuwait is the weathercock of the Gulf. It was the first of the minor states to terminate its treaty relationships with Britain, the first to erect a facade of constitutionalism, the first to enter into diplomatic relations with the Soviet Union and China. Most recently it has also become the first to acquire Russian arms and Russian military instructors. It was the earliest and most vocal supporter, as well as the principal financial backer, of the Palestine Liberation Organization, and of late years it has provided a haven for terrorists. It has been the foremost practitioner of the art of appeasement, paying Iraq to drop its claim to sovereignty over the shaikhdom and purchasing immunity from the unwelcome attention of the more extreme Palestinian groups by means of bribes.

Kuwait's voice has been the most shrill in denunciation of a Western imperalism, which served it very handsomely in the past, the most strident in demanding that the price of oil to Western consumers be raised ever higher. Yet for all this there is a remarkable persistence on the part of many Western commentators in viewing Kuwait as the most advanced of the Gulf states and in lauding its government as the most enlightened and able. It is a view as ill-considered as any conclusion about the shaikhdom's future, based upon its present appearance of stability, is unwise.

Bahrain

Like Kuwait, Bahrain is ruled by a merchant dynasty, the Al Khalifah, in whose hands political power ultimately still resides. The shaikhdom became independent in August 1971 when the former treaty relationship with Britain was ended. Two years later a constitution was introduced which, like that of Kuwait, declared Bahrain to be an Islamic state with the *sharia* as the principal source of legislation. It also provided for the setting up of a national assembly with limited powers, composed of appointed and elected members. The franchise was restricted to adult, male Bahrainis. Political parties were forbidden, as in Kuwait, so candidates had to stand as individuals. At the first elections for the thirty elective seats in December 1973 ten seats were won by candidates of Socialist leanings who had campaigned as the "Popular Bloc of the Left." They constitute a vociferous minority in the assembly which is, as a whole, a conservative body. Executive authority is vested in a council of ministers, which is directly responsible to the ruler. It is made up of members of the Al Khalifah family and some of the leading merchants in the shaikhdom.

Politics is a livelier affair in Bahrain than in Kuwait. Young Bahrainis are more accustomed to demonstrating in support of one cause or another than are their Kuwaiti compeers. The proportion of educated and semi-educated citizens in Bahrain is higher than in Kuwait, and the revenues of the shaikhdom are not sufficient to allow the Al Khalifah ruler to satisfy their desire for money and status by creating lucrative posts for them as government functionaries. These intellectual *sans-culottes* have long been avid consumers of whatever radical political ideas happen to be in fashion in the advanced Arab states, and the various recreational, cultural and sporting clubs which abound in the island serve as a forum for their interminable political discussions. Whether they will ever translate the hodge podge of Nasserist, Baathist, Marxist, and other notions which excite them into an effective political movement is another question. There has been a certain amount of tradesunion agitation in recent years, and attempts have been made to use the thousands of poorly paid Omanis and other immigrants who make up most of the labor force for riots and demonstrations. So far, however, the Al Khalifah and their supporters have remained firmly in control, and there is no evidence that the bulk of the population, from the wealthier merchants down to the peasant cultivators, desire any drastic change of regime, certainly not one of the kind envisaged by Bahrain's putative *enragés*.

Qatar

There has always been a certain vagueness about Qatar as a political entity. For much of the nineteenth century the peninsula was a dependency of Bahrain. Then the Al Thani clan, which ruled Dauhah, on the eastern side of the peninsula, declared themselves to be Ottoman subjects, a status which Great Britain, as the paramount power in the Gulf, refused to recognize. During the First World War the Al Thani entered into treaty relations with the British government which gave Qatar much the same legal standing as the Trucial shaikhdoms. Bahrain, Saudi Arabia, and Abu Dhabi have all preferred territorial claims of one kind or another upon Qatar over the past fifty years and more, and it was not until very recently that these fell into abeyance. When Qatar ended its treaty relationship with Britain and became independent in September 1971 the population of the shaikhdom was reputed to be about 90,000, perhaps half composed of immigrants. Much of the population is concentrated in and around the capital, Dauhah, and the remainder dwells in settlements along the eastern coast. All are sustained primarily, if indirectly, by revenues from oil.

Political power is firmly in the hands of the Al Thani ruler and his extensive clan. The Al Thani are the least distinguished of the ruling families in the Gulf, and their methods of government are somewhat rough and ready. They are by religious conviction strict Wahhabis, and many features of life in Qatar, though not their own, reflect their repressive inclinations. The Al Thani introduced a constitution in April 1970 which provided for a cabinet of ten ministers and an elected advisory council of twenty "citizens." There is not much doubt, however, where real authority resides and where it is intended to remain.

Thus far the only signs of disaffection that have been manifest have been among the Dhufaris and Omanis in the Qatar defense force. They have now been dismissed and their places filled by native Qataris. Some resentment of the Al Thani is expressed by the shaikhly families of other tribes in Qatar, and between different sections of the Al Thani themselves there is some ill-feeling. The immigrant population as a whole seems content to make its living from the country and not to harbor political ambitions. Of course, there are some restless spirits among them, especially among the *émigré* Palestinians and Egyptians, as well as among the minority of educated Qataris; but to challenge the supremacy of the Al Thani with any hope of success they would need the backing of the defense force, which at present seems well under Al Thani control. If the defense force should become involved in politics, it is more likely to be in support of one or other contending factions of the Al Thani than in support of a revolutionary *coup* designed to overthrow the dynasty. What can be predicted with some certainty, especially in view of the friendly relations subsisting between the Al Thani and the Al Saud, is that the Saudi government would not be indifferent to any attempt to change the internal *status quo* in Qatar.

United Arab Emirates

The federal constitution under which the United Arab Emirates was established in December 1971, when the seven Trucial states terminated their treaty relationship with Great Britain, was not intended to provide for any popular participation in government within the union. On the contrary, it was in essence a treaty of alliance among the rulers of the states, designed to preserve their position as the ultimate source of authority within their own shaikhdoms; and to underline the primacy of Abu Dhabi and Dubai as the richest and most populous states in the union. The only body set up by the constitution which enjoys real power is the federal supreme council, composed of the seven rulers, with the ruler of Abu Dhabi as president and the ruler of Dubai as vice president. They both possess a veto power over the council's decisions. The rights of the federal national council (or assembly) of forty members, nominated by the individual rulers, are limited to discussion and to the approval of the federal budget and draft legislation presented by the council of ministers, or federal cabinet. The cabinet, in its turn, is appointed by the rulers, and its composition again reflects the predominance of Abu Dhabi and Dubai in the federation: the prime minister and the ministers of finance, defense, foreign affairs and the interior are all nominees (and in most cases relations) of the rulers of these two states.

Historically, relations among the shaikhdoms have been an almost unbroken record of turbulence, feuding, and warfare. Throughout much of the nineteenth century the politics of the coast was dominated by a contest for supremacy between the Qasimi shaikhdoms of Sharjah and Ras al-Khaimah and the Bani Yas tribal confederacy of Abu Dhabi. A secondary cause of strife was the friction between Abu Dhabi and its neighbor, Dubai, where a dissident branch of the Bani Yas held sway. Both rivalries have endured to the present day, although in muted form. Abu Dhabi and Dubai, under the benign influence of wealth, have largely become reconciled to each other, but the very fact of their good fortune is a source of irritation to the Qasimi ruler of Ras al-Khaimah, who cherishes large ambitions but lacks the financial means to achieve them. His envy is shared to some extent by the other rulers, though none is rash enough to evince it openly, lest he should forfeit the financial subventions he receives from Abu Dhabi and, in lesser degree, from Dubai.

These and other strains within the federation have not yet endangered its existence, largely because the federal rulers have a mutual interest in staying together and submerging their differences in the face of hostile pressures from without and within. They are, for the most part, keenly aware of the dangers of subversion, and they realize that an attempt to overthrow any one of them is tantamount to an attempt to overthrow the whole institution of shaikhly rule in southeastern Arabia. For the five who do not possess any oil wealth of their own, the situation in their shaikhdoms presents no immediate problem. The case is different with Abu Dhabi and Dubai, where the sudden onset of wealth has disrupted the customary pattern of life and brought in thousands upon thousands of outsiders, to the point where these now outnumber the original inhabitants.

The social and economic changes within these shaikhdoms described earlier have brought political instability in their train, more noticeably in Abu Dhabi than in Dubai. Although the shaikhly system of government still prevails, and the rulers are, in theory at least, the ultimate source of authority, the very complexities caused by the material transformation of the two shaikhdoms into replicas of modern states are eroding the foundations of their rule. The chief agents of this erosion, more wittingly than unwittingly, are the "northern" Arabs who staff the growing bureaucracies, the schools, the hospitals, and the technical services. They, like their counterparts in Kuwait and Qatar, know little about the country or the people for whom they work. Their attention is fixed upon the countries from which they themselves came, upon the domestic politics of those countries, and upon the labyrinthine twists of the perennial Palestine issue. Conscious of their sophistication in comparison with the local Arabs, and confident of their superior political skills and sagacity, they find the spectacle of so much wealth, and consequently so much power, in the hands of backward Bedu a galling one, especially as they feel it could be put to so much better use in their own homelands.

For their part the rulers of Dubai and Abu Dhabi have sought to check the ambitions and activities of the *émigrés* by occasional dismissals and deportations, and by playing one national group off against another. Shaikh Rashid ibn Said Al Maktum of Dubai has shown himself to be more perspicacious and vigilant in this respect than the ruler of Abu Dhabi, Shaikh Zayid ibn Sultan Al Nahayan. He has also the advantage of being primarily interested in commerce, not in politics, at least not beyond his immediate purview. There is little doubt who rules in Dubai, and the *émigré* Arabs tread warily there. They are bolder in Abu Dhabi, and cluster more thickly about the person of the ruler, often obscuring his vision and even shutting him off from his own people. Zayid has greater need of their services than Rashid for he aspires to cut an impressive figure upon a wider stage. If Rashid has any grand design, it is to make Dubai a leading mercantile center: Zayid's hopes run in a political direction, which makes him more vulnerable to manipulation by outsiders.

While most of the *émigrés* from the larger Arab states have resigned themselves to existing circumstances, there are some who adamantly refuse to accept them. To these men the very existence of shaikhly rule is a constant affront. What they want is to see the whole apparatus of hereditary rule swept away and replaced by a form of government on the lines of those ruling in Cairo, Damascus, or Baghdad—or, in the case of a few, in Aden—in which they would occupy a prominent if not a dominant place. To aspire to such goals, however, is one thing; to attain them is another. The present regimes in the UAE will not be overturned without force, and to marshal the requisite amount of force the *émigrés*, alone or in combination with local dissidents, will have to raise a "street" force or enlist the support of the local armed services. There are certainly thousands of immigrant laborers in Abu Dhabi and Dubai from whom a "street" force could be recruited, but whether they would respond to an attempt to recruit them is problematical. The various agents and adherents of the clandestine Marxist and crypto-Marxist organizations which have been at work in the shaikhdoms over the past few years would seem to have had little success in stirring up popular feeling against the ruling families.

The local armed forces are another matter. The Union Defense Force (UDF) of something under 3,000 men incorporates the former Trucial Oman Scouts, which were raised and paid for by Great Britain and commanded by British officers on secondment. Although arrangements were made at the time of independence for the secondment of officers to continue, the proportion of Arab officers in the UDF has increased steadily, and with it the likelihood that the force will become before very long, if it has not done so already, a political instrument. Disaffection has also appeared in its ranks: early in 1973 it was reported that thirty-seven officers and men had been arrested for plotting and that a number of Dhufaris had been dismissed from the force. A question mark similarly hangs over the much larger and more powerfully equipped Abu Dhabi Defense Force, which has an air wing as well as armored support. Its British officers are rapidly being replaced by Arabs and Pakistanis, and both its reliability and its loyalty to the ruler can no longer be taken for granted. How far the scales may now be tipped in Abu Dhabi and Dubai, and therefore in the UAE as a whole, in favor of an eventual attempt at a military *coup d'état* it is impossible to say. What is perhaps more certain is that the local tribesmen, assuming that their fealty to their rulers remains unchanged, are now less capable of offering an effective resistance to such an attempt than they once were. And what is certain beyond the shadow of a doubt, in the light of the history of the former Trucial Coast and the customary way in which political changes, including changes of rulers, have occurred there, is that any such *coup* would be accompanied and followed by considerable bloodshed.

Oman

While few of the political conditions present in the oil states of the Gulf are to be found in Oman, the politics of the country is no less complicated, and in some aspects more complicated, than that of its neighbors. There are several basic dichotomies in Oman which threaten the unity of the country. The first is a religious schism between the Ibadi and Sunni Muslims. Another is the political factionalism between the tribes classed as Hinawi and those classed as Ghafiri, a factionalism which has deep historical, political, and religious roots. There is also an antipathy between highlanders and lowlanders, between the tribes which dwell in the Hajar mountains and those which inhabit the coastal plain and the desert fringes. Centuries of feuding have made the tribes rancorous by nature, and long isolation has made them hostile to strangers and foreign influences. They are, in short, a most fractious people to rule.

Traditionally, the ruling institution of Oman has been the Ibadi imamate, the *imam* being selected by the more powerful tribal chieftains and invested with spiritual and temporal authority over the Ibadi community. The authority wielded by an *imam* depended upon his personal standing with the tribes, upon his antecedants, his reputation for piety, and his ability to hold the balance between the Hinawi and Ghafiri tribal factions. With the accession to power of the Al Bu Said dynasty in the eighteenth century the imamate fell into desuetude. Successive Al Bu Said rulers from the turn of the nineteenth century onwards chose to reign as secular princes and to style themselves "saiyids," while by Europeans they were called "sultans." As the century wore on, the dynasty became increasingly isolated from its people, largely because its interests were maritime and mercantile rather than territorial and military, but also because it had forfeited the respect of most of its subjects by its neglect of the religious attributes expected of a ruler of Oman. Discontent among the tribes of the interior reached its height in the second decade of this century when several of the principal shaikhs elected an *imam* and launched a campaign to unseat the sultan at Muscat. He was saved by British intervention but in a settlement reached with the rebellious tribal leaders in 1920 he was forced to concede virtual autonomy to the interior of the country.

For the next thirty years or so the influence of the Ibadi *imam* and his supporters among the leading tribal shaikhs remained paramount in inner Oman, while the effective authority of the Al Bu Said sultan at Muscat was confined to the coastal region and the distant province of Dhufar. How long this *modus vivendi* might have lasted had Oman remained isolated from the outside world is a matter for historical speculation. Suffice it to say that it was brought to an end after the Second World War by the beginnings of oil exploration along the northern marches of Oman and by the attempted penetration of the area by Saudi Arabia. When the old Ibadi *imam* died in 1934 his successor, aided and abetted by Egypt and Saudi Arabia, tried to erect inner Oman into an independent state separate from the sultanate. The sultan of the day, Said ibn Taimur, responded by taking up arms against him, and with British military assistance he overcame him, drove him into exile, and established Al Bu Said authority over the interior for the first time in forty years. The eclipse of the imamate, however, did not in the eyes of many of the tribes automatically bestow the mantle of legitimacy upon the sultan's government; and the action of Said ibn Taimur after vanquishing his rival in retiring to Dhufar and never visiting Oman again did nothing to reconcile these tribes to his authority.

If Said ibn Taimur thought to escape the cares of state by shutting himself up in his palace at Salalah, in Dhufar, he was mistaken. A rebellion broke out among some of the hill tribes in the early 1960s, instigated by Dhufaris returning home after working in the Gulf oilfields. Some of them had been indoctrinated with radical politics in Kuwait, and given instruction in arms and guerrilla warfare in Iraq. They were reportedly also supplied with money, weapons, and transport by the Saudi government, which was still smarting from the setback it had received in Oman a few years previously. Although the Saudis later withdrew their support from the rebels, the latter found new patrons in the revolutionary government which came to power in Aden after the British withdrawal in 1967, the National Liberation Front. Under the NLF's influence the Dhufar rebellion acquired ideological overtones. Dhufaris were indoctrinated with Marxist-Leninist ideas by NLF agents. Arms and instructors were furnished by China via south Yemen, and picked recruits were sent to Peking and elsewhere for guerrilla training. Later, when the Chinese faded from the scene, the Soviet Union took their place as the principal supplier of arms and instruction in guerrilla warfare.

The rebellion might have been contained in its initial stages by a more enlightened policy towards the rebels on the part of the sultan. Said ibn Taimur, however, tried to crush it by intensifying the repressive measures which had provoked it in the first place. When these failed he turned to the British to get him out of his difficulties. British arms and troops were sent to Dhufar to campaign against the Popular Front for the Liberation of the Occupied Arab Gulf (PFLOAG), as the rebels now rather grandly styled themselves. For Saiyid Said, however, British assistance proved to be a poisoned chalice. As the price of continuing their help the British in 1970 demanded his abdication and the accession of his son, Qabus. The campaign dragged on and on, the British being joined early in 1974 by some 2,000 Persian troops, sent as the result of an understanding between Qabus ibn Said and the Shah. The Persians were reinforced in the next twelve months, and a modest contingent of Jordanian troops also arrived in Dhufar. Some considerable success has been achieved in reconciling the hill tribes to the young sultan's rule and the campaign now seems to be drawing to a close. Its eventual cessation will probably depend upon whether the NLF regime in Aden decides, or is forced, to desist from harassing the sultan in his southern domains.

Large claims have been made in several quarters for the significance of the Dhufar rebellion, but it is difficult to see it, despite its ideological trimmings, as anything essentially different from the tribal revolts with which the Al Bu Said have had to contend throughout their reign and which were usually brought on by their own incapacity. Such revolts were normally suppressed—where they did not simply die from boredom on the part of the rebels—by the application of substantial *douceurs*. Qabus ibn Said has adopted the same policy in Dhufar and in Oman generally, but he will need to show greater signs of resourcefulness if he is to rule Oman effectively. It is hard to see how the expenditure of half his revenues from oil on defense, and equipping his simple soldiery with Rapier air-defense systems and *Jaguar* fighter planes is going to solve his political problems. This expenditure, however, is part of the price he has to pay to keep his troops, as well as his armed gendarmerie, contented and loyal. On the other hand, if he follows the example of his fellow rulers in the Gulf states, as he seems to be doing, and increasingly replaces the British officers in his armed forces with Arabs and Pakistanis, contentment and loyalty, along with efficiency will be put sorely at risk.

To date there have been few ripples in Oman as a whole from the Dhufar revolt. Some PFLOAG cells and some minor seditious activity have been uncovered but the country as a whole seems unmoved. PFLOAG itself has shrunk in size, stature, and ambition. No longer does it aspire to "liberate" the Gulf shaikhdoms, its paymasters in Aden having themselves been paid by at least two of these shaikhdoms to curb their cat's-paws. Instead the rebels now refer to themselves modestly as the PFLO—the Popular Front for the Liberation of Oman. Whether the people of Oman will welcome the brand of liberation the rebels are touting is very doubtful. The Omanis have their own venerable bones of contention to gnaw upon, should the mood take them; they have scant need of the arid prolixities of Marxist-Leninist dogma to arouse them to a realization of their lot in this world. Where the real significance of the Dhufar revolt may lie, as indicated above, is in its function as a test of the capacity of Saiyid Qabus. If he succeeds in Dhufar, the tribes of Oman may come to respect him and to acquiesce in the continuance of the sultanate as the country's ruling institution. If he fails, or achieves only a stalemate, the future of the Al Bu Said dynasty may be at risk.

To the particular disquiet existing in each of the Gulf states must be added the general tension engendered by their involvement of late years in the Palestine question. Until the 1967 war little notice was taken of the Arab-Israeli dispute by the rulers and people of the Gulf. That the dispute existed they could hardly but be aware, whether from the vociferations of the *émigré* Palestinians in their midst or from the bombast ceaselessly broadcast from Cairo and Baghdad. The dispute, however, did not touch them or their lives, and their attitude towards it was correspondingly apathetic. Only in Kuwait and Riyad was much official notice taken of the question: in the former because of the large and active Palestinian minority, in the latter because Saudi Arabia had been drawn into the Palestine imbroglio as far back as the late 1930s.

The defeat of the Arab armies in 1967 did not of itself greatly disturb the Gulf Arabs, who in any case had little time for Egyptians, Syrians, and Iraqis. But it irritated some of their rulers, who felt the defeat offended their *amour propre*, and it severely upset King Faisal of Saudi Arabia. Because the rulers of the minor states either felt constrained to follow his lead or were eager to ape the example of Kuwait, they joined the clamor for revenge against Israel and embraced the cause of Palestine *irredenta*. Propaganda began to pour forth from local radio stations up and down the Gulf, most of it compiled and broadcast by "northern" Arabs, branches of the Arab boycott office were opened in the various shaikhdoms, organized demonstrations of the kind depressingly familiar in the Levant cities were mounted, and the leaders of the Palestine Liberation Organization were feted as heroes and given large subventions—as much, it should be added, to keep them away from the Gulf as to support them in their operations against Israel.

The consequences for the Gulf states of their involvement in the Arab-Israeli dispute have been without exception, unfortunate. The language of Gulf politics has been immeasurably coarsened by the introduction of the invective which customarily punctuates discussion of the Palestine question in the larger Arab states. Local standards of political conduct have not been improved by the example of the PLO's terrorist exploits or by the praise indiscriminately heaped upon them by the organization's supporters among the "northern" Arabs in the Gulf. There are signs, too, that the Palestine issue is being used, as it has long been used elsewhere in the Arab world, as a scapegoat for domestic ills and as a safety-valve for discontents originating, as often as not, in the incapacity of the local government itself. Yet for all the brouhaha raised about it, the Palestine dispute is an artificial one so far as the people of the Gulf are concerned, which is the reason why the arousal of popular feeling against Israel has only been achieved, and can only be achieved, by appeals to Islamic, and particularly Muslim Arab, sentiment.

Here again, it was Faisal ibn Abdul Aziz who set the tone. His public pronouncements over the years, and his actions even more, left no doubt of the depth and implacability of his hatred of Israel. For him the Arab-Israeli conflict was a *jihad*, waged to recover that portion of the *dar al-Islam* which had been usurped by the Israeli state. *Delenda est Judaea*, and as the world was to learn from his many pronouncements over the years he was determined not to rest until he had prayed in an undivided Arab and Muslim Jerusalem. He has now gone to his rest, and it remains to be seen whether or not his successor, Khalid ibn Abdul Aziz, feels as strongly about the question as he did. First indications are that he does not, although he is said to take his role as *imam* of the Wahhabiya seriously, and Faisal's sentiments, it should be recalled, sprang naturally from his Wahhabi beliefs and from that fierce intolerance not only of other religions, but also of other Muslim sects, which is a prime characteristic of Wahhabism. On the other hand, Khalid ibn Abdul'Aziz and, what is probably more important, his brother, Fahad, the new prime minister, appear to be well aware that the survival of the Saudi Arabian kingdom and of the Saudi dynasty itself depends in large measure upon the continued goodwill and approval of the United States. They are unlikely, therefore, to jeopardize that support by undermining the efforts of the United States to reduce the level of active hostility between the Arab states and Israel.

Faisal's invocation of the spirit of Islam militant in the struggle against Israel has left its mark on the Gulf states. Far greater prominence is given now than in years past in public life in the shaikhdoms to the observance of Muslim occasions and the expression of Muslim sentiment. One sign of the increased emphasis upon religiosity is the presence of a growing number of Muslim Brethren (*al-Ikhwan al-Muslimin*), most of them Egyptians from Saudi Arabia, where they had taken refuge some years ago from persecution by Nasser. The information disseminated in the shaikhdoms by the government-controlled press, radio, and television is strongly Islamic in tone and content. It is as much propaganda as it is information: everything is interpreted in Arab or Muslim terms, everything is seen from an Arab or Muslim standpoint. It is little wonder, therefore, that for most of the inhabitants of the Gulf states and Saudi Arabia the political map of the world seems to be constructed upon an Arab projection, that Cairo and Riyad, Damascus, and Baghdad are its principal reference points, and that the rest of mankind now acknowledges the resurgence of Arab power and the renewed triumph of Islam. Such euphoria presages little good for the West, or for the Arabs themselves.

Political Relations among the Gulf States

The dismantling of the treaty structure which had governed relations between Great Britain and the minor Gulf states largely destroyed the foundations of the states system which had existed in the Gulf since the early years of this century, and in some of its aspects for even longer. That system had ensured the prevalence of the rule of law in the Gulf's affairs over the natural disposition of the states around its shores to gain their way against each other by deceit, intrigue, subornation or the sword. Now that Britain has abandoned the role of arbiter of the Gulf's quarrels and guarantor of its peace, these states are without any means of regulating their affairs with one another peacefully. The United Nations is too unwieldy and ineffectual a body to be of practical use in the region, and the Arab League is now a much-tattered paper tiger—and a toothless one so far as Iran is concerned. With no one to guide the Gulf states or control them, all that the outside world can hope for at this time is that a sense of self-interest and responsibility will supervene to keep their relations amicable. It is, as will be seen, an exceedingly frail hope.

Saudi Arabia and the Gulf States

Ever since the foundation of the Saudi state in the eighteenth century the Saudis have been thorns in the flesh of their Arabian neighbors. At one time or another in the past two centuries they have taken up arms against every other principality in the peninsula, either in support of a territorial demand, or to levy tribute, or to enforce conformity to the Wahhabi practice of Islam. Despite the numerous vicissitudes of fortune suffered by the Saudi state in the nineteenth century, it emerged in its reconstituted form in this century, under the leadership of Abdul Aziz ibn Saud, with none of its earlier appetites abated. It has been, and still is, the conviction of the Saudi ruling house that it is destined to rule Arabia from the Gulf of Eilat to the Gulf of Oman, from the Straits of Bab al-Mandab to the Shatt al-Arab, and to bring the reformed faith to all the peoples of the peninsula.

The only power which successfully stayed the Saudi advance in southern and eastern Arabia was Great Britain, not only in the last century but in this century as well. It was British intervention in the interwar years which prevented Ibn Saud from overrunning Kuwait, Qatar, and the Trucial states, and the blanket of British protection over the petty shaikhdoms of south Arabia blocked the extension of Saudi influence south of the Rub al-Khali. After the Second World War the Saudi government successively quarreled with Bahrain over the location of their common maritime frontier, laid claim to southern Qatar and the greater part of Abu Dhabi, and tried to make a satrapy of the interior of Oman. On each occasion the accomplishment of its aims was frustrated by British opposition. Today nothing stands in the way of Saudi expansion southwards and eastwards, and it may only be a matter of time before such an expansion gets under way.

Qatar presents no problem: the Al Thani rulers are themselves Wahhabi by religious profession, and their relations with the Al Saud have long been amicable. Shaikh Zayid ibn Sultan, the ruler of Abu Dhabi, once the inveterate foe of the Saudis in eastern Arabia, has, since the British withdrawal from the Gulf, capitulated to Riyad and conceded its territorial demands. The settlement of the Saudi Arabia-Abu Dhabi frontier in the summer of 1974 allotted to the Saudis all the territory south of the Liwa oasis which had formerly belonged to Abu Dhabi, including the major portion of the Zarrara oil structure, which is itself part of a larger structure, the Shaiba field, discovered by Aramco in undisputed Saudi territory. A measure of the harshness of the settlement is the provision that Abu Dhabi may not exploit that portion of the Zarrara field lying in its own territory. The second major concession made by Zayid was the grant to Saudi Arabia of a strip of territory on the Abu Dhabi side of the shaikhdom's former frontier with Qatar, a concession which affords Saudi Arabia a corridor to the sea in the vicinity of the inlet of Khaur al-Udaid. In return for these substantial and unwarranted concessions the Saudis graciously withdrew their legally untenable and historically unjustified claim to the Buraimi oasis on the common frontier of Abu Dhabi and Oman.

The Saudi government has now achieved what the late Abdul Aziz ibn Saud in his lifetime sought and failed to acquire—an outlet on the lower Gulf east of the Qatar peninsula which would enable it, if the occasion arose, to cut off that shaikhdom and absorb it within the Saudi dominions. The Saudis have also placed themselves in a position to overawe the United Arab Emirates by sea as well as by land, and to menace, if they so wish, the UAE's maritime approaches, its offshore oil operations, and its rights to the territorial sea and continental shelf adjacent to its coasts.

While Saudi ambitions towards Oman may be of a less ambitious nature, nevertheless the sultanate is regarded as coming within Saudi Arabia's sphere of influence. At the close of 1971 Faisal ibn Abdul Aziz summoned Qabus ibn Said to Riyad and offered him aid of an unspecified nature against the rebels in Dhufar, in return for the recognition of Saudi territorial rights, again of an unspecified extent, along the desert frontiers of Oman. Although he does not appear to have afterwards pushed his pretensions regarding Oman any further, there is no reason to believe that Faisal in anyway abandoned them. On the contrary, the Ibadiya of Oman are objects of especial anathema to the zealots of Najd, who consider them little better than *kafirs*, infidels, and their subjection has been an object of Saudi policy for one hundred seventy-five years. What largely influenced Faisal in his treatment of Oman was his desire to isolate the Marxist regime in south Yemen, for which the cooperation of the Omanis as well as that of north Yemen (the Yemen Arab Republic) was required. It is highly likely that his successor will pursue the same tactics, especially as the course of Arabian history shows that whatever occurs in the southwest invariably influences the shape of events in the southeastern region of the peninsula.

Iraq and the Gulf States

Except for a brief period in the 1930s Iraq remained aloof from the affairs of the Gulf until the overthrow of the monarchy in 1958 and its replacement by a republican government. There was, as was to be expected, an antipathy from the outset between the revolutionary regime in Baghdad and the rulers of the Gulf states. The regicides of Baghdad were viewed with particular abhorrence in Riyad, despite the animosity which had previously existed between the Saudis and the Hashimites. The first overtly hostile move made by the Iraqi revolutionary junta against one of the Gulf states occurred in June 1961 when the treaty relationship between Great Britain and Iraq was terminated. The leader of the junta, Major-General Abdul Karim Qasim, immediately advanced a claim to sovereignty over Kuwait on the grounds that the shaikhdom had once been administered as part of the Ottoman *vilayet* of Basra, and that Iraq, as a successor state of the Ottoman empire, had also succeeded in full sovereignty to Kuwait. Qasim threatened to make good his claim by force, but he backed down when British troops were sent to the shaikhdom to defend it. Two years later Qasim was deposed and killed by his rivals in Baghdad and the new regime recognized the sovereign independence of Kuwait in return for a loan of some twenty-five million pounds sterling.

Iraqi activities in the rest of the Gulf in the early 1960s were confined to supplying arms to supporters of the exiled *imam* fighting in Oman, and to covert political agitation in Bahrain and one or two of the Trucial shaikhdoms. Soon after the Baathists came to power in Baghdad in the mid-1960s they began a propaganda campaign in the Gulf states designed to subvert the traditional form of shaikhly government and replace it with something more radical. The campaign had little success, partly because Iraqis were not greatly liked by the inhabitants of the Gulf, partly because it was so ineptly conducted. Money was the key to popular influence in the Gulf from the late 1960s onwards (as well as long before), and the Iraqis were hard put—as well as too parsimonious—to compete effectively.

The depths to which they could sink in their quest for influence were revealed in January 1972 when they facilitated the return to Sharjah of its former ruler, Saqr ibn Sultan Al Qasimi, who was bent upon murdering his successor and taking his place. He succeeded in the first aim but not in the second. Unabashed, the Baghdad regime continued with its efforts to spread sedition in the shaikhdoms and to overturn their governments. It found an ally in the People's Democratic Republic of Yemen and an instrument in the Popular Front for the Liberation of the Occupied Arab Gulf, which had established cells in most of the shaikhdoms. Dissidents and malcontents of one kind or another, but mostly of Marxist persuasion, were given guerrilla training in Iraq and sent back to the Gulf to do what damage they could. So far this has not amounted to very much, but it may become more pronounced if the Baathist regime devotes more attention, as it may well do in the near future, to the Gulf.

It was hardly surprising, in view of the Baathists' hostility to the Gulf's hereditary rulers, that the 1963 disclaimer concerning Kuwait should in due course have been renounced. The renunciation was made in March 1973 when

Iraq demanded the right to build pipelines and road and rail communications across Kuwaiti territory to the sea and to construct an oil terminal on the Kuwaiti coast. What lay behind the demand was Iraq's need for a better outlet to the sea than those afforded by the Shatt al-Arab and the port of Umm Qasr, which could not be used by large oil tankers, especially now that the North Rumaila field had come into production. What also prompted the demand, which was reinforced by an Iraqi attack upon a Kuwaiti frontier post, was Iraq's increasing political and military dependence upon the Soviet union, a relationship which had been formalized in a treaty of alliance in April 1972. Under the terms of this treaty the Soviet Union was accorded certain facilities at Umm Qasr for servicing Soviet naval vessels. The port, however, was of limited use to the Russians because of the shallowness of its approaches, which in any case lay through Kuwaiti territorial waters. The Kuwaitis rejected the Iraqi demand, and the question has remained unresolved since 1973, although periodic statements are made by one side or the other announcing its settlement, to be followed inevitably by denials that any such thing has occurred.

Iraq's need for a deep-water terminal for large oil tankers has sharpened as a consequence of the intensification of the Baghdad junta's quarrel with its fellow Baathists in Damascus over the consistency and ideological purity of their respective political beliefs. The Revolutionary Command Council in Baghdad is determined to reduce Iraq's dependence upon the pipeline through Syria to the Mediterranean for the export of much of its oil, and to ship as much as possible out through the Gulf. Construction has begun, accordingly, upon a new oil-loading facility some miles to the west of Fao, the small port at the entrance to the Shatt al-Arab. At first glance this undertaking would appear to diminish Iraq's need for an outlet for its oil through Kuwaiti territory, and to rob its demands upon Kuwait for such an outlet of much of their force. But the Iraqis are bent equally upon extending their shoreline upon the Gulf for another purpose, and this is to increase their share of the continental shelf and of any oil deposits it might be found to contain. For this reason they have resisted attempts by Iran and Kuwait to agree upon a median line in the upper Gulf between their respective coastlines.

The persistence of Iraqi designs upon Kuwait may also help to explain why the Kuwaiti government turned to the Soviet Union in the summer of 1975 for arms and military instructors. Even before the termination of the Kurdish rebellion in the spring of 1975 relations between the Russians and the Revolutionary Command Council (RCC) in Baghdad were considerably cooler than they had been in the rapturous days of 1972; and with the ending of the campaign against the Kurds the RCC no longer had the same need of Russian military advisers and specialists. Since the early months of 1975 the numbers of Russian military personnel in Iraq have been drastically reduced, and so, too, has the size of the contingent of engineers and geologists helping to run and develop the Iraqi oil industry. Further steps taken by the Iraqi government to extricate itself from the entanglements of the Soviet alliance have included the sale of oil to France in exchange for industrial goods, the purchase of arms from France and Britain, and negotiations with the Chinese government for closer economic and military ties.

Cold-shouldered by their erstwhile protégés in Baghdad, the Russians have found themselves, for that very reason, the objects of the Kuwaitis' attention. (The Kuwaitis themselves, of course, have been the objects of the Russians' diligent attention for some years past, as evidenced by the size of the Russian embassy in Kuwait and even more by the small army of KGB officers resident in it.) While it is all too clear why the Russians should be gratified by the invitation to supply Kuwait with arms and military instructors—one particular attraction is the greater potentiality of Kuwait Bay over Umm Qasr as a naval base—the reason why the Kuwaitis sought such a connection defies rational explanation. If they think it will secure them against interference from Iraq, they would do well to ponder the record of the Soviet Union's conduct in the Middle East and elsewhere over the past thirty years.

While the chances of Iraq's adopting a forward policy in the Gulf would appear to have been increased by the suppression of the Kurdish rebellion and the settlement of the long-standing quarrel with Iran over the location of the Perso-Iraqi frontier along the Shatt al-Arab, it is far from certain that the Baghdad government, in reality, feels secure enough to embark on such a policy. Relations with Iran, for all the recent show of cordiality, are still characterized by caution on both sides, and the situation in the Kurdish areas will continue to give rise to uneasiness in Baghdad. The rift between the Iraqi and Syrian Baathists constantly engages the regime's attention and energies, while within the regime itself there is an equally constant jockeying for power among the Baathists, the Communists, and others. Various discontents agitate the country's population. The Shii majority resents the Sunni supremacy in the government. Regional centers like Mosul in the north and Najaf and Karbala in the south chafe under Baghdad's edicts. Distracted by such vexations, the junta may find itself with little appetite for adventures in the Gulf.

Iran and the Gulf States

Although the figure of Muhammad Reza Shah arouses mixed emotions in the West, there is a general tendency to accept him at his own value as a progressive ruler who is determined in his lifetime to make Iran a modern industrial state and a military power without peer in the Middle East. Few Western governments question (at least publicly) the practicability or desirability of these aims. Instead they are content—or are constrained by the disarray in their own ranks—to humor his pretensions, sell him large quantities of arms and industrial goods, and pay him inflated prices for his oil. The irony of all this is that the shah himself poses a greater threat than anyone else to the stability of the Gulf and therefore to the security of the oil supplies upon which the West so heavily relies.

To take first his quarrel with Iraq. It was he, not the Baathists, who reopened the dispute over the Shatt al-Arab, and it was his action in April 1969 in denouncing the 1937 treaty defining the frontier along the waterway which began the war of nerves that eventually led the Baathists to conclude a defensive alliance with the Soviet Union which has given that power a *point d'appui* on the Gulf. The shah also afforded support and refuge to the Kurds in their revolt against Baghdad, not out of any sympathy for their cause but rather as a means of harassing his enemies. The Iraqi government responded in kind by encouraging a separatist movement in the Persian province of Khuzistan, adjoining the Shatt al-Arab, where a large part of the population is of Arab descent.

Now, apparently, all has changed, as a result of negotiations between Tehran and Baghdad begun in the spring of 1975. The shah has abandoned his support for the Kurds in return for the concession by the Iraqi government of his claim that the Perso-Iraqi frontier along the Shatt al-Arab should follow the median line of the river instead of, as in the past, the low-water mark on the Iranian bank. It can only be regarded in the light of what has subsequently befallen the Kurds, as a shabby compact. It cannot, moreover, given the character of the principals and their true feelings towards each other, be anything other than a truce. However, the shah, who not so long ago was describing the junta in Baghdad as "crazy, bloodthirsty savages," is now pleased to express himself as "astonished and delighted" by the leading figure of the junta, Sadam Husain al-Takriti, the Iraqi vice president, seeing him as "a young man with a bold imagination." Despite this, the shah knows full well that there are deep-lying and perhaps ineradicable sources of antipathy between the two countries—the distinction between Arab and Persian, the division between Sunni and Shii, the conflict between radical and conservative forms of government. If he really believes that a new era of mutual tolerance is now dawning in Perso-Iraqi relations, against whom, it might well be asked, is he arming so heavily, especially in tanks and aircraft? On the other hand, of course, he may merely be engaged in saber-rattling.

Towards the minor states of the Gulf the shah has so far acted with outward civility, although he has not bothered to disguise his conviction that they are fated to become Iranian satrapies. Too much has been made by Western commentators of his gesture in 1970 in withdrawing his claim to sovereignty over Bahrain as proof of his pacific intentions in the Gulf. As the claim had no foundation in law or in fact, its abandonment was a small price to pay for the political advantages gained at the time. A more accurate pointer to his real feelings and intentions (including his ultimate plans for Bahrain, when circumstances are favorable) was his seizure at the close of 1971 of the islands of Abu Musa and the Tunbs in the lower Gulf. These islands, situated in the vicinity of the Straits of Hormuz, were dependencies of the shaikhdoms of Sharjah and Ras al-Khaima. The shah's justification for seizing them was that he was anxious to prevent them from falling into the hands of extremists, who might use them as bases from which to threaten shipping, and particularly oil tankers, passing through the straits. Iran, he declared, could not permit its principal outlet to the world to be thus endangered. His action raised a certain amount of hubbub in the Arab world, but the only party to suffer from the affair was British Petroleum, whose holdings in Libya were sequestrated by Colonel Qadhafi in revenge for what he considered to be the British governments complicity in the shah's action.

Western reaction in general to the shah's move was indulgent. It was rapidly becoming part of the accepted wisdom that the guardianship of the Gulf formerly exercized by Britain had now passed jointly to Iran and Saudi Arabia. It is an impression that the shah has been happy to confirm by declaring, whenever the occasion arose, that the settlement of the Gulf's problems was exclusively the concern of the states around its shores and especially of its major powers. By this, of course, he meant himself, since control of the Gulf's waters depends upon naval and air power, and he has built up stronger naval and air forces than any other littoral state. How much justification there is for the present complacency in the West about the shah's plans to make Iran the paramount power in the Gulf is another matter. In the first place, it is difficult to see any advantages in allowing him to establish, as he has several times indicated he intends to establish, Iranian control over the Straits of Hormuz. The straits are an international waterway, a status which has been established, as the whole corpus of international law has been established, by Western nations, almost invariably against the opposition of Oriental powers. Already there have been dangerous indications on the part of some Middle Eastern states of a desire to exert the kind of control over the narrow seas adjacent to their coasts which is incompatible with international rights of free passage. No one's interests, not even the shah's in the last analysis, would be served if the international status of the Straits of Hormuz were to be eroded.

Secondly, there is nothing in Iran's past behavior in the Gulf to inspire confidence that the assertion of Iranian paramountcy would benefit anyone. For the greater part of the past two centuries Iran has been a source of irritation and disturbance in the Gulf. Successive rulers of Iran have cherished the illusion that they are fated to sway the destinies of Asia, to extend their dominion from the Tigris to the Indus, and to annex every inch of territory where an Iranian foot has trod. Their achievements, needless to say, never matched their aspirations, and the resultant sense of frustration frequently expressed itself, especially in the nineteenth century, in petulant refusals to cooperate with Great Britain in the suppression of piracy and the slave trade in the Gulf, and in continual and vehement protests about alleged, but wholly imaginary, infringements of Iran's sovereign rights. The fall of the Qajar dynasty and the accession of Reza Shah

Pahlevi, the father of the present shah, brought no change in the temper of the court at Tehran. Reza Shah entertained the same ambitions as his predecessors with respect to Iran's manifest destiny in the Gulf. His efforts to equip himself with a navy, however, foundered upon the resolute incapacity of his subjects to master the arts of seamanship and fighting at sea. His son has followed in his footsteps, with more apparent success, if the reports in the press about the fledgling Persian navy are to be believed. But to anyone acquainted with the history of Iran in the past two centuries it would come as a considerable surprise if this Gilbertian enterprise turned out to be anything but an expensive folly.

Some kind of understanding is said to exist between Iran and Saudi Arabia for the maintenance of peace in the Gulf and the suppression of elements hostile to the prevailing conservative political order. It would be exceedingly strange if such an accord actually existed, since these two states are more divided by their differences—religious, racial, cultural, historical, and political—than they are united by any apparent common interest in the preservation of the monarchical institution of government. The shah does not bother to pretend that he looks upon the Saudis as other than savage Bedu, parvenus and religious fanatics. The Saudis, for their part, regard the shah as a profligate, intoxicated with his own sense of importance, and the Iranian Shia as little better than *mushrikun*, polytheists.

The two states are expansionist by tradition and inclination, and it could well be that their ambitions will overlap and conflict in the southeastern corner of Arabia, in Oman and the United Arab Emirates. The shah has already, by the aid he has afforded the sultan of Oman in his campaign in Dhufar, signified his readiness to intervene militarily in the Arabian peninsula. He has also let it be known, in connection with his statements about controlling the Straits of Hormuz, that he is watching developments in the Musandam peninsula, where an improbable "liberation" movement has been reported among the wild Shihu who inhabit its desolate peaks and fjords. An outbreak there or an insurrection in any of the United Arab Emirates, directed against the ruling family or involving Iranian immigrants, would afford him the opportunity to intervene with force for the purpose of restoring the *status quo ante*. Saudi Arabia, with its pretensions to paramountcy in Arabia, could not allow such a move to go unchallenged, and the upshot could well be to embroil it with Iran, with incalculable consequences for them both and for the Gulf as a whole.

United States and Western Interests in the Gulf and Saudi Arabia

By a quirk of fate the world's principal and most readily accessible reserves of oil are located in one of its most barren and underdeveloped corners, so that the economic well-being of the United States, and even more so of Western Europe and Japan, is now subject to the whims and passions of a handful of Arab rulers and their retainers. It is a mistake to believe that any innate or acquired sense of responsibility will lead these rulers, or the leaders of any popular regimes which may succeed them, to use the economic power they now enjoy with discretion and moderation. Nothing in the history of the Gulf justifies comfortable assumptions in this regard, and to indulge in them is to ignore the rooted preference of the Arabs of the Gulf for immediate tangible gain over steady, long-term advantages, and their deep-seated, if half-concealed, antipathy for Western Christendom.

The United States, Western Europe, and Japan have one obvious, overriding objective in the Gulf, which is to secure access to the region's oil reserves in adequate quantities and at reasonable prices over the next two decades or longer. The realization of this aim depends upon the maintenance of political stability in the area and upon the avoidance of any strategic conflict there, in short, upon the Gulf's neutralization. Since a rough equilibrium exists in the Gulf today the achievement of this objective would seem to imply the preservation of the *status quo*, or at least the exercise of sufficient influence over whatever changes may occur to limit their disruptive effects. Yet all the factors in the present situation so far enumerated, and others which have not been considered or are not yet discernible, militate against the successful implementation of such a policy.

Until the picture with respect to alternative supplies of oil in the world, and alternative sources of energy, becomes clearer, no near-accurate forecast of the extent of the West's dependence upon Middle Eastern oil can be made. What can be predicted with a greater degree of certainty is that, unless the traditional laws of supply and demand assert themselves before long to bring down the price of oil, the financial disequilibrium created by its present high level will threaten the entire economy of the Western world and place it in pawn to Saudi Arabia, Iran, and the Gulf oil states. It has been made painfully clear since October 1973, when the Organization of Petroleum Exporting Countries doubled the price of oil and its Arab members imposed an embargo upon oil exports to the United States and the Netherlands, that the Muslim countries of the Middle East have found the weapon of retaliation for which they have been searching ever since Western Christendom established its predominance over the Islamic world in modern times. There is no mistaking the mood of exaltation which now grips Sunni Islam, and to a lesser extent, Shii Islam. Equally, there can be no doubt of the profound dangers to the West which this mood portends, dangers not only of economic subservience or collapse but also of the corruption of Western society and its institutions, social, political, and financial, by the deployment of the massive sums of money which the oil-producing states now have at their disposal.

Western governments, notably those of Britain and France, have been extremely slow or reluctant to acknowledge these dangers, preferring to seek refuge in optimistic arguments and predictions about the behavior of Iran and the Arab oil-producing states, arguments based not upon the actual behavior, modes of thought, systems of values, political ideas or religious beliefs of these states but upon Western notions of moderation and reasonableness, good sense and sober judgment, power, and responsibility, to none of which the Muslim states in question subscribe. The high prices demanded for oil by Iran and the Arab oil states are in reality nothing less than tribute, exacted from a supine West by a resurgent Islam. They are intended to place Western Europe in thrall to the Muslim East. Fanciful though this concept may sound to Western ears, it is nevertheless a reality to those who cherish long-standing grievances and resentments against Europe for having in the past overborne Islam. None feels this resentment more keenly than the Arabs, who deem themselves a chosen people, the repository of the true faith, the race of the Prophet, ordained by divine Providence to compel submission from others. Against such convictions, however farfetched they may seem in the West, the various nostrums prescribed by Western economists and governments for coping with the financial crisis besetting the West will prove, as they have proved to date, unavailing.

Nor, for all the sound and fury aroused by the issue, would any amelioration of the Arab-Israeli conflict bring relief from the present dangers. It is easy to contend—which is one reason why the contention has gained universal currency—that it was the war of October 1973 which prompted the embargo on oil by the Arab oil-producing states. But the threat of an embargo had been made before, as early as the Tripoli meeting of OPEC in December 1970, and again at the confrontation with the major oil companies at Tehran in February 1971. The object then was to force a unilateral rise in the price of crude oil, and so it was again in October 1973, when, as may be recalled, the announcement of the price rise took precedence over the promulgation of the embargo. The Yom Kippur War, in short, afforded an almost unique opportunity to the Arab oil-producing states to combine principle with profit, and at least one of those states, Saudi Arabia, apparently had advance knowledge of the impending Egyptian and Syrian attack upon Israel.

The further increases in the price of oil which have been made since October 1973, raising it to five and a half times its level before that date, have all been made without reference to the Arab-Israeli conflict. On the contrary, the excuse for these additional exactions has been the increasing cost of Western imports or some such equally disingenuous justification. Moreover, the shah has been in the forefront of those demanding ever higher prices, and it hardly needs mentioning that he has cheerfully been trading with Israel for years, and supplying that nation with oil, a practice he continued during the October 1973 war. It is also worth recalling that no Arab government has at any time linked conessions by Israel with a reduction in prices, not even the Saudi Arabian government's messenger, the peripatetic Shaikh Ahmad Zaki Yamani. The truth is that the oil weapon, especially in its financial aspects, has precious little to do with the Arab-Israeli conflict, in which, as argued earlier, the rulers of the Gulf states, have little real interest. Even if the conflict were to be resolved overnight, and to the Arabs' entire satisfaction, the price of oil would not drop, through that cause, by a fraction of a cent.

There is little point, in view of their record to date, in expecting the international oil companies to accomplish anything in the way of price reductions. As nationalization in the guise of participation erodes their power in the oil-producing states, reducing their functions to those of contract technicians and captive customers, their anxiety has become concentrated upon the simple securing of oil supplies, with cost as a secondary consideration. The depths of obsequiousness to which some of them are prepared to sink in order to safeguard their access to oil supplies were revealed by the depressing spectacle of Aramco, an American company, refusing for the duration of the embargo to supply oil to the United States Sixth Fleet. There is nothing to be gained either from hoping that Iran and the Arab members of OPEC will see reason and lower the price of oil to an economic level. As has just been contended, they march to the sound of a different drum. Their sights are fixed upon constant increases in price, even though they were forced by a variety of circumstances at the meeting of OPEC in Vienna in September 1975 to restrict their latest demand to a 10 percent rise. Since the price of crude oil has ceased to be determined by negotiation between the oil companies and the oil-producing states and is now fixed unilaterally by OPEC, the oil-importing countries have no safeguard against arbitrary price rises. It is pointless to trust OPEC to honor any commitments its members might make regarding price stabilization or the duration of new price levels. Since 1970 they have broken nearly every undertaking they have given in this regard, and there is no reason to believe that their behavior will change in the foreseeable future.

If the problem of price is to be tackled, the initiative wil have to come from the governments of the consuming countries, including those in Asia and Africa whose economies have been even more severely affected by the price increases of the past two years than those of the West. The OPEC cartel is not an indestructible monolith. None of its members is the natural partner of the other, not even the Arab oil-producing states. Already the facade of unity has begun to crack under the pressure of world economic conditions and as the tensions inherent in OPEC's own structure assert themselves. World consumption of oil has decreased markedly since the beginning of 1974, when its price was again doubled by OPEC, and some of its members, including Algeria, which has complained the loudest about alleged "imperialist exploitation" by the West, have tried to bolster their incomes by selling oil surreptitiously at prices below those set by the cartel. Algeria also supported Saudi Arabia at the OPEC meeting in Vienna in September 1975 in arguing for a smaller price increase against those members like Iran which wanted to impose a much greater rise. The clash which took place on that occasion between the Saudis and the Iranians was representative of something more than a difference of opinion over the additional amount of Danegeld that the West could be induced to pay without much protest. It was also an expression of the rivalry which exists between the two states over their respective spheres of influence in the Gulf region. Obviously, it is in the West's interests to encourage such dissensions within OPEC's ranks, with the object of eventually breaking the cartel's stranglehold upon the supply of oil, provoking competition among the oil-producing states for markets, and ultimately bringing the price of oil down to more realistic levels.

Yet the whole course of Western policy towards OPEC so far has run in a contrary direction—towards appeasement rather than defiance, towards accep-tance rather than rejection. Great ingenuity has been shown by professional purveyors of guilt and peddlers of self-abasement in the West in demonstrating that it is right and seemly for the West to atone for its past sins towards the peoples of hither Asia by lavishing its treasure upon them. Much contentment has been expressed that the surplus revenues of the oil-producing states of the Gulf have been absorbed in the international monetary system without wrecking it, and Western governments have virtually swooned with gratification at the lucrative contracts that have been concluded for the establishment of elaborate industrial complexes in Saudi Arabia and the Gulf states, and for the supply of inordinately large quantities of expensive armaments to them. None seems to question publicly the desirability or efficacy of these expedients, which appear the product less of reflection and calculation than of that fashionable despair which paralyzes the West today. Even if both shores of the Gulf were to be lined with petrochemical plants, dry docks and cement factories, and the armies of Arabia and Persia were to be arranged as Caesar's legions, the current level of oil prices ensures that huge surplus funds will still accrue of yet further control over Western Europe's economic destiny.

Present Western policy, in other words, seems almost deliberately designed to compound the dangers it is intended to avert. Not only is little heed apparently paid to the financial implications of continuing to adopt before the Middle Eastern oil producers the posture of the rabbit confronted by the stoat, but even less thought is given to the probable consequences of trying to soak up the excess oil revenues by the indiscriminate sale of arms to the major and minor Gulf states. When it is recalled that until the Second World War the arms traffic in the Gulf was tightly controlled and restricted to small arms for which the Gulf rulers could prove a need, the present spectacle afforded by the large-scale arming of Saudi Arabia, Iran, and the petty shaikhdoms is both ludicrous and shameful, not least because, given the technical backwardness and incapacity of these states, these large quantities of complex weapons, aircraft, and electronic equipment are destined to become nothing more than piles of expensive junk. It might also be asked against whom and for what purpose these states are arming themselves. The standard answers, involving references to Israel, the Soviet Union, the security of the Gulf and so on, are too well known to require further rehearsal here. The truth may prove to be something different, especially in the case of Saudi Arabia and Iran. If these two are tempted in the near future to embark upon military adventures, they will destroy the present uneasy equilibrium in the Gulf and place their own regimes in jeopardy.

Will the United States be able to influence or control the drift of events in the Gulf in the next decade or so? The answer to the question resides partly in the area of domestic American politics, partly in the matter of technique, and partly in the extent to which Western Europe and Japan can be associated with the United States in maintaining peace and security in the Gulf. It depends also upon whether the United States is prepared to reexamine the policy it has followed in the region since the Second World War. From that time until the British withdrawal from the Gulf at the end of 1971 this policy, broadly speaking, had two aims: to promote the paramountcy of Saudi Arabia in the Arabian peninsula and to give tacit support to Great Britain in keeping the peace in the Gulf. When, as often happened, these two objects conflicted, priority was usually given to the first. The predisposition in favor of Saudi Arabia seems to have been the product of a certain simplicity of thought and of assiduous propaganda on the part of Aramco. Starting with the premise that Saudi Arabia was the largest of the states of the peninsula, it was seemingly logical to assume that it was both natural and inevitable that the Saudis should eventually dominate their neighbors. From this assumption it seemed even more logical to conclude that such a consummation was also desirable, since the small littoral states under the British protection were considered to be little more than anachronisms in the modern age, hardly deserving of survival.

The deferential attitude adopted by Aramco towards the Saudi regime, and the considerable efforts it made over the years to present the regime to the outside world in a flattering light, only reinforced these assumptions. Aramco promoted the notion that there was not only an identity of interest between the United States and Saudi Arabia but a *natural* identity of interest, springing not just from obvious commercial considerations but also from an affinity between Americans and Saudi Arabs. It was plainly to Aramco's advantage to foster such a belief; it is less plain that its acceptance was to the advantage of the United States. Events have now shaken, if they have not entirely destroyed, the foundations of Aramco's faith. For the past twenty-five years and more it has been solemnly telling the world that it is not an American oil company but a Saudi company, operating in the interests of Saudi Arabia. Now the hyperbole has become the simple truth; the seeds of appeasement have yielded their accustomed fruit. An attitude of mind cultivated over twenty-five years, however, cannot be altered overnight, and the legacy of Aramco lingers on in the shape of continued readiness of the United States to support the paramountcy of Saudi Arabia in the peninsula, to supply it with arms, and to entrust it with responsibility for the peace of the Gulf.

Such a policy can only bear fruit as bitter as Aramco's harvest. It is not in the nature of the Al Saud to be content with the shadow of paramountcy: religious and dynastic, as well as political, compulsions have always driven them to seek the substance. Yet at the same time they are incapable by their own efforts of subduing the Yemen, south Arabia, and Oman. One has only to recall Egypt's ill-fated campaign in the Yemen to dispel any doubt about the difficulty of such an undertaking. The Saudis could overrun the minor shaikhdoms of the Gulf, but the upheaval this would cause would endanger the entire oil industry of the Arabian shore. It was precisely to prevent such an upheaval, as much as to protect British investments in the littoral shaikhdoms, that Great Britain in the past objected to and blocked Saudi efforts to absorb them. This objection still holds good today, and it is reinforced by other considerations.

It has been emphasized throughout this essay that the Gulf is a highly unstable area, its condition, despite a gloss of modernity, primitive, and its politics turbulent. The maintenance of peace and security there can be achieved only in one of three ways: either by the exertion of a hegemony by a strong local power, or by the imposition of a virtual protectorate by an outside power, or by the maintenance of the *status quo*, however uneasy it might be. No one local power is strong enough of itself to exert such a hegemony, and any attempt to do so by one of them would produce only chaos. The second possibility would appear to be ruled out, at least in an overt form, by the present climate in world affairs. Only the third means appears at all practicable at this time. Yet the maintenance of the *status quo* will require not only its acceptance by the three principal local powers, Iran, Saudi Arabia, and Iraq, but also the acquiescence of several outside powers, notably the other major Arab states and the Soviet Union. Whether or not Iran and Saudi Arabia will agree to the preservation of the *status quo* will depend, in large measure, upon the readiness of the United States to exert pressure upon them to do so. The chances of Iraq and the other Arab states agreeing to the exclusion of the Gulf from the arena of Middle Eastern politics are exceedingly slender, if only because its oil revenues bulk so large in the political, military, and economic calculations of these states.

The Soviet Union's intentions towards the Gulf are inscrutable, and any attempt to divine them depends upon the interpretation of a host of considerations too numerous even to list here, the greater part of which, in any case, have little or no direct connection with Arabia and the Gulf. Oil, it need hardly be said, is a strategic commodity of the first order, and control of the Gulf's oil fields is an object of prime strategic importance. It would not be in keeping with the past conduct of the Soviet Union if it were not to seek, by every means in its power, to acquire such control and with it the power to bring Western Europe and Japan to their knees, confident in the knowledge that, to judge from the record of recent years, Western Europe's ultimate response to such a contingency would be a supine and pusillanimous acquiescence.

Russia now has at hand for the attainment of this goal an instrument far more reliable and effective than transitory alliances with radical Arab governments or the clandestine support of the *soi-disant* liberation movements, viz., naval power, the means by which control of Arabia's coasts and seas has been acquired down the centuries. Should the Soviet Union decide to deploy its navy for this purpose, the West would have to choose between submission and resistance. Little purpose would be served in trying to avert such an eventuality by securing Russia's explicit or implicit agreement to the neutralization of the Gulf. The agreement would not be honored for long. The Gulf's oil is so glittering a prize that a struggle to possess it is inevitable, just as the Gulf's chronic instability ensures that opportunities for Russian mischief-making will be countless.

What happens in the Gulf in the next decade or so will be determined as much if not more by the resolution or irresolution of the West as it will by the Gulf's propensity for arbitrary and violent shifts of political fortune. So far Western Europe and Japan have shown only feebleness and fear in the face of OPEC's extortions and the Arabs' threat of an oil embargo, a reaction which has served only to increase the Arabs' and the shah's intransigence and arrogance. To the threat posed by the Soviet Union's naval presence in the Indian Ocean the industrial nations have, by and large, closed their eyes, presumably in the hope that thereby it will somehow magically disappear.

There are, needless to say, other responses open to them which would serve them better, now and for the future. The advantage in any economic contest between the West and the Middle Eastern oil-producing states lies with the former, not the latter, and whether by the instrumentality of a consumer's cartel or the imposition of trading sanctions or, if necessary, military intervention, the West would have little difficulty in demonstrating its superiority. Britain and Japan, and to only a lesser degree, France and Germany, have in the recent past been naval powers of the first rank. There is nothing intrinsic in their condition today, other than their will and sense of purpose, to prevent them in combination from becoming so again. If Russia, which has never been a first-class naval power, can become one in the space of a few years, so also can they, and much more readily. The burden of safeguarding Western and Japanese interests along and around the shores of Arabia should not rest upon the shoulders of the United States alone; and American diplomatic efforts might more rewardingly be spent in securing the direct support and cooperation of the Western European powers in ensuring Western naval supremacy in the Indian Ocean, the Red Sea, and the Persian Gulf than in trying to cajole the refractory and capricious regimes of the Gulf region into acting with a sense of responsibility towards the world at large.

XVI Iran: The Making of a Regional Power

Ali Banuazizi

Introduction

The widespread attention that Iran has received in the Western press over the past two or three years and the significance that is now accorded her by policymakers in nearly all Western capitals may be explained in terms of three interrelated factors. First, and perhaps foremost, has been the "energy crisis," with its various economic and political ramifications, leading to the appreciation of the hitherto unheralded role of the oil-producing countries in the world economy and the vulnerability of the West European, Japanese, and, to a lesser extent, American economies to fluctuations in the supply and price levels of oil. Iran's position among the Middle East suppliers has been a significant one, both in terms of its level of production (highest after Saudi Arabia) and the militancy with which it has championed recently the "cause" of the producing countries for higher prices.

The second factor has been the dramatic increase in Iran's military stockpiles and capabilities, starting in the late 1960s and intensifying after the British military withdrawal from the Persian Gulf in 1971, an increase the dimensions of which are yet to be fully apprehended. In the course of a few short years after the British withdrawal, an anticipated "power vacuum" has been filled by what promises to become the costliest arms race in history. To many observers, the character and magnitude of Iran's military build-up, as the major participant in this race, do not appear to be entirely commensurate with its defense needs—at least in terms of the more conventional criteria and parameters by which such needs are defined for small powers. They take quite seriously, therefore, what may at first seem like rhetorical statements by the shah to the effect that Iran's

463

defense perimeter extends into the Indian Ocean and that the security of the Persian Gulf and, by implication, the internal stability of its littoral states are among the country's primary foreign policy and strategic objectives.

Finally, there is the rather aggressive style with which the Iranian government—using its sudden, and initially considerable, riches—has embarked upon a course of spectacular domestic and foreign financial investments and economic ventures. In a period of less than two years, Iran placed one of the first advance orders for the British-French SSTs; bought 25 percent of the Krupp Steelworks; concluded a $6 billion deal with France for, among other things, the construction of five nuclear-power plants; shored up the English economy with a $1.2 billion loan; bailed out a foundering defense manufacturer in the United States with a $75 million loan; announced plans for the construction of the most extensive "New-Town" project of the century to be built in Tehran at an expected cost of $3 billion to $5 billion; and concluded a $15 billion trade agreement with the United States for the purchase of goods and services over the next five years.

The foregoing interrelated developments have greatly enhanced—both within and certainly outside the kingdom—Iran's image as an oasis of stability and reliable strength in an economically vital and strategically critical region of the world where turbulence and unexpected political upheavals are its all too familiar features. To understand Iran's current international behavior, however, requires a somewhat detailed review and analysis of the country's internal political processes by which the national interest is defined and national objectives are set and pursued. Such an analytical focus on the internal political processes is especially warranted where, as is the case with Iran, the society is not fully integrated, where the political system provides only limited channels for nonviolent political expression, and where the distribution of values, particularly political values, is often affected by the actual or perceived impact of external stimuli.

The present essay thus attempts to review and analyze Iran's postwar international behavior, particularly with respect to the United States, in the context of her internal political, social, and economic processes.

Background of the Present Situation, 1941-1953

The Allied invasion of Iran in the autumn of 1941, among other things, brought to an abrupt end nearly two decades of virtually total political independence and ushered in another era of open and often intense great-power pressures and rivalries in and over the kingdom. Furthermore, the abdication and departure of Reza Shah (the father of the present shah and founder of the Pahlavi dynasty), coupled with the disintegration of the central government's authority in the face of the occupying Russian and British forces, marked the end of a period in which the only major actor in the Iranian polity had been the monarch himself. The vacuum thus created by the collapse of an authoritarian regime prompted the reappearance of a number of hitherto isolated political figures and a proliferation of political parties and pressure groups.

In the decade following the Allied invasion, Iranian politics came to be shaped primarily by the nearly continuous, and at times fiercely competitive interaction among the shah, the aristocracy, the Communists, and the nationalists. While the first two represented the incumbents, the latter two typified the challenging elements of this quadrangle.

Despite his youth and relative political and administrative inexperience at the time he ascended the throne, Mohammad Reza Shah soon came to exercise a significant, and at times overriding, influence over the Iranian political system and particularly over the direction of the country's foreign policy.[1] This influence—often exercised with little or no public awareness—originated primarily in the support given the monarch by the upper echelons of the Iranian military and civilian bureaucracies, and was enhanced by his considerable personal popularity and by his reputation as a benevolent, compassionate, and constitutionalist king. In particular, the loyalty and support of the military appear to have been regarded by the shah as the most reliable and effective source of political security and strength. From the very beginning of his reign, therefore, the shah proceeded to ensure his personal command over the armed forces, while attempting to revive their morale and increase their capabilities— both of which had been drastically impaired by the Allied invasion of the country.

An early boost to the military's morale and the shah's control over it came with the decisive defeats of the secessionist movements in Azerbaijan and Kurdistan provinces. Under the tutelage of the Soviet Union, a Communist-inspired movement led by Ja'afar Pishevari had set up the Autonomous Republic of Azerbaijan in December 1945, while another Soviet-style Kurdish Republic was being declared by Mohammed Ghazi in a western Iranian province, Kurdistan. These developments represented the first direct threats to the country's territorial integrity in over two-and-a-half decades, and the Soviet support of the Azerbaijan movement rekindled amongst many Iranians the long-standing suspicion of the Russians' southward expansionism. Whereas the ground for the collapse of these regimes was prepared by the intensive diplomatic efforts of the Iranian government, aided by the public support of the American government (both in the Security Council of the United Nations and elsewhere), the actual reoccupation of these provinces in December 1946 and the subsequent reassertion of authority by the central government could be recounted as achievements of the Iranian army under the leadership of the young shah.

A further increase in the monarch's power, in this early period of his reign, occurred in 1949, when, following an attempt on his life, a constituent assembly paved the way for the establishment of a Senate, half of whose members were to be appointed by the monarch and the other half to be elected by the regular electoral process. In addition, the assembly invested the shah with the prerogative of dissolving both the Senate and the Majles (House of Representatives).

The Iranian aristocracy in this period was a heterogeneous body, consisting essentially of elements of the large landowners, tribal leaders, and remnants of the preceding monarchical dynasty. The political vacuum, created by Reza Shah's departure in 1941, was partly filled by the members of this aristocracy who constituted the majority of the Majles deputies until the early 1960s. Although the shah continued to enjoy the overall loyalty of this aristocratic majority, a chronic and at times intense struggle over a greater share of the political power took place, particularly during and shortly after the war years, between the monarch and a shifting alliance of this dominant group in Majles. The aristocracy as a whole was somewhat wary of the shah's reformist attitude toward the then existing socioeconomic system in the country. It was apprehensive, also, about the prospects of an increasing royal reliance on a reorganized and expanded military establishment for the restoration of an authoritarian monarchical regime.[2] This competition between the shah and his supporters, on the one hand, and the more ambitious elements of the aristocracy on the other, was gradually overshadowed by the growing strength of communist and nationalist challengers in the late 1940s.

The formation of the *Tudeh* (Mass) party in 1941 was the new organizational expression of the older Persian Communist party, which had played a prominent role in the establishment of the short-lived Gilan Soviet Republic in 1920. The party's platform, generally devoid of Marxist expressions, evoked a favorable response not only among the industrial workers but also among some members of the middle class and the intellectuals. Within a few years, it had turned into the only organized mass political party with an extensive network of cadres, particularly in northern Iran.

The height of the *Tudeh* party's political power was reached from 1944 to 1946, when it sent eight of its members to the Fourteenth Majles and held three cabinet posts in the cabinet of Ahmad Qavam during the Azerbaijan crisis. However, the withdrawal of the Soviet troops from Iran, followed by the collapse of the two pro-Communist separatist regimes in Azerbaijan and Kurdistan late in 1946, sent the party into a period of political and organizational decline which was accelerated after the abortive assassination attempt on the shah's life in 1949. It was only with the rise of the National Front to power in 1951 that the *Tudeh* party—primarily through a number of front organizations—came to gain new political strength and agitational capabilities.

The "nationalists" in the early postwar period comprised a loose conglomeration of individuals, parties and pressure groups that were held together by a common opposition to real and imagined foreign (mainly British) influence in Iranian affairs and a desire to curb the political power of the Shah and the aristocracy. They drew their strength from among the politically more articulate urban population, especially the Bazaar merchants, low- and middle-echelon civil servants, and university students.[3]

The figure around whom the nationalists rallied and who, in time became their most influential spokesman was Dr. Mohammad Mosaddeq. Having been confined during most of Reza Shah's reign, Mosaddeq resumed his political activities as the leader of the non-Communist opposition within the Iranian body politic in the early 1940s. The mounting anti-British sentiments, due mainly to economic grievances against the Anglo-Iranian Oil Company, provided Mosaddeq with the requisite political base, both within and outside of the Majles, to organize his National Front as the dominant force in Iranian politics in less than a decade after his reentry onto the political scene. In the brief, but tumultuous period of his premiership (1951-1953), most of his attention and effort was directed toward nationalizing the British-controlled oil industry and shaping a nonaligned foreign policy. The pursuit of these goals subjected Iran's relations with the Western powers, particularly Great Britain and the United States, to serious and unprecedented strains. Moreover, Mosaddeq's policies at home— notably his calling on the monarch to reign and not rule and to relinquish his control over the military, his liberal attitude toward the legally-banned *Tudeh* party's open political activity, and his defiant disregard of the traditional avenues of political bargaining in favor of direct and often intensely emotional appeals to the masses—alienated the traditional Iranian oligarchy.[4]

The nationalists' foreign policy was based upon two major premises. The first was that the cold war, as a political, economic, and ideological confrontation between the two world powers, would not adversely affect Iran's interests so long as the Iranian government pursued a neutralist stance and otherwise maintained friendly relations with both sides of the conflict on a nondiscriminatory basis. The second and related premise was that a direct and unprovoked Soviet threat to Iran's security was highly unlikely, and hence it could not be used as a reasonable justification for the build-up of the country's military capabilities. In regard to the latter premise, they maintained, furthermore, that in the absence of a credible external threat to Iran's territorial integrity, an expanded and strong military establishment could in itself imperil the very structure of Iran's constitutional system and fledgling democratic institutions. Similarly, the nationalists did not appear to regard the political threats posed by a growing internal Communist movement with any degree of alarm. They proceeded on the assumption that the institution of social reforms and acceleration of economic development would effectively meet such a challenge.

These assumptions, however—fraught as they were with both predictable and unforseeable challenges and internal consequences—were not acceptable to the monarch. Nor were they acceptable to the American policymakers of this period. The latter saw in Mosaddeq's dogged pursuit of a nonaligned foreign policy, the continued weakness of Iran's military and security capabilities, and the dramatic reduction of the shah's political power a high likelihood for Iran's collapse and her possible conversion into a Soviet satellite. It was in response to this perceived conflict between the American cold war strategy and the foreign and domestic policies pursued by the Iranian nationalists that the Eisenhower administration in August of 1953 actively welcomed the fall of Mosaddeq's government and the restoration of the shah's full authority. For at least the subsequent decade or so, not only the overall direction, priorities and tactics of Iran's foreign policy, but also the country's internal political processes (including the expectations, mood, and strength of the active and potential oppositional groups) continued to be affected by the choice that the American government made at that crucial juncture.

The Current Internal Political Environment

With Mosaddeq's fall, the main objective of the regime became the dissolution of all the actual or potential sources of political threat and the centralization of political power in the hands of the monarch himself. The political parties and pressure groups, which had come to have an increasingly discernible impact upon the course of governmental policies in the postwar period, were gradually eliminated. The *Tudeh* party was first in line. Soon after the 1953 coup (dubbed officially as the Twenty-Eighth of Mordad National Uprising), the government of General Zahedi initiated a vigorous and systematic crackdown on the *Tudeh* party organization, which led to its total dissolution, the imprisonment of many of its members, and the flight of some of its leaders to Europe. While the National Front supporters were treated with relatively more tolerance, they too were prevented from engaging in overt political activity.

With the shah beginning to assert himself increasingly as the major, if not the sole, repository of political power in the country, the important institutional components of decision-making, namely the Majles and the cabinet, which had been revived in the 1941-1953 period, were transformed essentially into mere instruments of political legitimization and policy execution. A constitutional amendment in 1957 entrusted the shah with the power to veto any measure adopted by the Majles relating to financial matters, thus providing further safeguards against the possibility of an unexpected revival of parliamentary assertiveness.[5] Indeed, since 1953, neither of the two chambers appears to have initiated any significant legislation or been willing or able to reject any of the major legislative proposals initiated by the executive branch. Also, no prime minister, and for that matter no cabinet member, has faced a vote of no-confidence during this period.

In the years immediately after the nationalists' fall, the monarch came to rely increasingly on the support of the military and attempted to regain his personal control over it. A potentially serious flaw in the armed forces' loyalty was cleared away when, in 1954, scores of pro-Communist officers were rounded up and purged. Moreover, some senior officers with detectable or suspected pro-Mosaddeq tendencies were either dismissed or forced into retirement. The shah's personal control over the military was further increased with General Zahedi's resignation in 1955 as prime minister. This control over the military and security agencies has since been enhanced by the monarch's skillful counterpoising of the authority, functions, and ambitions of the command personnel in various military and paramilitary services; by his selective, periodic retirement of senior officers when they have become apparently too indispensable to the regime's security; and by his attending to the personal and professional interests of the officer corps.[6] American military and financial aid in the 1950s and early 1960s, and increases in the flow of oil revenues in the last decade, have helped to sustain these efforts, particularly in regard to the expansion and modernization of Iran's military establishment.

In addition to the regular armed forces, the publicly-known agencies responsible for the maintenance of internal security are the national police force, the gendarmerie, and the State Security and Information Organization (known by its Persian acronym, SAVAK). The assignments of SAVAK seem to include: the detection of clandestine antigovernment activities both in Iran and abroad; the arrest, isolation, and otherwise intimidation of known or suspected political activists; the surveillance and censorship of the mass media; and the screening of applicants for government employment. The organization is thus engaged primarily in the more secretive and preemptive aspects of political control and coercion. Irrespective of the actual size of its personnel and methods of interrogation, intimidation, and suppression, it is by all accounts a widely feared agency. Clearly, its reputation for efficiency, ruthlessness, and general immunity to outside interference has added greatly to its strength.[7] The regular police force, gendarmerie, and the armed forces are held in reserve for more direct use or threat of force in the suppression of oppositional political activities, including street demonstrations, strikes and sporadic acts of terrorism and guerrilla-type movements.

By the early 1960s, the concentration of decision-making power in the hands of the Shah had reached a new high. Secure in his position as the undisputed source of all political authority and power, the monarch could now contemplate far-reaching reform programs from the throne with an almost revolutionary rhetoric and zeal. As he wrote some years later in his *The White Revolution* (1967),

The realization came to me that Iran needed a deep and fundamental revolution that could, at the same time, put an end to all the social inequities and all the factors which caused injustice, tyranny and exploitation, and all aspects of reaction which impeded progress and kept our society backward.[8]

The earliest indication of the impending reform came in 1957, when by royal decree a Western-style, two-party system was created in Iran. One party, *Hezb-e Melliyun* (Nationalists' party), representing the incumbent government and led by Premier Manuchehr Eqbal, was to present a "conservative" platform; the opposition party, *Hezb-e Mardom* (People's party), led by a long-time associate of the shah, Assadollah Alam, was to represent a more "liberal" and reformist position. The latter's platform listed some of the principles that were to be embodied, several years later, by the shah's own reform program. The choice between the two parties for the Majles deputies and various political functionaries had little or nothing to do with their ideological preferences or social and political positions. In many cases this choice was made even easier through prearranged assignment of membership.

This contrived experiment in party politics, however, proved to be a total failure. The party in power was widely accused of rigging the 1960 elections, and its leader, Premier Eqbal, had to resign under pressure from the "loyal opposition" and some independents who were beginning to mount a modest, but real, opposition. A new prime minister, Ja'afar Sharif-Emami, was chosen by the Shah to conduct a new round of elections in 1961. Within a few months after the formation of the new Majles, the new government came under attack in a highly tense political atmosphere. The immediate occasion was a nationwide teachers strike and the killing of one of the striking teachers by the police in the course of a minor skirmish that had developed during a demonstration in front of the Majles building. Sharif-Emami's cabinet could not withstand the political fallout of this relatively minor incident. His resignation and the naming of Dr. Ali Amini, a critic of the recent events and a more independent and reform-minded politician as prime minister in May 1962, ended the first phase of Iran's experiment with an imposed two-party system. Shortly thereafter, the Twentieth Majles was dissolved on the ground of its doubtful electoral origins and the likelihood of its opposition to the impending social reform measures.

In January 1963, the monarch formally unveiled his six-point reform program which was to form the basis for Iran's "White Revolution," later to be called the "Revolution of the Shah and the People." Its avowed goal was to promote social justice through a revolutionary, but peaceful, transformation of the country's social order. Two weeks after the shah's declaration, a national referendum was held on the objectives of the "revolution," and, not unexpectedly, they were approved by an overwhelming majority (99 percent) of those casting ballots. With eight new principles added later (7, 8, 9 in 1964; 10, 11, 12 in 1967; and 13 and 14 in 1975) to the original six-point declaration, the final charter of reform sets forth the following fourteen objectives:

1. Land reform;
2. Nationalization of forests and pastures;

3. Sale of shares in government-owned industries to finance the land reform program;
4. Profit-sharing in industry;
5. Reform of the electoral laws, including the granting of suffrage to women;
6. Formation of Literacy Corps to wage an anti-illiteracy campaign in rural areas;
7. Formation of Health Corps;
8. Formation of Reconstruction and Development Corps;
9. Convening Houses of Equity (parajudiciary courts) at the village level;
10. Nationalization of water resources;
11. National reconstruction and development;
12. Administrative and educational reforms;
13. Expansion of the ownership base of industry;
14. Equitable pricing.

In the wake of the announcement of the six-point "White Revolution," and despite its overwhelming referendum support, the regime faced its severest political challenge in almost a decade. The challenge came in the form of a series of massive riots that erupted initially in Tehran, but soon spread to Qum, Meshed, Isfahan, and Shiraz, during June 4-6, 1963. While these outbursts were quickly branded as "black reaction" (referring to the clergy's leading role in instigating them) by the government, it seems highly questionable that the opposition by the *ulema* could have formed the sole basis for the disorders. To be sure, the granting of suffrage to women and the implementation of a wide-scale land reform—and fear of its extension to the *awqaf* (charitable landed estates under the trusteeship of the clergy)—created considerable resentment among the more reactionary segments of the clergy. However, other less immediate causes also might have been at work. These include: (a) a more broadly based opposition to the increasingly decisive political role of the shah, evidenced most concretely in his government by decree since the dissolution of the Twentieth Majles in May of 1961; (b) renewed, though circumscribed, political activity by some National Front leaders with the tacit approval of the government; (c) a severe recessionary crisis in the economy which had pushed the government to the verge of bankruptcy; and (d) a number of violent confrontations between government troops and defiant tribesmen in the southern sections of the country.

The government's reaction to the June riots was prompt and, by all accounts, very harsh. This bloody quashing, together with the successful implementation of the land reform program, helped to break down the power of two traditionally dominant groups in the Iranian polity, the *ulema* and the landlords. And, with the defeat of the insubordinate tribal chiefs in the south, the authority of the central government was to be extended to all parts of the country without any viable challenge. What followed was an even greater monopolization of power and tighter control of the political process by the monarch. This highly centralized power was to be maintained and augmented by certain fundamental changes in the Iranian society, a successful economic recovery and growth, and the emergence of a new, more loyal political elite—changes that were to be brought about largely by the shah's own program of reform and style of leadership.

A new group of younger, more highly educated, Westernized, and reform-minded professionals and career bureaucrats has been gradually replacing the traditional political elite since the early 1960s. Personal wealth, as a basis for elite membership, has been largely replaced by education and proven loyalty to the regime. An early, and quite symbolic, indication of the rise of this new elite came in the summer of 1963, when the shah by a special decree chartered a recently formed "study group" of low-profile political aspirants (dubbed the "Progressive Center"), who had been meeting regularly to discuss Iran's social and economic problems, as the Economic Research Bureau to the Imperial Court. Later that year, a new political party, *Iran-e Novin* (New Iran), was formally founded to encompass and expand the membership of the Progressive Center. And, finally, the ascendancy of the erstwhile "study group" to the centerstage of the power structure was completed when, in March of 1964, one of its original members, Hassan-Ali Mansur, was called by the monarch to form a new government.

While strongly supporting the new party and giving its young leadership—within set limits—the reigns of government, the monarch stopped short of assuming its overall direction. Hence, in spite of the fact that the *Iran-e Novin* party had been organized to carry out the mandates of the "Revolution of the Shah and the People," Iran was not yet to have a single national party (such as those in the republican regimes of the Middle East and elsewhere) with the head of the state as its leader. The shah's commitment to a Western-style party system, with two major parties and a number of minor ones, seemed to be quite firm, and, at least in form, the two-party system was to be kept alive and officially encouraged. In reality, however, the loyal opposition groupings (including the *Mardom* party) did not find it opportune to challenge the incumbent party in any politically significant form until the late 1960s and early 1970s.

Mansur's term as prime minister lasted less than a year, ending with his assassination on January 21, 1965, by a member of a youthful and fanatic religious brotherhood which called itself "The Islamic Nations' Party." His death, however, did not alter in any way the shape of his cabinet or the fate of the *Iran-e Novin* party. As his successor, the shah promptly appointed a close associate of the late premier (and the minister of finance in his cabinet), Amir Abbas Hoveyda.

The major thrust of Hoveyda's government over the past decade has been the implementation of the socioeconomic reforms that were promised by the

"Revolution of the Shah and the People." The most fundamental and far-reaching, in terms of its social, political, and economic consequences, has been the land reform program. Since the early 1950s, various decrees had called for the transfer of royal estates to the peasants, increasing the peasants' share of income from the land that they worked, or limiting the dues and services that landlords could demand from their tenant farmers. These measures, however, could not—and perhaps were never intended to—effect basic structural changes in the highly exploitative economic relationship between peasants and landlords. Neither could they have had much impact on the quasi-feudal order which for centuries had relegated the peasants to an insecure, submissive sociopolitical status.

The major provisions of the land reform program, which had been enacted into law in 1962, were quite straightforward and pragmatic. They included: (1) limitation of landholding to a maximum of one village; (2) compensation payments to the landowners on the basis of land taxes paid prior to 1962; (3) transfer of the purchased land, whenever possible, to the tenant farmers; and (4) required membership in rural cooperative societies as a condition for the receipt of land by the peasants. The program was by and large executed efficiently and with dispatch by the ministry of agriculture. From the very beginning of the reform the government championed the cause of the peasants for economic and social justice with an unprecedented revolutionary rhetoric and zeal, while branding the landlords as a villainous class that was to carry the blame for many of the social ills and sufferings of the past. The absence of any organized resistance on the part of the landlords during the entire course of the reform was testimony not only to the newly consolidated power of the regime to initiate and carry through whatever measures that it deemed necessary, in general, but also to the popularity of the land reform program in particular.[9]

While the primary objective of the first two stages of the land reform program was the breakdown and distribution of large landholdings among the peasants, the third stage, begun in 1966 and continuing to date, has attempted to improve and modernize production and marketing methods in order to increase the productivity of the agricultural sector, stabilize food prices, and improve the living standards of the rural population. Thus, for millions of Iranian peasants the land reform program has meant greater control over their own affairs, modest improvements in their standards of living, and access to a variety of services provided by the government at the village level. Their dependence on middlemen, forward buyers, and moneylenders charging exorbitant interest rates has been considerably reduced by the formation of the "rural cooperative societies." By 1973, a total of 8,361 such cooperative societies, covering some 30,685 villages (more than half of the total number of villages in the country) and a total membership of 2,065,000 farmers, had been set up. In addition to cash and credit, these cooperatives provide their farmer-members with seeds, fertilizers, and farming equipment which would otherwise not be within the means of many farmers with small holdings.

Not all villagers, however, have reaped the benefits of the land reform. A substantial number, particularly in larger villages, are landless agricultural workers who compete for a shrinking supply of seasonal work at subsistence-level wages. The small size of the plots cultivated by most farmers after the land reform and the increased mechanization of agriculture have severely limited work opportunities for the landless villagers. Many of them have migrated on a seasonal or permanent basis to the larger cities in search of work. More often than not, however, their lack of any useful skills makes it impossible for them to find steady jobs, and thus they are forced to live in crowded squatter settlements. There, along with thousands of others who shared the same hopes, they try to eke out a day-to-day existence on low-paying, occasional and menial jobs.[10]

Aside from land reform, other programs of the "White Revolution" which have aimed at improving the lot of the rural population include literacy, health, and extension and development corps. Over the years, the tens-of-thousands of young people who have been recruited into these "revolutionary corps" upon graduation from high school or college have contributed their knowledge, skills, and much fervor for social change to the village communities. They have also symbolized and often actively promoted the regime's quest for social reform and for wider political support among almost three-fifths of the population that lives in the nonurban areas. In urban areas, the consequences of the rapid growth of recent years are evident in the vastly expanded industrial, commercial, and service establishments; in better housing, sanitary, transportation, and communications systems; in increased government activity in the health, education, and social welfare fields—all of which add up to much improved standards of living for the majority of urban residents.[11]

There are also glaring imbalances and inequities in the way in which the fruits of economic growth are distributed. While some of these economic inequities will be reviewed in the next section of this essay, a few words may be said at this point about their social consequences. A relatively narrow segment of the population, less than a fraction of 1 percent, residing in the exclusive sections of Tehran and a few other major cities stands out conspicuously as the direct beneficiary of the new economic prosperity in Iran. It is distinguished by the incredibly opulent life-style of its members. Its membership consists of an amalgam of the country's economic, political, and social elites, without the usual differentiations that separate these elite subgroupings in other, more developed societies. Directly beneath them in the socioeconomic hierarchy is a burgeoning middle class, comprised mainly of smaller businessmen, lesser professionals, teachers, middle-echelon government servants, and an increasing number of sales and managerial employees of large private concerns. A third and considerably larger stratum consists of manual workers in industries, construction, transportation, etc., lower-echelon government employees, and others in the services sectors, whose full-time wages are barely enough to meet their very modest level of living. Along with members of the middle class, they often find it necessary to carry more than one job to keep up with the recent inflationary spiral. At the bottom of the stratification hierarchy and forming perhaps 10 to 15 percent of the urban population are those who have yet to find any semblance of economic security within the system. Their ranks include scores of thousands of rural migrants, the unemployed, seasonal workers, peddlers, etc., most of whom live in abject poverty and are offered little or no services by the government.

The foregoing socioeconomic reforms of the past decade have so far made little, if any, visible impact on the country's political life. There has been little inclination to allow the emergence of genuine political institutions and parties. With the awesome increases in the state's power has come little recognition of the citizens' political rights, and often the government has regarded as elusive the distinction between political dissent—in any form—and treason. Hence, the use of coercive and extra-legal means have become accepted instruments of political control, and the usual guarantees of due process have all but vanished for those whose ideas are considered to be threatening to the security of the regime.[12]

Under these conditions, it is, of course, extremely difficult to assess the degree to which the regime enjoys the support of the various segments of the population or to estimate the size or strength of the opposition groups. In general, there is every reason to believe that the shah enjoys the support of the majority of the people. This is certainly true in the rural areas, where his land reform and associated programs have brought about considerable improvements in the lives of the peasants. It is also true in the cities, where the better-off and politically more sophisticated social strata attribute their improved level of living to the regime's success and view the monarch as the symbol of political legitimacy and stability.

Of those who are opposed to the regime—including a substantial proportion who are loyal to the present constitutional-monarchical system but are opposed to particular government policies—the majority are unable or afraid to express their opposition openly, as no politically legitimized mechanisms for such expression exist and great risks are attendant upon any effort to initiate them. The absence of such legitimate means has limited the options of the regime's adversaries to political passivity, episodic demonstrations and strikes (usually by university students and workers), leaving the country, or operating on a clandestine, underground basis. The major groups outside of the country include the central committee of the banned, pro-Soviet *Tudeh* party and a radically transformed National Front Organization, both of which used to operate primarily from Iraq from the early 1970s until the normalization of the Iran-Iraqi relations in early 1975. Several Maoist or independent leftist groups, whose avowed objective is the overthrow of the present regime, must also be included in this category. In addition, a vociferous minority of Iranian students in Europe and the United States has been active against the regime since 1960, thus serving as a major detractor of the regime's otherwise positive image in the

West. The radicalization of these students has usually taken place after they have left their homeland.

Within the country itself, the major opposition to the government has come in the form of loosely organized terrorist activities in the cities. In the past several years, these groups, whose ideological allegiances range from Marxism-Leninism to Islamic fundamentalism, have been responsible for a number of political assassinations, bank robberies, armed confrontations with the police, and acts of sabotage. Sporadic mass expression of political unrest and opposition to the regime—particularly in the form of strikes and clashes with the state security forces—have also been in evidence, especially in major universities and some industrial areas.

In March of 1975, in a surprising move which may give a new shape to Iran's political life, the monarch ordered the dissolution of the existing political parties and decreed the formation of a new, single-party system for Iran. The new party, to be called *Hezb-e Rastakhiz-e Mellat-e Iran* (the Iranian People's Resurgence party), will have the incumbent premier, Amir Abbas Hoveyda—who has the longest uninterrupted tenure of office in Iran's modern history—as its secretary-general for two years. Much more important than the reduction of the number of parties to one—which was more or less an affirmation of the existing state of affairs—were the implied sanctions in the monarch's historic speech. In declaring that the new party would belong to all Iranians, he made it clear also that all Iranians are expected to join. The only three criteria for joining, according to the shah, are belief in the country's constitution, loyalty to the system of monarchy, and support of the "Shah-People Revolution." Considering the fact that public rejection of any of these principles would be, under present conditions, tantamount to disloyalty and treason, the cost of political apathy may be expected to rise substantially in the coming years. Indeed, according to the monarch, those who do not join the party because of their rejection of these principles are "stateless" individuals for whom going to jail or leaving the country would be the only available options; those who subscribe to these principles, but choose not to join the party, will continue to enjoy their legal rights, although "they should expect no privileges."[13]

The Economy

The current upsurge in the Iranian economy, reflected in an unprecedented doubling of the gross national income over a period of slightly more than two years since 1973 and huge development and investment projects at home and abroad, is but the latest phase of an impressive economic performance which began in the early 1960s. No matter what set of criteria one chooses to apply in evaluating the performance of the economy over the last decade, the result is likely to be further testimony to a remarkable growth story with few, if any, parallels in the postwar world. Needless to say, the contribution made by the ever-increasing revenues from oil, both directly and through their multiplier effects in the economy as a whole, has been very considerable. However, it is unlikely that the growth of this sector alone could provide the sole basis for explaining the growth of the economy as a whole. Neither can one make a compelling case that economic planning and management in Iran, compared to other quasi-planned economies, have been exceptionally efficient. Any plausible explanation for the country's economic success, therefore, should take into account the contributive role of a host of political and economic factors beyond the inflow of oil revenues, as well as the nation's more-than-usual amount of luck in economic affairs.[14]

In the decade covering Iran's Third and Fourth National Development Plans, from 1963 through 1972,[a] the gross national product rose at an average compound rate of 10.5 percent per annum at *constant* market prices (or 13.4 percent at current market prices). As the population increased at an estimated annual rate of 3 percent during the same period (from 24 million to 31 million), an average per capita growth rate of 7.5 percent per annum was realized. With the exceptionally high increases in the GNP in the first two years of the Fifth Plan, mainly the result of the oil price hike of 1973, the per capita GNP showed more than a sevenfold increase in the twelve-year period under review, from $167 in 1962 to $1,274 in 1974. Moreover, until recently, this growth had been achieved with a remarkable stability in prices. Thus, from 1962 to 1972, the consumer and wholesale price indices rose at an average annual rate of 2.7 and 2.8 percent, respectively. A considerable erosion of this price stability, however, has taken place since the early 1970s, with a 27 percent increase from 1972 to 1973 and an approximately 20 percent per annum increase in 1974 and 1975.[b] While the government authorities have tended to blame this inflationary trend on "imported inflation," there can be no doubt that endogenous economic factors, including vast increases in government spending and greater consumer demand, have also been of greater significance in producing the recent inflationary pressures.

Table XVI-1 presents the growth rates of the major sectors of the economy and their share in the gross national product over the ten-year period (1963-1972) covering the Third and the Fourth National Development Plans. As shown in this table, oil, industries and mines, and services each registered growth rates that were higher than the rate for the GNP as a whole, while the agricultural sector grew at less than half of the GNP's rate. The sluggish

---

[a]Since, in the Iranian calendar, years run from March 21 to March 20, references to a given year cover the period that begins on March 21 of that year and runs until March 20 of the following year (e.g., 1963 = March 21, 1963-March 20, 1964).

[b]Thanks to an apparently successful campaign by the government to halt inflation, however, a clear downturn in the wholesale and retail price indices was in evidence starting in mid-summer of 1975.

Table XVI-1

Value-Added Growth Rates of the Major Economic Sectors and Their Relative Contribution to the GNP, at Constant Prices, 1963-1972

	Third Plan Period (1963-1967)		Fourth Plan Period (1968-1972)	
	Av. Annual Growth Rate	Percent. Share in the GNP	Av. Annual Growth Rate	Percent. Share in the GNP
Agriculture	4.6%	25.4%	4.0%	19.3%
Oil	15.3	15.3	15.2	18.7
Industries & Mines	13.0	20.9	13.1	22.8
Services	19.4	39.8	14.3	41.6
Net factor income from abroad (excluding taxes)	–	1.4	–	2.5
GNP (at Market Prices)	9.7	100.0	11.6	100.0

Source: Data adapted from the Central Bank of Iran.

performance of the latter sector led to a substantial decline in its contribution to the gross national product from 28.2 percent in 1963 to 16.0 percent in 1972. This decline was all the more disappointing as it occurred in spite of a number of major reform measures in this field by the government, including a major change in the land tenure system, the increasing adoption of crop-rotation system, the introduction of mechanized agricultural tools and chemical fertilizers, and substantial improvements in irrigation. While a slower growth rate for this sector is characteristic of most developing countries, the problem seems to have been somewhat more serious in Iran.

In addition to the changes in the output of the four major sectors of the economy, sectoral shifts may be noted also in the distribution of the labor force. The general trend in labor has been away from agriculture and toward industry and services. Thus over the ten-year period of the Third and the Fourth Plans, the percentage of labor force in agriculture fell from 53.5 in 1963 to 40.1 in 1972, while the shares of the industry and services in the total labor force rose from 21.9 percent and 24.1 percent to 29.4 percent and 30.0 percent, respectively. The relative number of workers in the oil sector remained at about 0.5 percent during this period. The total size of the labor force has grown from just over seven million men and women in 1963 to 9,129,000 in 1972, and it is expected to reach approximately 10.5 million by the end of the Fifth Plan in 1978.

The recent dramatic increases in the price of oil have brought about major changes in the Iranian economy. Late in 1973, following the October Arab-Israeli War, the posted price of crude oil rose from $2.99 to $11.65 per barrel, raising Iran's per-barrel take from $1.75 to $7.00. As a result, the country's oil revenues were quadrupled from $5 billion in 1973 to an estimated $20 billion in 1974. This new wealth has not only had a stupendous impact on the domestic economic situation, but it has enabled the government to engage in massive economic ventures abroad in an effort to establish, on a long-term basis, sources of foreign exchange earnings other than oil and to promote Iran's influence in the world economy.

Domestically, the impact of the increased oil revenues can best be seen in the substantial revisions that were made in Iran's Fifth National Development Plan (1973-1977). With the anticipated increase in the oil revenues from $24.6 billion to $98.2 billion for the Five-Year Plan period, a thorough revision of the plan's original allocations was necessary. For the first time in the twenty-five-year history of economic planning in the country, the limitation of financial resources was not apparently the primary constraint in setting planning objectives. Real limits on allocations were a number of major bottlenecks in the economy. These included: (1) the acute shortage of skilled manpower; (2) limitations in the infrastructural capacity of the economy, including electric power, roads and railways, ports, etc.; (3) inefficiencies within the executive agencies making it difficult to handle a heavy overload; and (4) the unquestionable inflationary impact of large domestic investments.

In spite of these limitations, the revised version of the Fifth Plan calls for a total fixed investment of $69.6 billion by the public and private sectors for the Five-Year Plan period. This is more than twice the allocation made in the original version. It may also be compared to the total investment of $10.8 billion in Iran's Fourth Plan. Almost two-thirds of the Fifth Plan's total investment ($45.5 billion) will be accounted for by the public sector, to which an additional $10.4 billion set aside for current development expenditures ($7 billion) and transfers to the private sector through loans ($3.4 billion) should be added.

Allowing for an inflation rate of 12 percent, the GNP is expected to rise at a staggering average rate of 25.9 percent at constant prices per annum, compared to the initial version's projected rate of 11.4 percent. This would raise the country's total output of goods and services from $17.3 billion in 1973 to $54.6 billion in 1978. Whereas much of this growth was expected to take place during the first two years of the plan period (32.8 percent in 1973 and 51.1 percent in 1974), the growth rate for the remaining three years was projected to be 16.5 percent per annum, which is still quite high when compared to the previous growth rates of the economy. If such rate of growth in the GNP were in fact to be achieved, Iran's per capita income would increase from $556 to $1,521 during the five-year period of the Fifth Plan.

The critical role of the oil sector in the GNP and the country's economic development in general can be seen in the projections for its growth and sectoral share during the present plan period. With an average growth rate of 51.5 percent (compared to 11.8 percent in the original version of the plan), the oil sector is expected to make up 48.7 percent of the GNP by the end of the Fifth Plan, compared to 18.7 percent at the end of the Fourth Plan.[c]

The average annual growth rates for the other main sectors of the economy over the period of the Fifth Plan have been projected to be as follows: agriculture, 7.0 percent; industries and mines, 18.0 percent; and services, 16.4 percent. Given these rates, the shares of the four major sectors will undergo substantial changes. By the end of the plan, the sectoral composition of the Iranian economy is expected to be as follows: agriculture, 8.0 percent; industries and mines, 16.1 percent; oil, 48.7 percent; and services 27.2 percent.

In addition to its far-reaching impact on the domestic economy, Iran's new oil wealth has enabled it to initiate a variety of trade agreements, joint ventures, and economic aid programs abroad. While the long-term benefits of these investments are expected to be the expansion and diversification of the country's industrial capacity and the ensuring of future foreign exchange earnings from sources other than oil, in the short run they have provided prudent investment outlets for current oil revenues which, if invested domestically, would seriously tax the absorptive capacity of the economy and add to the current inflationary pressures. In general, three types of investment and aid projects may be distinguished among the many that have been announced since the oil price increases of December 1973. These are: (1) normal trade agreements; (2) joint-ventures with other countries, including investments in already established major industrial concerns; and (3) economic assistance, including loans and credits, to developing and industrial countries and international agencies.

By far the largest of several recent trade agreements is one that was signed in March of 1975 between Iran and the United States. With a designated total of $15 billion, to be spread over a five-year period, it represents the biggest accord of its kind between two countries. Under the agreement—which excludes oil—Iran will spend $5 billion in military items (an actual reduction from the current figure), $5 billion in normal trade items, and the remaining $5 billion in actual disbursements for the development of its industries, food supplies, housing and public services. A major and controversial provision of the agreement is the construction of eight nuclear-power plants by American firms in Iran. Similar, though smaller, trade agreements have been signed recently with Canada, England, France, Germany, India, Italy, and Turkey as well as a number of Socialist countries.

A related category of investments by Iran has been that of joint industrial ventures with other governments and private foreign enterprises. Examples of this category include the purchase of a 25.04 percent share in the steel and engineering branch of West Germany's giant Krupp industries for an estimated $100 million; acquisition of a 25 percent share in West Germany's Deutsche

[c]Clearly, as a result of the recent drop in Iran's oil production (12 percent in the first half of 1975), these estimates may require major revisions.

Babcock and Wilcox, A.G. (a major manufacturer of power-generating machinery) for $75 million; and a number of other, less publicized ventures in Europe, Asia, the Middle East, and Eastern European countries.

Finally, in several significant credit and loan arrangements, Iran has begun to reverse her traditional recipient status to that of a creditor vis-à-vis several Western industrial nations and Socialist-bloc countries. In addition, she has made commitments for substantial economic assistance to a number of developing countries through bilateral arrangements and international organizations. In many of these arrangements, specific industries or projects in the recipient countries have been designated for development or expansion, with the expectation that Iran would hold favorable options in the purchase of their future products. In 1974 alone, according to government sources, Iran undertook credit and loan commitments totalling $8 billion, divided equally between the developing and industrialized nations. These commitments would obligate Iran to make annual disbursements equivalent to 6 percent of her GNP in "development assistance." Moreover, Iran has pledged support for the International Monetary Fund's "oil facility" fund to help alleviate balance-of-payment problems of Western nations. On several occasions the shah has proposed the creation of a special development fund for the less developed countries to which Iran, other oil-producing countries, and the industrialized nations would contribute.

It should be emphasized at this point that, with the exception of a relatively small number of firm and concrete agreements that have been concluded in the past two years or so, most of the aforementioned agreements are still no more than "letters of intent," for which final contractual arrangements are yet to be worked out. But even so, they represent an impressive investment portfolio for Iran, and, together with the dramatic growth that is predicted for the economy as a whole over the next decade, they should help secure a position of influence for the country in the world economy. In the long run, that influence may not rest entirely on Iran's oil.

Before ending this overview of the Iranian economy and turning to a closer examination of the recent developments in Iran's oil policy, a brief consideration of another aspect of the country's economic performance, the problem of income distribution, is necessary. As has often been the case in developing countries, the fruits of Iran's rapid economic growth have not been shared equally by the different segments of the Iranian society. In fact, there is sufficient evidence to show that the dramatic increases in the economy's output over the past decade, while improving the absolute living standards of virtually all Iranians, have at the same time increased the existing inequities along regional and social class lines. To take but one dimension of inequality, income, one finds major disparities between the income of urban versus rural households, with the former being six or seven times higher than the latter; wage differentials of three-to-one for workers in the modern industrial sectors versus those in traditional industries (e.g., rug-weaving, brick-making, fruit-drying, etc.); and management salaries that are several times higher than those of workers within the same industry in both the private and the public sectors.

As a result of this and other equally glaring disparities, the distribution of income in Iran is one of the most highly skewed in the world and appears to have become more uneven in the past few years. According to a regular survey of household budgets conducted by the government, the lowest fifth of all households in 1969 accounted for a mere 4 percent of the total consumption expenditures by all families, while the highest fifth of households accounted for 56 percent of the total.[15] These disparities have increased in subsequent years, particularly in the urban areas. During the same period, the distribution of *income* (which due to the lack of published data must be inferred from the family expenditure figures) has been even more skewed and growing in unevenness.

A number of measures—including subsidies for major food items, expansion of the ownership base of industries, construction of public housing for the low-income families, free education, tax exemptions to lower salaried employees, and recent legislations for comprehensive social security and for the provision of various social-welfare services to indigent families—have been initiated by the government in order to offer some relief to the lower-income groups in society. But these measures are not commensurate with the profound economic inequities in question, and at least so far the government has been reluctant to undertake more drastic redistributive measures to fulfill its own promise of "economic justice." The rationale for a more even distribution of economic opportunities and resources, it must be pointed out, does not derive from egalitarian concerns alone. Of equal significance is the fact that such profound disparities are bound to have adverse consequences for the development of the Iranian economy and the political stability of the regime in the future.

Oil: New Opportunities, New Outlook

The "black gold" of the Iranian economy, oil has long served as a ready source of foreign exchange earnings and the vitally necessary capital for the country's efforts toward rapid economic development. Furthermore, as the expansion of the nonoil industrial sector, which in recent years has become the major goal of the government, is almost entirely financed by the oil revenues, the dependence of the whole economy on oil is not likely to diminish in the near future. These economic realities, however, have not been the only factors shaping Iran's "oil policy" over the years. Of at least equal importance in determining that policy have been the country's domestic political conditions and the nuances of international power politics. A brief review of Iran's experience with this industry subsequent to its nationalization in the early 1950s may therefore shed some light on the nature of the country's present oil policy.

Whatever one's interpretation of the course of political events that led to the de facto failure of the struggle to nationalize the then British-dominated Iranian oil industry, the economic lesson of the nationalization effort was quite clear: given the acute dependence of the country on oil, the excess of supply over demand in the world oil market, and the firm monopolistic hold of the major Western oil companies over all phases of production and marketing, Iran's prospects for gaining full control over this national resource were extremely dim—at least for the near future. This was the reality that the new regime after Mosaddeq had to live by in the interest of economic recovery and political survival.

Following the nationalization crisis, the government entered into a new agreement in 1954, by which exclusive exploration, drilling, refining, and marketing rights were granted to a consortium of foreign oil companies. The agreement was for a period of twenty-five years, with renewal options for an additional fifteen years, and covered an area of 100,000 square miles in southern Iran. With the participation of American (40 percent), British (40 percent), Dutch (14 percent), and French (6 percent) oil companies in the new agreement, the monopolization of the industry by the former British firm, the Anglo-Iranian Oil Company (AIOC), was effectively broken.

Of particular significance in view of the future developments was the ushering in of a new phase in the relations between Iran and the United States in the course of resolving the nationalization crisis. Having decided to support the Shah and the British against Mosaddeq in the latter phases of the nationalization crisis, the American government played an active part in persuading the five somewhat reluctant "majors" to join in the consortium agreement. This was done through an offer of favorable tax provisions and of immunity from antitrust prosecution by the Department of Justice under directions from the National Security Council.

As for the consortium agreement itself, though recognizing nationalization, it did not differ substantially from other concession agreements that were in effect in the Middle East, or, for that matter, from the financial terms of the previous concession to the AIOC. According to its main financial stipulation, the consortium would pay the National Iranian Oil Company (NIOC) 12.5 percent of the posted price of the crude oil and 50 percent of the resulting profits. This was essentially the so-called 50-50 formula that was already in effect between Aramco and the Saudi Arabian government.[16]

In spite of some early signs of dissatisfaction with the consortium agreement by the Iranian government, a generally conciliatory attitude toward the oil consortium was adopted in the remainder of the 1950s and much of the 1960s. This seemed prudent on both economic and political grounds. Economically, a steady increase in oil revenues beyond their initial, postagreement level was vital to boosting a stagnant economy and to cope effectively with the country's mounting social needs. Politically, the substantial military and financial support of the United States was essential to the shah's efforts to bolster his fragile political base, particularly in the early years of this period. Any precipitous move to challenge the consortium over the issues of control and oil-pricing might have jeopardized the government's position vis-à-vis the oil companies and possibly the United States. Instead, as its primary strategy to increase oil revenues, the government concentrated on pressing, apparently successfully, the consortium companies to increase their production level in Iran. Thus, between 1955 and 1970, oil production in Iran showed an almost twelvefold increase from 329,000 to 3,829,000 barrels per day, with a corresponding increase in revenues (from the consortium) from $99.2 million in 1955 to $1,048 million in 1970.

Following the 1957 Petroleum Act, the Iranian government opened oil districts outside of the consortium's "agreement area" to competitive biddings, resulting in agreements with much more favorable terms than the 1954 consortium agreement. No longer would concession-type agreements be granted to foreign oil companies. Instead, the NIOC was made an active participant, in the form of a partner or contractor, in each new agreement, and Iran's royalties and share of profits were increased beyond those under the consortium's 50-50 formula. Exploration and development costs were to be absorbed, furthermore, by the foreign oil companies. This last stipulation, however, was modified by the 1961 Supplementary Petroleum Act. As an incentive to the foreign companies to take greater risks at the exploration stage, the 1961 act called for the NIOC to pay 50 percent of the exploration, development, and production costs incurred by a foreign oil company if it was successful in discovering oil in commercial quantities.

Two important agreements signed within a year after the enactment of the 1957 act showed clear advantages over the consortium concession. The first agreement was with Agip Mineraria, a subsidiary of the Italian state oil corporation (ENI); the second was with the Pan American Oil Company, a subsidiary of the Standard Oil Company of Indiana. In both cases, the NIOC was given a 50 percent partnership, which entitled it to 50 percent of the profits. Moreover, with the additional 50 percent tax paid by the foreign companies on their share of profits, the government's total take amounted to 75 percent of the profits. These accords set the pattern for several other "partnership agreements" that were signed in the mid-1960s.

Two developments in 1966 boosted the managerial control of the NIOC over the industry and the financial gains of the government even further. First, an agreement was signed between the French State Group (ERAP) and the NIOC, giving the latter almost total managerial responsibility over operations and a reported share of over 90 percent of the profits. Second, the consortium companies agreed to relinquish one-quarter of their 100,000-square-mile "agreement area" and to make available over the next five years a total of twenty million tons of crude on favorable terms to the NIOC. This latter provision enabled the Iranian oil company, for the first time, to enter into sales or barter agreements with a number of East European and Third World countries on an independent basis.

The present decade, marked by significant economic and political changes affecting the international oil market, has ushered in a number of major shifts in Iran's oil policy. The changes in the international market conditions have been most apparent, of course, in the new status of the Organization of the Petroleum Exporting Countries (OPEC) since the early 1970s. The once ineffectual OPEC, founded in 1960 by Iran, Iraq, Kuwait, Saudi Arabia, and Venezuela to pressure the international oil companies to give higher per barrel profits to the producers, has emerged as a powerful force in the world oil market. Undoubtedly, the most important change that has enabled OPEC to assume its new bargaining position— one which it had sought in vain to achieve for a decade—was the dramatic shift in the world supply-and-demand situation. Not only demand appeared to be substantially in excess of supply, but many of the producing countries had amassed sufficient foreign exchange reserves by the present decade so that they no longer had a very strong incentive to increase production. In fact, some of the producers were already contemplating production cuts in an effort to conserve their oil resources.

It was within this context that, in 1970, Libya decided to reduce its oil production, creating thereby a fairly serious shortage of oil supplies to European consumers, and later demanded higher tax payments from the oil companies operating in Libya. The importance of its oil exports to the world supply and its ability to reduce its level of production without great economic suffering, allowed Libya to pose credibly the threat of cutting off oil production if the companies did not comply with its demand for higher taxes. This was, in effect, the first instance in which a producing country used the threat of withholding oil in an effort to raise its per barrel take. It proved to be successful.

Soon after Libya's success, other producing countries, including Iran, began to make similar demands through OPEC, using the new tactic of threatening cuts in production if the posted crude price and taxes were not raised. Again the tactic was successful. The 1971 Tehran and Tripoli agreements provided for regular tax increases through 1975 for all OPEC members, representing the first major success of the producing countries, united within OPEC, to pressure the international oil companies for a greater share in oil profits.

The 1972 Riyadh agreement between OPEC and the oil companies greatly enhanced the position of the producing countries on yet another front, i.e., the fundamentally important issue of control over the various aspects of operations within the industry. According to this agreement, producing governments acquired a 25 percent share and far greater participation in the operations of the oil companies, with provisions for further increases until 1982, when the producers would gain a 51 percent share in the control of oil operations and in the same percentage of the oil produced.[17]

These dramatic developments on the international level, together with rapid economic growth and political stability at home, enabled the shah to embark upon a bold, new oil policy for Iran. What was once a comparatively conservative policy in regard to the international oil companies' control over the exploration, production, and pricing of oil, and a minor role within OPEC, was transformed into a policy that has catapulted Iran to a position of prominence among the producing countries and has made the shah himself the most influential spokesman for their cause.

The first objective of the shah's new policy was to gain full control over all the operations of the industry. His first move in this connection was to argue that the participation principles that were established by the Riyadh agreement were not appropriate for Iran or in its best interests. In an important speech before a National Congress marking the end of a decade of his "White Revolution" in January 1973, he declared that he had offered the international oil companies in the consortium a choice between the following two alternatives:

Since we are the kind of people who honor our contracts, one choice is to let the companies to continue their operations for the next six years, up to 1979, provided that the total earnings from each barrel of oil are not less than those earned by other regional countries, provided our export capacity is increased to eight million barrels of oil per day. . . . In 1979, this oil agreement will terminate and the present oil companies will have to stand in a long queue to buy Iran's oil without any privileges over the other customers.

Alternatively a new contract could be signed which would return to Iran all the responsibilities and other things which are not at present in Iran's hands. The present operating companies could then become our long-term customers and we would give them good prices and the kind of discounts which are always given to a good customer.[18]

After several months of intensive negotiations the oil companies chose the second alternative. On May 24, 1973, they agreed to replace the 1954 consortium concession with a new, twenty-year agreement with the following basic provisions:

1. All exploration, extraction and refining activities and installations are to come under Iranian control. A service company registered in Iran and subject to Iranian regulations will perform certain technical functions in relation to exploration and extraction for a period of five years only.
2. Control of all oil reserves is to be transferred from the former Consortium to Iran.
3. In the event of disputes arising out of the agreement, solutions will be reached on the basis of Iranian law.

4. Iran is guaranteed per-barrel profits at least equal to those secured by other Persian Gulf oil producing states.[19]

While the immediate or long-term consequences of this (re-)nationalization effort for Iran's oil income have not been fully assessed, in *political* terms, the agreement was a landmark victory for the shah and the NIOC. It was hailed by the government as a significant departure from all previous agreements signed between international oil companies and any producing country. And thus, twenty-three years after the original nationalization act, the sovereign could justly claim credit for its full implementation.

A second component of Iran's new oil policy has been the continuation of efforts, initiated in the early 1960s by the NIOC, to increase its participation in the "downstream operations" in the international oil industry—to become the "eighth sister" of the seven major oil companies—and to diversify its operations into related industries at home and abroad. Progress in the forward integration of the NIOC's operations from the production of crude to refining, transportation, and marketing has been achieved in joint ventures in refinery construction with other governments and companies (e.g., a major refinery with an annual capacity of two million tons per year in Madras, India, and another with a two-and-a-half-million-ton capacity in Sasolbur, South Africa) and recent agreements with international oil companies for participation in their down-to-the-pump operations. One such agreement was signed in 1973 between the NIOC and the Ashland Oil Company of Ashland's downstream operations; a similar, but much larger, agreement Ashland's downstream operations; a similar, but much larger, agreement was being negotiated in 1975 with Shell. Diversification into related industries has been carried out on a large scale and with considerable success in the fields of natural gas, petrochemicals, and tanker transport.

A third aspect of the new oil policy of Iran has been a vigorous push along with other members of OPEC for higher oil prices. Like other leaders of OPEC, the shah and other high Iranian government officials have steadfastly defended the fourfold price hike that took effect in 1974, arguing that the new price level was necessitated by the soaring prices of industrial goods and food imported by the oil-producing countries. In a recently published commentary, Premier Hoveyda wrote:

It should be noted that the oil prices manipulated by the international oil cartel were progressively reduced from $2.17 per barrel in 1947 to as low as $1.30 by 1970. On the other hand, between 1947 and 1973, the average price of 28 basic commodities—excluding oil—increased by more than 4.5 times in world markets.

When oil prices went down, it was conveniently labeled the law of supply and demand, and no one in the industrial world spoke of price rigging. It bothered no one that declining oil prices drained the oil-producing nations of their natural wealth and that rising prices of industrial products made it almost impossible for the non-industrial world to win its struggle for development.[20]

The shah argues, furthermore, that in reckoning future prices the oil-producing countries should take into account the cost of alternative sources of energy, which at present, in terms of both initial investment and operation, are much more costly than fossil fuels. But unless oil prices are maintained at a relatively high level, he believes, the world's major consumers would not attempt to develop alternative energy sources and/or use oil conservatively. Iran's oil reserves (estimated at 60 billion barrels or about one-tenth of the world's proven reserves) will be exhausted in less than thirty years at current production rates. This fact, coupled with the realization that the same oil can be used to produce as many as 70,000 different petrochemicals, has led Iran to invest heavily in nuclear power plants, to rapidly develop its petrochemical industry, and to reconsider its previous policy of seeking steady production increases. Thus, for the first time in recent years, crude production rates in 1975 were lower than the previous years, a fact which has been explained by some as a strategy to protect current price levels.

While rebuffing pressures from the consuming nations to lower prices, the shah has proposed that the price of oil be linked to a price index for twenty or thirty other commodities imported by OPEC countries from the industrialized nations. This "inflation index plan" has recently been endorsed by other OPEC members. It is seen as the only formula that would protect the purchasing power of the oil-producing states against the high inflation rates in the industrialized countries and it could presumably give the latter an added incentive to control their inflation. Less than 2 percent of the annual inflation of about 14 percent in these countries, it is contended, could be attributed to higher oil prices that went into effect in 1974.

Finally, in discussing Iran's oil policy it should be pointed out that, at least so far, the shah has refused to use oil as a political weapon against adversaries and their friends. Iran has not participated in the Arab oil embargo against Israel, neither did it participate in the embargo against the United States following the Arab-Israeli War of October 1973. Referring to this policy in a recent interview with C.L. Sulzberger, the shah remarked: "As for our own petroleum, we don't use it for political purposes, embargoes, pressures. . . . Thus we have not given any special assurance to anyone that Iranian oil would be made available to Israel if it returns the Sinai wells to Egypt in a further disengagement. No such assurances are necessary. Everyone knows our policy."[21]

Foreign Policy Objectives and Means

Iran's current international posture is perhaps best characterized as that of a status quo power. Particularly since the mid-1960s, the regime has been remarkably successful in normalizing its relations with several of its erstwhile enemies (including Egypt, Syria, the Soviet Union, China, and, recently, Iraq) and strengthening its diplomatic ties to an increasing number of other countries, allies, and international organizations. Making these diplomatic developments possible have been a combination of favorable external circumstances, including the atmosphere of détente between the two superpowers, and conducive internal factors such as continued political stability and an unprecedented economic growth. The role of the shah in the realm of foreign policy has been particularly decisive, with virtually every important move being either initiated or closely guided by him.[22] His effectiveness in enhancing Iran's international influence, prestige and image has been greatly aided by his widely publicized domestic reform programs and the prominent position that Iran occupies among the oil-producing states.

Since its gradual emergence in the early 1960s, the current phase of Iran's foreign policy (referred to officially as the "independent national policy") has been based on two general premises. First, it is believed that both domestic and international conditions have changed sufficiently since the parlous 1940s and 1950s to have rendered unnecessary Iran's virtually total dependence on an external power (notably the United States) for its own security, and that a more independent stance, within a broad pro-Western framework, is not only feasible but indeed desirable. Second, it is maintained that Iran's national interests, particularly its international trade and domestic economic development, are most effectively furthered in a context of regional stability and good relations with Western, Socialist and Third World countries.[23]

This striving toward a more independent or "neutralist" position in the international community has been evidenced by Iran's gradually changing posture vis-à-vis the United States and the Soviet Union. As noted earlier, following the restoration of the shah's power in 1953, the United States' influence in Iran increased enormously. This was reflected in part in the substantial military and economic aid by the United States, amounting to well over one billion dollars from 1953 to 1967, and in Iran's visibly pro-American stance in regional and world affairs. While the American support was crucial to the shah's efforts to build a more stable economic and military basis for his power, the strategic benefits of this friendship to the United States were also not inconsiderable. To ensure Iran's pro-Western orientation—which for the past three decades has been equated by the American policymakers with protecting the shah's regime against external or internal threats—was an important aspect of the American cold war strategy in the Middle East. The signing of the Baghdad Pact (subsequently CENTO) in 1955 by Iran, Iraq, Turkey, Britain and Pakistan (with the United States as an active supporter) could be seen as a major step in promoting that strategy by the creation of a "northern-tier" line of defense that would bridge the North Atlantic Treaty Organization (NATO) and South East Asia Treaty Organization (SEATO) alliances.

From the Iranian perspective, however, the multilateral Baghdad agreement was deemed insufficient as a guarantee of the country's security and internal stability. The violent destruction of the monarchical system in neighboring Iraq in 1958 gave a new urgency to the shah's demands for more direct and explicit commitments to the stability and security of his regime. In an astute and ultimately successful diplomatic maneuver, the shah, threatening to conclude a non-aggression pact with the Soviet Union, persuaded a reluctant American government, in March 1959, to enter into a bilateral defense agreement with Iran.[d] Read in its entirety, the agreement was meant to provide a formal basis for the American commitment to the security of the Iranian regime against both direct and indirect aggression.[24]

The agreement was only a further affirmation of the United States' commitment to preserve Iran's security, and, as such, its importance has rarely been played up by either government. Similarly, the termination of the American military and financial aid to Iran in 1967 was viewed by both sides as a sign of Iran's new economic strength and self-sufficiency. The relations between the two countries have remained close and extremely friendly for more than two decades without any interruptions or visible strains,[25] and their scope has continually expanded to include numerous economic, political, diplomatic, military, cultural, and scientific cooperations. Some recent examples of the diversity and scope of this friendship are the recently concluded $15 billion trade agreement, the largest such accord to be signed between any two countries; massive purchases by Iran of highly sophisticated weapons systems from American manufacturers; direct investments by the Iranian government in American industry; and negotiations currently underway between a number of major American universities and Iranian authorities for sponsoring joint academic and scientific projects and institutions. A joint Iranian-American commission was established by the two governments in 1974 in order to coordinate and further promote cooperation in various fields between the two countries.

The most important product of the new Iranian "independent national policy" has been the reorientation of its stance towards the Soviet Union. The earliest indication of a change in attitudes came in the fall of 1962, when Iran assured the Soviet Union that it would not permit the installation of foreign missiles on its territory. This diplomatic gesture signalled the reversal of the acrimonious relations between the two countries that had resulted from the breakdown of Soviet-Iranian negotiations for a long-term nonaggression treaty and Iran's bilateral defense agreement with the United States (1959). In the ensuing thaw between the two neighbors, Soviet propaganda attacks on the Iranian regime, which had reached an almost explosive pitch in 1959-1961, were halted, and the relations between the two governments were set on a diplomatically correct and at times quite friendly basis.

Significant expansion of trade relations, including long-term trade agreements and generous offers of credit and technical assistance, between the Soviet Union

---

[d]Pakistan and Turkey also entered into identical agreements with the United States at the same time.

and Iran were soon to follow. In 1965, after a visit by the shah to Moscow, the Russians agreed to make capital investments in a number of industrial projects in Iran. The most notable and symbolically significant among these was the construction of a steel mill near Isfahan. This was in exchange for Iran's abundant natural gas, which had been literally burned at the wellhead for decades, to be transported via a 700-mile-long pipeline from Iran's southern oil fields to the Caspian coast. Later, as if to underscore Iran's new independent posture, the shah made a $110 million purchase of military equipment (mostly nonsophisticated transport vehicles) from the Soviet Union. Over the past decade, the Soviet Union and other socialist countries have become the major importers of Iran's nonoil export commodities and have invested in a wide variety of industrial and agricultural projects.

In the political and diplomatic domains, also, indications of improved relations with the Eastern bloc countries abound. The shah has paid several official visits and played host to the top Soviet and East European leaders. The Soviet official statements and reviews in the Soviet mass media have been at pains over the last decade not to criticize Iran's international behavior or belittle its domestic social and economic advances. Similarly, the tensions and the periodic open clashes that had, until quite recently, marked Iran-Iraqi relations failed to drive the Soviet Union into open support of the Iraqi regime against Iran.

Undoubtedly, this marked improvement in the Soviet-Iranian relations has been greatly facilitated by the spreading atmosphere of détente that has permeated the Soviet-American relations. However, the improvement has also been a function of Iran's domestic social, economic, and political developments, which have altogether increased the security and stability of the shah's regime and contributed to its rising confidence. In the meantime, the enthusiasm displayed by practically all members of the Socialist world (including China) and particularly the Soviet Union to normalize and/or expand their relations with Iran—partly in order to compete with and reduce the Western diplomatic and economic influence—has clearly given some substance to the claim that Iran is pursuing an independent foreign policy.

Since late 1960s, the Middle East, especially the Persian Gulf, has been the principal and the most active arena of Iran's foreign policy. The government's diplomatic initiatives in this area may be examined with reference to (1) the non-Arab states of Afghanistan, Pakistan, and Turkey, all of which border directly on Iran; (2) the Arab states, including the littoral states of the Persian Gulf; and (3) Israel. In broad terms, common cultural roots with other countries in the region, lack of involvement in the Arab-Israeli conflict, a desire to prevent either of the two superpowers from becoming the controlling influence in the area, as well as its growing economic and military strength, have helped promote Iran's role as a major regional power in the Middle East.

In addition to normal diplomatic ties, Iran has joint membership with

Pakistan and Turkey in the Central Treaty Organization (CENTO), the successor to the Baghdad Pact, and in the Regional Cooperation for Development (RCD). The latter was established in 1964 as a supplementary organization to CENTO by Iran, Pakistan, and Turkey. Although the primary purpose of RCD was economic cooperation among its members, its formation also reflected some degree of disenchantment with CENTO and the United States' unwillingness to side with its allies within it in their regional disputes with their adversaries, particularly in the cases of the Pakistani-Indian conflict over Kashmir as well as Turkey in Cyprus.

The recent offers of economic assistance by Iran to the military regime in Afghanistan is illustrative of its "containment strategy" toward the Soviet Union. As a significant counterpoise to the increasing Soviet military and economic support to President Mohammad Daud's regime (which came to power after a successful coup against Mohammad Zahir Shah), Iran has made offers of aid, which by some accounts may be as high as $2 billion, for purposes of agricultural development, highway and railway construction, and a variety of joint industrial projects.[26]

In spite of cultural and religious affinities, Iran's relations with the Arab states have often been marked by some degree of tension and conflict. Political rivalries between the shah and individual Arab heads of state, Iran's economic and political ties with Israel (including de facto recognition since 1951), and its open quest for military superiority in the Persian Gulf may be cited as the main reasons for tensions between Iran and this group of countries. Furthermore, Iran's close military, diplomatic and economic ties with the United States were not entirely appreciated by most Arab governments which—at least until the recent developments—expressed open hostility toward the American government. The more recent trends in the Arab-Iranian relations, however, have been clearly towards normalization and greater friendship. Considerable wariness on the part of the Arab governments concerning the role of the great powers in the Middle East, together with Iran's willingness to offer economic assistance in various forms to Egypt, Jordan, and Syria, appears to have caused the Arab leaders to set aside their ideological differences with Iran—for the time at least—and pursue a pragmatic course in their relations with the Shah. Undoubtedly, Iran's prominent place in OPEC is an added incentive to both sides to maintain a modicum of political unity.

The most dramatic example of improvement in the Arab-Iranian relations is the recently initiated effort towards full reconciliation between Iran and Iraq—for years the major antagonists outside of the Arab-Israeli conflict in the Middle East. The agreement was reached at the OPEC summit meeting in Algiers in March 1975, between the shah and Saddam Hussein Takriti, the vice president of Iraq's revolutionary council and the country's effective leader. According to its major stipulations, the two countries would seek a definitive and durable solution of all their long-standing differences, including their border disputes and subversive infiltration from either side. As recently as February of the same year, the worsening relations between Iran and Iraq had caused severe clashes at their borders. At issue had been navigation rights by Iran in the Shatt al-Arab (a waterway shared by Iraq and Iran where the Euphrates and Tigris rivers converge to empty into the Persian Gulf), Iran's decisive military support of the Kurdish rebellion in northern Iraq, and Iraq's harboring of opposition elements to the Iranian regime since the early 1960s. Furthermore, the support by the Iraqi government to radical, antimonarchical movements in the Persian Gulf had for some time run in direct opposition to the Iranian efforts to preserve the status quo.

A direct outcome of the Iran-Iraqi agreement has been the effective crushing of the Kurdish struggle for autonomy in Iraq under the leadership of Mustafa Barzani. Especially since the spring of 1974, when, following a four-year truce, the Kurds rejected an offer of partial autonomy by the Iraqi government, Iran's military assistance to the Kurds had become the decisive factor in their ability to ward off the Iraqi army's attacks. According to estimates by observers and intelligence sources, as much as eighty percent of Iraq's 175,000-man army was involved in the Kurdish war. Within hours after the announcement of the Algiers agreement, the Iraqi government unleashed a major and apparently successful attack on the Kurdish strongholds, while the Iranian government limited its involvement to receiving the tens-of-thousands of refugees that were created by the new fighting. (The total number of Kurdish refugees in Iran from Iraq is estimated to be between 150,000 and 200,000.)[27]

For Iran the Algiers agreement has had both economic and political advantages. Economically, Iran has been assured of safe navigation rights in Shatt al-Arab waterway, on the eastern coast of which its largest petroleum refinery and a number of large oil fields lie. Iran has also closed ranks with Arab oil producers in preparation for future talks with the oil consuming nations. Politically, it has not only averted the possibility of an all-out war with its neighbor—a war that several recent border clashes had portended—but has silenced the propaganda attacks of several organizations of exiled opponents of the regime, including the *Tudeh* party apparatus that had been based in Baghdad for the past several years. In addition, improved relations with Iraq must also facilitate Iran's emerging role in the Persian Gulf.

It is indeed in the warm waters of the Persian Gulf and its southern shores that Iran's external concerns are currently focused.[28] The once passive role of Iran in the Gulf has been transformed into that of the dominant local power and a self-appointed guardian of regional stability and security in less than one decade. The extent of its commitment to the stability of the Persian Gulf may be seen in its extensive strategic penetration in the Gulf in such unprecedented actions for the Iranian military as the takeover of the islands of Abu Musa and the Greater and Lesser Tunbs in 1971 as well as direct involvement against rebel forces in the Dhofar region of Oman since 1973. The action on the three islands, located strategically at the mouth of the Persian Gulf, came just one day before the end of British responsibility for the defense of the trucial states (on November 30, 1971), apparently as the result of the belief that the islands, in unfriendly hands, could provide attack bases against vital Iranian shipping routes. Iran's stake in Oman has been much larger, and it reflects the shah's concern about the stability of the sultanates in the Gulf region. With an estimated total troop strength of 2,000 men, supported by its sophisticated air force, the Iranian military has been a decisive force in checking the rebellion in the mountainous Dhofar region of the sultanate. As elsewhere in the Middle East, the great powers are involved. The rebels are supplied with Soviet arms directly, or indirectly through the leftist government of Southern Yemen; the United States recently sought and was granted permission for its planes to use airfield facilities on the Omani island of Masirah, and after a visit to Washington by the Omani king, Qabus bin Said, in January 1975, it was disclosed that the United States is supplying Oman with the sophisticated "Tow" missiles for use in the Dhofar area.[29]

In its relations with Israel, while withholding formal diplomatic recognition, Iran has pursued a generally friendly course. In addition to economic ties, including the uninterrupted flow of oil and cooperation in a variety of agricultural and regional development projects, the two countries have maintained close ties in political, military, and intelligence spheres of mutual interest. The closeness of this relationship has not only been a source of irritation to the Arab governments, particularly during and shortly after the 1967 and 1973 Arab-Israeli wars, but it has stirred occasional domestic political opposition in Iran. Diplomatically, the shah has consistently supported the Arab states in their demand on Israel to relinquish areas that it occupied in 1967 and has affirmed the right of the Palestinians to have their homeland.[30]

The generally successful record of the Iranian government in attaining its major foreign policy objectives in the first half of this decade can, to a considerable degree, be attributed to the shah's paramount political power within Iran's body politic. The concentration of decision-making powers in his hands—with little discernible input from any other source—seems to have provided the Iranian regime with a measure of flexibility in its international behavior that is denied most liberal-democratic governments. Furthermore, the dramatic increase in Iran's military capability has been of great importance in enabling Iran to exert its increasing influence as a regional power. However, the sheer size and variety of Iran's recently acquired military hardware, as well as the rationale behind such a build-up, have become a matter of primary concern to many, both in Iran and abroad.

In tracing the development of Iran's military capabilities, it soon becomes apparent that while the country's stockpile of arms and military equipment increased substantially in the 1950s and early 1960s, it was only toward the end of the last decade that a dramatic build-up of sophisticated weapons systems was begun. Thus, between 1951 and 1967, when the United States terminated its military aid to Iran, the country's total annual military expenditures increased from $75.2 million to $435 million. Over the next four years, annual military expenditures were more than doubled to $976 million in 1971.

By the time of the British departure from the Persian Gulf in 1971, Iran had already emerged as a formidable military power in the area. Assessing the strategic significance of Iran's military capabilities in 1971, the Institute for Strategic Studies noted that the country's air force was "more than a match for the combined Arab air forces in the Gulf area," and its navy was far superior to any of her potential Arab rivals. Specifically, in terms of both equipment and manpower, Iran had established, by that time, a clear military advantage over its most prominent and active rival in the area, Iraq.[31]

In spite of its considerable size and accelerating rate, this military build-up was to be dwarfed, however, by Iran's purchases in 1973 and 1974, a period in which the country became the world's largest arms importer. In 1973, Iran's military purchases from the United States alone included: 202 AH-IJ helicopters, 140 F-5E supersonic interceptors, 108 F-4 *Phantoms*, 10 KC-135 jet tankers (making the refueling of the *Phantom* jets possible in midair, thereby increasing their range to 1,400 miles) 8 destroyers, 4 frigates, 12 high-speed gunboats, 2 repair ships, 14 Hovercraft (adding to what was already the largest Hovercraft fleet in the world), and 100 C-130 troop transports. In addition, orders were placed for 80 of Grumman's F-14 fighters (not yet deployed by any of the branches of the United States military) and 150 Hughes *Phoenix* long-range missiles (capable of carrying conventional or nuclear warheads). The latter two agreements represented the most sophisticated and expensive weapons systems ever sold by the United States to a foreign country.

In 1974, additional arms procurement agreements between the United States and Iran placed special emphasis upon the further expansion and modernization of the country's already powerful air force and navy. Six of the fast and expensive *Spruance*-class destroyers were ordered for the navy, and by mid-1974 Iran was considering the purchase of 250 F-17 lightweight fighters and an additional 40 attack aircraft, either Fairchild Industries' A-10 or LTV Aerospace's A-7.[32]

In all, it is estimated that Iran's military purchases (i.e., orders) in 1973 and 1974 from the United States amounted to over $6 billion. According to the Department of Defense figures, of the $8.3 billion in "foreign military sales orders" received by the United States arms manufacturers in fiscal 1974, $3,000 million came from the Iranian government. This placed Iran at the top of the list, with Israel ($2,100 million) and Saudi Arabia ($588 million) at second and third places, respectively. The Middle Eastern countries as a group accounted for $6,500 million, or close to 80 percent of the total foreign military sales by the United States.[33] Not only has Iran been allowed to purchase the most advanced equipment available, but in at least one case (Grumman F-14 fighter aircraft), a branch of the United States military, the navy, reportedly agreed to stretch its delivery schedule to give Iran equal priority in the receipt of a major new weapon.

Paralleling these arms procurements have been major investments for the construction and expansion of the country's military installations. Construction has been completed on a new base for the Hovercraft fleet on the Island of Khark (also a busy port for the oil tankers) and one for the *Phantom* jets in Kish. Current construction plans, some already underway, include the expansion of Iran's naval and air bases at Bandar Abbas (close to the strategically important Strait of Hormuz), additional naval gun emplacements on Abu Musa and Greater Tunb islands, a new naval base at Bushire, a military complex at Isfahan for a 10,000-man helicopter force, and a combined army-navy-air force base at Chahbahar, described as "the largest of its kind in all the Indian Ocean." In addition to these expansions in the military installations, part of the recent multi-billion dollar trade agreement with the United States calls for the development of an extensive and highly sophisticated communications network and automatic logistics system for the armed forces.

Although there will be an inevitable lag between the purchase dates and the time of effective operational deployment of these weapons and their support systems, it is generally agreed that by the late 1970s, when most of the current outstanding orders will have been delivered, Iran can duly claim the status of a major, nonnuclear military power. Her air force, for example, will have more fighter bombers (839), according to a recent account, than any NATO nation except the United States. Already, according to observers of the area and military analysts, Iran's navy can patrol the seas as far south as Madagascar; her air force has a strike capacity extending as far as Cairo; and, with over 1,000 helicopters and 3,000 armored fighting vehicles, the army is capable of landing a batallion of troops on the southern shores of the Gulf in less than two hours.

The issue of Iran's military build-up through purchases of enormous quantities of sophisticated weapons from the United States and with the help of hundreds of American military personnel and civilian advisors has created some misgivings in the United States. Some prominent members of the United States Congress, for example, deploring what they describe as "massive and apparently indiscriminate arms sales" to the Persian Gulf states, have even filed legislation to provide a six-month moratorium on arms sales (and deliveries) to these states. In Iran's specific case, the critics of the current American policy maintain that the continued arms purchases by the shah, at a time when his country's regional preeminence is well established, are indicative of his developing ambition for Iranian hegemony in the Persian Gulf and the Indian Ocean. Rather than ensuring the security of these regions, they contend, Iran's military build-up may in time become a major threat to their peace and security.

Furthermore, the critics contend that Iran's rapidly increasing military capabilities, which will soon reach those of the top nonatomic armies of the world, coupled with its rising economic strength, represent the emergence of a new political force at the international level. By design and necessity, Iran's interests and future policies, however justified from its own vantage point, may not always parallel those of the United States or of its own regional allies. The continued supply of arms to Iran will therefore exacerbate what has already become an unprecedented and potentially explosive arms race in the Persian Gulf, with consequences not only for those who are or will be directly involved but for the rest of the world as well. An added dimension to this debate in the coming years will undoubtedly be the concern that Iran—in spite of its being a signatory to the Nuclear Nonproliferation Treaty and its expressed desire to keep the Indian Ocean a nuclear-free zone—may in fact develop nuclear weapons.[34] Such a concern has recently been voiced in connection with the planned sale of eight nuclear power generators to Iran by the United States.

Mainly in response to the above criticisms, official and nonofficial Iranian sources have attempted to justify the country's military build-up on a number of grounds. Their reasons, although not systematically presented in any one document of forum, fall into three main categories. First, it is asserted that Iran's military expenditures, although exceeding those of her neighbors by a substantial margin in absolute terms, should not be considered excessive in view of its population size, economic resources, and growth potential. Furthermore, it is pointed out that the country's rapidly growing economy is increasingly dependent upon an uninterrupted flow of oil revenues, and hence Iran must be able to maintain, alone if necessary, the security of oil transportation routes through the Persian Gulf. In fact, it is argued that the country needs a strong military force to ensure not only its own interests in the Persian Gulf, but those of the oil-consuming nations as well. The shah has commented on more than one occasion that Iran has a national, regional, and international responsibility to act as "the guardian of 60 percent of the world's oil reserves." While the fulfillment of this responsibility appears to have necessitated, at least in part, the present level of military outlays, the precise nature of its genesis is far from clear.

Second, it is noted that a strong military force is essential for Iran as a credible deterrent to any possible future aggression by potentially hostile neighbors, including the Soviet Union. Indeed, based on the sheer magnitude of Iran's military build-up, as well as on the shah's thinly-veiled references to the issue, it may be assumed that the creation of a holding capability in any military confrontation with the Soviet Union has become a part of Iran's strategic planning.[35]

Third, it is believed that Iran's political stability and internal security require that it be prepared to intervene, if necessary by military force, to prevent any further expansion of Socialist-republican tendencies and/or revolutionary activities in the southern shores of the Persian Gulf. Such subversive activities, it is believed, pose a serious threat to the overall stability of the Gulf region, where the littoral states, with the exception of Iraq, are ruled by royal governments.

This common bond of kingship is seen to be critical to the maintenance of stable relations among the Gulf states, which has a long history of mutual distrust and rivalry which could otherwise erupt into armed conflicts. Not only, it is argued, would such conflicts have serious consequences for the Gulf countries, but they are also likely to prompt intervention by other countries with even more serious ramifications.

Apart from the foregoing official and semi-official justifications offered in defense of Iran's relentless efforts to build up its military might,[36] there are a number of other relevant factors that must be taken into account in an analysis of Iran's military posture. Boosting the morale and sustaining the professional interest of the officer corps have been of special importance in the shah's quest for sophisticated military technology, particularly since "training abroad [has] whetted the appetite of [the] officers for the latest and most expensive hardware."[37] The maintenance of the overall professional pride and satisfaction of the Iranian officer corps could only increase that group's interest in the survival of the present political structure and cement the officers' loyalty to the person of the monarch. Such interest and loyalty are clearly indispensable, for the army still remains the "final peacemaker and guarantor of the Shah's writ."[38]

Perhaps of equal relevance to Iran's spectacular military build-up are the less tangible and verifiable, but related, factors of ambition, prestige and image. There is little doubt that the shah currently believes that Iran must and will possess considerable power on regional and eventually international levels. That Iran will soon find itself in the ranks of the world's major powers has indeed become an article of faith, and perhaps a self-fulfilling prophecy at least in its military dimension. In this context, the revival of at least some aspects of Iran's historic imperial legacy seems to have become an incontestable part of the monarch's domestic and foreign-policy schemes. Clearly, both the reality and image of a modern and powerful military establishment are of indisputable value in achieving such ends.

Some Conclusions and Prospects

The purpose of this section is to present some inevitably tentative judgments about the short-run prospects of Iran's domestic situation and international relations. In making such projections, one is of course limited by one's present perception of events and by gradualist assumptions regarding the nature of change in the domestic spheres of both Iran and the United States as well as in the international situation in general. For Iran, if the events of the past two decades in the Middle East are any indication, rapid economic and political changes could easily void orderly and logical extrapolations from the present conditions.

To begin with the economy, it is generally agreed that, at the present rates of growth and industrialization, Iran will soon become the dominant economic power in the Middle East and Southwest Asia. By the late 1980s, Iran is expected to have significantly reduced the gap that currently separates it from the industrial countries of Europe in terms of trade, the size and diversity of industrial output, per capita GNP, and similar indices. These predictions are based, of course, on the supposition that Iran's revenues from oil will continue at or near their present level since a substantial drop in the price of oil would have a severe recessionary impact on the economy and delay many of its planned development projects. In addition to this critical dependence on the uninterrupted flow of oil revenues, the achievement of ambitious economic objectives will hinge on the government's ability to deal successfully with the current shortages in manpower, to keep the inevitable resurgence of inflationary pressures under control, and to expand the infrastructural capacity of the economy over the next few years. Moreover, unless the present wide disparities in the distribution of wealth and income are significantly reduced, they may constitute additional impediments to sustained growth and efficient development of the nations' human resources.

Politically, the already awesome power of the state is likely to increase even further as the regime continues on its present course, demanding active support from all segments of the society. Such support will come increasingly from the burgeoning urban middle class whose members, having enjoyed a full generation of economic prosperity, have come to regard the stability of the regime as a necessary condition for consolidating of furthering their gains.[e] To win the support of the workers and peasants, the majority of the population, the government is likely to launch new economic and social reform programs, with much of the impetus and dynamism for social change coming from the increasing demands and expectations of these groups rather than from the top leadership.

As the recent decision to establish a single party "for all Iranians" portends, organized democratic opposition to the regime will remain highly unlikely in the foreseeable future. And, while there is no reason to believe that the present clandestine oppositional groups, including those that have occasionally engaged in armed confrontation with the government or in acts of terrorism, will wither away, it is improbable that they could gather sufficient support and capacity to mount an effective challenge to the security of the regime. Excepting the regime's reaction to the more resolute and committed challengers of its authority—which is likely to continue to be decisively intolerant—coercive methods of political control are likely to give way increasingly to political socialization, indoctrination, and cooptation in order to ensure political allegiance.

---

[e]The possibility that at least some elements within this class may, under certain conditions, begin to press for a wider distribution of political power should also not be ruled out.

In its external relations, as long as the current atmosphere of détente among the great powers continues, Iran will find little reason to alter its highly successful "independent national policy" of the last decade. Under this policy, the government will continue to bolster and expand its diplomatic and economic ties to an ever-increasing number of Western, Socialist, and Third World countries. The pursuit of this active and pragmatic foreign policy, as has already become evident, will continue to yield both economic and political benefits. Economically, the advantages will include the transfer of technology from the industrialized countries, upon which Iran's own future industrial development will increasingly depend; creation of new markets for Iran's nonoil exports and of investment opportunities in other countries in order to increase and diversify Iran's foreign-exchange earnings in the future; and long-term barter agreements under which Iran's oil and natural gas are exchanged for industrial and agricultural commodities. Politically, the increased international recognition and influence that new friendships (particularly with some of its former enemies) will bring will no doubt be helpful in improving the regime's domestic and international image, legitimacy, and strength.

Regionally, having already become the paramount military power in the Persian Gulf, Iran is certain to want to extend its "peace-keeping role" into the Indian Ocean within the next few years. Its recently improved relations with Iraq—her major antagonist for over a decade-and-a-half—will perhaps help Iran achieve three major objectives in the Persian Gulf: (1) preserving the political status quo of the Trucial States, (2) assuming direct responsibility for the Gulf's security (a role similar to that played by Great Britain for a century-and-a-half), and (3) denying the world powers, including the United States (whose "presence" is currently limited to maintaining a naval base in Bahrain), a dominant position. Beyond the Gulf in the Indian Ocean, where India is the dominant power, Iran's strategy will continue to be one of encouraging the bordering states to develop a common "security structure" and an economic union.

Iran's relationship with the United States has been, with few exceptions, extremely cordial and friendly over the years. Indeed it would not be an exaggeration to state that with the exception of Israel's "special relationship" with this country, no other Middle Eastern government has had closer ties to the United States for as long a period as has Iran. While the origins of this friendship may be traced as far back as the first decade of this century, it has been since the Second World War, and especially after the restoration of the shah's power in 1953, that the relation between the two countries has assumed its present political, economic, and military significance. Furthermore, as noted earlier, the United States' influence in Iran has been significant not only in terms of the country's external relations and security, but also in the context of its internal developments and in guaranteeing the stability of the present regime.

Since the late 1960s, in part due to Iran's remarkable economic upsurge and political stability and in part due to its increasing military capabilities, a new phase in the Iranian-American relations has taken shape and will most likely continue over the next decade. Principally, this consists of the continuation of the already strong economic and military ties of the past, but with greater reliance on Iran's military capacity not only for the purpose of guarding its own national security, but also for preserving the overall stability of the Persian Gulf region. Though reflecting primarily changes in Iranian attitudes and policies over the past decade, this new phase in the Iranian-American relations may also be viewed as the consequence of the so-called "Nixon Doctrine." As such, it coincides with the United States' apparent intention to transfer gradually a greater part of the responsibility for the security of its allies, formalized in over forty bilateral and regional security pacts, to them directly or to regional powers that are willing to undertake such responsibilities. Presumably, such a policy would allow the United States to pursue global interests and strategies with greater flexibility.

There seems, therefore, little basis for the argument that Iran's pursuit of an "independent national policy" and/or its resolve to assume a greater regional role will—given the continuity of her present political system—pose any major dilemmas for the United States. The Irano-American relations in their unique and expansive sweep, seem destined to remain the cornerstone of Iran's foreign policy in the coming years. In its economic and trade relations; in its assessment of the imperatives of the global rivalries and of the international balance of power; in its determination to maintain the political status quo in the Persian Gulf; and in its extensive and expanding dependence on American military technology, Iran can ill afford to loosen its bonds of friendship and cooperation with the United States. And this despite occasional public expressions of pique and anger at specific American decisions or policies.

To be sure, Iran has long passed the phase of economic and political dependence on the United States. Normalization of her relations with the Communist countries, particularly the Soviet Union, and its willingness and ability to chart bold and clearly independent policies on a number of regional, and even global issues, certainly attest to its newly-found status as an active and independent actor in the international community. Its new status and capabilities have not, however, affected Iran's determination to look toward the United States as an indispensable and irreplaceable ideological, economic, political and military partner. Bonds of common regional and global interests, common values and ideological orientations necessitate such a partnership.[39]

In this context, it is perhaps more than a mere coincidence that the recent expressions of warmth and good will toward Egypt in Iran have followed a decided Egyptian swing toward the United States and away from the Soviet Union.

At this juncture, there seems to be no evidence to indicate that Iran is about to loosen either her Western ties or abandon the use of the "neutralist" strategy for which the continuation of peaceful relations with the Soviet Union are imperative. Thus, commenting on Iran's purchases of considerable quantities of Soviet arms (mainly armored personnel carries and artillery), the shah has recently pointed out:

I don't mind saying we are doing this to tell some quarters in the United States—quarters with masochistic tendencies who always try and hurt their friends and allies, those who wish to embargo the sale of all arms to the Middle East—to tell them that we have other sources of weapons, including Russia.[40]

Thus, the continuation of normal and by and large friendly relations with the Soviet Union must be viewed as simply the manifestation of Iran's desire to remain at peace with states of different sociopolitical orientation, and particularly with its powerful northern neighbor, rather than as evidence of its readiness to set aside its historic mistrust of Soviet ambitions and adopt a basically neutralist stance vis-à-vis the Soviet Union and the United States. Therefore, at least some of Iran's efforts to elevate Soviet-Iranian relations onto a new plateau may be best understood in this context. In the last two decades, it has indeed been the hallmark of Iran's policy toward the superpowers to take timely advantage of their ongoing rivalries while remaining essentially and firmly committed to the Western cause.

Notes

1. For a discussion of the nature and extent of the Shah's power in the war period, see Keyvan Tabari, "Iran's Policies Toward the United States During the Anglo-Russian Occupation, 1941-1946," Ph.D. dissertation, Columbia University, 1967, especially pp. 35-37, 57-58, 62-65, and 304.

2. See, for example, Joseph M. Upton, *The History of Modern Iran: An Interpretation* (Cambridge, Mass.: Harvard University Press, 1960), p. 100; and Tabari, "Iran's Policies," pp. 35-36 and 62-65.

3. For the nationalists' ideological orientation and sources of their political strength in the post-1941 period, see Richard W. Cottam, *Nationalism in Iran* (Pittsburgh: University of Pittsburgh Press, 1964), pp. 3-6 and 243-258; J.C. Campbell, *Defense of the Middle East: Problems of American Foreign Policy* (New York: Praeger Publishers, 1960), pp. 17-18; and T. Cuyler Young, "The Social Support of Current Iranian Policy," *Middle East Journal* 6, 2 (Spring 1952): 127-136.

4. For a detailed discussion of Iran's internal political processes and international behavior during Mosaddeq's premiership, see Hormoz Hekmat, "Iran's Response to Soviet-American Rivalry, 1951-1962: A Comparative Study," Ph.D. Dissertation, Columbia University, 1974, Chs. IV-VI.

5. On the precipitous decline of the parliamentary power and prestige in the post-Mosaddeq period, see Hekmat, "Iran's Response," pp. 136-141.

6. For the Shah's continuous attention to, reliance upon, and control over the Iranian armed forces, see Leonard Binder, *Iran: Political Development in a Changing Society* (Berkeley and Los Angeles: University of California Press, 1962), p. 144; Cottam, *Nationalism in Iran*, pp. 297 and 315; and George Kemp, "Strategy and Arms Levels, 1945-1967," in J.C. Hurewitz (ed.), *The Soviet-American Rivalry in the Middle East* (New York: Praeger Publishers, 1969), p. 29.

7. For various accounts and estimates of the nature, strength and functions of SAVAK, see, for example, *Newsweek*, October 14, 1974; *Atlantic* 234, 3 (September 1974): 28; and *Time*, November 4, 1974.

8. Mohammad Reza Pahlavi, *The White Revolution* (Tehran: Imperial Library, 1967), p. 15.

9. For a detailed description and evaluation of the first and second stages of the land reform program, see: Ann K.S. Lambton, *The Persian Land Reform, 1962-1966* (Oxford: Clarendon Press, 1969).

10. For an overview of the life conditions and some of the economic and social problems of this group of Iranian villagers, see Eric J. Hooglund, "The Khwushnishin Population of Iran," *Iranian Studies* 6, 4 (Autumn 1973): 229-245.

11. For an analysis of the consequences of the "White Revolution" on Iran's socioeconomic structure, see James A. Bill, "Modernization and Reform from Above: The Case of Iran," *Journal of Politics* 32, 1 (February 1970): particularly pp. 30-40; and Rouhollah K. Ramazani, "Iran's 'White Revolution': A Study in Political Development," *International Journal of Middle East Studies* 5, 2 (April 1974): 124-139.

12. For a detailed analysis of the nature and extent of active and potential opposition to the regime and the government's various techniques of challenge-management, see Marvin Zonis, *The Political Elite of Iran* (Princeton: Princeton University Press, 1971), pp. 39-74.

13. For the full text of the monarch's speech, in English translation, see *Kayhan International* (weekly overseas edition), March 8, 1975.

14. For recent surveys of the Iranian economy and the country's experience in economic planning, see Jahangir Amuzegar and M. Ali Fekrat, *Iran: Economic Development Under Dualistic Conditions* (Chicago: University of Chicago Press, 1971); G.B. Baldwin, *Planning and Development in Iran* (Baltimore: Johns Hopkins Press, 1967); Julian Bharier, *Economic Development in Iran, 1900-1970* (New York: Oxford University Press, 1970); Farhad Deftary, "Development Planning in Iran: A Historical Survey," *Iranian Studies* 6, 4 (Autumn 1973): 176-228; Charles Issawi, "The Economy: An Assessment of Performance," in Ehsan Yar-Shater (ed.), *Iran Faces the Seventies* (New York: Praeger Publishers, 1971); Robert E. Looney, *The Economic Development of Iran: A Recent Survey with Projections to 1981* (New York: Praeger Publishers, 1973); and various issues of the *Annual Report and Balance Sheet* of the Central Bank of Iran.

15. See *Employment and Income Policies for Iran* (Geneva: ILO, 1972), Appendix C (Income Distribution). (Mimeo.)

16. For an account of the background and terms of the Consortium Agreement, see, for example, Majid Tehranian, "Iran: Oil and the Struggle for National Power," paper delivered at the Conference on the Structure of Power in Islamic Iran, University of California, Los Angeles, June 26-28, 1969, pp. 14-24.

17. For an analysis of OPEC's present and coming financial leverage and of its impact upon industrial countries, see Thomas O. Enders, "OPEC and the Industrial Countries: The Next Ten Years," *Foreign Affairs* 53, 4 (July 1975): 625-637. Iran's views on these and related issues are reflected in Jahangir Amuzegar, "The Oil Story: Facts, Fiction and Fair Play," *Foreign Affairs* 51, 4 (July 1973): 676-689. See, also, Walter Laqueur and Edward Luttwak, "Oil," *Commentary* 56, 4 (October 1973): 37-43.

18. For excerpts from the monarch's speech on this occasion and from his other related speeches on oil, see "The Shah's Oil Battle," *Iran Almanac, 1975* (Tehran: Echo of Iran, 1975), p. 274.

19. For a brief report on the terms of the agreement, see "A New Oil Concept," *Iran Tribune* 8, 107 (August 1973): 6-7.

20. *New York Times*, February 5, 1975.

21. Ibid., March 23, 1975.

22. See, for example, Rouhollah K. Ramazani, "Iran's Changing Foreign Policy: A Preliminary Discussion," *Middle East Journal* 24, 4 (Autumn 1970): 427; and Shahram Chubin and Sepehr Zabih, *The Foreign Relations of Iran: A Developing State in a Zone of Great-Power Conflict* (Berkeley and Los Angeles: University of California Press, 1974), pp. 10-13.

23. For a detailed exposition of Iran's newly stressed independence in foreign policy, see Sepehr Zabih, "Iran's International posture: De Facto Nonalignment with a Pro-Western Alliance," *Middle East Journal* 24, 3 (Summer 1970): 302-318; and Ramazani, "Iran's Changing Foreign Policy," pp. 421-437.

24. For a somewhat detailed discussion of the shah's handling of the negotiations with the Soviet Union and the United States in this period, see Hekmat, "Iran's Response," pp. 173-181; and Chubin and Zabih, *Foreign Relations of Iran*, pp. 56-61.

25. The first two years of the Kennedy Administration must, however, be considered as a period of mutual suspicion and surface hostility. See, for example, Chubin and Zabih, *Foreign Relations of Iran*, pp. 100-103.

26. *New York Times*, February 3, 1975.

27. Ibid., March 7, 10, 11, 12, and 17, 1975.

28. On the rapidly expanding role of Iran in the Persian Gulf, see David Holden, "The Persian Gulf: After the British Raj," *Foreign Affairs* 49, 4 (July 1971): 721-735; and Chubin and Zabih, *Foreign Relations of Iran*, Ch. VII, particularly pp. 242-255.

29. *New York Times*, February 7 and 9, 1975.

30. See, for example, *Kayhan International*, December 24 and 28, 1974.

31. *The Strategic Survey, 1971* (London: The International Institute for Strategic Studies, 1972), pp. 39-45. See, also, Stockholm International Peace Research Institute, *The Arms Trade with the Third World* (Stockholm: Almquist and Wiskell, 1971), pp. 574-579.

32. For various estimates of the quantity and types of Iran's recent purchases of air, ground and naval weapons systems, see *The Strategic Survey, 1973* (London: The International Institute for Strategic Studies, 1974), pp. 42-45; Stockholm International Peace Research Institute, *Yearbook, 1973* (Stockholm: Almquist and Wiskell, 1973), pp. 307, 325-326; U.S. Congress, House, Committee on Foreign Affairs, *Hearings: New Perspectives on the Persian Gulf* (Washington: Government Printing Office, 1973), pp. 27-30, 40, and 47; *The Military Balance: 1974* (London: The International Institute for Strategic Studies, 1974); Frances Fitzgerald, "Giving the Shah Everything He Wants," *Harper's*, November 1974; *Guardian*, October 12, 1974; *Time*, March 3, 1975.

33. *New York Times*, April 14, 1975.

34. The shah has repeatedly stated that Iran will reevaluate her current nuclear policy the moment any other country in the Middle East develops a nuclear military capability. See, for example, *Kayhan International*, September 15, 1975; also see *Guardian*, November 30, 1975.

35. See, for example, his recent interview with Mohammad Hassanein Heikal in which he states: "I hold the conviction that armed forces are like a lock in a door. They will last for some time, at least [providing] our friends, all those who might want to help us, and ourselves, with an opportunity to move," *Kayhan International*, September 16, 1975.

36. The shah has recently, once more, reiterated his resolve to keep and, if warranted, to increase the pace of the military build-up. See the text of a recent and related speech in *Kayhan International*, September 15, 1975.

37. J.C. Hurewitz, *Middle East Politics: The Military Dimension* (New York: Praeger, 1969), p. 286.

39. The shah has repeatedly referred to these and other bases for Irano-American cooperative association. See, for example, his recent interview with the West German Television Network, quoted in *Kayhan International*, September 18, 1975. Also see Oriana Fallaci, "The Shah of Iran," *New Republic* December 1, 1973, p. 20.

40. Interview with C.L. Sulzberger, *New York Times*, March 19, 1975.

XVII Turkey: Problems and Prospects

Talat S. Halman

Introduction

Few nations defy generalizations and inclusion in categories as much as Turkey does. It possesses so many *sui generis*, even paradoxical, characteristics that it may be said to stand unique—and sometimes alone—in blocs, regions, and communities.

The United Nations and other international organizations include Turkey in the European community although 96 percent of its territory is in Asia. Not counting Albania, Turkey is the only Muslim nation of Europe and the least developed. In the Islamic world, it is one of the most Westernized countries—and certainly the most secular in government and education. In statistical terms, Turkey is classified as an economically underdeveloped nation, but it is far ahead of virtually all other underdeveloped nations judging by its social, political, and judicial institutions, its bureaucracy and armed forces, its cultural level and higher education. It is Europe's most Asian country and one of Asia's most Europeanized lands.

The paradoxes reveal themselves with compelling clarity in the economic domain: Turkey is a predominantly agricultural country, yet it is often forced to import food commodities. Its neighbors to the south and to the east have abundant oil resources while Turkey remains oil poor. Although it is Europe's most underdeveloped nation, it maintains a standing army which ranks as Europe's second largest after France.

In politics and diplomacy, too, Turkey has sometimes projected an image or engaged in action not conforming to norms or expectations. Although its predecessor—the Ottoman Empire—had collapsed partially as a result of the

507

hostility of major European powers, and the Turkish Republic came into being after waging a war of independence against European powers, all Turkish governments since 1923 have been staunchly pro-Western. Her population is 99 percent Muslim, yet Turkey has seldom, until recently, aligned itself with the Islamic community of nations, seeking rather a European identification. Its parliamentary democracy has suffered fewer setbacks since the end of World War II than has been true of the vast majority of the underdeveloped nations. Turkey has escaped such vicissitudes as entrenched military dictatorship, one-party rule, totalitarian regimes, and police state in the postwar period, unlike most countries. Significantly, even the 1960 coup d'état and the 1971 military intervention were presumably undertaken for the purpose of "strengthening democracy." In both cases, in sharp contrast to the sequence of events in other nations, the military resisted the temptation of staying in power and placed the reins of government in the hands of a freely elected parliament and civilian cabinet.

Affinities rather than disparities characterize Latin American, South Asian, Balkan, African, and Islamic countries both within and among their regions or communities. Yet Turkey, irrespective of its similarities to the Third World, has been exceptional if not unique in many areas of its history. Its problems and prospects, therefore, must be assessed within the special context of Turkish realities and without strong reliance on the formulas and the diagnoses which are frequently applied to the underdeveloped countries in general. United States policies to be applied to Turkey should similarly take cognizance of the *sui generis* aspects of Turkish politics and cultural values. The synthesis which has evolved in the Turkish Republic since 1923 calls for a multiplicity of perspectives and a dynamic or fluid approach.

This report reviews modern Turkey and previews the next decade of Turkish politics, economy, foreign relations, and social-cultural life. It analyzes the dominant themes of Turkey's internal and international politics. It explains how the current Turkish political and economic situation evolved from the events of the past and explores the outlook for the coming decade on the basis of present-day domestic and worldwide developments. The fundamental approach is analytical and interpretive rather than expository and directs itself to the critical issues that may emerge by 1985.

In its entirety, this report endeavors to determine and assess the critical choices confronting the United States with respect to Turkey, an ally of long standing, which holds a significant and perhaps unique place in U.S. foreign relations from a geopolitical (strategic; defense) and ideological standpoint.

Glimpses of the Past

The Turkish Transformation: 1923-1938

Very few nations in modern times have witnessed changes as drastic and as swift as those that took place in Turkey from the early 1920s to the early 1930s. Even in countries where Fascist or Communist regimes have applied draconian measures to carry out ambitious ideological programs of action, the scope of revolutionary change has seldom equalled what Turkey was able to accomplish under Mustafa Kemal Atatürk.

Although the process of modernization based on European models had started in the Ottoman state in the closing years of the eighteenth century, it was in the second and third decades of the twentieth century that the Turkish nation undertook its first systematic, if not comprehensive, effort to join the mainstream of the West. The transformation was cataclysmic: The Ottoman Empire, a sprawling state made up of diverse ethnic, linguistic, and religious communities, gave way in 1923 to a new homogeneous nation-state. The House of Osman, the dynasty which had reigned for more than six centuries, was replaced by representative government. Sovereignty was transferred from the constitutional monarchy to the republic.

In order to launch what was to become this century's first successful nationalist-modernist revolution, Mustafa Kemal Pasha was forced not only to remove the sultan's ruling establishment, but also wage a war of independence on three fronts—against the Italians in the south, the Armenians in the east and the Greeks in the west. The Turkish war of independence constituted the prototype of the anti-imperialist struggles for national liberation. The patriotic spirit it required and regenerated gave impetus and fervor to the progressive reforms Mustafa Kemal Atatürk initiated once the Turkish Republic came into existence in 1923.

Vigorous innovations in Turkish life were introduced in quick succession. Education became secular. The hold of Islam over social institutions and culture was broken. European-style hats replaced the fez, which Atatürk saw as a symbol of Oriental backwardness. The caliphate, the supreme leadership of the Muslim community of the world, a title held by the Ottoman Sultans for more than four centuries, was abolished. Women's rights were broadened and women actually brought into the country's vital sectors to an extent still hardly matched by any underdeveloped country. The determination to make Turkey a secular state brought about the divorce from religion of the legislative, executive, judicial, and administrative branches of the government. With the swift adoption of the Swiss Civil Code and the adapted versions of the German Commercial Code and the Italian Penal Code, a wholly new legal system came into being. In 1928, Atatürk undertook the most difficult of reforms: Turkey abandoned the Arabic script and adopted its own Latin alphabet. Under the aegis of the Turkish Language Society, created by Atatürk, an energetic campaign was started to rid the language of its Arabic and Iranian words and to replace them with revivals of old Turkic words or new coinages. The language reform, which miraculously took root within months, eventually made much of the Islamic Ottoman heritage inaccessible to the younger generations, facilitated adult literacy programs and accelerated primary schooling, helped redirect Turkish scholarship and culture from their Islamic Arabo-Iranian character to a predominantly European outlook.

The moving spirit—perhaps the "ideology"—of the Turkish transformation was Kemalism (later called Atatürkism). Its six main tenets were "republicanism, nationalism, *étatism*, populism, secularism, and reformism." Although not listed among the fundamental principles, Westernization constituted a major goal. Kemalism seemed to equate its ideals and models of social progress, economic development, and cultural renewal with the norms and values which evolved as part of European civilization. Wholesale imitation of the West, however, was not encouraged by Atatürk. He articulated the need for an authentic Turkish personality not patterned after other nations, big or small, Eastern or Western.

In emphasizing Turkey's unique character, Atatürk endeavored to create a new sense of identification with the pre-Islamic achievements of the Turks while introducing his nation to Western technology and culture. He had considered the Islamic Arabo-Iranian impact on Ottoman life too objectionable to preside now over the complete Westernization of Turkey. At any rate, despite his admiration, he probably found the European powers, against whom he had waged a hard-fought war of liberation, suspect in their motives. He was unwilling to deliver his sovereign country into a web of economic or cultural imperialism. He stressed the need to steer an independent course in foreign policy and to maintain dynamic relations without bloc alignments which sometimes put small countries at a disadvantage or even in danger. In the economic domain, too, the Kemalist policies withstood the temptation of conversion to the Communist or capitalist system. Instead, a mixed economy was preferred in keeping with Atatürk's statement that Turkey is neither a Socialist nor a capitalist country but rather a "nation that resembles no other nation except herself."

The bold and sweeping transformation of Turkey could have been possible only through massive popular support. Predictably, there were uprisings, acts of sabotage, criticism, and revolts in a country where the entire political system changed, a new script was adopted, the religious establishment and education came to an end, etc. At different stages of his presidency, Atatürk faced, and crushed, numerous opponents and insurgencies. The most critical was the Kurdish rebellion of 1925, which was broken by the army. Other forms of opposition were also removed if and when they threatened the Kemalist regime: a number of would-be assassins of the president were hanged, many intellectuals and politicians critical of Atatürk were sent into exile, and some Marxists served jail sentences.

Kemalist Turkey was ruled by a one-party regime in which the parliament and the cabinet generally acted in accordance with the principles and guidelines set by Atatürk. Two opposition parties were formed, presumably as loyal opposition, to serve as a platform for critical views and to constitute a step toward parliamentary democracy. The first, after six months of existence, was suppressed because of an alleged connection with the Kurdish uprising in 1925. The second, which achieved strong popular support as soon as it came into being, was dissolved within three months in 1930.

The Turkish Republic under Atatürk was hardly a democracy, but it would be wrong to characterize it as a totalitarian regime. Nor does it really lend itself to the term "military dictatorship." The best definition might be "authoritarian presidential system with a one-party parliament." The armed forces remained loyal to their heroic commander-in-chief, the nation's liberator, who never wore his uniform in fifteen years as president and who painstakingly secured the noninvolvement of the military in politics. The public knew, however, that the Kemalist regime based itself on the effectively organized, nationwide, and unified support of the armed forces. The slogan "The Army is the Guardian of the Reforms" served as a succinct expression of this fact of Turkish life.

The Kemalist reforms were the high ideals and initial achievements of the republic. The revolution of the 1920s settled down to consolidation and gradual evolution in the 1930s. Turkey strove to establish a balance between *étatism* and the emerging free enterprise system. The First Five Year Plan for Industrialization, inspired by the Soviet model, spurred development efforts. Literacy increased from less than 9 percent in 1923 to more than 30 percent in 1938. Close to 500 People's Houses and more than 4,000 People's Rooms were established to give impetus to culture and adult education throughout the country.

Fifteen years of Atatürk's presidency, ending with his death in November 1938, left a legacy which has shaped the politics, economy, social forces, and culture of Turkey. The same legacy is likely to influence Turkish life in the decade 1975-1985, and perhaps through the twentieth century. Among the fundamental Kemalist principles at work in Turkey are the commitment to progressive democracy based on representative government, the emphasis upon a pragmatic foreign policy, the preference for a mixed economy, the focal significance of the military, the vital role of education and culture, and sustained modernization patterned after Western models.

Out of World War II into Democracy: 1938-1950

Ismet İnönü, who acceded to the presidency at Atatürk's death in November 1938, upheld Kemalist principles and, in large measure, furthered them. Under him, social economic development might have gained momentum, but World War II imposed severe strains and burdens—diplomatic pressures, high cost of maintaining an enormous defense system, scarcity of foodstuffs and manufactured goods, and other economic hardships—although Turkey remained neutral and escaped the scars of war. Partly because of these constraints, but mainly because of his personal approach, which had manifested itself when he served as Atatürk's prime minister, he stressed *étatism*, the state bureaucracy, a flexible foreign policy based on national interest rather than treaty obligations, and autocratic rule.

Miraculously Turkey succeeded in avoiding entry into World War II. Its geopolitical position obviously made it particularly vulnerable and its treaty commitments to France and Britain (in return for their acquiescence with Turkey's annexation of Hatay in July 1939) might have dragged it into the theater of action. But Inönü's astute and adroit diplomacy, which involved manipulating the major powers, succeeded in sparing Turkey from destruction, loss of lives and territory and prevented vast damage to its economy. Turkey declared war on Germany virtually as a *pro forma* act after the Allies had already crushed and invaded Nazi Germany. The declaration enabled Turkey to qualify as a charter member of the United Nations and to become eligible for United States aid.

A year after the end of the war, the Soviet Union demanded part of Eastern Turkey and special rights of passage through the Turkish Straits. Stalin had already made these claims at Potsdam, but the overt demands caused widespread alarm in the United States and Europe as well as in Turkey itself. Turkey, faced with the danger of being sucked into the Soviet zone of influence as well as the possible loss of some of its territory, perhaps even of its sovereignty, decided to abandon its de facto neutrality and gravitated toward the Western community of nations, principally the United States. The close relations between the United States and Turkey began with the Truman Doctrine, grew with the Marshall Plan, and were solidified with Turkey's participation in the Korean War and its membership in the North Atlantic Treaty Organization (NATO) in 1952.

No sooner was Turkey forced to cast its lot with America than it decided to adopt a multi-party system. According to one view, the transition to a democratic system constituted a major concession President Inönü had to make to the United States for military and economic aid. Another view holds, however, that even at the height of the one-party rule, the Republican People's Party, to which Atatürk and Inönü belonged, felt uneasy and embarrassed, if not guilty, about its absolute power and that a transfer to a multi-party parliamentary regime had always been the aspiration and an ultimate goal. Although the motivation has yet to be determined, it was probably a combination of these two phenomena—American expectations finding receptivity in the Kemalist ideal of establishing a true democratic regime.

The hastily held elections of 1946, which had given the opposition parties little chance to get organized, drew criticism for the prevailing atmosphere of governmental oppression and irregularities favoring Inönü's ruling Republican party. But the following four years enabled the major opposition party, the Democratic party, to strengthen its nationwide organization and gain support. In May 1950, Turkey held its first truly universal elections, which were remarkably free of irregularities. The Republican party suffered a crushing defeat and, after nearly three decades of power, transferred the reins of government to the Democratic party.

The Inönü presidency from 1938 to 1950, spanning the tragic years of World

War II and the emergence of the cold war, left behind an unfortunate legacy of austere and authoritarian rule, suppression of left-wing and right-wing intellectuals, arrested social and economic development, an anachronistic bureaucracy, and setbacks in rural education (mainly because of the closing of the remarkably successful network of institutes for village teachers on grounds of Marxist infiltration).

The period also established some fundamental facts of Turkish life which have continued into the mid-1970s and are likely to continue in the decade 1975-1985: The commitment to basic rights and freedoms, an abiding faith in free elections and a multi-party parliamentary system as the framework of the democratic way of life, the ability to conduct foreign policy in accordance with the national interest and in a flexible and pragmatic fashion, the preference for military and economic alignments with the West, a determination to avoid loss of sovereignty at the hands of excessively dominant allies.

The Democratic Decade: 1950-1960

The Democratic party came to power with a resounding victory at the polls in 1950, increased its popularity and plurality in 1954, encountered serious difficulties and setbacks in 1957, and toppled in 1960 when a junta gained control of the country. Led by President Bayar and Prime Minister Menderes, the Democrats seemed to differ very little in their foreign policy and economic orientation from the Republicans. In the early 1950s, they reaped great benefits from massive U.S. aid and from the large quantities of agricultural products exported at the unusually high prices that prevailed during the Korean War. While the Democratic party's platform stressed the primacy of the private sector whereas the Republican party appeared to advocate the significance of the public sector, the Democratic record shows that in the ten years from 1950 to 1960, although Turkish private enterprise made gains in investment and "know-how," the state sector registered an unprecedented growth and accounted for the country's vital economic activities.

The Democratic decade, starting with wide freedoms, became less and less free as inflation grew, particularly after 1955, stimulating vehement criticism in the press and causing disgruntlement among the lower and lower middle classes. The armed forces, many of whose officers felt the economic pinch, responded to the mounting dissatisfaction with the Democratic regime which appeared, by the decade's end, to have made a fiasco of the economy and a mockery of democracy. The Democratic party fell because of the economic setbacks for which it was largely responsible and the repressive measures it introduced in its desperate efforts to remain in power.

The decade marked the consolidation of United States-Turkish alliance. Turks in all walks of life, with the exception of a handful of Marxists, seemed to cherish the cooperation. To many, friendship with America meant the survival of Turkey's sovereignty and territorial integrity as the cold war continued to cast on the Turkish soil the long shadow of Russian domination. From 1946 on, politicians, private citizens, and the press heaped praise on Americans, always referring to them as "friends and brothers." Criticism of the United States was considered tantamount to Communist links or leanings. "Westernization" had been a Turkish ideal since the mid-nineteenth century: Now America became the model. Some prominent Turks expressed the hope that their country would some day turn into "Little America."

In the 1950s, it appeared that Washington had virtually taken over the management of Turkey's economic, diplomatic, and military affairs. In the United Nations, the Turkish delegation voted exactly the same way as did the U.S. delegation. American bases proliferated on Turkish soil and as many as twenty thousand U.S. military personnel were stationed there. In 1959, when President Eisenhower arrived in Ankara on a state visit, he was astonished to observe that the Turkish President Celal Bayar opened their official meeting "with the remark that we really had nothing to talk about, since we all knew that our views were identical in every respect."

In return for its aid and investment in Turkey, the United States seemed to be reaping numerous benefits: presence in one of the world's most strategic countries, a triumph for the democratic system (Turkey was often referred to as "the showcase of democracy"), a fairly large and promising market and, perhaps above all, the cooperation of Europe's largest standing army. "The bulwark of the Western defense system," as Turkey was often described by Western statesmen and journalists, came to be considered a "big bargain." In 1952, General William Arnold, head of the Military Mission to Turkey, told a congressional committee: "I know dollar for dollar you are getting more in Turkey than you are in any place in the world." In a conversation with C.L. Sulzberger of *The New York Times* in Izmir in May 1954, Lt. Gen. Paul Kendall echoed the same idea: referring to the Turks and Greeks as "the best damned mercenaries I know."

The Turks, from the president to the man in the street, seemed totally committed to America. This devotion might have resulted from fear of the Soviet Union and its designs on Turkey, or from a genuine admiration for the achievements of Western technology, of which the United States was the most successful example, or perhaps from a combination of these attitudes. The fact remains that, throughout the 1950s, Turkish officialdom and public maintained an uncritical attachment to the United States. The fidelity, which was unprecedented, lost ground in the 1960s and was kept alive by a small segment of the Turkish nation in the 1970s.

The final years of the decade also saw the Greek-Turkish conflict over Cyrpus resolved when all parties agreed to have an independent Republic of Cyprus established. The agreement gave the Turkish minority of the island broader rights than their numerical strength might have entitled them to under different circumstances. But these paper rights were to prove unworkable in the first three years of the new Republic, and bore out the critical view advanced by some Turks in the 1950s and later that the Menderes government should have pressed hard for either an independent Turkish Cypriot Republic or for annexation of a part of Cyprus into the Turkish state and that it yielded to United States and NATO pressures in agreeing to the establishment of the Cyprus Republic.

Revolution/Democracy Restored: 1960-1971

On May 27, 1960, following four weeks of student uprisings, the Turkish armed forces, led by thirty-eight officers, overthrew the Democratic party regime. Menderes and his party stood indicted for policies which allegedly violated the Constitution and endangered democracy. The junta of thirty-eight (reduced to twenty-four in November 1960 when fourteen members were dropped) called itself the "National Unity Committee," celebrated the new age as a "Revolution" and "The Second Republic," and promised to introduce significant reforms.

From its first references to foreign policy onwards, the committee reiterated and maintained its adherence to Turkey's Western alliances including NATO, Central Treaty Organization (CENTO), and United States ties. It ruled the country until the latter part of 1961 when it transferred power to a civilian government following free elections. Its two major contributions were the establishment of the State Planning Organization, which since then has prepared three five-year development plans, and a new Constitution (adopted in 1961 by a national referendum), which expanded freedoms and endeavored to strengthen both the rule of law and the social institutions.

The junta served the country well by making sincere efforts to revitalize democracy for the future. It shared its authority with a civilian cabinet, with consultants from the academic world, and with technocrats. It created a Constituent Assembly as a transitional legislature and for the drafting of the new Constitution. By means of the smooth transfer of governmental power to a civilian parliament and cabinet, it emphasized the primacy of the national will expressing itself freely through representative government.

On the debit side, the National Unity Committee proved inefficient in administration, committed the judicial and political error of holding arduous trials as a result of which the deposed Prime Minister Menderes and two of his cabinet members were hanged, meted out stiff penalties to several hundred legislators, and suppressed the Democratic party. Various ill-planned purges in the armed forces and at the universities stirred extensive criticism.

Shortly after the elections of 1961, which gave no party a clear majority making it necessary to form a coalition of the Republican People's party and

DP's heir apparent, the Justice party, it became obvious that a new constitution and various swift reforms do not necessarily secure stability or the effective functioning of democracy in an underdeveloped country beset by massive economic problems.

Planning, introduced with fanfare as a panacea, gave Turkey clarity of economic goals and improvements, but fell short of the expected giant leap forward. The progressive Constitution, a rather impressive document, provided the framework for a welfare state based on a mixed economy, strong freedoms, including guarantees of the freedom of speech, assembly, etc., but even the well thought-out checks and balances including an independent judiciary, and other provisions and protections often proved unable to offer solutions to political crises in the 1960s and particularly in the 1970s.

By 1965, coalition governments, including two formed by former President Inönü, an autocrat turned democrat, had failed to create political stability. Parties were locked in strife. The Cyprus issue, which erupted in late 1963, made Turkish public opinion realize that the West, principally the United States, would not necessarily stand by Turkey in matters vital to Turkish interest. In 1964, Turks were outraged when President Johnson sent Prime Minister Inönü a communiqué threatening United States sanctions if Turkey intervened militarily in Cyprus. The "honeymoon" that had started in 1946 came to an abrupt end—and relations have never been the same. The disillusionment gave rise to rapprochement with numerous socialist countries, including Turkey's "traditional enemy" Russia.

In 1965, the Justice party was swept into office under the leadership of its young pro-American chairman, Süleyman Demirel, who became an energetic premier with a strong majority in Parliament. He won reelection in 1969 despite vigorous opposition.

Throughout the 1960s, ideological debates raged on the Turkish political and intellectual scene. The 1961 Constitution, buttressed by governments which have upheld and protected it, provided for wide freedom of political activity. The decade witnessed widespread strikes, student uprisings, two averted plots (by the same colonel who was tried and executed) to overthrow the regime and to establish military dictatorship, clashes in the streets, political murders, "sit-ins," and violent protests.

Beginning in 1965, Turkey enjoyed unprecedented freedom of expression and public criticism. Many ideas and creeds, which had been repressed for decades, and many types of overt demonstration against governmental authority emerged with telling effect. The press, the universities, and the literary and intellectual publications became a battleground for ideologies. Marxist views and strategies clashed with the capitalist pressure groups and with the liberal thinking of the government. Islam, on the ascendancy since the advent of universal suffrage, grew into a formidable political force.

Although extremist parties failed to score much success in national elections, the rumblings on the far left and the far right were heard loudly and clearly throughout Turkey. For the first time in Turkish history, a full spectrum of ideologies emerged: the right-of-center Justice party was in power; the left-of-center People's Republican party, advocating a West European type of socialism, served as the major opposition; Fascists, fanatic Islamists and ultra-conservatives comprised the far right; Kremlin-type, Balkan-style, and Maoist Communists composed the far left. Although the Constitution rules out extremist ideologies, a quasi-Nazi party operated under the name of Nationalist Action Party and a Communist program was offered by the Turkish Labor party. Among the moderate programs and platforms of the centrist parties were a mild brand of socialism, American-influenced liberalism, and neo-Atatürkism.

In the second half of the decade, much of the upheaval that marked and shook the Turkish political scene was the result of anti-American and anti-capitalist agitation by Marxists. The shock waves had started in 1964 with "The Johnson Letter." Capitalizing upon it, the leftist press and large groups of Marxist graduate students conducted a vehement campaign against both America and the Turkish private entrepreneurs. Their propaganda, abetted by the negative image America created by the war in Vietnam, and such mistakes as sending to Ankara an ambassador who had just completed a stint as the Director of the Pacification Program in Vietnam and the visits of the U.S. Sixth Fleet to Turkish ports, took hold over a growing segment of the population. The tide had turned: in 1946, a prominent poet, Fazil Hüsnü Daglarca, had written a long poem entitled "Missouri" in which he welcomed the "brotherly presence" of the U.S. battleship in the port of Istanbul and referred to "brave America." Twenty years later, the same poet admonished the Turkish president, General Cevdet Sunay, on the eve of his state visit to the United States, not "to set foot on their airplane." There were widespread anti-American demonstrations in Turkey's major cities where "Yankee Go Home" and "Down with United States Imperialism" signs, once almost inconceivable, were now a common sight. Terrorists burned Ambassador Komer's car, harassed U.S. officials, planted bombs in U.S. office buildings, roughed up sailors of the U.S. Sixth Fleet, kidnapped American servicemen and killed Israel's Consul in Istanbul. Peace Corps volunteers, enthusiastically invited by the Demirel government and numbering about six hundred in 1966-67, were charged with being CIA agents by some Turkish parliamentarians and forced to terminate their work in Turkey.

Leftist propaganda accused private industry and other entrepreneurs of serving American interest as "compradores." Premier Demirel and his associates—also the Justice party in general—were criticized for catering to capitalist and imperialist interests. The armed forces were shown as being so Americanized that they had little capability for independent military action.

The electoral results of 1965 and 1969 seemed to belie the effectiveness of the sustained propaganda from the Left. The Justice party showed solid strength while the moderately socialist Republican party lost ground and the Turkish

Labor party suffered major defeats in the 1969 elections. The weakness of the Republican party was partially a result of a cleavage which led to the birth of another party. But the setbacks of both the Republicans and the Labor party were significant as well as baffling since they made a poor showing, particularly among the lower classes, the industrial workers, and the urban poor.

It was in the 1960s that the Turkish Republic became truly pluralistic—not only in terms of social stratification but also in its political modalities. Predictably, it felt the acute crisis of the feverish quest for ideas and ideologies, of disenchantment with many traditional values, of the consternation caused by the vulnerability of social institutions. As a burgeoning pluralistic society, it lacked the resourceful apparatus to cope with disruptions and tensions.

As the decade neared its end, the Justice party government appeared incapable of formulating imaginative programs of action to combat poverty and to establish more balanced economic development based on the precepts of social justice. It was under severe criticism for failing to divorce Turkish foreign policy from its European and American orientation. The economy maintained a rate of growth of about 7 percent per annum, which was the rate chosen as the plan's target as early as in 1961. Turkish workers in West Europe had started funneling funds into the Turkish economy. But inflationary pressures and trade deficits forced a major devaluation of the Turkish currency in 1970. The agitation for Kurdish nationalism, supported by many leftists including some prominent members of the Turkish Labor party, caused consternation in political and military circles. When terrorist kidnappings, robberies, murders, etc., and uprisings by students and workers became frequent and frightening occurrences in 1970, the Demirel government was forced to establish martial law in certain areas. But the commanders of the armed forces became increasingly displeased about what they considered was Premier Demirel's inability to deal with the riots, violence and terrorist acts. In March 1971, they asked the Demirel cabinet to step down, whereupon Mr. Demirel resigned.

"The Revolution of 1960," which had sought to restore a strengthened democracy, came full circle with the military intervention of 1971, which also articulated the same concern of making democracy safe for Turkey. In the intervening eleven years, democratic institutions and freedoms, on the whole, gained much ground. The rule of law and the independence of the judiciary became stronger than ever. Higher echelons of the bureaucracy attained an unprecedented level of efficiency and were able to keep the state machinery running even during the height of the political crises. Many sectors of Turkish life—private enterprise, the universities, professional organizations, unions, cultural establishments, etc.—showed impressive resourcefulness. But, because of the upheavals which were often simplistically attributed to freedom, because of the way the Turkish democratic system was identified with an American model, because of the inability of democracy to accelerate economic development and social justice, there was a reversion to a more disciplined regime to launch extensive reforms. Democracy itself had become somewhat suspect, and the military commanders felt the need for a more vigorous response to the revolution of rising expectations.

The commanders had the "option"—as the collective leadership of the country's largest single organized power—to establish military dictatorship. But they chose a new formula—a "military-civilian caretaker" arrangement. The decision demonstrated that the Turkish armed forces, when feeling compelled to intervene, tend to find solutions which do not necessarily conform to the patterns of military interference prevailing in underdeveloped countries. It proved once again that Turkish generals have a strong sense of the supremacy of the national will which they recognize as a preference for a free democratic system. The two major coups d'état in Turkey (in 1960 and 1971), dissimilar in many respects, had the common purpose of strengthening the country's economic and social structure, seeking to institute reforms which an elected government might have found more difficult to undertake and serving as a transitional administration before the return to a stronger democracy.

Military-Civilian Caretakers: 1971-1974

As the Turkish Republic entered the 1970s and began its second half-century, it was beset by political instabilities which hampered economic growth and made the future of democracy uncertain. In the four years from early 1971 to early 1975, six prime ministers (Demirel, Erim, Melen, Talu, Ecevit, and Irmak) formed seven cabinets in which close to one hundred fifty individuals served as ministers.

The military intervention of March 12, 1971 installed a national coalition of parliamentarians and technocrats without dissolving the Parliament. The new prime minister, Professor Nihat Erim, a jurist who had served as a cabinet member in the late 1940s and as an MP since that time, undertook the task of formulating and launching reforms in vital areas, including land. Martial law authorities maintained order. The legislature continued its normal legislative activities. The chief of staff and the commanders of the armed forces participated in some of the basic policy decisions of the civilian government. It was hoped that this realignment of powers would secure a creative and dynamic structure. Although no action had been taken against prominent politicians, unlike the arrests of 1960, various repressive measures were implemented, particularly at the beginning of the new regime, including the closing of the far-left Turkish Labor party and the arch-conservative Islamic National Order party, the banning of numerous periodicals and a large number of books, and the arrest of many prominent intellectuals and journalists.

During the first few months of the Erim government, two significant foreign policy decisions were taken: Official recognition of the People's Republic of

China and the ban on the cultivation of opium. The former was a logical extension of the new approach of maintaining good relations not only with the Western community but also with the Socialist bloc and the Third World countries, but had the appearance of having been inspired by Washington because it came just a few days after America's recognition of China.

The ban on opium cultivation was to have a major impact on United States-Turkish relations in 1974. From the mid-1960s on, Washington had urged Turkey, the source of up to 80 percent of the illegal heroin used in the United States, to impose a ban. The appeal was based on considerations of friendship and alliance. Premier Demirel was sympathetic, but fearful of the political consequences of an act which would have left tens of thousands of farmers and peasants without a source of income. He would also have risked fulminations from the leftists, nationalists, and other critics about his willingness to abrogate national sovereignty. Some colleagues and commentators urged Demirel to drive a hard bargain with Washington to secure large amounts of compensation in the form of aid and credit. As a politically acceptable compromise, Demirel reduced the number of poppy-growing provinces from twenty-one to seven in 1970, and to only four in 1971.

Erim's total ban, which he announced in July 1971, came after the same, if not more intense, pressure from America. He explained that his decision was based on humanitarian reasons. The White House and the media praised the decision. President Nixon issued a statement affirming that "the agreement represents by far the most significant breakthrough that has been achieved in stopping the source of supply of heroin in the worldwide offensive against drugs."

Although he had referred to humanitarian reasons, Prime Minister Erim had assumed that Washington would pay Turkey substantial compensation, warning some U.S. officials about the possibility of a future government rescinding the ban if adequate compensation failed to come through. But Washington seemed determined to obtain the ban that it had once considered vital at the lowest possible price. Following long and difficult negotiations, involving occasional blows to Turkish pride, Washington agreed to pay a total of $35.7 million in installments within two years. A more substantial payment might have secured a binding treaty, but Washington proved unwilling to seek a long-term or permanent solution. Less than three years after Erim's decision, the coalition cabinet of Bülent Ecevit lifted the ban and resumed cultivation. In the process, America was faced once again with the danger of illegal Turkish opium and United States-Turkish relations again plummeted to a very low point.

The so-called "Reform Cabinet" of Nihat Erim, after eight months in office, found it impossible to launch any reforms in the face of intensive opposition from the Parliament, the private sector, groups of vested interest, etc. Accusing Erim himself of having compromised his own original goals, most of the technocrat members of the cabinet resigned. Erim's second cabinet showed little interest in reforms. The subsequent cabinets formed by Ferit Melen and Naim Talu were essentially transitional caretaker governments, which did not seek to achieve much and in fact achieved virtually nothing, other than the provision of political continuity.

For America, these stopgap and makeshift cabinets meant a continuation of the military alliance and the opium ban, as well as economic cooperation, etc. The commanders who had a strong say in major decisions from March 1971 to October 1973 started out as reformists but, within a few months, submitted to the lobbying of the private sector which they came to equate with democracy. In retrospect, the military intervention of March 1971 appears to have solved none of Turkey's problems, nor has it achieved any of its initial objectives. The disruptions it has caused in the country's political and intellectual life and the damage it has inflicted on the national economy have been too big to justify any aspect of such an intervention.

When Turkey observed its fiftieth anniversary as a republic, it could rightfully boast of many achievements, but seemed embarrassed about its experiences of the early 1970s, and could only hope for a better future than the last few sterile years.

Turkey in the Mid-1970s: Cross-Currents and Crossroads

The general elections of October 1973 gave no party a clear majority to form a government. Politicians and observers had virtually unanimously expected Mr. Demirel's Justice party to win easily, but the Justice party barely won one-third of the seats in Congress. The People's Republican party, running on an explicit Socialist platform, obtained nearly 190 seats to the amazement of most of the pundits, but it needed a partner in order to form a coalition cabinet. For more than three months, numerous formulae and combinations were considered, yet no coalition seemed feasible. Finally, with some pressure from the commanders, Bülent Ecevit's Republican party entered into a coalition with the arch-conservative Islamic National Salvation party of Professor Necmettin Erbakan. The two partners, which were satirized as "strange bedfellows," had very little, if anything, in common—perhaps only a common belief both in the need for swift industrialization and the concept of social justice.

This uneasy coalition, with Ecevit as prime minister and Erbakan as deputy prime minister, encountered strong opposition from the Parliament, with which it could have coped, but its own internal struggles were a greater threat to its existence. Erbakan and his colleagues systematically tried to block cabinet decisions and the legislation that Ecevit and his party wanted to pass. Conversely, Erbakan had virtually no ideas that appealed to the majority wing of the cabinet.

The event which suddenly made a national hero out of Bülent Ecevit was the

Cyprus intervention of July 1974, followed by a further gain of territory in August. Earlier in the year, tension had arisen between Turkey and the United States because of Ecevit's lifting of the opium ban, and Greece and Turkey had been exchanging threats over oil exploration rights and the question of territorial waters in the Aegean Sea. The coup arranged by the dictatorship in Greece against Cyprus President Makarios and the installation of Nikos Sampson, a hated killer of Cypriot Turks, as the new president gave Turkey the justification it needed to invade part of the island republic.

Since 1963, Cypriot Turks had suffered economic deprivation, injustice, discrimination, and displacement. Many of them had been killed or wounded or maimed. Although all Turkish governments had taken an active interest in the plight of the Cypriot Turks, no solution had been possible. Feeble attempts at military intervention in 1964 and 1965 were aborted either by lack of landing vessels or by United States interference or both. At the United Nations, Turkish diplomats had failed to get any favorable resolutions passed except the resolution establishing the United Nations Force in Cyprus. The intercommunal talks between the leaders of the Turkish Cypriots and Greek Cypriots had yielded no results after several years. Consequently, at least twenty thousand Turks lived as displaced persons. Suddenly, a new national leader took a firm decision and undertook decisive military action to change the situation in Cyprus.

Ecevit's action gave Turkey effective control of nearly 40 percent of the territory of Cyprus, brought about the removal of Sampson, who had been described in the world press as a gangster and a thug, contributed to the downfall of the dictatorship in Greece and the establishment of a democratic regime. For Turkey, the success of its military intervention gave a tremendous boost to the national pride, a sense of achievement and destiny, and a renewed faith in the armed forces, which had not seen action since the Korean War twenty years before and which had lost prestige because of its unfortunate involvements in domestic politics. Ecevit emerged as the great hero, the leader that the nation had been yearning for; even some of his long-time foes felt obliged to sing his praises. References were being made to him as "The Second Atatürk."

To most Turks, Bülent Ecevit seemed the best leader Turkey could hope for: young, energetic, honest, consistent, author of a very promising Socialist platform which deals fairly with the private sector, a man of vision, a Western-oriented statesman who would protect Turkey's interest and integrity vis-à-vis the West, at the same time that his nationalism would prevent the danger of excessive Soviet influence over Turkey. The capable, amiable man who appeared in early July 1974 had become in August 1974 the strongest leader in Turkey—probably in the present and the foreseeable future. The military blunder which caused the Turkish air force to sink a Turkish destroyer during the Cyprus action prevented the emergence of any one of the commanders as a national hero, and perhaps eventually as a dictator. Ecevit received all the priase and none of the blame.

His new stature gave Ecevit the opportunity of consolidating his political power. He attempted to rid himself of Erbakan's National Salvation party and to have new elections held so that he could come to power on his own with a solid parliamentary majority. But the man who had achieved a military and diplomatic victory in Cyprus in mid-summer found that his political strategy failed in the fall. He resigned with the hope of forming a temporary coalition with the Democratic party and holding elections soon. But the Democratic party refused—or reneged. In the ensuing period of crisis, a national coalition cabinet (composed mainly of technocrats, a few members of the small Republican Confidence party, and some independent legislators) with Sadi Irmak as prime minister took office. It received only 17 votes of confidence from the 450-member Parliament, but held office as a lame duck caretaker government. In the face of strong opposition from all other parties, Bülent Ecevit and his People's Republican party found it impossible to press for new general elections. Ecevit held the hope of winning a clear majority at the polls while his rivals feared setbacks and losses.

After protracted negotiations, in April 1975, ex-Premier Süleyman Demirel formed a coalition cabinet (commonly referred to as the "Nationalist Front") with the participation of his Justice party and three small parties—the National Salvation party, the Confidence party, and the National Action party—whose chairmen became deputy premiers and who obtained powers beyond their parliamentary strength.

By remaining out of office, Ecevit has escaped the political blame for rampant inflation and deepening economic crisis. Yet, Demirel has gained the opportunity of demonstrating that he too is capable of responding to challenges in an impressive way. All of Ecevit's adversaries actually are hoping that developments might show Ecevit as less the hero who triumphed in war than a mere recipient of the benefits of the Cyprus affair. Premier Demirel seems to have adopted political stances and programs of action which are more than faintly reminiscent of the policies pursued by Ecevit to good advantage in 1974. Not the least of these is the firm stand Demirel took against the United States on the matter of the military bases in the summer of 1975. He demonstrated effectively that he was not, contrary to the generally held belief, pro-American, that he could stand squarely against Washington.

The by-elections for forty-nine senate seats and six congressional vacancies were held in mid-October 1975 in a tense atmosphere. Political leaders leveled bitter charges against one another and many bloody incidents occurred. Although the by-elections could not have been conclusive in determining the fate of Demirel's coalition cabinet, they were considered a major test for the two major parties. A resounding victory for Ecevit might have paved the way for general elections soon—prior to the general elections, which, normally, will take place in October 1977. Another litmus test was the relative strength of the arch-conservative National Salvation party.

The actual results, though far from dramatic or conclusive for any leader or party, gave Demirel enough success to continue in office while indicating that Ecevit is gaining ground as Turkey's future leader. The Justice party and the Republican People's party each won twenty-four Senate seats. In terms of the size of the popular vote, Ecevit's party showed greater strength. The National Salvation party, which won only a single seat, suffered a major setback. Of the six congressional seats, four went to the Justice party and two to the Republican People's party.

An analysis of the votes seems to indicate that Demirel reaped the benefit of his anti-United States stand and of the appeal he made to the supporters of centrist and rightist voters not to split their ballots but to vote en bloc for the Justice party. Conceivably many voters cast their ballots for Justice party candidates simply to avoid Ecevit's coming to power. Whether or not, the same centrist-rightist front can be mobilized in the general elections is a matter of conjecture.

Two clear conclusions may be drawn: (1) The electorate seems inclined to restore the two-party equilibrium; (2) Ecevit's party has become the clear choice in urban and industrial areas. These two factors will probably play a paramount role in the next general elections.

Demirel and his associates, in the wake of the elections, undertook energetic effots to persuade some of the small parties and independent MPs to join the Justice party. Such a consolidation would have political and psychological advantages for Demirel and his party although it could not enable Demirel to form a new government. He appears anxious to eliminate the National Salvation party, but can hardly afford to, because this party holds the balance in Parliament. He needs a minimum of 226 seats in the lower house. Of the total of 450, Ecevit's Republican People's party has 190 and Erbakan's Salvation party, 48. Even if Demirel can rally behind him all the other votes in addition to the 150 held by the Justice party, he would still fail to muster enough strength. His only other alternatives would be to form a minority government or bring about a split in the Salvation party. These prospects are highly unlikely; so is the possibility of a Justice party-Republican People's party coalition which has been suggested and urged by many influential individuals.

The party alignments, however, are fluid or flexible in many cases. Although strife among parties is intense, sudden and inexplicable reversals, arrangements, and alliances are not rare. Consequently, one cannot dismiss any possibility as unrealistic.

In the ideological spectrum, leftist views are embodied in the Republican People's party. The Marxist-Leninist doctrine is represented by two parties organized in mid-1975. So far there has been no indication as to how much strength these tiny parties might gain in time. The extreme left-wing of

Republican People's party has been exerting intense pressure on Ecevit to adopt a Marxist platform, but Ecevit has so far preferred a Socialist platform which does not bear direct allegiance to Marxist-Leninist views. The centrist and rightist doctrines held by the Justice party, Democratic party, and the Republican Confidence party are essentially the same, with differences in degree and emphasis. The National Salvation party maintains a platform which could be described as "Islamic socialism." The National Action party of ex-Colonel Alpaslan Türkes projects the image of an old-style national socialist or fascist organization, and has often been accused of supporting the "commandos" who have been responsible for various acts of violence and raids.

Throughout 1975, Turkey has witnessed intense political conflict, maneuvering and machinations exacerbated by mass demonstrations and bloody clashes particularly during the election campaign and at the polls.

In the midst of turmoil, numerous factors seem to inspire confidence and help to avoid Turkey's drifting towards chaos. Since his election in 1973, President Fahri Korutürk, a retired four-star admiral who served as commander-in-chief of naval forces until 1960, a former ambassador to Moscow and an ex-Senator, has used his prestige to work out compromises among politicians. His stature and influence have probably held some generals and admirals at bay when they felt the time had come to assume power. The military, in general, maintains an internal balance which makes it difficult for a single commander to exercise control over the armed forces. In recent years, top-level bureaucrats have performed an impressive function by keeping the administrative and executive machinery running even at times of political stress or crisis. At such times, however, there is a slowing down of investment activity both in the public and private sector—from which the economy suffers gravely.

Since the mid-1960s, the growing participation of technocrats, university professors, and intellectuals in the political process either as part of the body politic or from the outside has contributed to a more effective solving of problems. The press, although still quite partisan and circulation-oriented, frequently provides constructive criticism and serves as a staunch defender of fundamental rights and freedoms. In the 1970s, Turkey projects the image of a country whose institutions and social dynamics are capable of solving or, at least, alleviating most of the problems confronting it without recourse to a fascist regime, military government or totalitarian communism.

In 1974 and 1975, Turkey was faced with the decisions of the U.S. Congress to place an embargo on arms to Turkey because of the continuing Turkish involvement in the affairs of Cyprus. The reaction from the Ankara government and public opinion has been very strong: it was particularly powerful in the summer of 1975. The embargo, which was the result of intense pressure by the Greek-American lobby, has brought United States-Turkish relations to the lowest point ever. Resentment in Turkey resulted from the punitive aspect of the congressional decision and the breach of faith it signified for those Turks who had considered America a friend and ally for nearly three decades. Particularly irksome was the fact that the embargo encompassed military equipment which the Turks had already contracted to purchase and for which partial payment had been made. Also, the danger of the immobilization of some segments of Turkey's armed forces arose.

There were strong protests and denunciations. The press, including all pro-American newspapers, sternly criticized the U.S. Congress. *Hürriyet*, a pro-Western paper which enjoys by far the largest circulation in the country, published a front-page lead editorial entitled "For Turkey there is no longer an America."

Demirel retaliated by announcing the take-over of twenty-five American bases that are considered crucial to America's intelligence surveillance of the Soviet Union and to any U.S. military intervention in the Middle East—particularly support of Israel.

It was only after intense lobbying by the Ford administration that Congress finally lifted the arms embargo in early October 1975. But the anti-American sentiment caused by the affair is likely to persist in the foreseeable future. American presence in Turkey will be renegotiated; consequently, some of the bases may have to be vacated and the U.S. government may be asked to pay some compensation for those bases that will be retained.

The embargo episode seems to have made the Turkish public realize that excessive reliance on America for defense purposes and for military supplies should be avoided; Turkey should seek closer cooperation with the Socialist countries, including the Soviet Union, as well as with the Arab nations, Iran, and others; a domestic arms industry should be developed.

In 1975, Turkey's political circles and public opinion experienced the deepest possible disenchantment with United States-Turkish cooperation, after nearly three decades of staunch alliance.

The Shape and the Forces of the Decade 1975-1985

Domestic Politics and Foreign Relations

The Turkish nation has traditionally been responsive to strong benevolent leaders even if they do not necessarily belong in the gallery of democratic statesmen. Some of the proudest achievements of the Turks have been attained under the leadership of charismatic, heroic or legendary figures. In the mid-1970s, Bülent Ecevit started—mainly as a result of his Cyprus action of 1974—to protect the image of a leader who shares most of these qualities and who is also a democrat. These attributes will probably secure for him a parliamentary majority when general elections are held by October 1977.

It seems highly probable that Süleyman Demirel, head of the Justice party and premier of the four-party centrist and rightist coalition commonly referred to as the "Nationalist Front," will continue in office in the foreseeable future. But the government's parliamentary balance is so precarious and alignments change so rapidly that no prediction is possible. What appears certain is that both Demirel and Ecevit will play a major role in Turkish politics in the decade 1975-1985, provided that democracy does not give way to some form of dictatorship.

If Ecevit holds power, his success will inescapably depend on his cabinet, consultants, appointees, and circle of colleagues. In the history of the Republic, no leader except Atatürk succeeded in both enlisting and using the talents of the country's best minds, administrators, and technocrats. Ecevit, as a party leader and prime minister, came under severe criticism for not having task forces worthy of his leadership and programs. The success of his future leadership will depend on a stronger cadre.

If and when Ecevit returns to the office of the prime minister with a parliamentary majority or as the head of a harmonious coalition, he will probably seek to continue to pursue his policy lines of 1974. These include: greater independence and flexibility in external relations, decreased reliance on NATO and the United States for military needs, formation of urban-rural localities to ease the problems of unintegrated urban and rural configurations, acceleration of industrialization, expansion of cooperatives, tax reforms, the creation of a third sector called the "people's sector" to operate in rural as well as urban areas, etc. It could also reasonably be expected that the Ecevit government would place greater emphasis on *étatism*, reduce the proportionate share of foreign capital, increase taxes on the private sector, etc., and probably formulate a new land reform bill.

Although it is conceivable that centrist or rightist governments would also undertake some of these programs of action, none would be likely to implement the entire repertory, choosing rather to adhere to the essentials of traditional platforms with considerable emphasis on foreign and domestic private enterprise.

The swift progress of industrialization and urbanization will enhance the strength of the People's Republican party. The five million young adults who will join the electorate in the next ten years will also lean in the direction of Ecevit's party rather than any other party—provided of course that the Ecevit regime is basically successful, that centrist and rightist parties fail to form a broad-based alliance more responsive to social problems, and that no new party emerges to rival Ecevit's Socialist programs.

In the event of major crises, a military intervention or a long-term dictatorship is a possibility, but if Turkey's problems are not insuperable the armed forces are likely to continue their watchfulness without getting politically involved. It would be realistic to expect, however, that, in view of their experience of direct involvement in the past fifteen years, some measure of participation on their part is inevitable. Since the early 1960s, hundreds of officers of all ranks have leaned toward various ideologies. Some of them actually uphold and defend a specific ideology. An economic breakdown or a major political upheaval might well cause groups of officers or an aspiring dictator to attempt a *coup d'état.*

Aside from far-reaching socioeconomic problems, terrorist activities or acts of violence—even peaceful demonstrations by students—could pave the way for a military take-over.

Whether the high command of the armed forces will have any definite ideological orientation in the next decade is difficult to tell. Most high-ranking officers at the present time appear to be in the mainstream of Kemalism whereas younger officers reportedly lean in other directions, but mainly towards socialism. If Ecevit and his party succeed in inculcating in the public at large and the armed forces the belief that socialism may be regarded as the culmination of some of the basic Kemalist principles—which they have yet to achieve—their position in Turkish political life will undoubtedly be solidified.

In the early years of the decade, the Cyprus issue may continue to have wide repercussions in the world, cause greater strain between Greece and Turkey and perhaps inflict some economic burdens on Turkey. The Turkish Republic of Cyprus, proclaimed in February 1975, might remain independent, but it will conceivably become an offshore province of mainland Turkey. The idea of federation is more of a palliative offered to the Greeks than an objective of the Turks. Even if a federal system is actually formed on the island, it will not work, it will not be allowed to work, as most observers of the Cyprus scene know. Limited war between Turkey and Greece over Cyprus and/or rights in the Aegean Sea is not outside the realm of possibility, but it will probably be averted if the danger arises.

In the 1975-1985 period, any Turkish government is likely to review and revise its NATO ties. Depending on a wide variety of factors, Turkey may well decide to withdraw entirely from the North Atlantic defense system. This does not mean, however, that it will automatically gravitate to the Socalist bloc or any bloc. Yet, it seems almost certain that she will strengthen its ties with the Third World, including the Arab nations and the Balkan countries. Its relations with Israel, which Turkey recognized as early as in 1947, might be severed if the Arab nations exert intense pressure. The decade might see the dissolution of CENTO, but RCD (Regional Cooperation for Development) is likely to continue.

Kurdish nationalism could pose a threat to the southeastern part of Turkey. At least three million Kurdish-speaking citizens live in the region. If a Kurdish state is established on Iraqi territory, many Turkish Kurds might voluntarily resettle there, lessening the problem for the Turkish government. But, more likely, there will be agitation among them before, during, and after the establishment of an independent Kurdistan. This could create enormous difficulties for Turkey, particularly if the Kurdish minority demands, and fights for, secession and annexation of Turkish territory. The conflict would probably lead to much bloodshed and destruction. American support of Kurdish nationalism might conceivably put an end to American-Turkish alliance and friendship for a very long time.

The Economy

Unless a revolutionary change establishes a Communist regime, Turkey may be realistically expected to maintain its traditional synthesis of *étatism* and private enterprise. Controls, and checks and balances will continue to be implemented by the bureaucracy and the State Planning Organization. Depending on the economic orientation of political leadership, there might be shifts of emphasis in favor of the state sector or the private sector. A strong Republican People's party government would almost certainly expand the role of the state in the national economy, perhaps nationalize certain industries, mining, banking, and import-export activities, and impose heavier taxes on the private sector. A right-of-center government would most probably lean towards the liberal policies designed to develop private enterprise and to attract more foreign investment. A centrist cabinet, particularly if constituted as a broad-based coalition, is likely to retain the present composition of the mixed economy.

The shape of the Turkish economy could of course undergo drastic and unforeseen changes because of cataclysmic crises in the world economy—like the present oil crisis which erupted with alarming suddenness, and without warning. Barring such international problems and assuming continuity of regime, Turkey will probably maintain and further develop its mixed economy in the decade 1975-1985. Whether or not it can continue to do so until the end of the century will depend in large measure upon a substantially improved performance of the system itself.

The fundamental problems confronting Turkey in recent times are likely to frustrate development efforts during the coming decade.

The population, which reached forty million in 1975, will increase to nearly fifty-five million by 1985, and to seventy million by the end of the century. The rate of growth, averaging about 2.5 percent per annum, is well above world average. It is not expected to drop substantially below 2 percent in the near future. Population increase, consequently, will strain resources and arrest development particularly in view of the fact that the population younger than fifteen years of age now constitutes about 50 percent of the total population. This segment, which makes virtually no productive contribution while accounting for massive consumption and requiring extensive government services, will become a huge majority by 1985. Without a drastic drop in the birthrate, it should be impossible for Turkey to achieve rapid economic development. Family planning, initiated in 1965, has been losing momentum since the early 1970s.

The rate of economic growth in Turkey, projected at 7 percent for 1963-1973 and realized at about 6.6 percent, is too slow to bring about major improvements in national life. The target of 7.9 percent per annum stated in the Third Five Year Plan (1973-1977) will probably prove overoptimistic. In 1971, per capita national income was approximately $350. If the Third Plan achieves its objectives, the figure may rise to about $475, which still represents a very low level of economic development. Under ideal circumstances, Turkey's per capita income may rise to about $1,500 by the end of the century, bringing the country to the present level of Italy.

Currently, inflation is rampant: Prices rose at the rate of 25.5 percent in 1974, higher than in Italy and Greece, according to OECD figures. In 1975, there has been an upward trend—to 30 percent. The pattern of income distribution continues to be flagrantly unjust, with nearly half of national income controlled by almost 20 percent of Turkish families. Each year, the trade deficit grows and will probably get bigger in the next decade. Soaring oil prices are likely to exacerbate the situation. If the United States ceases to be a supplier of military hardware, Turkey will be forced to purchase arms abroad which will further strain its capabilities. The added burden of maintaining thirty to forty thousand troops on the island of Cyprus and the military requirements created by the tense political situation will continue to pose financial problems. In addition, the Turkish government is obligated to high expenditures and substantial investments in Cyprus. It is estimated that the first year of Turkey's military presence in Cyprus entailed an expenditure of about £T35 billion or 2.5 billion U.S. dollars, which was the equivalent of 40 percent of the annual national budget of Turkey.

Turkey's external debt must be paid at an annual rate of $150 to $200 million. This sum is not far short of the total foreign aid Turkey receives each year. Although various deferments have eased payment pressures in the past few years, the accumulated indebtedness will add to the foreign payments problem in the last two decades of the century.

U.S. economic aid since 1946, including loans and grants, total close to three billion dollars by 1975. In 1974, AID assistance was a mere seven million, and military aid has been reduced to virtually nothing. The Consortium (consisting of the United States and nine West European nations) continues to extend credit to projects envisaged in the Five Year Development Plans. The nine European Economic Community countries will give Turkey 267 million EEC "units" until 1976 in loans to industrial projects.

Despite liberal privileges granted to foreign capital, the Turkish economy has achieved medium success at best in attracting investments from abroad. In the twenty-year period from 1950 to 1970, total foreign capital invested in Turkey barely exceeded $100 million. In the same period, American investments in the world (exclusive of the United States itself) totaled more than $70 billion. Considering the amounts invested abroad by other industrial countries as well, it is fair to assume that Turkey received less than one-thousandth of the global flow of capital.

The year 1975 was marked by mounting trade deficits. Imports increased at the rate of 45 percent while exports decreased by about 35 percent. Foreign exchange transfers by Turkish workers abroad fell by more than 20 percent. The trade deficit approached the $3 billion mark by the end of 1975. An OECD report forecast that, if present trends continue, Turkey's foreign debt will rise to about $10 billion by 1980. This amount is additional to the outstanding foreign indebtedness of nearly $4 billion.

Among the heaviest burdens on the national economy are military expenditures, which increased by 55 percent in 1975 and which run as high as 30 percent of the national budget, and the losses of the State Economic Enterprises. The vast network of state enterprises, the first one of which was established in 1934, encompasses public and semi-public corporations active in a broad variety of fields (railways, insurance, paper mills, advertising, iron and steel works and banks). Some of them have registered substantial losses and incurred huge debts in spite of the virtual monopoly they have enjoyed of their respective markets. The First Five Year Plan stated that "some of the State economic Enterprises are seen to be short of working capital and investment capital, to have insufficient liquidity and a tremendous burden of debt. Their net worth accounts for a very small portion of assets." The Second and Third Plans have tended to accentuate the positive aspects by referring to the role the enterprises "have played as an effective tool for development by virtue of industrialization . . . their pioneer work . . . constructive contributions in production, employment, use of advanced technology, and protection of price stability." During the first ten years of planned economy, the State Economic Enterprises accounted for about 40 percent of all public investments. The State Planning Organization admits that "there are serious questions about their productivity and the need for their reorganization remains."

The government made earnest attempts to develop plans for the reorganization of these state enterprises in the early 1960s and early 1970s. There have also been numerous projects to sell some of the corporations to the private sector. So far none of these endeavors has yielded results. The government seems to have no alternative but to carry the financial burden of the network which had been envisaged as the bulwark of *étatism* but which has come to embody its inefficiency and failure. The system is a monument to Parkinson's law, although it has been praised for having served as the training ground for experts and managers employed by privately owned industry. Much of its capacity is underutilized or even mismanaged. An overhaul undertaken not as a mere administrative reorganization but as a program of economic revitalization could conceivably eliminate most of the liabilities of the State Economic Enterprises. Conversely, unless some drastic solution is found to transfer them to the private sector or to transform them into profit-making industries, the national economy will continue to suffer, falter, and sustain losses.

The total number of unemployed workers in Turkey rose to about two million in 1975. This figure is expected to reach the three million mark by 1985. There are 800,000 workers abroad, three-fourths of whom are employed in West Germany. There are definite signs that there will be drastic changes in Bonn's policy of employing foreign workers. If the German job market shrinks or closes to Turkish employment, the economic consequences for Turkey could be frightening: The transfers of foreign exchange by Turkish workers to their homeland will drop from an average of one billion dollars a year in the 1970s (the record amount was close to a billion and a half dollars in 1974) to substantially less. As a result, Turkey's foreign exchange reserves will diminish in corresponding amounts and less money will be available for investment in the private sector.

Another serious consequence of workers returning en masse will be the swelling of unemployment figures. Furthermore, since these workers, on the whole, return with a new sense of labor and living, joblessness or a lower level of life style will engender strong dissatisfaction among them. If conditions in West Germany, Holland, Australia, Belgium, and other countries lead to massive layoffs of Turkish workers, who return to find no jobs in Turkey, one might expect critical labor versus government confrontations, massive demonstrations and strikes, and widespread upheaval in Turkey in the next decade. Such convulsions could even lead to the establishment of a military dictatorship with Fascist leanings or a regime which could be characterized as "the dictatorship of the proletariat."

The magnitude of the problem is expressed by the fact that nearly a million and a half workers, eligible and already registered, were waiting to go to West Europe in 1972-1973. In the peak year, 1973, the actual figure for those who went came to 136,000. The authorities predicted that 70,000 would go in 1974, but the economic crisis in Europe caused this figure to stay at 17,500. In 1975 there was a mere trickle to Austria and several Arab countries. Unless the present trends are reversed, it seems highly unlikely that an additional one million Turkish workers will be gainfully employed abroad by 1995 as the State Planning Organization projected. If the crisis is protracted or if there are further major changes in the employment policies of some European countries, particularly West Germany, the present total will probably decrease or at best remain steady.

The possible opening of some Arab job markets to Turkish manpower—if it actually takes place—will involve substantially fewer numbers. Libya, for instance, has announced in early 1975 that she could employ up to 60,000 Turkish workers and technicians. The Arab demand might create special problems for Turkey since, unlike the employment of unskilled labor in West Germany and elsewhere, it will draw on Turkey's limited skilled manpower.

The State Planning Organization hopes to solve Turkey's basic problems in the area of employment through swift industrialization, projecting that the problem will be solved in the last decade of the century. Turkey has fallen short of many of its plan targets: In the first ten years of planned economy, 1963-1973, it came close to the projected 4 percent increase in agricultural production, exceeded the 6.5 percent expected rise in services, but maintained a level of industrialization far below the target of 12 percent. Whether the Turkish economy will generate sufficient dynamism and strength to reach the 12 percent level in the decade 1975-1985 will depend on a variety of factors internal and external, economic and political—not the least of which is political stability. In 1974, the private sector investments exceeded plan projections by 23.8 percent, but only 83.2 percent of the public sector investments were achieved. Since 1974 was a year of political uncertainties and the Cyprus problem, the performance of private enterprise, which often slows down its investment activities during periods of crisis, looks impressive. Needless to say, higher investment activity in the public sector is a natural corollary of a stable administration. Hence, one could assume that, once governmental stability is achieved, the pace of industrialization will increase to the level hoped for by the State Planning Organization. This will, however, be possible only if most of the other economic factors are virtually ideal.

Urbanization will create problems and pressures which could hardly find solutions in the next few decades. The State Planning Organization estimates that the number of Turkish cities with populations exceeding 250,000 will rise from eight in 1975 to sixteen in 1985. By the same year, more than half of the total population will live in cities with a population of at least 10,000. Istanbul will reach the five million mark, and the ratio of urban-rural populations will be reversed from 40-60 percent in 1975 to 60-40 percent in 1985. By the year 2000, the urban population will rise to about fifty-six million from the present sixteen million while the rural population will fall from about the present twenty-four million to sixteen million.

Although such extensive urbanization will eventually have beneficial corollary effects by reducing the cost of communications, education, and various social services, the short-term problems it will create in such areas as urban infrastructure and municipal services, including housing, electricity, city transportation, hospitals, water supply, etc., are likely to exacerbate the present difficulties. Already four million people, one-tenth of the population, live in shantytowns the vast majority of which are in a substandard condition.

Major cities, Istanbul and Ankara in particular, have been experiencing overcrowding, chronic shortage of running water, pollution, garbage disposal problems, health hazards, etc. Power failures and cutoffs are frequent occurrences. Officials foresee the possibility of cutoffs up to four hours a day starting in 1978. The urban problems of the next quarter century are likely to have convulsive effects on the economy and society.

Prospects for agricultural growth seem limited because the vast majority of arable land is already under cultivation. Erosion continues to pose a severe threat. The average annual increase of agricultural products of 3.9 percent from 1968 to 1972, and the expected 4.5 percent increase in the period 1973-1978, fall short of the requirements for feeding the rapidly growing population. There is no critical shortage of foodstuffs. Turkey has never experienced famine although undernourishment and malnutrition are constant problems. If the food industry succeeds in increasing its output at the rate of 6 percent per annum, as anticipated by the State Planning Organization, Turkey may escape serious food shortages in this century. It is susceptible to the danger of setbacks because of adverse weather conditions, and there is the strong possibility that the planners are overly optimistic about the agricultural sector. As in the past, it will undoubtedly be necessary for Turkey to import some staple food items at times, but its food exports will probably equal or even exceed food imports in the next ten years. Normally the country should be confronted with no famine condition comparable to the disastrous situation that exists in some Asian and African nations.

If the trends of recent times continue, Turkey will probably be forced to devalue its currency quite sharply at least once, possibly even twice, in the coming decade. As a result of two minor adjustments made in 1975, the value of the Turkish lira went down from $1 = £T14 to $1 = £T15. More drastic devaluations may be expected in the not too distant future.

Since the early 1960s, when the question of Turkey's becoming a member of the European Economic Community first arose, economists and politicians have held intensive debates on the possible benefits and disadvantages of the Common Market for Turkey. Turkish participation will take place in stages culminating in full membership in 1995 subject to its attainment of an economic level acceptable to the Common Market. The conclusion one can draw from a broad spectrum of opinion expressed by supporters and critics is that Turkey has little to lose and a little to gain during the transitional stage, particularly as an associate member. The country benefits both from certain tariff exemptions on the textiles and agricultural products it exports and from advantageous imports such as manufactured goods. The easy access of Turkish workers to EEC job markets has also been a substantial gain. But if it is admitted to full membership having fulfilled the minimum requirements without truly strengthening its economy, Turkey's Common Market ties will, on the balance, tend to work against its economic interests.

Irrespective of full EEC membership, Turkey's commercial and industrial relations with the United States, which have not been as extensive as left-wing propaganda has led the public to believe, could be expanded in the coming decades to the benefit of both countries.

In the field of education, despite some gains, the record of the past forty years has not been impressive. About half of the adult population is illiterate. In 1975, according to figures revealed by the minister of public education, there are more than 700,000 boys and girls at primary school age who have no opportunity to go to school. The growth of the population at a rate which has never dropped below 2.5 percent per annum has created a massive young population (twenty million below the age of fifteen in 1975). The demands on the government and public funds for the education of the young are enormous. The problem at the higher educational levels is also assuming serious proportions. Each year, well over a hundred thousand secondary school graduates are finding it impossible to enroll in the universities. Many who are admitted must specialize in fields other than those of their choice. Far too many university graduates find no employment in the fields of their own specialization: Government offices, banks, and commercial establishments have a depressingly large number of clerks and minor functionaries who hold degrees in the humanities and the sciences although the same jobs could and should be performed by secondary school or high school graduates. The Turkish educational system has so far failed in organizing itself according to specialization requirements and employment structure.

By 1980, it is expected that the number of secondary graduates who want to enroll in the universities will exceed half a million. The growth of graduate studies has been swift and substantial. In the academic year 1965-1966 there were about 100,000 students and 6,200 faculty. Both figures more than doubled in ten years. The student-faculty ratio is healthy compared to many other nations. The Turkish ratio of one teacher to fourteen graduate students compares favorably with Norway's (one to seventeen), Canada's (one to eighteen), and Greece's (one to thirty-two), is equal to Italy's (one to fourteen), and is slightly less favorable than Germany's (one to twelve). This indicates a capability for the expansion of the student body, but a lack of other facilities will constitute a "bottleneck." There can be no realistic expectation of meeting the enormous demand for graduate studies in the near future.

Meanwhile, various imbalances and deficiencies continue: University graduates engaged in work in Turkey constitute only 1.7 percent of the working population, whereas the European average is 3.4 percent. The ratio of professionals and technical workers within the active population is barely 3 percent; this compares quite unfavorably with Greece (5 percent), Canada, and France (10 percent), and Yugoslavia (15 percent). There is one physician to 2,300 persons in contrast to one for every 650 people in Greece, one for 700 in France, and one for 500 in West Germany. Nearly two-thirds of all physicians live in the three major cities while in the underdeveloped eastern part of the country, there is one doctor for every 10,000 people.

In the mid-1970s, Turkey began to establish closer ties with the Arab countries as well as other Muslim nations. The economic consequences of Islamic cooperation may give numerous Turkish products favorable and profitable markets. But the obvious advantage would be financial aid, credit, and investment funds from the OPEC countries. An agreement concluded with Libya in January 1975 is significant, perhaps even typical of what might be expected of

the new era of Turkish-Arab cooperation: The agreement calls for the establishment of a Turkish-Libyan investment bank which will pump Libyan oil funds
into joint projects; Libya's agreement to hire up to sixty thousand Turkish
workers; the creation of a joint tanker fleet; Turkish-built roads; the construction of a 1000-kilometer railroad in Libya; the establishment of joint armaments
industry and the sale of three million tons of crude oil to Turkey in 1975 "at
favorable prices," as well as other economic and technological projects. Iran will
give Turkey a loan of $1.2 billion for roads, railways, and industry. Arab funds
might become available in substantial amounts: They will undoubtedly prove
quite useful to the Turkish economy, but such financial ties may involve
Turkey's military commitments to the Arab world and Turkey might consequently become involved in a Middle Eastern or North African conflict which it
might have escaped otherwise.

In view of the problems and the prospects, both Turkey and the United
States would derive substantial benefits from expanded economic and commercial cooperation.

Washington would be well-advised to develop a new economic blueprint for
commercial, industrial, technological, and financial relations with Turkey on the
basis of mutual benefit and profitability. The Turkish governments of the next
decade are quite likely to respond with goodwill, reason, and perhaps enthusiasm.

The economic progress of Turkey since the end of World War II has been
notable for some solid achievements. The revolution of rising expectations,
however, has often outdistanced the accomplishments. Turkey is hardly a typical
underdeveloped country. Its social, political, and economic institutions seem
strong enough to give new impetus to development. A stable government, which
provides solid leadership and has the capability of carrying out reforms, will
probably usher in a period of relative prosperity and wider social justice by
1985.

Policy Recommendation

Long-term projections about Turkey and policy recommendations regarding
United States-Turkish relations are obviously subject to the effects of worldwide
and regional developments. Although such cataclysmic events as a holocaust or
invasion by a superpower, etc., are not outside the realm of possibility, this
report bases its suggestions on the assumption that Turkey will remain a
sovereign independent state in the foreseeable future. It is assumed, by the same
token, that the United States will maintain its present importance in world
affairs, without undergoing drastic changes in its domestic life and foreign
policy. If the world trends of the 1970s continue, détente will probably grow,
bloc divisions and regional alignments will lose ground, foreign policies will be

guided less by ideologies than by practical economic considerations, a less lopsided relationship will emerge between the industrialized countries and the Third World, and interdependence will become more entrenched than ever.

Assuming that both Turkey and the United States experience the normal growth of their present prospects and problems during the next ten years, within an international context not reshaped by vast unpredictable changes, the two countries will continue to find it mutually beneficial to maintain their cooperation in many spheres of activity. In particular, if Middle Eastern oil and the Arab-Israeli conflict remain as significant as they are at present, the United States will regard Turkey as vital to its interest, because if Turkey makes her territory neutral and open or if Ankara shifts its alignments, the Soviet Union would immensely benefit from acquiring access to the rest of the Middle East. Turkey, on its part, values its sovereignty and independence too strongly to expose itself to Soviet domination which would come in the wake of a rupture of United States-Turkish alliance. Although the traditional Turkish distrust of the Russians was excessively emphasized during the cold war, the fact remains that Turks, even the majority of pro-Soviet Marxists, certainly the Socialist Republican People's party, are resolved to protect their national integrity against any power—big or small, Communist or Western. In the next ten years, unless Turkey installs a Communist regime or becomes a satellite as a result of armed aggression, Turkish foreign policy will probably be based on the view that a distant superpower makes a less dangerous ally than a contiguous superpower.

The United States government can solidify its relations with Turkey if its policy takes cognizance of the special characteristics of the Turkish situation. The problems which have weakened Turkish-American relations from the mid-1960s on, after nearly two decades of strong alliance and broad cooperation, are notable for their psychological dimension. Rather than substantive issues, official postures and attitudes seem to have caused varying degrees of anti-American feeling among the Turks who had been pro-American virtually en masse.

The primary reason for the negative sentiment was, as it happened in most other countries as well, the obtrusive presence of U.S. military and civilian personnel. The special privileges and immunities, the affluent life, the quasi-colonialist detachment from local realities, etc., which marked the American presence alienated the Turks over the years. The more decisive anti-American attitudes, however, resulted from a series of blunders: In 1964, at the height of the Cyprus conflict, President Johnson sent the Turkish Premier Inönü a very strongly worded message threatening sanctions against Turkey, including intervention by the U.S. Sixth Fleet, if the Turkish armed forces engaged in any action against the island republic. In 1971, when the Turkish government banned opium production, and in 1974, when a new government permitted partial cultivation, Turkish public opinion was incensed that Washington was treating Turkey as less than a sovereign independent nation.

It was only at the time of the Turkish military intervention in Cyprus in mid-summer 1974 that the State Department began to act in a manner which most Turks found acceptable, but the good impression created through the avoidance of repeating President Johnson's mistake of 1964 was dispelled when Congress, overriding the efforts of President Ford and Secretary of State Kissinger, decided to cut off military aid to Turkey. The arms embargo of 1975 has done almost irreparable damage to United States-Turkish relations.

United States-Turkish relations, if they are to continue on a mutually beneficial basis, must be predicated upon the recognition of certain realities, concepts, and principles: Turks are essentially thankful for U.S. aid programs totaling well over four billion dollars, but have come to view them not as charity but as America's investment in its own security. The dominant feeling on the part of the politicians and the public is that "America needs Turkey just as much as Turkey needs America—if not more." Some patronizing attitudes on the part of American officials must be avoided at all cost. In the past, particularly in the 1950s, some Turks were themselves responsible for these attitudes because of their feeling of inferiority and their sychophancy. By 1975, however, national pride demanded that all relations must be conducted as between two equal partners in dignity. The insistence is on Turkey's independent foreign policy. For nearly twenty years, Turkey voted in the United Nations in the same manner as did the United States. It fought in Korea beyond the call of duty, with the largest contingent and the biggest casualties, second only to the Americans. It followed the American and NATO policy guidelines well into the 1970s. In recent years, however, Turkey's conduct of foreign affairs has become increasingly pluralistic, flexible, and pragmatic.

Turkey will probably maintain closer ties and have broader cooperation with the Soviet Union and other socialist countries in the next decade. Relations with the People's Republic of China, which Turkey recognized in the summer of 1971, may be expected to get stronger—particularly if Turkey leaves the United States-NATO axis and seeks to avoid becoming a Soviet satellite. Iran, various Arab countries, and Turkey might easily come together, after decades of aloofness in some vital matters, to pursue some common economic, diplomatic, and military interests. In consideration of Turkey's military might, which could help the Arabs in a Near East confrontation, Turkey could receive from the oil-producing countries substantial amounts of funds, aid and credit. If U.S. corporate investments and military assistance to Turkey come to an end for any reason, the vacuum will probably be filled by West Germany, Arab countries, the Soviet Union, Iran, France, Japan, and China.

It is logical to assume that if NATO continues, Turkey will continue to be a member during the next decade. In the early 1950s, joining NATO was considered by the Turkish leaders as virtually a matter of life and death. In the mid-1970s the new leaders are reconsidering the benefits from the alliance. But no alternatives seem to have been formulated for maintaining Turkey's defense against the potential aggression of the Soviet Union which, although it has far better relations with Turkey than any time since the early 1930s, still harbors hopes of acquiring Turkish territory, control over the Straits, and access by land to the entire Middle East.

Unless a new constructive formula is found, it appears certain that Turkey will ask the United States to vacate its military bases and withdraw its military personnel. Confiscation or nationalization of American investment is less of a possibility but could happen if relations deteriorate or if a far-left government comes to power.

The Turkish economy, notwithstanding gains, is likely to experience massive problems in the period 1975-1985. The only panaceas one can imagine are discovery of oil and billions of dollars in aid and investment—both improbable prospects. The decade, then, forebodes widespread unemployment, trade deficits, balance-of-payments difficulties, commodity and food shortages, perhaps even an occasional famine, etc. Social problems will probably cause upheavals and political instability at times. Until 1985 Turkey is likely to experience vast problems which cannot be solved or alleviated until the end of the century.

Problems and prospects provide strong indications that the United States and Turkey stand to reap mutual benefits from their interdependence. A new era of American-Turkish cooperation is feasible and full of promise. Having Turkey on her side would safeguard the United States defense and economic interests in the Middle East, ensure better protection of Israel, indirectly help America's relations with the Muslim world, and ideologically strengthen the prospect of success for Turkey as a "showcase of democracy." Turkey would benefit from America's protective shield, from its commercial and industrial investment, military aid, technological and educational expertise, etc.

Both countries recognize the validity and see the basic value of United States-Turkish cooperation. Now that the arms embargo has been lifted, the time is ripe for negotiating a new set of agreements or perhaps a comprehensive treaty. In fact, preliminary talks have started in Ankara. The objective should be to conclude a series of agreements, independent but interrelated, or a full-fledged treaty encompassing a defense pact, trade agreements, economic and technological aid, educational cooperation, opium cultivation, etc.

In addition to their joint commitments in NATO, Washington and Ankara can formulate a new bilateral agreement or pact to determine the long-term status of U.S. bases and military personnel in Turkey, to regulate military aid, to establish the principles and the *modus operandi* of joint defense, Turkey's purchases of military equipment, weapons, etc.

In the economic sphere, Turkey will probably be highly receptive to an expansion of American-Turkish corporate investment activity in the industrial fields most essential to domestic consumption and those areas which are most lucrative for export purposes. Such investments, as in the past, would amortize themselves in very brief periods and continue to yield high profits for a long time. The United States has yet to realize Turkey's impressive potential as an exporter of industrial goods produced at competitive prices as a result of lower manufacturing costs and cheap labor.

By creating employment, new American-Turkish enterprises would ease Turkey's awesome problem of spreading unemployment. They would also lessen trade deficit and balance-of-payments problems and accelerate industrialization. It might be advisable for Ankara and Washington to negotiate the purchase of all or some of the Turkish State Economic Enterprises by a new American-Turkish corporation or a multinational corporation which would overhaul them and operate them efficiently and profitably. If this huge network of industries can be made to function properly through better management and advanced expertise, the U.S. investors and the Turkish economy would reap great benefits.

Direct economic aid will not be forthcoming to Turkey unless overall Washington policy undergoes drastic changes, but occasional humanitarian assistance, mainly in foodstuffs and medical supplies, may be sent to Turkey in the event of disasters or special hardships as in the past. In negotiating a multifaceted agreement, economic aid could constitute a crucial element to secure acceptance of concessions regarding military bases, opium, etc.

An American education, particularly in the technical fields, is generally held in the highest esteem among the Turks. In recent years, U.S. scholarships to foreign students have decreased. An increased number of grants to Turkish students would be considered exceedingly attractive and advantageous by the Turkish government, which is faced with an enormous demand for higher education and spends large sums to send students abroad. An agreement might be reached to exchange graduate students. In many fields, interested American students could obtain free tuition, stipends for board and lodging, travel expenses, etc., from the Turkish government in exchange for Turkish students studying in the United States on American grants. If such exchange programs can be worked out with many countries, America would greatly benefit from having increased numbers of foreign students gaining knowledge of the United States and from thousands of young Americans becoming experts in the life, language, and history of other nations. An exchange program could also be negotiated on the following bases: For each foreign student studying in the States on an American grant, the foreign government would hire a qualified American as a teacher of English or other subjects at regular salaries plus travel expense, stipend for residence, etc. This is a variation on the Peace Corps idea, but it would be far more acceptable to many countries including Turkey.

Two problems have contributed to anti-American feeling among Turks since the mid-1960s—the brain drain and art plunder. An estimated one-fifth of all Turkish physicians work in the United States, while there is a critical shortage of doctors in some parts of Turkey. The growing awareness of the loss of valuable archaeological objects and wide publicity about the availability of many items of Turkish origin in U.S. museums have caused official and public anger. There have even been announced intentions of terminating the excavation privileges of the United States and other countries. If Washington is interested in concluding a comprehensive new agreement with Turkey, making some provisions regarding the brain drain and art plunder would generate goodwill and secure some benefits in exchange.

United States policy on Turkish opium, although seemingly successful from 1971 to 1973, when cultivation was effectively banned, has proved faulty, causing widespread public ire and ultimately failing. The fallacy of United States negotiations in 1971 was the willingness to forego a long-term ban which would have required more than $35 million in compensation. A larger amount in cash which could have been given in the form of an investment, or a donation of a series of schools or hospitals or an educational TV network, might have elicited a permanent ban from the Turkish government. The possibility still exists and could be renegotiated independently or as part of a more comprehensive United States-Turkish agreement or independently.

State Department policy vis-à-vis the Cyprus issue since July 1974 has pleased Turkey's political circles and public opinion. The congressional decision to cut off military aid, by the same token, has caused dismay and anger. If the State Department changes its policy and adopts a line less favorable to Turkish interests in the Cyprus conflict, the reaction in Turkey would be so vehement that United States-Turkish relations would probably deteriorate to their lowest point ever and might not be restored to normalcy for many years. Washington's attitudes in the case of a possible Kurdish insurgency will likewise be crucial.

The United States can hardly afford to lose Turkey as one of its staunch allies located one of the world's most strategic places. Turkey, on its part, would expose itself to grave dangers if she severed its relations with the United States and the Western defense system. In recognition of this interdependence, the two countries should enter into new dynamic arrangements based on equal and dignified as well as mutually beneficial relations.

Index

Index

About the Authors

A.L. UDOVITCH is chairman of the Department of Near Eastern Studies at Princeton University. His major scholarly interest is the social and economic history of the Medieval Islamic World and it is in this field that he has published a book and numerous articles. He has been on the Board of Governors of the American Research Institute in Turkey since 1969. He is also a trustee of the Northeast Pooled Common Fund and chairman of the Committee on Islamic Studies, American Oriental Society. Professor Udovitch is a member of the Board of Editors of the Journal of Inter-Disciplinary History and of the International Journal of Middle East studies and is Co-Editor of *Studia Islamica*.

ALLAN G. HILL is currently the regional representative (Demographic Division) for the Population Council in Western Asia. He lives and works in Amman, Jordan where he is a visiting professor at the University of Jordan. Professor Hill was a Commonwealth Fund Fellow at Princeton University from 1973-1975 and lecturer in the University of Aberdeen, Scotland. He has contributed to books and periodicals on the subject of populations of the Middle East.

CHARLES ISSAWI is a professor in the Department of *Near Eastern Studies* at Princeton University and one of the leading scholars on the economics of the modern Middle East. Twice a Guggenheim Fellow, Professor Issawi has also been a Social Science Research Council Fellow and a Fellow of the Middle Eastern Institute. He is the author of *The Economic History of Iran* (1971), *Oil, The Middle East and the World* (1972) and *Issawi's Laws of Social Motion* (1973).

BENT HANSEN, professor of economics at the University of California at Berkeley, has spent several years in Egypt as an economic advisor to the Egyptian government. He is the author of *Short and Long Term Planning in Underdeveloped Countries.*

MORROE BERGER is professor of sociology and director of the Program in Near Eastern Studies at Princeton University, where he has taught since 1952. Professor Berger was the first president of the Middle East Studies Association and has been a consultant on Middle East affairs to several United States governmental agencies and private foundations. His works on the Middle East include *Bureaucracy and Society in Modern Egypt* (1957), *The Arab World Today* (1962), and *Islam in Egypt Today* (1970). Several of his works have been translated into Arabic and published in Cairo and Beirut.

P.J. VATIKIOTIS is professor of politics with reference to the Near and Middle East in the School of Oriental and African Studies in the University of London where he also served as chairman of Middle Eastern Studies from 1966 to 1969. A Guggenheim Fellow in 1961-1962 and educated in Greek and English schools in Palestine, at the American University in Cairo and at the Johns Hopkins University, Professor Vatikiotis has taught at Indiana University, University of California at Los Angeles, and Princeton University. He is the author of *The Fatimid Theory of the State* (1957), *The Egyptian Army in Politics* (1961, reprinted 1975), *Politics and the Military in Jordan* (1967), *The Modern History of Egypt* (1969), *Conflict in the Middle East* (1971), *Greece, A Political Essay* (1975), *Egypt Since the Revolution* (Ed. 1968), and *Revolution in the Middle East* (1972).

ELIE KEDOURIE, professor of politics at the London School of Economics, University of London, was educated there and at St. Antony's College, Oxford. He is a Fellow of the British Academy and serves as editor for the journal *Middle Eastern Studies.* Professor Kedourie is the author of *England and the Middle East, Nationalism in Asia and Africa, Afghani and Abduh: An Essay on Religious Unbelief and Political Activism in Modern Islam.*

SHIMON SHAMIR is head of the School of History at Tel Aviv University, and formerly director of the Shiloah Institute of Modern Middle East Affairs. He is the author of *A History of the Arab East.*

BOUTROS BOUTROS-GHALI, professor of political science at Cairo University, was born and educated in Cairo and at the University of Paris. In addition to serving as head of the Department of Political Science, Professor Boutros-Ghali is professor of international law and international relations at Cairo

University, Editor of *Al-Siassa Dawlya*, an international affairs quarterly and of *Al-Ahram Iktisadi*, an economic and political bimonthly. He has lectured in universities throughout the world and is the author of numerous articles and books in English and French which include *Foreign Policies in a World of Change* (1963), *L'Organization de l'Unité Africaine* (1969), *La Ligue des Etats Arabes* (1972) and *Les Conflits de Frontières en Afrique* (1973).

WALTER LAQUEUR is director of the Institute of Contemporary History and the Wiener Library in London, chairman of the Research Council of the Center for Strategic and International Studies in Washington, and professor of history at Tel Aviv University. He is also Editor of the *Journal of Contemporary History* and the *Washington Papers*, and the author of several books on modern European, Russian and Middle Eastern history, including *The Fate of the Revolution* (1967), *Road to Jerusalem* (1969) and *A History of Zionism* (1972).

ALBERT H. HOURANI of St. Antony's College, Oxford served as director of the Middle East Centre at Oxford from 1958 to 1971. He has been visiting professor at the University of Chicago, Harvard, University of Pennsylvania, American University of Beirut and is the author of a number of studies on the Middle East, including *Arabic Thought in the Liberal Age* (1962).

JOHN WATERBURY, the Middle East representative of the American Universities Field Staff in Cairo, is the author of *The Prince of the Believers*.

BEN HALPERN is Richard Koret Professor in Judaic Studies in the Department of History at Brandeis University and a member of the editorial board of *Midstream*. Formerly at the Harvard Center for Middle Eastern Studies from 1956 to 1961, Professor Halpern has written extensively on the problems of modern Israel, including *The Idea of the Jewish State* (1961, 1969).

MALCOLM H. KERR is dean of social sciences and professor of political science at the University of California, Los Angeles. Formerly at the American University of Beirut, he has also spent periods of residence doing research in England, France, Egypt and Tunisia. A leading expert on the contemporary politics of the Middle East and North Africa, Professor Kerr is the author of *Lebanon in the Last Years of Feudalism, 1840-1868, Islamic Reform* (1965), *The Arab Cold War* (1971), co-author of *The Economics and Politics of the Middle East* and edited *The Elusive Peace in the Middle East*.

JOHN B. KELLY, a leading specialist on the Persian Gulf and Arabian peninsula, was formerly professor of history at the University of Wisconsin, the University of Michigan and Oxford University. Born in New Zealand and educated there and at the University of London, he is presently engaged in historical research and writing in London. He is the author of *Eastern Arabian Frontiers* (1964) and *Britain and the Persian Gulf, 1795-1880* (1968).

ALI BANUAZIZI, a specialist on Iran, is professor of social psychology at Boston College.

TALAT S. HALMAN teaches Turkish studies in the Department of Near Eastern Studies at Princeton University. An eminent Turkish writer, in 1971 he served as Minister of Culture on Turkey's National Coalition Cabinet. He has served as a political columnist for the Istanbul dailies *Milliyet* and *Aksam* and is the author or translator of fifteen books in Turkish and English including *Eski Uygarliklarin Siirleri* (Poetry of Ancient Civilizations, in Turkish).